BL
4 volset
25/131-

THE CORRESPONDENCE OF

George, Prince of Wales 1770–1812

VOLUME I 1770-1789

We the undersigned do witness that
George Augustus Frederick Prince of
Wales was married unto Maria Fitzherbert
this 15th of December 1785 ———

George P ———
Maria Fitzherbert
———

Maria Fitzherbert's marriage certificate
Original size 9″ × 7½″

THE CORRESPONDENCE OF

George, Prince of Wales 1770-1812

VOLUME I 1770-1789

EDITED BY

A. Aspinall, M.A., D.Litt.

CASSELL · LONDON

CASSELL & COMPANY LTD
35 Red Lion Square · London WC1
and at Melbourne · Sydney · Toronto
Johannesburg · Cape Town · Auckland

© A. Aspinall 1963
First published 1963

Made and printed in Great Britain by
William Clowes and Sons, Limited
London and Beccles
F. 763

Editor's Preface

In 1938 three volumes of George IV's correspondence, edited by the present Editor, and covering the period of the unrestricted Regency to the King's death (February 1812–June 1830) were published by the Cambridge University Press. The series of which the present is the first volume, will cover the earlier years of George IV, as Prince of Wales and as Prince Regent during the twelve months of the restricted Regency. Those familiar with the 1938 volumes will recall the introductory remarks of Sir Charles Webster in which he referred to the unsatisfactory character of the King's Papers: 'Some were destroyed by Knighton immediately before, or soon after, the King's death. Others must have been lost in changes of residence. Others were taken away by McMahon and Bloomfield. That there should be many more we know from other collections and by references to the letters themselves.' This can be said, too, of the pre-1812 correspondence. That the King had a very vulnerable past is common knowledge, and many letters which would have thrown a somewhat lurid light on his more dubious connexions during his early years were naturally destroyed by his executors or by others. For very different reasons, practically all his correspondence with Mrs. Fitzherbert was burnt by Wellington as his executor in the drawing room of Mrs. Fitzherbert's house in Tilney Street on 24 August 1833 in the presence of her old friend Lord Albemarle. Some idea of the bulk of the material may be formed from the Duke's remark to Albemarle after several hours' burning: 'I think, my Lord, we had better hold our hand for a while, or we shall set the old woman's chimney on fire!' The few papers which Mrs. Fitzherbert insisted on retaining for the sake of her reputation with posterity, and especially her marriage certificate, remained secreted in Coutts's Bank until 1905 when they were handed over to King Edward VII, and, by his orders, subsequently bound and placed among the Private Archives. Whether the Duke of Wellington destroyed any portion of the general correspondence we shall never know. There is internal evidence that he read the MSS., which remained in the possession of his family at Apsley House until 1912, for his docket appears on some of them, but he was very meticulous about preserving his own papers, and there is no reason to suppose that he did away with anything beyond what he deemed necessary for the preservation of the reputation of the King whom he so loyally served, and of the Monarchy itself.

Despite these losses the collection still retains much correspondence of a private and family nature hardly calculated to add to the reputation of King George IV. Historians and the wider reading public have particular reason to be grateful to Her Majesty the Queen for her generosity in granting permission for its publication. Nothing of substantial historical importance, however objectionable from a personal point of view, has been omitted. The main omissions are a few letters or passages of slight interest whose text is obviously unsuitable for publication, and letters containing birthday greetings. In addition a number of purely official documents which are doubtless duplicated in the Public Record Office, together with some formal notes from Ministers, such as requests for an audience for themselves or for foreign diplomats, will be omitted from later volumes. Many additional letters from the Prince of Wales, preserved in other archives, public and private, have been or will be included as necessary to the understanding of the whole.

Writing in 1938 Sir Charles Webster referred to the difficulties encountered by the present Editor in preparing the 1812–30 correspondence for publication, 'where there are many gaps and where the reference to persons is often allusive'. The difficulties with these earlier letters are very much greater. There is a very much larger number of undated, inadequately dated and wrongly dated letters to tease and harass one, and no amount of effort will always provide a solution. And the Prince, and occasionally his brothers, wrote much-needed apologies for their 'horrid scrawls', whilst fading ink and damp-stained paper add to deciphering troubles. Moreover, until the official or semi-official correspondence begins in 1811, the letters contain references to a far greater number of obscure individuals, and much time has been spent in seeking information about them, often without result. The annotation, then, though on a generous scale, like that of the Editor's *Later Correspondence of George III* now in progress, and including much new material from MSS. in private hands, is, inevitably, not exhaustive. In view of the fact that about eight more substantial volumes in this and the complementary Cambridge Series remain to be published, and that, after almost forty years of University teaching, failing eyesight is bringing the Editor's working life towards its close, he has deemed it best to push ahead as quickly as possible with the remaining volumes, in spite of possible objections from critics that some obscure individual is given no footnote.

The original spelling has been retained except in the case of copies which are in no recognizable hand, for there seems little point in preserving the bad spelling of mere clerks. The formal beginnings and endings of letters have been omitted, except for specimens which throw light on personal relationships—and changing relationships. Some of the Windsor letters have no folio number; most of these belong to the Princess of Wales's MSS.

'Add. Georgian' are MSS. in the Royal Archives which were acquired, or else numbered, after the microfilming of the main collections at the beginning of the second World War. They are easily distinguishable from the British Museum Additional MSS., which are quoted simply as 'Add. MSS.' (*Egerton MSS.*, of course, are also B.M. MSS.) The curious grammatical constructions and the vagaries of the fantastic spelling (and there is no consistency even in a single letter) are to be attributed, partly at any rate, to the extreme haste in which the letters were written and to the fact that the thoughts of the writer ran ahead of his pen. But the use of *sic* has been kept down to the minimum. The spelling of Prince Adolphus deteriorated so sharply after 1793 when he left Hanover to fight the French, that one wonders whether his earlier letters were written under supervision.

It is hoped to print a comprehensive index at the close of the series. The Editor would be grateful for the correction of any errors that may have crept into the footnotes. Such corrections will be incorporated in subsequent volumes.

He would also like to take this opportunity of expressing his gratitude to Her Royal Highness the Princess Royal and the Earl of Harewood for permission to quote from the MSS. at Harewood House; and thanks are similarly due to Captain C. K. Adam, the Marquess of Ailesbury, the Duke of Devonshire, the Duke of Dorset, Earl Fitzwilliam, the Marquess of Hertford[1], Lord Kenyon, the Earl of Lonsdale, the Earl of Minto, Earl Mountbatten, and Mrs. Sinclair of Thurso, Caithness.

The Syndics of the Cambridge University Press have kindly consented to the reproduction of all the letters passing between the King

1. Letters from the Ragley MSS. were added at a very late stage in the preparation of this volume, and the first footnote reference to Lord Hugh Seymour-Conway is on page 281.

and the Prince of Wales which were first published in Volumes I and II of *The Later Correspondence of King George III.*

Finally, the Editor would like to thank Mr. R. Mackworth-Young, M.V.O., Her Majesty's Librarian, Miss Price-Hill, the Registrar of the Archives and her staff, Mr. Oliver Millar, M.V.O., F.S.A., the officials of the British Museum, the Public Record Office, the National Library of Scotland, H.M.'s General Register House, Edinburgh, the Huntingdon Library, and Mr. E. A. Smith, Lecturer in Modern History in the University of Reading, for most valued help and advice.

Contents

Genealogical Tables

Illustrations

I   C.1770-1780

As one would expect, the Prince of Wales's correspondence whilst he was a boy was practically restricted to the family circle, including Lord Holdernesse, who was in general charge of his education from 1771 to 1776. The correspondence during these early years would have been even more meagre but for Holdernesse's prolonged illness, which kept him abroad for a considerable time. There is little to be learnt about the kind of education the Prince and his brother Frederick received at the hands of their tutors, but we know that the Prince, at any rate, acquired a fair knowledge of the Classics, and of French, German and Italian. He never learnt, indeed, to spell correctly, but then his tutors were similarly incapable. The King, who was doubtless hard to please, complained in August 1780 that his eldest son had made insufficient progress with his studies. According to tradition, the discipline was fairly strict; even on one of Frederick's birthdays (his fifteenth) lessons went on as usual throughout the morning. At 8 p.m., when they normally ceased, he and his brother were customarily allowed to make up the Queen's commerce party, which lasted until ten, or thereabouts.

We have to rely on Horace Walpole for an account of the quarrel between Lord Holdernesse and his subordinates which ended in his resignation in 1776. It was said that they had taken advantage of his absence abroad to prejudice the minds of the two Princes against him, with the result that he lost all control over them. Horace Walpole was prejudiced against Holdernesse, whose abilities were admittedly second-rate, but he was not without sense and penetration, and he was thoroughly devoted to the performance of his duties. He may have been as sententious as old Polonius, but he gave the Prince of Wales excellent advice, and the Prince's reputation would have stood immeasurably higher had he taken it to heart. It was perhaps as well that Holdernesse died when he did: had he lived a few years longer he might well have been broken-hearted at the ruin of all his hopes of an heir-apparent endowed with all the moral qualities of his parents.

The year 1780 saw the Prince separated from his brother Frederick, to whom he was much attached, and who, in December, was sent to Hanover to complete his education and start his military training. They were not to see each other again for six and a half years. Having attained the age of eighteen, the Prince of Wales was at last emancipated from the irksome control of his tutors, and was free to enter the world of gallantry. He threw himself into it with reckless abandon, encouraged, no doubt, by the example of his dissolute and contemptible uncles, the Dukes of Cumberland and Gloucester; and, carrying on the Hanoverian tradition, he developed political as well as personal friendships with such Whig politicians as Fox and Sheridan who were in opposition to the King's Ministers, and whose private lives were as scandalous as those of the Royal Dukes. Surprisingly enough, the King so far relented in his hostility to his brothers as to receive them (but not their wives) at Court, but it was not until Fox was almost in his grave, more than a quarter of a century later, that the King more or less forgave *him* for having both led his son astray and opposed the Ministers of his own choice.

In December 1780, then, the Prince was given a very modest establishment, but until he came fully of age, he remained subject to restrictions. He was still to live under his father's roof, at Buckingham House; he was given practically no pocket money (Prince Augustus, as a young man, had only a guinea a week); if he went to the theatre it had to be with his father's consent; he was not allowed to attend Balls or Assemblies at private houses, and Masquerades were absolutely forbidden; and he was required to attend church every Sunday.

These restrictions proved to be unenforceable. They have been described as stupid, odious and German in character, but the inescapable facts are that the King was well aware of the essential worthlessness of his son's character, and that he was making a vain effort to save him from perdition. Whether he was aware of Frederick's loose way of living in Hanover remains uncertain, but, rightly, he had much more respect for the character of his second, and favourite son who, despite youthful excesses, and unlike his elder brother, was determined above everything else to devote himself wholeheartedly to the service of his

3

country in his chosen profession of arms. (The obituary notices, forty-seven years later, admitted that the Duke of York had not observed the moralities of private life, but suggested that there was nothing un-English, nothing un-princely, in his failings.)

Already, at the age of seventeen, the Prince of Wales confessed to the lovely Mary Hamilton, one of the Princesses' attendants, and whose virtue was as unblemished as her beauty, that he was rather too fond of both women and wine. From her he turned, baffled, to the actress Mrs. Robinson, the famous Perdita of *The Winter's Tale*, and engaged with her in an intrigue which became public property. Like Harriette Wilson at a later date, she was determined to profit from the connexion, and she extorted from him a promissory note for £20,000, payable on his coming of age. The King's indignation when he heard of this scandalous affair and discovered that *he* would have to find the money which would save his son from public exposure, can well be imagined. 'My eldest son', he wrote (28 August 1781), 'got last year into a very improper connexion with an actress and woman of indifferent character through the *friendly* assistance of Lord Malden. A multitude of letters passed, which she has threatened to publish unless he, in short, bought them of her. . . . I have thought it right to authorize the getting them from her, and I have employed Lieut.-Col. Hotham, on whose discression I could depend to manage this business. He has now brought it to a conclusion, and has her consent to get these letters on her receiving £5,000, undoubtedly an enormous sum, but I wish to get my son out of this shameful scrape.' The King apparently knew nothing about the bond, believing that the securing the letters ended the affair. Fox was called in to arrange this other matter, and he succeeded in recovering the bond in return for an annuity of £600 settled on her, and to be extended (to the amount of £200) to the life of her daughter, Maria Elizabeth Robinson.

I THE PRINCE OF WALES TO THE QUEEN[1]

[c. 1770]

My dear Mama, nothing could have made me so happy as your Majesty's letter, and I will always endeavour to follow the good advice you give me in it being your Majty.'s most dutiful son, George P.   (41727)

1. The Prince's first letter to be preserved; undated, and in a very childish hand. So is the next specimen of his writing, which reads, simply, 'In the hand of God is the prosperity of man—George.' (41728)

4

QUEEN CHARLOTTE TO LADY CHARLOTTE FINCH[1]

12 Aug. 1770

My dear Lady Charlotte, I beg you will deliver to the Prince of Wales the pocket book, wherein I have put a letter which you will open and read unto him, desiring him to remember the contents thereof, but not to mention it to anybody. I must beg the same of you, as my intention is not to shine but to do real good, and after all not to have anything to reproch myself with hereafter.

The book opens on the left side of the lock.   (36348)

3 QUEEN CHARLOTTE TO THE PRINCE OF WALES

12 Aug. 1770

My dear son, the demand of a pocket book furnisheth me with an opportunity of stating to you my wishes concerning your future conduct in life. Time draws near when you will be put into the hands of governors, under whose care you will study more manly learning than what you have done hitherto. My advice will be short but sincere, & therefore I flatter myself, not less serviceable to you. Above all things I recommend unto you to fear God, a duty which must lead to all the rest with ease; as His assistance being properly implored will be your guide through every action of life. Abhor all vice, in private as well as in publick, and look upon yourself as obliged to set good examples. Disdain all flatery; it will corrupt your manners and render you contemptible before the world. Do justice unto everybody and avoid partiality. The first will acquire to you happiness in this world as well as hereafter: the latter will make you unhappy, because it leaves after it an unhappy conscience—a situation which seems to me the most wretched in life, as it deprives us of the greatest enjoyment of life, that is, peace of mind. Love and esteem those that are about you. Confide in and act with sincerity towards them, as that alone will be productive of a lasting friendship. Treat nobody with contempt, for that will deprive you of it. Be charitable to everybody, not forgetting your meaner servants. Don't use them with indifference, rather pity them that are obliged to serve, and do unto them as you would be done by. I mean by that you should not think yourself above doing good unto them. The contrary will make you appear vain, and vanity is the root of all vice and a sure proof of ignorance. For what is man to man? We are all equal and become only of consequence by

1. Governess to the Royal Family, 1762–92 (1725–1813). She was the daughter of Thomas, 1st Earl of Pomfret (1698–1753), and mother of the 9th Earl of Winchilsea and Nottingham. Horace Walpole described her as 'a woman of remarkable sense and philosophy' (*Last Journals*, i.125 [1910]).

setting good examples to others, and these must be given with a view of doing our duty but not with the idea of superiority, for then the action loses its merits.

Lastly I recommend unto you the highest love, affection and duty towards the King. Look upon him as a friend, nay, as the greatest, the best, and the most deserving of all friends you can possibly find. Try to imitate his virtues, and look upon everything that is in opposition to that duty as destructive to yourself. After this I am sure you can't be unacquainted with what belongs to me as I am the next to the King. Keep in love and friendship with your brothers and sisters, for I am sure they will deserve and require it of you: and as you ought to seek your happiness in that of others, I am sure you will contribute to that of your own family. I, for my part, can safely say, you will contribute greatly towards mine, in following the advice of your most affectionate mother. (36346)

4   THE EARL OF HOLDERNESSE[1] TO THE PRINCE OF WALES

Walmer Castle[2], 27 June 1771

I want words to express the tender sensations which the great honour of your Royal Highnesses letter gave me. A life devoted to your service is only to be rewarded by the King's approbation, and your Royal, kind & gracious acceptance of my dutifull attachment.

Nature, Sir, has done her part in forming your heart and mind with endowments fit for a great Prince. Your Royal Highness must compleat her work by cultivating those happy talents and virtuous dispositions implanted in you. That your Royal Highness may become the comfort of your Royal parents, an honour to your country, a blessing to his Majesty's subjects, is the daily and most ardent prayer of [etc.].   (41729)

5   LETTERS FROM THE EARL OF HOLDERNESSE TO THE PRINCE OF WALES AND PRINCE FREDERICK[3]

Aston [Yorks.], 15 Sep. 1771

I avail myself of the permission your Royal Highnesses gave me of addressing you both in the same letter. My best thanks are due for the great

1. Robert D'Arcy, 4th Earl of Holdernesse (1718–78), Governor to the Prince of Wales, 1771–6. He had been a Lord of the Bedchamber, 1741–51, and Secretary of State in the Pelham and Newcastle Ministries. Horace Walpole referred to him as 'that formal piece of dullness'.

2. He was Lord Warden of the Cinque Ports, 1765–78.

3. The King's second son (1763–1827). Created Duke of York, 27 November 1784. K.G., 1771. Colonel in the Army, November 1780; Colonel of the 2nd Troop of Horse Grenadier Guards, March 1782–October 1784; Major-General, 1782; Lieutenant-General, 1784; Field-Marshal, 1795; Commander-in-Chief, 1798–1809, 1811–27.

honour of your letters. If a faithfull discharge of the duty I owe the King and your Royal Highnesses in executing the trust his Majesty has confided to me, can merit such a reward as the very kind expressions contained in those dear letters, I will venture to lay claim to it, and shall certainly merit the continuance of your Royal Highnesses good graces by the most constant and affectionate attachment. I rejoice to hear by Mr. Smelt's[1] letters that Prince Frederick's slight indisposition will probably neither be painfull nor of long duration. I saw with infinite pleasure that while that Prince was confined one day by physick, the Prince of Wales preferred his brother's satisfaction to his own amusement and staid at home to keep him company. These endearments, as they tend to lay the foundation of the most lasting freindship, will be a constant source of happiness to both brothers thro'out their lives.

As Frederick asks me for a description of this place, tho' a small one, it would take too long a space for a letter & more of his time than he can afford to spare from his studies and amusements; I shall reserve it till I have the honour of attending him at Kew.

Your Royal Highnesses will regularly be informed of my motions by Mr. Smelt. I shall pursue the business that brought me into Yorkshire with all possible diligence, as I impatiently wish for the moment of returning to my duty.

The pride of my life and the wish of my heart is your Royal Highnesses welfare and happiness. The path of virtue is the road to both. That you may continue in that track is the daily and fervent prayer of [etc.]. (41730–1)

Hornby Castle[2], *3 May 1772*

Permit me, dear Princes, to adress myself to your Royal Highnesses on the anniversary of the day when I entered on the important office of superintending the education of his Majesty's eldest sons. I felt and still feel how arduous a task the King imposed upon me, how important the trust, how nice the undertaking. I have severely scrutinized my conduct towards your Royal Highnesses for twelve months past, and conclude I must go on as I began; on your part, dearest Princes, I think I see a fair year's improvement (you know I never flatter) yet still much is to be done, and whether the return of this day in future years is to be honourable and pleasing, or disgracefull and wretched to me depend upon you.

You are and ought to be the chief objects of my sollicitude. I have

1. Leonard Smelt (1719?–1800), Sub-Governor to the Prince of Wales and Prince Frederick, 1771–6.

2. His seat in Yorkshire. He was Lord-Lieutenant of the North Riding, 1740–77.

devoted myself to your service. I have not only given up to that sole duty my time and thoughts but even my little reputation, for if you do not turn out those aimable Princes nature intended you to be, I shall and perhaps I ought to be blamed.

This adress shall not close with the formality of a letter. No expressions of duty, affection and respect can express what is lodged in the breast of your faithfull Holdernesse.   (41733)

6   THE PRINCE OF WALES TO PRINCE WILLIAM[1]

Londres, le 20 de Janvier, 1773

Je me flatte que vous vous portez bien aprez le cercle. Je vous prie de faire mes compliments à Edoüard[2], a Messieurs Budé[3] et Hook[4]. Je suis fort aise d'apprehendre que vous faites mieux vos leçons. J'espere que vous me ferez le plaisir de me répondre. Mon cher Guillaume, je suis votre bon frere.   (Add. MSS. Georgian 4, f.13).

7   LETTERS FROM THE EARL OF HOLDERNESSE TO THE PRINCE OF WALES

Hertford Street, 16 Mar. 1774

Your Royal Highness has opened a private correspondence that gives me as much pleasure as it does me honour. I hope you will continue it, and write with frankness your own genuine thoughts. Permit me likewise to open myself in like manner without formality or reserve, thus a free and freindly intercourse once established between us will increase confidence by the easy conveyance of questions, hints or opinions.

1. The King's third son, afterwards (1830) William IV (1765–1837). Created Duke of Clarence, 20 May 1789. K.G., 1782. Post Captain in the Navy, 1786; Rear-Admiral, 1790; Vice-Admiral, 1794; Admiral, 1799; Lord High Admiral, May 1827–August 1828. Ranger of Greenwich Park, 1794–7; Ranger of Bushey Park, 1797–1830.

2. The King's fourth son (1767–1820), and the father of Queen Victoria. Created Duke of Kent, 24 April 1799. K.G., 1786. Colonel in the Army, 1786; Major-General, 1793; Lieutenant-General, 1796; General, 1799; Commander-in-Chief in North America, 1799–1800; Governor of Gibraltar, 1802–20.

3. General Budé (c.1736–1818) was Instructor (later Governor) to Prince William and his younger brothers. He was of Swiss origin, and he served in the Hanoverian Army. Later, he was the Duke of York's private secretary (c.1736–1818). 'His person', wrote Fanny Burney in 1786, 'is tall and showy, and his manners and appearance are fashionable. But he has a sneer in his smile that looks sarcastic, and a distance in his manner that seems haughty' (*Diary*, ii.97 [1876 ed.]).

4. The Rev. Mr. Hook was one of Prince William's instructors.

8

The greatest regret I have had during the course of my illness has been my necessary absence from my dear Princes. Doctor *Warren*[1] flatters me I shall soon be able at least to receive them here, it will be an happy moment, as it will ever be the pride and pleasure of my life to prove my faithfull attachment. (41734)

London, 18 Mar. 1774
I observe with great pleasure a visible improvement in my dear Prince of Wales's second letter, tho' still with some little faults arising from want of thought. For instance, a word is left out at the bottom of the first page, that leaves the sense ambiguous. I don't wish your Royal Highness to make your letters lessons, but a little thought is necessary to make yourself understood. Your promises of docility and of freindship towards me are real cordials to me. I hope you will never forget that promise once made is sacred and must be kept. *Truth* is the first quality of a man; the higher the rank, the more to be adhered to. It is with *such truth* I profess the most affectionate and faithfull attachment to my dear Prince. (41735)

8 THE EARL OF HOLDERNESSE TO THE PRINCE OF WALES
AND PRINCE FREDERICK

À Rheims, le 22 Mai 1774
Vous m'ordonnez de vous ecrire, mes chers Princes, et vous daignez m'y exciter par les aimables lettres que je recus au moment de mon depart; je n'entreprendrai pas d'exprimer l'exces de ma sensibilite sur tout ce que Vos Altesses Roiales me disent d'obligeant, ma vie vous est consacré mes chers Princes, la continuation de cette amitie dont vous daignez m'honorer doit faire le prix de mon assiduité a remplir aupres de vous le devoir penible mais flatteur que le Roi m'a imposé. La nature vous a donee de ses plus precieux dons, c'est a vous, mes chers Princes, de perfectionner ses presens par votre application et de vous rendre le bonheur des peuples, le soutien de votre Roi et pere qui vous montre l'exemple de la vertu. Mo[nsieu]r Smelt rendra un compte exact a vos Altesses Roiales du progrez de notre voiage dont je lai envoye le journal, vous trouverez les details que je supprime dans l'etat de la France par Mor. Piganiol, *en Suisse* mes lettres deviendront plus longues, elles n'en seront peutetre pas plus interressantes. Adieu, mes aimables Princes, vous scavez la tendresse et l'etendue de mon attachement. (41736)

1. Richard Warren (1731–97), physician to the Royal Family.

9 THE COUNTESS OF HOLDERNESSE[1] TO THE PRINCE OF WALES

Dijon, 31 May 1774

La lettre[2] dont votre Altesse Royale a bien voulu m'honorer fait le sujet de mon admiration, tant par la beauté de l'ecriture que par la pureté du stile et l'élegance de sa tournure, mais ce qui me frape et me flatte davantage sont les sentiments de bienveillance dont elle daigne nous honorer Milord et moy, si le plus veritable attachement puisse meriter un tel honneur, votre Altesse Royale peut-etre assuré quelle n'est pas deplasée, elle scait en n'en pouvoir douter que Milord lui a consacré sa vie, et que son bonheur depend de la maniere dont elle recevras ses conseils, mais indepandament de ses liaisons le merite personel de votre Altesse Royale lui attireroi de ma part le respectueux devouement avec lequel j'ay l'honneur d'etre [etc.]. (41737)

10 THE EARL OF HOLDERNESSE TO THE PRINCE OF WALES

À Dijon, le 4 Juin 1774

Vous etes bien aimable, mon cher Prince, de me donner de vos nouvelles; vos lettres me font d'àutant plus de plaisir que j'y remarque le developpement de votre esprit, et que vous m'y donnes des preuves de cet excellent caractere qui me fait augurer tout ce j'espere de votre coeur et de vos talens. Je ne puis trop vous le repeter, mon cher Prince, la nature a tout fait pour vous, il ne s'agit que de perfectionner par votre assiduité ses pretieux dons.

Voici un aniversaire[3] bien interessant pour tous les Anglois; nous le celebrons ici de notre mieux, mais surement avec des coeurs pleins de devoir et de reconoissance. Je me transporte avec vous a *St. James's*, je vous y vois avec votre air gracieux accoster ceux qui vous entourent,

1. Lord Holdernesse married (1743) at the Hague, Mary (1721 ?–1801), daughter of Francis Doublet, of Groeneveldt, Member of the States of Holland.

2. Dated, Kew, 18 May: 'Vous ne pouvez pas concevoir le plaisir que j'ai de savoir que vous avez en un bon pas sage, & que My Lord se porte mieux. La joie que j'ai eu de vous voir encore une fois étoit tout à fait inattendue. J'ai été bien faché de n'avoir pas aussi le plaisir de revoir My Lord avant qu'il partit, mais je m'en console par l' ésperance de le revoir le jour de ma naissance parfaitement rétabli. J'ai bien des compliments à vous faire de la part de mes freres. Ils sont fachés aussi bien que moi, qu'il n'yait point de bal jeudi, mais il y aura en revanche des feux d'artifice. Je vous prie, madame, de faire mes tendres compliments à My Lord. Je souhaite que le beau temps & la gaieté vous accòmpagnent pendant vôtre voyage, & je vous prie de me croire très sincerement et avec toute la reconnoissance que je dois à vos bontés, votre très affectionné ami' (Add. MSS. 33132, f. 21). There are a few more letters from the Prince and Prince Frederick to Lady Holdernesse in Add. MSS. 33132, all in French, and probably written with some assistance.

3. The King's birthday.

distinguer les personnes selon leur rang et leur merite, j'y vois briller votre politesse pour les Dames, et votre affabilité envers tous. Je crois entendre vos propos, du sens dans tous que vous dites, la vivacite tempere par la prudence, et un soin exacte a eviter de faire des questions qui pourront embarasser ou donner de la peine a ceux auxquels elles sont adresser, voila le rapport auquel je m'attend par la poste de Mardi.

Vous faites bien de l'Honneur a ma fille mon cher Prince de la regretter dans vos parties de *plaisir* que je voudrois bien etre en etat de participer avec elle, et si vous regrettez de n'etre pas de notre voiage daignes croire que je vous y souhaite bien sincerement: le moment viendra peut-etre ou le Roi permettra quelque petite excursion au moins en Angleterre, recevez en attendant mon aimable et bien aimé Prince les voeux sinceres que je fais pour votre bonheur et pour votre prosperite. (41738)

I I   THE COUNTESS OF HOLDERNESSE TO THE PRINCE OF WALES
AND PRINCE FREDERICK

Geneva, 17 July 1774
L'interet que vos Altesses Royales daignent prendre a La Santé de Milord m'est garant quelles m'excuseront de se que mon assiduité aupres de lui a retardé jusqu'a present ma reponse au lettres dont vos Altesses Royales m'ont bien voulu honorer, Les même raison Messeigneurs vous porteront aussi a m'excuser de ce que je m'adresse conjointement a tout les deux. Je suis flatté de ce que le fruit de Sion Hill nous ait retracé dans la memoire de vos Altesses Royales le moment heureux viendra ou je pourés avoir l'honneur de leurs en presenter moimême. Le Prince Frederick me demande des nouvelles de la France; je ne suis guere en etat de lui en donner d'ici. La voix publique nous assure que tout est heureux sou le nouveaux regne[1] que le chancelier[2] est exilé et l'ancien Parlement retabli. Comme je ne vois que peu de monde voila tout ce qui est venu a ma connoissance; nous avons ici et au environs une Colonie Angloise, Le Duc de Hamilton[3], Milord

1. Louis XVI (1754–93) succeeded his grandfather Louis XV (1710–74) on 10 May.

2. Nicolas Augustin de Maupeou (1714–92) had succeeded his father as Chancellor in 1768 and incurred great unpopularity by suppressing the *Parlements* and establishing new Courts. His place was taken by Maurepas (1701–81).

3. Douglas, 8th Duke of Hamilton (1756–99). He resided on the Continent from 1772 to 1776 under the care of Dr. Moore, father of the famous soldier Sir John Moore. Dissipation ruined his constitution.

11

Chesterfield[1], Lumley[2], Monsieur Harvy neveux du General Monsieur Clive et bien d'autre jusqu'a nombre de soisante. Nous avons Laissé a Lausanne Milord Linsey[3] et Midleton[4] le premier me parroit considerablement grandi et fortifié. Monsieur Brydone[?] connu par les lettres qu'il a donné au public est avec lui. Milord et Milady Carmarthen[5] continue encore avec nous et nous esperont les posseder encore quelque tems, comme ils ont eu la complaisance de nous sacrifier la plus grande parti du tems qu'ils ont destinée a leur excursion d'outremer. Au reste Messeigneurs les plaisirs de la Suisse me sont asséz inconnu. Je ne sors que pour faire quelque courte promenade dans les charmants environs de cette ville; nous avons aussi essuyes des jours de pluye et de froit, le tems est a present remis au beaux ce qui rejouit beaucoup les habitans vue que la recolte est deja commencée.

Je filicite vos Altesses Royale du sejour du Prince Ernest[6] a Keu; j'ai apris avec bien du plaisir des nouvelles de sa santé comme j'ose prendre le plus vif interet a tout ce qui le regarde.

Milord continu tout doucement a se retablir, son entier retablissement ne peu l'operer qu'avec le tems apres une aussi forte maladie et l'etat de foiblesse auquel ses soufrances et sa diete l'on nessessairement reduit; il a été levé pendant quelques heures hier et aujourd'huy en tout etat il est devoué le plus sinserement a vos Altesses Royales, elles me permettront d'y joindre les mêmes sentiments de ma part et daigneront recevoir les assurances du profond respect aved lequel j'ay l'honneur d'etre [etc.]. (41739)

1. Philip, 5th Earl of Chesterfield (1755–1815) succeeded his cousin in the peerage in 1773. Ambassador to Spain, 1784–7; Master of the Mint, 1789–90; Joint Postmaster-General, 1790–8; Master of the Horse, 1798–1804.

2. Possibly a son of the Earl of Scarborough.

3. Robert, 4th Duke of Ancaster (1756–79), styled Marquess of Lindsey, 1758–78. He succeeded his father as Duke in 1778, and died of scarlet fever eleven months later.

4. George, 4th Viscount Midleton [I.] (1754–1836), succeeded his father, 1765. M.P. for Whitchurch, 1774–96. Created Baron Brodrick [G.B.], 1796.

5. Francis, 5th Duke of Leeds (1751–99) was styled Marquess of Carmarthen, 1761–89. Succeeded his father as Duke, 23 March 1789. M.P. for Eye, 1774; for Helston, 1774–5. Lord of the Bedchamber, 1776–7; Lord Chamberlain to the Queen, 1777–80. Foreign Secretary, 1783–91.
He married: (1) in Nov. 1773, Amelia (1754–84), daughter of the 4th Earl of Holdernesse. She eloped from her husband in December 1778 and was divorced in May 1779. (2) in October 1788, Catherine (1764–1837) daughter of Thomas Anguish: 'a most pleasing woman, and ... most certainly a far prettier Marchioness than she was as a girl' (Minto, *Life and Letters of Sir Gilbert Elliot, Earl of Minto* [subsequently cited as *Minto*], i.235).

6. The King's fifth son (1771–1851). Created Duke of Cumberland, 1799; King of Hanover, 1837–51.

12

THE EARL OF HOLDERNESSE TO THE PRINCE OF WALES
AND PRINCE FREDERICK

Geneva, 11 Aug. 1774
I am too well apprized of the good hearts of my dear Princes to doubt of
the kind reception a few ill written lines in my own shaking hand will
meet with.[1] I cannot express how much I lament that a birthday con-
gratulation should be thus conveyed to my aimable Prince of Wales.[2]
Your Royal Highness now enters upon your *teens*, the first step to
manhood. May I be a true prophet when I foretell that riper years will
improve those early buds of virtue I have seen with joy. Yes, dearest
Prince, I shall live to *see* you, what I *wish* you, an ornament to your
country & a comfort to your parents; such is my daily prayer.   (41741)

THE COUNTESS OF HOLDERNESSE TO THE PRINCE OF WALES

Geneve, 12 Aoust 1774
Je ne scaures jamais asses remercier votré Altesse Royale de la corespondence constante dont elle m'honore; je m'en fais honneur parmi le
peu de personnes que je frequente ici, en leur faisant admirer la beauté
de l'ecriture de ses lettres; vous interessé trop Monseigneur les etrangers
sensé pour qu'il ne voient point avec le plus vrai plaisir le developement
de ses talens; et le merite de votre Altesse Royale est deja en partie
connu a Geneve; je recoit de toute part des compliments sur l'heureuse
anniversaire de ce jour, mais je me vante interieurement de les surpasser
tous dans les voeux que je fais pour la prosperite de Votre Altesse
Royale, daigné les croire Monseigneur des plus sinsere, et qu'independam-
ment de toute autre consideration, mon attachement personal sufiroit
pour de tels sentiments.

Milord auroit fort souhaité d'assister a nos rejouisances et d'etre du
moin present quand on boiroit a la santé du jour; mais sa foiblesse ne
lui permet pas cette satisfaction, ne lui etant pas possible de se trainer
jusqu'a notre salle a manger; quoique sur le même etage que son ap-
partement, il s'est fait un effort pour ecrire quelque ligne a votre
Altesse Royale et a Messeigneurs vos freres, la languer de son corps ne
le rend pourtant pas moins ardant dans les prieres qu'il ne cesse de faire
pour le bonheur de ses eleves Royaux, daigné recevoir Monseigneur les
voeux reuni de toute ma famille, et me croire en particulier avec le plus
veritable attachement, et le plus profond respect [etc.].   (41742-3)

1. For the Earl's illness in 1774, see Horace Walpole's *Last Journals*, i.327, 556. 'Lord
Holdernesse, who had had a violent humour in his face, which struck in and had fallen on his
hearing and his breast, had been to seek relief in the south of France, whence he had returned
in the last autumn, a little mended in his health, but still very deaf' (May 1776).

2. His birthday was on the 12th.

À Genève, ce 12 Aoust 1774

Monseigneur, Je viens de recevoir une nouvelle preuve des bontés dont Votre Altesse Royalle m'honore et c'est avec le plus grand empressement que je me hâte de lui en témoigner ma reconnoissance. Elle me permettra de saisir l'occasion de cet heureux anniversaire pour lui renouveller les assurances des voeux que ne cesserai de faire pour son bonheur, et j'ose me flatter que Votre Altesse Royalle est persuadée du plaisir avec lequel nous nous reunissons tous pour célébrer un jour si intéréssant pour nous. Nous éprouvons ici une chaleur extrême et qui surpasse de beaucoup ce que j'ay jamais senti en Angleterre, heureusement que mon papa[1] n'en souffre que mediocrement, permettez moi, Monseigneur de vous témoigner combien je suis sensible a l'interèt que vous voulez bien prendre à la santé d'une personne qui m'est si chere, et je puis dire avec assurance qu'il le mérite par l'attachement sincere qu'il a voué a Votre Altesse Royalle. Sa santé se fortifie quoiqu'avec moins de promptitude qu'il ne le souhaiterois, il est levé presque toute la journée et se trouve fort bien jusqu'ici du nouveau regime qu'il à commencé et qui consiste en poulet et en légumes.

La vie que nous menons ici est si uniforme qu'elle me met dans l'impossibilité de rien mander d'amusant à Votre Altesse Royalle toute la compagnie que nous voyons ici consiste en l'assemblée des Sindics de cette ville dont le plus *Macaroni* à aumoins soixante et dix ans. Il y a aux environs d'ici une troupe de comediens qui est celle du Prince de Condé[2], comme elle est assez bonne nous y allons souvent; Mr. de Voltaire[3] y doit être ce soir et malgré la chaleur je m'imagine qu'il y aura un très grand concours de peuple pour le voir, on y donne une de ses pièces nommée Les Lois de Minos, c'est une de ses derniers dont je n'ay pas grande opinion ce qui joint à la chaleur m'empechera d'y aller.

My lord Carmarthen est très sensible a l'honneur du souvenir de Votre Altesse Royalle et me prie de lui presenter ses très humbles respects. Comme mon papa et maman ont l'honneur d'ecrire eux mêmes, je n'importunerai pas davantage Votre Altesse Royalle que pour la suplier de recevoir l'assurance du profond respect avec lequel j'ay l'honneur d'être [etc.]. (41744–5)

1. Lord Holdernesse.

2. Louis, Duc de Condé (1756–1830), who married (1770) Marie Louise (1750–1822), daughter of Philip, Duke of Orleans.

3. The French *philosophe* (1694–1778), who lived at Ferney, near Geneva.

Geneva, 29 7bre [Sep.] 1774

Si j'etois capable d'envier le bonheur de ma fille[1]; c'auroit été dans le moment qu'elle se mettoit aux pieds de leurs Majestés, et quelle eut le bonheur de faire sa cour a Votre Altesse Royale, je me crois sure de l'accueil gracieux dont elle l'auras honoré; votre coeur est trop bon Monseigneur pour ne pas se resouvenir de ceux qui comme elle on l'honneur de lui etre attaché, c'est avec le plus veritable regret que nous abandonnons l'esperance de jouir d'un pareil bonheur cet hiver; rien que la plus urgente nessessite auroit pu nous y determiner; Montpellier est l'endroit que nous avons choisi pour notre retraite, des que la santé de Milord poura lui permettre de s'y transporter, elle se retablit visiblement depuis sa derniere operation qui aura ete a ce que j'espere la fin de ses souffrances et le moyen de sa convalesence permanante; J'ay fait vendredi passé une petite excursion a la campagne chez Monsieur de Boisy, par un tems detestable, ayant eu de la pluye toute la journée, mais quoique prisée du plaisir de la prommenade, j'ay trouvé des resources dans la reception cordiale qu'on m'i a fait, et dans la gaiêté de cette aimable famille; nous etions dixsept a table sans autres etrangers que ceux que j'ai mené avec moi. Les enfants de Monsieur de Boisy sont tres aimable et bien elevés; Lady Carmarthen qui les a vue poura en rendre compte a votre Altesse Royale; nous avons apris avec le plus sensible plaisir la naissance du fils du Prince Charle[2]. Je vous felicite Monseigneur de votre nouveau cousin; cet evenement doit faire bien du plaisir a la Reine[3]. Pensez quelque fois aux absens, Monseigneur, et daigné croire qu'on ne peut rien ajouter a l'attachement sinsere et au profond respect avec lequ'el j'ay l'honneur d'être, Monseigneur [etc.]. (41746–7)

Geneva, 10 8bre [Oct.] 1774

J'ay bien des excuses a vous faire Messeigneurs d'avoir tardé si longtems a remercier vos Altesses Royales des jolies lettres dont elles mont honorée. La vie retiré que je mene ici ne me fournit aucun matiere qui

1. Lady Carmarthen.

2. Queen Charlotte's brother, Prince Charles of Mecklenburg-Strelitz (1741–1816), who succeeded as Duke in 1794, married (1768) Frederica (1752–82), daughter of the Landgrave of Hesse-Darmstadt. Their fifth child, Frederick, was born on 1 September 1774, but died in November.

3. Queen Charlotte.

auroit pu leurs servir d'amusement, et je craignois de les importuner avec les steriles exspressions de ma reconnoissance, j'ay trop de vanite pour avoir entierement caché l'honneur d'une telle corespondence et n'ai pu m'empecher de montrer des lettres dont j'admirai le stile et l'ecriture; vous en avez tout l'honneur, Messeigneurs, tous ceux qui les ont vu se sont recrié sur des talens superieurs a l'age de l'un et de l'autre Prince, enfin, Messeigneurs, vous avez deja des admirateurs et des partisans dans un pais ou le merite de vos Altesses Royales n'est connu que par le raport.

Nous nous preparons serieusement a partir d'ici dans le courant de la semaine prochaine, nous feront de bien petites journeés au moins au commencement, je crois que nous metront neuf jours de voyage pour arriver a Montpellier sans compter le sejour a Lyon; Je ne dis rien de Milord comme je scais qu'il a l'honneur d'ecrire au Prince de Galles lui même; je me flatte d'avoir le plaisir de voir Mademoiselle Schwellenberg[1] ici avant notre depart, et que nous la possederont quelque tems a Montpellier cet hiver tel etoit son plan du moins la deniere fois que je l'ai vu en attandant j'ai les mellieures nouvelles de sa santé comme les Etats du Languedoc s'assemblent a Montpellier le mois qui vient ils attireront quantité de noblesse, la nouvauté de la scene pourra peut-etre donner lieu a quelque evenement assez amusent pour en entretenir les Princes je les suplie en attandant d'etre persuader de l'attachement sincere et du profond respect avec lequel j'ay l'honneur d'etre, Messeigneurs [etc.]. (41750–1)

17   THE EARL OF HOLDERNESSE TO THE PRINCE OF WALES
AND PRINCE FREDERICK

Geneva, 2 Nov. 1774
As I am now in hopes of being able to maintain a regular correspondence with my dear Princes I wish it not to have to take too serious a cast, that my letters may not always appear to come from a censor of small blemishes (for no black spots have hitherto appeared) but from one who, if in duty he is sometimes obliged to find fault, wishes at the same time to contribute to your Royal Highnesses reasonable amusement. I shall be happy if my letters can furnish a moment's pleasant avocation from essential study.

I have just been reading over again all the productions of my dear

1. 'Mrs.' Schwellenberg was the Queen's Keeper of the Robes. She 'had been with the Queen from her infancy'. She 'was a shrewd, ambitious woman'. She styled herself Madame, 'as a distinction from her companion', though she was unmarried (Mrs. Papendiek, *Court and Private Life in the time of Queen Charlotte*, i.14). Fanny Burney thought her disagreeable and found her very difficult to work with.

16

Princes since I left them, and am much delighted to find in course of date a visible improvement in their compositions. I say nothing of the tender feelings the expressions of their kindness excite in my mind; if they could look into my heart they would find gratitude and dutifull affection too deeply impressed there to be ever effaced.

I hear of their accomplishments from many quarters, but should be cautious of too hasty a beleif of what I so ardently wish, were not those pleasing accounts confirmed from those who, by a daily intercourse and anxious observance, are the most competant judges, and who, I am sure, would not deceive me. But above all I have the highest authority, the impartial, tho' indulgent sanction of a parent who founds his judgement upon truth and reason, nor suffers his fondness for his dear aimable children to mislead his understanding. I have too good an opinion of the hearts and heads of the dear Princes to fear their knowing these commendations or that they can have any other effect than to stimulate their desire to deserve them.

I adress this letter to both Princes. My future ones shall be adressed to each in particular, to *one* at a time, and I beg that *both* would not for the future give themselves the trouble of writing by the same post. I will also avoid professions, as they cannot but be convinced of the affectionate love and faithfull attachment of their ever faithfull Holdernesse. (41748)

18 LETTERS FROM THE EARL OF HOLDERNESSE TO THE PRINCE OF WALES

Geneva, 10 Nov. 1774
Nothing is more striking than the contrast between the appearance of the little territory of Geneva, and that of their great neighbours, France and Savoy. The first has an air of ease, happiness and plenty, the second that of poverty & wretchedness. On the one the buildings are in repair, the fields cultivated with industry, the people well cloathed, neat and employed; on the other the inhabitants naked, dirty & idle, the villages in ruins, the lands neglected. Such, my dearest Prince, are the effects of a free or an arbitrary government. In my short airings round Geneva I have had frequent occasion for this remark; it struck me more forcibly in my short journey of about fourteen miles to Boisy. Your Royal Highnesses eye has never yet contemplated the misery which a great part of the human species endure; under the King's mild and happy government everyone around you breaths affluence, and if some of my deluded countrymen are discontented with their lot, they should come abroad to judge by comparison of their own felicity that would be compleat if they knew how to enjoy it.

But à propos de Boisy; I was delighted with my expedition, and tho'
I was unfortunate in the weather, which prevented me from stirring
abroad, I was charmed with the cordiality of my reception & with the
freindly harmony of a numerous family of different age and sex;
the chearfull happiness that arises from virtue and innocence, and the
chearfull practise of every moral and religious duty is visible in that
blessed society. I never met with more aimable people, or that enjoy
affluence in a more reasonable manner; the poor for many miles around
feel the effects of their charity. Your heart is too good, my dearest
Prince, not to partake the satisfaction I felt in this pleasing scene, and I
will not at present draw your attention from it.

I omitt the formal close of a letter.   (41749)

Montpellier, 9 Dec. 1774

Upon my arrival here I found myself honoured with a letter of the 17th
Novr. from my aimable Prince of Wales, and was particularly flattered
with the close of it, and shall make it the study of my life to deserve the
very honourable appellation of his Royal Highness's *freind*.

I found by the last letter to Lady H[oldernesse] the Prince was
inspired with caution upon the report that the late Pope[1] came to an
untimely end by poison. I know but one person of whom the Prince
should be diffident upon that account; I mean *George Prince of Wales*,
who, by giving a loose to his appetite, may be his own enemy and hurt
an excellent constitution by *slow poison*. Do not therefore, dear Prince,
look with an evil eye upon those who preach moderation in your diet.

I cannot name a virtue that does not bring your royal father to my
mind. Abstinence is one among the many that adorn his Majesty; equally
master of his passions and his appetites, he enjoys the greatest of all
blessings, *mens sana in corpore sano*. In this point I wish the Prince may
rival the King.

But there is another species of poison against which the Prince cannot
be too much upon his guard & which will require all his attention and
caution. I mean that most deadly of all, which is poured in at the ear,
and is the more dangerous as it is pleasing in the first sensation, tho'
followed by ruin & destruction; I need not explain myself farther at
present. The Prince's sagacity will tell him what I allude to, and his

1. Lorenzo Ganganelli, Clement XIV (1705–74), Pope since 1769; famous for his dissolution
of the Jesuit Order in 1773. The poisoning story was widely believed, in spite of the testimony
of his physician and his confessor. The Prince wrote to Lady Holdernesse: '. . . Papa m'a dit
l'état dans lequel on avoit trouvé le corps du Pape, cela m'a fait d'abord faire la reflexion que
les Princes devroient toujours prendre garde a ce qu'ils font et avoir une conscience nette,
pour partir pour l'autre monde, quand il plaira a notre Seigneur de les appeller . . .' (Add.
MSS. 33132, f.32).

18

good sense will prevent him from calling those who shall make the attempt *his freinds*. This is one of the prayers of his faithfull Holdernesse. (41752)

19 THE COUNTESS OF HOLDERNESSE TO THE PRINCE OF WALES AND PRINCE FREDERICK

Montpellier, 13 Jan. 1775

Si j'avois suivi mon inclination Messeigneurs, il y a longtems que j'aurais remercié vos Altesses Royales de l'honneur de leur correspondence[1]; mais je craignois d'empieter sur des moments precieux remplis par l'ettudes ou les plaisirs; Milord est sensiblement touché de tout ce que leurs lettres contiennent d'obligeant pour lui, et leur bonté augmente son impatience de les revoir; nous ne pouvont l'un et l'autre leurs etre plus attachés en 1775 que nous ne l'etions deja precedament, la saison me permet pourtant de renouveller nos voeux pour leur bonheur et prosperité, et nous esperons d'etre a même de contribuer un peu plus a leur amusement a l'avenir que nous n'avons pu faire par le passé.

Depuis la separation des Etats notre facon de vivre retombe presque dans l'unison de celui de Geneve, nous gardons il est vrai Monsieur et Madame de Perigord[2], qui attendent les ordres de la cour pour le retablissement de l'ancien Parlement de Toulouse, mais la representation qu'exige leur Etat est cause qu'on ne les voit que dans une cohue de monde presque aussi nombreuse que les assemblés de la Duchesse de Northumberland[3], Je fais parmis les Angloises une petite parti de Loo de tems en tems, ce qui ne derange pas nos heures comme elles sont tout valetudinaires, nos promenades jusqu'ici ont eté bornées aux portes de la ville, a l'exception d'une petite excursion a *cette*, dont Milord me dit qu'il rend compte a Monseigneur le Prince Frederick; mes expeditions vont s'alonger au moyen d'une nouvelle monture (car je vais devenir *cavaliere*) c'est sur une bonne Bourique Messeigneurs que je

1. The Prince had informed Lady Holdernesse on 30 December 1774: '... My Lord Mahon a épousé Lady Esther Pitt. My Lord Chatham n'étant pas assez riche pour lui donner une dot, sa mere y a supplié en parties en lui donnant tous ses bijoux, et My Lord Temple, son oncle, lui a fait present de mille guinées pour s'habiller' (Add. MSS. 33132. f.36).

2. For him see *Lady Bessborough and her Family Circle*, ed. Lord Bessborough and A. Aspinall, pp. 24-5, 27.

3. Hugh, Duke of Northumberland (1714-86), who succeeded his father-in-law as Earl of Northumberland in 1750, and who was created Duke in 1766, married (1740) Elizabeth (1716-76), daughter of the 7th Duke of Somerset. She succeeded her father as Baroness Percy in 1750, and was a Lady of the Bedchamber to the Queen from 1761 to 1770. He was a Lord of the Bedchamber, 1753-63; Lord Chamberlain to the Queen, 1762-68, and Lord-Lieutenant of Ireland, 1763-5.

compte me promener, et je suppose que Milord le Baton a la main maccompagnera a pied en imitation des anciens patriarches; peut-etre que vos Altesses Royales gattées par l'habitude de monter a cheval n'auront pas pour mon aimable animal tout le respect qui lui est du, et quelles riront de l'idée de ses oreilles; voila ce que c'est que le prejugé. Miladi Clermont[1] s'en sent tout les jours et personne n'y trouve a redire; je vous defie pourtant Messeigneurs d'en rire plus que n'en ay fait moy même. Miladi Clermont c'est mise an Amazone pour faire honneur a sa bête, moy par economie. Je me contente de mon deshabillé ordinaire avec un grand bonnet noir pour me garantir du soleil. Voila un petit detail qui mettra j'espere vos Altesses Royales de bonne humeur.

Et pour ne pas l'interompre par d'autre propos, je me hâte de les assurer du profond respect avec lequel j'ai l'honneur d'etre [etc.]. (41753-4)

20   LETTERS FROM THE EARL OF HOLDERNESSE TO THE PRINCE OF WALES AND PRINCE FREDERICK

Montpellier, 10 Feb. 1775
If I am again in arrear of correspondence with the dear Princes it is my misfortune not my fault. Frequent returns of nervous giddiness has made writing impossible at times, and as my phisical advisers abridge me in the use of pen & ink even when I am most free from my disorder, I hope their Royal Highnesses will jointly accept my thanks for their last kind letters.

1. Lady Clermont (*c*.1734-1820) was the daughter of Col. John Murray, M.P. for Co. Monaghan. In 1752 she married William Henry Fortescue (1722-1806), who was created Baron Clermont [I.] in 1770 and Earl of Clermont [I.] in 1777. He was on very friendly terms with the Prince of Wales and Fox. According to Wraxall the Countess 'was formed, like her lord, for the atmosphere of a Court. Endowed with no superior talents, though possessing a cultivated mind; her manners subdued, yet exempt from servility; with an agreeable person, but destitute of beauty; uniting consummate knowledge of the world to constitutional serenity of temper.... I have scarcely ever known a man more fitted for a companion of Kings and Queens than was Lord Clermont. . . . Such was his passion for the turf that when menaced by his father to be disinherited if he did not quit Newmarket, he refused, preferring rather to incur the severest effects of paternal indignation than to renounce his favourite amusement. His understanding was of the common order, but though his whole life had been passed in the sports of the field or among jockeys, yet he wanted not refinement.... Inhabiting as Lord Clermont did a splendid house in Berkeley Square, maintaining a table at once delicate and luxurious, choice in the selection of his wines and in every accompaniment of taste or opulence, the Prince of Wales used frequently to make one of the number of his guests. He enjoyed, indeed, the privilege of sending at his pleasure to Lord Clermont, of commanding a dinner and naming the persons to be invited of both sexes, a permission of which H.R. H often availed himself' (*Wraxall*, v.25-8).

20

Mor de Périgord's military command is lately extended beyond the limits of this province. The distemper amongst the cattle having made great ravages in Guienne, every possible precaution is taking to prevent the infection from spreading. Lines of troops are formed, & some regiments of infantry are moving southward to reinforce those already in these parts, and Mor de Périgord commands the whole. He leaves us on Monday to make a progress into Guienne, and it is supposed that chemin faisant he will re-establish the old Parliament of Toulouse. Madame de Périgord remains here.

The marriage of the Prince of Piedmont with *Madame*, the King of France's sister, is said to be settled.[1] Nature has not been bountifull to this Princess in her outward form, but I am told that her mind, improved by a most excellent education, make her ample amends for want of figure.

Pardon, my dear Princes, this uninteresting letter. The recluse uniform life I lead furnishes me with no subject of amusement, and I think it will be no news to your Royal Highnesses to hear that I ever am [etc.]. (41755)

Montpellier, 14 Apr. 1775
As I now count the remaining time of my residence here by days and no longer by months and weeks, I try to sum up the beauties and defects of this place and its environs; your Royal Highnesses will perhaps not dislike to know the result of my observations.

The town itself is far from being an handsome one, the scite of it very uneven, the descents and risings inconveniently rapid, the streets narrow and crooked, few that can admitt a carriage and scarce any where two can pass without difficulty, yet it contains an innumerable quantity of fine houses built with an excellent grey coloured stone with decent tho' not elegant fronts, but within they are ill disposed, dark and melancholy; there is scarce such a thing as a garden, a little yard with four chesnut trees behind our house is called one, and is admired, indeed we rejoice at the sight of a few green leaves which are not very common, and render my Lady's apartment pleasant. There are no publick buildings worth notice within the walls. Your Royal Highnesses are already acquainted with the *Peyron* and the aqueduct, a most magnificent as well as usefull work; here we constantly take our morning and evening walk and discover three kingdoms and the sea, the view is indeed wonderfully fine, the country all round interspersed with villages and

1. Princess Clotilda (1759–1802) married Charles Emmanuel, Prince of Piedmont and later (1796) King of Sardinia (1751–1819), on 6 September 1775. He was the son of King Victor Amadeus III (1726–96).

country houses, fine gentle risings in the fore ground, larger hills at a distance, and the mountains of the Cevennes, the Alps and the Pyrenees to bound the prospect; but it wants our verdure to make it pleasing. I am always surprized, never delighted with the scene before me. Want of trees, the colour of the soil and of the buildings cause a glare of light insuportable to the eyes; the heat of sun is scalding, the wind commonly boisterous, often cold, raises a dust that choaks and blinds one; we have scarce had a drop of rain these three months. As to the productions of the earth we can see the corn in full ear, the hay harvest begun etc. and the trees in all their beauty, if the olive and mulberry deserve the apellation. Perhaps I should be more partial to the place were I less impatient to return to dear England. A cordial welcome from my aimable Princes is the fond hope of their ever devoted Holdernesse. (41756)

21 THE EARL OF HOLDERNESSE TO THE PRINCE OF WALES

Lyons, 30 Apr. 1775

Upon my arrival here I found myself honoured with my dear Prince's letter of the 14th inst. by which I find he has misaprehended the meaning of one of mine to Mr. Smelt. I never meant, in my criticism upon the confidential correspondence of both brothers, to give a preference to the compositions of either, but to shew that the stamp of *character* appeared in their letters; that one should *make sail*, the other *increase his ballast*. My observation went farther than a remark upon stile in wh. both are so visibly improved as to give me infinite satisfaction. But I am delighted beyond measure at the manner in which your Royal Highness receives what appeared to you a reproof. Goodness of heart superior to all elegance is evident in every expression upon that subject, & leaves me no room to doubt you will be that aimable Prince my fond heart wishes to see you. (41757)

22 THE EARL OF HOLDERNESSE TO THE PRINCE OF WALES
AND PRINCE FREDERICK

Lyons, 4 May 1775

Monsieur de Cordon[1] and his lady passed thro' this city the 2d inst. & did us the honor to sup at our *auberge*. He made me very happy with the

1. The Sardinian Minister in London. His chapel in Lincoln's Inn Fields was gutted during the Gordon riots in 1780. 'On pense ou plutot on se flatte que M. Cordon reviendra ici', wrote the Queen on 7 October 1783 (to Budé), but he was succeeded in October 1784 by the Chevalier de Pollon.

account he gave me of his accidental interview with my dear Princes, and sung the praises of their politeness & affability in a manner that does them credit, and was a lucky omen for the following day, the anniversary of one of the most important epochs of my life.[1] You, my dearest Princes, will make it the happiest; you will improve in merit with approaching manhood & give me room to bless the hour when I devoted myself to your service.

Prince Frederick will allow me to return my thanks for his obliging letter of the 21st April, which gave me infinite pleasure, tho' I had some difficulty to reconcile the date with the account it brings that their Majesties were to pass the CHRISTMASS holidays at Kew, but whether Christmass or Easter was to be celebrated, I rejoice to find the Princes were allowed to partake the pleasures of the festival. The next set of red letter days, I hope, will bring me into the royal presence, and enable me to tell the dear Princes *part* of what I feel, for no words can express the extent of affection, duty, & attachment of their ever faithfull Holdernesse. (41758)

23 THE EARL OF HOLDERNESSE TO THE PRINCE OF WALES

Hornby Castle, 17 Oct. 1775

I hope I need not tell my dear Prince the sincere pleasure every kind mark of his remembrance gives me. Your Royal Highness knows my devoted attachment too well to doubt of it. Our society here has lately been augmented & embelished by Mrs. Lockhart's appearance amongst us. Her visit indeed was short, but long enough to leave the most favorable impressions upon those amongst us who did not know her before. She left us this morning.

Fishing has been a fashionable amusement with our ladies. My new waters furnish an immense quantity of perch that bite so freely, they come home loaded with spoil. The weather has favoured their sport, and they are so eager at it that I am forced to ring the alarm bell (an antique peice) to summon them home at dinner time. I should have left them with regret upon any other occasion than that of offering my respects to the Prince of Wales. If the weather continues fine tomorrow I think of a jaunt to view Middleham Castle in Wensleydale.[2] I hold this place under a grant from the Crown. It has been in the two branches of the family above five centuries; I think the first date is in 1263. It had a park and was a place of some note, but destroyed in the last civil wars; 'tis now only a ruin.

1. See his letter of 3 May 1772 (No. 5).

2. Like his predecessors he was Constable of Middleham Castle.

On Thursday morning the fox-hunters have their rendez-vous here. I shall set out a breakfast in the hall, with a jug of amber and a brown loaf, but I fear the modern sportsmen will preferr tea, coffee and chocolate. I beleive the meeting will be numerous. Tho' I never was fond of the sport myself I always loved the gaiety of the outset and can speculate upon the enthusiasm with which the real adepts follow it. I shall accompany them in a carriage to the cover.

We leave this place on Saturday & I hope to attend the dear Princes on Tuesday. I have no doubt of finding them in their usual bloom of health, or of meeting that reception from them which is the reward expected for all the anxiety of their ever faithful Holdernesse.[1] (41759–60)

24   THE PRINCE OF WALES TO THE KING

1 p.m. 24 June 1776
I take the liberty of sending these translations to yr. Majesty, as they met with yr. approbation this morning in the foul copy[2], and permit me Sir, at the same time to thank yr. Majesty for yr. most gracious present of books. (41761)

25   THE PRINCE OF WALES AND PRINCE FREDERICK TO THE KING

Kew, 11 a.m., Wednesday[3]
I hope your Majesty will have the goodness to excuse our presenting to you this trifle, as a small mark of our sincere affection & duty. We are your Majesty's most dutiful sons. (41764)

1. Holdernesse resigned his appointment in May 1776. A few days later, Lieutenant-Colonel George Hotham succeeded Smelt as Sub-Governor, and the Rev. William Arnold succeeded Cyril Jackson (later, the famous Dean of Christ Church) as Sub-Preceptor to their Royal Highnesses. 'No reason was assigned for so great a revolution', wrote Horace Walpole. 'All that got out at first was, that Lord Holdernesse had been quarrelling with Jackson for three months, and had said he could not serve with him' (Walpole, *Last Journals*, i.555). 'On his return [from France, in the autumn of 1775] he found great prejudices had been instilled into the mind of his pupils . . . against him; and it had grown so bad that from last November [1775] they had treated his authority with contempt, and often ridiculed him to his face. This he imputed to Jackson' (*Ibid.*, i.556). 'Lord Hertford told me besides that Salgas, son of a French refugee, and one of the Prince's tutors, insisted on retiring too, from the ungovernable temper of the Prince. All his servants, even to valets de chambre, were changed' (*Ibid.*, i.558).
    This is Holdernesse's last letter. He died on 16 May 1778.

2. There is little point in reproducing a translation from the Classics.

3. Endorsed, 'Supposed 1776'. It seems unlikely that the 'trifle' was a birthday present in 1776, for 4 June that year was a Tuesday.

Portsmouth Dockyard, 3 May 1778

My dear sons, for I look on this letter as addressed to both of you, I trust the account of [the] Queen's and of my safe arrival at this place will give you pleasure. We accomplished our journey[1] in seven hours, which is half an hour less than when I visited my friends here five years ago.[2] From the rising of sun untill near Petersfield the day was warm, and neither dust nor dirt to be found; the road from Epsom to Guilford is extremely beautiful. I was received with every demonstration of joy at this place, to which at Godalmin was joined a certain degree of affection that a feeling heart is sensible of but cannot find terms to express. The rain became so violent on Portsea Down that Spithead could not be seen. On quitting the carriage I instantly took every step necessary to quicken the sailing of part of the fleet, and trust my directions will expedite the service. From the change of wind we hourly expect the Ruby and America, each of 64 guns, and by the order sent for putting 100 men out of the Medway into the Robust, 74 guns, may arrive on Monday from the same place. By the account arrived from Sir John Lindsay[3] there is a well grounded hope the Victory may join us on Wednesday, which has made me resolve to pass that day here.[4]

By this sketch you will see I have not been idle; before three I had the eight Admirals whose flags are flying at Spithead, the Governor of this garrison[5], the Commissioner[6], the five gentlemen who attend the Queen and me, Lord Sandwich[7] and Lord Amherst[8] to dinner. After a glass of

1. From London. They left the Queen's House at 6 A.M.

2. See Horace Walpole's *Last Journals*, i.239-40.

3. Rear-Admiral Sir John Lindsay (1737–88) took part in the French War of 1778–83. He was appointed Commander-in-Chief in the Mediterranean, 1783, and Rear-Admiral, 1787. He was Lord Mansfield's nephew.

4. The King had inspected the *Victory* (later famous, of course, as Nelson's flagship) on 26 and 27 April at Chatham.

5. Lieutenant-General Robert Monckton (1726–82). Gazetted Governor, 20 April 1778. M.P. for Portsmouth, 1778–82.

6. Samuel, 1st Viscount Hood (1724–1816). Lieutenant, 1746; Captain, 1756; Rear-Admiral, 1780; Vice-Admiral, 1787; Admiral, 1794. He had been Commissioner of the Navy at Portsmouth since January 1778, and was created a Baronet, 20 May 1778, on the occasion of the King's visit. For his share in the victory of Rodney over the French fleet under De Grasse, off Dominica, on 12 August 1782, he was created Baron Hood [I.]. He was M.P. for Westminster, 1784–8; for Reigate, 1789–90, and for Westminster, again, 1790–6. Commander-in-Chief at Portsmouth, 1786–9, and 1791–3; a Lord of the Admiralty, 1788–95; Commander-in-Chief in the Mediterranean, 1793–4. Created Viscount Hood [G.B.], 1796.

7. John, 4th Earl of Sandwich (1718–92), First Lord of the Admiralty, 1771–82, after having held many offices from 1744.

8. Jeffrey, Baron Amherst (1717–97). Fought in America in the Seven Years War, and was Commander-in-Chief 1778–82, and 1793–5. Peerage, 1776. Field-Marshal, 1796.

champaign to the success of the fleet, I retired and drank my coffee with the Queen, and went to the top of the house. The sun was shining and with my glass saw the fleet at Spithead. After giving the gentlemen a little time for the bad custom of toasting, I sent them word five was a good hour to visit the Yard. I observed the ships building, those fitting for sea and those repairing, saw the new ships, and about five of acres [sic] of well-paved ground that when last here was a marsh over flowed each tide, now well stowed with timber for the use of this yard. I also saw the smiths work and visited the boat builder's branch. I should not forget to mention that shipwrights as usual sang the two songs they performed the last time; the one of which was of their own composition, and without the partiality I have for them, really a better style of musick than any patronized by *His Honour*. As I left them they sang 'Briton, strike home', which instantly stopped me, and was glad to see a company of at least 3,000 seem by their countenances equally with me zealous on this occasion.

This morning I am going quietly with L[ieutenan]t G[eneral] Carpenter[1] whilst all the rest are in their beds, to walk over the Yard, which is in a perfect state of solitude. At ten the Queen and I go to the Governor's chappel to hear divine service, after which I shall receive the Corporation and have a Levée. The evening I hope will be dry; if that be the case I shall conduct the Queen on board of the Sandwich, 90 guns, which lyes not twenty yards from shore in the harbour, by which means she will see a ship of the second rate without any trouble.

I cannot conclude without just adding that I know very well I have a difficult time to steer the helm, but the confidence I place in Divine Providence, the attachment I have for this my native country, and the love I bear my children, are insentatives sufficient to make me strain every nerf to do my duty to the best of my abilities. My dear sons, place ever your chief care on obeying the commands of your Creator. Every hour will shew you that no comfort can be attained without that. Act uprightly and shew the anxious care I have had of you has not been misspent, and you will ever find me not only an affectionate father but a sincere friend. May Heaven shower the choicest blessings on you both and on the rest of my children is the first and last prayer of each day of him who will ever remain, my dear sons, your most affectionate father.

1. An Equerry since 1761; Clerk-Marshal of the Mews, 1771 (1713-88). 'A particular favourite of the King' (Horace Walpole's *Last Journals*, ii.318). He drowned himself in the Serpentine on 8 March 1788.

P.S. The D. of Montague[1], the Bishop[2], L.Col. Hotham[3] and Mr. Arnold[4] may be curious to hear how we are in this place. You may read this unto them and add to the Duke that anything that marks a feeling heart cannot but be acceptable to him; and to the excellent Bishop, that I did not want to encroach on his line in those overflowings of my heart concerning Divine Providence. 'Tis the religion of the heart I only touched upon. Revelation, the greatest of all blessings, I am certain will be masterly explained by him to you, who possesses with not less superiority every qualification that deserve the epithets of religious, moral, learned and good man.[5] (41765–6)

27 THE PRINCE OF WALES TO THE KING, AND THE REPLY

Queen's House, 4 May 1778
It is impossible for me to express the feelings of my heart and the sentiments of gratitude with which I was filled, upon receiving your Majesty's most gracious and affectionate letter. I flatter myself that by the pains I shall take in imbibing your Majesty's admirable principles of virtue and religion, and in following your excellent advice of looking up at all times

1. George Brudenell [Montagu], Duke of Montagu (1766) and 4th Earl of Cardigan (1732), (1712–90). Governor to the Prince of Wales and Prince Frederick, 1776–80; Master of the Horse, 1780–90. His 'formal coldness of character' was said to render him 'uncommonly well fitted' for his post as Governor.

2. Richard Hurd (1720–1808). Bishop of Lichfield and Coventry, 1774–81; Bishop of Worcester, 1781–1808. In June 1776 he was appointed Preceptor to the Prince of Wales. According to Horace Walpole, he 'had acquired a great name by several works of slender merit, was a gentle, plausible man, affecting a singular decorum that endeared him highly to devout old ladies' (*Last Journals*, i.555).

3. George Hotham (1741–1806), fifth son of Sir Beaumont Hotham, Bart.; Sub-Governor to the Prince of Wales and Prince Frederick, June 1776; Treasurer and Secretary to the Prince of Wales, December 1780.

4. *See* No. 23n. 'Poor Arnold', wrote Prince Frederick from Hanover on 3 January 1783, 'little did I think the last time I saw him that he would have been in so dreadful a situation.' He had become mentally deranged. He died at Leicester in the summer of 1802.

5. Ramus, one of the King's servants, was sent down to Portsmouth in advance of the Royal family, to make preparations for their visit. He returned to London on 24 April, and, in a letter to the King, the Queen thus referred to his activities: 'He finds the house at Portsmouth extreamly neat. All rooms furnish with "very elegant cutton beds" [*sic*]; this is his expression, but no bedding for the servants' beds. The kitchen so very indifferently stokd with furniture that the greatest part must be taken from hence. Ramus also wishes to know whether the *epargne* from Windsor is to be sent or not, there being no wont of a desert; he is of opinion that would make the table look better. . . . Portsmouth town was so full on Thursday night that no lodgins could be found, and a great many of the ladies were obliged to set up all night; the scarcity of post horses immense. It was owing to this that Ramus came so late [at 10 P.M.], for he says the poor beasts are so fatigued, nobody can't get along with them.' (36349–51)

to our great Creator, you will not find all the care and trouble you have been at in my education misspent, but that on the contrary you will find me hereafter not only worthy of your affection as a child but of your esteem as a friend. It shall always be the principal object of my life to deserve your Majesty's expressions of tenderness and affection, and to do all in my power to contribute to the happiness you receive from the most excellent of women.[1]

I am always happy to hear of the loyalty and attachment of the people to your Majesty, as it convinces me that their sentiments agree so perfectly with those of, Sir, your Majesty's most affectionate, most humble and most devoted son and subject.

P.S. Pray, Sir, be so gracious as to present my duty and love to the Queen.[2] (41769)

THE KING'S REPLY

Portsmouth Dockyard, 6 May 1778
Nothing could have given me more real joy than the receipt of your letter filled with sentiments of affection to the Queen and me, but above all as it contains the only true foundation on which I can depend on the truth of that or any other good in you. I mean on your constantly having before your eyes that everything we have, indeed, that we exist an instant, is the effect of an All-wise, Gracious and Beneficent Creator, to whom every secret thought as well as action is known. Keep that always in your mind, and you will find strength to meet all the vicissitudes of this life and an ardour from principle to do your best whilst it pleaseth Him to let you remain in this world.

I flatter myself things begin to bear a more favorable aspect. I have declared I will not move till the part of the fleet under Rear Admiral

1. In all his letters to the King the glaring contrast between promise and performance is notable.

2. Prince Frederick too replied to the King's letter—on the 4th: 'Words can hardly express what my feelings were when we received your Majesty's most gracious letter. It was an honour we could not have expected, particularly at a time when you are so much employed by the publick affairs. I am sure for my part that it will always be my greatest ambition to deserve your Majesty's and the Queen's affection. This instance of your singular goodness towards us, Sir, requires our most dutifull acknowledgements. I had no doubt that the people, wherever you went, would testify their joy at the view of their Sovereign, and I am sure that the whole nation must perfectly agree with these in their sense of your paternal care of the State.

'I would not have dared to intrude upon your Majesty's leisure had not I thought it incumbent upon me to assure you Sir, that I am, and ever will be [etc.].' (43360)

Parker[1] is reported ready in every particular to sail; and should the wind be fair as late as Friday I will remain to see him get out, but should that not I shall certainly return on Saturday to town.[2]   (41770)

28   THE QUEEN TO THE PRINCE OF WALES

Portsmouth, 6 May 1778

Mon tres cher fils: Par negligence de la poste j'ai risqui de perdre votre chere lettre a la fin je priai Lord Carmarthen d'envoyer quelqun pour demander si par hazard le maitre de poste n'avoit point reçue des lettres pour lui, & heureusement j'avoit bien jugé & a neuf heure ce matin la lettre me fut porté. Je vous en fait dabord mes remerciments & vous professe que vos lettres sont en verité le seul amusement dont je joui ici.

Pour vous dire quelque chose qui puisse vous faire plaisir je me hate a vous mander que votre lettre & celle de Frederick ont pris un très grand effet sur le Roi; il en est extrèmement *content* & me dit '*I am proud of my two boys' letters*'. Aussi a t'il raison & je vous conseille en amie de continue dans ses sentiments dont vous faites profession dans votre letter au Roi & vous vous en trouverez bien pour toute votre vie ces deux lettres je comte employer pour vous procurez ses amusements doux. Nous parlames avant mon depart, je me flatte de quelque succès & je me trouverai heureuse si je pourroit etre regardée par vous comme l'instrument de vos plaisirs, il n'y est pour le moins personne qui souhaite plus de vous en procurez que moi.

Le Roi s'employe toujours a faite les ouvrages necessaires pour les differents flottes quils doivent partir, il marche pour le moins huit heures par jour & s'amuse bien avec ses compaignie, quant a mon individue je me trouve vis a vis de Lady Egremont[3] & nous sommes egalement ennuyé de nos personnes & j'avoue que de me trouver dans une maison remplie de companie dont je n'ose point pas profiter me rend tout a fait meloncolie & je croi qu'un outre séjour a Portsmouth me tuerai car j'ai l'ame trop sociable pour vivre comme je fait. Le vent ne nous favorise point de tout, il n'ya personne qui est plus interessé

1. Sir Hyde Parker (1714–82). Lieutenant, 1745; Captain, 1748; Rear-Admiral, January 1778; Vice-Admiral, September 1780; 5th Baronet, 1782. He was second-in-command in the squadron which, under Vice-Admiral Byron, sailed for America in the summer of this year.

2. Their Majesties left Portsmouth at 8.30 A.M. on Saturday the 9th, and reached London at 4.30 P.M.

3. Charles, 2nd Earl of Egremont (1710–63), married (1751) Alicia Maria (*d*.1794), daughter of George, 2nd Baron Carpenter. In 1761 she was appointed one of the Ladies of the Bedchamber. In 1767 she married Hans Moritz, Count von Bruhl, of Saxony.

29

dans ce changement du vent que moi car je sçai qu'alors je doit retourner chez vous ou je souhaite d'etre, depuis hier au matin deux vaissaux ont due faire voila pour joindre Admiral Byron[1] a Plymouth, mais cela ne peut point s'executer. Je ne peut me loué assez de attentions de Lord Sandwich, tous ce que depend de lui pour rendre mon sejour agrèable, il le fait, il me soigné dans le yacht & ma expliqué tous ce qui me fait necessaire a scavoir, domage qu'il avoit a faire a une guarante. Les habitants de Portsmouth paroissent etre fort content de revoir leur Souverain parmie eux; cest an pays loyale & leur joi se laisse sentir mais pas exprimer cetoit de même par tout ou le Roi a passé & je croi quon le trouveroit ainsi dans tout le royaume si le Roi y voulut allé; car j'ai toujours jugé le peuple de ce royaume attaché au Souverain, honnette & verteux en general, & il mest absolument impossible de juger toute une nation apres la conduite de quelquez seigneurs mal intentionnees.

Je vous prie de faire mes compliments au Duc[2], le Colonel Hotham & le reste de vous messieurs, continuez moi votre chère amitie, soyez persuade de la mienne & croyez moi jusqua la mort, votre tres affectionné amie & fidelle mère. (36355–6)

29   THE PRINCE OF WALES TO THE KING, AND THE REPLY

Kew, 12 June 1780
Dear Sir, I think it my duty to acquaint your Majesty yt. upon our return through Hyde Park, the Duke & Duchess of Cumberland[3] passed us in

1. The Hon. John Byron (1723–86), second son of the 4th Lord Byron, and grandfather of the poet. Captain, 1746; Rear-Admiral, 1775; Vice-Admiral, 1780. He was the last survivor of the crew of the *Wager*, one of Anson's squadron, shipwrecked on an uninhabited island in the South Seas (not more than ten of the crew of 160 lived to return to England).

2. The Duke of Montagu.

3. Henry Frederick, Duke of Cumberland and Strathearn (1745–90), fourth son of Frederick, Prince of Wales, and, therefore, the King's brother. On 2 October 1771 he married a young widow, Mrs. Anne Horton, *née* Luttrell (1743–1808), she being the daughter of Simon, 1st Earl of Carhampton, and he an illegitimate son of the disreputable Colonel Henry Luttrell. She was described as being 'vulgar, noisy, indelicate and intrepid, though not accused of gallantry, one who set modesty and decency at defiance', and it was said that after hearing her talk one should go home and wash one's ears. A thoroughly disreputable man, 'an idiot Prince' (Lady Louisa Stuart), he was for long not received at Court, and his marriage resulted in the passing of the Royal Marriage Act in 1772. 'Cumberland House in Pall Mall,' wrote Wraxall, 'might then be considered as the central point of elegant amusement in the metropolis. . . . A crowd of distinguished persons, male and female, filled the apartments once every week. That the Duke was a very weak man the circumstances attending his unfortunate connection with Lady Grosvenor and his marriage with Mrs. Horton sufficiently attest. . . . The King held her [the Duchess] in great alienation, because he believed that she lent herself to facilitate or to gratify the Prince of Wales's inclinations on some points beyond the limits

their carriage. The Duke alighted, & sending the Duchess forward, joined us and accompanied us through the Park. His Royal Highness expressed that he had been under some embarrassment in what manner to behave on meeting us, but hoped that what he had done was for the best, & said at the same time that if yr. Majesty disapproved of the step he had taken, that you would please to suppose it never had passed. I thought it my duty to acquaint yr. Majesty with what had happened, & shall reserve further particulars till I have the honor of seeing you tomorrow.

P.S. My humble duty attends the Queen.[1]   (41771)

THE KING'S REPLY

[12 June 1780]
The more open you are in your conduct towards me, the more cordial will always be mine in return. Nothing could be more proper than your writing me word of your meeting this day in Hyde Park with the Duke of Cumberland. Your conduct has been most proper; I say nothing of others.

The Queen desires I will make her compliments to you and that you will acquaint Miss Goldsworthy[2] that she is to bring your three sisters at the same hour tomorrow that Mr. Lyte[3] is to bring the three boys. (41772)

of propriety, Carlton and Cumberland Houses communicating behind by the gardens' (iv.321).

When, on 19 January 1787, the Duke heard of the death of Lord Carhampton, his father-in-law, he inquired of the King whether he might not wear mourning 'as an indispensable act of propriety' and be allowed to pay his duty to the King in black. The King replied, rather coldly: 'I have received the Duke of Cumberland's letter. He must be the best judge how to conduct himself on an occasion that does not in the least concern me.'   (54484-5)

1. The Queen wrote to Prince William on 28 July: 'The report of the King's being reconciled to his brothers is true. It seems to give universal satisfaction in public, but makes no difference in our way of living at Windsor. The Duke of Cumberland comes to Court, and walks Sundays upon the Terrace. The Duke of Glocester's bad state of health will not permit him to do either.' And see Horace Walpole's *Last Journals*, ii.313-15.

2. The young Princesses' sub-governess. Mary Hamilton thought her '*most praiseworthy* and indefatigable in the duties of her station, but she wants softness of temper and manner— nor do I think her either qualified by education or birth to be sub-governess to the daughters of a Monarch'.

3. Henry Lyte (*d*.1791) was gazetted Master of the Robes and Privy Purse in the Prince's Household, 29 December 1780, and was appointed the Prince's Treasurer and Secretary in May 1787.

26 June 1780

I hope you will be as glad to hear as I am to inform you, that all of us here are perfectly well.[1] I think seabathing makes us much stronger. I begin now to like it very well. I am now able to jump in by myself, tho' at first I did not relish it much.[2] I shall be happy to hear that you and Frederic are perfectly well, if you can spare me a line. I wish you joy of the good news from America.[3] Mr Bruyeres[4] has told me that he had acquainted Colonel Hotham of the great joy we all felt when we heard of the late happy reconciliation in our family.[5] I dare say you felt the same. Pray give my best love to Frederic and my compliments to the Gentlemen of your Establishment, particularly to the Duke of Montague.

P.S. Mr. Bruyeres desired me to make his most dutiful respects acceptable to both your Royal Highnesses.   (45698)

Seahouses, 8 Aug. 1780

I am very happy to congratulate you upon the return of your birthday, & wish you a great many happy ones. I should have been much more so, if I could have been with you to pay my compliments in person. I am glad to hear that all the family is perfectly well; I suppose you will begin your hunts about the beginning of next month, which I know will give you great pleasure.

I bathe now every day, but I have not been able to make any progress in swimming, for the sea has been extremely rough for more than a week, so much that on Sunday a boat was overset which was carrying a cargo of beer to one of our ships; no lives however were lost, but all the cargo went to the bottom. We have now two vessels, the Surprise cutter, & the Shark sloop, the latter of which is a three-masted one. We are all

1. Prince William wrote to the King on 18 October 1779: 'I have received a letter from my brother Edward in which he tells me that the family have lived very happily at Windsor; but, above all things, I am pleased to find that your Majesties have received more satisfaction from him this summer than you have at any time. I am glad that this has been the case, on another account, for it must have given the General pleasure.' (44604–5)

2. 'All at Eastbourn are well', wrote the Queen on 28 July. 'Edward learns to swim & is delighted with this amusement.'

3. The news of Rodney's victory over the French fleet under De Guichen in the West Indies in April, and the capture of Charleston in May had recently arrived.

4. Prince Edward's Instructor.

5. 'The reconciliation of the King to the Dukes of Gloucester and Cumberland is now made public,' wrote Mary Hamilton in June. 'They were introduced on Tuesday to the Princes and Princesses with the restriction that their Royal Highnesses were not to enquire after the Duchesses of Gloucester and Cumberland. They are to be at the Drawing Room today, and the elder Princes are to meet them.'

King George III and his Family
by Zoffany c. 1770

The Prince of Wales on horseback
by Stubbs 1780

very well, & have received much benefit from the sea air & bathing. The house where I live, having been formerly a horizontal mill, is round; one half gives us a noble view of the sea, the other a fine view of the Downs & meadows. We have been twice to the noble old Castle of Pevensea; it is not more than five miles from our houses. Once we went to HirstMonceaux, a very fine old castle belonging to Mr Hare[1] who has pulled down all but the walls to get materials for building a new house, & indeed it is a great pity.

Pray be so good as to give my love to Frederic as well as to all my sisters and young brothers; with my compliments to his Grace the Duke of Montague & to all the gentlemen with you.

May I beg leave, that you will make my duty acceptable to my uncles, the Dukes of Gloucester[2] & Cumberland.

P.S. Mr Bruyeres desires me to present his most humble respects; he says that he regrets much his not having the opportunity to pay his homage in person to your Royal Highness on the auspicious day which he hopes for a long series of years to come will be kept & blessed by millions. He prays for your health, happiness, & the completion of all your wishes, & begs to offer his most humble respects to Prince Frederic; He says we shall all celebrate the 12th of August. (45699–700)

31   LETTERS FROM THE KING TO THE PRINCE OF WALES, AND A REPLY

Windsor Castle, 14 Aug. 1780

No one feels with more pleasure than I do your nearer approach to manhood, but the parent's joy must be mixed with the anxiety that this period may not be ill spent, as the hour is now come when whatever foundation has been laid must be by application brought to maturity, or every past labour of your instructors will prove abortive.

This has made me think it my duty to state on paper what I trust the goodness of your heart and no want of penetration will make you thoroughly weigh; the contents of this are known to the Queen, whose conduct as a wife as well as mother even malevolence has not dared to mention but in the most respectable terms.

The numberless trials and constant torments I meet with in public

1. Francis Hare-Naylor (1753–1815). Much of his property was sold to pay the debts of his stepmother, and he remained in embarrassed circumstances until his death.

2. William Henry, Duke of Gloucester (1743–1805), third son of Frederick, Prince of Wales, and therefore the King's brother. Major-General in the Army, 1767; Lieutenant-General, 1770; General, 1772; Field-Marshal, 1793. Chancellor of the University of Dublin, 1771–1805. In 1766 he secretly married a widow, Maria, Lady Waldegrave (1736–1807) the illegitimate daughter of Sir Edward Walpole; her mother, Dorothy Clements, had been a milliner's apprentice.

life must certainly affect any man, and more poignantly me, as I have no other wish but to fulfill my various duties. The experience of now near twenty years has convinced me that however long it may please the Almighty to extend my days, yet I have no reason to expect any diminution of my public anxiety. Where am I therefore to turn for comfort but into the bosom of my own family?

As to your mother I can with truth say that in nineteen years I have never had the smallest reason but to thank Heaven for having directed my choice among the Princesses then fit for me to marry, to her; indeed I could not bear up did I not find in her a feeling friend to whom I can unbosom my griefs.

As the eldest of my children, and the one on whom, whenever it shall please Divine Providence to put a period to my existence in this world, the prosperity of my dominions as well as of the rest of my progeny must greatly depend, it is natural that I should be most excessively anxious for your becoming worthy of the station you, according to all human foresight, must fill. Your own good sense must make you feel that you have not made that progress in your studies which, from the ability and assiduity of those placed for that purpose about you, I might have had reason to expect; whilst you have been out of the sight of the world that has been kept under a veil by all those who have cirrounded you, nay your foibles have less been perceived than I could have expected; yet your love of dissipation has for some months been with enough ill nature trumpeted in the public papers, and there are those ready to wound me in the severest place by ripping up every error they may be able to find in you.

God has bequeathed to you enough quickness of conception, whenever you will allow yourself calmly to reflect that you must acknowledge the truth of the position that every one in this world has his peculiar duties to perform, and that the good or bad example set by those in the higher stations must have some effect on the general conduct of those in inferior ones.

You may certainly be of the greatest assistance to me as you advance in life, if you will connect yourself only with those young men who seem to be of worthy characters and to wish to make themselves of utility and ornament to their country. Such a respectable line of conduct would perhaps from interest at first, but at length from example restore this country to its former lustre.

I fear your religious duties are not viewed through that happiest of mediums, a gratitude to the Great Creator, and a resolution to the utmost of your power implicitly to obey His will as conveighed to us in the Scriptures. It is this alone that gives man a well-grounded superiority in merit to the brute creation. No one can entirely escape errors, but those shields will prevent their degenerating into habitual vices.

34

Let it be the constant practice of your life at least once in every day coolly to examine your own conduct, and it will be impossible for your good heart not to check many evils that otherwise must give you many unhappy days. I own fairly it is to that constant habit that I have often corrected myself, and that I have ever found self-deserved approbation a much happier state than any indulgence which met with self-condemnation.

Latin and French you have learnt, and with a moderate degree of attention those languages may be kept up; as to German your proficiency is certainly very moderate, yet in Germany you will have possessions that will place you in one of the superior stations in that great Empire. You cannot do your duty unless more master of that language; besides, you must acquire a knowledge of its Constitution and more particularly of that of your future dominions, whose prosperity must chiefly depend on the fatherly hand of its Sovereign, and the conduct of those subjects but too well deserve every attention, from their unalterable attachment to their Princes.

You have read cursorily some historians, by which you may have acquired a general view of the principal facts in Antient and Modern History, but as yet no insight into the springs which caused them, or any comprehensive knowledge of the Constitution, laws, finances, commerce, &c. of these Kingdoms, and of the relative situation as to these points of our rival neighbours, and of the other European States.

I certainly shall think it right to make some new arrangement concerning you, but as it is a matter involved with difficulties, I trust you will rest contented when I say that I mean to do it with no greater delay than what must naturally arise from them. Believe me, I wish to make you happy, but the father must, with that object in view, not forget that it is his duty to guide his child to the best of his ability through the rocks that cannot but naturally arise in the outset of youth, and the misfortune is that in other countries national pride makes the inhabitants wish to paint their Princes in the most favourable light, and consequently be silent on any indiscretion; but here most persons, if not concerned in laying ungrounded blame, are ready to trumpet any speck they can find out. (41774-5)

THE PRINCE OF WALES'S REPLY

Windsor Castle, 15 Aug. 1780
I had not the honor of receiving your Majesty's most gracious and affectionate letter till late last night, or else should certainly have answered it before this evening. Permit me to express how extremely sensible I am of the parental attachment & kindness you profess towards

me, and allow me to assure you it will be my principal object thro' life to merit them, & to convince you how truly I remain, Sir, [etc.]. (41776, and [draft] 38048)

Queen's House, 22 Dec. 1780

I last week communicated to you the having sent to Lord North[1] the plan of the expence that forming your family will cost me, as well as what is absolutely necessary for Frederick and for taking the three boys out of the nursery. It amounts to what is certainly rather inconvenient to me, and can only be boren by every one keeping scrupulously to their quota, and my reducing every possible expence in my own establishment.

It becomes therefore necessary, on placing you in this middle state between manhood and childhood, that you should exactly understand my intentions. I have chose to convey my thoughts on paper, as you will then have it in your power at any time to recurr to them; besides, on a subject wherein my happiness as well as pride is so much concerned as in your making a respectable figure in the world, I can reason more coolly on paper than in conversation, but should you at any time wish to talk on the subject, you will never find me unwilling to enter into it. Indeed, I wish more and more to have you as a friend and in that light to guide you, rather than with the authority of a parent.

The letter I wrote to you in August must have shewn you that my mind was engrossed by the arduous task before me. The Governour's part now ends, my attention and anxiety must be redoubled. From your childhood I have ever said that I can only try to save my country, but it must be by the co-operation of my children only that I can effect it. If you become zealous in fitting yourself for the thorny situation you most probably will fill, and will consider that it is your duty to countenance only those young men whose morals are praiseworthy, and whose inclinations to inform themselves and become useful members of the community by their conduct is apparent, you will take an immense load off my shoulders. So exemplary a part in you will prepare instruments that may enable me to pave a path for you more pleasant and undisturbed than it has been my lot to enjoy; besides, it will redouble my endeavours to put some vigour into this country, as I shall then feel a probability of success. If I can think you will be happier and can restore this country to its proper tone after my demise, I shall not repine at the difficulties and trials I have met with, but this great object of my wishes can alone be

1. First Lord of the Treasury, 1770–82; succeeded his father as 2nd Earl of Guilford, 1790 (1732–92). Home Secretary, April–December 1783, in the Coalition Ministry; Lord Warden of the Cinque Ports, 1778–92.

attained by application on your part, and a guard on your behaviour, which are indispensably necessary to gain you the good opinion of men of worth and deserved reputation.

My inclination is to grant you all the rational amusement I can, and keep you out of what is improper, and so to steer you, that when arrived at the full stage of manhood, you may thank me for having made you escape evils that ill become a young man of rank, but in your exalted situation are criminal: for Princes must serve as examples to others, and though not perhaps always so much copied in their virtues as might be wished, yet if they deserve praise it will in some degree check the improper career of others.

I have in my plan of your Establishment (which I will in a day or two communicate to you as well as the names of the persons I have fixed upon)[1] granted as much for your expenditure under the heads of Robes and Privy Purse as I was allowed by the late King[2], and as to horses I have allowed infinitely more. I never had but three saddle horses. I have allowed as far as sixteen between road horses and hunters for you. The Household expences fall on me, therefore that is omitted.

As you may at times be desirous of dining with some of your attendants, I shall consent when I am in town that you may have a dinner in your appartment on Sundays and Thursdays, but I cannot afford it oftener, to which any of your Lords, Grooms, Equerries and those who have formerly dined with you may be invited.[3]

You may very naturally chuse to go oftener to Plays and Operas than I may. I shall not object to it when I am in town, provided you give me previous notice that we may not expect you in the evening, but then you must go in your box attended by your regular attendants, as all Princes of Wales have heretofore done. Whenever you are desirous of dancing, on an intimation to the Queen or me, we shall very readily forward it, and shall have no other wish on such occasions but to make the Ball

---

1. The following appointments to the Prince's Household were gazetted on 29 December 1780:

Groom of the Stole	Lord Southampton
Gentlemen of the Bedchamber	Earl of Courtown, Lord John Clinton, Viscount Parker
Treasurer and Secretary	Lieut.-Col. Hotham
Master of the Robes and Privy Purse	Henry Lyte
Grooms of the Bedchamber	Hon. Mr. Legge, Hon. Stephen Digby, John Johnson
First Equerry and Commissioner of the Stables	Lieut.-Col. Lake
Equerries	Lieut.-Col. Hulse, Lieut.-Col. Sir John Dyer, Lieut.-Col. Stevens.

2. His grandfather, George II (1683–1760).

3. The Prince was to remain under his father's eye at Buckingham House.

agreeable to you; but I shall not permit the going to Balls or Assemblies at private houses, which never has been the custom for Princes of Wales. As to Masquerades, you already know my disapprobation of them in this country, and I cannot by any means agree to any of my children ever going to them.

Of course you will come every Sunday to church and to the Drawing Room at St. James's when I appear there, as also at the Thursday Drawing Room.

When I ride out of a morning I shall ever expect you to accompany me. On other days I shall not object to your doing it also, provided it is for exercise, not lounging about Hyde Park. Whenever you ride out or go in a carriage, one of your attendants must accompany you.

When I mentioned your not going to private houses, I should have added the impossibility of going either in town or the country to those of your uncles[1], had you not known that on my reconciliation with them in the beginning of the summer, the saying the women will not appear will not be admitted by me as a reason to relax on this head.

I shall try to make the evenings when you do not frequent Plays or Operas, pass agreably to you by inviting by degrees variety of company, when you shall ever have your choice of playing at cards or conversing, if you think it less constrained, in the musick room. Be but open with me and you will ever find me desirous of making you as happy as I can, but I must not forget, nor must you, that in the exalted station you are placed in, every step is of consequence, and that your future character will greatly depend in the world on the propriety of your conduct at the present period.

I cannot conclude without assuring you that I shall ever remain[2] [etc.]. (41780–1)

1. The Dukes of Cumberland and Gloucester. The former had recently been enjoying some very good hunting in Sussex, and he would have been even better pleased had the Prince of Wales and Frederick been with him. (54452)

2. The original draft (41777–9) contained the following additional paragraph:
'I know very well you do not love labour, therefore should wish to have instruction instilled into you with as much ease as possible. If you wish without wading through books to get a knowledge of the finances, of the trade and commerce of this country, persons shall be found to come and give the information in conversation at your own hours, but though I ardently wish that you would incline to this, I shall not press you farther on the subject than you may be inclined.'

II   1781-1782

At the beginning of 1781 Prince Frederick was on his way to Hanover, and a few weeks later the Prince of Wales lost the company of his brother William, who again went to sea, for the first time, in the summer, to a foreign station. Frederick was a much more reliable correspondent than his eldest brother, who was repeatedly reproached for neglecting to answer letters. Frederick wrote regularly, too, to the King, nor did he neglect his young sisters, to whom, from time to time, he sent small presents. Though Hanover was a dull place after London, he came to like the life there, as he was wholly absorbed by the task of perfecting himself in the duties of his profession. He rather disliked his Mecklenburg uncles, suspecting them of tale-bearing.

The Prince of Wales was still only nineteen when, in March 1782, Lord North, after being Prime Minister for nearly twelve years, was forced to resign after his unsuccessful conduct of the American War lost him the confidence of the House of Commons; and the King was compelled to fall back on the Rockingham and Chathamite Whigs, and, in consequence, to take Fox as Foreign Secretary. The ministerial changes are barely reflected in the Prince's scanty correspondence, though the King in his letter of 30 March, referred to his being 'harassed by many disagreeable events', and the Prince thought that the new Ministry seemed 'to wish me better than the former one'. His friend Gerard Lake, wisely advised him to steer clear of party politics: politicians, he suggested, were only too anxious to make use of him for their own advantage, and to become connected with party would mean that the Royal Family would become a house divided against itself. And Prince Frederick repeatedly advised him to improve his relations with his father, who complained of his 'want of even common civility to the Queen' and to himself; of his 'total disobedience'; of his notorious neglect of every religious duty, and of his connexion with loose women like 'Perdita' Robinson. Madame Hardenburg, with whom the Prince had a notorious intrigue, was not quite a woman of the town, but very nearly so, as her subsequent conduct showed. The seduction, described at some length in the Prince's letter, had highly important political repercussions. Hardenburg, it will be remembered, had married the Countess Reventlow, and had come to England from Hanover in the hope of being appointed Hanoverian Minister in London, but, so great was the scandal caused by the Prince's entanglement with Madame Hardenburg, he was forced to leave the Hanoverian service for that of the Duke of Brunswick. His wife's conduct there, too, however, was so equivocal that he was compelled to divorce her and he found it expedient to enter the Prussian service, in which, ultimately, he so greatly distinguished himself as one of the Liberators of Europe.

32 PRINCE FREDERICK TO THE PRINCE OF WALES [1]

Ostend, 3 Jan. 1781

We arrived here yesterday after a voyage of fifty hours owing to the haziness of the weather. The ship tossed and rolled so horribly that everybody was sick, even some of the sailors who had been all their lives at sea. I shared the common fate, but yet was less so than anybody else, for after the first four and twenty hours I recovered. On Monday

[1]. 'The brothers were separated because they were great friends,' said Horace Walpole (*Last Journals*, ii.341). But that was one of his many doubtful statements. Prince Frederick, who had been gazetted a Colonel on 1 November 1780, was on his way to Hanover to study French and German and to complete his military education. Accompanied by Colonel Richard Grenville, he left Buckingham House on 30 December 1780. 'Nothing could be more affecting than the parting between the Prince and the rest of the royal family. Their Majesties both wept severely; and the Prince of Wales, in particular, was so much affected with the misfortune of being deprived for so long a period of the sole companion of his youth, that he stood in a state of entire insensibility, totally unable to speak or to express the concern he felt so strongly' (*Annual Register*, 1781, Chronicle, p.161).

Frederick arrived at Margate that night. He wrote next day: 'We had at first intended to have stopped at Canterbury, but finding ourselves so early there we resolved to push on here. The road, upon the whole, is very disagreable, being exceedingly hilly and in parts exceedingly heavy, but the post from Dartford to Rochester is remarkably beautifull, on account of the many views of the river which was very luckily for us yesterday filled with vessels, among the rest two East Indiamen which were going round to the Downs. . . .' (43361)

evening we heard a good many cannon fired, and have since found it was the Bellona, Captain Onslow[1], who was engaging a Dutch ship of fifty-eight guns, which he took.[2] There is a very strong report here, which I hope is true, that there has been a very great riot at Amsterdam, that the Stadt House and one quarter of the city has been burnt, and two or three of the magistrates murdered, and that the rest have been obliged to abscond; in short, that everything is in the greatest confusion there.

I have been employed all the morning in walking about the town, which is very inconsiderable. We visited the three convents, which, never have [sic] seen anything of the kind before, I was very desirous of seeing. One of them is of Capuchines. We went into the convent and found them all at dinner. They appeared very contented, they wear no shirts, they are dressed exactly as the monks are represented in the Duenna[3], except that these are in brown, and the others in black. The other two convents are of nuns, the one of Beguines, who are allowed to quit the convent whenever they please. This convent is very ugly and not worth speaking of. The other is of Conceptionistes. They wear a white dress. We desired to see the sœur Jecole [?] who speaks English. She is a woman about forty, and has the most sanctified face I ever saw. I have just this moment seen a very famous man, Major Tyler, who was concerned with Laurens. Monsieur de Welderen[4] arrived here last night and sets out tomorrow for Ghent. He sent us his best respects thro' our Consul and said he should have been very happy to see us, but thought it might not be proper for him in his present situation to do so. I have had a visit this morning from the Commandant, Mons. Dreve, who told me that they expected the Emperor[5] soon in this part of the world, from whence, he thought he might be certain that he would pass into England.

I cannot close my letter, dear brother, without desiring you to give my duty to the King and Queen, and my love to my brothers and sisters, as well as my best compliments to all our friends at home. (43362–3)

1. Admiral Sir Richard Onslow (1741–1817). Captain, 1761; Rear-Admiral, 1793; Vice-Admiral, 1794; Admiral, 1799. Created Baronet, 1797.

2. England was at war with Holland and the Bourbon Powers in alliance with the Americans.

3. Sheridan's comic opera (1775).

4. 1725?–1807. For many years, until the outbreak of war in 1780, he was the Dutch Minister at the Court of St. James's. He died at his London home.

5. Joseph II (1741–90), Emperor since 1765. He visited the Netherlands in June 1781.

Clarges Street, 19 Jan. 1781

It is impossible for me ever to reconcile the idea of departing from this country without begging your Royal Highness's permission to trespass upon that goodness, you have always shewn me, to request the favor of you to present, in the most respectful & grateful terms, my duty to the King & Queen, & to assure their Majesties that I greatly lament I have not an opportunity to pay my duty to them in person, & that I shall always retain the highest sense of gratitude for the great goodness & kind attention both myself & family have experienc'd from them upon all occasions.

Allow me now, Sir, to offer your Royal Highness, what I do with the greatest sincerity, my most hearty wishes for your prosperity & happiness & that you will believe me to be, with the truest respect [etc.].   (38050)

34   THE PRINCE OF WALES TO PRINCE FREDERICK

Queen's House, 20 Jan. 1781

I have been waiting with anxious expectation for a letter from you; one of our packet boats was obliged to throw the mail overboard, and I fear there were some letters in that to yr. friends here. Alas!, my dearest Frederick, I have been obliged to part with my best friend, Lake. He is set off for America, The ships, as soon as the wind is favorable, are to sail to Cork. He is still at Portsmouth expecting every hour to be summoned on board. Our parting, as you may suppose, was a very severe trial to us both, especially as we had received so great a shock in our late separation from you. You know how much I love him, & therefore will easily conceive what a loss he is to me at the present moment, more especially as I have not you, my dear brother, with me, from whom I could always meet with disinterested advice. . . .

I am to see Warwick Lake² tomorrow about buying two fresh horses for you. I am packing up yr. writing box with a few new things wh. I think you will like to have abroad when you see ym. I have ordered you

1. Gerard Lake, Viscount Lake (1744–1808), of the 1st Regiment of Foot Guards, one of the Prince's earliest friends; his First Equerry, 1780–6 and 1787–96, and Gentleman attendant on the Prince from 1796 until his death. M.P. for Aylesbury, 1790–1802, and for Armagh [I.], 1799–1800. Fought in the Seven Years' War, and in America during the last stages of the War of Independence. Commanded a Brigade of Guards in Holland in 1793; Commander-in-Chief in Ireland for a short time in 1798; Commander-in-Chief in India, 1800–7; Baron Lake, 1804; Viscount Lake, 1807. Major-General, 1790; Lieutenant-General, 1797; General, 1802.

2. Gerard Lake's younger brother (*d.*1821). He looked after the Prince's racing stables.

two plain frocks & some black breetches wh. will go by the messenger. Pray present my best love & affection to dear Joan[1] & tell him he may expect a letter from me in a post or two when you receive yr. next from me, wherein I shall treat him comme il faut. Adieu, my dearest brother. I have not another moment to spare to write to you for I must attend our usual circle of old tabbies. . . .

P.S. I forgot to mention to you yt. I wish you wd. enquire what will be the best method for your phaeton to travel over to you. (43373-5)

35 LIEUTENANT-COLONEL GERARD LAKE TO THE PRINCE OF WALES

Portsmouth, 23 Jan. 1781
I cannot leave England without once more returning you my most sincere thanks for your great friendship & wonderful kindness towards me, & at the same time to beg your indulgence in suffering me to express the sentiments of a heart warmly attach'd to your service, & full of the most anxious & best wishes for your future happiness & welfare. Relying upon your goodness, I will endeavour to point out some few things from which, in my poor opinion, you are likely to suffer. In the first place I think your great good nature is liable to be impos'd upon by people who have not the smallest pretensions to your civility or attention, & who will presume upon that goodness & become troublesome to you. I mention this as I know it has been thought your good nature makes you too condescending, & trust me, it is absolutely necessary to make proper distinctions between men, as the surest way to gain the esteem & regard of the most sensible & valuable part of mankind. Beleive me, a knowledge of the world & of men is very necessary, & the most difficult to be acquir'd. Allow me to say it is more so for you, as the retir'd & private education unavoidably chalk'd out for a Prince has prevented you from knowing so much of them as young men who have reap'd the benefit of a publick school in general do at your age; besides, your situation is such as to make people very anxious to be upon the best footing with you, & I am sorry to say that too many there are in this world who, to gain your favor, will acquiesce & encourage you in doing things that they themselves would perhaps be the first to condemn, & when they find the world disapproving your conduct, will lay the blame entirely upon yourself.

As to politics you well know I have ever, except once in the Great

1. Colonel Richard Grenville (1744–1823), one of the Prince's friends, was the brother of Lord Glastonbury and nephew of George Grenville, the Prime Minister. Colonel, February 1779; Major-General, November 1782. For many years he was at the head of the Duke of York's Household. Fanny Burney described him in 1787 as 'a silent, reserved valetudinary' (*Diary*, ii.398).

Park at Windsor, studiously avoided talking about, nor do I, at this time, wish to enter upon the subject farther than to entreat of you before you lend yourself to any party, to consider well what you mean. Your own good sense (of which no one has a greater share) if properly employ'd, will prevent your becoming the dupe of those who have no other design than to make use of you for their own advantage. I mean to speak of no particular sett of men, but my great anxiety for your future ease perhaps leads me to say more than I ought. If you reflect a moment you will see that any engagements of this sort will lead you into difficulties which it may be impossible for you to extricate yourself from, so long as you live. Recollect what a large family yours is, and you will see how necessary it is for you *all* to live well together, & I am thoroughly convinc'd that it is for your own interest so to do, & that you will by that means not only enjoy more real comfort, but that you will be more at your ease in every particular. I make no doubt of a most excellent & sensible speech of the Duke of Cumberland's having struck you as forcibly as it did me; it was, let our family stick by each other, we need not fear the world.

I fear you will think me impertinent & troublesome for plaguing you with this letter. However, I must still intrude upon your good nature by adding one wish more, which is to beg that you will not write any more letters to a certain sort of ladies, & I should hope that what you have already suffer'd will be a sufficient warning. . . .

I do most heartily wish you may be pleas'd with the manners &c. of your present establishment, which appears to me to be compos'd of good men, tho' many of them entirely unknown to me. Lord Southampton[1] very kindly call'd in Clarges Street on Friday to take leave of me. We had of course some conversation about you, & I am clearly convinc'd that he not only wishes but is determin'd to do everything in his power that can afford you pleasure or comfort, & it is my firm opinion that he will be perfectly faithful, & is too much the man of honor to say or do anything but what is perfectly upright & fair towards you. I know that so much averse is he to tittle tattle that he is absolutely determin'd, should any one person be detected in bearing tales about your family, to make a point of having him dismist your service, let him be of whatsoever rank he will.

I have taken the liberty of setting down some regulations & recommendations which Col. Stevens[2] is so obliging as to undertake to shew

1. Charles Fitzroy, 1st Baron Southampton (1737–97); third son of Lord Augustus Fitzroy and grandson of the 2nd Duke of Grafton; peerage, 1780; the Prince's Groom of the Stole, 1780–95. He had been Groom of the Bedchamber, 1760–2, and was Vice-Chamberlain to the Queen, 1768–82.

2. Lieutenant-Colonel Stevens, Equerry and (February 1784) Groom of the Bedchamber to the Prince of Wales.

to you, & I flatter myself if you have no objection to them, you will order them to be comply'd with. At the same time let me beg of you to alter the whole or any part of them entirely to your satisfaction, as nothing would make me more unhappy than thinking any arrangement of mine should be in the smallest degree disagreable to you, for beleive me my only wish is to promote the good of your service, & to do all in my power to put everything upon best footing.

Will you permit me, Sir, to trouble you with my duty to the Duke of Cumberland & return him my best thanks for his great civility & attention to me, & assure him how much I lament not having had it in my power to pay my respects in person to both their Royal Highnesses.[1] Accept, my dearest friend (if you will allow me to call you by that name) my best thanks for your picture, which you are, I flatter myself, well convinc'd is the most valuable present you could have given me, & that I never will part with as long as I live. Adieu. God bless you, & that you may enjoy every blessing & happiness in this life is the real & sincere wish of one who begs leave to subscribe himself, your most truly attach'd friend and servt. (38051–2)

36   PRINCE FREDERICK TO THE PRINCE OF WALES, AND THE REPLY

Hanover, 27 Jan. 1781
I have received your letter which I will answer next post as I am obliged to write to the King and if possible to the Queen tonight. I have only time to desire you will send us over regularly the *Morning Herald*, the *Morning Chronicle* and Almond's paper[2], and to say that I am, dear brother [etc.].

Joan desires to be remembered to you and says he will have the profound and high honor of writing to you next post. (43372)

1. The other being the Duke of Gloucester.

2. John Almon (1737–1805), the London bookseller and journalist. In a letter dated 14 December 1780, the journalist William Woodfall refers to Almon and 'his mischievous *Courant*' (i.e. the *London Courant*, of which, however, he does not appear to have been the registered proprietor). According to Almon's own account, his paper, the *General Advertizer*, was being subsidized by the Whig Opposition to the extent of £300 a year, in 1784, and earlier (A. Aspinall, *Politics and the Press* [Home & van Thal, 1949], pp. 271, 435; and *Engl. Hist. Review*, April 1948, pp. 201–32 [*Statistical Accounts of the London Newspapers in the Eighteenth Century*]).

Q[ueen's] H[ouse], 6 Feb. 1781

I received ye day before yesterday yr. little short letter & wait in anxious expectation for the next post. The King told me he had written you an account of ye little dispute yt. has so lately happened between him & our friend ye Duke of C[umberland].[1] Ça ne nous fait pas le moindre honneur ici à la maison de la Reine, mais tout au contraire. Dear Lake continues vastly well at Portsmouth. I forwarded yr. two letters to him. Ye convoy, together with ye fleet, expects to sail every day. William goes to join ye great fleet on Saturday, when they also expect to set sail for Gibraltar. I have nothing more to add unless it be that I shall send you some frocks & a few other things by ye messenger on Friday. Dear brother, adieu.

P.S. Pray tell Joan I will certainly before next Tuesday write him an account of ye meeting between his brother & me, who appears to me to be now in perfect good health. My best compliments to yt. facetious little rogue Joan. Tell him I wait with great impatience for a letter from him, & yt. he has found his snug piece.   (43380)

37 PRINCE FREDERICK TO THE PRINCE OF WALES

Hanover, 9 Feb. 1781

I have many thanks to return you for your very kind letter, which I received this moment. . . .

As for my advice, you know, dear brother, that upon whatever subject you want it, it shall always be at your service to the full [extent] of my power. I was shooting last Tuesday but never fired my gun off once, for owing to too much caution all our game got away. I have practised five or six times with a rifled barrelled carabine at a butt, at which I succeeded better than could have been conceived; it is very difficult thing.

1. On 31 January the Duke of Cumberland wrote to his brother, the King: 'As I supposed that every mark of attention on my part to the Prince could not but be agreable to your Majesty, it was with the utmost astonishment and mortification I learnt your Majesty had forbiden the Prince's Establishment to accept my invitation to dine at Cumberland House.

'After this publick proof of your Majestie's intention to exclude me from the benefits of society enjoy'd by the rest of mankind, it is impossible to receive with satisfaction those attentions (however flattering) all your Majestie's subjects wish to pay me when I am conscious they thereby incur your Majestie's displeasure.

'Thus, Sir, condemned by your Majesty to a situation so repugnant to my own feelings, all that remains for me is to request permission to withdraw from your Majestie's dominions and as a citizen of the world seek an asylum in some other part of the globe.' ([Draft] 54454 & 54455)

Grenville and all say that I have the steadiest hand they ever saw. Last night we had our Masquerade again; I danced every dance but one. When I return to England I must teach you two different kind of dances from what we have the least idea of, the quadrilles and the valtzies. The first is a kind of cotilion but with English steps. The other is a kind of Allemande, but much prettier. They generally introduce the valtzy into the quadrille. I beg you will send me over by Busch[1] some hats, for it is a thing we cannot get in the least here. Give my compliments to all friends at home, particularly to Miss Hamilton[2] and the Duke of Cumberland. . . .

Our post goes out so early that I must finish my letter. I shall therefore only sign myself [etc.].

P.S. I forgot to tell you that my phaeton must be sent over in a neutral bottom to Hamburg or some other seaport near here. I believe my horses must come the same way, for the roads are so excessive bad all the way from Ostend that they will be all spoilt before they arrive here. Tell William if he is still at home that I would have wrote to him this post but really have not had time. If there is anything new in London in the buckle way I shall be very glad to have it. You must take care [to send] some more whips with the phaeton. Adieu.   (43381–2)

38   THE PRINCE OF WALES TO PRINCE FREDERICK

Q[ueen's] H[ouse], 9 Feb. 1781
I send you enclosed with this ye kee of yr. writing box wh. is gone by ye messenger, as well as some papers wh. I have sent in ye box. I hope you will approve of my having sent ym., for in opening yr. case to get out some things for you, I saw one paper laying upon ye rest wh. began, 'My dearest Angel', or something to yt. effect, I do not justly recollect what; upon wh. I took ym. all up & sent ym. directly to you, for fear if ever yt. case should by chance be opened in yr. absence, someone more anxious than me should chuse to fumble ym. over. Everyone here desires to be remembered to you. You shall have a longer letter from me next week, as well as Joan, to whom I beg you will present my most respectful & dutiful compliments. Give ye little mulatto a kick on the backside for my sake. Lord, when shall I receive yr. next letter? I

1. Lieutenant-General George William von dem Bussche, one of the Hanoverian Generals.
2. Mary Hamilton (1756–1816), one of the Attendants on the Princesses from 1777 to 1782. The Prince of Wales fell violently in love with her in 1779, when he was sixteen. Her father, Charles Hamilton, was the son of Lord Archibald Hamilton and grandson of the 3rd Duke of Hamilton. In 1785 she married John Dickenson of Taxall. See her *Correspondence*, edited by Elizabeth and Florence Anson (1925).

King George III
by Gainsborough 1781

Queen Charlotte
by Gainsborough 1781

believe ye winds are determined I never shall. In my next to you I will entertain with a most ridiculous adventure wh. has lately happened to yt. little pugfaced rascal Mills[1], much to his dismay. Adieu, my dearest Frederick.

[*P.S.*] Ye newspapers I hope come regularly.   (43383)

39   LETTERS FROM PRINCE FREDERICK TO THE PRINCE OF WALES

Hanover, 12 Feb. [*1781*]

. . . I forgot to mention to you in my last letter that I wanted some more gloves of both sorts. Do not send me less than half a dozen hats, three of each sort. I wish also you would desire Warwick Lake to buy for me ten couple of small foxhounds for our pack here, which is, considering all things, better than I could have expected. I have subscribed to it. As for the carriage of these hounds over, I shall leave that totally to him.[2]

Our messenger is going. I must therefore close my letter by desiring my best compliments to the Duke of Cumberland, Miss Hamilton, &c., &c.

P.S. Since I wrote this, I have received a letter from the King by which he appears to me to be much pleased with your conduct in his dispute with the Duke of Cumberland.[3] Remember dear brother that I shall always be happy to be of the least use to you, either by giving you my advice or by any other means whatsoever. Adieu.   (43384–5)

1. J. Mills was one of the Prince's Pages of the Backstairs.

2. Frederick had not taken his horses over with him, and he wanted them, too, to be sent. He wrote to the King on 9 March (43394): '. . . I have enquired about the best means of bringing over my horses, and everybody to whom I have applied have advised their being sent in a neutral ship to Bremerlee, because if their passage is good it will only last four days and they will have a very short journey by land, but if they were to be landed at Ostend, their journey would take them above three weeks and the roads are so excessively bad in Flanders as well as all through Westphalia that they would probably be quite spoilt before they arrived here. Your Majesty orders me at the same time to acquaint you what kind of town Hanover is; in general it is not well built, and I must confess the Palace is the worst house in the whole town, but however there are some houses which are certainly very fine, particularly Prince Charles's; it belongs to little Busch, and as he as Écuyer, lives at the stables, he lets it to Prince Charles. . . .'

3. Frederick wrote to the King next day: 'I have many thanks to return your Majesty for your gracious letter which I have this moment received. The cause of it I own I much lament, but however am happy that your Majesty is pleased with my brother's conduct in the affair. I have no doubt but that he will do everything in his power which he thinks will be agreable to you. . . .'   (43386)

Hanover, 13 Feb. 1781

Everybody here says that you have been ill, but as nobody has wrote me word of it I hope in God at least that it is nothing of consequence. I have nothing particularly new to tell you except that I pass my time pretty well. Our Carnaval ended last Saturday, and now no more publick Balls or Masquerades till after Easter. . . . Pray for God sake why have not you wrote to me for so many posts? I had a great mind not to have wrote to you this time, but however, my great good nature made me condescend to send you these few lines. I have nothing more to add except my best compliments to the Duke of Cumberland to whom you will please to say that I have received his letter, to which I will if possible answer this post, if not certainly the next, as well as to Miss Hamilton, and all other friends in England.   (43389)

Hanover, 21 Feb. 1781

It was impossible for me to execute the promise I made you of writing to you last post, for I have had so much to do since our arrival here that I have hardly had a moment unemployed. Sunday morning Prince Ferdinand[1] arrived here in order to stand Godfather with the Duke of Brunswick[2] and myself to Prince Charles's[3] youngest son. He is in figure very like the late Duke of Cumberland[4]. On Sunday evening all the ladies were presented to me. Out of about fifty there was not above five that I thought the least pretty. On Tuesday I saw all the sets of horses. It is impossible to conceive finer horses for parade. The set which I make use of, and which certainly is not the finest by a great deal, is yet infinitely handsomer than the Queen's set in England. In my opinion, the prettiest set, tho' not the tallest, is the white horses. What is very particular in this set is that they are folded perfectly white, all but their noses and eyelids which are red. I also saw all the stallions and saddle horses, but it will take up too much of my letter to give you a description of them. The first time I write to the King, which I am affraid I have not time to do today, I will tell him as much as I can how

1. Brother of Frederick the Great of Prussia (1730–1813).

2. Charles William Ferdinand, Duke of Brunswick (1735–1806), Duke since 1780. His daughter Caroline married the Prince of Wales in 1795.

3. Prince Charles of Mecklenburg-Strelitz (1741–1816), Queen Charlotte's brother. He succeeded his brother Adolphus Frederick as Duke in 1794, and took the title of Grand Duke in 1815. His ninth child, Frederick (1781–3) was born on 7 January. In the spring of 1786 Prince Charles planned a visit to England. Amongst other things he wished the King to agree to be 'guardian to his children'. According to Lord Ailesbury the Queen kept her brother's letter referring to his proposed visit in her pocket three weeks before she showed it to the King (Ailesbury MSS. *Diary*, 9 April 1786).

4. William Augustus, Duke of Cumberland (1721–65), third son of George II.

they are. I have road about eight of them. I was last night at the Masquerade which was exceedingly pretty. I went there at six and did not come away till three. I had almost forgot a commission Prince Earnest[1] has begged me to give you, which is to order for him a pair of silver buckles like the last I had before I set out, and a pair of broad silver spurs like those I have. Give my best compliments to the grave Duke of Cumberland and tell him I shall not forget his advice. Tomorrow we are going out a shooting dogs, cats, rats, mice, bucks, does &c. &c. &c. On Tuesday if possible we are to have a bear hunt. I am to subscribe to the hunt here which is better, if one may believe what they say here, than I should have supposed; at least it is better than nothing.[2] (43376-7)

Hanover, 27 Feb. 1781

I am affraid you will think me very troublesome in giving you so many commissions, but however, you must expect a good many particularly in this letter, which will be in a manner composed of nothing else. In *primis* I have to beg you will order me a Vandyke dress of white sattin waistcoat and breeches with a pink cloak; the hat must be white sattin with a fine plume of feathers, and trimmed in the dernier gout. I forgot to say that there must be the shoes and everything for I did all in my power but it was impossible to get it made here. Secondly you must get just such a sword as Grey[3] made for us. Thirdly, you must send me over by the next quarterly messenger another edition of gloves of both sorts, and as for shoes and boots Rhymer has already got his orders about them, only I forgot to add a dozen pair of the accoutrement leather soaled shoes.

I pass my time very well here; to be sure it is not England. However, taking everything together, I do very well. I am luckily not very difficult.

1. Frederick's uncle; brother of Prince Charles (1742-1814). 'Prince Ernest had wished to marry the great heiress of the North, Miss Bowes, whose fortune exceeded that of the heiress of the South, Miss Tylney Long; but the King objecting to his being united to a subject, his Royal Highness left England and never returned. Most certainly such a fortune in Germany would have made him a Prince indeed, but as he was a younger brother it might have disturbed the harmony of the House of Mecklenburg-Strelitz, of which the reigning Duke was not married' (Mrs. Papendiek, *Court and private life in the time of Queen Charlotte*, i.75).

2. Replying to the King's suggestion that he should take more exercise in the form of walking, Frederick wrote (19 April):

'. . . Instead of taking a long walk I go out a snipe shooting which is pretty good exercise, as I always go a-foot and generally walk two German miles or more before dinner, but that never interferes with my studies, which begin always at eight o'clock and last till eleven, because I chose to have my German master as well as Monsieur Falk in a morning as I thought that I should gain more in a morning than in an evening. . . .' (43412-3)

3. Robert Gray (*d.*1788), the Bond Street goldsmith and jeweller. His son William succeeded to the business.

I am four hours at my studies like a good boy. I think, having nothing better to do, I will give you a little specimen of the way of passing my time. First of all I get up so as to have breakfasted at eight; I then go to the ingeneers and learn geometry and to draw military plans till ten. I then have a drawing master till eleven. I then either walk or ride till one. At one I dress and we dine at half an hour after one. At four I have my German master till five, and then I amuse myself vastly well the rest of the day. But I am affraid I shall bore you with this stuff. I shall therefore only beg my compliments to Miss Hamilton and the rest of my friends at home.

P.S. I forgot to desire you would send the Collars of the Garter and Bath over for I understand that it is the custom to wear them here on the King's Birthday, New Year's Day and such days for the people being given much to prayer in this country tho. not to fasting. By the rules of all Orders we must put these on view.[1]   (43392–3)

40   THE PRINCE OF WALES TO PRINCE FREDERICK

[*Qu.H. 19 Mar. 1781*]

... I flatter myself you attribute my silence to nothing but ill-health, for I think you are too thoroughly convinced of my unalterable affection to attribute it to anything else. I say nothing more concerning myself or England in general, as I reserve everything concerning us *all* here till a very long letter next post. The true reason of my writing to you is to recommend to you in ye strongest manner poor Busshe as a friend of mine; so far from being the gentleman that took poetical licence, as we supposed, he is a very honest, agreable, chearful man; in short, more like an Englishman than any man of Ger-ma-ny than ever I yet saw. He has been infamously ill treated by yt. old rascal Alvensleben[2], ye whole of wh. you will hear from him. Hardenberg[3] witnesses ye truth of everything he says & ye old Field Marshall is acquainted with it; they are both I understand from Busshe, very honorable, respectable men. Everything yt. concerns his department he wishes should pass between you and ye King, & indeed it is much better it should be so, for the

1. Prince Frederick had been invested a Knight of the Bath in 1767, and a Knight of the Garter in 1771.

2. Baron d'Alvensleben, the Hanoverian Minister in London. His nephew, M. d'Alvensleben, was the Prussian Minister at Dresden.

3. Karl August von Hardenberg (1750–1822), the Prussian statesman, had married the Countess Reventlow, who became entangled in an intrigue with the Prince of Wales. The scandal compelled Hardenberg to quit the Hanoverian service in 1782 and enter that of the Duke of Brunswick. He entered the service of the King of Prussia in 1792.

King attends to nothing they say and says he will not concerning ye horses, but will wait till he hears from you. He now begins to be convinced of ye truth of many things Busshe says, & wh. Alvensleben had assured him to be false. In short, I shall be personally obliged to you, dear brother, if you will take these too worthy people as much by ye hand as possible. You will find her especially every thing yt is amiable & I am convinced you will be pleased with her society, & for heaven's sake beware of yt. two [. . .] uncles, I mean particularly Ernest & George[1]; they have made stories & talk'd all sorts of nonsense wh. is come round to us here ever since you have been at Hanover. They will be ye first to take part in any little jollity with you & ye first to repeat it, & to accuse you of it; they will live & hang upon you unless you cut them. Pardon me, my dearest brother, what I write to you; you know I promised to write everything yt. came round to me concerning you; you know how much I love you, & therefore hope you will look upon this in ye right light, I wish you to be very civil to them, but no intimacy.

Adieu, dearest Frederick. I had promised you a short letter, but when I once have my pen in hand writing to you I know not when to stop. May every happiness Heaven can afford center upon you is ye. constant prayer of yr. ever affectionate George P.

P.S. I shall answer Joan next post as well as you & give you an account of all yr. commission wh. I hope I shall have performed to yr. approbation. Once more adieu, dearest Frederick; would to Heaven I was with you.   (43397–8)

41   LETTERS FROM PRINCE FREDERICK TO THE PRINCE OF WALES

[Hanover, 24 Mar. 1781]

Dear brother, I cannot describe how much I have been alarmed with the account of your illness, which, however, luckily I did not hear without being told at the same time that you were now in a manner well, which I pray God heartily may be true. I write you this little scrawl first to desire you to put my tradesmen in mind that the quarterly messenger will soon come and that therefore they must begin to make my things. You must tell Fitch to make me two pair of huzza breeches quite down to the ancles with a strap under the foot of white ram's skin, but not to count them in the half a dozen pair which I ordered him to send every quarter; and also order Blaymer a dozen pair of accoutreman leather soaled dancing pumps and two pair of half boots of the shining leather; all this is besides the usual complement which I ordered to be sent quarterly before I

1. Prince George of Mecklenburg-Strelitz (1748–85).

quitted England, and also some hats. Everything else I shall leave to your taste, wisdom and care, and therefore shall only add my compliments to Miss Hamilton and all other friends in England, and repeat my most hearty prayers for your thorough recovery, and sign myself most sincerely your most affectionate brother. (43399)

Hanover, 30 Mar. 1781
I cannot help again most sincerely congratulating you upon your recovery because since my last letter to you I have had a more distinct account of your illness, which I am affraid arose principally from being over-heated. You know, my dearest brother, that I hate a sermon as well as you, but my affection for you forces me to entreat you for God's sake to take care of your health. You cannot stand this kind of life, and I am affraid it is the Windsor Lodge Duke[1] who leads you into it. I have no doubt but that he means you exceedingly well, but believe me, he is not the best adviser you can follow. You know me, I hope, my dearest brother, too well to think me a preacher, but as you told me upon our dearest friend Lake's going away that you begged I would give you my advice, I could not refrain from saying so much, as my affection for you would not permit me to pass it over in silence.[2]

Now that I have done with my long sermon I shall tell you first of all that I send over a number of trifles to the Queen and my sisters by the courier, but as I did not know what to give you I have sent you a painted fur lining, which I hope you will like. It is the dernier gout at Paris. You will think I believe that I am going to set up a shop here, but I must beg you will send over another steel sword like the one Gray made for us, so that I must by the next courier have two over. But I shall tire you with this long scrawl.

P.S. Let nobody see this letter. Do not forget my commissions. Give my compliments to Lyte and to Miss Hamilton as well as all other friends in England. Adieu. (43402–3)

42 LETTERS FROM THE PRINCE OF WALES TO PRINCE FREDERICK

Queen's House, 30 Mar. 1781
I last night received yr. buckles and yr. letter. I will take care you shall have yr. buckles immediately, & now I will set down to write a volume to

1. The Duke of Cumberland. He was Ranger of Windsor Forest and Great Park, 1766–90.
2. He wrote to the King, the previous day: 'I shall certainly in the first letter which I write to my brother express as forcibly as I can what your Majesty wishes.' (43400–1)

you. In primis, to make use of yr. own expression, I must tell you, as I already have done in a letter I have sent you by Busche, yt. ye only reason of my not writing to you was yt. I have been upwards of a month under Sir Richard Jebb's[1] hands, so ill yt. for two days he was very much alarmed for me. . . . I remained cooped up in my bedchamber an entire fortnight without ever tasting anything but barley water or some damned wishy washy stuff of that sort. I was sensible of my danger for those two days when ye disorder was at its crisis, and I cannot say I was much affected with any idea except when I thought I never should see either you, my dearest Frederick, or my dear friend Lake again. Whilst I was so ill I received three letters from you, all wh. arrived together as well as one from Joan Grenville. I cannot express to you how happy they made me. . . .

I am become a tolerable good whip & have given those orders concerning yr. phaeton wh. you desired me to give in one of yr. preceding letters. You will now have it very soon. Would to Heaven I could come over in it, for you cannot form to yourself an idea how happy I should be to see you soon again. It is my principal & constant wish, but no matter, I hope our separation will not last long. . . .

We heard very bad accounts of poor Winchelsea[2] who was arrived at Lisbon. Lady Charlotte Finch, her two daughters[3] & John Conyers[4] set out directly to see him, but since they are gone we have heard much better tidings of him wh. promise a speedy recovery. I hope he will soon recover, for a more truly worthy, honorable man I believe does not exist.

I flatter myself you will be pleased with ye manner in which yr. commissions are executed, as I have taken infinite pains with ym. all. I hope you liked ye frocks I sent you over, & by ye next messenger I will send you two new uniforms at least, with ye dress and undress of my hunting uniform. It is called so & is universally admired thro'out London, tout ce qui s'appelle ton, has made it up by way of handsome Ranelagh frocks. If there are any other cloaths of any sort or kind besides these & yr. Vandyke dress, wh. you wish to be sent over, I will take care of it. I shall also send you some new buckles together with ye sword you ordered. Grey humbly begged to make some alterations & improvements

1. The Prince of Wales's physician since 1780. Created baronet 1778 (1729–87).

2. George Finch, 9th Earl of Winchilsea (1752–1826), who succeeded his uncle in 1769. Lady Charlotte Finch was his mother. He was a Lord of the Bedchamber, 1777–1812, and Groom of the Stole, 1804–12. In May 1789 he acted as second to Lieutenant-Colonel Charles Lennox, later, 4th Duke of Richmond, in his duel with the Duke of York on Wimbledon Common.

3. Frances, who married Charles Feilding R.N.; and Henrietta (1750–1818).

4. Possibly the son of John Conyers of Copthall, Essex (d.1775) who had married Lady Charlotte Finch's sister Henrietta (1727–93).

in it, to wh. I most graciously assented. He has sent it home; 'tis excessively pretty, a mixture of gold & steel beads. However, tho' it is so pretty I made him take it back immediately, as it was not near so pretty or so elegant as yr. sword, nor was it anything in yt. taste. You will therefore have another, time enough to go by ye messenger, as elegant & as handsome as hands can make it.

No news passing here in particular. . . . I am now going to write a line to Joan, & therefore will conclude, dear brother, with assuring [etc.].

P.S. I have begun my letter to Joan, but since I began it I have cut my finger so deep yt. I cd. only add these few lines to plead my excuse. But he shall have yt. & you shall have another letter from me by Tuesday's post. (43404-7)

Queen's House, 10 Apr. 1781
I receiv'd yr. most affectionate letter[1] the day before yesterday, & I cannot express to you what delight & satisfaction it gave me. Yr. sermon, as you call it, is merely ye advice of one friend to another & a proof of that excellent heart I have always known you to possess. Believe me, dearest Frederick, if we always preach so to one another we might be ye best of friends thro'out life, & God grant we may ever continue so. Nothing on my part shall be wanting to encrease if possible this happy union. You mentioned in yr. letter as if you apprehended yt. the D[uke] of C[umberland] had in some manner been ye cause of my disorder, by raking & rioting & other things of ye same sort. You are really much mistaken. I have never seen ye D. ever since you have been gone; when anything of that sort has been going forwards, quite ye contrary. He has acted as my firmest, staunchest & best friend would have done, as you or Lake would have done, had you or he been present, in an affair wh. I wanted ye advice of such a friend, wh. has lately happened, & wh. I hope now will be speedily put an end to. It originated from ye old infernal cause Robinson[2]. . . . You shall hear everything concerning it the moment it is settled, but it is too long to be mentioned now. You will therefore perceive how much you are mistaken concerning [him], when so far from rioting and raking with me, he is always advising me to take care of my health. . . .

Let me a little into ye whole scene of everything yt. passes at Hannover, as I will do in my next, concerning everything yt. passes here. Yr. commissions I have executed. I have got both yr. swords, tho' different from each other, I think them both handsome. Buckles I send you as

1. No. 41 (30 March).

2. Mary Robinson (1758-1800), 'Perdita', the actress and mistress of the Prince of Wales. She had married Thomas Robinson in 1774.

usual, as well as a watch & chain wh. I hope you will like & wear for my sake. Ye hair in ye chain is mine. Yr. Vandyke dress is compleat & beautiful; ye hat for it I have ordered of Cater; it was made by ye tailor to Covent Garden Theatre. Ye ruff belonging to it is separate from ye whole & ties with two little white strings & tassels. I do not mean it is a ruff, but lace; it is an imitation only, but very beautiful in ye shape of our shirt collars, only deeper. Remember yr. shirt collar or stock must not appear in this dress; you had therefore best not wear any stock at all & tuck yr. collar down or under. I flatter myself you will find all these things executed with yt. dernier gout, wisdom & propriety you attribute to me in propria persona, & yt. being ye case I remain [etc.].

P.S. Best compliments to dear Joan. He will excuse my not writing to him as yet, as I want to make up for lost time to you. Ten thousand thanks for ye present you say you send me by ye messenger. (43408–9)

43 LETTERS FROM PRINCE FREDERICK TO THE PRINCE OF WALES

Hanover, 18 Apr. 1781

... I must give you the commission to distribute a few trifles which I have sent directed to you to be given among my four sisters, one fausse montre is for Princess Royal[1], and the other with her sypher upon is for Puss[2]. The other two little things are for Mary[3] and Sophia[4], and a fan for Elizabeth[5], the finest is for her and the plain one is for the Queen. As for you, as I wrote you word before, not knowing what to send you, I desire your gracious acceptance of a fur lining which is made at Liège, and which I was told there was the ton at Paris. I have two commissions

1. Charlotte Augusta Matilda, the Princess Royal (1766–1828), afterwards Queen of Württemberg.

2. Princess Augusta Sophia (1768–1840), the King's second daughter.

3. Princess Mary (1776–1857), afterwards Duchess of Gloucester; the King's fourth daughter. Princess Amelia's first letter to the King which has been preserved, referred to her sister Mary. It was inadequately dated 22 July: ' ... Miny feels pain when she puts on poultice. I allways do hold her hand, and a warm napkin is put over the flannel with the fomentation' (Add. Georgian 14/2). Princess Mary was too young to merit much comment in these early letters, but on 31 July 1787 the Princess Royal wrote to Prince Augustus: 'Mary is wonderfully grown this year and I think her face improved her hair is turned up which makes a very great alteration: but as for my poor little Sophia I am afraid that she will never be very tall for she is so much shorter than her sister that one should take her to be four years younger at least: they have begun to learn German but the measles have put a stop to all their lessons for some time; which I am very sorry for as I think every hour that they loose of consequence.'

4. Princess Sophia (1777–1848), the King's fifth daughter.

5. Princess Elizabeth (1770–1840), afterwards Landgravine of Hesse-Homburg, the King's third daughter.

more to give you which you will think very extraordinary ones. The first is to send over some of the Ormskirk medicines for the bites of mad dogs. You will give my compliments to Keate[1], and tell him from me that I am not mad myself but that there being none of this medicine to be got here, I must beg he will let you have a good parcel for me. Joan is particularly anxious for this, which will really very possibly be necessary, for you have no idea how we are pestered with dogs here. The other is for some coss lettuce seed of which they have none here.

I forgot to acquaint you that I am growing one of the best whips here. Last Saturday I had the most ridiculous accident here that can be imagined and which makes me the more impatient for the arrival of my phaeton from England. There is one phaeton here of the King's which is the most Christian-like equipage he has here, & which I always drive. Last Saturday I drove Prince Charles[2] out in it, just as we had got in the middle of the street smash goes the hind axle, by which means off went our hind wheel and down we came all on one side. I burst out laughing but Prince Charles was badly frightened tho' he was the uppermost. But the worst of the whole was that he fell upon my arm and so I could not stop, and we trotted on slowly all on one side for above fifty yards till somebody stopped the horses. As soon as they were stopped I rolled out without being the least hurt, and thus ended our ridiculous tumble. Luckily it was in the straight road or otherwise people would have said that I had done [it] thro: bad coachmanship. But I must finish my letter, I shall therefore only beg my compliments to Miss Hamilton. I cannot however conclude without wishing you was here with me.
Since this was wrote I have two more commissions. The first is to send us a turtle whenever it is possible, and the other is for a tabor and pipe, which are very much wanted for our country dances. Adieu. (43410–1)

Hanover, 24 Apr. 1781
Dear brother, I have no time to write to you now, but I cannot help thanking you for your kind letter, which I shall answer as fully as I can the first opportunity; you shall have the full account of everything that is done here. Many thanks for your having executed all the commissions. (43414)

Hanover, Apr. [1781]
I am waiting with impatience for the letter which you promised me. We have now two English posts due, and you may easily conceive how eager

1. Thomas Keate (1745–1821), surgeon to the Prince of Wales.

2. His uncle, Prince Charles of Mecklenburg-Strelitz.

we are for any news that comes from dear England. Busche, who arrived here the beginning of last week, brought me your letter as well as the things you was so good as to send me. By what he says I find many things are altered since I quitted England. I shall certainly do what you desire me about Busche, and had very luckily before I read your letter already told him that if there was anything that he wished should be done, and thought that I could be of any use to him by writing to the King, I should certainly be very happy to do it. I can write you, when I have more leasure, many more instances of that rascal Alvensleben, but I wish you would not mention them. I only tell you one now.

General Wallmoden[1], whom you must remember and who is an exceedingly clever man, having been fourteen years Minister from Hanover at Vienna, which is always regarded as a step towards being in the Cabinet, wished to quit the Army and enter as Minister. He is without a doubt the fittest man of this country for that office, and besides it was his due, but however, Alvensleben as had weight [sic] to get him refused and it is supposed that he intends to appoint his own nephew Hacke, a Minister whom you remember in England; he used to talk so badly & is of all the stupid and tiresome fellows the stupidest. Wallmoden feels this so much that he says he will go back to Vienna for a year, and if in the course of that year the King does not chuse to appoint him Minister, he shall resign and return to Hanover. Walmoden did not indeed tell me this himself, but he told it to the person who told it me, but at the same time begged it might never be mentioned again. I beg therefore you will never mention it to anybody whatsoever, because it can do Walmoden no good, and would certainly do him a great deal of harm. I beg you will give my duty to their Majesties and tell them that as I had nothing particular to write to them, I should not do it this post, but that they might each of them depend upon a letter by the quarterly messenger who sets out Thursday sennight. Pray give my compliments to Miss Hamilton and tell her how much I am obliged to her for her kind remembrance of me. I must beg you will send me by the courier four cricket bats and two dozen of balls, for we have no such things in this country. I think you will be tired of reading this scrawl. I shall therefore only add that I am and ever shall be [etc.]

My compliments to the Duke of Montagu, and to little Mrs. Privy Lyte[2]. (43415–6)

1. The reputed son of George II (1736–1811).
2. Henry Lyte was the Prince's Privy Purse

Hanover, 4 May 1781

I have not time this post to answer your last letter fully but shall certainly very soon. I wish you [would] send some more new country dances, for people are vastly fond of our country dances here. I do not know why, but very luckily I am hardly upon decent terms with Prince Ernest[1] or with Prince Charles. As for Prince George[2] he is, the Lord be praised, gone back to Prague. I have a great many pretty stories to tell you about these three pretty genius's as well as about many other people, but which will be too long to add here. Give my compliments to Miss Hamilton and to all other friends in England. . . . (43417)

44 THE KING TO THE PRINCE OF WALES

Queen's House, 6 May 1781

You must be too thoroughly acquainted with my sentiments to be surprised at the pain I received from the communication Lord Southampton made me last night at your request. Indeed, it would be great injustice not to allow that he executed it in the most delicate manner, and tried to state your sorrow at having taken a step that you are conscious must displease me, and a resolution of in future conforming yourself to that line of conduct which will make me more happy as more becoming a Prince of Wales. It is the hopes of this, and your having conveyed it to me before it had reached me by any other means, that can make me in the least pass over what has happened. I do not doubt that the last evening papers, or those of tomorrow morning will have the whole business fully stated in it. Indeed it is now allmost certain that some unpleasant mention of you is daily to be found in the papers, and grieved enough as I am by those transactions, it would be greatly aggravated if I did not trust that malevolence greatly adds on these occasions.

Do read over the letter I wrote to you a few days after your last birthday[3], and the one in December[4] previous to the appointment of your family. You confessed they gave you pleasure and satisfied you. Examine yourself and see how far your conduct has been conformable to them, and then draw your conclusion whether you must not give me many an uneasy moment. I wish to live with you as a friend, but then by your behaviour you must deserve it. If I did not state these things I should not fulfill my duty either to my God or to my country. I say as little as

1. Frederick's uncle, Queen Charlotte's brother.

2. Another of the Queen's brothers (1748–85).

3. No. 31, 14 August 1780.

4. No. 31, 22 December 1780.

possible, from an hope that your reason will begin to act. Whenever it does, I do not doubt but instead of pain you will give me pleasure.

The real kindness I have shewn by the assurances I gave you through Lord Southampton of my intention to come to your assistance in [a] shameful transaction ... (on which subject I will be silent till the business is nearer a conclusion) made me flatter myself you would have redoubled your intentions of acting in a manner worthy of my approbation. That a little eased my mind, but now I hear of your going to sup at Lord Chesterfield's[1], which whilst contriving you knew would be displeasing to me. If you felt as you ought, you could not enjoy any pleasure which you are conscious that parents who deserve your affection as well as respect, when they hear it, will meet with their displeasure. Nothing you can do can be long a secret; the very companions of your follies ever repeat what happens. Indeed it cannot be otherwise; those who can partake of them must be wanting in judgement, and therefore pride themselves in shewing their habitudes with you, or from design wish to give all those whose good opinion is worth having a mean one of you.

Who is the person to whose house you have chose to go contrary to a general injunction of mine but Lord Chesterfield, who the last summer was your object of dislike? Is it right to abuse a man one hour and make him your companion the next? You may easily believe I am greatly offended at him, therefore I will not say more concerning him; but believe me, the conduct that makes all good men despise a St. Leger[2] and a Windham[3] is more criminal in the Heir Apparent of the Crown, who ought to be a means of restoring decency in this Kingdom; besides, this whole business has so much the air of those manoeuvres that discredited the Duke of Cumberland and a continuance of which have rendered him certainly neither a creditable adviser nor companion for you.

When you read this carefully over, you will find an affectionate father trying to save his son from perdition; one who knows any evil you have acquired is not owing to bad example at home, who wishes you may

1. 'One night', wrote Horace Walpole, 'as soon as the King was gone to bed, the Prince, with St. Leger and Charles Windham [Wyndham], his chief favourites, and some of his younger servants, the Duke of Cumberland and George Pitt, son of Lord Rivers, went to Blackheath to sup with Lord Chesterfield, who, being married, would not consent to send for the company the Prince required. They all got immediately drunk, and the Prince was forced to lie down on a bed for some time' (*Last Journals*, ii.361 [1910], 4 May 1781). Chesterfield 'has as little good breeding as any man I ever met with!' wrote Fanny Burney. Yet he was the King's Master of the Horse, 1798–1804, and a K.G. (1805).

2. Colonel Anthony St. Leger (?1759–1821) one of the Prince's boon companions. He was appointed a Groom of the Bedchamber to the Prince in February 1784.

3. Charles William Wyndham (1760–1828), brother of the 3rd Earl of Egremont; M.P. for Midhurst, 1790–5; for New Shoreham, 1795–1802; for Sussex, 1807–12.

become worthy of the situation that Divine Providence probably intends for you, who knows you are not wanting in natural tallents if you will exert them, and hopes you have an heart to feel what is owing to those who have from your tenderest infancy treated you with kindness, and are desirous of continuing it.[1]   (41789-90)

45   THE PRINCE OF WALES TO PRINCE FREDERICK

Queen's House, 11 May 1781

I ought to have answered by ye preceding post yr. very kind letter wh. ye messenger brought me, as well as to thank you in ye name of ye whole little family for ye presents you was so good as to send ym. With regard to me you know ye sincere and warm feelings yt. exist in my bosom respecting everything yt. concerns you, & therefore I think you will not doubt how agreable even the merest trifle yt. comes from you would prove to me, but really & truly I think ye lining beautiful. I have punctually executed all yr. commissions & have ordered something else for you wh. I think you will like when you come to see it, & yt. is, another Vandyke dress besides the one you desired me to order for you. The one you gave me an order for was to be white sattin & pink, wh. I accordingly had put in hand immediately, but ye tailor yt. made it at Shee's direction made ye whole of the dress white satting, with pink puffs & knots. It is beautiful. Ye hat is made by Cater, but then we considered yt. if there was to be a masquerade in ye summer season you could not well wear yt. dress. I ordered you another wh. is lyloch silk ye whole, with pale buff puffs & knots. I think you will admire it when you see it. Yr. phaeton will set off this week or ye next for Hamburgh. You must send somebody for it. I drove it & it follows exceedingly well. I have driven it 22 miles with four in hand within ye two hours at a trot, wh. is reckoned pretty good driving. . . .

Yr. phaeton is shipped on board of a Hambro' ship, with particular marks upon it with a direction for someone else, for should ye ship be taken, & were they to see ye direction for a subject of England, they wld. seize it, but being directed to somebody yt. has nothing at all to do with England, they wld. let it proceed on its voyage. I therefore send you ye marks & directions by wh. you must send for it. You will see them written in ye enclosed paper in Lukin's [?] hand. Part of yr. commission only ye

1. The *Morning Chronicle* reported on Friday 4 May that the Prince attended a masked Ball at the Pantheon on the 2nd, dressed in a black domino; that he sometimes walked about with Lord Cholmondeley, the Hon. Mr. Wyndham and Mr. St. Leger; and that he frequently passed the lovely Perdita, dressed in regimentals under a black domino.

messenger can bring with him. Yr. cloaths & a few other things I believe ye hats to yr. dresses & two or three round hats; the swords with some other trifles & with ye watch I send you are all packed together in a long wooden box, another box full of bats & balls, & another box full of brushes & other things wh. Sam wrote over for to order, a box of saddles, & General Freytag[1] will take care shall be safely embarked by ye next Hambro' ship wh. is to sail a fortnight hance. We intend yr. hounds should go by ye same conveyance. I hope I have now executed everything to yr. satisfaction, so that I shall be for ye future employed upon ye like occasions, for believe me, dear Frederick, nothing can afford me more pleasure than doing anything yt. can give you satisfaction. I also send you ye Extraordinary Gazette with excellent news from Lord Cornwallis[2]. My best compliments to Joan & Busche. I will really write to ym. both by next Friday's post. Adieu. It is very late.   (43420-3)

46   LETTERS FROM PRINCE FREDERICK TO THE PRINCE OF WALES

Hanover, 5 June 1781

I suppose you must have heard of my accident[3], and therefore will excuse my long silence. I have a thousand things to say to you but have not time at present to write them. My arm is so far recovered that I shall set out tomorrow for the Hartz. I shall be absent about a fortnight but you may depend upon receiving a long letter from me upon my return. I have not time to add only to beg you will send over by the post some fresh books of country dances.

1. Field-Marshal William von Freytag (1711-98), the Hanoverian General.

2. Charles, 1st Marquess (1792) and 2nd Earl (1762) Cornwallis (1738-1805), second-in-command of the King's army in America. Capitulated at Yorktown, 1781. Governor-General of Bengal, 1786-93 and 1805; Master-General of the Ordnance, 1795-1801; Lord-Lieutenant of Ireland, June 1798-May 1801; Plenipotentiary to Amiens, September 1801.

   The *London Gazette Extraordinary* (10 May) gave the news of Cornwallis's rapid advance through North Carolina and of his victory over the Americans at Guilford.

3. Frederick explained what had happened, in a letter to the King (25 May): 'I hope your Majesty will excuse my long silence but as I acquainted you about a week ago I had the misfortune in going downstairs to strain the back of my knee, and two days afterwards as I was lifting myself out of the phaeton, the servant upon whom I was leaning, thought that I was tumbling and therefore tried to ketch me, by which he strained my right wrist so violently that I have been under the surgeon's hands ever since. I had before intended to have asked your Majesty's permission to go to Pyrmont for my amusement, but I have now the additional reason that the surgeon recommends my going to pump my wrist with the water there, which is remarkable good to fortify any weakness, because he adds that having already strained the same wrist violently twice if I do not get it cured thoroughly now, there may remain a weakness there for life. . . .'

[*P.S.*] If William is returned tell him my love [*sic*] and tell him upon my return he shall receive a letter from me.[1]   (43429)

Clausthal, 15 June 1781

I could not let General Fawcitt[2] set out without writing you a few lines. I have been at Solingen, Gottingen and the Hartz. You can have no idea of the country here, it is so exceedingly mountainous and covered all over with wood. At Gottingen I saw the young gentlemen valt, which is exceedingly pretty. They also rode a *carousel*, which is in its way equally pretty. I have been quite at the bottom of two mines here, which are about 1,300 feet perpendicular under ground; it is excessively amusing to see the whole process of the working the ore.[3] But Fawcitt is in a hurry to go away. When I return to Hanover I shall certainly fullfill my promise in writing you a very long letter.   (43432)

Hanover, 3 July 1781

I have not yet had time, nor shall I this post be able to fulfill my promise of a long letter to you. Most of the things are arrived from Hamburg; the swords are very handsome but the watch is beautifull. . . .

1. Writing from Portsmouth on 21 May 1781, the Duke of Cumberland sent the Prince news of his brother: 'I have made every inquiry after Prince William; they left the Fleet three days ago & are cruizing about Brest, they are in want of wine & water & therefore I believe they will be in about the middle or end of the next week. While the Fleet were at Gibraltar the Spanish gunboats were throwing shells on the Tower & have entirely destroyed the house, so that nothing remains but the fortifications, the inhabitants being obliged to move to the southward & have made up huts for their present reception. . . .'   (54456)

2. Sir William Fawcett (1728–1804). Served in the Seven Years' War, the American and French Revolutionary Wars; Adjutant-General of the Forces, 1781; K.B., 1786; Lieutenant-General, 1782; General, 1796.

3. Frederick wrote to the King on the 19th: '. . . The night of our arrival at the Hartz there was a kind of an assembly of all the different trades such as miners, carters &c. They gave us a feu de joi of whips, which is one of the most extraordinary things that can be seen or heard, the noise of it is not to be described. We went down on Wednesday into the Dorothea, and came up by the Caroline. Each of them are about thirteen hundred feet deep. We were six hours under ground. Nothing can be more amusing than the seeing them. The next day we went to see the forges; we saw the whole process of preparing the ore, of casting it, and of at last coining it. The Friday we went and saw the new work called the Georgstoll, which is one of the most curious things that can be conceived. It will take as they told us eighteen years more before it is finished. On Saturday we went to see the view from the Broken [*sic*]; on our journey we stopped to see the silver mines at Ramelsberg, which are quite different from those at Clausthal for at the Ramelsberg they do not blow up mines as at Clausthal but loosen the ore by the violence of fire; the heat is not to be described; the miners are obliged to work quite naked except a small leather belt around their loins. . . .'   (43433–4)

I have not time to add any more but hope you will be so good as to write soon because it is now near two months since I have heard the least word from you. (43437)

47   THE PRINCE OF WALES TO PRINCE FREDERICK

Tuesday evening, 17 July 1781

You will not wonder at my long silence when you know the cause of it. Ye misery yt. I suffer is not to be believed. However, you must give yr. word & honor as a gentleman before you begin to read ye sad tale I have to unfold, yt. it must be buried in ye strictest silence, for reasons wh. will strike you, & for others wh. I will mention to you. What I have suffered ever since last Saturday was sennight, is beyond ye power of man to describe. However, I will now begin.

Soon after I recovered my violent illness in ye winter [*sic*] I went to Court. There I saw Monsieur Hardeng Madame was there also, but whether on account of the crouds there were ye two ensuing Drawing Rooms, I never saw her either yt. Drawing or any of ye other two, but being at St. James's ye ensuing Thursday, someone, upon my asking, shewed her to me at ye other end of the room. I bowed to her but could not get up to speak to her before ye. Court was over. However, I met her in ye evening in ye. Queen's appartment, at a great concert we had there. I then was introduced to her. After having conversed with her some time I perceived yt. she was a very sensible, agreable, pleasant little woman, but devilish severe. I thought no more of her at yt. time. Busche having desired me to take notice of her husband as a very sensible honest man, I invited him to dinner, with a grande société, in order to shew him every civility & attention yt. was in my power, by introducing him to several people, in short, to as many as I possibly could, in order to encrease his acquaintance & make him known to some of ye. people of ye. first fashion here. He dined with me once or twice before I met him, *alone*, at ye. Lodge at Windsor, in order to hunt with our pack of hounds ye. next morning. The King invited him down twice in this manner in order to hunt. However, ye. third time he was invited down, he was ordered to make up ye. King's hunt, & desired to bring Madame with him. I had seen & met Madame only once since ye. first time I mentioned meeting her at ye. Queen's House, in ye. Queen's appartment, when I was set down to whist with a set of very good and consequently very grave players. She was set down at ye next table opposite to me to a commerce party with my sister, a thing I could easily perceive by her looks she disliked very much, not particularly because she was to play with those

65

girls, but because, as I have since learnt from her, she hates all games at cards, as I do, unless they are games of chance, merely for ye sake of gambling. That night I thought her devinely pretty. My attention was naturally taken from the cards, & in short, I could not keep my eyes off her. One of my sisters who had undertaken to teach her ye. game, with wh. she was totally unacquainted, played her cards for her, & I observed her to be equally inattentive to her play, as I was, but I thought I met her eyes too frequently to fancy yt. it proceeded from inattention or common curiosity only. However, at yt. moment I was too much taken up with looking at her myself to be so observant, tho' it struck me after-wards. From that moment ye. fatal tho' delightful passion arose in my bosom for her, wh. has made me since, ye. most miserable & wretched of men. With whom should I so soon place my whole confidence & all my cares & misfortunes wh. have now brought me to ye. utmost pitch of misery, as with him who is ye. friend of my heart, who has always proved himself deserving of ye. confidence I have placed in him, my dearest brother? Yes, my beloved Frederick, with you I know this un-happy secret will be buried in eternal in eternal [sic] silence. O did you but know how I adore her, how I love her, how I would sacrifice every earthly thing to her; by Heavens I shall go distracted: my brain will split. But to return to our subject. I went down to Windsor. I met Mme. Hardenberg there; she was to stay & did stay a fortnight there with us. During ye. first three or four days I shewed her every attention possible, & did not mention a word of love to her. However, within a day or two I said to her, after having shewn her very particular attentions, yt. it was a pity after having met so often at Windsor I could not have ye. satisfac-tion of seeing her so frequently in London, & asked her if she was not to be seen in town sometimes after eleven o'clock when her husband was out. She resented this with very great spirit saying she believed I had forgot whom I was speaking to, but, upon my making her strong excuses & saying I really did not mean to give her ye. smallest offence, she said she would forget all. But in order to shorten my dismal tale & not to stick upon minutiae I will tell you yt. [I] dropped every other connexion of whatever sort or kind, & devoted myself entirely to this angelick little woman. I grew more & more fond of her, & to so violent a degree did I doat upon her, yt. it impaired my health & constitution very much. Jebb was obliged to attend upon me. I have spit blood & am so much emaciated you would hardly know me again. This had a strong effect upon her. She began then to perceive how truly I was attached to her, & one morning when I called upon her at her house at Old Windsor while her husband was absent, after I had complained much of her coldness & cruelty to me, she thus spoke to me, "I certainly am very much attached to you, & do love you most sincerely, & it affords me great delight to think yt. you are attached to me, but I must tell you yt. I was once very much attached to another person, & did think yt a woman never could love but once very sincerely during her life. If, after such a declaration, you can attach yourself to me, it will be an additional proof of your love, but should you not, for God's sake let us drop all thoughts of love & part very good friends''. I assured her yt. what she had said, so far from lessening my affection, encreased it if possible, & made me entertain a higher idea of her honor. I then continued visiting her two or three times more before she would consent to listen to any idea of compleating my happiness. However at last she did. O my beloved brother, I enjoyed beforehand ye. pleasures of Elyssium; but this is a secret wh. no one but Hulse[1] & you know of. Thus did our connexion go forward in ye most delightful manner yt. you can form any idea to yourself of, till an unfortunate article in ye. *Morning Herald* appeared, saying yt. ye. German Baroness who had been imported by ye Queen, had taken a house next door to Perdita's in Cork Street, & yt. my carriage was seen constantly at her door. Ye. confusion wh. caused this article is yt. a Polish Countess, Countess Raouska, has taken ye. house next to Mrs. R[obinson]'s, & ye. Duke of Gloucester's carriage is very often, nay even every day seen at her door. Be this as it will, her husband, who had been put upon his guard by some servant in his family, came to her & told her yt. unless she immediately wrote a letter to me saying she would drop all connexion with me he should suppose she had cuckolded him. She endeavored to convince him concerning his absurdity about ye. newspaper, & at last grew angry. However, he intim[id]ated her so much by his brutality yt. she was in a moment of fright weak enough to confess I had made proposals to her, tho' never had succeeded, & forced her to write ye. letter I have already mentioned to you, to me. He also wrote one to me wh. accompanied it. I almost fell into fits when I received the packet from him, & augured no good from it, but upon opening it I thought I should have run distracted, as I conceived her to be guilty of ye. blackest ingratitude & cruelty to me. However, I immediately sat down & wrote to them both saying to him yt. it was very true I was very strongly attached to his wife, but yt. I should be ye. most infamous of human beings if, after the proposals I had made her I should have a single doubt concerning his wife's character, for yt. she had always treated me with ye. utmost coolness & yt. I was ye. only person yt. he [*sic*] was to blame in ye. whole of this affair. As to her, I wrote her ye. most passionate of letters. I thought everything was then at an end, & I sent an express for Lord Southampton & desired he wld. go into ye. King & ask his permission for me to go abroad, as an unfortunate affair had of late happened to me wh. made me excessively miserable, & I wished by yt. means to try if I could not a little dissipate my thoughts; yt. it was not an affair yt.

1. The Prince's Equerry. See No. 171.

would ever come to ye. King's ears & yt. therefore I flattered myself I should receive his Majesty's leave to set out as soon as possible. The answered [*sic*] Southampton brought me was yt. the King cld. not at present think of my going abroad as it was during ye. war. This was on Sunday sennight in ye morning, & on Sunday at noon I received a letter from her, yt. she was forced to write ye. preceding one to me, reminding me of her attachment, saying she hoped I had not forgot all my vows, & would run off with her yt. night. Adoring her as I do, judge of ye. different combats my heart had to endure, ye. idea of ye. noise my flight would cause in ye. world, then ye. idea of being in possession of her who alone forms all my happiness. For some time I in a manner lost my senses entirely. However, I chanced to meet her & consented to ye. plot, but as soon as I had, reflection crouded itself on my mind. Ye. thought wh. then occurred to me was yt. although she was unhappy, nay miserable, with her husband, yet she would live as a woman in her situation in life ought to do; at least she could eat & she cld. drink & live, but had she been with me, you know our father's severe disposition; everything yt. was shocking is to be expected from him; & ye. very thought yt. I should perhaps see ye. object of all my tenderness, of all my love, in short, ye. only woman upon earth I can & do only love, perishing for want, is such an idea yt. it stabbed me to ye. very heart & staggered my resolution. I need not desire you, dearest Frederick, to feel for my sufferings. Yr. generous heart will sufficiently share ye. pangs & conflicts I have & still do endure; in short, my misery was such yt. I went under ye promise of ye greatest secrecy & threw myself at my mother's feet & confessed ye. whole truth to her. I fainted. She cried excessively & felt for me very much. There was then but one thing to be done, & we sent Hulse to Mme. H. to tell her yt. nothing but an unforeseen accident wh. had happened cld. prevent my coming. Upon this ye. Queen only begged me to allow her to tell ye. King upon condition he took no part in it, what had been ye. subject of our conversation. Whether she was quite true to me or not I cannot say. However, all yt. I have now time to tell you is yt. my father sent for Hardenberg & yt. he went off with my little angel to Bruxelles on Thursday night, leaving me to all ye. agonies of misery & despair. I have not time, my best friend, to explain anything more to you at present, but will certainly by ye. very next post. I only now have to add yt. I trust so much to yr. honor (yt. supposing her to [be] capable of allowing of it, wh. I believe impossible but I say supposing yt. possible) yt. you would not add to my misery by making up to her or making love to her even in ye. most distant. If ever I should hear it you wld. be ye. cause of my death, but I cannot help upbraiding myself for want of confidence in yr. honor, so you are incapable of it, you wld. not hurt yr. brother who loves you so tenderly, in ye. most distant manner, however you must allow for ye. feelings of a lover. You

68

will see ye. necessity for yr. secrecy. I will tell you & explain to you much more in my next, concerning all my plans & views wh. are ye. only things wh. now keep me alive. With regard to the King, you will not make any comments, I hope, upon any part of ye. business to him, only say you are sorry to hear of the affair & promise yr. secrecy upon ye. occasion. Adieu, dearest of brothers, my heart is ready to burst.

Queen's House, Friday, 20 July 1781
P.S. You will perceive my agitation by ye. horrid style & scrawl. You shall hear from me again almost immediately, as I have scarce any other satisfaction left than yt. of knowing I have a friend who will feel most truly for me. Once more, adieu, my dearest Frederick.   (43440–5)

48   PRINCE FREDERICK TO THE PRINCE OF WALES

30 July 1781
I cannot let General Freytag return to England without writing to you to thank you for your last letter, though I am sorry it was on so dismal an occasion. You, I am sure, are too fully persuaded of my affection for you not to know how much I felt upon reading your letter. As for the promise which you ask of me, I most willingly give it, for if you knew her as well as I do ... you would be completely cured of any particular affection for her. Next letter I shall write to you, when I suppose your grief be a little subsided, I will send you an exact account of her behaviour to me, of which I have no doubt she spoke to you, though very possibly with not so exact a regard for truth as I will have. There is also another story of her which I know for a fact & which I will also send you, but which you must never mention.

I am just returned from a very agreeable party to Pyrmont, which is a sweet spot.

Pray send me back by the courier the new Army List. I have not time to add any more, only that I am, [etc.].

Pray write soon.   (43448–9)

49   LIEUTENANT-COLONEL GERARD LAKE TO THE PRINCE OF WALES

Yorktown, Virginia, 25 Aug. 1781
By my letters dated the 4th of April I find myself as usual under the necessity (contrary to your express commands) of returning my thanks

to you for some fresh mark of favor. What I at present mean is the high honor her Majesty was pleas'd to confer upon my family from being so extremely kind as to stand godmother to my little boy[1] with your R.H. & Prince Frederick. It is impossible for me to express how much I feel oblig'd to her Majesty for this strong mark of kindness shewn to Mrs. Lake[2] at a time when she was so particularly circumstanc'd. May I beg your R.H. will take an opportunity of expressing the thorough sense I have of the obligation conferr'd upon me, & how sincerely I wish it may be in my power to convince her as well as the rest of your family [of] the sincerity with which I am attach'd, & how much I wish my future conduct may prove my sentiments as they have hitherto done, will ever induce me to do that which appears to me for the good of your interests, & I flatter myself your R.H. will do me the justice to acknowledge that I have constantly endeavour'd to perform the duties of the very honorable & flattering situation his Majesty had so graciously & unexpectedly plac'd me in,[3] to the best of my abilities, ever wishing to establish that regard, friendship & confidence so necessary to form an agreable intercourse between parents & their children for the ease & happiness of a family, & surely is none more so than your Royal Highnesses, to which the world will of course look up for example from considering how immediately concern'd they are in your family living well together.

Col. Conway[4], who will in all probability deliver this letter to you, is very well able to inform you of what is going on & we have been doing in this part of the world, & I do assure you no one can give you a more exact account, as he has taken the utmost pains (in which he has succeeded) to be wherever anything was to be seen, & has prov'd himself to be a very cool, determin'd man & excellent officer. He is, beleive me, a most honorable & worthy man. I have liv'd much with him & shall very severely feel the loss of his society. He will tell you I command the Light Company which is still remarkably fine, notwithstanding the great loss of men they have sustain'd. I may without being accus'd of partiality, as I can have had no hand in making them what they are, be allow'd to say there is nothing superior to them in the world either for discipline, zeal or spirit. Capt. Dundas of the 1st Regt., who was with them all through the Carolinas, commanded them from the time of Col. Hall's death, who fell when they so gallantly cross'd the Catanba, has prov'd himself a most imcomparable officer. He is a young man of the greatest merit in

1. His second son, George Augustus Frederick Lake (1781–1808), who was killed in the Peninsular War.

2. In 1770 Lake married Elizabeth (1751–98), daughter of Edward Barker.

3. That of First Equerry to the Prince.

4. Colonel the Hon. Robert Conway (1748–1831), Aide-de-Camp to General Sir Henry Clinton, who despatched him to England to represent the desperate state of affairs in America. He was the third son of the 1st Marquess of Hertford.

his profession, & I am certain no one is more convinc'd of it than Ld. Cornwallis, who, upon seeing me posted with the company, congratulated me upon being at the head of the best & finest in the world, at the same time expressing his great approbation of the conduct, skill & gallant behaviour of Capt. Dundas upon every occasion. Gen. O'Hara[1] who, as the Gazette has already told you, has commanded this Brigade most wonderfully well, & establish'd the best discipline & good order imaginable, has shewn me every attention possible & I understand means to put the Grenadiers to my Company and give me the command of both. This you may be certain makes me feel very happy & oblig'd, more especially as he will do it in so handsome a manner. You will easily conceive I feel most exceedingly happy at being under Lord Cornwallis, an officer so distinguish'd for his abilities & so universally ador'd by the Army, which is not to be wonder'd at when one reflects upon his conduct being so uniformly meritorious & great in all his undertakings. I most sincerely wish his exertions may be crown'd with the success they so justly deserve, tho' I fear, from what cause I do not pretend to say, this war will never be finish'd in the way we have all so much reason to wish it should, as I have no doubt that every American is so entirely averse to a reconciliation with the mother country, so exasperated against us, at the same time so fertile in resources, that it is not possible this country ever can be conquer'd, tho' I do presume England never was possess'd of a more zealous, spirited or gallant army than is at present in this part of the world, & that nothing they can do will be wanting to end it gloriously.

So much for *politics*. You well know how little I interest myself about them in general, & feel half inclin'd not to mention what I have, but thinking you might expect some intelligence, I determin'd to give you the opinion of most people in this part of the world in the fewest words possible, & those I think strictly true. I have not the smallest idea of what the next campaign will be, whether active or otherwise. It is imagin'd we shall not be quite idle; we are at present throwing up works to protect our shipping which are to lie here the winter, as it is the finest bay & best calculated for their safety during the hard weather in all America.

I grow very impatient to hear how you are amusing yourself, & long much to know if everything turns out to your expectation. If it does as compleatly as I wish, you are by many degrees the happiest man in this world. Let me know how you proceed, in a few lines from your own hand, which will, you may be certain, add much to the comfort of him

1. Charles O'Hara (1740?–1802); commanded the Brigade of Guards in America; wounded at Guilford Courthouse, 15 March 1781, and captured at Yorktown, 19 October following. Major-General, 1782; Lieutenant-General, 1793; General, 1798; Governor of Gibraltar, 1795–1802.

who wishes to assure you at all times how much he is your oblig'd faithful servt. & sincere friend.

[*P.S.*] May I trouble you to make my best respects to the Duke of Cumberland, who has been so very kind as to think of me occasionally in your letter. I flatter myself you will not shew *one part* of this letter to anyone. (38053–4)

50 PRINCE FREDERICK TO THE PRINCE OF WALES, AND THE REPLY

Mont Brilliant, 28 Aug. 1781

I now sit down to fulfil my promise of writing to you what passed between Madam de Reventlau & myself, which I have no doubt but you have heard from herself, but very possibly with not so much regard to the truth, as upon my honour I will have. When I first arrived here, you know very well I was not acquainted with a single person. For the first two or three days I could make no difference between people, but as his Majesty had particularly ordered me to pay attention to the Field Marechal it was natural I should also pay attention to his family. But I am certain that I was not at all particular to her. On the Thursday after my arrival there was a masquerade at which I asked her to dance the first dance with me. I never could stir in the room but she followed me & in so very striking a manner that everybody remarked it, particularly after supper was over, for as I was standing talking with somebody else she came behind me & took hold of my arm & asked me to walk about in the room with her, & a little time afterwards as I was dancing with her she said to me that she had got the headache & would sit down. And immediately after whispered me that if there was nobody in the next room she would go with me there. Now I humbly think that is speaking in pretty plain terms. As for me, I desired no better fun but unluckily the room was full. Well, she immediately afterwards quitted me & went up to a lady there & said that I was the most tiresome fellow she had ever seen & that I never would leave her alone & a number of other pretty things. Now I do assure you that I have not added the least thing in this story, which I am afraid you will think very long, nor would I have wrote it to you if I had not thought it would be of use to you for showing what a woman she is. I know also other stories of her still worse than this, but I do not think it necessary to mention them to you as I think this is sufficient.

I have many thanks to return you for the many fine things you have sent me by the courier. I see you have had very fine doings on your birthday at Windsor. I suppose you have had many congratulations on the day, but none can have been more sincere than that of, dear brother, [etc.]. (43454–5)

Windsor Castle, 18 Sep. 1781

Ten thousand thanks for yr. last kind letter, for I have not wrote to you since I received yr. two last letters. I could not have thought Mme. H— capable of such conduct as you have told me of. Il ne faut pas se laisser mourrir de douleur. My spirits are greatly better, but I never can think of her without ye. strongest love & regard, as I really am of opinion her conduct was of ye most generous kind towards me. I cannot but confess to you, my dear Frederick I had some doubts about her whilst our connexion lasted, as she appeared to me to be very capricious & very singular in some things, & very chearful & agreable in others. In short it was a very miserable & unhappy affair alltogether, most compleatly so. However, I should be vastly obliged to you if, as soon as you have received this, you wld. write me word back again how she behaves at Hannover, & whether you have seen her, & supposing you have, what passed between you & her, what report says, &, in short, let me beg of you to tell me openly & freely as I am sure you will as I desire it, everything you know concerning her.

The K. is excessively cross & ill-tempered & uncommonly grumpy, snubbing everybody, in everything. We are not upon ye very best terms; however, I will defer all yt. to be ye. subject of another letter to you. Good God, what wld. I give either to have you with me or to be with you for a little time. I litterally, as I have already told you, lost half myself in being separated from you. Old Johnston & I drink your health together very cordially every evening; there never passes a day yt. you are not present to my mind. Would to Heaven yt. you was again here. I cannot help repeating it over & over again, & indeed I am thoroughly convinced, my dearest Frederick, you are too well acquainted with my heart to doubt its sincerity. Yr. birthday[1] did not pass without my offering up ye. sincerest prayers to ye. Almighty for ye. continuance of yr. prosperity & happiness thro' a long course of years. I was not the person yt. was ye least joyous on yt. occasion. I must conclude now, as I fear I am already too late for tea, but I cannot finish without desiring you to give my best compliments & remember me in ye. most affectionate manner possible to my friend Joan. Tell him I hope I shall ere long have ye. satisfaction of shaking him by ye hand. Tell him if he wants any I hope he will send to me to execute ye. commissions. Ask him if he knows who this is. I have almost forgot his black appearance; if I am not much mistaken he looked a good deal like a ravelin.

P.S. You will be happy to here [*sic*] yt. Gerard[2] arrived safe in America & joined Lord Cornwallis, & was in ye. last engagement. He continues

1. 16 August.

2. Lieutenant-Colonel Lake.

perfectly well, & agrees vastly well with Conway, whom he speaks of in ye highest manner.   (43458–9)

51   PRINCE FREDERICK TO THE PRINCE OF WALES, AND THE REPLY

Hanover, 12 Oct. 1781

I take the first opportunity of answering your last affectionate letter. As for Madam de Hardenberg's behaviour since her return here it has been very much like the injured Lucretia, so much so that she would not do me the honor of speaking to me. However, at last she deigned to pester me from the beginning of dinner to the end with questions about England. As I hate her almost as much as I do the devil I only answered her questions without chusing to enter farther into conversation, which she took so ill that she did not chuse to speak to me for a fortnight afterwards. However, one day she spoke to me and appeared as if she intended to mention to me what had passed in England, which I carefully avoided. In short, dear brother, I think you ought greatly to rejoice that you have got off so well as you have done. . . .

I am sorry to hear what you say about the King's not being in good humour. Let me entreat you to do everything possible to set all right again as it only plagues both of you without answering the least end in the world. I suppose you are now hunting almost every day, as by the papers I see that you have been out with the Duke of Cumberland's hounds. We are now going to begin our shooting parties here. I am become one of the best shot here, both with shot and with ball, so much so that I can shoot hares in their full speed with a ball at an hundred yards distance.[1] You can have no idea of stag shooting. I have often run five or six miles as hard as I could on foot with my gun on my shoulder after a stag. I do not think the stags here much larger than they are in England, but here a stag is never to be shot till he is twelve years old and in England they are always shot at six.

I forgot to tell you that a short time ago a letter from England with hints that Mr. Gray's bill on my account were very high; I must therefore beg you, dear brother, to send me some things but not too many; however I must beg you will not forget the commissions which I sent you.

I have not time to write more; I shall only beg you to write often and to believe me, [etc.].   (43467–8)

1. On 13 March he had written to the King: 'We have had three shooting parties, in which I have had very great success, because, having very good eyes I am already a good shot.' (43395–6)

74

THE PRINCE OF WALES'S REPLY

Windsor Castle, 22 Oct. 1781

I cannot help seizing ye earliest opportunity of acknowledging yr. very kind letter; it gave me more real satisfaction than I can express to you, indeed it delighted me beyond measure. The love I have for you, dear Frederick, is so great yt. it will always render me happy in hearing from you, but I confess you made me peculiarly happy by yr. last letter, as I feared by not having heard from you for some time, yt. some cursed letters from England had endeavoured to break thro' yt. boundless confidence & affection wh. ever have subsisted in our intercourse. Indeed, my dear Frederick, I am sorry to tell you yt. ye unkind behaviour of both their Majesties, but in particular of the Queen, is such yt. it is hardly bearable. She and I, under the protestations of ye. greatest friendship, had a long conversation together. She accused me of various high crimes & misdemeanors, all wh. I answered, & in ye vulgar English phraze gave her as good as she brought. She spoke to me, she said, entirely without ye King's knowledge. Now I am thoroughly convinced from ye language she used & ye style she spoke in she must previously have talked ye subject over with ye King, who wanted to try whether I could be intimidated or not, but when she found I was not so easily to be intimidated she was silent; after having tried various topicks in order to vex me, finding yt. yt. was a very difficult task, she at last began talking about us both, & abused you monstrously, as well as me; in short, I cannot imagine what could have put her so much out of humour. I am certain you never will repeat again what I mention to you in this way as it is of the utmost consequence to us both yt. our family disputes should be as little known in publick as possible. . . .

You mentioned hunting in yr. last letter to me. No man is so much altered in his method of pursuing yt. almost divine amusement as I am; I have plenty of excellent & beautiful horses, & ride ym. well up to ye [*sic*]. I have taken plenty of all ye rural amusements this autumn. I am become an exceeding good shot, & have some extraordinary good pointers. Ye first time I ever fired a fowling piece off I shot at a sheet of paper at 60 yards distance & covered it full of shot; I then shot ball with a rifle gun & fired twice following thro' ye. heart of a sheet of paper. I hope you will allow yt. to be an extraordinary thing for one yt. had never let off a gun before, & I still continue to keep up a very good character. I now hunt 4 times a week, twice with ye. King & his hounds & twice with our friend ye. Duke of Cumberland & his hounds, who desires his best love & affection to you. I will mount you in a capital style if you will but come. If it only depended upon you I flatter myself my wishes would not be long without being fullfilled. You are well convinced, dear brother, at least I hope so, of ye sincerity of those wishes. Heaven is

75

witness yt. I wld. give almost all I am worth upon earth to have you here again; you cost me many a sigh & many a serious moment. I am not surprised at what you write concerning Gray's bill, as the King is grown so stingy with regard to himself yt. he will hardly allow himself 3 coats in a year. Remember me in ye. kindest manner to my friend Joan; desire him to write to me & tell him I wld. have written to him tonight had I not written so long a letter to you, but he *really* now shall have a letter from me soon. Let me hear from you frequently, as I shall scrawl much to you.   (43469–71)

52   LETTERS FROM PRINCE FREDERICK TO THE PRINCE OF WALES

Hanover, 26 Oct. 1781

As the quarterly courier sets out today I must give you a number of commissions. First of all, I suppose Davis is by this time returned to England and will certainly therefore have told you in point of cloaths what I want and what I cannot wear. I must with all convenient speed desire some frocks and three uniforms, as also leather breeches and boots. I must besides put you in mind of a sword in the style of the Turkish saber Bland[1] made for us but not so fine; if there is anything else I have forgot you may supply it out of your own noddle. I had almost forgot to desire you would also send me over some indian ink and the best sort of lead pencils because we have no such good things here. I have not time to add anything more but you may depend upon another letter soon.

P.S. Pray write here; Joan begs to be kindly remembered to you. Adieu. (43474)

Hanover, 8 Nov. 1781

I have many thanks to return you for your kind letter, which I received last Friday. What you ask me about Madam de Hardenberg is impossible, for first she has abused you so terribly by all accounts here that I am thoroughly persuaded she is completely cured of her love for you, if she ever had any. Excuse me, dear brother, if I say so, but really if one may judge by her behaviour here, she cannot have had much. At present, however, she is not here & I hope she will not return soon. It is impossible for you to write to her, & I am sure if you was, she would show them about. In short, the more I see of it the more I think you ought to rejoice at having got rid of her. . . .

1. The King's Sword-cutler.

76

I have just heard that the King has ordered over twenty stags from hence. Tomorrow we intend to catch some. Pray let me again entreat you to be upon as good a footing as possible with the King, for really it is of so much consequence to yourself that it appears to me quite ridiculous that you do not at least attempt. You see, dear brother, I write exactly what I think, because I see so much vexation to yourself as well as to him, that it must be every way for both your goods. I have not time to add more, dear brother, except to beg you would send us over a tabor and pipe. (43475)

Hanover, 1 Dec. 1781
You will receive this letter by the person who always accompanies me to the chasse and whom I must particularly recommend to you as very much attached to me. He is of that rank among the chasseurs that upon all shooting parties he dines with us. I wish therefore you would take care that he dines with your pages and that if it is necessary he may also dine with the King's pages. I am sure if you tell Ramus[1] from me that I wish he would invite him if he comes to Windsor that he will do it. I beg also you would tell Santhaque[2] from me that as he is his countryman he would take him under his protection and among other things carry him to Twigg's where I have given him orders to buy a number of things for me. I believe you will find the stags exceedingly fine; there is but two of them which are aged, the others are all of about three years old. By the by, if you have anything to send me which you do not think should be seen and which is not of such consequence as to want an immediate answer, you may trust it to him. We had last week a great chasse where we killed forty two wild boars, which are very few, considering the trouble they were at in preparing it.

As this will certainly be longer reaching you than it would be if I was to send it by the post I shall only add that I shall ever remain [etc.].

P.S. When he brings you this letter pray first see him and make faces at him, for I do not suppose you can speak, for he talks nothing but German. There will also come over for you at the same time a boar's head pickled. I forgot to tell you that his name is Clous. Adieu; my compliments to all friends in England. (43478–9)

1. William Ramus was one of the Pages of the Backstairs.
2. Santhague, another Page of the Backstairs.

Hanover, 20 Dec. 1781

I cannot let the courier set out without writing you a few lines. When the stags are in England you will receive a letter from me which will be brought to you by one of the chasseurs who accompany them; it contains a recommendation of him. I have wrote to Mr. Warwick Lake to desire him to send me over a brace of good pointers; when he has got them you will be so good as to let them be delivered to the care of this chasseur, who is really as honest and good a fellow as ever existed. I am going tomorrow to a great chasse about five and twenty miles off; we expect to find there a great deal of game. I suppose you will have passed the Christmas holydays at Windsor. We intend to be exceedingly merry here; now the carnival begins we shall begin our masquerades the third of January. I have not time to add any more. I shall therefore only beg my best compliments to all friends in England. Pray write often, dear brother, and believe me [etc.].

[*P.S.*] I forgot to wish you a merry Christmass and a happy New Year.[1] (43480–1)

53 THE PRINCE OF WALES TO PRINCE FREDERICK

Windsor Castle, 24 Dec. 1781

It is now almost a year since I had the happiness of seeing you, & it has I do assure you appeared to me to be ye. longest twelvemonth I ever passed. There is nothing I would not do to see you, did I think it lay in my power to gratify my pleasure, my satisfaction, my happiness in beholding my best & dearest friend in you, my dear Frederick. Our dear Gerrard[2] has come off, as we always thought he would do, with flying colors. He commanded ye. sally at York Town, & received Lord Cornwallis's thanks in ye. publick Orders for his gallant & sperited conduct. He is now upon his return, & I flatter myself I now shall have ye. satisfaction of seeing this excellent man soon again. I should have written to you some time ago, only I wish'd to defer it till I was able to acquaint you with our friend's arrival, but finding it was likely still to be some time before he would arrive, I could not delay any longer what is always a pleasure to me, ye writing to you.

Davis & I have hit upon a method, if you approve of it, of sending you over all yr. things regularly by Ostende, as ye messenger is for ever making difficulties, & if he does take anything he looks upon it as conferring ye. greatest favor. By some confusion among ye. tradespeople

1. The King himself disliked these seasonal greetings, though he had no objection, apparently, to birthday wishes.

2. Lieutenant-Colonel Lake.

you did not receive, I have heard, yr. things regularly, but that was before Davis arrived, & he will now take care you receive everything punctually. I am happy to hear from him how well you look & that there never was anybody so thoroughly liked & beloved in Germany as you are. There is nothing new going forward here. We have had some prodigious good day's sport lately. I hunt constantly & I find myself much the better for all the exercise I take. I have sent you over a wax model of me wh. is reckoned by everybody yt. have seen it remarkably like, except its being too fat, & especially about ye chin. . . . (43482–3)

54 LETTERS FROM PRINCE FREDERICK TO THE PRINCE OF WALES

Hanover, 30 Dec. 1781

I cannot let General Fawcett return without sending you a few lines by him. Today is the anniversary of my having quitted you; how very much everything is altered during that time. By all accounts that I have heard the King and you are not upon over-good terms, which I am sincerely sorry for. For God's sake do everything which you can to keep well with him, at least upon decent terms; consider he is vexed enough in publick affairs. It is therefore your business not to make that still worse. He may possibly be cross, but still it is not your business to take that too high. You know, my dearest brother, I hate *preaching* full as much as you do, and constraint if possible more, but still for both your sakes I entreat you to keep as well together as possible. I know you will excuse what I write to you because it comes from the heart.

We have at present here an Italian Opera which plays every other night[1] and our masquerades begin on Thursday next, so that during the carnaval we shall be very gay. Pray write often; it is neer two months that I have not received the least line from you, and I am sure you ought to have a great deal more to say. I do not think you will see the stags in England before the end of February, if they live so long, which I almost doubt, as they have already been in their cases.

Pray give my best compliments to all friends in England and also congratulations in the New Year. You are too fully persuaded of my affection for you to make it necessary for me to repeat the same compliments to you on this occasion. Excuse my sermon and believe me, dear brother [etc.]. (43486–7)

1. Frederick was rather concerned about the condition of the Opera House, 'because at present', he wrote, 'there is but one passage out, so that if the House was to take fire the people would be either burnt or crushed to pieces'. (43395–6)

Hanover, 18 Jan. 1781 [*1782*][1]

I have many thanks to return you for your last kind letter which I would have answered sooner, but I rather chose to delay it till the courier set off. I have not yet received one single thing which Davis sent. I shall therefore beg you will send me a couple of frocks by the courier and also my heron's feather. Grenville[2] has a number of things coming over by the courier, so you must not load him too much. I think in general it is much better to send everything, as Davis says. We have been exceedingly fine at our second Masquerade, here, seven and twenty of us were masqued in characters and it succeeded very well. I suppose you will now have done hunting; the stags will not arrive these six weeks in England, for the Elbe is froze up.[3] As for the Hardenbergs I can give you at present no particular account. They returned here last Monday, from the Hardenberg, their house in the country, but as I have not seen him since, I cannot tell what plan he means to follow. I am curious to know whom you will have as Lord of the Bedchamber, in the place of Lord John Clinton[4], and in the place of Digby[5]. By all accounts you and Digby did not hit it well together. . . .

Pray give my compliments to all friends in England. We have got here Lord Bathurst's[6] son who is a charming fellow. We are great friends. Joan begs to be remembered to you. You must excuse this scrawl for I have not had time hardly to write at all. Dear brother, pray write often and believe me [etc.].[7]   (43368–9)

1. Both this letter, and Frederick's letter of the same date to the King, are apparently wrongly dated. First, Lord John Clinton died in November 1781. Second, there is the further reference to the stags on 15 February 1782. Third, Frederick informed the King on 28 October 1781 that Lord Apsley had been in Hanover two months.   (43472–3)

2. Richard Grenville's brother.

3. 'Nothing can have been more unlucky than the poor stags, which have not quitted Bremen. They have once been to the mouth of the river, but it was impossible for the ship to proceed on its voyage, as the wind was contrary, and now it will probably be the middle of February before they will again be able to sail. . . .' (Frederick to the King, 18 January [43366]).

4. The fourth son of the 2nd Duke of Newcastle; M.P. for East Retford, 1778–81. He had died, at Lisbon, on 10 November 1781 (1755–81).

5. The Hon. Stephen Digby (1742–1800), grandson of the 5th Baron Digby. Groom of the Bedchamber to the Prince of Wales, 1780–2, and then Vice-Chamberlain to the Queen, to 1792.

6. Henry, 2nd Earl Bathurst (1714–94), Lord Chancellor, 1771–8, had two sons: Henry, who succeeded as 3rd Earl (1762–1834); and Apsley (1769–1816). The reference is to the elder. He was M.P. for Cirencester, 1783–94; a Lord of the Admiralty, 1783–9; a Lord of the Treasury, 1789–91; Commissioner of the India Board, 1793–1802; Master of the Mint, 1804–6 and 1807–12; President of the Board of Trade, 1807–12; Foreign Secretary, October–December 1809; Secretary for War and the Colonies, 1812–27; and Lord President of the Council, 1828–30. He was styled Lord Apsley, 1775–94.

7. Frederick wrote to the King that day (the war with the Bourbon Powers was still in progress): '. . . Last week two more Companies of the Sixteenth Regiment pass'd thro: here,

Queen's House, 28 Jan. 1782

I cannot think of writing two formal letters over to Germany without scribbling three or four lines to you to thank you for your very affectionate letter, & flatter myself yt. ye. not having been well for some time will appear a sufficient excuse for my silence. Thank God I am now almost quite well again. It has been nothing but a little feverish cold wh., having [been] neglected for some time, became so strong at last as to oblige me to take care of it, but nothing of any consequence; however, fully sufficient to make me very unwell. I will execute any commissions you may want, & have ordered some new buckles & other nick nacks to be sent over to you. You may expect a very long letter from me during ye. ensuing fortnight; indeed I only wrote now for fear you should be uneasy at my long silence. I will therefore conclude, dearest Frederick, with assuring you yt. I still am what I ever was, & what I ever shall be [etc.].

P.S. Pray tell me how Mme. Hardenberg is & what she is about now. Dear Lake continues perfectly well.[1]   (43488–9)

Hanover, 15 Feb. 1782

I have not hardly a moment's time to write to you yet I cannot let the courier set out without thanking you for your last kind letter, and telling how sorry I am to hear of your indisposition. We have had here sledge parties for this last week, which are exceedingly amusing. I am arrived at a very great proficiency in driving a sledge, which I do not find more difficult than driving a phaeton only the horses grow very often resty. It is particularly amusing by torch light. I suppose by this time you have seen the stags which have been sent from hence, but I am affraid they

the Light Infantry and the Colonel's Company; they are exceedingly fine and a much more equal body of men than the Fifteenth as well as considerably younger, by all accounts nothing can be finer than the Grenadiers of this Regiment, they as well as the rest of the Regiment will pass thro: here the fifth of the next month.

'Our weather here is the most extraordinary I ever saw. We have one day a violent frost, and the next, a violent rain. This can never be wholesome and indeed the whole town experiences it, for there is hardly a single person here who is not sick. . . .' (43366–7)

1. Frederick wrote to the King on 4 February: '. . . You are too well acquainted with my affection for Lake not to conceive how rejoiced I am at his return, after having gained to himself so much credit, and I have no doubt but that he will do everything in his power to make my brother behave in such a manner as to please your Majesty. . . .' (43491–2)

are quite spoilt on account of the time they have been pent up in those cases.

As for what you want to know about Madam de Hardenberg, she is going away in about three weeks into the country, and how long she is to stay there I cannot tell. You must excuse this short scrawl but for fear the snow should not last I must make the best use of my time. Adieu dear brother, you may depend upon a letter from me very soon again. Pray give my best love to Lake, and tell him I could not perform my promise of writing to him by this messenger but that he may also be sure of one the first opportunity.   (43493)

Hanover, 1 Mar. 1782

You must not expect a long letter from me, but I could not let the courier set off without just writing a few lines to you to tell you with how much impatience I wait for the letter which you promised me. The next six weeks will be exceedingly tiresome, for we are not allowed either to have any masquerades or balls; in short, the town is as dull as it is possible. All our snow is gone, so that we can have no more traineaux parties. I am sure if you was ever to be of one of those parties you would like it above all things. I cannot express to you how happy the news of Lake's promotion made me.[1] News you cannot expect from us here. I hope you have taken care of everything which I desired of you in the letter which you received by the chasseurs.

Dear brother, I have nothing more to add except my love to Lake and to beg you would write often, and that you would believe me [etc.].

P.S. Joan desires his best respects to you.   (43496–7)

57   LETTERS FROM THE PRINCE OF WALES TO PRINCE FREDERICK

Queen's House, 1 Mar. 1782

I this morning received yr. kind letter, for wh. I am most exceedingly thankful. Now I have returned you my thanks for this great favor I will begin my letter by telling you yt. I have done everything in my power to shew Mr Clouse every attention possible. I have had him three times with me; he has dined with my Pages, but could not dine with the King's & Queen's Pages, as he was not down at Windsor while we were there.

1. Lieutenant-Colonel Lake was promoted to be Colonel on 16 February, and he was also appointed Aide-de-Camp to the King. 'Your Majesty', wrote Frederick, (1 March) 'is too well acquainted with my affection for him not to conceive the joy I felt upon receiving the news of his promotion.'   (43494–5)

He is to come to me again tomorrow, when we are to try three rifle barrel guns, one yt. he brought over, one yt. Freytag got over from Germany for me, & one wh. was made by ye. best workman we have here; he is a Swiss German, & his name is Egge. This gun is made after Furgeson's rifle, it is almost ye. neatest peice of workmanship & one of ye. best guns yt. ever was made. It is not perfectly new, for he made it about three years ago for my friend St. Leger, who is one of ye best fellows yt. ever lived, & a great favorite of Gerrard's, wh. I am certain will be very much in his favor with you; he never made use of it but only carried it over to the West Indies & brought it back with him again. Egge saying yt. he could not get one finished by ye time prescribed for Signor Clouse's departure, I desired my friend St. Leger to give his up to you, wh. he has done most readily, & Egge is to make him & me to [sic] new ones upon the same construction. Ye gunsmith himself says he could not possibly turn out of his hands a better gun than this. I therefore after all these preliminaries, beg yr. acceptance of it, I have ordered him to send with yr. Büxen spanner a remarkable good pair of pistols wh. I also beg yr. gracious acceptance of in token of yr. great kindness & affection to me. I have some things for you from Gray wh. Davis will take care to have safe delivered to you soon; may I ask, have you received yt. wax profile wh. I sent? I am particular about this, as I wish to know what you think of it.[1] I have had painted for you a picture ye same as one I have given Gerrard; it is a half length painted by Gainsborough[2] & reckoned remarkably like by every[one], I wish to know wh. you think will be ye best way to send it over, as I will not have it sent till I receive yr. answer. I dare not in these letters write anything particularly secret, but will endeavour, if I can catch a moment before Clouse sets off, to write you a great deal of news, wh. I hope will be very interesting & entertaining. It is now time for me to go upstairs; at least Gerrard says so, & is hurrying me to conclude. I therefore with reluctance close this as I do every other letter to you, for I could write, scribble & chatter for ever when you are ye. subject. Adieu, my dearest & best of brothers; may Heaven shower down its choicest blessings upon you & hasten the moment of our meeting again, is ye constant & fervent prayer of [etc.]. (43498–9)

Queen's House, 15 Mar. 1782
I have not time now to write you a long letter on very interesting subjects as I had promised, must therefore defer it, when you may depend upon having it by ye. next post or ye. post after. As I had promised Clouse to

1. See No. 53.

2. Thomas Gainsborough (1727–88).

83

send you a letter by him, I cld. not let him go without three lines to you. I have sent you over a whole parcel of buckles from Gray, I have also sent you a pair wh. I wish you wld. present to his Highness or Littleness Ernest[1], & one pair for my old friend Joan Grenville. They are ye. two smallest pairs & I believe are marked. Adieu, I cannot add any more except yt. I am [etc.].

P.S. I have given Clouse a couteau de chasse with a belt. (43502)

58   PRINCE FREDERICK TO THE PRINCE OF WALES

Hanover, 25 Mar. 1782

I have a thousand thanks to return you for your two last letters, the one of which I received by Clous who seems quite delighted with his journey and with the kindness with which you treated him. I am also extremely obliged to you for the gun and pistols which are charming and which the very first opportunity I shall try. I am very impatient for the letter which you promised me in which I am to here how everything is in England. The Lord be praised Lent is now over, so that we shall again return to our amusements. We have had such a fall of snow during the last four days that it is in some places in the country near six foot deep.

You, in your last letter, desired to know if I had received the things which Davies sent. I have not received those even which he sent last Christmass. About three weeks ago a merchant here received a letter from a correspondent at Brussels to say that they had passed through that place and that they would probably arrive here in a fortnight, but they are not come yet.

We have no news here which can possibly interest you as you will very easily conceive. As for Madame de Hardenberg, she is at present here, but will set out in a very few days for her husband's estate with him where she is to remain all the summer. She at present is upon a plan of retirement, so much so that she has not been at more than one assembly this fortnight.

I think I have given you as full an account as I can of her and as it is late I shall close my letter by wishing you, my dearest brother, all health and happiness and begging to be remembered in the kindest manner to Lake, and by signing myself, dear brother [etc.]. (43503-4)

1. His uncle, Prince Ernest of Mecklenburg-Strelitz.

Tuesday, 26 Mar. 1782

I have but a moment to scribble this unintelligible epistle to you, to wish you most sincerely joy of having been appointed Colonel of ye. Horse Grenadiers.[1] No one can feel more true satisfaction than I did, or more heartfelt joy than when I first heard this agreable peice of news. But I also heard something of you wh. has given me great uneasiness & pain; yt. you have a return of yr. old bleeding at yr. nose & of yr. old cough. For Heaven's sake for yr. own sake & for my sake more particularly, take care of yourself as I cannot express to you what I have felt concerning you. I have no more time at present, but you shall have a very long letter next post. I cannot conclude without once more beseeching you to take care of yourself; you do not know of how much consequence you are to us all here. Once more adieu, dearest of brothers. May Heaven shower down its choicest blessings on you, & may you long continue to enjoy every happiness this world can afford, is ye. constant prayer of [etc.].

P.S. The King had only ordered you the full uniform. I have also ordered you the frock.

P.S. ye 2ᵈ Dear Joan, I hope you are well, & congratulate you most sincerely on ye. appointment of ye. Colonel of ye. Grenadiers.   (43505)

60   PRINCE FREDERICK TO THE PRINCE OF WALES

Hanover, 29 Mar. 1782

Though I wrote to you by last post yet I cannot help writing you a few lines to acquaint you that all the things which Davies sent last December are at last arrived, just the day after I had wrote you word that I did not know what was become of them; but unluckily the thing of all others I wished for the most was quite spoilt, which was your bust in wax; it was all brok[e] into a thousand pieces; luckily however the face was not injured. I wait with impatience for the letter which you promised me and which I was in hopes you had intrusted to General Fawcitt, but alas my hopes were in vain. He tells me you are and look exceedingly well, which I was very happy to hear. We are agoing to lose Lord Apseley which I am exceedingly sorry for; he is excessively agreable and we have been great friends all the time he has been here.

1. Prince Frederick was Colonel of the 2nd Troop of Horse Grenadier Guards from 23 March 1782 to October 1784, when he was appointed Colonel of the Coldstream Regiment of Foot Guards.

I have not time to add any more; therefore, my dearest brother, I hope you will excuse this scrawl. Write often and believe me [etc.]

P.S. Grenville [sends] his best respects to you. Adieu. (43508–9)

61 THE KING TO THE PRINCE OF WALES, AND THE REPLY

Queen's House, 30 Mar. 1782
The Prince of Wales could not be ignorant of the displeasure his absence[1] this day would give me, and his stooping to direct one of my pages yesterday to keep that intention to himself and come this morning and notify the Prince of Wales being gone at four this morning, shews he took the step not inadvertently. I must insist on the like not being done again and must add that at a time when I am so harrassed by many disagreable events[2], any improper behaviour of the Prince of Wales is doubly severe to me.

He must know his conduct in general is so different to the plan I chalked out and to which he said he perfectly acquiesced, that I shall soon be obliged, if he does not amend it, to take steps that certainly will be disagreable. (41792)

THE PRINCE OF WALES'S REPLY

30 Mar. 1782[3]
I am excessively sorry that my behaviour should in any manner be displeasing to yr. Majesty, especially at this period. As to taking this step inadvertently I certainly did not, as I mentioned it to her Majesty near three weeks ago; and I could not conceive there could be any impropriety in communicating my intention to yr. Majesty thro' yr. page, whom yr. Majesty has so frequently sent to me on similar occasions. With respect to my conduct in ye world, I flatter'd myself it had merited ye strictest approbation, tho' in great measure different from the limited plan your Majesty had originally chalk'd out for me, wh. from my youth & inexperience I then inconsiderately acquiesced in. Had I in pursuit of my reasonable amusements selected any but ye best company in this nation, I should have justly merited your Majesty's displeasure, but as I

1. From the Levée. He set off with Colonel St. Leger for Northamptonshire to hunt foxes.

2. Lord North, having by his mismanagement of the American War lost the confidence of the House of Commons, had resigned the premiership, and the King had been compelled to resort to the Whigs, who formed a Ministry under the Marquess of Rockingham.

3. The date is slightly suspect: it seems unlikely that he would return to London from Northamptonshire in time to write this reply on the 30th.

have not behaved in a manner to reflect the smallest discredit either on yourself or upon me, I thought yt. in pursuing a line of conduct ye most likely to gain ye good opinion of the world, I should have been fortunate enough to have obtained your Majesty's, for whom I shall ever be happy to testify ye profound respect with wh. I am, Sir, your Majesty's most dutiful son and subject. (41794)

62 LETTERS FROM PRINCE FREDERICK TO THE PRINCE OF WALES

Hanover, 12 Apr. 1782

I have but a moment's time to return you a thousand thanks for your kind congratulations as well as for your goodness in ordering my uniform, which I shall beg you will send at latest with the courier if you cannot send it sooner, for though Davies's way is very sure, yet it is very slow, but as probably by none of these means I shall be able to get my uniform for these six weeks I shall beg you will send me over by the post a very full description of both the uniforms which, if Master Shee can write he can very easily do, as well as two sets of the buttons, and at the same time I humbly beg that you will take care that I may receive by the courier both the swords, the sash, the cap, the clasp, the furniture, in short, everything which belongs to the cloathing. I think you have enough to do to fullfill all these commissions, but I must beg that as for the description of the two uniforms and the buttons you will send them by the very first post or courier which sets out from England.

I have not had time to add any more. I shall therefore only beg my best love to Lake and that you would believe me, dear brother [etc.].

P.S. I believe you will hardly be able to read this scrawl, but you must excuse it on account of haste. Joan begs to be remembered to you. Adieu. The first time you see General Budé and General Freytag pray give them my compliments and tell them I am very sorry that it is not in my power to answer the letters they were so good as to send me by this messenger, but that they may depend on the very first occasion. Once more adieu. (43512–3)

Hanover, 26 Apr. 1782

I have been awaiting with the greatest impatience for the letter which you have so long promised to write to me and which is not yet arrived. As for the commissions which I gave you in my last letter, I shall again beg you will particularly take care of them and if possible send them sooner over than by the courier. The things which Davies sent last February are

87

not yet arrived. If you will be so good therefore to let somebody inquire when a Hamburgh ship sails and let everything be directed to Monsieur Van Axen, merchant at Hamburgh, by which means the things will come the quickest. Lest you should have forgot any of them I shall send you inclosed a list of them which I hope will be clear.

News you can not expect from us here nor anything else which would particularly please you. I shall therefore, dear brother, conclude my epistle by begging my compliments to all friends in England, by desiring that you would write often and that you would believe me [etc.].

P.S. Joan begs his respects. Adieu.   (43518–9)

[Enclosed list]
List of the things which I want from England.
1. The full uniform.
2. The frock uniform
3. The cap
4. The two swords, viz., the large one and the frock one.
5. The clasp.
6. The tassle.
7. The full furniture.
8. The frock furniture.
9. At least four sets of buttons which I must beg may be sent over immediately in small parcels like letters by the courier who goes every fortnight.

N.B. As both the furnitures will be wanted for the camp at Lunenberg which begins the beginning of June I must beg to have them over as soon as possible.

N.B. The uniform & bits[?] must also come with the furniture.   (43520)

63   THE PRINCE OF WALES TO PRINCE FREDERICK

Queen's House, 10 May 1782
I am almost ashamed after so long a silence to write to you at all, but I hope for yr. forgiveness when you know the reason. *I have had a great deal of business of late, & some of such consequence* that it has almost prevented my attending to anything else. I dare not express myself so openly in a letter, but I think you will easily guess & understand what I mean when I tell you that the new Administration seem to wish me better than the former one. With respect to news there is nothing at present yt. hardly merits yt. name. If there is any, allow me, dearest Frederick, to refer you to our dear friend Lake, who will give you an

entire & ample account of anything that passes here. I hope I shall be able to do so soon myself. Would to Heaven I were able to communicate with you by word of mouth. You cannot form to yourself an idea how impatient I am to see you again, & how delighted I shall be to see our old triumvirate resume its former strength & stability. All yr. commissions I have taken proper care of, but have unfortunately forgot thro negligence ye. direction of ye. mertchant at Hamburgh, but shall endeavour to find yr. last letter in wh. it was among all ye. other letters wh. I have received from you. Pardon this scrawl, dearest brother, as I write in ye. utmost hurry for fear ye. post shd. go out before I can deliver my letter. You may really depend upon hearing from me soon again; till then, dearest Frederick, believe me [etc.].

P.S. Dear Joan you shall also be troubled with a letter from me. I hope Speedimans and analepticks, anti cook & butlers &c. &c. &c. do preserve you from disorders of all sorts & kinds. Dear Frederick, yr. little Herne mare in fole by Highflyer has dropped a colt. I will mention something about this colt to you in my next. (43523–4)

64 LETTERS FROM PRINCE FREDERICK TO THE PRINCE OF WALES

Hanover, 24 May 1782

I cannot express to you how happy you made me by your last letter which I received on Monday. I confess it was so long a time since I had heard from you that I could not conceive what the reason was.

I received last Friday the buckles &c. which have been near three months upon the road. The buckles are beautifull. I gave Joan his and I also sent Prince Earnest those which you had intended for him. However we have now a weapers mourning so that I shall not be able to wear them so soon. I am exceedingly happy to hear that you have done all my commissions which I hope will arrive here very soon. By the by I have mentioned that we have a weapers mourning and have totally forgot to say who it is for. It is for Prince Charles's wife who died here last Wednesday.[1] But pray do not speak to the Queen about it till she tells it to you, as I have been desired to entreat the King to break it to her.

1. The Queen's brother, Prince Charles of Mecklenburg-Strelitz, married (1768) Frederica (1752–82), daughter of the Landgrave George William of Hesse-Darmstadt. She died on 22 May. On 28 September 1784 he married her sister Charlotte (1755–85). Frederick referred to the Princess's death in a letter of the same date to his father: 'She was taken ill last Monday was sennight with the disorder which reigns here to a violent degree, but what was very surprising, would never take the least medicine or do the least thing which could tend to her cure. The efforts which she made on account of her cough were such as to make her lie in on Sunday evening full six weeks before her time. This made the fever return with redoubled violence and at last killed her on Wednesday morning.' (43527–8)

89

You have no idea how dull it is here at present; everybody is gone out of town or *so* sick as not to be able to stir out, so that we live quite retired. I have not time to add more but you may depend upon my writing soon again. I shall therefore only beg to be remembered to all friends in England and to sign myself, [etc.].

P.S. I forgot to tell you that Grenville returns a thousand thanks to you for his buckles on which to cut a flash on the very first occasion. As for Prince Earnest, he means to thank you himself. Once more adieu.

P.S. I forgot to beg you to send me some hats, particularly those for my uniform, the same number as last time, only, instead of sending three round hats send me but one round hat and four uniform and four plain hats. Once more adieu.   (43529–30)

Lunenburg, 14 June 1782
As it was out of my power to write to you before I quitted Hanover I shall send this, hoping that Fawcett is still there, who has undertaken to deliver it to you. We left Hanover at seven o'clock in the morning, and arrived here at seven in the evening, which considering the distance, which is fifteen German miles, and the roads which are worse than can be conceived, is exceeding good going. The camp was formed on Tuesday morning; it consists of nine batallions and sixteen squadrons. They began on Wednesday morning with their first evolution, which, considering all things, went off pretty well. Yesterday we had the Parade Review but before we had got have [*sic*] along the line the rain was so violent as to wet us all through in an instant. One terrible inconvenience however of this camp is that it is at such a monstrous difference from this town where the Head Quarters are, as well as all the rest of the Generals, near eight English miles, so that all our old Generals here [*sic*], it is quite a journey there and back again.

   I think I have given you a proper dose of this camp, but having nothing else worthy your notice to relate to you I was resolved I would give you a high idea of how much I am improved in my profession. If you please afterwards I will give you an exact account of every manoeuvre as well as of all the faults which have or shall be committed here. The evenings are as dull as anything can be, for there is not a single soul in the town whom I know except the Generals, who, though exceeding good men, yet being with them continually for four and twenty hours, even the very best things will grow tiresome. I must close my letter as we are now going out to inspect the Cavalry man by man and horse, which is what I am very curious to see. I shall therefore only beg my love to Lake and that you would believe me [etc.].

N.B. You will easily conceive after having read this that I wrote it in my uniform booted and spurred ready for the feats of the day. Adieu.[1] (43531-2)

Hanover, 19 July 1782

As the courier sets off this evening I cannot help writing to you to scold your [*sic*] for your excessive long silence; it is above two months since I have had a single line from you. Pray for God's sake write often, you must have so much to say, every little particular is interesting to me. I have received the two swords and the hats which you was so good as to send, and the other boxes will arrive by the waggon from Hamburg by tomorrow morning. I am infinitely obliged to you for the buckles which you was so good as to send me by the Duc d'Aremberg; they are beautiful.

Pray excuse the shortness of this scrawl, but really having nothing to say which can interest you, for I do not suppose you would like to hear of the births, marriages and deaths here, I shall therefore conclude by assuring you, dear brother, that I am most sincerely [etc.].

P.S. Pray write often. I forgot to beg you would give my best compliments to Freytag and tell him that I am much ashamed I have not as yet answered his last letter but that he may depend upon a letter the very next occasion. Adieu. (43533)

Hanover, 30 Sept. 1782

I have been waiting very impatiently these four weeks for the letter which you promised me thro' Lake, but unluckily I have been disappointed. I believe you have quite forgot me, for I have not received a line from you since May last. I am sure I do not ask too much when I only humbly entreat for a line now and then when you have nothing better to do, to say that you are well.

I must give you the commission to order two lottery tickets to be bought for me and to send me over the numbers. Now pray do not forget this; if you think it too great a trouble to send them over yourself, pray give them to Lake to send them over. I have not time to add any more except that I am most sincerely [etc.]. (43536)

1. During the next three weeks Frederick was ill, suffering from 'the terrible disorder which has raged all over Europe, of which many old people have died'.

3 Oct. 1782

Monsieur, mon très cher fils, Il est bien vrai que l'arrivé de little Stovel [?] nous a causé quelques alarmes pour vous, mais Dieu soit loué, votre lettre me met tout a mon aise, & je souhaite bien sincerement de vous revoir bientot quand même votre visage ne seroit pas tout a fait dans son beau, car il faut sçavoir que les *grandes beautée* paroissent toujours plus a leur *avantages* quand ils sont en *negligé*. Quand aux cherurgiens je ne croi jamais que la moitie de ce qu'ils disent & il me semble que c'est la autant[?] qu'ils peuvent pretendre raisonnablement.

Nous avons fait ce matin une visite a l'école de Eaton ou les Docteurs Roberts[1], Davies[2] & Langton nous ont recue poliement j'ai demandé pour le jeune Leake mais il n'y etoit point, et en revange j'ai vue un garçon Irlandois qui avoit la tête remplie d'une grosse & pesante cavalerie ce qui me fit une si grande peur que je n'ai point manqué de me retiré tout de suite dans la bibliotheque de Dr. Davies pour etre a l'abri de ses petits ennemies quadrupedes. Une certaine demanguison m'est survenue, mais je me flatte cependant que l'imagination y a plus de part & que pour la realité il n'en est rien.

Je ne manquerai point de faire vos excuses au Roi, il est a present occupée a lire les dépeches, il sera surement bien aise de vous revoir aussitot que possible.

Vos freres et surtout vos deux soeurs ainées sont bien sensible de votre bonté et la petite Sophie ce cher petit ange m'assure *that she loves that dear little dog Waly*. Oh! le joli peti[t] very very much.

La Princesse & le Prince de Mecklenbourg vous offre bien des compliments et moi comme la derniere de la compagnie je vous assure de mon tendre attachement avec lequel je suis votre tres affectionné amie & fidele mère.

P.S. J'ai bien mes deux yeux & non obstant cela j'ai mal écrit.   (36360–1)

1. William Hayward Roberts (*d.*1791), an assistant Master at Eton, and a Fellow. In December 1781, by the King's wish, he was elected Provost. It was said that whilst he was a Fellow he gave great card parties 'which filled the College court with carriages and tumult, not much to the edification of a place of education'. He was described as 'a person of the largest size and bulk with great red eyebrows'. 'The Provost', wrote Fanny Burney, 'is very fat, with a large paunch and gouty legs. He is good-humoured, loquacious, gay, civil and parading.' 'The King and Queen', she added, 'are always well disposed to show civility to the people of Eton and Windsor' (*Diary*, ii.241).

2. Jonathan Davies (1736–1809), Canon of Windsor 1781–91; Provost of Eton, 1791. When Roberts was elected Provost, Davies, who was then Head Master, and as such had strong claims to the succession to the highest office in the College, was consoled for his disappointment with a Canonry of Windsor. However, he succeeded Roberts as Provost in 1791.

Windsor Castle, 15 Oct. 1782

You cannot form to yourself an idea how much I feel myself concerned & hurt that you could even for a moment suppose it possible yt. I cld. either have forgot you, or yt. anything you cld. employ me in cld. appear troublesome. Indeed, my dearest Frederick, you injure me very much, for I can assure you that tho' my laziness may appear very great & really is quite inexcusable, yet my affection never has varied from you ye. least; it is so strong & of yt. firm kind yt. it will never cease but with my existence. Did not I feel yt. tender love for you (wh. I always have done, & now do in a still greater degree than ever) as a brother, the friend of my youth & the companion of my childhood, my gratitude to you for ye. numberless marks of yr. friendship would recall you to ye. recollection of a heart wh. is as strongly attached to you as it is possible for ye heart of one man to be attached to yt. of another; & I flatter myself yt. yt. friendship, wh. has ever subsisted between us since the moment of our birth, will as years multiply over our heads in proportion be tied in a still firmer knot. I hope you are sufficiently acquainted with the sincerity of my heart to beleive yt. ye. expressions I have made use of in this letter are its genuine sentiments & that they proceed from the very bottom of my soul. Let me now entreat yr. forgiveness, as I can assure you you shall no longer have any reason to complain of me upon this score, & indeed I hope you will not have any upon any other. Yr. Lottery tickets shall be bought directly & sent over to you if possible in my next letter, & I beg you will send me over all the commissions you have to send to England except just what relates to *pails, brushes, combs, forks, curry combs, common saddles & bridles*, in short tout l'attirail nécessaire, & tout les petits minutiae of ye. stable, but as to the fine furniture and *every commission of every other sort & kind*, I beg and entreat I may have ye. *satisfaction* of executing them, as I can assure you, my dearest brother, nothing upon earth can give me more pleasure than the idea yt. I am doing any thing yt. can be agreable to you, & I flatter myself you will find ym. executed with yt. punctuality & regularity you will approve of. I intend sending you among other things by ye next messenger a portrait of me painted by Gainsborough & reckoned by everybody to be a remarkable strong likeness. He is to pack it up himself. It will be rol'd up & sent in a tin case. You will therefore make yr. servants take care how they unpack it. I was very much astonished when I saw Col. Diepbrock, I think yt. was his name, by his telling me yt. you are at least an inch & a half wider over ye. shoulders than I am. I wish you wld. send me an exact measure of yr. heighth as I wish to compare it with my own, in order yt. I may form to myself some idea what sized person I may expect to see when I have ye. long wish'd for happiness of seeing you. I will not buy yr. Lottery tickets myself, as I am such a damn'd unlucky dog myself in every instance yt. I shd. be very sorry to intail ye. same ill luck upon you. We have no news stirring here at present except yt. ye. Duke & Duchess of Schwerine[1] are just arrived & yt. I am to have ye. honor of being introduced to their Durchlauchtenships on Wednesday next. For Heaven's sake write me ye. next letter; you write one of yr. facetious, lively, giddy letters, & no more of yr. scolding ones, car je vous assure qu'elles me coupent jusqu'au fond de l'ame, je ne suis du tout point content de ce que je vous ai dit dans cette lettre. Mon coeur sent beaucoup qu'il ne sait exprimer.

P.S. Compliments & kind remembrances to dear Joan.   (43537-9)

PRINCE FREDERICK'S REPLY

Hanover, 28 Oct. 1782

I have a thousand thanks to return you for your kind and affectionate letter which I received last Friday, and which I would have answered immediately if the post had not arrived so late as to put it totally out of my power. I will take care not to write any more scolding letters, which really I thought you had deserved. I shall wait with the greatest impatience for your picture, for which I am exceedingly obliged to you. I must beg you will take care, when the courier comes back, to send the things which you like and not let him chuse as he used to do, by which means I was sometimes above four months without receiving my things, and also to take care that the rest be sent as soon as possible and in the most expeditious manner, because I have not yet received the things which ought to have come by the last courier. News you can expect none from us here. We have had Prince Charles of Hesse Cassel[2] here who appears a very agreable man, but most infernal formal. By the by, whenever you are to be married let me recommend to you the daughter of the Hereditary Prince of Cassel[3] who is said to be one of the greatest

1. Frederick, Duke of Mecklenburg-Schwerin (1717-85) married (1746) Louisa Frederica, daughter of Frederick Louis of Württemberg (1722-91). On 11 October the newspapers reported that their Serene Highnesses the Prince and Princess of Mecklenburg-Schwerin had arrived in London on the 9th with a grand retinue.

2. (1744-1836). He was the third son of Frederick, Landgrave of Hesse-Cassel (1720-85), who married Princess Mary (1723-72), daughter of George II, in 1740. Prince Charles married Princess Louisa (1750-1831), daughter of Frederick V of Denmark, in 1766.

3. William (1743-1821), second but first surviving son of Frederick, Landgrave of Hesse-Cassel (1720-85). Like his brother Charles, he married a daughter of Frederick V of Denmark (Princess Caroline [1747-1820]). Princess Frederica (1768-1839), the Hereditary Prince's elder daughter, married the Duke of Anhalt-Bernburg (1767-1834) in 1794. The younger daughter, Caroline, was only eleven.

beauties ever seen. She is only fourteen years old, which is so much the better, and I think the sooner you marry the better. Adieu my dearest brother, I have not time to add more. Give my best love to Lake, and believe me [etc.].

P.S. Pray write often and long, once more adieu.
A thousand excuses for having blotted the paper but it is impossible to write it over again. (43540–1)

67 CHARLES JAMES FOX[1] TO THE PRINCE OF WALES

St. James's Street, 18 Dec. 1782
Your Royal Highness will easily conceive that I want words to express the gratitude I feel for the very kind manner in which your Royal Highness is so good as to express yourself towards me. I am afraid that your Royal Highness has understood more from the few words that I dropt to Colonel Lake than I meant to convey. What I meant to say was only that I thought from the appearance of things that there was a great probability of change[2], and that on that account I wished very much for an opportunity of conversing with your Royal Highness in order to know your wishes upon matters in which (in any situation) it would be my happiness to obey your commands. I am still of opinion that change is probable, & should be very happy to have the opportunity of learning your Royal Highness's wishes upon some subjects, but am afraid that I must be at the House of Commons at the hour at which it is probable your Royal Highness may leave the Drawing Room tomorrow. Your Royal Highness may depend upon my attending your commands at any hour Friday or Saturday which you may be pleased to appoint.

Permit me, Sir, to repeat the assurances of my gratitude for the distinguished marks of kindness with which your Royal Highness has so repeatedly honoured me, and of the perfect attachment with which I am, Sir [etc.]. (38059–60)

1. Third son of Henry Fox, 1st Lord Holland (1749–1806). He had been Foreign Secretary in the Rockingham Ministry, but had resigned, on Rockingham's death in July 1782, rather than serve under Shelburne. By this time he had acquired an unbounded influence over the Prince of Wales; and the King, regarding him as chiefly responsible for having led the Prince of Wales astray morally as well as politically, detested him.

2. A change of Government; but it was not until Fox and North coalesced in February 1783 that the Shelburne Ministry resigned after being defeated in the House of Commons.

Hannover, 20 Dec. 1782

I have a thousand thanks to return you for your picture which I think exceedingly like except the nose, which is certainly not shaped like yours. I suppose long before this you are thoroughly recovered from your accident, which, however, by all accounts might have been a very bad one. We are all here in expectation of news about the Peace, which I most sincerely hope may not take place, as it cannot but be an ignominious one, and I do not think that we are reduced so low as to make that necessary.[1] So far for politicks.

I shall go about the end of next month to the fare at Brunswick to make the acquaintance of the Prince and Princess of Mecklenbourg[2]. The fare is amusing enough as there is generally a good many strangers there, and I like the Duke of Brunswick exceedingly. He is extremely polite, and behaved to me, particularly the last time that I was there, with a degree of affection which one seldom finds in such great people. We have not been able to have a party in sledges as yet this year; unluckily all our snow and frost is gone, which I am exceedingly sorry for, as I think this a very great amusement.

As I have nothing more to write to render this scrawl in the least amusing, I will finish by assuring you [etc.].

P.S. Pray write often. It is now above six weeks since I received a line. (43548–9)

1. Preliminaries of Peace between Great Britain and her former Colonies were signed on 30 November 1782, and Preliminaries of Peace with Spain on 30 January 1783.

2. Frederick Francis, Hereditary Prince of Mecklenburg-Schwerin (1756–1837) who succeeded his uncle as Duke in 1785, and who married (1775) Louisa (1756–1808), daughter of John Augustus of Saxe-Gotha.

III   1783

The year 1783 saw two 'total' changes of Government. In February the
two Opposition leaders, Fox and North, formed their much-criticized
alliance to turn out Lord Shelburne and 'force the Closet'; and after the
country had been without a Government for five weeks the King, after
momentarily contemplating abdication in favour of his eldest son and
retiring to Hanover with the rest of his family, capitulated to the
Coalition. Fox always protested that it was never his object to deprive
the King of his constitutional prerogatives, yet it was his settled conviction that the House of Commons should have a negative control over
the appointment of the Ministers. In March 1783 he seemed to be
quite genuinely anxious to keep on good terms with the King and to
uphold the King's position.

According to Wraxall, Ministers received 'a prodigious accession to
strength and consideration' from the avowed junction of the Prince of
Wales, who came of age on 12 August. Therefore it fell to his friends,
again in office, to settle the question of a separate Establishment. It was
said that Shelburne had promised him the magnificent income of
£100,000 a year. How, then, could his own friends be less generous?
At first they were ready to be generous, even extravagant, though
Portland and Keppel were the only two Cabinet Ministers to support
Fox with any enthusiasm, and as soon as the rest heard of the King's
violent reaction to the proposal, which he considered to be 'a shameful
squandering of public money', especially at a time when his subjects

were 'much loaded with taxes', they beat a hasty retreat and came out strongly in opposition to it. Fitzpatrick thus outlined the course of the negotiations:

'The King originally agreed that the whole business of the Prince of Wales's establishment should be settled by the Duke of Portland, and his first plan was that Parliament should be applied to for the whole £100,000. This was consented to. But upon further conversation it was thought that a part from Parliament, and a part from the Civil List, would be more palatable in the House of Commons. The Duke of Portland apprised the King of this . . . [on 15 June], in answer to which he wrote a very angry letter, complaining of the departure from the first proposal. In answer to this the Duke of Portland wrote, that he did not mean the latter should supersede the first plan, which he was ready to propose to Parliament. The King answered this by saying that he had not changed his opinion of their (his Ministers') conduct by this letter; that he totally disapproved of the whole of their proposal; that he could not think of burdening the public, but was ready to give £50,000 a year from the Civil List, which he thought sufficient; and that he found, notwithstanding all the professions of the present Ministers for economy, they were ready to sacrifice the public interests to the wishes of an ill-advised young man; that he would never forget or forgive the conduct of the present Ministers towards him. This, we suppose, has been settled with the enemy, and no measures are yet determined upon, but as we have a good attendance of friends in town, the wish is to do something tomorrow [18 June], and at least to die handsomely.'

The 'enemy'—the Shelburne Whigs led by Shelburne in the Lords and the young Pitt in the Commons, were certainly aware of the King's violent quarrel with his Ministers, but, as they were in a minority in the House of Commons, they felt unable as yet to come to his assistance and advised him not to dismiss the Coalition 'unless some very particular opportunity presented itself'. So he had to compromise and bide his time. The Ministers too had to retreat, for they had pledged themselves to the Prince that he should have £100,000 a year, and, without his consent, they could not honourably recede. In the end, giving way to the advice of his dear friend the Duchess of Devonshire, he released them from their promise, behaving, as Fox acknowledged, 'in the handsomest manner'. The final arrangement, then, was that the King should allow his son £50,000 a year from the Civil List, and this, with the Duchy of Cornwall revenue, would bring his income up to £62,000; and that the only demand to be made on Parliament was for £30,000 for the payment of the Prince's debts, and a similar sum for his outfit. 'The truth is,' wrote Fox, 'that, excepting the Duke of Portland and

Lord Keppel, there was not one Minister who would have fought with any heart in this cause. I could see clearly from the beginning, long before the difficulties appeared, that Lord North and Lord John [Cavendish], though they did not say so, thought the large Establishment extravagant, and ... to fight a cause, where the latter especially was not hearty [he was Chancellor of the Exchequer], would have been a most desperate measure.'

By Christmas the Prince, finally emancipating himself from parental control, had moved into Carlton House, though the extensive, and highly expensive, alterations he had planned were still unfinished. They went on, in fact, for nearly thirty years, and, after enormous sums had been spent, the house was pulled down.

Before the close of the year, the introduction of the famous India Bill, which proved as unpopular as Walpole's Excise scheme had been, gave the King the opportunity of getting rid of Ministers who had forced themselves upon him, and, after the Bill had been rejected by the House of Lords, the Coalition was summarily dismissed on 18 December. The Prince himself, who had taken his seat as recently as the first day of the Session (11 November) had voted with his Whig friends in the first division in the Lords, but, acting on the advice of Fox, who had no wish unnecessarily to inflame the King against his son, he subsequently stayed away.

69   LETTERS FROM PRINCE FREDERICK TO THE PRINCE OF WALES, AND A REPLY

Hanover, 17 Jan. 1783

I find I must again write you one of my scolding letters, having lost all patience. You must remember that after a silence of near six months you promised me in your letter of the 10th of October that you would never be so negligent again, but alas I have not ever since that moment received one single line from you. I am affraid that having been so very long absent I am quite forgot.

I shall set out in about six weeks for Brunswick, which is about the time that the Prince and Princess of Schwerin mean to be there. Our Masquerades are begun here, but if I am to judge of all them by those which are passed I must confess I believe they will be very dull. We have as quiet a life here as is to be conceived. I shall find myself quite out of my element when I return to London, being so totally unaccustomed to racketing and noise. I will give you as exact an account as possible of my manner of life here. I get up in the morning about seven, and breakfast; at nine I go to my lesson in fortification; at ten, I have my German Master; from eleven till one, I ride sometimes out a doors, and sometimes in the manege, in which, by the by, I am grown a great proficient. At one I dress, at two dine; dinner is hardly ever over before four, when I go into my room again. If there is any Assembly, which happens very seldom, I go there at half after five, and play at cards, till nine, otherwise I sit at home quite alone. About a little after nine sup; after supper is over I generally go up into my room and read, till between twelve and one when I go to bed. Thus have I lived from the 27th of January 1781 till this present moment. I am so thoroughly accustomed to it that I can do everything without a clock.

I have given you as thorough and exact a description of our mode of living here as I could, which I have no doubt, you will shudder with the very thought of it. I am affraid at the same time I shall also have compleatly bored you with it. I shall therefore only add my best compliments to all friends in England [etc.]. (43554–5)

FROM THE PRINCE OF WALES

Queen's House, 17 Jan. 1783
Thank God I am now perfectly recovered from my accident, & should certainly have acknowledged yr. two last kind letters, but we have really been lately employed so much in hunting & other rural amusements yt. I have hardly had time to eat & drink, so far from having a moment to myself, but whenever I have, beleive me, the pleasantest I pass are those wh. I dedicate to you. In yr. former letter, you mentioned a young lady whom you thought wd. make a very good spouse for me. In the first place I understand there is an unfortunate madness in the family. In the second place I do not intend to marry till I am near the aera of thirty; & in the third place, my dear jocose Frederick, I do not know how I can turn such a number of younger brothers as I have to a better use than by making ym. take ye load of matrimony off my shoulders.

People talk very much & very strongly indeed, of a Peace today; they even go so far as to say that it is come over & signed, but God knows whether there is any truth in it or not, for one day we talk of peace & ye. next of war. The Queen has received a letter from New York concerning William, with exceeding good accounts. He is out upon a cruize under Lord Hood, having entirely left Digby[1]. Indeed I cannot express to you ye. satisfaction I have received lately concerning him. In ye. accounts I received of him from Elphinstone[2], who was his Captain in

1. Robert Digby (1732–1815). Captain, 1755; Rear-Admiral, 1779; Vice-Admiral, 1787; Admiral, 1794.

2. George Keith Elphinstone, Viscount Keith (1746–1823), fifth son of the 10th Lord Elphinstone. Captain, 1775; Rear-Admiral, 1794; Vice-Admiral, 1795; Admiral, 1801. M.P. for Co. Dunbarton, 1781–90, and for Stirlingshire, 1796–1801. Commander-in-Chief

the Warwick all last summer, he says there cannot be a more gallant or a better officer than our dear William is already & promises to be; that nothing can equal his steadiness or the knowledge he has already acquired, wh. is quite incredible; in short, yt. he is now a remarkable good Officer, & in all probability will be one of the best in the whole Navy. I think, my dearest Frederick, yt. this account cannot fail of pleasing you, as I know ye. great affection you have for him as well as me.[1]

You shall know the success of yr. lottery tickets in a letter next week, but Desnoyer being ill prevents my seeing him in order to examine his books. Pardon me if I break off my letter thus abruptly & conclude here for I am in the utmost hurry; you shall hear again for certain next week. I will therefore now close my epistle with wishing you many & many happy New Years. (43556-7)

PRINCE FREDERICK'S REPLY

Hanover, 4 Feb. 1783

Though I have not much to tell you, yet as Lord John Russel[2], who is returning to England, has undertaken the conveyance of a letter to you, I cannot let him set out without writing a few lines to you to thank you for your very kind and affectionate letter which I received last Friday. You are totally mistaken about the Princess whom I recommended to you as a wife.[3] I have enquired about the idea which you have of there being madness in the family, and find it totally groundless. In the family of Hesse, there never was the least suspicion even of such a disorder. She is by all accounts beautiful and wonderfully accomplished.

I was at Brunswick last week for five days, and past my time very

in the Mediterranean, 1799–1802; at Plymouth, 1803; in the North Sea, 1803–7; of the Channel Fleet, 1812. Created Baron Keith [I.], 1797; U.K. Barony, 1801; Viscount Keith, 1814. Prince William later (1811) wished to marry Lord Keith's only daughter, the heiress Margaret Mercer Elphinstone, afterwards Comtesse de Flahault, and who was Princess Charlotte of Wales's bosom friend.

1. William received no letter from the King between September 1782 and the middle of April 1783, 'in which,' wrote William, in reply, 'you was pleased to express your approbation of my conduct. This is the first time I have had that pleasure of receiving a letter from your Majesty as from a tender parent to his son grown up. You was likewise pleased to say I should not return immediately, which is another mark of your great affection, because it is my good fortune to have already served so much of my six years abroad that it was my wish to stay out till my apprenticeship was completed.'

2. Lord John Russell (1766–1839) succeeded his brother Francis as 6th Duke of Bedford, in 1802. Ensign, 3rd Foot Guards, 1783–5. M.P. for Tavistock, 1788–90, and 1790–1802; Lord-Lieutenant of Ireland, 1806–7.

3. See No. 66.

agreably. As we are now very well known there, there is much less ceremony, so that there is no great gene. We had a great Masquerade there, when there was above twelve hundred masks. I suppose that hunting goes on as usual twice a week; I shall have quite to begin afresh, it is so long since I have heard the tongue of a hound. In short I shall be totally out of my element when I return, after having lived so long so very quiet a life. I must beg you will order that the next liveries which are sent over for my grooms be made with white cloath waistcoats and breeches instead of green ones, which I think will look infinitely better, besides which the green fades so terribly. Give my best compliments to all friends in England.

P.S. My best love to Lake. Pray write often. Adieu. Excuse this scrawl; it is written in a monstrous hurry. (43560–1)

70 CHARLES JAMES FOX TO THE PRINCE OF WALES

St. James's Street, Tuesday night [4 Mar. 1783]

I should have written to your Royal Highness last night, if Mr. Townshend had not undertaken to see you at the Masquerade,[1] & acquaint you with all the particulars of what had happened. L⁴ North wrote to his Majesty this morning to let him know that we had absolutely declined acting unless the Duke of Portland[2] was appointed to the Treasury.[3] The King desired to see him, & Ld. North waited upon him accordingly this evening. His interview with his Majesty was short, and the substance of the conversation was merely this: that as we could not give up the point of the Treasury, and as Lord North could not take it nor act without us, that his Majesty had no further commands for his Lordship. This negociation is therefore entirely at an end, and not only the country is now without a Ministry, but there does not appear at present any prospect of making one. I understand his Majesty appeared in perfect good humour & easy, from whence one might imagine that he has some other scheme in view, but I do not learn from any quarter that this is the case.[4]

1. On 22 December 1780, the King, it will be remembered, had absolutely forbidden him to go to them.

2. William Henry Cavendish Bentinck, 3rd Duke of Portland (1738–1809); Lord-Lieutenant of Ireland, April–August 1782; First Lord of the Treasury, April–December 1783, and March 1807–September 1809; Home Secretary, 1794–1801; President of the Council, 1801–5.

3. Lord North's letter is in Fortescue, *Correspondence of George III*, vi.260–61.

4. The King vainly offered the Premiership to the young Pitt, made unsuccessful overtures to Lord Gower, tried to detach Lord North from the Rockinghams, again urged Pitt to form a Government, made overtures to Lord Temple (Lord-Lieutenant of Ireland) and to Chatham's nephew, Thomas Pitt; and finally, on 2 April, having no other resource, capitulated to the Coalition after drafting an Abdication Message to Parliament.

I really think this is a moment when those who wish well to his Majesty & to his authority in this country ought to advise him not to delay any longer taking those measures to which he must be driven at last, for it is impossible but the greatest dissatisfaction must arise from the present unsettled state of affairs. I trust to the goodness which your Royal Highness has repeatedly shewn me that you will consider this letter as written in the utmost confidence, but I really think the King's situation extremely critical unless he can make up his mind to trust those who have the most unfeigned attachment to his person and family, & who alone are capable of serving him at this juncture.   (38065–6)

71   THE KING TO THE PRINCE OF WALES [draft]

[?*March 1783*]

The situation of the times are such that I must, if I attempt to carry on the business of the nation, give up every political principle on which I have acted, which I should think very unjustifiable, as I have always attempted to act agreable to my duty; and must form a Ministry from among men who know I cannot trust them and therefore who will not accept office without making me a kind of slave. This undoubtedly is a cruel dilemma, and leaves me but one step to take without the destruction of my principles and honour; the resigning my Crown, my dear son, to you, quitting this my native country for ever and returning to the dominions of my forefathers.

Your difficulties will not be the same. You have never been in a situation to form any political system, therefore are open to addopt what the times may make necessary; and no set of men can ever have offended you or made it impossible for you to employ them.

Your mother, whose excellent qualities appear stronger to me every hour, will certainly instantly prepare for joining me with the rest of my children. You may depend on my educating the boys in a manner that, if called into the British service, they shall not be undeserving of any marks of brotherly affection you may be inclined to shew them.[1] (41795)

1. See Fortescue, *Correspondence of George III*, vi.314-17, for the King's draft of an Abdication Message to Parliament, *c*.28 March 1783.

72 THE EARL OF AILESBURY[1] TO COLONEL COSBY[2]

14 Apr. 1783

Lord Ailesbury sends his compliments to Colonel Cosby & wishes to prevent his having the trouble of calling in Seamore Place in consequence of a message Miss Jeffries was desired to give him from Lᵈ A., who sees nobody at present. The chief thing he had to tell Col. Cosby he knows perhaps already, viz. about a letter the K— has received lately from the Nabob of A[rcot][3] in which he expresses no small anxiety about the event of a certain ring commission to the success of which Col. Cosby was so instrumental that Ld A— has desired Lord North to do him all the justice that is possible to the Nabob, to whom the Queen, in her immediate letter of thanks to him, mentioned having received the ring in question since Col. Cosby's arrival in England.[4]   (38067)

73 THE DUKE OF PORTLAND TO THE PRINCE OF WALES

5.25 p.m., Wednesday, 30 Apr. 1783

The Duke of Portland has the honor of acquainting his Royal Highness that he had the pleasure of receiving his Majesty's full & most ready approbation of Dr Jackson[5] as a successor to the Deanery of Christ Church in case the Bishop of Bristol[6] shall incline to be translated to the

1. Thomas Brudenell Bruce, 2nd Baron Bruce (1747) and (1776) 1st Earl of Ailesbury (1729–1814). He was Lord Chamberlain to the Queen, and had been Governor to the Prince of Wales and Prince Frederick for a short time in 1776, when he was succeeded by his elder brother, the Duke of Montagu.

2. Sir Henry Augustus Montagu Cosby (1743–1822). He had served in India under Clive and Coote, and had been appointed commander of the Nawab of Arcot's cavalry in 1778. Towards the end of 1782 he returned to England on sick leave, bearing with him despatches concerning the war with Hyder Ali of Mysore. He was knighted in January 1784.

3. Wraxall considered Muhammad Ali 'one of the most able Asiatic Princes who has reigned in our time'. He 'maintained a perpetual conflict either with the insatiable avarice and rapacity, or against the more oppressive policy and tyranny of successive Governors of Fort St. George' (iv.83).

4. The King wrote to Lord North on 8 April: 'In December the Queen received the diamond ring Sir Thomas Rumbold [Governor of Madras 1777–80] had been entrusted with, and had secreted till Col. Crosbie [*sic*], who came in the autumn from Madras, obliged him to deliver it, since which time the Queen has wrote to the Nabob to acknowledge the receipt of it' (Fortescue, *Correspondence of George III*, vi.348).

5. Cyril Jackson (1746–1819), Sub-preceptor to the Prince of Wales and Prince Frederick, 1771–6. Later, he declined offers of several bishoprics.

6. Dr. Lewis Bagot (1740–1802), Bishop of Bristol, 1782; translated to Norwich, 1783; and to St. Asaph, 1790.

See of Norwich.[1] The Duke of Portland takes the liberty of giving his Royal Highness the earliest information of this possible & very probable event in consequence of having been told by Mr. Fox that Dr Jackson had the honor of possessing a considerable share of his Royal Highness's good opinion.[2]   (38068)

74   PRINCE FREDERICK TO THE PRINCE OF WALES

Hanover, 12 May 1783

I cannot set out on a long journey without first of all taking leave of you, and at the same time putting you in mind that there is such a person living as me, which [you] really appear to have compleatly forgot, at least if I am to judge of your [silence], which has been for the last ten months. Indeed it is a little hard during so long a time not to receive a single line from you. I shall set out tomorrow for Berlin where I shall see the Reviews. I shall not be long away as I intend to be back for his Majesty's birthday.[3] I was yesterday evening at a concert given by two French horns. Nothing can be conceived finer than their tone, besides which they have wonderful execution. They mean to go to London in about four months. They are, if I am not much mistaken, in the service of the Duke de Rohan[4]. Pray let me recommend them to your protection. I am certain you never heard anything equal to them.

As I have not time and I do not think you deserve a longer letter, I shall only repeat to you, my dearest brother that I am [etc.].   (43571-2)

75   THE EMPRESS OF RUSSIA[5] TO M. SIMOLIN [6] [translation]

Sarsko Selo, [?Old Style] 18 May 1783

I wish to take into my service Captⁿ John Knowles[7] with the rank of Rear Admiral; you will let him know it, and after having acquainted

1. See Fortescue, *Correspondence of George III*, vi.382–4.

2. See the Prince of Wales's letter to Fox, 30 April 1783, in Lord John Russell, *Memorials & Correspondence of C. J. Fox*, ii.109.

3. 4 June.

4. He died at an advanced age in 1816.

5. Catherine II (1729–96), Empress of Russia since 1762.

6. The Russian Minister to the Court of St. James's.

7. Lieutenant, R.N., 1759; Captain, 1780; Rear-Admiral, 1799 (*d.*1801). He remained in the Royal Navy.

yourself with his terms you will fix with him the time of his departure; meanwhile, as my intention is to procure for my service some able sea officers who you suppose may be found among the Lieutenants and other Officers of that country, I give you leave, with the advice of people at your place who are acquainted with those matters, and that of said Captain Knowles, to invite them thereto, and agreeing with them about the terms; you will let me know the sum necessary for their passage. (38070)

76 THE PRINCE OF WALES TO PRINCE FREDERICK

Queen's House, 27 May 1783

I have just received yr. kind letter for wh. I am very much obliged to you, & I shall not begin by apologizing for my fault but confess it tout uniment & sue for mercy. But to tell you the truth I have had a great many things upon my mind of late, pleasant ones mixed with unpleasant ones, but do not think of whatever kind or sort they may be, they could any of them even for an instant make me forget my dearest friend & brother. I am in great hopes, but I tell you this as a thing I do not wish generally to be spoken of, yt. I shall soon be in a situation by an Establishment being form'd for me such as I ought to have, to receive you with open arms next year, & in a manner yt. I shall be able to testify to the world ye. affection I have hitherto always borne you, & wh. I shall constantly cherish thro'out life.

The town is at present much enliven'd by ye. arrival of ye. Duc de Chartres[1] & a large party of French both men & women, who thank God are going away next week, yt. is to say, all ye. gentlemen & ladies except ye. Duc de Chartres & two gentlemen yt. are attending upon him. Monsieur de Conflans, a man yt. distinguish'd himself very much last war with the light troops, & is an exceedingly sensible, agreable, well bred man, & Mr. de Fitz James[2], indeed all the French yt. are here, seem to be exceeding pleasant, civil, polite people, but the Duc de Chartres, tho' he does not at all want for sense, on the contrary is rather clever, but I think he is a great beast; in short, I cannot bear him. We

1. Until he succeeded his father in 1785 as Duke of Orleans, Louis Philippe (1747–93) bore the customary title of Duc de Chartres. Notorious as *Égalité*, he was guillotined during the Revolution in spite of his democratic professions. His son, Louis Philippe (1773–1850) became King of the French in 1830 after the July Revolution. Horace Walpole referred to the Duke's arrival in England in a letter of 8 May (Toynbee, *Letters of Horace Walpole*, xii.443).

2. Charles, Duc de Fitzjames (1712–87). He owned a château at Clermont. 'The Duke of Orleans and Fitzjames seem as much at home at Brooks's as Hare, Fitzpatrick or Fox', wrote Eden's friend Storer, in 1786 (Auckland, *Journal and Correspondence*, i.369).

are very civil to one another but yt. is all. My reason for saying I was glad ye. French were going, is not because I disliked ym. but because we have had so many parties & fêtes & assemblies & suppers upon their account, yt. everybody is grown quite tired of ym.

I cannot conclude my letter to you, my dearest Frederick, without condoling with you for the loss of our poor dear little brother.[1] Had you known what a sweet child he was you wd. have felt his death as severely as I did, & indeed for yt. reason I am glad you did not know him, but setting aside his loss, I cannot express to you what I felt for our poor dear mother, who is now I beleive within about six weeks of her laying in,[2] & I am happy to tell you yt. she is in perfect health & seems to have got up her spirits most astonishingly, infinitely beyond what anybody cd. have expected, especially in so short a time.[3]

I have sent you two canes, I hope you will like ym. I understood from Gerrard yt. you wanted ym. to go by ye messenger. I cannot say I quite approve of them myself but they were ye best I cd. get made in so great a hurry. However I will take care you shall have two better by ye. next messenger, for I will bespeak ym. directly.

Adieu my dearest Frederick, you *may really* depend upon hearing from me soon again. Wd. to Heaven I cd. see you as soon as this letter will reach yr. hands; vous savez bien que ce n'est pas manque de volonté mais de moiens. If you have any other commissions pray send ym. to me & I will execute ym. to ye best of my poor endeavours. Pray think of seeing old England's shores again as soon as possible. Beleive me, no one is more impatient, my dearest Frederick, for yt. long wished for & long expected moment of yr. arrival here, than he who [etc.].

P.S. I forgot to tell you yt. I have been fortunate enough to have it in my power to do a piece of service to a very old friend of our's, I mean Dr. Jackson, by getting him thro' my interest ye. Deanery of Christ Church. He desires to be remember'd to you in ye. warmest manner as one of the oldest of yr. friends & servants. Pray remember me in ye. kindest manner to my old friend Joan.   (43573-5)

1. Prince Octavius (1779-83) died on 3 May 'of an hereditary humour which the Princess Dowager of Wales had brought into the family, and of which she herself and some of her children and grandchildren died' (Horace Walpole, *Letters*, xiii.7n.).

2. Princess Amelia (1783-1810), the King's youngest child, was born on 7 August.

3. The King too, deeply mourned the loss of his little boy. 'There will be no Heaven for me', he said, 'if Octavius is not there.' In misfortunes and afflictions he was firmly supported by his religious faith. 'It has pleased the Almighty', he wrote to William, 'to put an end very unexpectedly of the most amiable as well as attached child a parent could have. May I find those I have, as warmly attached as he was, and I cannot expect more. I will not add more on a subject that very much fills my mind, and I own as [sic] strongly convinced me how very transitory all enjoyments are in this world, but it the stronger convinces me that the fulfilling every duty is the only real comfort, and that our rewards must be looked for in another, not this world' (14 June 1783).

Downing Street, 6 p.m., Friday, 6 June 1783

The Duke of Portland has the mortification of acquainting his Royal Highness that his Majesty's ideas respecting the amount of his Royal Highness's Establishment do not *as yet* seem exactly to correspond with those which were submitted to his Majesty by the Duke of Portland as the unanimous opinion of the King's confidential servants. His Majesty however did not appear to have formed any such resolution as to preclude further representations upon that subject, & the Duke of Portland is much inclined to beleive that his Majesty's affection for his Royal Highness will dispose him to concede what his regard for the circumstances of his people induces him more maturely to consider. The Duke of Portland is unwilling to detain his Royal Highness with the particulars of what passed in his Majesty's Closet, but will be ready to attend his Royal Highness for that purpose whenever he shall have the honor of receiving his Royal Highness's commands. (38073)

Downing Street, 5 p.m., Wednesday, 11 June 1783

It is with very great pleasure that the Duke of Portland acquaints his Royal Highness that he has received his Majesty's commands to prepare the draught of a Message to both Houses of Parliament for their assistance in making a suitable provision for his Royal Highness's Establishment, that his Majesty has signified his approbation of the proposition which the Duke of Portland has the honor of transmitting herewith to his Royal Highness, & that his Majesty's Message will be sent to the two Houses on Tuesday next. As it has been the constant custom in all cases which concern the Royal Family to make the communication to both Houses on the same day, & as in a matter of such high moment it has been also usual to give notice of his Majesty's gracious intention, the adjournment of the House of Lords to next Monday unavoidably occasions this delay, which is the only interruption which the Duke of Portland flatters himself his Royal Highness's satisfaction may ever suffer.[1] (38074)

1. It was not until the 23rd that the Royal Message was presented to the House by Lord John Cavendish: 'His Majesty, reflecting on the propriety of a separate Establishment for his dearly beloved son the Prince of Wales, recommends the consideration thereof to this House; relying on the experienced zeal and affection of his faithful Commons for such aid towards making that Establishment, as shall appear consistent with a due attention to the circumstances of his people, every addition to whose burthens his Majesty feels with the most sensible concern' (*House of Commons Journal*, xxxix.500).

Hanover, 13 June 1783

A thousand thanks for your kind letter which I confess was quite an unexpected pleasure. We are just returned from a very pleasant excursion to Potsdam and Berlin where we have been to see the troops reviewed; we have been received by the King[1] and the Prince of Prussia[2] in the most gracious manner. As for the troops, it is impossible to conceive anything finer; I confess I never was so struck with anything in my life. In short, were I to begin upon that subject I should never have finished; I therefore will excuse you and not trouble you with a description of the manoeuvres.

I believe you would like Berlin vastly; it is a beautiful town and the society is very agreable. We also found there a parcel of French just freshly imported, but I do not think they seemed in the least to please at Berlin. By all accounts Monsieur de Chartres must be a terrible brute, always drunk and very fond of low company. As for Monsieur de Conflans, some speak well of him and others ill of him; as an Officer I do not think people speak much in his favor. At least he was at Berlin when he did not shew off to his advantage.

I think you will find some difficulty in decyphering this scrawl, but I have got a most horrid pen and I have not time enough to get another. I will therefore spare your eyes the trouble of reading any more, by concluding and assuring you that I shall ever be [etc.].

P.S. You may depend upon hearing from me soon again; pray write often. Adieu.[3] (43582-3)

1. Frederick the Great (1712–86), King of Prussia since 1740.

2. Prince Frederick William (1744–97), Frederick the Great's nephew, who succeeded him as Frederick William II.

3. Frederick wrote at greater length about his visit to Potsdam, on the 6th (to his father): '... We arrived on the fifteenth in the evening at Potsdam. The town is exceedingly fine the streets very broad, and the fronts of the houses exceedingly handsome. His Majesty the King of Prussia has laid out immense sums in beautifying the town. People who report that he had knocked down many houses without asking the leave of the proprietors are very much mistaken; the manner of his doing it is this; whenever he sees a house whose appearance he dislikes, he immediately sends to the proprietor and offers to rebuild it at his own expence. There have been many instances of the proprietors refusing this offer, and then he does nothing; if the offer is accepted he rebuilds the house with a very fine front, and as for the inside of it, he allots a certain sum, which is sufficient to fit it up plainly and neatly, but if the proprietor chuses to have it more elegantly arranged, he may if he desires it receive that sum and add what he chuses to it.

'The next day we were presented to his Majesty who received us in the most gracious manner. He is short and small but wonderfully strong made, not very well upon his legs, but on horseback, your Majesty would be astonished to see him. One of the days we were with him, he was from three o'clock in the morning till near eleven without ever getting off his

horse. I cannot say his Majesty's wardrobe is the best I ever saw; he always wears the uniform of the Army, as it is called, which is a blue coat, with red cape and cuffs and a large shoulder knot. His coat is always buttoned quite down to the bottom, a very bad old uniform sword, a pair of black velvet breeches very greasy and dirty, and pair of boots which, never being blacked, are become quite red. However, with all this he has exceedingly the air of a gentleman and something exceedingly commanding in his look. The Prince of Prussia is a very large man, but of a very good person. He appears very clever, and has a very disagreable and difficult part to play, which to all appearance he does with great prudence. He has his foibles as well as other men; his behaviour towards me was exceedingly kind. He appeared to me to have a hearty enmity for the French and a great affection for us. His Majesty dines at twelve o'clock and sits near four hours at table except when he has strangers, but to the great astonishment of all his Gentlemen, during the whole time that we were at Potsdam, Berlin and Magdebourg, he continued sitting the four hours at table, which is a mark of kindness which he has never done to any other strangers but us. On the 17th began the Reviews. The Regiments which were reviewed were the three Batallions of Guards, the Regiment of Rhodig of one Batallion, which were formerly the late King's Guards being known by the name of his tall Potsdam Grenadiers, the Prince of Prussia's Regiment and General Zettwitz's which is a Fusiliers Regiment. These two Regiments are each of two Batallions, of five Batallion Companies and one Company of Grenadiers by Batallion, upon which plan all the rest of the Army are. They are also compleated up to the last augmentation and were therefore fifty one file in each Company and fifty six in the Grenadiers, ten non-commissioned Officers, one of whom is Pfahn Juncker who must always be a man of family, and who after he has served three or four years, as non-commissioned Officer becomes Ensign, indeed no Officer is received into the service before he has been Pfahn Juncker, except the Kings Pages and four Officers. The Grenadiers, are always formed into Batallions, each Batallion consisting of four Companies, there were four of these Batallions at Potsdam. The three Batallions of Guards and Rhodig's are recruited out of all the Regiments of the Army each being obliged to send three men a year of a particular size. The Prince of Prussia and Zettwitz's are upon the plan of the rest of the Army, each regiment has its particular District which they call Canton, from whence they draw half of their men, the other half must be strangers. Ten months in the year those of the country are allowed to go upon furlough, the other two they must be at the exercise. It is impossible however to see the least difference between, those who are continually with the Regiment, and those who are so long upon furlough, because they are at first so exceedingly well drilled. The Prussians never put a man into the ranks till he has been a whole twelvemonth at the drill during which time he is not allowed to receive a single blow and indeed the idea we have of the wonderfull severity of the Prussians is not in the least founded. During the exercise you never see a single blow given. The first Serjeant of each Company, whom they call Feld Weber, stands in the rear of the Company and marks down each fault that is committed, those men who have made these faults are exercised again in the afternoon, and then for the least fresh one they are thoroughly thrashed. It is impossible to describe the care that is taken of the health of the soldiers among the Prussians. They are only allowed to mount guard every tenth day so that they are five nights in bed and one up, and the Serjeants are obliged to see that the men are properly fed and indeed it is wonderful the air of health, which all the Regiments have. They exercise often, and but a little at a time. They seldom exercise above two hours, by which means the men are never over fatigued. The order and discipline of them, is too well known, for it to be necessary for me to mention it; indeed it is very surprising, and one Regiment is so exactly like the other, that it strikes one very much. They are obliged to load and fire six times and what is very surprising, is how exceedingly well they aim. They always say what is certainly very true that if a man knows how to fire fast one can always make him fire slow, but that upon many occasions firing fast is very necessary particularly against Cavalry, so that it is done with regularity. . . .'
(43578–81)

111

Windsor, 15 June 1783

Colonel Hotham, the punctuality with which you have always performed every minutest part of your duty during the time I have had the pleasure of personally knowing you, added to your discression and the attachment you have ever shewn to the real good of my children, makes me pitch on you to acquaint the Prince of Wales with what I should have done by word of mouth had he on Thursday mentioned the affair of his seperate Establishment to me; but I find from the Queen that though he came for that purpose, he begged her to thank me and declined doing it in person least it might drawn [*sic*] on a conversation with me. I am not surprised he avoided that, as his conscience, if not entirely put to sleep as well as his knowledge of my sentiments, must have made him expect that on such an occasion I should have uttered very homefelt truths; perhaps the present method has the advantage, as it leaves no room for misapprehensions.

You will therefore tell him that from the first formation of the present Administration I had authorized the D. of Portland to consult with the other Ministers and propose what Establishment could be made for the P. of Wales when he came of age; indeed Ld. Shelburne[2] had had similar directions before the change. That Duke a few days past mentioned to me that, including the income of the revenue of Cornwal, Parliament should be applied to for a sum of £100,000 per annum. This I thought, however I might wish to have my son settled with comfort, the weight of taxes my subjects labour under and his granfather having had that sum with a wife and nine children, that the proposal might with reason be thought unreasonable, and therefore directed the Ministers to reconsider it. On Wednesday the D. of Portland reported to me that they persisted in the opinion that they could venture to propose this sum to Parliament, as it was understood that whenever the P. of Wales married, no encrease would be made to his revenue, and that every sort of expence at setting out, whether furnishing or altering any house he may reside in, must be taken out of this annual income. Upon which, though I did not depart from the opinion that a less sum would have been sufficient for every reasonable purpose and an addition to make it up the £100,000 whenever he married, yet when the Ministers chose to propose the larger sum on the above conditions, I should not object to it.

You will further acquaint him that having in my possession the late

1. This letter, together with a few others not addressed to the Prince, is included because it refers to his Establishment.

2. William Petty, Earl of Shelburne and (December 1784) Marquess of Lansdowne (1737–1805). Prime Minister, July 1782–April 1783. He had succeeded his father as Earl of Shelburne in 1761.

house my mother[1] inhabited in Pall Mall, I am willing to grant him the use of it, but on condition that he does not give any of the ground away, namely, by enlarging the passage the D. of Cumberland has at the bottom of the garden, and that he takes on himself all repairs, taxes, and the keeping of the garden; he must find stables for his horses in town and conveniences for his carriages, I have no room for them; besides, an interference of seperate servants is very inconvenient. As to a country house, I have none for him: the appartment he occupies at Windsor shall always be kept ready to receive him; if he wants any other habitation he must provide it himself.

I certainly do not mean to recommend any additional servants, but strongly recommend that the fewer sallaries are added, the more will remain for other expences, and the less he will have to retrench whenever the day comes that he may think it right to propose to me the wish of marrying.

I cannot conclude without mentioning that his own good sense must convince him how little reason I have to approve of any part of his conduct for the last three years; that his neglect of every religious duty is notorious; his want of even common civility to the Queen and me not less so, besides his total disobedience of every injunction I had given, and which he, in the presence of his brother and the gentlemen then about him, declared to me he was contented with.

I hope he will now think it behoves him to take up a line of conduct more worthy of his station, that he may regain the good opinion of men of religion, decency and worth, and that a continuation of levity may not shorten his days and make him too late repent the not having followed the advice of an affectionate though distressed parent.[2]   (16391–2)

1. Frederick Louis, Prince of Wales (1707–51) married (1736) Augusta (1719–72), daughter of Frederick of Saxe-Gotha.

2. The King redrafted his letter, and actually sent it to Hotham on the 21st. The revised draft runs as follows: 'Colonel Hotham: the punctuality with which you have always performed every minutest part of your duty during the time I have had the pleasure of personally knowing you, added to your discretion and the attachment you have ever shewn to the real good of my children, makes me pitch on you to acquaint the P. of Wales with what I should have done by word of mouth had he not, when he came here to mention the affair of his seperate establishment, changed his mind and from what I learnt from the Queen, begged her to thank me, declining doing it in person least it might draw on a conversation which might embarras him. I am not surprized he avoided it, as his conscience, if not entirely put to sleep, as well as his knowledge of my sentiments, must have made him expect that on such an occasion I should have utter'd very homefelt truths: now that the business is fully in train I desire you will acquaint him that not thinking it advisable to apply to Parliament for any further assistance than such as may enable me to allow fifty thousand pounds pr. annum which, with the revenue of Cornwal, will make his income about twenty seven thousand more than the late King thought sufficient for me in a similar situation, which will, I am fully perswaded, enable him, with proper attention, and oeconomy, to live handsomely, but not with the shameful extravagance he has shewn till now, which appears the stronger by an

Downing Street, 15 June 1783

The Duke of Portland, having had the honour of humbly representing to your Majesty on Friday last that the reason of his not being prepared to submit to your Majesty's consideration drafts of Messages similar to those which it has been usual to send to the two Houses of Parliament in all cases which affect the interests of the Royal Family consisted in the variety of modes which had occurred for making a provision for the establishment of his Royal Highness the Prince of Wales, has now the

intimation he has sent me through the D. of Portland that he has debts to the amount of above twenty nine thousand pounds, to which I might add what I gave him on a former very improper business. He must therefore recollect that this is the last time his debts can be paid and that therefore he must live on the sum allotted and that I do expect an assurance through you from him of his intentions to keep within bounds. What I mean to apply to Parliament for his debts and for fitting up his house, stables and any other necessaries upon this occasion, is a sum of sixty thousand pounds. I mean to let him have the use of the house my late mother inhabited in Pall Mall, but on condition that the premises be not damaged, particularly that the passage my mother granted to the late D. of York be not widened, and that he shall take all repairs, taxes and the expences of keeping the garden on himself; he must also find stables in Town for his horses, and houses for his carriages, I having no room for them; besides an interference of seperate servants is very inconvenient.

As to a country house, I have none for him; besides it would draw on so many additional expences that I think it best avoided. His apartments at Windsor shall alwaies be kept ready to receive him, yet should he wish another he must provide it himself. But I here again repeat, he must, if he means not to lose the good opinion of this nation, avoid debts. I do not mean to propose any addition to his attendants except those of an inferior kind which a seperate house and table naturally require. Whenever he shall think it right to express to me the wish of marrying I shall look on myself authorised to apply to Parliament that his annual income may be encreased to one hundred thousand pounds.

I cannot quit this subject without just saying that a plan must now be prepared under his inspection for the expences of his housekeeping, stables, Privy Purse, keeping back a sum for extraordinaries which should be exactly kept to, or he will soon be obliged to retrench, or do worse: now is the hour to put the whole on a proper footing. As to furnishing and repairing the house, buying or hiring stables, estimates should be first made that the expence do not exceed the means of effecting them.

I cannot conclude without mentioning that I am convinced the P. of Wales on the smallest reflection must feel that I have little reason to approve of any part of his conduct for the last three years; that his neglect of every religious duty is notorious; his want of common civility to the Queen and me, not less so; besides his total disobedience of every injunction I had given and which he in presence of his brother and the gentlemen then about them both declared himself contented with. I must hope he will now think it behoves him to take up a fresh line of conduct more worthy of his station, that he may regain the good opinion of men of religion, decency and worth, and that a continuation of levity may not shorten his days and make him too late repent at not having followed this advice of an affectionate though distressed parent.' (16366)

honour of transmitting them to your Majesty in obedience to your Royal commands.

In the two Messages to the House of Commons, your Majesty will observe a difference, the cause of which the Duke of Portland begs leave with all humility to state to your Majesty, on the consideration of which he presumes to hope for the signification of your Majesty's pleasure concerning the one or the other being prepared for your Royal signature.

Upon a very attentive consideration of the subject, it was conceived that it should be submitted to your Majesty that Parliament should enable your Majesty to allow fifty thousand pounds, part of the one hundred thousand pounds which it is most humbly presumed may be requisite for the Prince of Wales's establishment, by granting to your Majesty out of the Sinking Fund an annual sum to that amount until the Exchequer Bills which have been issued for the discharge of the Civil List Debt are wholly paid off, when the disposal of that sum would revert to your Majesty, and that the remaining sum of forty thousand pounds which, together with the revenues of the Duchy of Cornwall, will make in the whole the sum of one hundred thousand pounds, should be advanced to your Majesty, out of the Aggregate Fund, unless it should be your Majesty's pleasure to order this sum to be paid to his Royal Highness out of the present Civil List revenues. But as it is obvious from the numerous Royal Family with which Providence has blessed your Majesty that it will be impossible for your Majesty to provide a suitable mainten- ance for the younger Princes and Princesses out of your present revenues, the propriety of alluding to that happy circumstance is most dutifully submitted to your Majesty in case your Majesty should judge it expedient to call upon your Parliament for the whole of their assistance on the present important occasion.

Your Majesty may possibly be the rather induced to consider this latter mode not wholly unworthy of your attention by your Majesty's being informed of a communication which has been made to the Duke of Portland by the Prince of Wales's order, and which his Royal High- ness, who has expressed in the strongest terms his determination to conceal nothing from your Majesty, has directed him to lay before your Majesty. It appears, upon a very strict scrutiny into the state of the Prince of Wales's expenditure, that there remain due to tradesmen various sums amounting in the whole to somewhat more than twenty-nine thousand pounds, for the discharge of which there is no resource but in the great liberality of your Majesty, who may direct them to be included in the arrear of debt which Parliament was apprized of at the opening of this session by your Majesty's most gracious Speech from the Throne, from which it is most reasonably to be expected that the Civil List should be exonerated, or who may order it to be paid out of such part of your revenues as your Majesty has heretofore graciously condescended to

115

appropriate to the use and maintenance of his Royal Highness. The Duke of Portland thinks he ought not to close this subject without laying before your Majesty the assurances of his Royal Highness that he is not more or otherwise indebted than as the Duke of Portland has had the honour of representing to your Majesty.

The Duke of Portland most humbly ventures to hope that his Majesty's goodness will be so far extended to him as to forgive his having presumed to offer his poor thoughts to your Majesty upon a subject which he most anxiously solicits your Majesty to believe he most devoutly wished never to have occasion to mention to your Majesty or to have been otherwise employed upon but as the instrument of carrying your Majesty's gracious intentions into effect.   (16358–9)

THE KING'S REPLY

Windsor, 10.59 a.m., 16 June 1783
It is impossible for me to find words expressive enough of my utter indignation and astonishment at the letter I have just received from the D. of Portland. These words are certainly strong and would be inexcusable if not authorized by the following facts. When the D. of Portland desired I would turn my thoughts to fixing on a sum for the separate establishment of the P. of Wales when he arrives at the age of twenty-one years, I desired he would with the rest of the Efficient Ministers[1] consider what proposal should be made to me on that subject. About a fortnight since, he acquainted me that it was their unanimous opinion that a sum of one hundred thousand pounds, including the revenues of the Duchy of Cornwall, should be obtained from Parliament. I instantly shewed my surprize at so lavish an idea, and the more so when my subjects are so much loaded with taxes, and said I thought fifty thousand pounds in addition to the revenue of Cornwall, which would nearly exceed twenty seven thousand per annum of what the late King thought sufficient for me in a similar situation, was all that could with any reason be granted, and consequently desired that Duke to acquaint the Ministers with my opinion and of my wish that they should reconsider this business. On the 6th of this month the Duke of Portland told me they continued to think it right to propose that sum to Parliament, from whom they meant the whole sum should come; that the reason of putting it so high arose from a knowledge that the Prince of Wales has debts which must be paid out of his annual income, besides the expense of fitting himself out, and that they meant to acquaint him of this and that no addition could be made whenever he married. I did not deny that I still thought the sum too large, though I acknowledged if no

1. The Cabinet Council.

116

increase was made whenever he married that I would make no further objection.

I therefore was surprised on the 13th to find the Duke of Portland had not the drafts of the Messages, but that they would soon be sent to me, from which time I have been in expectation of them, but this suspense is now fully explained, for the whole proposition is changed. I am to be saddled with the whole odium of the measure, and the expense at the same time ultimately to fall entirely on me, who am not, from my numerous progeny, in a situation to bear it, though I had been assured no part was to be paid by me; and in addition I am pressed to take twenty-nine thousand pounds of debt on myself which I have not incurred, that the public may blame me, and the Prince of Wales with so unreasonable an income not be subject to this sum which can alone have arisen from shameful extravagance. I therefore must declare that unless the proposal is brought back to the mode in which the D. of Portland first stated it to me, and that all expenses are thrown on the P. of Wales, I cannot proceed in this business and shall think myself obliged to let the public know the cause of the delay and my opinion of the whole transaction.

I cannot conclude without saying that when the D. of Portland came into office I had at least hoped he would have thought himself obliged to have my interest and that of the public at heart and not have neglected both, to gratify the passions of an ill advised young man. (16360-1)

FROM THE DUKE OF PORTLAND

Downing Street, 5.30 p.m., Monday, 16 June 1783
The Duke of Portland should feel himself too much oppressed by the signification of your Majesty's displeasure if he could not acquit his own conscience of every idea of having intentionally incurred it. He therefore with the utmost humility implores your Majesty to be graciously pleased to reconsider the propositions which he had the honour of submitting to your Majesty, not with the view to the adoption of either of them, but in the humble hope of its being possible that your Majesty may be so indulgent as to allow that such ideas might not have appeared to him totally inconsistent with the plan first proposed to your Majesty's consideration. But as your Majesty seems to prefer a direct application to Parliament for such a sum as, together with the revenues of the Duchy of Cornwall, will amount to one hundred thousand pounds per annum, it only remains for your Majesty's servants to give effect to that preference and the Duke of Portland most readily recurs to it as the mode distinguished by your Majesty's approbation. Your Majesty will forgive the Duke of Portland's presuming to take the liberty of representing to your Majesty that the proposition respecting the Prince of Wales's debt

rested entirely upon the idea of the Civil List's being exonerated from the allowance your Majesty has heretofore made to his Royal Highness or by Parliament's taking the payment of it upon themselves, but in this he concludes himself mistaken and is ready to acknowledge his error; at the same time he cannot but request your Majesty's permission to disavow every idea of escaping from the odium which any measure may be subject to which he may feel it his duty to recommend to your Majesty. It has always been his opinion that such blame should fall entirely upon those who have the honour of being advised with by your Majesty [sic] and from those sentiments your Majesty will never find him deviate in the least degree. He also must beg leave to declare that however he may have been mistaken in the propositions he had the honour of laying before your Majesty for your Majesty's choice of the mode in which your liberality was to be extended to the Prince of Wales and not as a substitute for the plan first submitted to your Majesty, he never had any other motive but his regard to your Majesty's honour and the interests of your people, which he knows it so essential to attend to entitle himself to any share of your Majesty's approbation [sic].

The Duke of Portland takes the liberty of offering to your Majesty's consideration the Messages he had the honour of transmitting to your Majesty this morning and of again availing himself of the opportunity of repeating his declaration that it never was his intention or that of your Majesty's servants to attempt to influence your Majesty to deviate from the plan originally proposed, and that what was suggested to your Majesty was implicitly submitted to your Majesty's option, which was to be considered by them as the rule of their conduct. (16361–2)

THE KING'S REPLY

Windsor, 10.22 p.m., 16 June 1783
The letter I have this instant received from the D. of Portland does not in the least alter my opinion with regard to the one I have received this morning and to which I wrote the feelings of my heart. If the Pr. of Wales's Establishment is to fall on me, it is a weight I am unable to bear; if on the public I cannot in conscience give my acquiescence to what I deem a shameful squandering of public money, besides an encourage-ment of extravagance, and likely to prevent the P. of Wales at a proper time wishing to marry, as it would be lessening his expenditure. To shew that my ideas do not arise from any other motive than duty towards the public I make the proposal on the adjoining sheet. (16362)

118

Windsor, 16 June 1783

Not thinking it advisable to apply to Parliament for an Establishment
for the Prince of Wales till he chooses to marry, my subjects being so
much loaded with taxes, I have examined the Civil Lists, and having put
every expense upon the lowest possible establishment, only fifty
thousand pounds remain which I am willing to allow the P. of Wales in
addition to the revenue of the Duchy of Cornwall which will make his
income twenty-seven thousand pounds more than the late King thought
expedient to grant me in a similar situation, but then I do not mean any
increase should be made of his attendants but those of an inferior kind,
which the having a separate house and table will require; and if he will
promise to avoid running again in debt I will apply to Parliament for a
sum to pay his present ones and for furnishing his house and other
expenses, which articles together shall amount to fifty thousand pounds.

Therefore all that is required is a Message to both Houses of Parliament for a sum to pay the debts of the P. of Wales and to fit him out on
the present occasion; the sum to be moved for will be fifty thousand
pounds. Thus he will be comfortably but not extravagantly settled.
(16362–3)

82 THE KING TO LORD NORTH [copy]

Windsor, 11.35 a.m., 16 June 1783

Lord North, the treatment I have received from the D. of Portland, if
the other Ministers are not equally privy to the transactions concerning
the Establishment of the P. of Wales, is such that I have thought it
necessary to send an immediate answer to the letter I have received from
the D. of Portland, of which the inclosed is a copy. I can scarcely suppose
you and Lord Stormont[1] can have known the whole and acquiesced in
it. I therefore send this for the persual of both & that you may exculpate
yourselves, though it may not be necessary to assure you of the truth
of every syllable of my letter, yet as it is so strong it may be wrong to
add that I could take an oath with regard to every circumstance. (16363)

1. David Murray, 2nd Earl of Mansfield (1727–96). Succeeded his father as Viscount
Stormont [S.], 1748, and his uncle as 2nd Earl of Mansfield, 1793. Secretary of State for the
Northern Department, October 1779–March 1782; Lord President of the Council in the
Coalition Ministry, April–December 1783, and again from December 1794 to his death.
Scottish Representative Peer, 1754–96.

83 LETTERS FROM LORD NORTH TO THE KING [copies]

Whitehall, 16 June 1783

Lord North has had the honour of receiving his Majesty's commands, which he will immediately communicate to Lord Stormont.   (16363)

Monday night, 16 June 1793

Lord North has the honour of informing your Majesty that Lord Stormont was at Wandsworth Hill when he sent your Majesty's letters to him and did not arrive in town till late in the evening. Upon recollecting what had passed upon the subject of the proposed Establishment for his Royal Highness the Prince of Wales, they have set down to the best of their remembrance the exact state of the fact; many reasons might occur after the Cabinet sufficient to induce the Duke of Portland to think it his duty to submit the alterations in question to your Majesty's consideration.   (16364)

Monday night, 16 June 1783

Your Majesty having done Lord Stormont and Lord North the honour of communicating to them your Majesty's letter to the Duke of Portland, and having been pleased to command them to acquaint your Majesty whether they were informed of the alterations made in the first plan proposed for the Prince of Wales's Establishment, beg leave, in obedience to these your Majesty's commands, to submit to your Majesty that the said alterations were made since the last meeting of the Cabinet and consequently without their knowledge, but they imagine that the Duke of Portland, finding a difference of opinion among those he had conversed with, thought it right to state the matter to your Majesty in all its different views.   (16364)

84 CHARLES JAMES FOX TO THE PRINCE OF WALES

Brooks's, Monday, 16 June 1783

I have not heard anything material since I had the honour of seeing your Royal Highness, but the more I reflect upon what has passed the more I am convinced that with respect to your Royal Highness's interest in the business, there is not the least reason for apprehension. Whenever an answer comes from Windsor it shall be sent to your Royal Highness, and I should be glad to know where you are to be found tonight in case an answer should come so soon, which, however, I do not think probable.

Will your Royal Highness pardon me if I presume to offer my advice against sending for Lord Herbert[1], if the measure is not already taken? As he has had thoughts of belonging to your Royal Highness's family, I beg leave to submit whether sending to him might not be considered as something more of an engagement than would be desireable. I must again entreat your Royal Highness to forgive my offering my advice upon this occasion, but the great goodness and condescension with which your Highness has always treated me have made such an impression upon my mind that whenever I think your Royal Highness's dignity may be in any way concerned, I feel too much interest to be silent. The same objection does not hold in regard to Mr Luttrell[2], whom I would advise your Royal Highness to send for by all means. I think upon the whole that this storm is likely to blow off; if it does not I need not assure your Royal Highness that it will be a great comfort to me that in this short Administration I should have been able to settle your Royal Highness's Establishment to your satisfaction, and that in every situation I shall esteem your Royal Highness's protection, and (if I might venture to use such a word) friendship as the first honour of my life. I trust your Royal Highness will easily believe I would not use this language if I were not determined in every situation to be at your Royal Highness's commands.   (38075–7)

85 THE PRINCE OF WALES TO [?] THE DUKE AND DUCHESS OF CUMBERLAND[3]

4.15 p.m. [*?16 June 1783*]
My dear friends, I mean to do myself the pleasure of dining with you today as business of consequence has happened wh. has prevented my going down to Windsor. Pray send an express for James to come ye instant he receives yr. letter & desire him to croud all the sail possible. I have ye honor to be ever most sincerely, your dutiful nephew & friend. No answer is requisite.   (41796)

1. George Augustus Herbert, 11th Earl of Pembroke (1759–1827); styled Lord Herbert until his father's death in 1794. M.P. for Wilton, 1780–5, and 1788–94. Vice-Chamberlain of the Household, 1784–94. At this time he was Lieutenant-Colonel in the 2nd Dragoon Guards.

2. James Luttrell, (c.1751–88), M.P. for Stockbridge, 1775–84; for Dover, 1784–8. Surveyor-General of the Ordnance, 1784–8. He was the fourth son of the Earl of Carhampton.

3. Endorsed 'Monday the 16th, '83'. In November the Duke and Duchess set off for the Continent, remaining abroad, in France, Italy and Germany, until 1786.

Downing Street, 2.15 p.m., Monday, 16 May [should be June] 1783

The Duke of Portland has the honor to inform his Royal Highness that he has this moment received his Majesty's answer, in which his Majesty expresses his highest displeasure at the mode of making the provision for his Royal Highness & at the idea of taking upon himself to discharge his Royal Highness's debt—& his Majesty declares that unless the proposition first offer'd to his Majesty is adopted by his servants & all expenses thrown on his Royal Highness, his Majesty shall think it necessary to acquaint the publick with his opinion of the whole transaction.   (38069)

Downing Street, 1 p.m., Tuesday, 17 June [1783]

His Royal Highness having been informed by Mr. Fox of the very unexpected determination which his Majesty has thought proper to adopt, the Duke of Portland will not detain his Royal Highness by a repetition or any discussion of a subject which the Duke of Portland has such particular reason to be mortified at & to lament. He only means to acquaint his Royal Highness that he has just done himself the honor of writing a note to his Majesty in which, after very shortly expressing his concern at finding the representation he submitted to his Majesty of none avail, he requests the honor of paying his duty to his Majesty as soon as his Majesty shall think proper to order him.   (38079)

Downing Street, 6 p.m., Tuesday, 17 June [1783]

The Duke of Portland will not fail to obey your Royal Highness's commands the moment that it is in his power. The messenger is not as yet returned. The Duke of Portland is too sensible of the anxiety your Royal Highness must suffer in the present very extraordinary moment not to think it his duty to offer you the most immediate relief. (38078)

Downing Street, 7.30 p.m., Tuesday, 17 June 1783

The Duke of Portland has the honor to acquaint your Royal Highness that he has this instant received his Majesty's answer in which his Majesty expresses great surprize that no notice had been taken of his proposal for your Royal Highness's Establishment, which he is determined not to extend—and that his Majesty will be in town tomorrow at half-past twelve o'clock when he is graciously pleased to say he shall be ready to hear the Duke of Portland's ideas on the mode which his Majesty thinks the only one he can with justice to his people propose. (38080)

87   THE KING TO LORD NORTH [copy]

Windsor, 7.30 a.m., 17 June 1783

I have just received Lord North's letter stating what he and Lord Stormont remember concerning the transactions on the proposal of a separate Establishment for the P. of Wales, and it is so much less explicit than I should have expected from, to a degree, their joint production, that it convinces me they have not been thoroughly apprized of the whole & rather than avow that, evade the question, for it is impossible they can seriously think that if persons objected to the largeness of the provision, made it right to increase it by paying his debts. I have received a second letter from the D. of Portland which certainly does not set his conduct in a more favourable light in my eyes, to which I have wrote an answer, a copy of which I herewith enclose as well as of my proposal. This whole business shews who has the interest of the public at heart and who has virtue enough to cast aside all private feelings where that interest is intended to be sacrificed. I desire all these papers may also be communicated to Lord Stormont. Believe me, no consideration can ever make me either forget or forgive what has passed, and the public shall know how well founded the principles of economy are in those who have so loudly preached it up, who have most shamefully on that supposed principle diminished the peace establishment, yet, where they think it will answer their own wicked purposes, are ready to be most barefacedly lavish. (16364–5)

88   THE DUKE OF PORTLAND TO THE KING, AND THE REPLY [copies]

Downing Street, 1 p.m., Tuesday, 17 June 1783

The Duke of Portland is extremely concerned to find by the commands he has had the honour of receiving from your Majesty that your Majesty's opinion remains unaltered by the representation he humbly submitted yesterday to your Majesty's consideration. It is impossible for him to presume to trespass upon your Majesty's presence at this moment, and he has only most humbly to request your Majesty's permission to have the honour of attending your Majesty as soon as your Majesty may think proper to order him. (16365)

123

Windsor, 4.17 p.m., 17 June 1783
I have this instant received a letter from the D. of Portland, but to my great surprize no answer on the proposal I sent him last night for such an Establishment as on the maturest reflection I can think fit for the Prince of Wales on the present occasion; and he may depend on my not agreeing to one of farther extent. I shall be in town by half hour past twelve tomorrow when I shall be ready to hear the Duke's ideas on the mode which the circumstances of the times makes me think fully adequate to the only one I can, with justice to my people, propose. (16365)

89 PRINCE WILLIAM TO THE PRINCE OF WALES

Hanover, 12 midnight, 17 June 1783
Dear George, I cannot let Dalrymple[1] go without writing to you. This is only a letter of introduction for him to tell you from me everything I have to say. Ever believe me to be, yours sincerely.[2] (44643)

90 THE DUKE OF CUMBERLAND TO THE PRINCE OF WALES

Queen['s] Palace, 4.50 p.m. [? c.17 June 1783[3]]
My dear Prince, the Duke of Portland acquainted the House that the papers not being ready to be laid before the House he had nothing

1. William Dalrymple, Colonel of the 2nd Foot Guards, November 1782.

2. The King had complained of William's 'unhappy disposition to resist control', and, in general, of his unsatisfactory conduct at sea. 'Your judgement', he told him, 'does not ripen so fast as I could wish. To be fit to command, the knowledge of obedience must first have been obtained, without which, self-control cannot be gained.' He added: 'You seem to wish to copy Frederick, but there is one very considerable difference; he, though two years older, is perfectly compliant to every advice the Officers about him give him.' And he had concluded: 'I shall certainly send you to the Continent as soon as you return from sea, that your manners and behaviour may be formed fit for shore, and that you may be in time an Officer. Lord Howe, who certainly is a scientific Officer, assures me that he thinks in our Service the attention is carried so long alone to seamanship that few Officers are formed, and that a knowledge of the military is necessary to open the ideas to the directing large Fleets.' It was necessary, then, that William should have some military training in Hanover which would enable him to acquire 'that politeness and decorum which is but little to be met with on service in the Navy and in headquarters on shore, though essential in a Prince, a gentleman, and an Officer.'

3. This seems a likely date, especially if the letter refers to the King's Message to Parliament on the subject of the Prince of Wales's debts. On 17 June 1783 'the Duke of Portland said that, as he understood the business which had been expected to come before their Lordships,

further to trouble their Lordships with. Ld. Mansfield[1], being previously apprized of it, immediately adjourned the House, therefore no word was said in reply.

The Duke of Pd. & I had a great deal of conversation, as I had also with Ld. Keppel[2] & Ld. Loughborough[3]. We all agree, I believe, the messenger will be back with the D. of Pd. by six this evening. My opinion is the K. will write word he will not trouble the D. as he shall see him tomorrow at St. James's.   (38062)

91   THE DUCHESS OF DEVONSHIRE[4] TO THE PRINCE OF WALES

[? c.17 June 1783]

In case I shd not have time to tell you all, my d[r] brother—these are the heads of what I collected from the D. of P[ortland]'s conversation.

He seems to think that the attempting to carry this thro by force would be impossible—as neither L[d] North or L[d] John[5] would support it or go out on it—& in the case that it was attempted to be carryd thro'

and for which they had been summoned, was postponed, he should move for the adjournment of the House, which he did, and the House adjourned accordingly' (*Parliamentary Register*, xi.236). Lord Mansfield presided over the deliberations of the House, there being no Lord Chancellor whilst the Coalition was in power (the Great Seal was in commission). 1783 is the only possible year.

1. William Murray, 1st Earl of Mansfield (1705–93), Lord Chief Justice, 1756–88.

2. Augustus, Viscount Keppel (1725–86). Rear-Admiral, 1762; Vice-Admiral, 1770; Admiral, 1778. First Lord of the Admiralty, March 1782–January 1783, and April–December 1783. Peerage, 1782.

3. Alexander Wedderburn, Baron Loughborough and Earl of Rosslyn (1733–1805). Solicitor-General, 1771–8; Chancellor to Queen Charlotte, 1771–80; Attorney-General, 1778–80; Lord Chief Justice of the Common Pleas, 1780–93; created Baron Loughborough, 1780; First Commissioner of the Great Seal, April–December 1783; Lord Chancellor, June 1793–April 1801. Earldom, April 1801.

4. Georgiana, Duchess of Devonshire (1757–1806), first daughter of John, 1st Earl Spencer, and sister of Henrietta, Countess of Bessborough, married the 5th Duke of Devonshire (1748–1811) in 1774. The Prince of Wales was among the many admirers of both these lovely sisters, but it was to Lord Granville Leveson-Gower that Lady Bessborough ultimately surrendered, whilst Charles Grey, later 2nd Earl Grey and Prime Minister, became the accepted lover of the 'beautiful Duchess', and gave her a child, who was named Eliza Courtney (1792–1859), and who married (1814) General Robert Ellice. The unsuccessful Prince never forgave Grey. He habitually addressed the Duchess as his 'dear sister', and she styled him her 'dear brother'.

5. Lord John Cavendish (1732–96), fourth son of the 3rd Duke of Devonshire. Chancellor of the Exchequer in the Rockingham and Coalition Ministries, March–July 1782; April–December 1783.

in these circumstances it must put an end to the Administration in 3 days. The thing therefore to be considered is whether it is not in the power of the present Administration to serve you more by staying in than going out—& whether the destruction of a Ministry, *qui vous est devoué* is not more likely to be detrimental to your interests than trusting to them to serve you in the best way they can.[1] But Mr Fox looks upon himself as bound in honour to carry it thro for you & will go out rather than give it up, unless you release him; but great delicacy must be us'd in releasing him—& you must do it, if you think it right, as if it was of your own accord, for he does not know the D. of P. knows about it. I find from the Duke that they imagine the K— will perhaps agree, as it seems as if he fears more the éncrease of the Establishment than of the money.

If, after you have consulted him, you think it for the good of y^r service to speak to Mr Fox, pray, d^r. b^r, do it soon—tomorrow. God bless you. (38071-2)

92 THE PRINCE OF WALES TO THE DUKE OF PORTLAND [copy]

[18 June 1783[2]]
I am very uneasy to find the difficulties that still remain in forming my Establishment, and I beg leave to observe that when your Grace and the Cabinet unanimously agreed that the sum of 100,000 p^{ds} was a proper allowance for that purpose I was perfectly contented, and should you now find it necessary to lessen that sum I must and shall abide by your decision, but y^r Grace must know that 50,000 a year granted by Parliament will put me in a worse situation than I am at present, and if you leave me circumstanced as I am now I must have reason to think myself very unfortunate that this business has been entered upon at present. Whatever may be the event of this transaction (which I leave entirely to the Cabinet to decide upon) I cannot but be equally sensible of y^r Grace's good intentions towards me, and remain [etc.]. (38082)

1. 'There is great reason to think', wrote Fox on 17 June, 'that our Administration will not outlive tomorrow. . . . The immediate cause of quarrel is the Prince of Wales's Establishment, which we thought perfectly agreed upon a week ago' (Russell, *Memorials and Correspondence of C. J. Fox*, ii.114).

2. The date appears from the Prince's letter to Fox on the 18th (Fitzgerald's *Life of George IV*, i.39).

St. James's Place, Wednesday evening [*18 June 1783*]

Lord Stormont is gone out of town, which makes it impossible for the Cabinet to be tonight. I have the less regret in giving your Royal Highness this information because I am perfectly convinced that this little delay is likely to be rather advantageous than detrimental. I beg leave to repeat again that I think myself bound by every principle of honour as well of gratitude to take whatever part your Royal Highness chuses to prescribe me in this business, but all that I hear inclines me to the opinion that it is your Royal Highness's interest as much as ours to temporize in some degree.   (38081)

St. James's, Friday, 20 June [*1783*]

After a good deal of conversation last night it seemed to be the general opinion that his Majesty's Ministers had no part to act in the business of your Royal Highness's Establishment but to submit it entirely to the King's pleasure. The Duke of Portland however will not fail to take an opportunity of suggesting to his Majesty how very desireable it would be to give such an allowance as may be in some degree agreeable to your Royal Highness's wishes, and will endeavour to render this idea the more palatable to the King by so shaping the proposition that the more your Royal Highness is to receive the less his Majesty will be to pay; for if the scanty allowance is adhered to, the King must pay it all, for nothing shall make me go to Parliament to ease the Civil List unless I see at the same time that such a provision is to be made for your Royal Highness as may be tolerably satisfactory. But notwithstanding the way in which it will be put to his Majesty, I must fairly own that my opinion is that he will still adhere to the small allowance, in which case your Royal Highness will certainly be in a worse situation than before. I need not say how much I have felt for the manner in which yr. R.H. has been treated. I do not wonder that you should be so sensible to it, but do let me conjure you, Sir, to bear it with calmness & with constancy, and, whatever you may feel, to conduct yourself so as to put the world on your side. I have suffered many misfortunes & disappointments in my life (God forbid that your Royal Highness should ever know any) and I have always found the pride of bearing them with dignity to be the best consolation. If I did not feel the attachment which I do for your Royal Highness I should not presume to advise you upon such delicate points, but I feel that much of your Royal Highness' reputation in the world will depend upon your conduct in this trying occasion. Where the world thinks that duty is owing, believe me, it is always right to shew duty, and if anyone forgets what he owes to you, there is no conduct so dignified, there is no revenge so noble as to shew that you do not forget what is owing to him. I am afraid your Royal Highness will think I am presuming very much upon the condescension you have shewn me in venturing to write in this manner, but if this letter should appear too much like a sermon it comes at least from one who does not wish to be serious more than is necessary, and whose attachment to Your Royal Highness makes him as solicitous for your reputation as he could be for his own.   (38083–5)

94   THE PRINCE OF WALES TO COLONEL GEORGE HOTHAM, AND THE REPLY

Queen's House, 22 June 1783

In the letter that you yesterday shewed me from the King, there are many points which give me extreme concern; that in particular where his Majesty is pleased to mention that I have been wanting both in duty and common attention to him and the Queen. Nothing, I can assure you, ever was more distant from my thoughts; indiscretions I may have been guilty of, but of none with a criminal intent. A real sense of my duty too, added to a most affectionate regard for their Majesties, with a sincere inclination to shew it upon all occasions has, and I hope ever will be the constant rule of my conduct. Upon these principles I am persuaded that you will do me the justice to believe I acted, in my ready acquiescence to accept the present proposals for my future Establishment, notwithstanding I had received assurances that his Majesty had graciously consented that an application should be made to Parliament for a far more ample allowance. However I may in this instance feel my disappointment, I desire that you will assure his Majesty for me in the most dutiful and affectionate manner that as far as it lays in my power my intentions are not to exceed my income. At all times their Majesties shall find me a dutiful and affectionate son, and I trust that whatever unfortunate misunderstanding may have unhappily subsisted between us, it will hereafter be buried in oblivion.   (41800)

COLONEL HOTHAM'S REPLY [copy[1]]

Windsor, 22 June 1783

Sir, I have the most sincere and heartfelt satisfaction in informing your Highness that his Majesty's perusal of the letter you did me the honour of delivering me this morning was attended with every good effect I could expect.

1. In the King's hand.

I have his Majesty's commands to acquaint your Royal Highness that your reception on his part, on your coming to Windsor tomorrow, shall be such as may leave your Royal Highness no room to doubt of his paternal affection, and, from a principle of delicacy, not a single word shall be mentioned by his Majesty relative to any past unhappy misunderstandings.   (16397 and 41802)

95   PRINCE FREDERICK TO THE PRINCE OF WALES

Hanover, 18 July 1783

It is with the greatest pleasure I sit down to wish you most sincerely joy of your Establishment being now settled. I hope it is fully to your mind, and that now all those little differences and bickerings which have hitherto existed will be totally over.[1] I am just returned from a tour which I have made to Strelitz and Schwerin. You can have no idea of the quantity of all kind of game one sees in that country, particularly at Ludewigs Lust, the country residence of the Duke of Schwerin, because he will not allow any game to be shot for above a German mile, which is near six English miles, round his Palace, so that when one drives along one may see a hundred stags and hinds together, and they are so tame that they will let you come quite close to them. You know the Prince and Princess of Schwerin[2] who were in England last year; they are exceedingly lively and good humoured. Everybody belonging to this place are in the country so that at present the town is quite a desert. There is nothing going forwards; we pass whole days here without seeing almost a single soul. I suppose that at present there is not much amusement in London, as most of the publick places of diversion are shut and all the nobility in the country. I have no doubt but that you will find this a very stupid scrawl, but I am really in so very lazy a humour that I can hardly keep up my attention to write. I shall therefore ease you from the trouble of reading any more and only sign myself [etc.].   (43589–90)

1. Frederick wrote to the King on 14 August: '. . . William brought me from your Majesty the copies of the letters which passed about my brother the Prince of Wales's Establishment. I hope you will pardon me, Sir, in saying that it has only confirmed me in the idea I have ever had of the gentlemen who form the present Administration, who having forced themselves into power against the will of your Majesty, have at last thrown off the mask and shewn to the world the real motives of their actions, without their being viewed through the false mirror of modern patriotism. . . .' (43600–1)

2. See No. 66, where the Prince of Wales referred to them as the Duke and Duchess. If he (or his brother) was referring to the Duke's heir, then Frederick Francis (1756–1837), who succeeded his uncle as Duke in 1785, is indicated. He married Louisa of Saxe-Gotha (1756–1808) in 1775.

Windsor Castle [*endorsed 'Middle of July 1783'*]
I seize ye opportunity of Monsieur de Linsing[en]'s going to Hannover to
scribble a few lines in a hurry to you just to tell you yt. I am alive au
milieu de mille travers et de mille malheurs. I wish you was here, dearest brother, I cd. then perhaps find some relief, some support amidst
everything that I have to undergo. I will write you a long letter wh. you
may depend upon on the return of the messenger; my heart is too full
& I have too much to say to be able to write to you at present. I can only
press you as I have always done of late to come over here in ye. course of
[the] year, be it for ever so few weeks, as I wish vastly to see you & talk
over several subjects with you wh. from the intimacy wh. has always
subsisted between us, it is impossible for me to confide at least so much
in any body else as in you. I can add nothing more at present except just
to assure you how truly & sincerely I am [etc.].   (43591)

Queen's House, 31 July 1783
I take ye opportunity of my steward's & Maitre d'Hotel's going over to
Germany to write a few lines to you. I beg leave to recommend him to
yr. princely notice. I beg you will see him & speak to him; he is a great
favorite of Gerrard's, & I do not think when I say this to you, I am
giving you a bad impression of him. His name is Weltjie[1], he has kept a
great Club in St. James's Street for some time & I beleive is a very
honest good fellow. He was originally in ye. Duke of Brunswick's
kitchen, & is going to see his old friends & countrymen at Brunswick for
a few weeks. I therefore beg of you, my dearest brother, yt. you will
favor him with a letter of recommendation to ye. Duchess[2], be it but of
three lines only, saying who he is & what [h]is office is about me, &
desiring her to honor him on that account with her gracious protection.
I wd. have troubled her with a letter on ye. occasion myself, but it being
so long since I had ye happiness of being personally acquainted with her,
& you being so great a favorite of hers, & having seen her so lately, I had

1. Louis Weltje was Comptroller and Clerk of the Kitchen and Cellars in the Prince's Household, 'an employment', as Wraxall remarked, 'that demanded great gastronomic talents'. He
added, 'Weltje was a German of no ordinary bodily dimensions, not distinguished by the
humility of his deportment or manners, and fully impressed with the importance of his post.
Though he had resided some years in England, he spoke no language except a barbarous
Anglo-Westphalian jargon, which generally provoked laughter' (*Wraxall*, v.307). He became
a naturalized British subject, by Act of Parliament, in 1786.

2. The Duke of Brunswick married George III's sister Augusta (1737–1813) in 1764. 'We
used to think her, though not handsome, a good figure, but she is now grown so fat and plain
that, though covered with jewels, I never saw a woman that looked more unfashionable'
(*Diaries of Mrs. P. L. Powys*, p. 152 [18 Jan. 1772].

rather it came thro' you than immediately from me.[1] I shd. not say so much on this occasion, my dearest Frederick, if I did not wish this poor fellow very well. I therefore once more beg you wd. be very kind to him.

As to yr. kind expressions & wishes concerning my Establishment you are excessively kind & affectionate as you always are upon every occasion to me, but I wish, my dearest brother, ev'ry thing had gone as you say you wished it had, but I dare not say anything more at present, vous saurez tout en temps & lieu, je m'exprimerai plus au large bientot. My best compliments & love to our dear little blasted seaman.[2] Do not tell him what I call him upon any account. I beg you will write me yr. opinion of him immediately, as I will write mine of him, in order yt. I may see whether our discernment has been alike. I am afraid you will be tired to death of this long, tiresome & dull epistle. I therefore will not give you any further cause for complaint, but will conclude with assuring you, yt. I shall ever remain [etc.].

P.S. I hope you approved of ye things I sent you over by William from Gray's. I have just written to William.   (43594–5)

97 PRINCE FREDERICK TO THE PRINCE OF WALES

Hanover, 25 Aug. 1783

I have a thousand excuses to make to you for not having sooner answered your kind letter which I received by Welkie[3], but really I have been so

1. Frederick visited the Duke and Duchess in August 1781. He wrote (17 August): '. . . I cannot express how very polite every body was to us, the Duke in particular. I never saw anybody more pleased to see another than the Duchess was to see me. She could not refrain from tears. I was not so much questioned as I believe I should have been, if I had not always pleaded ignorance or at least given such answers that it was impossible to make any thing of. The Duke is exceedingly agreable, and did every thing that could possibly amuse us. The country about Brunswic is exceedingly beautifull. The Duchess was so good as to give us a Ball, at a house which belongs to her at about a league from the town, which she calls Little Richmond. The house is very odd, but the situation very pretty; it is situated upon a little hill, with a river running at the bottom. . . .' (43450–1)

And Frederick informed the Queen: 'I must say I found it much more agreable than I thought beforehand I should, as everybody appeared really glad to see me and did everything in their power to render our stay there pleasant to us. I was much afraid I should have to undergo much questioning, but I luckily escaped that. The Duke is exceedingly agreable, and treated me not only with great politeness but also with great affection. As for the Duchess I say nothing about her because your Majesty knows her very well, only that I do not see the east likeness between her and Princess Amelia' (the King's aunt—George II's second daughter [1711–85]).

2. Their brother William.

3. Weltje.

very much employed, being now of age here, that it has been totally out of my power. I gave him according to your desire a letter of recommendation to the Duchess of Brunswick and I believe he has been thoroughly contented with his stay there.

As you are now arranging your own Household I shall offer my services to you to send you over Rhenish wine which it is impossible you can buy good in London, nor indeed can any wine merchant get it for you [as] good as all the wines which are to be sold at Hambro and at Breman are made. If you want to have any from hence it will be very easy for me to provide you with very excellent genuine wine and which I can easily send over to England by the gentleman who is so good as to do any commissions for me at Hambro. I shall set out tomorrow on a tour to the different Courts in the Empire which will take me up about a month; in my return I shall stop for a short time at Osnabruck in order to settle the affairs there and then shall come back here.[1]

You ask my opinion of William: I find him certainly in some points much improved, but he is so excessively rough and rude that there is no bearing it. He has tried once or twice to play his manuel jokes upon me but as I returned them to him fourfold he has given over. However, I have no doubt but that he will in time get the better of this as he will soon see that it is not at all liked in this country.[2]

I will not trouble you this time with a longer letter as I really have not time, but you may depend upon having a long one upon my return. Pray give my best compliments to all friends in England and believe me, [etc.].   (43602–3)

98   PRINCE WILLIAM TO THE PRINCE OF WALES

Hanover, 29 Aug. 1783
My dear Eyes, Your favour came safe to Hanover thro' the hands of your bandy-legged maitre d'hotel[3], who is now at Brunswick. . . . Send me over a horse & a groom.

1. Frederick would have been present at the Imperial Reviews during the autumn but for the necessity of going to Osnabrück to take possession of the government of his Bishopric (so General Grenville informed Lord Cornwallis on 22 August).

2. Frederick thus referred to his brother in his letter to the King, 14 August: '. . . I purposely avoided mentioning William in my letter of last Friday as I did not think it safe to do it by the post. I find him very much grown and considerably altered for the better. To be sure he is as yet a little unpolished, but I have no doubt that his good sense will soon make him alter in this respect, and I am sure I will do everything in my power to assist in making him act according to your Majesty's wishes. . . .'

3. Weltje.

Has Cater put my name up yet? Tell him to send me over for myself a hat just like those I have, two more cocked ones with the German General's button & a half dozen round hats. Tell Gray to send me over some shoe buckles & a pair of stone knee buckles. You will say I am always begging, but you must send me a very elegant watchchain, & now ask for anything you please, & it shall be granted. . . .

Miss Keppel & the whole tribe of handsome & pretty girls are well. (44647)

99 THE NAWAB OF ARCOT TO COLONEL HENRY AUGUSTUS MONTAGU COSBY

Chepauk, 6 Sep. 1783

It gave me real satisfaction to perceive by a letter I have lately had the honor of receiving from her Majesty the Queen of Great Britain that thro' your interposition and exertion the ring which I gave in charge to Sir Thomas Rumbold[1] as a small testimony of my respect and esteem for her most gracious Majesty was ultimately presented and delivered into her Royal hands, and I regard this mark of attention in you as a test of friendship and attachment.

We have written to the Company[2] and to our Minister, Mr. Macpherson[3], to settle an arrangement between us and the Company by which our creditors will be secured in a regular annual payment of a certain proportion of their just claims till the whole shall, according to an agreement we have lately made with the Bengal Government, be finally liquidated, and as the justice and propriety of this measure must be obvious to everyone it will we doubt not be adopted without hesitation.

1. Governor of Madras, 1777–80; created a Baronet, 1779 (1736–91).

2. The East India Company.

3. John Macpherson (1745–1821) was created a Baronet in 1786. He was at this time a Member of the Governor-General's Council at Calcutta, but, earlier, he had been employed by the Nawab on a secret mission to England. Muhammad Ali had borrowed large sums of money at high rates of interest from the Company's servants at Madras, and Macpherson had procured large loans for him. Macpherson succeeded Warren Hastings as Governor-General *ad interim*, 1785–6, pending the arrival of Lord Cornwallis. He was M.P. for Cricklade, 1779–82, and for Horsham, 1796–1802. 'Soon after Sir John Macpherson's return from Bengal', wrote Wraxall (iv.237), 'the Prince of Wales commenced an intimacy with him which lasted above fourteen years, from 1788 down to 1802, when it became suddenly eclipsed and never revived. During that time few individuals enjoyed more distinguishing marks of his Royal Highness's favour. Sir John communicated constantly with him by letter while travelling on the Continent. When in London, he was admitted to Carlton House at almost all hours, frequently when the heir-apparent was in bed.'

133

I shall be always happy to hear of your health, and should you return to India, to render you every service in my power. May all happiness attend you. What can I say more? (38086)

100   THE PRINCE OF WALES TO PRINCE FREDERICK

Queen's House, 7 Nov. 1783

I am most excessively alarmed & terribly uneasy at understanding yt. you have again been seriously ill. For Heaven's sake, dearest brother, take care of yr. health, you know not of how much consequence it is to us all, at least it is to me, yt. you shd. preserve yourself. You are the greatest comfort I expect in ye. world, ye dearest & ye. best friend I possess in ye. universe. You cannot form to yourself an idea of ye. endless happiness I expect to enjoy again one day or other in your society, therefore let me once more entreat of you, for Heaven's sake, to take care of your constitution. I saw Apsley yesterday in town, & I was talking to him of you; he says you are very subject to coughs, therefore it is ye. more incumbent to be careful of the slightest attack you may receive upon yr. chest. Pardon, my dearest Frederick, if I appear to have been preaching a sermon; beleive me, it only proceeds from the sincere affection I ever have & ever shall cherish in my heart for you.

Now let us have done with such grave subjects. I am hard at work upon my mansion at Carlton House, where I hope to take possession ye third or fourth of next month, tho the house will then be very far from being finished. I am adding & building considerably to it, & hope on yr. return you will not think me a bad architect. You will ever find there a warm heart & thorough wellcome. Pray write to me soon again or else I shall begin to think yt. you have quite forgotten me, especially as I hear of yr. writing frequent & long letters to the King. Indeed I shall grow quite jealous of his Majesty if it goes on in this manner much longer, but to be serious, pray write to me frequently & above all things never let me remain in ignorance concerning ye. state of yr. health. There is no news stirring about here at present except yt. I am to take my seat[1] next Tuesday. My best compliments to dear Joan.

P.S. Not got as yet into Carlton House. (43619–20)

101   PRINCE WILLIAM TO THE PRINCE OF WALES

Hanover, 7 Nov. 1783

Dear George, again I trouble you with commissions, not for myself but for my uncle Prince Charles, who would be very much obliged to you

1. In the House of Lords.

134

if you would send him over a saddle & everything relating to it with the bitts & briddles marked with his name. Do not forget the dog to be brought over by the courier.

I am sorry to say you are a bad correspondent, but it is really true, for I have wrote to you since my arrival in Germany four times at least & I have not as yet received an answer. Your occupations are so many & so great I suppose that you cannot find time to answer your brothers.

I am really so tired I can write no more but to assure you that I am, dear George, your most affectionate brother.   (44649)

102   THE PRINCE OF WALES TO THE QUEEN

Carlton House, 11.50 a.m., [*?11 Nov. 1783*]
I hope you will forgive the liberty I am taking in troubling you with this epistle, but it is owing to my anxiety to be perfectly right with respect to the robes I am to wear in the House of Lords this day[1], having understood some time ago from you that the King disapprov'd of those I commonly wore, thinking that they should appear on State Trials or occasions when he is NOT in the House, & that I had a Royal robe which I ought to wear whenever his Majesty was on the Throne. I accordingly rummaged the old trunk which contains the robes this very morning with Stone the robemaker, & we found an old & very rich velvet robe, to the full as long & large as the King's, which he insists upon it never could have been a Parliament robe but made for some Prince of Wales whether it was ever worn or not, either my grandfather[2] at the late King's coronation[3], or for the late King at King George the First's coronation[4], but he positively insists that it is a coronation robe for a Prince of Wales & not a Parliament robe. He then told me that the robes I wear now are perfectly different to every other Peer's even to those which *my* brothers & the King's brothers wear; that in the first place, all Dukes have four rows of ermine as their distinction, which is call'd the powdering, that the King's brothers as well as mine have six rows of powdering, & that I have seven rows to my robes. Nothing but my wish to do what is most dutiful & agreable to the King makes me take the

1. On that day the Prince of Wales was introduced into the House of Lords, shortly before the King read the Speech from the Throne on opening the Session. He was supported by the Dukes of Cumberland, Richmond and Portland, and he took his seat in the Chair of State on the King's right hand.

2. Frederick Louis, Prince of Wales.

3. George II was crowned on 11 October 1727, four months after his accession.

4. George I (1660–1727) was crowned on 20 October 1714, eleven weeks after his accession.

135

liberty of boring you, my dear Madam, on such a dull occasion & subject. However, if you will be so good just as to state this to the King before he goes down to the House, to know what his pleasure is upon the subject I shall be extremely oblig'd to you to let me instantly know his Majesty's commands, as we have not much time to spare. If you should chuse or think it would be best to shew the robes for the King to decide upon them I will send old Santhague with them in my coach, as I fear I shall not be dress'd myself, to your Page or the King's, whichever you shall please to direct. Pray forgive, my dearest mother, any inaccuracies should there be any in this letter, as I write in such a hurry that I hardly know what I am scribbling. (41798–9)

103 THE DUKE OF CUMBERLAND TO THE PRINCE OF WALES

Calais, 25 Nov. 1783

We arrived at Dover between nine & ten, the road exceedingly heavy & hilly, together with the carriages being very much loaded made our journey so long. We embarked Monday morning at half pt. eight for Calais & arrived here by half pt. twelve; very fine weather but rather too little wind; everybody in good health & hardly sick, myself not at all. This day we set out for Paris & shall arrive there on Sunday, from whence you shall hear again what the place affords.

So much for the manner of passing our time. Believe me, dear Sir, that nobody could feel more than *we* did at parting with you & were melancholy enough on the road. Your kindness & politeness to us on all occasions can never be forgot. Whenever you have a leisure moment of reflection, consider there is not one more sincerely attatched to you then [*sic*] myself & that my greatest wish in life is your honor, happiness & prosperity. I cannot help writing the very feelings of my heart to you. Your conduct at all times has been so remarkably good to me that whenever I have it my power to be of service to you, you have a right to command to me. We are just getting into the carriage & both hope we shall not be forgot. (54460–1)

104 PRINCE FREDERICK TO THE PRINCE OF WALES

Hanover, 28 Nov. 1783

A thousand thanks for your kind and affectionate letter, as well as for your enquiries after my health which is, God be praised, now pretty well re-established. I received a number of things by the courier, for

136

which I return you many thanks; indeed they are beautifull. The cameo of you is wonderfully like, and I am desired by Grenville and Budé to tell you they think it very shabby of you not having sent each of them one also. You tell me to write often, which I will do with a great deal of pleasure, but you must also be more regular in your correspondence with me, for for [*sic*] the last six months I have received only two letters from you. I have here a long account in the papers of your having taken your seat in the House of Lords, and I wish you most sincerely joy of it, as I have no doubts it will have given you great pleasure. If you have not better weather in England then we have here, hunting will not go on very well this year, for we have had for these last three weeks continual rains, and now we have a violent frost, so that it is impossible to ride out of the town. William is at present pretty well accustomed to the manner of living here. At first he could not bear it[1], and during the whole time that I was absent led a very uncomfortable life. Now however he goes on very well, particularly as our amusements are begun again for the winter.[2]

Having no subject very amusing or entertaining to write to you about, I am affraid you will be sufficiently bored with this scrawl by the time you will have got so far. I will therefore, conclude by begging you to believe me [etc.]. Pray write often.   (43623–4)

1. William conveyed a rather different impression to the King, to whom he wrote on 10 October: '. . . My brother Frederick is just returned [from Cassel], & as I suppose he will write to your Majesty, it is needless for me to say anything about him, but that the demonstrations of joy upon his arrival show how much the people are attached to your Majesty. I wish I could say as much for my countrymen. I have every day more & more reason to be thankful at my being sent to Hanover, for everybody loves my brother & me & wish to make our stay agreeable to us. This [is] another instance of fatherly affection that your Majesty has sent me, where I can get nothing but what is good; therefore I am in duty bound to behave me so as to convince my affectionate father that I am [etc.].' (44648)

2. Unlike Frederick, William did not care for hunting. Frederick wrote to the King on 21 November: 'We have had last Wednesday a very great chasse in which we killed thirty six boars. William was not of the party as he is not a very great admirer of that amusement; besides which, his shoulder hinders him from ever being a good shot, as he cannot bear the least recoil of the gun.' (43621–2)

IV 1784

There are few references to the rapidly changing political situation during the early months of 1784 in the Prince's letters to his brothers. He was too lazy, too negligent or too preoccupied to write regularly to Hanover. In any case his letters, unless sent by the courier or the quarterly messenger, were liable to be opened in the post. He and Frederick did not see eye to eye in politics. Frederick had the sound instinct of keeping the family united, aloof from the party conflict, but the Prince of Wales, ignoring the promise he had made in December 1783 not to oppose the Ministers of his father's own choice, persisted in Opposition politics, with the result that he and the King were hardly on speaking terms. His father doubtless heard of his revellings with Fox and his other Whig intimates. 'In the quadrille which he danced in honour of Mr. Fox's pretended victory [at the Westminster election and the parliamentary discussion over the scrutiny which followed], he was so far overcome by the wine he had drunk,' wrote Thomas Orde, 'as to fall flat upon his face in the middle of the figure, and upon being raised from the floor, to throw the load from his stomach into the midst of the circle.' With justice the King complained of his 'reprehensible conduct', and matters came to a head on 24 August when the Prince informed his father that the state of his finances compelled him to economize and go abroad.

Already on 6 July he had written to Frederick saying that his financial situation and his unpleasant relations with their father had made him decide on this step. He would meet Frederick in Vienna and spend the winter either there or in Paris. But the real reason why he contemplated living on the Continent was carefully concealed: he was reluctant to commit himself on paper.

He had put an end to his connexion with Lady Melbourne, and Mrs. Hodges, another 'flirt', had left London. 'Her brother', declared the Duke of Devonshire, 'behaved vastly well about it, and said if her husband would not take her out of town, he would, for he did not choose his sister should be talked of in such manner.' By this time Mrs. Fitzherbert had become the object of the Prince's most ardent attentions, but, being virtuous as well as beautiful, she refused to add to the number of his mistresses.

The facts about her are well known. She was the elder daughter of Walter Smythe of Brambridge, near Winchester, and a Roman Catholic. When she made the Prince's acquaintance, probably in 1783, she was a twenty-seven year old widow, and childless. In 1775 she had married Edward Weld of Lulworth Castle, Dorset, who died the same year at the age of forty-five or thereabouts; in 1778 she married Thomas Fitzherbert of Swynnerton, Staffordshire, and he died three years later at the age of thirty-four.

The Prince was determined to marry her, but the Royal Marriage Act of 1772 barred a legal union, and, even if one had been possible, the Act of Settlement would have deprived him of his right to the succession to the throne. Two days after he had written to Frederick, having worked himself up into a state of frenzy, he made a half-hearted attempt to commit suicide. Keate the surgeon, Lord Southampton, Edward Bouverie and Thomas, afterwards Lord Onslow, arrived at Mrs. Fitzherbert's house in Park Street, near Park Lane, with the alarming news that the Prince had stabbed himself with his sword and that only her immediate presence would save his life. She refused, however, to accompany them to Carlton House until they agreed that she should take with her a lady of high character, and she chose the Prince's close friend, the Duchess of Devonshire. They called at Devonshire House for the Duchess, and, arriving at Carlton House, they found the Prince in bed, pale and covered with blood. 'The sight so overpowered her faculties that she was deprived almost of all consciousness. The Prince told her that nothing would induce him to live unless she promised to become his wife and permitted him to put a ring round her finger. . . . A ring from the hand of the Duchess of Devonshire was used.' A deposition of what had occurred was drawn up, and was signed and sealed by the Duchess and Mrs. Fitzherbert. It ran as follows:

'On Tuesday the 8th of July 1784 Mr. Bouverie and Mr. Onslow came to me and told me the Prince of Wales had run himself thro' the body & declar'd he wd. tear open his bandages unless I wd. accompany

Mrs. Fitzherbert to him. We went there & she promis'd to marry him at her return, but she conceives as well as myself that promises obtain'd in such a manner are entirely void—9th of July 1784.'

The Duchess had repeatedly warned him that a marriage was out of the question, but, she said later, 'any remonstrance from me was always follow'd by threats of killing himself'. After signing the deposition she set off for the Continent the following day, and there she remained until the autumn of 1785.

Without the King's consent the Prince could not have gone in pursuit of her, but even as late as 24 August, when he informed his father of his intention to go abroad, he was apparently unaware that he could be prevented from leaving the country. Ostensibly, he was going on account of his financial situation; consequently, his letter to the King marked the beginning of a lengthy correspondence on the subject of his debts which was concluded only in 1787. Warned by his father that his going abroad would bring discredit upon the entire Royal family, and that it would occasion a final and irrevocable breach between them, the Prince, as always when it came to the point, lacked the courage to cut himself off from his family, and decided that it would be easier to win Mrs. Fitzherbert by renewing his threats to commit suicide unless she came back to him.

105 PRINCE WILLIAM TO THE PRINCE OF WALES

Hanover, 2 Jan. 1784
Dear brother, I am afraid you will accuse me of laziness; it is true, & I will for the future never do the like. My brother & I were both of us alarmed at your late indisposition; however it is, thank God, all over now. Do, I beg of you, take more care of your health, for tho' you are a young man & you have a good constitution, yet by repeated attacks it must be weakened & you will easily conceive what we all should feel if it was to take a serious turn.

You are right respecting the groom & horse; my stay on the continent will probably be too short to make it worth while sending them over, but at the same time I shall require both when I come to stand on my own bottom as I shall also expect other assistance from you then which I make no doubt you will do in the most affectionate way a brother can do.

To say I preferred Germany to England would be false, yet at the same time I must allow I pass my time very agreeably & the people seem & are really desirous to please Frederick & me. I at first, like so many of my countrymen, abored everything that was German for no other reason in the world than because it was not English. I now begin to see things in general with different eyes from what I did at first. An honest man, whether an Englishman or a German, is still an honest man & there are a great many such here; therefore it is my own fault if I keep company with bad ones. You will very likely say that is an hipocritical letter; by no means, I assure you. I have two reasons for writing in this manner; the one is to show you that when I chuse I can write as sensible letters as anybody; the other is to give you a just idea of his Majesty's subjects at Hanover, for they are indeed very worthy people.

You have, I have seen by the papers, taken your seat in the House of Lords. To advise you on this subject would be at the same time foolish as well as misplaced; however, you will, I hope, as a brother, let me make you two wishes which really proceed from my heart; they are that you would be cautious, & that everything may turn out for the better.[1] I am afraid I have already tired you with my advice, yet I hope that when you come to consider the reasons for my having done thus much without your permission, you will put it to the true one, which is that I most heartily love you & wish you well.

My compliments to all your gentlemen, & ever believe me to be, dear George, your most affectionate brother and most sincere friend.

P.S. Do not forget the spaniel for Prince Charles.   (44650-1)

106   THE EARL OF AILESBURY TO SIR HENRY COSBY [2]

Seamore Place, 16 Jan. 1784
Lord Ailesbury sends his compliments to Sr Henry Cosby, & is obliged to him for the satisfaction he receiv'd from receiving the inclosed, by which he has the pleasure to find that the Nabob[3] has receiv'd the Queen's thanks for his valuable present, & her Majesty's acknowledgments of Sr Henry Cosby's service on that delicate occasion. L^d A—

1. His uncle, the Duke of Cumberland, also referred to the political situation at home, in a letter to the Prince of Wales from Strasbourg on 28 December 1783: '. . . We [the Duchess and himself] both lament that the present critical situation of publick affairs does by no means assist in making you happy. . . .' He added: 'You know best whether North is steady. If he does not join the other side they will find it a very hard struggle indeed. . . . I know they will try to get at Loughborough, I suppose Thurlow will be Chancellor. He is the *great favourite* of all. . . . Every event that makes so many changes at home does *us* the greatest harm abroad & shews that when we have not other enemies to cope with we must quarrel among ourselves. . . .' (54465-6)

2. He had been knighted a few days earlier.

3. The Nawab of Arcot.

141

will trouble Sr Henry tomorrow with his letters for India, & with his best wishes for a prosperous voyage to & from that part of the world. (38093)

107 PRINCE WILLIAM TO THE PRINCE OF WALES

Hanover, 21 Jan. 1784

I beg leave to recommend to your protection Doctor Blaine¹, phicisian to the fleet in the West Indies during the late war: he wishes vastly to have the title of your phicisian. I shall be happy if you will do him that service. I am, dear George, your most affectionate brother.   (44652)

108 THE PRINCE OF WALES TO THE EARL OF HERTFORD ²

Carlton House, 26 Mar. 1784

My Lord, In consequence of your Lordship's application, I am ready to assure you of my good wishes to the late members for Coventry³, & your Lordship may depend yt. before I give my consent to the renewal of my lease I will attend to whatever your Lordship may represent to me on behalf of the citizens of Coventry.⁴ I remain, my Lord, most sincerely yours.   (Egerton MS.3262, f.1)

1. Sir Gilbert Blane (1749–1834). Physician at St. Thomas's Hospital on his return to England, 1783, until 1795; Physician to the Prince of Wales, 1785. Created Baronet, 1812.

2. Francis Seymour-Conway, 1st Marquess of Hertford (1719–94). Created Earl of Hertford, 1750; Marquess, July 1793. Lord of the Bedchamber, 1751–64; Lord-Lieutenant of Ireland, 1765–6; Master of the Horse, September–November 1766; Lord Chamberlain of the Household, November 1766–April 1782, and April–December 1783. He supported both Lord North's Government and the Fox–North Coalition, and was said to have refused Pitt's offer of a dukedom in December 1783, but by 1793 he was supporting Pitt. In 1783 he had five members in the Commons: his four sons and Whitshed Keene.

3. One of them was William Seymour-Conway (1760–1837), Lord Hertford's son, M.P. for Coventry, 1783–4; for Downton, 1785–90; for Orford, 1790–6. He was in the Army, and became a General in 1804.

The other was Gibbon's friend, John Baker-Holroyd, Lord Sheffield [I.], (1735–1821), also in the Army. M.P. for Coventry, February–July 1780, and November 1780–84; for Bristol, 1790–1802. Irish peerage, January 1781; U.K. peerage, July 1802. Earl of Sheffield [I.], 1816. Supported the Fox–North Coalition, and consequently lost his seat at the 1784 general election. Later, he supported Pitt.

4. Coventry, though a 'very open' constituency, was to some extent under the influence of the Seymour-Conways. The King wrote to Pitt on 28 March: 'No candidates have yet started at Coventry against the late Members, which is the more extraordinary, as I am told two new men might certainly, at not more than £2,000 each, succeed, the town is so desirous of a

142

Carlton House, 28 Mar. 1784

I had intended writing you a very long letter by ye. return of the messenger, wh. I understood was not to have been till ye end of the week, descriptive of the present situation of our politicks here, & of my motives for pursuing ye line of conduct wh. I follow'd thro the whole winter, & of yt. line wh. I intend now to pursue, but the courier is just come to say yt. he is to set off at eight o clock this evening, therefore it is totally impossible. However, I determined not to let this opportunity slip of recalling myself to your recollection after so long a silence, wh. has been in part occasioned by a long & severe fit of illness, from wh. I am now, thank God, perfectly recovered. I am very anxious to explain my conduct to you, & my reasons for acting as I have done, & I think you will beleive me when I say yt. I have acted from principle, but I really do not know how to write safely to you unless by the quarterly messenger. However, as I have missed this opportunity of opening myself fairly to you, you may depend upon my seizing ye. very first opportunity of doing so yt. offers itself. Gerrard[1] has bought you a charming horse, one of Sir Harry Featherstone's[2] called Standby, got by Prophet; very handsome, has raced very well, & is a very good hunter. He is a dark chestnut & about fourteen hands three inches high, & I beleive he has bought another for you but I know not what he is, & I am not quite sure yt. he has bought another, but I only beleive he has. I just crossed Standby in ye. ride at Gill's & I think he is a charming pleasant horse. I bought two at ye same sale, but they are only geldings, & hunters, but I gave an enormous price for ym. My best compliments to Joan & to all friends at Hannover. Pray present my best respects when you write, or when you see ym., to the Duke & Duchess of Brunswick. I am going to write to William. Adieu my dearest brother, beleive me in every situation, & at all times [etc.].

I like Sam very much.   (43635–6)

---

change of representatives.' John Robinson, who had 'managed' the elections in 1780 for Lord North, and who drew up elaborate plans for the 1784 elections on Pitt's behalf, thought that the Seymour-Conway influence there, if it could be joined to that of the Government, might turn the scale; but Lord Hertford, contrary to expectation, went into opposition. However, Lord Sydney, the Home Secretary, was able to write: 'Coventry is carried by Sir Sampson Gideon and Mr. Wilmot against Lord Sheffield and one of the Conways' (H[istorical] M[anuscripts] C[ommission], Rutland MSS., iii.89).

1. Lake.

2. Sir Henry Fetherstonhaugh, 2nd Baronet (1754–1846). Succeeded his father, 1774. M.P. for Portsmouth, 1782–96. A well-known country gentleman, he possessed estates in Sussex, Essex and Northumberland. He voted with the Prince's friends on the Regency question.

Hanover, 9 Apr. 1784

The quarterly courier who arrived this morning has brought me your kind and affectionate letter of the 28th, and I expect with impatience the long letter which you have promised me soon which you may send with the greatest safety by the common messenger, as I am very certain that no letters are opened which come by him. You know I have never mentioned politicks to you. Let me, however, my dearest brother, give you one piece of advice, which is to take care what you are about, that is to say, to beware doing those things which you may hereafter repent every day of your life.

I am exceedingly sorry to hear of your indisposition, but hope that you are now thoroughly recovered and that you will take care of your health. Remember we have all of us a right to insist upon your taking care of yourself. I will not add more at present, my dearest brother, but you may depend upon hearing from me soon. Pray write often.

P.S. Grenville and Budé beg their duty to you and that I will return you their humble thanks for your kind present of the buckles and of the ring, which they think beautifull. (43639-40)

110 LETTERS FROM PRINCE WILLIAM TO THE PRINCE OF WALES

Hanover, 9 Apr. 1784

I have just received your letter of 28 for which I return you my thanks, particularly for the ring, & shall have the pleasure to answer it by the courier this day fortnight. (44657)

Hanover, 23 Apr. 1784

I am happy now to be able to discharge the debt you have so agreably laid me under. I return you my sincere thanks for the horse & for everything else you sent me, & believe me when I say it is not ill disposed of, for nobody has a greater regard for your welfare, my dearest brother, than I have. I cannot sufficiently thank you for the very affectionate terms you express concerning me in your last kind letter.

I hope your time has been spent agreably this winter. Mine has been neither one thing or the other, neither agreable nor disagreable. This town is very full or totally void of publick amusements; however, since I have introduced myself into the private parties of the women I spend my time much more pleasantly than I did. I take my place in the private houses

144

just like any other & go away when I please. I find it best to go alone or with the faithful Merrick[1].

Genl. Budé desires to be remembered to you & says Quaker is in good health. Merrick likewise presents his compliments & desires to be laid at your feet as he cannot go lower. I am happy to find that Sally is in such a good condition; tell her from me that I expect a stroke of her at my return, as it was by my means she got her place.

Your wish to me was such a good one that I return the compliment of the beggar's benison, and I am [etc.].

P.S. I shall be obliged to you if you will order Gray to mend the steal sword I send over; pray let me have the two prints of Windsor. (44658-9)

I I I   LETTERS FROM PRINCE FREDERICK TO THE PRINCE OF WALES, AND A REPLY

Hanover, 23 Apr. 1784

I cannot let the quarterly courier set out without sending you a few lines to tell you how impatiently I wait for the letter which you have promised me. We are here so quiet and so totally out of the way of the noise and bustle which are continually going on in the world that we know little or nothing of politicks, and was it not for the English post we should not think that there existed any other people in the world but ourselves. You know not therefore the pleasure that it is to us to receive letters from England. I am sure if you did you would write oftener. I have been sitting for my picture to a young painter here in crayons which being reckoned like, I send you a copy of it.

I am affraid I shall miss the courier if I write longer. I shall therefore conclude by assuring you that I am ever [etc.].   (43643)

THE PRINCE OF WALES'S REPLY

16 May 1784

I have but a few minutes to write to you as Colonel Abercromby[2] is in a hurry to set out. I beleive him to be one of the very best officers in any service whatever. I therefore am certain yt. you will shew him every

1. Captain William Augustus Merrick (*d.*1785). The King had written to Major-General Budé on 25 July 1783: 'I have, through the recommendation of Lord Hood for that purpose, nominated Captain Merrick also to accompany him' [i.e. Prince William, to Hanover].

2. Lieutenant-General Sir Ralph Abercromby (1734–1801). Colonel of the 103rd Foot, 1781–3; Major-General, 1787; Lieutenant-General, 1797. M.P. for Clackmannanshire, 1774–80 and 1796–8; K.B., July 1795. Commanded the British army in Egypt against the French; mortally wounded in the battle of Alexandria, March 1801.

attention possible in yr. power, but let me also entreat of you to do it upon my account. William knows him well & will be glad to see him. Tell him his friend & mine George Hanger[1] is coming over on purpose to see him, by whom I shall write to you both; he will follow Abercromby in day or two furthest [*sic*]. I am excessively obliged to you for yr. picture, but I do not think it half so well looking as you are. I can trace the likeness & yt. is all. I am keeping t[w]o places in my house, on purpose for portraits of you & Billy. Tell my Uncle Ernest yt. I shall certainly write to him to thank him for his present by Hanger, & you shall certainly have by Hanger ye. letter I promised you. Pray give my love to William & to all our friends at Hannover, I have only time to subscribe myself, my dearest Frederick [etc.].

P.S. I have some very extraordinary business wh. I cd. wish to see you in order to talk over with you, as it is impossible for me ever to trust it to paper, & as no friend upon earth but you my dearest Frederick shd.ever know anything of it, but pray keep this perfectly to yourself.   (43646-7)

PRINCE FREDERICK'S REPLY

Hanover, 17 June 1784
As Colonel Dalrymple means to set off for England tomorrow I take this opportunity to thank you for your very kind letter by Abercromby, to whom you may be sure I shall be exceedingly happy to shew every civility in my power. Hanger passed through here last week and delivered me your message. I think that you may with all safety send me either a letter or anything whatsoever either by the courier who goes every fortnight, or by the quarterly messenger, as no letter or packet of mine have ever been opened. If however you do not like that your name and seal should appear to it, desire any one of your Gentlemen to write the direction and seal it and then I am certain it will arrive safely into my hands. I mean to set out soon upon a tour to Vienna in order to see the

1. George Hanger, 4th Baron Coleraine (1751–1824); one of the Prince's boon companions. Succeeded his brother in the peerage, 1814, but did not assume the title. He retired from the army in 1776, but served as a Captain in the Hessian Jäger corps in the American War. He was a prisoner in the King's Bench for debt, June 1798–April 1799, and he lived for some time in Paris to avoid his creditors. Raikes said he 'was a *beau* of the first water, always beautifully powdered, in a light green coat, with a rose in his buttonhole. He had not much wit or talent, but affected the *vieille cour* and the manners of the French Court. He had lived a good deal in Paris before the Revolution, and used always to say that the English were a very good nation, but they positively know not how to make anything but a kitchen poker.' Wraxall said that he 'might rather be considered as a humble retainer of Carlton House than justly numbered among the friends of the heir-apparent. Poor even to a degree of destitution, without profession or regular employment, subsisting from day to day by expedients, some of them not the most reputable, he was regarded as a sort of outcast from decent society' (v.311).

Austrian camps, after which I shall go to Dresden and from thence return here. My new carriage arrived today. I think I never saw a neater one. It has however unluckily not been well packed, as it is exceedingly scratch-ed. News you cannot expect from us here, at least none that you care about, so that I am affraid it is totally out of my power to render my letter amusing, I shall therefore conclude by assuring you that I am ever [etc.].   (43652–3)

112 THE DUC DE CHARTRES TO THE PRINCE OF WALES

[Paris, 26 June, 1784]

Ne m'accusez pas je vous en prie, mon cher Prince, de negligence ni de legerté. Je serois au desespoir que vous me soupconassiez de l'une ou de l'autre envers vous; la seule raison qui m'ait empeché de vous ecrire jusques ici est la certitude ou j'étois que 2 ou 3 têtes couronnées au moins auraient pris lecture de ma lettre avant qu'elle vous parvint et quoique je n'eusse pas de secret d'état a vous mander, je vous avoue que pour eviter cette espece d'inquisition et peutêtre queslques plaisanteries sur la manière dont je vous ecrivais, he me suis refusé le plaisir de me rappeller a votre souvenir aussitot que je l'aurois desiré, et j'ai attendu une occasion sure telle que celle du Duc de Lauzun qui est mon ami depuis 25 ans dont j'ai eu l'honneur de vous parler quelques fois, et qui vous certifiera que j'ai toujours présente l'amitié que vous m'avez témoignée, et un bien grand desir de me trouver a porter d'en recevoir encore de nouvelles marques. La raison qui m'a empeché de vous ecrire par la poste m'engage a vous prier d'en user de même pour moi: je desirerois cependant bien savoir dans quel temps vous comptez arriver à Brighthelmstone et combien vous comptez y rester. Si vous voulez bien charger Lauzun de me le mander il me le fera savoir exactement, et je m'arrangerais en conséquence. Il n'est rien arrivé dans ce pays ci d'assez gagni d' assez interessant pour vous être compté, ainsi pour ne pas vous ennuyer plus longtemps. Je me bornerai, mon cher Prince, a vous prier de penser quelques fois a moi, et de m'ecrire quand vous trouverez des occasions vous pouvez être sur de faire beaucoup de plaisir a un homme sur l'amitié duquel vous pouvez compter et qui comme vous voyez profite de la permission que vous lui avez donnée de vous écrire sans aucune ceremonie.[1]

(38094)

1. The Prince's uncle, the Duke of Cumberland, met the Duc de Chartres in Paris at the end of November 1783: 'A visit passed from him at my door [*sic*] & I waited on him yesterday morning—very civil, but no offer to entertain, nor mentioned the D[uches]s of Chartres. So far for his civility to us after our amusing him in London!' (54462). 'Be on your guard',

Carlton House, 6 July 1784

I have just received yr. very kind letter by Dalrymple, & was excessively happy to hear yt. you had entirely recovered [from] ye. indisposition you had when he first saw you. I had him with me a considerable time, & as an old friend & acquaintance was able to gather more information from him than from any one else concerning yr. way of life, & in short concerning everything respecting you & William. I confess to you I am very unhappy at understanding you have no idea of returning to England the ensuing winter, as I had flattered myself you wd. have done, & I assure you I had not built a little upon it. However, since you will not come over & see us, I am determined to come over & see you, but this I bind you under ye. most solemn promise of honor never to reveal. I know not how soon this project will take place, but I shd. think certainly within these six weeks. My reasons for undertaking it are, partly ye. enormous expence wh. ye buildings in addition to my house, & wh. the fitting up of it have put me to, partly ye. wish of travelling for ye. sake of dissipation, & partly *ye. very very unpleasant situation I am in at home*; & my last & principal reason of all is, ye desire of seeing you. Indeed, my dearest brother, being so long used from my earliest childhood to live upon ye. footing of ye. most perfect intimacy & friendship with you, I can no longer bear ye. idea of passing another year without seeing you. In short, my determination is taken, & I intend in a day or two to write to the King to acquaint him with my resolution. Luckily he cannot prevent me. Tho' I respect him & use him with all possible duty, deference, & respect, I think his behaviour is so excessively unkind yt. there are moments when I can hardly ever put up with it. Sometimes not speaking to me when he sees me for three weeks together, & hardly ever at Court, speaking to people on each side of me & then missing me, & then if he does honor me with a word, 'tis either merely ' 'tis very hot or very cold', you yourself must feel in any situation how unpleasant this must be, but particularly so in mine, & then sometimes when I go to his house never taking any notice of me at all, as if I was not there. With regard to the Queen I cannot enough say what I feel for her, her goodness to me is such yt. I wd. bear anything to save her a moment's uneasiness, but this really goes too far. My intention is to join you, be it but for three hours in order to converse with you, wherever you are. I mean at once

wrote the Duke to his nephew, from Strasbourg (28 December 1783), 'if the D. C[hartre]s comes to England, & do not be too civil, for I think, considering the attention I shewed him, he ought to have given us a fete or at least as much attention as to a private English gentleman how [*sic*] goes a hunting' (54465–6). He wrote again on 14 April 1784: 'I find by the paper the Duke of Chartres is come to England. He is quite done up at Paris & has been obliged to leave the D[uches]s of Chartres but £4,000 a year after the great fortune she brought him. He is in very bad repute in his own country.' (54468)

to go to Vienna, & then follow you if you shd. have left yt. City. I bring Lake with me, & mean to winter abroad either at Vienna or Paris, I an not clear wh., but I rather beleive ye. latter. Respecting ye. secret I sent you word by George Hanger I intended to communicate it to you, I think it safest to preserve it in petto till I have ye. happiness, my dearest brother, of once more seeing you, wh. period I think is not now very far distant. I fear, my dearest Frederick, I have tired you with my long prose. I mean to write to William by ye. same post. I will therefore conclude this long & tedious epistle with assuring yt. in every situation thro' life you will ever find me [etc.].

P.S. I have been confined to my house for ye whole week by a very violent & nasty fever, & am still very much out of order, tho' I flatter myself I am something better. I am grown so thin, yt. I think you cd. not possibly know me. Best compliments to Budé & Grenville. I direct this to Hannover tho' I know you to be at Vienna.[1]   (43659–60)

114 LETTERS FROM THE QUEEN TO THE PRINCE OF WALES

Windsor Lodge, 9 July 1784

My dearest son, after our parting I considered the pleasure of your long wished for present, but upon mature consideration I find it more *prudent* for myself to *decline* accepting it, as the expence attending the dear little intelligent creatures will not suit my finances. I flatter myself I am in time to prevent your putting yourself to any further inconvenience about them, as I shoud grieve that your pretty attention to me should be attended with any trouble to you. I desire you will be persuaded that this mark of your affection is very sensibly felt by your very affectionnate mother & friend.   (36362)

Queen's Lodge, Windsor, 11 July 1784

Having recovered my senses a little after a long & painfull operation of three full hours performed upon one of my fore teeth by Monsieur Dumirgue[2], I take up my pen to thank you for your pretty letter & cadeau which malgré bon gré I must accept, notwithstanding all my

1. George Aust (Under-Secretary of State for Foreign Affairs) wrote on 10 July: 'The Prince of Wales, by the advice of his physicians, is soon to set out for Spa, having obtained leave to travel for three months. Vienna is mentioned as one of the objects of his curiosity, though it will be wonderful if he should not take a peep at Paris' (Add. MSS. 35622, f. 273). And on 2 August: 'The excursion to Spa seems now doubtful' (*Ibid.*, f.306).

2. Dumergue was the Royal family's dentist.

boasted prudence. Alas! *you know Pope*[1] *says, Wee woman [sic] have no character at all*, to which I subscribe only *so far* as concerns the little steeds, for my unsteadiness was only occasioned by delicacy, not want of inclination: for you little know how much I feel any attention from you. I shall make it my chief study to establish the household of this new acquired *little family* & shall not forget *appointing* some of the *physical tribe* to prevent the appoplexy you threaten them with. I shall only desire you will keep them in your stables till I come to Kew on Wednesday when we will settle about them.

My pen is very inadequate to express my feelings on this occasion, but still more so to convey to you la vraye tendress avec laquelle je suis jusqu' au tombeau mon tres cher fils [etc.].

I beg pardon for having kept the groom so long, but indeed my head is now hardly clear enough to say any thing very reasonable.

Your sisters vous font mille amitiées.   (36363)

115   THE PRINCE OF WALES TO THE DUCHESS OF DEVONSHIRE

Kew, 19 July [1784]

My dearest Friend, For such I shall still call you altho' your letter to Mr. Onslow[2] last night makes me doubt whether or not you wish me to look upon you any longer in that light. Conscious as I am of my own innocence, and of my having no intention even in the smallest instance to deceive you or her that is dearer to me than life[3], and having endeavoured to convince you thro'out the whole of my late proceedings, of the irreprochable integrity which has ever actuated me (excepting in one instance, for wh. you know I sufficiently suffered) and wh. I flatter myself will ever be the principles of my conduct thro' life, you will not I hope be surprized at the feelings which so severely occupy my whole mind. I commissioned Mr. Onslow to inform you, and he tells me that he fulfilled my desire, that I was perfectly ignorant of the step your Grace was persuaded to take upon my account, and very much distressed at finding you did so. I also commissioned him to assure you that however painful it might be to me making this unhappy affair still more publick, and tho' it would be most exceedingly disagreable to me to put myself under the hands of a surgeon to whom I am perfectly unused, that I was still willing to do so, if your want of confidence in a man to whom you had ever expressed yourself as looking upon him as yr. best

1. Alexander Pope (1688–1744), the poet.

2. Thomas Onslow (1754–1827), succeeded his father as 2nd Earl of Onslow in 1814. M.P. for Rye, 1775–84; for Guildford, 1784–1806.

3. Mrs. Fitzherbert (1756–1837).

and dearest friend, could make you wish to subject him to so mortifying as well as degrading a situation. I do not therefore solicit my
acquittal upon this subject as a favor, but I demand it as a justice due
to me. For these reasons you will not be surprized at my saying yt. I
think your conduct in conveying your ideas to me thro' a third person,
and in saying yt. ye letter was intended more *for me than for him*, was
both unkind and ungenerous. If you are not convinced of my innocence,
say so to me. Why did you fear writing to me to tell me so? Beleive me,
I have too much self regard and too much pride, notwithstanding the
true affection and great friendship I bear you, to live in any society,
where my character is in the least degree suspected, but more particularly
in one where I have so long had the good fortune to be esteemed and
received upon so very different a footing.

Excuse me if I now advert to some particular passage in your letter to
Mr. Onslow. You say you wish me to look upon you as a real friend, and
not as a confidente. When did I ever put you in any situation but that of
a real friend? The communications I made to you upon this subject were
in the character of my friend. Where is the use of a real friend but to
express to them what you have nearest to your heart? When did I ever
entertain thro' the whole of this affair either a single dishonorable or
unworthy idea? I refer to your own recollection. I appeal to your own
integrity. Have you not yourself told me that my conduct thro'out
towards this most amiable of women (and who ever must be trans-
cendently the dearest to me thro' life, whose character to all who knew
her must be most unblemished and respectable) has ever been perfectly
honorable? Nay, so much so that when I expressed my uneasiness to
you upon my situation respecting her, you did, unknown to me, in
justification of my sentiments and from the embarrassment you felt on
yr. own account, submit the whole business to the Duke of Devonshire's[1]
opinion. You know what his answer was. Need I therefore ask was my
conduct irreprochable or not? With respect to the present transaction
before us, I have both said enough and taken sufficient pains to set you
right upon the subject. You will not, I flatter myself therefore, be astonished if I say that till I hear from you yourself that you are satisfied upon
the facts I have stated, it must be impossible for me to have the happiness of seeing you. If such is to be my case, however much I may
lament it, I never can be brought to think I deserve it. I need not recall
to your mind, I am certain, what my affection and what my friendship
has ever been to you. You know that I frequently have told you, and
especially of late in moments wh. I not only thought but hoped

1. William, 5th Duke of Devonshire (1748-1811), succeeded his father as Duke, 1764. He
married (1) Georgiana Spencer (1757-1806) in June 1774; and (2) Lady Elizabeth Foster
(*c*.1760-1824) in October 1809, she being the widow of John Thomas Foster (*d*.1796) and
second daughter of the 4th Earl of Bristol.

would be the last of my miserable existence, that excepting her who was present, you was the next dearest object to me in life. Have I ever entertained even for an instant towards you a single sentiment wh. the tenderest of brothers might not entertain for a sister?

Excuse me for having thus long trespassed upon your patience, but having me with so many *false friends* of late in the world, it is but too natural for me to be over anxious in securing one who has ever proved themselves so much otherwise towards me, and the continuation of whose esteem is so essential to my happiness. As to this letter you may shew the contents of it to the Duke, whose opinion I respect, and to the whole world if you please, as it contains sentiments both towards yourself as well as my *ever beloved Maria, wh. I am not only not ashamed of but must ever glory in.*

I really am so fatigued, I can say no more except that I flatter myself you will allow me to conclude with calling you, as I ever have done, and hope I ever shall, my ever dearest friend and sister, and that you will allow me to subscribe myself, Your ever affectionate friend and brother.[1]
(Chatsworth MSS.)

116 PRINCE WILLIAM TO THE PRINCE OF WALES

Hanover, 23 July 1784

I am much obliged to you for your friendly letter of the 7; it has put me out of apprehension concerning your health, particularly as Dalrymple has wrote me an account of your late indisposition. Do, my dear brother, begin to take more care of yourself, for health is with difficulty lost, but when lost, is irrecoverably gone. Besides, a person is but half a man when his constitution is ruined. You may very likely be as old at thirty as you ought to be at sixty years of age.

As in your letter to me you express a desire of learning how I am situated in this part of the world, I will now endeavour to do it in as few words as possible. You may remember I told you, when I set off for Germany, that it was likely Budé and I should fall out, as he never has enjoyed my confidence. The affair has happened, & we are now on such terms that must be very disagreeable to both of us. He has acted, or rather wished to act, in the same stile he did formerly. He was displeased if I went out alone. However, I soon cut him short & have done

1. On the 17th the Prince wrote an eighteen-page letter to Mrs. Fitzherbert, who had hurriedly left the country after the fantastic happenings at Carlton House. He again threatened to end his life if he could not live with her, informed her that he had broken off his connexion with Lady Melbourne, and signed himself 'not only your most affectionate of lovers but the tenderest of husbands' (Shane Leslie, *Life and Letters of Mrs. Fitzherbert*, i.24).

exactly as I liked best, & in measures where I wanted advice I have always taken Merrick's. Being thus situated with Budé, & not being pleased with the phlegmatick way of the Germans, I wished to return, not to stay in London but to do my duty again at sea. I accordingly wrote to Lord Hood & expressed my desire of his mentioning the matter to the King. His Lordship declined, as it would be a dangerous subject to speak to his Majesty. Somehow or other it got to the royal ears, & I was informed my father did not approve of my coming home, nor of the tricks I have plaid here, though God knows I have not plaid many. Do, my dear brother, I beseech you, consider how disagreeably I am situated in this damned country, and let me know your advice. Will mentioning it to the Queen do any good? Pretty qualifications to be sure for any young man like me, smoaking, playing at twopenny whist & wearing great thick boots. Oh! I wish I was returned: England, England for ever, & the pretty girls of Westminster. . . .

Do, my dear brother, I beseech you, consider how disagreeably I am situated in this country, & whether it is not possible for me to return to sea next autumn. I must trouble you with another request, not to forget me when the quarterly messenger returns, but not too expencively, as my money matters are not in the most flourishing stile. . . .   (44664–5)

117 LETTERS FROM PRINCE FREDERICK TO THE PRINCE OF WALES

Vienna, 28 July 1784
I have many thanks to return you for your last kind and affectionate letter, to which I take the very earliest opportunity of answering [*sic*]. You may easily conceive how happy it would make me to see you. Our having always been brought up together and the affection which has always subsisted between us makes me exceedingly impatient for the moment of our meeting, but at the same time I never can think of returning without the King's express commands; besides, my education and the learning of my profession require still my remaining some time in these parts. I am exceedingly sorry to hear of the very unpleasant difference between you and the King. For Heaven's sake do everything in your power to put an end to it, for it would be a dreadfull calamity not only for us, but for the whole country if it was to continue. Let me also entreat of you, my dearest brother, to give up the idea of travelling. Indeed, you know not all the inconveniences to which you would be subjected, and as for saving money I can assure you you are very much mistaken if you think that you will be able to do that.

We arrived here last Friday after having had a very agreable journey, and have been received very graciously by the Emperor[1]. I am obliged to dress this moment for a great dinner. I have therefore not time to add more except to assure you that I am ever [etc.].   (43664–5)

Vienna, 12 Aug. 1784
I could not refuse the bearer of this a few lines of recommendation to you. Her name is Paradis; she became blind at a very early age, in spite of which she plays upon the harpsicord in the most surprising manner. As I know that you are fond of musick I am certain you will be much pleased with her.   (43666)

118   PRINCE WILLIAM TO THE PRINCE OF WALES

Hanover, 12 Aug. 1784
It is with the most sincere affection & brotherly regard that I take up my pen to congratulate the best of brothers on his birthday: a day that must [be] & is ever dear to me, after the repeated & frequent marks of your kindness & affection for me.[2] Believe me, dear brother, nobody has a greater friendship for you than I have. You have always treated me in the way that a younger brother can wish from an elder. I am by no means an ungrateful wretch. I have not forgot your affection for me, & shall be happy if it will ever be in my power to serve the best of brothers, to whom I pray God may grant health & happiness.

I have a very worthy & respectable friend to recommend to you, my dear George, who, I am sure, would have the honour to please you if you was better acquainted with him, & would be most highly flattered if you would employ him in your household; if I was not sure of him I would not recommend him: I mean our old Windsor acquaintance Dalrymple, of the Queen's Regiment. He is really a worthy man & pleasant person in society, universally respected by all his acquaintances, particularly by me, & reckoned one of the best officers in the service. Do, I beg, my dear brother, consider if you could not serve him. I should

1. Joseph II.

2. The Duke of Cumberland wrote to the Prince of Wales from Strasbourg on 23 August: 'Ld. & Ly. Clive have been here for a few days. She talks in raptures about the balls & parties you have given them. . . . My last letters from England I recevd. yesterday, of Friday the 13th, which mentions your having dined the day before at Windsor, which was your birthday, of which I wish you most heartily joy & renewal of health & pleasure. [I] am glad to hear you are got well again & hope Brighton divert[s], yet I do not think it is a kind of life that will entertain: there is too much sameness. London is the only place that can afford you various amusements.' (54469–70)

consider it as a favour conferred upon me, & I am sure you will find him very deserving your friendship, & what will give you pleasure is that the public will approve it. I beg & entreat again that you would do me this single favour, the first I have ever asked. Do, my dear brother, consider about it, & do it out of affection for me.

I yesterday morning received a set down from the two persons that were concerned in begetting me. The female was more severe than the male. I do not mention names for fear the letter should be opened. I have not done anything I know of to merit such a rebuke: patience however in all things. . . . (44666–7)

119   THE PRINCE OF WALES TO THE KING, AND THE REPLY

Brighthelmstone, 24 Aug. 1784
It is with the utmost reluctance I now sit down to communicate anything to yr. Majesty wh. may in the smallest degree tend to anything like uneasiness either to yourself or the Queen, whose mutual good opinions & approbation I shd. ever think the most flattering sanction to any measure I shd. judge fit to adopt. I therefore think it my duty to inform your Majesty of a resolution I have been induced to take, from the peculiar and very embarrassed situation of my affairs, arising from the necessary expenses I incurred during the course of last year; I mean the putting in full practice a system of economy by immediately going abroad, & wh. nothing but my absenting myself from this country for a certain time can possibly effectuate. The unwillingness I naturally & sincerely feel to inconvenience your Majesty, especially at the present moment, upon my account, can be equalled only by that wh. you yourself expressed to me sometime since at ye. idea of yt. object being excluded by laying any additional burthen upon ye. country. I therefore beg leave to repeat yt. I think it encumbent upon me to give your Majesty ye. earliest information of an event wh. it is absolutely necessary for me to put in immediate practice.   (38110, and, with trifling changes, 41812–3 and 31858)

THE KING'S REPLY

27 Aug. 1784
The Prince of Wales, if not void of every degree of reflection and of those feelings which a good heart must experience, need not be told the unpleasant sensations the letter Lord Southampton delivered from him on Wednesday has occasioned, in addition to what I constantly suffer

155

from his reprehensible conduct, which has grown worse every year, and in a more glaring manner since his removal to Carlton House.

To be more explicit, the Prince of Wales must remember that after voting in the House of Lords in a manner that he felt must be displeasing to me, he came and voluntarily declared his resolution of not opposing any persons I might at any time judge right to employ; that if I did not trust to his heart he hoped I did not think him such a fool as not to know his interest was inseparable with mine; he is certainly a judge whether his behaviour has coincided with this declaration.

After assuring me when his establishment was settled, a large sum allowed for furnishing the house I have given him the use of, and for purchasing other necessaries, and an equal sum for paying off the debts he had contracted, that he would be careful to avoid again getting into difficulties; I owne I had hopes he was sincere, as on my going to Carleton House he proposed the only painting it and putting handsome furniture where necessary; but in very few weeks this was forgot, and large additional buildings erected; and least [sic] these should not waste enough money, the most expensive Fetes given, and at this hour considerable additional are [sic] again begun; yet the Prince of Wales chuses to term his difficulties as occasioned by necessary expences, when I am sensible that with the income he receives and the large sum granted him at setting out last year might have afforded him every reasonable elegance and enabled him to live with magnificence; but then sense, not every frivolous and irregular passion, must have directed his conduct.

If he has deranged his affairs he ought to take a manly resolution to diminish his expences and thus establish a sinking fund by degrees to clear those debts, which would in some measure palliate with the public for an extravagance which everyone but his flatterers have universally blamed; the Prince of Wales ought to know that every step he takes is of consequence, that if he once loses the good opinion of this nation it is not to be regained.

I have found myself under the disagreable necessity of shewing the Prince of Wales's letter to the Queen, who is as much hurt as me, and coincides in the opinion that if his improper plan was put into execution his character would be forever blasted in this country, and also in all Europe. I therefore insist on his giving up a measure that would be a public breach with me; to save him has been my only reason for putting up with many unpleasant things; but if he is resolved to ruin his character, at least I will not bear any part of the blame, and my people shall know that this shameful flight is in defiance of my express prohibitions both as King and father; but if this representation brings the Prince of Wales to a recollection, and makes him take the honorable path I have proposed; when I see by an uniformity of conduct it is acted up to, and that a certain sum is employed annually to pay off his incumberances and fresh ones not incurred, I will see whether I can contribute towards getting it sooner effected, for which reason as yet except the Queen I have not mentioned the strange plan to anyone but Lord Southampton.

I am certain if the Prince of Wales will consult the different gentlemen of his establishment on their particular branches, that they can form a plan, and that he, like a rational being, will conform to it, he will find things much easier arranged than he may imagine; but if he acts otherwise he must remember these last words of a much distressed parent, he will in every sense be ruined and lose the affection and protection of him who as yet remains his very affectionate father.   (16460–1)

120   LETTERS FROM LORD SOUTHAMPTON TO THE PRINCE OF WALES

Stanhope Street, 8.30 p.m., Friday, 27 Aug. 1784
I have the honor to send your Royal Highness the King's answer to your letter. His Majesty was graciously pleased to read it to me. I think it puts the whole of your R.H. future prospect under your eye, & submits it to your understanding to decide upon. I need not observe that the King expects an answer to his letter.

I hope that you will permit me the honor of seeing your R.H. when you come to town, as there are many things that I could explain, de vive voix, which are not easily written.   (31881)

[Fitz Roy] Farm, 10 a.m., Monday, 30 Aug. 1784
I am honor'd with your Royal Highnesses commands, and propose reaching Windsor between one & two o'clock, so that I may see the King upon his return from his morning ride. According to your orders I send back the copy of your R.H.'s letter to the K— which I have read, & find it does not hold out any offer of staying your intended voyage under any stipulation; which I own I wish it had, because the K— letter makes a conditional proposal which gives me an opening for anything that your R.Hs might ask in answer. With submission to your R.H., that part that you give to me in commission to ask whether the K. chuses that you should take leave before your departure, I likewise wish had been in the body of your R.Hs letter, as it would have been an addition to the terms of respect in which you couch your determination of going abroad, convinced as I always have been that the K— can & will prevent your leaving the Kingdom.

Your Royal Highness will be so gracious as to order your servant by whom I am to send an account after my return from Windsor, to be in Stanhope Street at five o'clock. (31883)

Stanhope Street, 8.15 p.m., Monday, 30 Aug. 1784
I have deliver'd your R.H.'s letter to the King, who was much hurt that no notice was taken of his proposal, or any particular answer made to his letter. H.M. remains in the same opinion about your going abroad & will not consent. Her Majesty seems equally hurt, & anxious that you should not go. As to the question about taking leave, no direct answer was made except that the K— did not see it possible for you to take leave when you was acting in defiance of his wishes. Your Royal Highness will probably have a letter from the K— in a day or two, more explicit.

I must just add that the K. was remarkably quiet, & I saw a strong inclination to have everything settled well if your R.H. would but yield to his wishes & speak out. (31882)

121 THE PRINCE OF WALES TO THE KING

Carlton House, 30 Aug. 1784
I am more shocked than I can possibly express at the contents of your Majesty's letter, as I am fearful that you have misunderstood both my conduct & intentions. With regard to any retrenchments that could be of material service in point of effectually lessening the incumberances alluded to by your Majesty in your letter, I find that by staying in England, that object is perfectly unattainable, & that nothing but my going abroad can possibly put me in the situation I should wish. Your Majesty must easily conceive how truly hurt I must feel at a publick breach with you, Sir. I therefore hope that as your Majesty must be conscious that my view in going abroad is to relieve myself from embarrassing difficulties, *not* to incur the censure of acting with the smallest disrespect towards you, that you will for these reasons not be induced to bring this affair to so cruel or so painful an issue as that of an open rupture, or think of placing me in so injurious or so unjust a light as that of being guilty of a shameful flight, while I have taken every possible & respectful means of previously acquainting your Majesty with my intention. I therefore think it my duty to inform your Majesty that I have an idea of residing for some time at Brunswick, which I hope will meet with your Majesty's approbation, as I see no fresh reason for altering my resolution of travelling, a resolution formed upon the most mature deliberation & upon the thoroughest conviction of the necessity of its taking place. (41815–6; 41817, 31860, 31862)

Brighton, 1 p.m., 1 Sept. 1784

I am very much obliged to you for your l̅re, but am very much hurt and surprised that neither the King nor your Lordship should think my letter an answer to his Majesty's. If your Lordship remembers, his M-y. says in his letter to me (which I suppose is the proposal you allude to as not being answered) ỵt. if I came to to [*sic*] my senses and make proper retrenchments, & ỵt he sees an annual sinking fund laid aside for ye payment of my debts, *he may then perhaps see* whether he can anyhow alleviate the burden, but then, there is another clause in the proposal which I had forgot to mention, namely, ỵt no new debts sḥd be incurred. God bless my soul, how can you now say ỵt in my letter I take no notice of his Majesty's proposal? I think I must undoubtedly have answered it in ỵe fullest manner possible. I therefore send you again the copy of my l̅re to the King, and have marked where I have answered his Majesty for fear it sḥd *again escape your notice*. I beg ỵr Ldshp. will be so good as to keep ỵr copy till I have ỵe pleasure to see you in town, which will be witḥt fail on Thursday.

How can I, my Lord, make any retrenchments out of my annual expence that would in the least tend to extricating me from my present embarrassed situation? It would be merely a drop of water in the sea! But allowing ỵt there ẉd be retrenchments made out of my income ỵt could be of material service to the payment of my debts, would ỵr Lordship, with your ideas of propriety, have the Prince of Wales, the Heir of Apparent [*sic*] to the Crown of Great Britain, dismiss his servants, sell his horses, and part, in short, with every magnificence annexed to his situation in life? A moment's reflection will I am sure convince ỵr Lordship of ỵe absurdity as well as impossibility of adopting so ridiculous as well as indecent a measure.

Your Lordship very well knows and feels ỵt it would be improper for me to live with a less degree of magnificence than I hitherto have done, and ỵr Lordship very well knows that *it is impossible for any sum to be laid aside out of my income ỵt could be of any material service to the payment of my debts*. I therefore am astonish'd that his Majesty can any longer continue to entertain such an idea, or ỵt your Lordship has not as yet attempted to convince him of ỵe absurdity of it. With regard to the King's proposal for opening, as ỵr Lordship calls it, I am sure ỵt upon reading ỵe copy of my l̅re to his Majesty you will see ỵt I have answered him most fully. As to asking anything of his Majesty, I have nothing to ask of him. I do not wish to put his My. either to the expence or the trouble of paying my debts, I therefore acquainted his M-y. with my resolution of going abroad as ỵe only means I have of extricating myself, & wh. I am determined most strictly to adhere to. Proposals cannot come

159

from me; *it does not become me to stipulate with his Maj. They should come from him.* My residing abroad is y͏e only method I have of clearing myself, as I think I have now pretty plainly demonstrated to y͏r Lordship. This plan, therefore am I resolved to adopt, as I am convinced it will appear more creditable and more honorable in y͏e eyes not only of this Kingdom but of all Europe, & more satisfactory to myself, than pursuing y͏t line of conduct pointed out to me in his M-j's letter, and which would involve me in still deeper difficulties. Every circumstance therefore y͏t I have mentioned to y͏r Lordship in this l͏re will tend to convince you how fully and thoroughly I answered his My. in y͏e letter I had the honor of writing to him, as well as y͏e necessity of my putting my plan in immediate execution.

I am fearfull y͏t y͏r patience is exhausted in reading this long epistle, I therefore conclude with assuring you, that I truly remain [etc.].   (31885)

LORD SOUTHAMPTON'S REPLY
Fitz Roy Farm, 9.30 p.m., Thursday, 2 Sept. 1784
I went to town according to your Royal Highnesses commands this morning, & returned upon receiving notice that you did not intend coming to town until tomorrow to dinner. Upon my return here I found a messenger with the inclosed from the King, with a note to myself. Pray let me have the honor of seeing you immediately upon your R.H.s coming to town.   (31887)

123   THE KING TO LORD SOUTHAMPTON
Queen's House, 2 Sept. 1784
Lord Southampton having intimated that the P. of Wales meant to set out on his improper journey as tomorrow, I send the enclosed message to be either sent to Brighthelmstone or delivered to him on coming to town, whichever Lord Southampton may find necessary. I am confirmed in the opinion of being able to prevent the P. of Wales's departure, but chuse to take this method of doing it. Ld. Southampton will find no lawyer hardy enough to deny the power.   (16464 and 16466)

[Enclosure] THE KING'S MESSAGE TO THE PRINCE OF WALES
Queen's House, 2 Sept. 1784
An open breach with me is but one among the many and still greater mischiefs which the step the P. of Wales seems misled enough to take

Augustus, Duke of Sussex
by Gainsborough 1783

The Princesses Charlotte Augusta, Augusta, and Elizabeth
by Gainsborough 1784

probably leads to. The precipitation with which he has been advised to preclude all communication with me on the subject of his leaving this Kingdom or of the circumstances and manner of doing it, and the abrupt and offensive manner which has been recommended to him of announcing this purpose, could not fail, in the first instance, of producing that effect. The consideration of the farther evils which I foresee from the P. of Wales executing this design makes me think it necessary as his father and his Sovereign strictly to charge and command him by this paper not to leave the realm without having obtained my particular leave.   (16465 and 16467)

124 THE PRINCE OF WALES TO THE KING

Brighthelmstone, 5 Sept. 1784

As I still continue apprehensive that your Majesty has throughout this business misunderstood both my conduct & intentions, I again presume to trouble your Majesty upon the subject of my intended plan. I have already informed your Majesty that my reason for going abroad arises from the impossibility of remaining here situated as I am. With respect to your Majesty's proposal, which I understand from Lord Southampton as well as as [sic] from your Majesty's own letter you did not think I had taken sufficient notice of, I beg only to request your Majesty to refer to the letter I had last the honor of writing to you, in which I mention'd to your Majesty the impossibility of such retrenchments being made out of my income as could effectually tend to relieve me, & which I had flattered myself would have appeared to your Majesty as a sufficient answer to what you had recommended, as well as an adequate reason for my absenting myself for some time. Your Majesty therefore I hope must be convinc'd that it is necessity alone that drives me abroad, & by no means an inclination to act in contradiction to your Majesty's wishes. Impressed with the recollection of [the] letter which your Majesty wrote to Colonel Hotham last year, & which I saw at your own immediate desire, your Majesty may conceive that I could not presume to do more than humbly & simply to represent my situation as well as the only means I have of extricating myself from my difficulties.   (41818–9, and 31868)

125 LETTERS FROM LORD SOUTHAMPTON TO THE
PRINCE OF WALES, AND A REPLY

London, Monday, 6 Sept. 1784

I deliver'd your Royal Highnesses letter to the King this day; likewise had the honor of communicating to her Majesty that passage given in command, in your letter to me.

161

The King does not answer your R.H^s letter immediately, as you continue resolved not to ask anything, which makes it difficult how to act, but your R.H. may expect one soon. In the meantime H.M. has enquired of me the sum that will be wanted to pay your debts, and finds that it exceeds his M.-s means of paying them without assistance from Parliam^t What consideration that would require before it is agitated, your R.H^s will easily judge. I obeyed your orders in stating to H.M. the substance of your former letter to me wherein you prove the impossibility of making such a saving as would be effectual, & how improper it would be for the Prince of Wales to be reduced to live beneath the dignity of the Heir Apparent. All this H.M. received with uncommon attention; & he is now fully informed of everything relative to your Royal Highnesses circumstances.

The Queen commands me to say to your R.H. that she is extreamly sensible of your kind expressions & intentions towards her, that you know her own good wishes for your happiness, & that she trusts you will not venture to go abroad at the risque of offending the K— for ever. (31888)

FROM THE PRINCE OF WALES [copy]

Carlton House, 17 Sept. 1784
My Lord, I am excessively obliged to you for the communication of his Majesty's letter[1] and as I think by his manner that it may be his gracious intentions to extricate me from my difficulties, I must desire your Lordship to order Colonel Hotham to make out as near a state as he can of my debts in order that you may transmit them to the King. I also take this opportunity of informing your Lordship that till I am acquainted thro' you with his Majesty's intentions I shall postpone my departure, as I should of course ever be desirous of acting in conformity with his Majesty's wishes as far as in my power. (16374, 31893 and 41821)

LORD SOUTHAMPTON'S REPLY

Stanhope Street, Wednesday, 17 Sept. 1784
I had the honor to send your Royal Highnesses letter in to the King before the Levée; which was returned to me during the Levée, together with the original of the inclosed copy. With humble submission I

1. Dated 17 September. 'I thank Lord Southampton for the communication of the letter he has this morning received from the Prince of Wales, which I take this method of returning.' (31892)

162

thought your R.H^s letter too cold towards the King; & his Majesty's answer confirms me in that opinion. When Col. Hotham makes out the statement of your R.H. debts, I most ardently wish that they may be carry'd to his Majesty with a warm & affectionate letter from yourself to him; it will do more good than all the messages upon earth, & must draw from his Majesty a warm & affectionate answer in return. There is but one person on earth of whom Y.R.H. can ask favors. It raises your dignity to ask of him openly and with the same good grace which is so conspicuous when you grant them to others. I beg pardon for intruding my humble opinion. I trust to your R.H^s goodness in attributing it to my faithfull attachment to your person.   (31890)

126   PRINCE WILLIAM TO THE PRINCE OF WALES

Hanover, 15 Oct. 1784
I take the liberty to recommend by Lord Hood Doctor Blaine, our late phisician of the fleet, to your protection & I shall take it as a favour if you will give him the title of your phisician.   (44671)

127   PRINCE FREDERICK TO THE PRINCE OF WALES

Hanover, 15 Oct. 1784
I take the very earliest opportunity to acquaint you with my safe return here. This journey has been most exceedingly amusing particularly the sejour of Vienna which is delightfull. The manner of life there is exceedingly agreable and there is not the least gene. During the time I was there there was a fête every evening which lasted so long, particularly the Balls, that I was hardly ever able to get away before six oclock in the morning, and as I was occupied the whole morning in seing everything which is remarkable about the town, I had hardly a moment left for repose. One week particularly I went to bed on the Monday, and I never saw my bed again till the Sunday night following. During the camps however we led quite a different life as we always went out with the troops at four o'clock in the morning. I cannot say however that I am sorry after so very long and boisterous a journey to be at last returned to my own fireside. I am affraid you will think me grown very old for talking in this manner, but I can assure you from experience that home has many advantages which it is impossible ever to find in other places.

I am affraid I should tresspass upon your leisure were I to add more to this letter. I shall therefore conclude by repeating to you again and again that I am ever most sincerely [etc.].

P.S. Pray write often.   (43675–6)

163

27 Oct. 1784

Sir, this is the first day on which I am enabled to have the honour of transmitting to your Royal Highness, in obedience to the comments I some time ago received, an estimate of your debts which I do herewith enclosed.

It was my earnest wish to have stated to your Royal Highness the exact state of every part of your debts with precision, but I soon found that was impossible: every day brought on some charge in every department which I could neither account for nor control. All I could do, therefore, after much delay, has been to collect what can only be called an *estimate* of your Royal Highness's present debts, and those ostensibly contracted by your orders, which must be calculated as such, though they do not yet appear. I should be glad to send you *more* than an estimate, because I know how very fallacious all estimates are whatever; and I should have done so, had not the greatest part of it come under other regulation than mine. But your Royal Highness must be sensible how little I have been communicated with in matters of your expence by those whose duty it was to have constantly communicated with me. Your stables is the only article in the account I have now the honour of presenting to your Royal Highness, which comes properly from *me*. I give that, and *can* give it, on a rough calculation only, for the Christmas quarter; for in this, as in every other department, such fresh expence arises from one hour to another, from quarters in which it is so little to be expected, that it is utterly impossible for me to give more than a random guess for a week forward, a circumstance which, as your Treasurer, I should be truly ashamed of, had I either the confidence or the power, which every Treasurer of your Royal Highness's ought, for your own security, to be vested with. As I have unfortunately enjoyed neither, my feelings are not those of shame but of sorrow, which will never prevent my doing the utmost in my power to retrieve your Royal Highness's finances from the wretched and the disgraceful state in which they stand at present.

Having transmitted to your Royal Highness the enclosed paper, my duty, in strictness, ought to cease, but I was so long, formerly, in the habit of pointing out dangers to you that I cannot, in my own conscience and for my own ease of mind, forbear it now.

It is with equal grief and vexation that I now see your Royal Highness (in matters of expense I mean) totally in the hands, and at the mercy of your builder, your upholsterer, your jeweller and your tailor. I say totally, because these people act from your Royal Highness's pretended commands, and from their charges there is no appeal. I leave Mr. Lyte to account to your Royal Highness concerning his own feelings about the two latter. The two former have neither of them been employed with any previous consultation with me. They have undertaken, and are carrying works through, to an enormous amount, without a single care or enquiry from whence money was to arise for their discharge; neither my advice, my expostulations, nor my representation of there being no fund whatever for this purpose, has been regarded. They have thus plunged your Royal Highness into difficulties so great that it has long been out of the power of your own treasury to extricate you from them, and you are now driven from necessity, painful necessity, to trust to events for other means of doing so. My own correspondence with Mr. Holland [1] may sufficiently shew what my uniform opinion has been on that subject, and demonstrate, I hope to your Royal Highness's satisfaction, that I at least have done my duty.

Mr. Holland's estimate of future works amounted, some little time ago, to £18,000, which was to cover the purchase of all houses, &c., &c. What he gives in at present, as included in the paper I have now the honour to enclose, comes to £30,250. The increase is a rapid one, and though additional orders from your Royal Highness are pleaded in extenuation of it, it still may give you to judge how little an *estimate* can be depended upon.

For my own part, I deliver in M. Gaubert's, amounting to £35,000, merely because he sends it to me and I have no right and still less inclination to make the smallest addition, but from my own experience of what has passed, I have little doubt but that the expense to you will, at last, be greatly *beyond* that sum, and if measures are not taken very different from what have hitherto been made use of; if Mr. Gaubert is allowed carte blanche, as he has been, and if your Royal Highness's orders, so constantly alleged to be given to *him*, are to supersede every direction and care that those much higher in office than himself think proper to make use of for your interest and service, your Royal Highness will find your self involved in fresh distresses, the very moment after you are extricated from the present ones.

I have repeatedly had the honour of representing the amazing expense of your stables. The last quarterly account will shew your Royal Highness clearly that it amounted to the quarterly proportion of above £31,000 per annum; double what Col. Lake thought would be sufficient sixteen months ago! Your Royal Highness has been pleased to express yourself sensible of their enormity, but instead of finding (as I had ground for supposing I should) a contraction in that article, I discover, to my great mortification, that the keeping running horses is to enhance it beyond all kind of calculation whatever!

I will not, Sir, conceal from you that your last orders, brought me by Colonel Lake, gave me equal surprise and concern. I paid obedience to them with much greater reluctance than I ever did to any commands of

1. Henry Holland, the architect (1746–1806).

your Royal Highness's because I know it cannot be for your credit and your honour that so many people should be left unpaid, as there must be by these means. Were I inclined to interest your Royal Highness's passions on this subject, I could easily paint to you the distress this must occasion to numbers, but I need only address myself to your justice, not to your compassion.

Your Royal Highness knows the whole of your income; £12,500 each quarter is what you receive from Government. That, and the precarious supply your Duchy of Cornwall can afford you half yearly, is *all* you have to answer the demands of your household for salaries and wages, your table and living, your stables of each kind, with all their appurtenances; your Privy Purse, your buildings of every sort, your furniture for those buildings; all your tradesmen, and all allowances and acts of charity and beneficence that your very elevated situation calls upon you to make.

How inadequate these two streams are to furnish so many torrents of expense, your Royal Highness cannot but be as good a judge as myself.

I humbly beg pardon for having taken up so much of your time, but the station I have the honour of holding in your Royal Highness's Household requires me to conceal nothing from you; if I did, I should be most highly culpable. It is painful to me to make a representation to you of your distress; it is equally painful to your Royal Highness to make your own reflections in consequence, but there is a duty incumbent on us both.

I have the honour to be [etc.].   (16476–7, and 41822–3)

DEBTS

In Mr. Lyte's department		£30,000
Stables on calculation 25 Dec. 1784		12,000
Balance due for the old works at Carlton House in Mr. Holland's Department		7,743
Balance due on Mr. Gaubert's department do.		8,700
		£58,443
Mr. Holland's estimate to complete the new works in his department	£30,250	
Deduct money paid Mr. Birch[2] for purchase of houses	1,400	
	£28,850	
Mr. Gaubert's estimate for completely fitting and furnishing the inside with furniture for two seasons, &c.	35,000	63,850
		£122,293
Money borrowed by H.R.H. on the 22 Dec. 1784 of which Col. Hotham was informed by H.R.H. on the 14 Jan. and received application about from Mr. Birch on the 11 Feb. 1785, Security on houses near Carlton House	£4,000	
To be paid off in one year by quarterly instalments, the 1st payment commencing 25 March 1785	6,000	
	£10,000	
Money likewise borrowed, the particulars of which H.R.H. has not yet been pleased to inform Colonel Hotham about	15,000	25,000
Total estimate of debts and engagements		£147,293

(f.16377)

1. This is a fuller account than the one in 41824, where the total is only £118,293.
2. William Birch was one of the Clerks of the Council to the Duchy of Cornwall.

PRINCE FREDERICK TO THE PRINCE OF WALES

Hanover, 30 Oct. 1784

As I know how much you are a lover of musick I could not refuse the bearer of this letter of recommendation to you. His name is Lolle and he is reckoned one of the most capital performers on the violin in the world. I heard him play this evening and was quite astonished at his skill. (43677)

THE QUEEN TO THE PRINCE OF WALES, AND THE REPLIES

Windsor, 11 Dec. 1784

Mon très cher fils: Après une gelée si forte et un temps si sain, j'espère de reçevoir des bonnes nouvelles de votre part pour le moins égale a celle d'hier. J'ai prié le Chevalier Dyer[1] de vous dire mille joli choses de ma part & je me flatte qu'il s'en est bien acquitté; j'ignore absolument *his gift of speech*, ainsi j'aurai tort de doute de ses talents, je suis sure de son zile de sorte que je fie a lui.

Il est bien propre que votre petit esculape vous tient un peu en prison; votre mal quoique point dangereux demande à être soigné, et comme vous ete *naturellement si prudent et si attaché a une vie solitaire* il n'y a aucun doute que vous en serez quite en très peu de temps. Je recommende surtout la diète du bon Jebb comme le meilleur remède de tout, car il faut avouer que c'est après tout le remède le plus efficace.

Le Roi me charge de ses amitiés pour vous; vos soeurs grandes et petites font des veux pour votre retablissement à moi quoique la derniere je ne me sens pas la moins tendrement attachée et interressée au retour de votre santé et c'est avec ces sentiments que je suis de coeur et d'amé votre très affectionnée amie et fidelle mère. (36364)

THE PRINCE OF WALES'S REPLY

Carlton House, 11 Dec. 1784

Ma chère Mère, Je viens de recevoir vôtre cher billet, & je ne puis pas en vérité vous exprimer quel plaisir il m'a fait. Mon petit esculape c'est montré très digne du titre dont vous l'avez honoré, il est vrai qu'il ne me tourmente pas beaucoup de medicines, et jusqu'ici pas une seule saignée, mais de l'autre côté il me fait observer un régime très exact, & même qui me paraitrait un peu dur, si j'étais en parfaite santé,

1. Sir John Swinnerton Dyer, 6th Baronet (1738–1801), a Colonel and Captain of a Company of Guards. Groom of the Bedchamber to the Prince of Wales. Succeeded his father as Baronet, 1780. He committed suicide by shooting.

car je n'ai pas gouté depuis avant Hier quoique ce soit de solide pas même le plus petit morceau de pain; mais je m'en trouve beaucoup mieux, je n'ai pas la moindre fièvre, & les vilains gros boutons commencent déjà a se sécher. A vous dire la verité, ma chère mère, d'ecrire en général dans une indisposition pareille fatigue beaucoup les yeux, & principalement par un temps pareil a celui qu'il fait, je me flatte donc que vous me pardonnerez si je ne rends pas cette épitre si longue que je l'aurais autrement faite, principalement si je n'avais pas les yeux un peu incommodes. Mettez moi aux pieds du Roi, embrassez mes chers frères & Soeurs de ma part, & quand a vous même ma chère mère *tho' last not least in love,* croyez qu'il n'y a personne au monde qui vous est plus sincèrement & fidèlement attaché, que [etc.].   (41825)

FROM THE PRINCE OF WALES

Carlton House, 16 Dec. 1784

Aiant appris par My Lord Southampton que vous aviez eu la bonté de dire aujourd'hui, que vous aviez dessein de me venir voir demain, j'ai été pendant quelque temps a considérer par quel moien vous pourriez arriver a Carlton House, sans risquer de vous enrhumer; pour cette raison il m'est entré dans la tête que le plus sur moien d'y venir sans attrapper de rhume serait de venir en chaise a porteur tout le long du Parc, jusqu'a la porte du jardin ou il y a les sentinelles & ou vous trouverez du monde pret a vous recevoir, & pour vous conduire a travers le jardin. Je me flatte aussi d'avoir le bonheur de voir mes soeurs, pour cette raison si vous voulez prêter une chaise a porteur a l'une, j'envoierai la mienne pour l'autre avec mes gens, ils seront tous prets chez moi, ou plutôt à la maison de la Reine a quel qu' heure que vous voudrez, et lorsque vous aurez la bonté de me dire a quel heure je dois me tenir pret pour avoir l'honneur et le bonheur de vous recevoir, j'envoierai ma chaise a porteur et mes laquais une bonne heure d'auparavant pour être d'abord a vos ordres lorsque vous en aurez besoin. Pardonnez moi, ma chère mère, si je vous ennuie un peu de tous ses détails, mais comme je vous aime toutes, tant vous ma chère maman, que mes chères soeurs, et que je suis extrèmement impatient de vous revoir toutes, et même peutêtre si vous êtes toutes bien bonnes de vous faire quelque petit cadeau, il était absolument nécessaire que je vous ennuiasse d'une prolixité de langue, pour laquelle il n'y aurait pas d'excuse, si l'affaire ne demandait beaucoup d'explication ce qui est en vérité le cas. Adieu, ma chère mère, que le bon Dieu vous garde et vous protége long temps est la prière continuelle du plus sincèrement attache [etc.].   (41826–7)

Paris, 27 Dec. 1784

Lady Elisabeth Foster[1] a eu la bonté de me remettre la lettre que vous m'avez écrit, cher Prince, vous voyez que je profite de la permission que vous me donnez d'agir avec vous amicalement, rien ne m'a jamais été plus agreable que les nouvelles assurances d'amitié que vous voulez bien me donner; de peur de vous ennuyer de ma reconnoissances je ne vous en parlerai plus, comptez je vous en prie sur moi a jamais comme sur une personne qui vous est tres dévouée et qui vous aime veritablement beaucoup, encore une fois je ne vous en parlerai plus pas même à la fin de mes lettres quoique ce soit un usage consacré. Je me suis acquitté de vos commissions pour Ld. Malden[2], Lauzun [?] et Conflans, ils sont bien sensibles aux marques de votre souvenir; Malden seulement se plaint qu'il y a deja longtemps qui vous lui promettez de lui écrire sans avoir effectué jusques ici cette promesse. J'espere que le mois de Fevrier ne se passera pas sans que je vous fusse ma Cour j'en ai je vous jure un desir extreme, j'espere que vous serez parfaitement retabli dans ce temps la je sais que vos convalescences ne sont pas longues mais en vérité vous ne devriez pas pour les gens qui vous aiment les répeter aussi souvent voila tout mon sermon mon talent n'est pas de prêcher sur la continence it faut meme que j'aime beaucoup les personnes pour m'engager a leur en dire autant. Quand a votre voyage en France certainement personne ne l'auroit plus desiré que moi mais je suis charmé que vous ni l'ayez pas éffectué. Sans savoir les dispositions où notre Cour étoit à votre égard, dont je vous parlerai plus en detail dans le mois de Février, et dont je vous rendrai compte dans touts les temps si elles changerient quand je trouverai des occasions sures de vous écrire, parceque la maniere de vous annoncer ici vous mettra à l'abry detoute gene et de tout inconvenient je vous instruirai de tout si vous voulez

1. Lady Elizabeth Foster (1760?–1824), second daughter of the 4th Earl of Bristol, married (1) John Thomas Foster (*d.*1796) who deserted her, leaving her to bring up two children on £300 a year. She was befriended by Georgiana, Duchess of Devonshire, who engaged her as a governess to 'Miss W'—the daughter of a *liaison* between the Duke and Miss Charlotte Spencer. She soon ceased to be governess, remained an inmate of Devonshire House, became the Duke's mistress and gave him two children: (*a*) Sir Augustus William James Clifford (1788–1877), and (*b*) Caroline St. Jules, who in 1809 married George Lamb, the youngest son of the 1st Viscount Melbourne and brother of Lord Melbourne the Prime Minister. Clifford entered the Navy in 1800, became a Captain in 1812, and subsequently an Admiral. He was knighted in 1830 and made a Baronet in 1838. On 19 October 1809 the Duke married his mistress (see page 151*n.*).

2. George, 5th Earl of Essex (1757–1839), styled Viscount Malden until he succeeded his father in 1799. M.P. for Westminster, 1779–80; for Lostwithiel, 1781–4; for Okehampton, 1785–90; for Radnor, 1794–9.

bien me prevenir quelques semaines d'avance et pour lors vous choisirez ce qui vous conviendra le mieux.

Adieu cher Prince j'usque au mois de fevrier car j'espere que les apparences de guerre ne m'empecheront pas d'aller passer quelques temps avec vous, si je ne le pouvois pas j'en serois bien contrarié je vous le jure.   (38097–8)

V   1785

The negotiations for the payment of the Prince's debts, started in 1784, made no further progress in 1785 because he refused to make a full disclosure, and the King suspected that his son had been spending money for political purposes. A settlement might well have been reached had the Prince agreed to set aside a portion of his income for the payment of his debts and been willing to break with the Opposition. Fox and the Duke of Portland, to do them justice, had often said that a Prince of Wales ought to be unconnected with party, but the Prince told Sir James Harris, 'I cannot abandon Charles and my friends.' Harris, who was shown the correspondence between the Prince and the King, had to admit that the King's letters were 'harsh and severe, constantly refusing every request the Prince made, and reprobating in each of them his extravagance and dissipated manner of living'. He hit on the expedient which was ultimately to be adopted to extricate the Prince from the financial bog into which he had sunk. If only the Prince would marry, Parliament would gladly place him in a state of 'affluence and comfort'. To this the Prince replied, vehemently, 'I never will marry! My resolution is taken on that subject. I have settled it with Frederick . . . Frederick will marry, and the Crown will descend to his children.'

It had long been the avowed ambition of the Hereditary Prince of Prussia, who succeeded his uncle Frederick the Great in August 1786 as Frederick William II, to marry his eldest daughter Frederica, of whom he was dotingly fond, to the Prince of Wales. Lord Dalrymple, the

British representative at the Court of Berlin, would have welcomed the alliance, partly because it would have strengthened the political connexion between the two countries which had been in some measure re-created when George III, in his capacity of Elector of Hanover, had joined the Fürstenbund, formed in 1785 by Frederick the Great to resist the alleged aggressive designs within the Empire of Emperor Joseph II. Dalrymple wrote to Lord Carmarthen, the Foreign Secretary: 'If the Prince of Wales has no other view in marriage but domestic happiness, I do not believe that he will find anywhere a woman more likely both from her merit and personal accomplishment, to contribute towards it.' He suggested that one of the conditions of such an alliance should be that the Hereditary Prince's eldest son (who succeeded his father in 1797 as Frederick William III) should marry one of the King's daughters, of whom the Princess Royal, Augusta and perhaps the fifteen-year-old Elizabeth were now old enough to be seriously considered. But, to this double-marriage project there seemed to be one serious obstacle. It was believed (wrongly, as the event showed) that the Hereditary Prince intended to marry his eldest son to the only daughter of the Stadholder, William V, Prince of Orange. And Dalrymple might well have felt it necessary to abandon the whole idea had he known that in December 1785 the Prince of Wales was already married—to Mrs. Fitzherbert. The King would have welcomed the match with Princess Frederica and Parliament would willingly have paid the Prince's debts, but the Prince was then determined to marry no one but his beloved Maria, who, whilst she was abroad, heard that a marriage was being suggested between the Prince and the fifteen-year-old Princess Frederica of the United Netherlands. (Five years later she married the Duke of Brunswick's son Charles, whose sister Caroline was destined to become the wife of the Prince of Wales.)

The Prince would have followed Mrs. Fitzherbert to the Continent in July 1784 but could not leave the country without his father's permission, and this permission the King, who knew well enough the hollowness of the pretext that his son wished to go abroad in order to cut down his expenditure, naturally withheld. The Prince had no other resource than to bombard her with long, impassioned letters in which he repeatedly threatened to end his life unless she returned to England to marry him. The Duke of Orleans was said to have been the medium of this remarkable correspondence. 'The speed of the couriers exciting the suspicion of the French Government, three of them were at different times put into prison. Wrought upon and fearful, from the past, of the desperation of the Prince, she consented, formally and deliberately, to promise she would never marry any other person; and lastly she was induced to return to England and to agree to become his wife, on those conditions which satisfied her own conscience, though she could have no legal claim to be the wife of the Prince.' Lord Holland's account of the state of the Prince's mind, communicated to him by Mrs. Fox, is probably not excessively exaggerated. 'He cried by the hour . . . he testified to the sincerity and violence of his passion and his despair by the most extravagant expressions and actions, rolling on the floor, striking his forehead, tearing his hair, falling into hysterics, and swearing that he would abandon the country, forego the Crown, sell his jewels and plate, and scrape together a competence to fly with the object of his affections to America'—where, presumably, he could defraud his creditors of a quarter of a million.

A final letter, extending to forty-two pages, brought Mrs. Fitzherbert to terms. She returned to London early in December, and the marriage took place, in the greatest secrecy behind locked doors, at her house in Park Street, in the evening of the 15th. After some difficulty an Anglican clergyman had been found, reckless enough to perform the ceremony— the Rev. Robert Burt, who was brought out of the Fleet Prison. His debts, amounting to £500, were paid; he was appointed one of the Prince's chaplains and was promised a bishopric when the Prince succeeded to the throne. (But this ultimate reward he never received: he died in 1791 at the age of thirty-five, as Vicar of Twickenham, twenty years before the Prince was in a position to redeem *post obits* of this sort.) After the conclusion of the ceremony (and the clergyman confessed on his deathbed to having performed it) the bride's uncle, Henry Errington, and her brother, John Smythe, signed as witnesses the certificate which the Prince himself wrote out. Then he handed it over to her for her signature, and told her to keep it to her dying day. The names of the witnesses were cut out by Mrs. Fitzherbert herself, to save them from the peril of the law, when, at Queen Caroline's trial in 1820 Brougham threatened to summon her as a witness.[1] Concluded in defiance of the Royal Marriage Act of 1772, the marriage was illegal, though canonically valid, and such children as there were were legitimate in Canon Law though illegitimate by the law of England. After the ceremony the couple set off on their short honeymoon to Ormeley Lodge, on Ham Common, near Richmond, their carriage breaking down on the way.

All references to her children were subsequently destroyed, and their number remains conjectural. It has been thought that her adopted niece, Marianne Smythe, was in reality her own child (though she may have been her brother John's illegitimate daughter); and that there was a son too.

That some sort of ceremony had taken place was soon widely believed. Sir Gilbert Elliot heard that a Catholic priest had officiated, that Mrs.

1. The marriage certificate, cut by Mrs. Fitzherbert, is reproduced as the frontispiece to this book.

Fitzherbert was to be given £6,000 a year for life and to be created a Duchess. George Hardinge, the Queen's Solicitor-General, was saying at Court in April 1786 that the Prince's marriage would occasion civil war. At the end of April 1787 Fox declared in Parliament, by authority from the Prince, that there was not the smallest foundation of any sort for the story of the marriage. 'Rolle hinted at the distinction between a *legal* marriage and some ceremony that might satisfy the consciences of some persons, but Fox rejected any such distinction, and asserted again that there never had been the slightest ground for this slander, either legally or illegally, and, in a word, denied positively from the Prince himself the whole of this slander, in words so strong and so unqualified that we must believe him.' 'I own', added Sir Gilbert Elliot, 'I was much rejoiced to hear this story so completely contradicted, as I thought it both mischievous in the highest degree to the country, and in the same degree dishonourable to the Prince.' He might well have added that the marriage story was mischievous in the highest degree to the prospects of the Whig Opposition. If the Prince had married he had forfeited his right to the succession to the Crown. He would no longer have been in a position ultimately to make his friend Fox Prime Minister.

Fox was quickly made aware that the Prince had misled him. After making his statement in the Commons he met Errington in St. James's Street, and was bluntly told, 'You have been misinformed. I was present at the marriage!' Mrs. Fitzherbert never forgave Fox for thus damaging her reputation, and declined to become a Duchess when Fox and his friends came into office in 1806.

133   THE PRINCE OF WALES TO THE KING

Carlton House, 5 Jan. 1785
Several months have now elapsed since your Majesty encouraged me to hope that you might releive me [*sic*] from my present very unpleasant situation by having express'd a wish that an account of my debts should be submitted to your consideration, which would have taken effect much earlier had it been in my power to have obtain'd a sufficiently exact amount of them.

Your Majesty may conceive how sensibly I regret the largeness of the sum, but I will hope that you may consider that the chief part of the debt I have incurred has been in objects which, in general, have been deemed necessary, & which from their nature cannot be again repeated. I mean of course the expences I have been at in making my house more adapted to the residence of a Prince of Wales. I hope your Majesty will do me the justice to believe that I shall feel the obligation of any releif

175

[*sic*] from your hands as gratefully & as naturally as I ought to do, & I flatter myself your Majesty will not be offended at the mode I have taken of laying this matter before you, & that you will allow me to have the honor of subscribing myself with all possible respect [etc.].   (41835, also 31854 and 31896)

134   THE EARL OF AILESBURY TO SIR HENRY COSBY

London, 10 Mar. 1785

I am much obliged to you for your polite letter & particularly for having represented my conduct upon a certain delicate occasion so favourably to his Highness the Nabob of Arcot & the Carnatic to whom I beg you to express better than I have been able to do the grateful sense I have of his Highness's very gracious attention to me by a letter which I have shewn their Majesties, to whose tender feelings for the sufferings described by his Highness I cannot do sufficient justice. I am very thankful to you for your intended civilities to Lt Anstey as I shall be for any shewn Lt Walker[1], who is patronis'd by the Queen & is a very deserving young gentleman of the 73d Regiment. I was rejoiced to hear of your safe arrival in India & my daughters join me in every good wish to you & Miss Cosby. I shall be entertain'd & instructed by the accounts you favour me with from Madrass & I shall be certain of their being *authentic* which it is difficult to get about Indian affairs.[2]   (38106)

135   THE KING TO LORD SOUTHAMPTON [copy]

Queen's House, 13 Mar. 1785

Lord Southampton having on the 5th Jany. delivered to me a letter from the Prince of Wales inclosing what he calls the state of his debts, which was merely saying they amounted to £150,000, though in the Prince's letter to Lord Southampton of the 17th of Septr. he directed Colonel Hotham to make out as near a state as he could of his debts; I have till

1. Lieutenant-General Sir George Townshend Walker (1764–1842). Captain, 1791; Lieutenant-Colonel, 1798; Major-General, 1811. K.C.B., 1815. Lieutenant-General, 1821; Commander-in-Chief at Madras, 1826–31. Baronet, 1835.

2. The letter was endorsed: 'Sir Henry Cosby being in command of a considerable detachment of the Madras army at the time he rec'd the foregoing letter, immediately appointed Lt Walker mention'd therein, as patronised by her Majesty, upon his Staff, and is the present Majr Genl Sir George Walker.'

The Duke and Duchess of Cumberland,
and her sister Lady Elizabeth Luttrell
by Gainsborough 1784

On Tuesday the 8th of July 1784 Mr Bouverie and Mr Onslow came to me & told me the Prince of Wales had run himself thro' the body & declar'd he wd tear open his bandages unless I wd accompany Mrs Fitzherbert to him. We went there & she promis'd to marry him — at her return but she conceives as such as —

that promises obtain'd in such a manner are entirely void.

G Devonshire

M Fitzherbert

9th of July 1784

Georgiana, Duchess of Devonshire's Memorandum, signed by Mrs Fitzherbert

now been waiting for such a statement, but none being arrived, I have wrote the inclosed to the Prince of Wales which I desire may be deliver'd to him. (16375)

[Enclosure] THE KING'S MESSAGE TO THE PRINCE OF WALES

Queen's House, 13 Mar. 1785
Private

On the 25th Augt. last the Prince of Wales gave me notice of his resolution to leave the Kingdom, driven to it, as he suggested, by his necessities. A project so replete with mischief and disgrace of course drew from me a peremptory command that he should not quit the Kingdom without my express leave, together with a recommendation of some plan for retrenchment and payment of his debts by a reserve out of his revenues.

On understanding afterwards that the Prince considered what had passed as an implied application to me for the payment of his debts, and that although he thought such a request made to me directly would lay him under no obligation to any other person, he would not make it, but rather persist in his resolution; I sent him word that if he had any application to make on account of his debts he ought to state the amount for my consideration, and the security against future excesses, without which it would be impossible for me to engage at all in the business.

On the 17th Sept. the Prince of Wales ordered Colonel Hotham to make out as near a state as he could of his debts to be transmitted to me, and said he should postpone his departure till he was acquainted with my intentions. At the end of four months, on the 5th Jany., I received from the Prince the following note (sum total of my debts £150,000), and to this moment, I have received no farther particulars, nor any sort of explanation. This which he calls a state of his debts was enclosed in a letter where he refers the chief part of that sum to refitting Carlton House, for which purpose as well as for enabling him to begin his Establishment and discharge such debts as he had then contracted, the sum of £60,000 was allowed him. He had at the same time an annual income assigned him of £50,000 together with the Dutchy of Cornwall. This was more than any of his predecessors unmarried had ever enjoyed; yet his expences appear to have been nearly four times his income.

Upon this I forbear to make any reflection; the impossibility of continuing such profusion will strike his own good sense, and the impropriety of extorting such supplies, if that were possible, from the good will of an affectionate country, will equally strike his generosity. In the confidence that these must be his feelings, I should anxiously adopt his wishes to be delivered by any practicable mode from a situation so

177

mortifying to himself and so distressing to the honourable support due to his rank.

But whether I can take any measure for this purpose consistent with his credit and my own, or what those measures could be, cannot be decided without the fullest examination into the source and extent of the evil. An exact statement of his expenditure, and the management under which it has issued, is the ground on which any plan must be conceived for establishing a stricter œconomy, and for creating a security fit to be relied on against [future excesses]. Without these, the payment of his present debts would be of little avail; instead of satisfying his honour, it would only compromise it with other parties, and involve him deeper by raising a new credit liable to be abused in the same manner. Such a statement is equally necessary for examining the nature and extent of the Prince of Wales's engagements; for it would be an unpromising commencement of reform, if debts supposed to be contracted in a state of mismanagement and dissipation beyond any visible fund for payment or any probable expectation of such a fund, should be taken on general suggestion only, without full investigation.

This examination is also necessary to distinguish the preference and priority of payment which may be due to them; as after every reduction which may be effected, their amount must probably require on any possible supposition some tract of time to discharge them. (41836–7, and 31864)

136 THE PRINCE OF WALES TO THE KING [copy]

Carlton House, 14 Mar. 1785
Sir, I seize the earliest opportunity of returning your Majesty my most grateful thanks for your gracious letter and have desired Lord Southampton to wait upon your Majesty with the particulars of the estimate I had the honour of sending your Majesty some time ago, and which I should already have done had I not understood that it was the amount only your Majesty wished to receive. I have the honour to subscribe myself with all possible respect [etc.]. (16377, 31866 and 41838)

137 THE KING'S MESSAGE TO THE PRINCE OF WALES

Queen's House, 21 Mar. 1785
The estimate delivered to the Prince of Wales by Colonel Hotham 27th October 1784 by no means answers what the paper delivered by Lord

178

Southampton on the 13ᵗʰ of March 1785 from the King to the Prince of Wales requires. Indeed it shews there are debts, but no ways points out that the works at Carlton House have been conducted with oeconomy, that what is still to be compleated is void of profuseness, nor it is any explanation of the sums borrowed and for what purposes. Besides there is no plan for reduction of expences, to avoid future embarassments, and to establish a reserve for gradually clearing the inordinate debts that have been permitted to exceed every reasonable hope of being discharged.   (31867 and 16489)

138   THE KING TO THE PRINCE OF WALES[1]

Windsor, 29 Mar. 1785
The Prince of Wales is sufficiently aware that his letter of the 14th Mar. is by no means a satisfactory or suitable answer to my proposal of the 13th.

It contains a paper, dated the 27 Octʳ 84, intitled, an Estimate of Debts and Engagements the first being the amount of debts already contracted, £58,440; the second of debts, he is still resolved to contract, £63,850; in all £122,293. This paper, it should seem, was drawn out in consequence of the Prince's orders to Col. Hotham of 17 Septʳ; of wh. he gave me notice by Ld. Southampton on that day. On the 5th of Jaⁿ the P. of W. had represented the gross amount of his debts to be £150,000, without further explanation.

By way of further explanation, the above mentioned paper is sent me, with a note subjoined to it, of money borrowed on the 22 Decʳ 84, £25,000; wh. added to the former sums, makes £147,293.

The paper does not purport an account of his present debts; nor even mention the names of his creditors, the conditions of loan, or other particulars respecting the nature of his engagement; for wh., in the last article of £15,000, Col. Hotham makes this apology, *that his R. H. has not yet been*

1. The letter is in *The Later Correspondence of George III* (Cambridge University Press, 1962), edited by A. Aspinall, i.147. The letter here printed is the Lord Chancellor's draft, with Pitt's marginal emendations and comments.

pleased to inform him thereof. In short, it corresponds so little with the avowed object of my enquiry, that these particulars would not be worth observing, if they did not derive some importance from an assertion in the P. of W.'s letter of the 23 of Mar., that EVERYTHING, *which either he or Col. Hotham knows, concerning every debt, has already been submitted to me.*

That letter proceeds to insist on the impossibility of making any abatement of his income; *as it* [is] *with the greatest difficulty, that he is able to go on with it at present.* ˣ(*Considering, that his expenses exceed treble the amount of his present income, I can only understand this, as an express declaration, that he will suffer no bounds to be set to his profusion. If this will admit of qualification, the P. of W. would do well to explain it.*)

(*Upon this he infers,*) ⋌ that I find myself unable to assist him *so far as I could wish ;* and thereupon, expressly declining all further communication upon the business, he concludes with a menace to run away from his situation, in direct defiance of the solemn injunction, I have laid upon him, not to leave the realm without my express permission.

(*Upon the menace to disgrace himself, I shall only observe, that it is but an awkward and inefficient means to attain any purpose, particularly an improper one.* But) the immediate consequences of executing such a threat (if that step were really to be taken) both to the P. himself, and to any person who might bear a part in it, make it of some importance, that ⋌ (*even*) this correspondence should be rightly understood.

I have hitherto said nothing either of my power or intention to assist in delivering the Prince of Wales from the embarrassments, into which he is daily drawing himself; nor of the proportion, in which his present means ought to be applied to that end. But I have frequently said, and I now repeat, that my concurrence in any plan for that purpose must depend on its being formed with sufficient regard both to his honour and mine. It

ˣ *Perhaps this may without impropriety be omitted and*

⋋ *from my having stated to him the necessity of his adopting some plan of retrenchment*

This sentence also may perhaps be omitted.

⋋ *whatever has passed in*

is, in my judgement, essential to both, ⋏ that some scheme of oeconomy should be settled for reducing his expense within a certain measure; and that the observance of it should be secured, as far as the nature of the occasion will permit. To reform the profusion of his present expenditure, that expenditure and the management, under which it has issued, must be examined. The excesses in one must be retrenched, the abuses in the other corrected, and a settled application of his income must be made to a measured rate to necessary expense. This must be further secured by making his servants responsible, in their several departments, for their diligence and fidelity in the observance of it. To this end, their accounts should be submitted to due examination from time to time. That no future debts may be contracted (*beyond the sphere of this scheme*,) the examination and payment of the present debts should be so ordered, as to cut off all temptation to borrow, or lend in an improper manner.

⋏ *that considerable expence should not either now or hereafter be entailed on the public, on this account,*

This, or some other plan, equally adapted to the avowed principles, upon which ⋏ *I am inclined to* interpose, must be adopted. For it is extreamly obvious, that to advance £150,000, and leave things as they are, would only reproduce the same situation a year or two hence, with additional reproach to the wisdom and honour of all parties concerned. To look into the detail of pocket expenses is no part of this object. ⋏ (*And, that*) no articles material to the avowed principles of this inquiry can be buried under loose denominations, ⋏ (*I shall readily trust to the good sense and honour of the gentlemen, from whom I expect the explanation.*) (P.R.O., Wm. Dacres Adams MSS.)

⋏ *alone I can ever*

⋏ *On the other hand it is plain that*

⋏ *without defeating altogether the object proposed*

139 LORD SOUTHAMPTON TO THE PRINCE OF WALES

30 Mar. 1785

I beg leave to express my thanks for the very gracious communication of the contents of the King's letter, which I had not seen, H.M. having sent it seal'd up. Without seeing the letter, I cannot so well judge of

181

the endeavours to oblige your Royal Highness to yield in certain points. If they are proposals they remain open to your answer, & I should suppose them coupled with some indications of a disposition to pay debts; should that be the case, I humbly think your Royal Highnesses hastening your departure would not be a prudent measure. May I be allowed to express a wish that you would postpone your plan either until you have seen the utmost the K. intends doing towards assisting you, or that your R.H. may obtain his M. consent to your leaving the country; and that you would not break off a negotiation which his M. seems to have renew'd notwithstanding your last letter, which certainly left him at liberty to talk no further about debts. (31879)

140 PRINCE WILLIAM TO THE PRINCE OF WALES

Hanover, 1 Apr. 1785
It is a very long time since I have wrote you a single line. I did not like to do it, for what should I say? My amours . . . can be no amusement to a young man in the great pleasures of London nor can my private disputes with Budé amuse you; in short, Hanover is a dull place & very much given to scandal, which I unfortunately feel most extremely. The noblesse here are haughty and proud; my free tongue with my English oaths would not go down with the *Vons*, so I left them short there & associated myself with the second class; people in England would receive them everywhere, but the German etiquette does not allow it. However, I was determined to amuse myself; I frequented their houses & forsook the Barons, which gave great offence in this town. Now as I do not care what people say about me I laughed at the envious fools of the first class & lived in a very agreeable society. The Hanoverian rascals were not content with abusing me here, but they made the blasted spies write false accounts to the King, from whom I have lately received a most serious & alarming letter. He says that if I do not alter my conduct he will put one of my younger brothers over my head in my profession. What an event! I am thus ruined in my father's opinion by the damned Hanoverian rascals. I am sure, dear brother, you will always stand my friend & I hope to God I shall ever prove grateful to you. One of the greatest crimes is ingratitude & cannot be allowed in the family of Brunswick. So far I am a German that I glory in being sprung from that illustrious House & so long as I live I hope never to dishonour it by any vice. These same sentiments will make me quit the Navy directly if I find the King puts anybody over my head & not remain a disgrace to my profession, like the Duke of Cumberland[1]. I have myself wrote to their

1. The Duke of Cumberland had entered the Navy in 1768, becoming Rear-Admiral, 1769; Vice-Admiral, 1770, and Admiral, 1778.

Majesties & have made Frederick interpose with the King in order to have my situation changed. I beseech you to speak to the Queen upon the subject, for you know well we two are our mother's favourites, & let me have an answer by the return of the messenger.

I take Freytag to be one of the spies; this son of a bitch has taken a disliking to your regiment of Light Dragoons in this service on account of your being upon bad terms with the King.[1] He desired the Queen to send her regiment a neat sett of instruments with her name on them. I am the protector of your regiment on account of my intimacy with you & of my antipathy for that rascal. I wish you would send them a sett of instruments in black, ornamented in silver with P.W., & I will give them in your name to the regiment.

I beg you will give Dalrymple my compliments & tell him I will write this day senight.   (44674–5)

141   THE PRINCE OF WALES TO THE KING

Carlton House, 7 Apr. 1784 [1785]

I am very much concerned that your Majesty continues to persist in wishing me to adopt a plan wh. I have all along thought & think still more from having reflected upon it farther perfectly impracticable, I mean the reducing my expences while my residence is in England.

As to the particulars of the account which I had the honor of transmitting to your Majesty, I still must beg with submission to repeat yt. I have delivered in not only ev'ry item I know of, but that they have been made out in the most explicit manner I was able.

The part of the statement I conceive your Majesty principally alludes to, is to that of the £25,000 I borrowed. It was impossible for me to communicate either to Colonel Hotham or anybody else the names of the people who advance'd me this money, & feeling the obligations I am under towards them I cannot abuse the confidence they have placed in me by exposing their names upon this or any future occasion.

Before I conclude I beg leave to assure your Majesty that the plan I have laid down for myself has not been formed with views of gratifying any desire I might have of seeing foreign countries, but simply & honorably to clear myself from the confin'd, embarrassing & truly improper situation I at present feel myself in.   (41810–1 and 31872)

1. Prince Edward too disliked Freytag. He wrote (24 May 1788): 'Our worthy Commander-in-Chief, according to my last letters, is also amazingly fallen off, and seems to draw near to the conclusion of his days. Alas! None will feel his loss as much as me, for in him I lose the best of my friends, and the man who has constantly taken my part; and Heaven knows what I have to expect from the man whom we all must believe will be his sucessor, Genl. F——g.' (45758)

Queen's House, 12 Apr. 1785

While the Prince of Wales persists in rejecting *as perfectly impracticable any plan to reduce his expences during his residence in England*, that determination renders the payment of his present debts an object of no importance to his future happiness or honour.

Whenever the Prince of Wales changes his mind so far as to look upon a plan for measured expence and settled oeconomy as an article of conduct which he owes both to himself and to his country, it will be time enough to take up the consideration of his present debts, of none of which any particular explanation has yet been given, but one part of which to the amount of £25,000 the Prince describes as debts which it would not be honourable to his creditors to avow.

Upon the Prince of Wales's plan, as he terms it, *simply and honourably to clear himself from his present situation*, I shall only refer it to himself to reconsider the whole force and extent of that phrase. It requires looking but a little way forward to foresee how much he may risk of his present situation, the moment he should act on such an idea as that of leaving the kingdom against my express command. (16510 and 16499–500 [draft by Pitt])

143 THE PRINCE OF WALES TO THE HONOURABLE HUGH SEYMOUR–CONWAY

Newmarket, Monday night, 12, 18 Apr. 1785

My dearest Hugh, I must absolutely dine *tête a tête* with you tomorrow as I have very particular business of consequence to talk over with you. I shall be in Town so as to dine punctually at six, or a little before six o'clock, with you. Pray do not take any notice to any living creature of my having written to you to tell you yt. I was coming to London, tho' you may perhaps hear it from some other quarter or other. I write to Bouverie by the same messenger, but not for the communication of the same business as to you.

Adieu, my dearest friend, beleive me even most truly & affectionately yours.

P.S. I find, my dear Hugh, I have written to you upon a half sheet of paper instead of a whole one. I hope you will excuse the great incivility, but I am really to[o] *Georgelike*, alias lazy, to write it over again. My best compliments to Jacko & George.[1] (Ragley MSS.)

1. Presumably Hugh's brother (1763–1848). 'Jacko' must have been a pet name.

Hanover, 7 June 1785

I write these lines to return you many thanks for the very handsome present which you was so good as to send me by Goldsworthy[2]; indeed it is most beautiful. I find Edward most exceedingly grown and improved in every respect. His figure is infinitely better than ever could have been expected when I left England.

News you cannot expect from us here unless it is that we are in dayly expectation of the Emperor seizing upon Bavaria.[3] His Imperial Majesty seems to have a wonderful mind to swallow up that country. I will not trouble you longer with the politicks of this country which will not, I believe, amuse you much. There is another subject upon which I should be very glad to write to you but I do not think it safe to mention it in this letter which goes by the post. I shall however take the very first opportunity of writing very fully to you about it.

I will not tresspass longer upon your leisure and shall therefore conclude by assuring you how sincerely I am ever [etc.]. (43719–20)

145 LETTERS FROM THE PRINCE OF WALES TO THE DUKE OF YORK

15 June 1785

I am desir'd by the Duchess of Devonshire to recommend to your notice Mr. Beddingfield, who will have ye honor of delivering this to you. I know nothing of him personally myself except yt. he has certificates he wished to shew you from several Generals, of his having serv'd remarkably well. (43724)

Carlton House, 22 June 1785

I received yr. last kind letter on Friday last. I cannot express to you how anxious I am to hear from you what business of consequence it is you want to talk over with me. Beleive me, there is nothing you can wish me

1. Prince Frederick was created Duke of York on 27 November 1784.

2. Colonel Philip Goldsworthy (c.1738–1801), the King's Aide-de-camp. Colonel 1784; Lieutenant-General, 1799. M.P. for Wilton, 1785–8, and 1794–1801. He appears rather infrequently in the Royal correspondence, but on 14 April 1788 Princess Elizabeth referred to his suffering from gout. 'Indeed,' she added, 'I pity him most sincerely, for I cannot bear to hear people congratulated upon such a misfortune.'

3. His plan was to exchange the Austrian Netherlands for Bavaria. The Elector, Charles Theodore, agreed to give up Upper and Lower Bavaria, the Upper Palatinate, Neuburg, Sulzbach and Leuchtenberg in return for the whole of the Netherlands, except Namur and Luxemburg, but Frederick the Great led the opposition in the Empire to this grand design, and formed the *Fürstenbund* which compelled Joseph II to abandon it.

to do or attend to for you yt. I shall not be most anxious to execute to yr. satisfaction. I have also many affairs & much business I wish to talk over with you. I wish to God you cd. devise some method for our meeting; if you will settle any place where you think we can meet with any sort of convenience I will instantly come & join [you] wherever it is. My particular friend Colman (who has had ye. pleasure of being introduced to you last year at the Margrave of Anspach's[1]) will deliver this to you. Let me seize this opportunity of recommending to you for yr. protection his son who, I beleive, really is a very good & a very promising lad. Shd. it be in yr. power soon without breaking thro' any promises you may have bound yourself under to recommend him to the King for one of the first Ensigncies in the Guards, I shd. look upon myself, my dearest Frederick, as under very particular obligations to you. William has just sail'd.[2] I think he is a very good hearted boy, lively, spirited, perhaps a little too boisterous, poli, mais peu maniéré. I have not time to add anything more than to express how anxious & impatient I shall feel till I hear from you again, as I am excessively curious to know what it is you wish to say to me. And now Adieu, my dear Frederick, beleive me [etc.].

P.S. Pray excuse this scrawl as I am writing to you off the back of my travelling box as I am going to set off for Brighthelmstone.   (43725–6)

Carlton House, 20 July 1785
It was not in my power to write to you by my friend Lord Cornwallis, being prevented by business of the utmost consequence to me & wh. I will inform you of by letter very soon.[3] My reason for writing to you at present is to recommend in the strongest manner possible to you a particular intimate friend of mine, Frederick St. John, Lord Bolin-

1. Christian, Margrave of Brandenburg-Anspach (1736–1806), who sold his Principality to the King of Prussia, and settled in England at Brandenburg House, Hammersmith. He married, as his second wife, at Lisbon (13 October 1791), sixteen days after the death of her first husband, the 6th Lord Craven, Elizabeth (1750–1828), daughter of the 4th Earl of Berkeley, and she became well known in London society as the Margravine of Anspach.

2. On account of the impropriety of his conduct William was informed in May that he was to quit Hanover and to be sent to sea again. He was very happy to leave 'that damned country'.

3. In the summer Cornwallis was invited to attend the Prussian military review, and the Government asked him unofficially to confer with the Prussian King, Frederick the Great, on the state of Europe. Cornwallis's account of his audience on 17 September is in Ross, *Cornwallis Correspondence*, i.208. He described the Duke of York as having 'a great deal of good nature and a very good heart'. He added: 'His military ideas are those of a wild boy of the Guards, the uniforms and promotions of that corps, about which he is vehement to excess. One cannot, however, help loving him. . . . There is no chance of any good coming but by his being kept abroad and of the English being kept from him' (*ibid.*, i.211).

broke's second son[1]. I am sure when you are well acquainted with him you will like him excessively, you will find him uncommonly gentlemanlike & well-bred & degree of naiveté in his character yt. really is quite charming; in short I think he is one of the most aimiable young men I know.

Adieu my dearest Frederick, I have not time to add anything more except to assure you how truly I ever shall be [etc.]. (43734)

146 LETTERS FROM THE DUKE OF YORK TO THE PRINCE OF WALES, AND A REPLY

Osnabruck, 25 July 1785

I take the opportunity of Freemantle's return to England to return you many thanks for your kind and affectionate letter by Colman. You may easily conceive how happy it would make me to do anything to please you. As therefore there is at present an Ensigncy in the Coldstreams to be given away by the death of Colonel Broderick[2], I have written to General Lyster[3], that if the King has not given it already away to one of his Pages, which I am affraid of, he should recommend Mr. Colman for it. I am under a prior promise to Lake that as soon as Mr. Frank is old enough for a Commission, I am to have him. This vacancy however he is too young.

I had meant by this opportunity to have wrote to you about many things but I have not time enough. I must therefore wait for some other safe occasion. I shall set out at the latter end of next week for Silesia in order to be present at the King of Prussia's review of his troops there. He has formed this year one camp of them all so that we shall see at least betwixt sixty and seventy thousand men together. I shall as soon as the camp is over make a tour all through Silesia and Lusatia in order to see the different Prussian fortresses, after which I shall go to Berlin

1. Frederick, 2nd Viscount Bolingbroke (1734–87), who succeeded his famous uncle, the 1st Viscount, in 1751, was a Lord of the Bedchamber, 1762–5 and 1768–80. He married (1757) Lady Diana Spencer, daughter of Charles, Duke of Marlborough. (His second son, Frederick St. John (1765–1844), became a General. Ensign, 1779; Lieutenant, 1780; Captain, 1780; Major, 1783; Lieutenant-Colonel, 1791; Colonel, 1795; Major-General, 1798; Lieutenant-General, 1805; General, 1814. He served in Ireland during the Rebellion and with Lake against the Marathas. He was M.P. for Oxford City, 1818–20.) Lord Bolingbroke and his two sons were jointly in receipt of a secret pension of £1,200 a year. It was suggested in 1782 that if the pension was transferred to the public list, it would not have to appear in Lord Bolingbroke's name, 'otherwise his creditors would seize it'.

2. Henry Brodrick, third son of George, 3rd Viscount Midleton. He was a Lieutenant-Colonel in the 2nd Foot Guards, and died at Lisbon in June.

3. Lieutenant-General Henry Lister, of the 2nd Foot Guards. He died in November.

and stay there till the autumn manoeuvres at Potsdam, from whence I shall return back to Hannover.

Adieu, dear brother, you will have had enough of this scrawl. I shall therefore conclude by repeating how sincerely I am [etc.].   (43735–6)

FROM THE PRINCE OF WALES

Brighton, 2 Aug. 1785

Major Symes[1] will deliver this to you. He has plagu'd me to death to recommend him to you. He is a Gentleman Usher in my family, & I know little or nothing at all of him. He comes with Col. Musgrave[2], Aid de Camp to the King, & whose merit as an Officer is universally known. Adieu.   (43738)

THE DUKE OF YORK'S REPLY

Hanover, 5 Oct. 1785

I take the opportunity of Grenville's going to England to return you many thanks for your two kind letters by Colonel Sims and Mr. Beding-field. They appear both of them very good kind of people, particularly Sims, who seems very fond [of] and very attentive to his profession. I am just returned from my expedition into Silesia, from whence I went to Berlin to see the autumn manoeuvres. The manner in which I was treated by the King and the Prince of Prussia was more flattering than I can possibly express. The troops are astonishingly fine, particularly the Cavalry. In Silesia I saw seventy five squadrons together. They charged in two lines en muraille five and thirty in the first and forty in the second line; it succeeded perfectly and was the finest sight I ever saw in my life.[3] But enough of military matters, least you should accuse me of being Prussian mad. There are other subjects upon which my affection for you would make me wish to touch but as, when I mentioned them to you, you did not appear to take the hint, I suppose you do not wish me to do it. I shall therefore conclude by repeating to you how sincerely I am [etc.].

P.S. Pray write often. You may be sure I shall be very exact in answering.   (43749–50)

1. Lieutenant-Colonel Richard Symes of the 52nd Foot. Lieutenant-Colonel, 1782.

2. Thomas Musgrave; Colonel, 1782.

3. Cornwallis's opinion was very different. The manœuvres 'were such as the worst General in England would be hooted at for practising; two lines coming up within six yards of one another, and firing in one another's faces till they had no ammunition left: nothing could be more ridiculous' (Ross, *Cornwallis Correspondence*, i.212).

Brighton, 10 a.m., Thursday, 13 Oct. 1785

As this is the last day yt. the whole of the present party will be able to meet in this place, I flatter myself you will allow me to expect ye pleasure of yours & Lady Beauchamp's company at dinner, & I hope to be able to make such a party as will be agreable to you. I trust too much to yr. goodness on every occasion not to excuse the liberty I take in asking you at so short a notice.   (Egerton MSS. 3262, f.3.)

148 THE PRINCE OF WALES TO MRS FITZHERBERT

3 Nov. 1785

I hardly know, *my dearest & only belov'd Maria*, how I am to begin this letter to you; such a train of extraordinary & wonderful events have happened lately (wh. at first created the greatest apprehensions & alarms in my bosom & since have tended to the facilitating & entire arrangement of our plan, so that nothing now is wanting but the arrival of my adored wife in this country to make me the happiest of men), that I can hardly persuade myself I have not been in a dream for these ten days past.

I shall now begin with endeavouring to give you as concise an account as I can of the most interesting & principal events, & wh. are most material for you to be inform'd of. However, before I enter entirely upon an account of the whole of this business I must beg leave to preface my narration with desiring you to observe when you have read this letter thro', whether my attachment to my Maria has ever varied even in the most trifling instance from the first moment I reveal'd my passion to her to the present period, & in the next place, when you are thoroughly acquainted with the train of events I am going to relate, whether my conduct has not been worthy of yt. attachment she express'd to me in

1. Francis Seymour-Conway (1743–1822), styled Viscount Beauchamp from 1750 to 1793, and Earl of Yarmouth, 1793–4, succeeded his father as 2nd Marquess of Hertford on 14 June 1794. M.P. [I.] for Lisburn, 1761–8; for Co. Antrim, 1768–94; for [G.B.] Lostwithiel, 1766–1768; for Orford, 1768–94. Chief Secretary to the Lord-Lieutenant of Ireland, 1765–6; a Lord of the Treasury, 1774–80; sent on an Embassy to Berlin and Vienna, 1793–4; Master of the Horse, 1804–6; Lord Chamberlain of the Household, 1812–21.

He married, as his second wife (1776), Isabella Anne (1760–1834), daughter of Charles, 9th Viscount Irvine [S.], and, later, the Prince's reputed mistress (until, in 1819, she was supplanted by Lady Conyngham). Wraxall wrote: 'Before he completed his 34th year he [Lord Beauchamp] had married two of the richest heiresses of high birth to be found in England. . . . The second had such a degree of beauty as is rarely bestowed upon woman; the empire which she maintains at this hour [1818] over the Regent . . . depending, however, from the first moment of its origin, more on intellectual than on corporeal qualities, and reposing principally on admiration or esteem' (*Memoirs* [1884], iv.138).

her last letter & of the consent she then gave me, & last of all, whether I have not acted in every circumstance yt. has lately happen'd most strictly up to the character of *her lover & of her husband*, titles I would not change for the possessions of the whole universe.

Immediately after the last letter I wrote to you we sent over to Holland & we receiv'd about a week ago the following answers to our questions, of wh. I have sent an exact copy inclos'd in this letter, but of wh. I shall take no notice at present, & not till very late in the course of this letter, as there are many other circumstances much more interesting to us wh. preeceded our receiving this answer from Holland, & wh. I am now going to enter upon.

A few days after I had written to you, a gentleman[1] (whose name I will make known to you when I see you), who had liv'd upon some sort of intimacy with me at Brighthelmstone & who really is a very gentlemanlike man, both in his disposition & manner, but to whom I had never ye. least idea of mentioning anything in the way of business, as we were walking out one morning together, ask'd me if I had never had any intention or desire of going abroad. I answer'd I had, & yt. I beleiv'd I shd. from the total ruin'd state of my affairs be oblig'd to put yt. plan soon in execution, & I added yt. as there was no secret in yt. I made no scruple of talking very openly of it. He lamented very much ye. reason wherefore I was to leave this country, but said he thought it might tend very much to my advantage & amusement. Here our conversation ended that day without going any further; however, I observed from yt. moment he more & more sought my society & particularly if he saw me either walking or riding alone. Some days after the conversation I have just been relating to you had pass'd, he began mentioning politicks to me & asking me my objections to the present Administration. I said it was too long & too old a story to be reviv'd, & in short yt. I had too many to be able to explain ym., yt. my aversion was rooted upon good grounds, & yt. it was not a little yt. cd. eradicate it. He then ask'd me if I had ever applied to the present Ministers about the arrangement of my affairs, & if I had not, why I had not. I told him that they had always slighted me upon every occasion & that I was above paying my court to any earthly being whatever, yt. I trusted I shd. be able to extricate myself as an honorable & honest man without the assistance of any one but my own. He then went on saying, but if the Ministers shd. be inclin'd to do what you cd. wish, wd. you feel yourself oblig'd to ym? I said, certainly, yes indeed, yt. I shd. look upon myself as a perfect madman was I to throw away an opportunity of extricating myself out of my difficulties, especial-

1. Hugh Elliot (1752–1830), the diplomatist, and Sir Gilbert Elliot's younger brother. Minister to Bavaria, 1774–6; Envoy to Prussia, 1777–82; Envoy to Denmark, 1783–9; Minister to Saxony, 1792–1802; Minister to Sicily, 1803–6; Governor of the Leeward Islands, 1809–13; Governor of Madras, 1814–20. See *Wraxall*, v.185–8.

ly if it was not at the expence of my honor, but yt. if the Ministers suppos'd yt. I shd. cringe to ym. in order to make ym. do it, or yt. after they had done it I shd. desert my old staunch friends, & throw all the support I cd. into ym., they were very much mistaken, for yt. I had rather be an indigent[1] independent man whose principles & honor wd. be respected than one wallowing in riches & affluence & upon whose integrity the slightest reflection might be cast; but enough, said I to him, has passed upon this subject: you are not acquainted & never cd. be from yr. situation with the present Ministers or with their views, & therefore cannot at all be a judge of how I am situated respecting them. How do you know yt?, said he immediately; know then yt. ye First Minister[2] is the person I know the best & yt. I respect ye most, as I beleive him to be a perfectly honorable & disinterested man. I then stopped him short & said yt. I thought it was very ungenerous of him to lead me on to find out what my sentiments were without previously acquainting me with the circumstance of his regard for the First Minister; however, yt. I was not in the least asham'd of my sentiments & yt. I had already & frequently express'd them in publick, yt. I beleiv'd & flatter'd myself everybody yt. had ever heard my name mention'd had heard ym. also. He said yt. they were sentiments yt. did me the greatest credit & honor & were worthy of yt. character for honor & integrity wh. he had always understood I gloried in. He then ask'd whether he might relate the conversation yt. had pass'd between us to the Minister. I absolutely refused yt., as I thought it wd. appear yt. I either wanted to insult him or to draw on some sort of a communication between us, neither of wh. I wish'd. There everything rested yt. day. However, ye. next morning he came & breakfasted with me & said yt. he cd. not help thinking over all night what had pass'd the preceeding day between us, & yt. it was a pity yt. something cd. not be done to set me at perfect liberty to shew me in the proper light I deserv'd to the people not only of my own country to whom I was the greatest glory possible, but to other European nations, for he was sure they wd. adore me whenever I came to be known by them, compliments & words that went in at one ear & out at ye. other. I detest flattery from the bottom of my soul & therefore prevented his going on any further as soon as I possibly cd. I said it was very true it might be a great pity yt. nothing cd. or wd. be done for me by the nation & by my father, but yt. as there was not the smallest probability of any plan being adopted upon my account yt. cd. give me the smallest satisfaction, & as I myself did not see the possibility of it, we had better talk no more upon yt. subject. He said he must beg my pardon but he must proceed a little further. He then began with putting ye. following question to me. If the Ministers shd. have form'd any plan, wd. you give it a patient hearing & consider it

1. 'man' follows, but is scored through.   2. Pitt.

191

well over? Stop, said I immediately, I shd. imagine from what you mention'd yesterday of yr. great regard to the First Minister yt. you are inform'd of his secrets wh. if you are determin'd to mention to me I shall certainly not keep, & therefore I will not hear ym. or else yt. you are employ'd by the Minister to sound me, neither of wh. will I admit of. I will have nothing to do with any underhand work nor will I lend my name to it, but if the Minister has anything to propose to me, let him speak out himself or let one of his emissaries, you or anyone else, speak out, as coming from him to me with his authority to lay any plan or plans he may wish'd [*sic*] to lay before me & I will give ym. a proper consideration, & I will then return him an answer when my resolution is taken without exposing him either to the world or to my father; in short, in order not to detain you too long, my Maria, before we come to what is most essential, he acknowledged yt. he came directly from ye. Minister to me, yt. there were two plans wh. had been thought over, ye. one arising from my father, the other from the Minister, but yt. ye. Minister was greatly offended with my father's conduct of late to him & yt. therefore as he had always wish'd to instill me with a good opinion of him, knowing that most likely in the common course of things one of these days I shd. be his Sovereign, he wish'd to adopt yt. plan yt. wd. be most agreable to me, relinquishing both his own plan & yt. form'd by my father, wd. I but let him know any one I had form'd myself before I sent it in to my father, yt. he might be able to back it with all his might & main. I said I was very much oblig'd to ye. Minister for this declar-ation but yt. I must entreat & insist yt. he did not put himself in the least in a perilous situation respecting my father upon my account, a man who neither had it in his power or his inclination to support him hereafter, for I once repeated yt. I cd. at no time alter my sentiments with respect to my own friends or my conduct towards them. He de-clared yt. this was very noble in me & that he shd. relate what had passed in conversation between him & me to the Minister, yt. he was only at present at liberty to say yt. there were two plans, as I have already said, the one arising from my father, ye. other from ye. Minister; yt. ye. Minister's plan was for my travelling, but of how or where he de-clar'd himself perfectly ignorant; yt. this plan was to be communicated to my father ye. next day by the Minister & yt. afterwards it was to be explain'd to him in order yt. he might communicate it to me; that as to my father's plan, he was perfectly in ye. dark. Now the plot will begin to thicken. I have been oblig'd to detain you, my Maria, thus long to shew you ye thorough good grounds I had to begin upon, & how entirely I have held thro'out the same candid, plain, firm line of conduct to the Minister, my father, & to thee; was I capable of acting otherwise in any one instance I shd. be unworthy of the character of your husband, a name I never will part with till I am unworthy of it, or till death shall tear me from thee. But to proceed. Ye next day I saw nothing of my man; however, the second day he came with a long face, ready made up for the purpose, saying he had a great deal to communicate to me yt. was of the utmost consequence; yt. he wish'd very much to have an hour's conversation with me if I cd. find a moment in the course of the day when we shd. not be interrupted, as what he had to say required a good deal of explanation & consideration. I immediately said, most undoubtedly, & yt. as I had always made it a maxim never to postpone business of consequence if I cd. possibly help it, I was ready to hear anything he had to say & wd. order that no one shd. be let in to interrupt us. He then began with saying yt. he had had a long conference with the Minister who had had a long conference with my father, & that if I wd. allow him he wd. relate as concisely as possible what he understood to have passed in these two different conferences respecting the two plans he had previously & antecedently mention'd some days before to me. I stopp'd him & said yt. if he wd. remember there was one plan, namely my father's, concerning wh. he said he was perfectly in the dark; he said he remain'd so still but he thought he cd. guess what was the drift of it. He then began with saying yt. ye. Minister, after having ask'd an audience, beg'd leave to open his plan to him, that my father said he was very ready to listen to any plan he had to propose to him, but yt. he had also a plan of his own to talk over. The Minister's plan wh. he then acquainted me with, was for me to travel for a certain time but under certain restrictions, & yt. any debts I might have shd. then be liquidated during my absence. My objections to this plan were only relative to ye. restrictions, such as yt. any man who had ever tasted liberty & ye. sweets of ease cd. never consent to any restraint. However, my objections to this plan were nothing I found, as my father had already stated his, & the principal of wh. was yt. there had been a report & an idea yt. some time back, a year or so, I had only wish'd to go abroad in order to marry an English lady whose name my father did not then recollect, & he gave the Minister leave to give yt. as a reason for his objecting to this proposal. I shall take no more notice of this plan or of my answer to it till I have told you what my father's plan was, wh. he desir'd might not be carried formally from him to me as a message, but plainly stated as having been mention'd by him to the Minister, & yt. whatever answer I made to it shd. be instantly carried back to him. Well then, this proposal was yt. provided I wd. marry the Prince of Orange's daughter[1] an immense increase of income with a perfect clearing of all debts.

You are too well acquainted with my heart, *my dearest wife*, & with its

1. Princess Frederica (1770-1819), the only daughter of William V (1748-1806), the Stadholder, married (1790), Charles, Hereditary Prince of Brunswick, the son of Charles William Ferdinand, Duke of Brunswick (1735-1806), and therefore became the Princess of Wales's sister-in-law.

193

way of thinking to suppose yt., had I been without any attachment whatever, I shd. have risked the sacrificing my happiness & liberty to any pecuniary or interested view, but being bound by all ye ties wh. love & honor can render forcible, wh. were confirm'd by the solemn vow I made unto you & unto Heaven in the most sacred manner & at the most aweful of moments, wh. was then register'd in the books of eternity, & since has been ratified as mutual by the consent you so lately have given, how cd. I act otherwise than by instantly rejecting a proposal so repugnant not only to everything yt. is both divine & human but to my own feelings. I therefore immediately said yt. I was excessively sensible of my father's goodness but as I had frequently declar'd my sentiments yt. I never shd. marry unless it was the woman I cd. prefer to all the world (for I did not hold marriage in such slight estimation as some people did), he must excuse me if I declin'd his offer, yt. as I understood it was his desire to marry my brother I begg'd yt. my declining to enter ye. holy state might not be ye. means of thrusting any bar or stop to what concern'd him; on ye. contrary yt. so far from wishing to impede the happiness of any one of my family I shd. always be the first in endeavouring to promote yt. of all my relations, but yt. I did not see why I was to sacrifice myself for ye. rest of the family. This was the answer I return'd to my father's proposal.

The gentleman then who brought these two proposals said yt. this was very well & very handsome on my part, but that my father was desirous of knowing whether I had any other reasons at ye. bottom than those wh. I had assign'd wh. stimulated me to decline this offer, as he had always thought yt. I shd. be inclin'd to refuse it; in short, whether if I went abroad my motive for so doing wd. not be in order to see you, & last of all whether my attachments being secured to you were not the reasons for my not accepting this proposal. It immediately struck me how much persecution I shd. be able to save myself, & in the second place yt. the means were now thrown into my hands of acting in a manner I always wished to do, I mean candidly & openly, with the spirit yt. becomes not only a gentleman but a man, & last of all of publickly avowing, at least to my father, the sentiments wh. I profess to my beloved wife & wh. I glory in, & wh. I told thee, my Maria, thou shouldst one of these days see me do. Cd. I do better, can I, could I, ever enjoy a moment's happiness, a moment's joy, a moment's comfort without thee? No, thou art my life, my soul, my all, my everything. But enough; I will proceed. I said my father knew me well enough to be certain yt. no view upon earth, particularly an interested one, cd. ever tempt me was I disengaged from any[1] attachment whatever to risk my happiness or comfort in ye smallest instance, but yt. I cd. not but confess, since he was so inquisitive & so desirous of knowing ye. true state

1. 'particular' is at this point scored through.

of my affection, yt. I was attach'd for life & had long been so to the most amiable of women, yt. nothing now cd. alter either my sentiments respecting her or my affection for her; yt. I assur'd him had yt. not been in ye case I shd. have return'd the same answer to the proposal, & yt. I flatter'd myself as I had been thus candid with him he wd. be equally candid & fair with me, & that he wd. therefore not in future press me to do what I never cd. comply with. Thus ended the conversation that day. However, I was greatly surpriz'd at seeing ye *gobetween* (a name I have coin'd just now) arrive two or three days after; he desir'd to say a few words in private. I instantly complied with his request & attended him into another room. He then said he was commissioned to ask me should I wish to go abroad, & if I did, whether any idea of a marriage with you was or would be my motive for travelling. I told him yt. those were questions wh. neither he nor anyone else, not even my father, had any right to ask. Now, Sir, said he, will you allow me to put another question to you wh. I think almost too indelicate to be ask'd you by anyone else but yr. father & almost too indelicate to be put to you in yr. situation by him: however, in order to be perfectly true to ye. trust I have undertaken of having ye. honor of waiting upon you, I cannot help asking it according to my orders, but as I flatter myself you think yt. tho' so entrusted & so commission'd I wd. do nothing yt. was dishonorable or what I conceiv'd contrary to yr. interest, I request of you not to answer ye. question unless you perfectly wish it, or think yt. you are oblig'd to answer it any way in ye world, except by saying I do not choose to answer it, or if you intend to answer it, I must beg of you to take time to consider well over what answer you intend to make. I have already declar'd to the Minister after some time hesitating whether I shd. come with such a question to you, yt. if I did I shd. first of all entreat & supplicate you not to answer this interrogation unless you entirely wish'd it, & yt. if you did I shd. desire you to take time to consider it thoroughly well over first before you returned any answer whatsoever. I told him yt. ye. question startled me a little at first as it was an extraordinary one, tho' not an unexpected one; however, yt. as I always acted but with one motive & upon the same grounds in everything, I wd. after præfacing yt. I thought such an interrogation perfectly unhandsome & unfair, return such an answer as I thought perfectly honorable, & yt. was "That what was done in this affair cd. not be undone". He begg'd me to explain myself further, but added at the same time yt. he had most fully got his answer. I then said yt. he might torture his brain to find anything more out for I wd. not answer him, but yt. if my father wanted to be inform'd of further particulars I was ready to satisfy him, but no one else. He then left me. However, he again return'd the next day & said he was order'd after having made pretty near ye. same apologies the preceeding day, to put ye. same question as he had the day before, to wh. I return'd the same answer, still assuring him yt. I was ready to give my father any further satisfaction. He then said yt. tho' none of ym. wanted to learn anything more, yt. they were perfectly satisfied, yt. they were thoroughly convinc'd I was married or at least they were certain from what I said yt. if I was not married (wh. they did not beleive to be ye. case) I shd. be soon, & yt. I never shd. marry any other woman but you. This was said with a sort of interrogating look, to wh. I bowed assent. Think not, my Maria, my beloved wife, yt. I have deceived ym. or mean to deceive ym. in the least by what I have said. No, I have look'd upon myself as married for above this year & half, ever since I made to thee & thou madst to me in the face of Heaven, a vow mutually to regard one another as man & wife, & never to belong to anyone else but to each other, & wh. vow thou hast so lately confirm'd by ye. consent thou hast given to *become mine*. Dost thou think, thou only beloved of my heart, yt. if it had been possible for thee to disregard such bonds, to have broken yr. vows & to have thrown yourself into the arms of another, first of all I neither cd. nor wd. have survived it, but supposing I cd. have born the seeing you in ye. arms of another, & yt. knowing you had broken thro' all ye. laws both human & divine, yt. yt. wd. have been a reason for my doing ye. same; no, because you have done wrong yt. is no excuse, no palliation to me for acting wrong. I have principles wh. I glory in, principles of honor & justice, from wh. I can at no time deviate; on the contrary, to wh. I must ever most steadfastly adhere, especially when they are strengthen'd by love & the consciousness of acting right. One more question before we parted did I ask ye. emissary yt. was then with me, & yt. was whether my father was very violent at ye. idea of my being married. He said no, yt. he had said what was decreed in Heaven cd. not be subverted on earth; in short, yt. ye. only way for my father now to act was entirely to connive at it, wh. he beleiv'd was his intention. There our meeting ended & nothing more has pass'd since except an intimation yt. something wd. be propos'd to me soon, as there was something in agitation wh. was not as yet brought to perfection but that it was nothing yt. cd. hurt my feelings by wishing me to sacrifice an amiable woman to whom I was so sincerely attach'd, & wh. they knew I shd. refuse. My information tells me it is quite of another kind & wh. I must explain to you for many good reasons.

Were I to marry a woman of any other nation but a German, such as a Princess of France or Spain, had I any children by such a marriage, they wd. not after my decease succeed to the German dominions. They cd. not at any time hereafter inherit ym. unless their mother was a German. Now then, my brother (who I begin by saying is the best freind I have in ye. world, & to whom I am more attach'd then to anything else upon ye. face of the earth excepting yourself) has always been my father's favorite & always has been treated as such, (tho' yt.

never made ye least alteration in my brother's conduct to me) I understand yt. it is my father's wish to marry him to the King of Prussia's great niece[1], a daughter of the Hereditary Prince of Prussia, or of Prince Ferdinand of Prussia[2], who are both the King's nephews, I do not know exactly to wh. of the two she is daughter, & yt. ye. proposal he intends to make to me is this: yt. as my children, if I have any by my marriage with you, cannot succeed after my demise to ye. Hanoverian territories by ye. German Law, yt. if I will consent to give up *my* succession, I mean by yt. all right in my person, shd. I survive him, to ye. Hanoverian dominions, & transfer it to my brother at his death in order to make him un meilleur parti, yt. he will then in yt. case be ready to do anything I chuse respecting you, such as either acknowledging you as my wife or anything else I may please. This my private authority tells me to be ye. case. I may be mistaken but I do not think it likely, & shd. yt. be ye. case I shall instantly subscribe to those terms, after having, yt. is to say, the proper assurances respecting you, for there is no sacrifice, *my beloved wife*, yt. I have not & will not make for thee; thou art a treasure to me I never can part with, & I never can go too far to testify yt. love wh. never can end but with my life. Such are the principal events yt. have passed as yet.

I must now proceed to tell you how I have conducted myself since, what has passed in an interview I have had with yr. Uncle[3]. I wrote to him instantly to come to me upon receiving the papers from Holland. However, upon all these other affairs happening I sent him another letter much more pressing, desiring to see him immediately, & we agreed to meet half way upon ye. road between Red Rice & London. The moment I saw him I put the papers respecting Holland into his hands, & when he had read them I then told him everything I related to you & insisted upon it he shd. name it to nobody but to your mother. I then explained to him yt. from the enquiries I had made, to be sure we might be married two years hence in Holland when I am 25 years of age, but then yr. situation wd. be just the same here or there as if married in England, yt. therefore a marriage in England, witness'd and attested in ye manner I will inform you of presently, was much more to be wish'd than a marriage abroad, yt. situated as I was & as yr. situation in either case whether married in Holland or England was exactly ye same, we did not conceive yt. that wd. make any difference to me of yr. sense &

1. The Hereditary Prince of Prussia (1744–97), who succeeded his uncle Frederick the Great as Frederick William II on 17 August 1786, had only one marriageable daughter at this time— Frederica (1767–1820), who married the Duke of York on 29 September 1791. Her sisters were born in 1774 and 1780 respectively.

2. Prince Ferdinand of Prussia (1730–1813) was Frederick the Great's brother, not nephew. His daughter Louisa (1770–1836) married (1796) Count von Radziwill (1775–1833).

3. Henry Errington, the brother of Mrs. Fitzherbert's mother, Mrs. Mary Smythe.

feeling, & yt. considering what had passed between us now upwards of eighteen months ago, & ye. consent you had so lately given, wh. caused me with reason to give ye. answer I have done, & ye manner in wh. yt. answer was taken, & ye. idea they have taken yt. we are perfectly married, wh. in reality we certainly are, yt. there was but one thing for us now to do, & yt. was to be married as soon as possible & yt. can only be done by yr. immediate return to this country, in wh. there wd. appear nothing particular as you have already declar'd yr. firm intention of so doing, & I beleive it was in yr. last letter to your mother, but not only in yt. letter but in several others; in short, ye. only thing for you to do is to set out for England almost ye very next moment after you receive this express, & to be married ye. very night of yr. arrival, & not to say a word either of ye day of yr. return or of our marriage to yr. family till it is over, as you will then be received by ym. all with open arms. This was yr. uncle's advice to me as man to man, to send ye. enclosed plan to you instantly by express & to make you follow it back to England as fast as possible, as ye. thing must now absolutely be done, ye sooner it was done under the present circumstances the better, as your family are acquainted with the consent you have given they wd. not be offended when they knew it was over, but rather be pleas'd with you for the delicacy of yr. not acquainting ym. with it till we were bound in due form to each other, in order yt. they might have it to say if ever they were called upon, that they knew such a thing was in agitation but they were not inform'd of its having taken place till after everything was over. All this passed in conversation with yr. uncle & a great deal more, wh. I cannot trust my memory with. However, I supp'd last night with yr. friend Lady Anne[1] with whom I had already talk'd a great deal respecting you, & finding she knew everything respecting our situation I made no scruple of talking over our affairs very freely with her. It has been ye. whole delight of my life for above these three weeks last past, as she has been with her sister almost every day during yt. time at my house in order to meet the Duke & Dss. of Cumberland, & we have by yt. means had constant opportunities of talking ye. subject over with each other. I related to her most circumstantially everything yt. is included in this letter as well what was relative to the proposals as to what past in conversation between yr. uncle & me, &, in short, everything I have gone thro' upon your account, & then ask'd her opinion what she thought you wd. do. Do, says she, she has nothing else to do but to act exactly as you have desir'd her. Were she not absolutely compel'd by the urgency of both your situations & biass'd by her affection (wh. she said she really

1. Lady Anne Lindsay (1750–1825) was the daughter of James, 5th Earl of Balcarres. In 1793 she married Andrew Barnard, and, when he was appointed Colonial Secretary to Lord Macartney, Governor of the Cape, she accompanied him to Cape Town, returning to England in 1807. When Mrs. Fitzherbert went abroad in July 1784 Lady Anne went with her.

beleiv'd to be very sincere) as well as what had previously passed eighteen months before between us, as the consent you had so lately given, she said yt. gratitude alone (from what she knew of ye. generosity of your disposition) to a man who had made every sacrifice upon earth for you & wd. if there had been as many more have made them all to you, wd. make you act in ye. manner I wish'd. As to the two former I said I had great reason to flatter myself, at least I hop'd so, with success, & if love was to ensure success I might then I beleiv'd be pretty certain of it, as no man ever has loved & does love woman as I have, & do, love thee. But as to ye. last reason she gave for yr. coming, I mean gratitude for the sacrifices yt. I have made to you, I denied having any right to claim any; you might have it but I had no right to claim any. It was true I had made many & great sacrifices to you, at least what ye. world wd. call so, but when I felt a delight, a pleasure yt. I had it in my power to testify my love & my attachment in so strong [a] manner yt. my principles led me to act right, & I had a pleasure in so doing, & ye. consciousness of being right after having acted in this manner, I thought I had no right whatever to claim any merit for acting in a manner yt. was most agreable to myself.

I shall say very little more before I put a conclusion to this volume, for a letter I cannot call it. Well, then, I thought it right & honorable by you as soon as I found what was my father's way of thinking upon this business to acquaint those of my family yt. I knew to be my friends, & yt. I cd. rely upon, & yt. happen'd to be just at the moment upon the spot, I mean the Duke & Dss. of Cumberland, with everything respecting my situation with you. They have behav'd in ye. handsomest manner possible, & tho' they had settled their departure for Tuesday next & have business of the utmost consequence of their own, they have said yt. if it was for my happiness they wd., if they possibly cd., postpone their journey till after ye. return of ye. courier from Paris with yr. answer, & yt. if you intend to follow very close they will endeavour to remain here in order to give a sanction by their presence to our happy tho' secret union. Everything will be done as private as possible; no one else besides the Duke & Dss. will be present unless it is the Duke & Dss. of Devonshire; in short, everything is settled. We want nothing but yr. arrival.

When Hunter[1] returns, if he brings yr. consent, wh. I will not in ye. least call in question, & ye. account what day you set out, ye. moment I have read it I shall send him back to Dover immediately to wait there, either to bring me instantly an account of yr. arrival & how soon I may calculate yt. you will arrive, or else to attend upon you wh. ever you please to ye. last post before London, & then to come forwards in order to acquaint me with ye. approach of all ye. happiness I have in life. I then shall either meet you in a hackney chaise by myself between

1. The Prince's courier.

Rochester & London, or wait till I hear of yr. arrival in Park Street[1], to wh. place I shall fly upon ye. wings of love ye. moment I know you are come. I think I had better come into the house ye. back way thro' the stables & ye. garden, you know ye. way I mean. However, you shall not be arriv'd ten minutes before I am with you. I will not trust even to yr. sending. Whichever of these two plans you approve of most, either of meeting you on ye. road or waiting till you are arriv'd, I will follow, as I must see you ye. moment you arrive in order to settle where you chuse to be married, as we must be married ye. night you come, before anything is known of yr. being in England; as to ye method of our being married, I will acquaint you with yt. when we meet, & when we settle where we are to be married. One thing more I have to say respecting yr. arrival & then I will draw this letter, tedious as it is, to a conclusion, & yt. is yt. I hope when you do come you will endeavour to come to London, you will contrive to come early in ye. evening, but not till it is dark.

And now, my Maria, my beloved wife, (for such you really are) represent to yourself one moment my situation. I have made every sacrifice yt. was in my power to make to you. There is but one more sacrifice I cd. make to you & yt. is my life, wh. I certainly will do & shall think you mean me so to do if you have again deceiv'd me & have held out false hopes, but I do not think you capable of such a conduct, such cruelty, such insensibility. Think one instant how I am situated & yt. my fate is at present in yr. hands, & I think you will hesitate. By coming you make me ye. happiest of men; by staying or doubting one instant you not only make me think yt. you are dead to feeling & to everything I have undergone for you, but you ruin & blast my reputation in ye. world & with my friends. You stamp me with the epithets of a liar & a scoundrel, wh. they will have a right to think me & will think me, if you do not acknowledge I have told ym. ye. truth by yr. coming, tho' I am conscious of having acted strictly consistent with honor & truth, they will never think yt. can be ye. case, if ye woman I profess ye. truest & firmest love to, does not fully act up to my assertions, especially when they know yt. she has given her consent & by yt. means has declar'd her affections; they will immediately conclude yt. I have deceiv'd ym., & do you think, my Maria, yt. were it possible for me to survive ye. losing you, I wd. consent to live in ye. world with the slightest imputation cast upon my honor? No, yt. I wd. not, especially under the epithets of a liar & a scoundrel wh. are synonymous expressions, as the one never can exist without ye. other, wh. I must & shd. appear to be were you now to leave me, & consider to whom I shd. appear such, & innocently too, to my father, my family & ye. world in general.

I shall not add another syllable, but leave ye. decision of this affair to

1. Mrs. Fitzherbert's house no longer exists.

what you may think my merits are respecting you, to ye. sincerity of my attachment & to my not having a wish nor a desire in life yt. does not center in you; in short, I trust ye. whole to yr. generosity. Come then, oh! come, dearest of wives, best & most adored of women, come & for ever crown with bliss him who will thro' life endeavour to convince you by his love & attention of his wishes to be ye. best of husbands & who will ever remain unto ye. latest moments of his existence, *unalterably thine.*

P.S. I send you a parcel & a letter from Lady Anne, & I send you at ye. same time an eye, if you have not totally forgotten ye. whole countenance, I think ye. likeness will strike you.[1] (50237-50258)

1. There is an inaccurate version of this letter in Shane Leslie's *Life and Letters of Mrs. Fitzherbert.* The following letter is printed as revealing the identity of the 'go-between'. Hugh Elliot's secret letter to Pitt, dated Brighthelmstone, 17 October 1785, is endorsed at the end, 'Shewn to the King'. He wrote:

'Encouraged by the very flattering attention you have given to my verbal communications upon a subject of a most delicate nature, I do not hesitate to take up the pen to convey to you in writing the real state of a business in wh. I at present find myself engaged, & wh. I must either drop or prosecute as you shall be pleased to direct.

I need not recapitulate the circumstances that have induced the Prince of Wales to honor me with a considerable share of H.R.H.'s confidence since my arrival at Brighthelmstone where I came solely with the intention of bathing in the sea, & of profiting of those moments of leisure in wh. I have been permitted to cultivate yr. acquaintance. But I think myself bound to assert that, totally unconnected with H.R.H.'s attendants & society, I am indebted entirely to the Prince's own condescension & indulgence for the frankness with wh. he has been pleased at different times to converse with me upon the inconveniences of his present situation, or his desire of being relieved from them.

As an honest man & loyal subject, I cd. not refrain sometimes from expressing with zeal those sentiments to wh. you, Sir, are not a stranger, & of combating, to the utmost of my ability, some prejudices to wh. I sd. have thought myself culpable in having yielded. So far however, from having incurred H.R.H.'s displeasure by this conduct, it has led to his choice of me to open a communication with the King's most confidential servants, & I am empowered to speak to those whom I thought the most likely not to oppose his wishes, but to convey the knowledge of them in the properest manner to the King.

There is so much difficulty in putting upon paper the secret circumstances I have learnt, or in detailing the imminent danger to wh. H.R.H. is exposed from a manner of life that can be thoroughly understood but by those who are eye-witnesses of it, that out of respect to the Prince I shall be justified in not dwelling upon so distressing a subject, but that I may be allowed to advance that in my opinion H.R.H. risks being lost to himself, his family & his country if a total & sudden change does not take place. I will even venture to add that the Prince is at this moment not insensible that such a change is necessary, & that it is one of the motives wh. make him desirous of visiting the Continent under such restrictions as the King may think proper to advise. His own desire is to go to those places wh. shall be approved of, with no other retinue than Cols. Lee & Sloughter, or to join me to the party if the King sd. honor me with a sufficient degree of confidence to justify me in accepting so flattering an offer. As H.R.H. does not wish to travel as P. of Wales, it is not apprehended that any addition to his income wd. be necessary for the purpose of travelling, & it is with pleasure I observed that the Prince expects that his future relief from his present embarrassments might

Palais Royal, Paris, 20 Nov. 1785

La perte que je viens de faire de M. le Duc d'Orleans, mon tres honoré pere qui est mort le 18 de ce mois apres une maladie douloureuse, me plonge dans la plus vive douleur, je me fais un devoir d'en informer votre altesse Royale dont les bontés et l'amitié qu'elle me temoigne sont pour moi un sur garant de la part qu'elle voudra bien prendre à ma juste affliction. C'est une consolation que j' ose esperer que votre Altesse Royale ne me refusera pas. Je la prie d'être aussi convaincue de ma reconnoissance que du tres respectueux avec le quel j'ai l'honneur d'être, Monseigneur, de votre Altesse Royale tres humble et tres obéissant Serviteur. (38107)

Portsmouth, 25 Nov. 1785

I take this opportunity of writing to you a confidential letter as young O'Brion will deliver it in person. The money I desired you to send me was necessary, for as my allowance is but small, I am not always enabled to pay my bills at sight. A distressed brother Officer of mine was the reason I drew for so large a sum. I am under very particular obligations to this man, & as he has but me for his only friend, I was more under the necessity of helping him. I give you my word of honour I do not intend to touch a farthing & it is all intended for this unhappy person. You are my last resource. I sent an express to my agent; he refused me the money, so I beg therefore you will send it me down in notes by my servant. Excuse me if I do not mention the Officer's name: I must likewise beg you will not mention this circumstance to O'Brion.

be the consequence of the satisfaction the King & country wd. receive from his conduct abroad. A complete break in rooted habits of life & opinions can only be produced by a strong remedy. I fear the effects of bad example & prejudice will with difficulty be got the better of except at some distance from the source of them. In this view I do not hesitate to recommend to yr. serious attention the purport of this letter. H.R.H.'s own expressions were, "*I am certain the King will be better pleased with me when I return*", & dare I add that it wd. be the greatest ambition of my life to contribute to so desirable an event. I wave entering into any further detail of this important concern untill I shall have learnt yr. pleasure concerning it.

    I have too great confidence in the indulgence of a Royal master to apprehend any displeasure from the part I have ventured to act in so very delicate a position, & I trust that you will do justice to the motives wh. have prompted me to venture thus far without previous orders.' (50201-2)

You will have heard I asked Lord Howe[1] for the Phaeton & that I was refused her. My motives you are sufficiently acquainted with: it was my desire to oblige your worthy friend Lord Keppel. My present wish is to be Lord Hood's Captain next summer if he has the command at Portsmouth. I have every reason to wish it: particularly family ones. The coolness that subsists between the King & you would always make my stay unpleasant at home, therefore my happiness will depend upon my being employed. I preferr the Portsmouth station on many accounts: particularly as during the summer months I shall be frequently able to enjoy your society. The Mediterranean would be too expensive, as I do not believe my allowance will be the greatest. My present situation is as happy a one as I can wish; whenever the ship is in port I am on shore at Mr Martin's[2] in the Dock Yard. I am treated as if I was one of his family; he has two daughters about my own age: we dance & amuse ourselves vastly well: when at sea I am very well satisfied. I am upon the best terms with Capn Thornbrough[3], who is a very worthy man & does everything to make me happy. The only uneasiness I now feel is the visible coolness my father shews me. I have not upon my word received more than two letters from home, & I have been six months absent. I am regular in my correspondence; I write whenever the ship sails. I have wrote everything that is in my heart. I do not beleive I have another secret in the world. I trust you will answer me as kindly & as openly explain yourself in this letter, as there is no danger of anybody's seeing our correspondence as O'Brion is to bring me back your answer. I must again beg you will on no account shew this letter & do not speak about it. O'Brion is a very good boy, but he is very young: therefore pray be very cautious in your questions particularly about Martin's family.

I have only one more wish to make that you would come down for four & twenty hours only to Portsmouth. Our conversation, tho' only for a few minutes, would be to me of much greater advantage than writing for six months. I have many things to say to you, my dear brother, that I cannot possibly write. I have now nothing more to say except that you would be kind enough to send me down by O'Brion a lockit for my shirt with your hair & a pair of buckles. After the many kind actions you have done me I should be the most ungrateful of beings was I not to be

1. Richard, Earl Howe (1726–99), Admiral of the Fleet. M.P. for Dartmouth, 1757–82. Captain, 1748; Rear-Admiral, 1770; Vice-Admiral, 1775; Admiral, 1782. A Lord of the Admiralty, 1763–5. Commander-in-Chief in the Channel, 1782. Created Viscount, April 1782, and Earl, August 1788. Popularly known among the sailors as 'Black Dick', from his dark complexion.

2. Henry (afterwards Sir Henry) Martin, Commissioner of Portsmouth Dockyard.

3. Sir Edward Thornbrough (1754–1834). Captain, 1782; Rear-Admiral, 1804; Vice-Admiral, 1805; Admiral, 1813; G.C.B., 1825.

attached to the tenderest of brothers by more than an ordinary brotherly love: you will therefore beleive me when I subscribe myself [etc.]. (44690–1)

Portsmouth, 27 Nov. 1785
Nothing can induce me to the step I now take but the thorough knowledge of the tender regard you have always professed for me. You well know that my circumstances are very narrow, & I at present have absolutely not a farthing. I could wish you would, dear brother, send me two £500 banknotes by the return of my servant. As I know you are not in the pleasantest circumstances do not send me more than what you can with ease spare, as I shall be equally obliged to you for part as for the whole. Tomorrow I sail & shall return soon, so send my man down in the course of next week. (44687)

151 THE PRINCE OF WALES TO THE DUKE OF YORK

Brooks's, 3 Dec. 1785
I cannot let the opportunity slip of my friend Whitworth's[1] going to Hanover, in order to write to you. I beg you will shew him ev'ry attention possible, not so much *on my account*, as I am sure when you know him you will like him on his own account & as much as we all do here; a more gentlemanlike, liberal-minded man never existed. I have known him long & think I can answer for his meeting with yr. approbation. I do not mean he is a man I have ever had an opportunity of placing any confidence in, but a man supposing I had had such an opportunity, yt. I shd. never have scrupled to have plac'd yt. confidence in. We have liv'd in great intimacy for a considerable time & I have a very great partiality for him. C'est assez pour mon ami. I flatter myself you will like him as well as you have Mr. Beddingfield, ou autrement çe ne sera pas grand chose du moins moi je pense comme cela. I am writing to you from our Club at Brooks's where there are a great many people playing at whist & making such a noise yt. I hope will appear to you a sufficient excuse for any inaccuracies there may be in this letter.

1. Charles, Earl Whitworth (1752–1825). Having retired from the Army in 1783, he entered the diplomatic service. He was Minister to Poland, 1785–8, obtaining this post (according to Wraxall) through the influence of the Queen of France and the Duke of Dorset, afterwards his future wife's first husband. He arrived at Warsaw on 21 January 1786. Envoy to Russia, 1788–1800; K.B., 1793; created Baron Whitworth [I.], 1800; Minister to Denmark, 1800; Ambassador to France, 1802–3; Lord-Lieutenant of Ireland, 1813–17. Created Viscount, 1813, and Earl, 1815.

Things here are very much in ye. state they have been for some time past, & London is as dull as anything can possibly be. Nothing new stirring, wh. I am afraid will be ye. case till after ye. meeting of Parliament. In short, I am afraid, my dearest Frederick, yt. this epistle will appear a very great *bore or boar* whichever you please to term it. I will therefore release you as soon as possible from so dull an occupation as reading my nonsense, & conclude with assuring my dearest brother of ye. truth with which I ever shall remain [etc.].

P.S. I forgot to tell you yt. Whitworth is remarkably fond of a good dinner, & will have no objection to yr. giving him one every day whilst he stays at Hanover. N.B. one, two, three, or four bottles of wine will be no objection. If you can avoid his taking a stroke before he gets to Warsaw he will be much obliged to you. Once more, my dearest brother, Adieu. Write soon, pray do. (43755–6)

152 PRINCE WILLIAM TO THE PRINCE OF WALES

Portsmouth, 28 Dec. 1785
The short stay Doctor Blaine made in this part of the world prevented me writing: & as amusements are pleasant to seamen when it is in their power to enjoy them, I make no doubt you will excuse my not writing when the ship is at Spithead. I always have my letters ready to send to the post as soon as we arrive. I therefore do not know if Mr. Martin has as yet received a letter for me: if he has I will own the receipt by the next post.

In my last letter I mentioned to you my intentions about my future employment. I should wish to have a guardship for many reasons. You know I cannot live with any comfort at home: I must therefore be employed. It is dull work cruizing in a frigate, particularly in winter time. It would be by far too expensive to have a station in the Mediterranean: besides I never wish to leave England during the peace. The only thing that remains is a guardship. I must own I have set my heart on one. They are the first ships sent abroad upon the breaking out of a war, & I shall always prefer serving on foreign service to being employed in the Channel during a war. Was I not afraid of tiring you, I could give you many more reasons.

About money matters I am going to surprize you. The day before I sailed, one of my old shipmates came to me in the greatest distress for money. I put my hand into my purse & gave him two guineas, which was & is still every farthing I have in the world. I contrive somehow or other to make it out pretty well. Do not suppose by this I want money. I would not have asked you last time had it been for myself; my allowance is enough for my present wants. I have £125 a quarter: in general I cannot spend it, but particular business has obliged me to give away 90 guineas, which you will allow make a great hole in that sum. Next quarter I shall go on in the old way. The only favour I have to beg of you is that you will be kind enough to let my German servant live in town with you. I wish you would take him. I can recommend him as a sober honest man. I have an English servant, so that this man is of no use to me. If you do not chuse to take him, I hope you will allow him to stay where he is: in which case pray pay him his wages 4 guineas a quarter & half a guinea a week. We will settle that matter when we next meet. I am afraid you are tired with this long dry letter. I will now therefore have done & finish by subscribing myself [etc.].

P.S. I wish you would give this letter for Dalrymple to Lord Cholmondeley[1] with my compliments & desire him to enclose it to Gibraltar. (44694-5)

153 THOUGHTS ON THE KINGDOM OF IRELAND WRITTEN DURING THE DEBATES ON THE IRISH PROPOSITIONS IN THE YEAR 1785[2] [unsigned]

When national bodies of men are disturbed from their ordinary habits of tranquility and shew general indications of discontent, it is the part of true policy not to disregard such tokens as can never arise, or exist, in a State without danger. If any case of injury exists or is supposed to exist, the dangers which may result from thence become evident and the causes being open and proclaimed, either the redress of the grievance or the suppression of the complaint comes to decision, according to the accustomed mode between nations which from the want of some superior tribunal is too frequently referred to the fate of arms. But the case of injury is not the case of Ireland. No such charge is imputed. No

1. George James, 4th Earl and 1st Marquess of Cholmondeley (1749–1827). Captain of the Yeomen of the Guard, April–December 1783; Chamberlain to the Prince of Wales, 1795–1800; Lord Steward of the Household, 1812–21. Succeeded his grandfather as 4th Earl, 1770; created Marquess, November 1815.

2. In 1785 Pitt tried unsuccessfully to bring about the commercial union of the British Isles, his scheme being embodied in Eleven Resolutions. Import duties on foreign goods should be the same whether imported into Great Britain through Ireland or imported into Ireland through Great Britain. Where the duties on English or Irish goods were different on importation into the other country, these duties were to be reduced in the kingdom where they were the highest, to the lower scale. And Ireland was to purchase the advantages of free trade with England and the colonies by an annual contribution to the cost of the Navy, whenever the hereditary revenue of Ireland should exceed £656,000 in any year of peace. But the opposition of British traders and manufacturers caused the scheme to be so considerably modified as to compel the Irish Parliament, which had at first welcomed it, to reject it.

injury has been committed. The Government of the country for many years past has been administered with lenity and national moderation; nevertheless there exists unequivocal tokens of a disturbed public mind. But as there is no basis of inveterate anger, founded on national injury, no malignance can exist in the case. If Ireland has felt herself aggrieved by some latent and incommodious part of her Constitution the extent of her complaint towards England does not amount to any charge of injury.

The Constitution of Ireland is a mixt monarchy, similar to that of England, and all its parts are equally ballanced for internal peace. The Crown is in the possession and exercise of all its constitutional prerogatives, not only without envy or ill-will, but it is fortified by other branches of the Constitution wch. are combined in concurrent interests with the Crown. There is a nobility and landed gentry, which in every country are the natural and constant supports of a throne. The pride of birth, hereditary honours, and the ambition of the nobility in public employments, attach them to the Crown. Similar principles in gradation affect the body of the landed gentry, and one common interest of all those persons, whether nobility or gentry, who possess fortunes unequal and superior to the property of the multitude ranges them on the part of the Crown against any republican principles of equalization.

The proprietors of land in Ireland are more bound to the support of quiescent government than any landed proprietors in any other kingdom in the world. The reason is because the great landed fortunes of Ireland have at some time or other been acquired under the banners of English settlements, and altho' much time has elapsed since these first settlements, yet even the most antient titles might be shaken if any general convulsion were to happen. Besides these obsolete claims against the oldest settlements and landed titles, which nothing but general confusion could now revive, it is to be considered that there are other lurking claims of more recent date against which a very great body of Irish landed proprietors can have no protection but in the stability of their government. To go no farther back than the reign of King James the first, and from thence to the end of that century, viz., to the settlements of Ireland after the Revolution, where are the title deeds which, within that period, have not been harrowed up again and again by inquisitions, confiscations, settlements, revocations of those settlements, resettlements, &c., &c., together with numberless acts of fraud and violence attendant upon all these changes? All proprietors of lands who are conscious to themselves of being under these circumstances must be sensible that any searching times of confusion might drive them from their possessions into the wide world. As this class constitutes the body of the Protestant interest in Ireland it is acknowledged by all parties that the Protestant interest cannot subsist but by the support of a

Protestant Government, and of a Protestant throne. The Protestant Church of Ireland, which may be called a class of spiritual nobility and gentry, are doubly interested in the support of the foregoing principles. All these parties can only secure themselves by combining their own interests with those of the Crown. They have one common cause to support, viz., the present Constitution of mixt monarchy without any biass or private interest leading towards republican independence.

There is another interest growing up in Ireland which is at present considerable, the partially distributed, viz., the manufacturing and commercial interest. This is a Protestant interest, and as far as it extends, it coincides in views with the foregoing interests. Peace is the harvest of commerce and manufactures. Of all wars those w[ch.] are most destructive to their interests are domestic wars entailing unquiet possessions and turbulent Governments, thereby destroying both the exertions and objects of pacific industry. Besides these obvious interests by w[ch.] commerce is attached to quiet government, it is to be observed that commerce partakes of the soil where it is planted. Commerce accumulates property and therefore in these kingdoms where the acquisition of land and every gradation of ascent is in course of time open to the merchant or the manufacturer, they feel themselves ultimately upon the same bottom with the landed interest. They are impatient to acquire settlements in land; they partake of all its interests; they entail their acquired estates upon their families, and in every respect occupy the places of those who have left them, and thus they fill up a succession of persons still grafted upon the same system of landed interest, and by this succession they are assimilated from time to time into the Constitution of a landed kingdom of which, after their adoption they become similar and concordant parts.

The consideration of these points is essential in discussing the present state of Ireland, to shew that altho' Ireland has claimed and acquired to herself an independence of the Legislature of the English Parliament, yet they have no wish or tendency to become independent of the Crown. There [sic] only object has been to acquire the rank and Constitution of an independent kingdom in every respect similar to the mixt monarchy of her sister kingdom. The Crown is therefore now become the bond of union between the two nations.

Ireland has hitherto been a province to the Crown and Parliament of England. The original settlements of Ireland were made by joint adventures of Kings of England and of English subjects. The famous laws in the reign of Henry 7th, commonly called Poynings Laws, w[ch.] have lately been repealed to give independence to Ireland with respect to its own Legislature[1], were originally passed for the protection and security of the English Pale and settlers in Ireland. The English settlements in

1. By the Rockingham Ministry, 1782.

208

Ireland were at that time in a very crude and hazardous state. It had been found impossible, by the principle of conquest alone, to exterminate the old native interests of the original Irish. Several parts of the country were therefore united from time to time with the English interests by compromises of treaties and alliances. Such compromises were substituted in default of power, and the effect wch. they produced was that of enabling the native interests to contend with the English interests in Councils as well as arms. It was to defend the settlers against this consequence as well as to secure the dependence of the settlers themselves upon the Crown of England that the famous law of Poinings was enacted for notifying the causes of Parliament to the Privy Council in England. It was both an act of union and protection to the settlers.

In the subsequent periods, from the reign of Henry the 7th to William the 3rd., altho' the native interest of the antient Irish was gradually obliterated, yet a constant succession of national troubles, producing perpetual changes and uncertainties in the state of landed property, there was no permanent body of landed proprietors receiving and transmitting their landed properties in hereditary succession who could claim the character of the hereditary people of Ireland. From the period of the Revolution to the present time a continued state of civil tranquility and of undisturbed possessions for nearly a century has organized and drawn forth into form the inherent spirit and faculties of a nation ambitious to acquire the co-ordinate rank and constitution of that mixt monarchy from which the settlements of Ireland are derived and under one united Crown to become an independent kingdom.

It is thus that the Irish nation has arrived thro' various fortunes and successive gradations to the claims of an independent kingdom. But if it be an honorable ambition which has prompted Ireland to aspire to independent empire, the same ambition will not permit them to stop there, or to leave the corresponding parts of that system unfinished. If from a province they are become an independent kingdom, their first attentions ought to be directed to prepare a new and splendid rank for their sovereign, now no longer the sovereign of a province, but wearing the national crown of an independent kingdom of Ireland. Having requested a separation from the Parliament of England, wch. heretofore has acted in concert towards the government and protection of Ireland, it is a debt wch. they owe to themselves as well as to their Sovereign to strengthen his hands by an additional civil establishment suitable to royalty, and similar to the civil establishment of the Crown of England. A royal Household, a Court, a marine, ministers, ambassadors, &c., which would again return to themselves in offices of honour and trust conferred upon the nobility and gentry of Ireland.

If their Sovereign, having been for many years attached and wedded to a sister kingdom, should condescend to adopt his eldest son and heir

209

apparent as the partaker of his thrones to receive the first coronation of an Irish Crown in Dublin, would not the ambition which has called for a King give him the reception of dignity and honour which would be due to such a King, being the son and heir apparent of the Sovereign and his representative?

But any such step or the most distant thought towards it must alone proceed from the will and pleasure of the Sovereign. It could not, however, be considered as any derogation to the Sovereign. *Collega Imperii* was a title well known and frequently in use with the Roman Emperors. The occupancy of an united throne by the heir apparent would extend the stability of the reigning family upon a broader basis. It would be an augmentation of the dignity of the Crown without endangering the liberty of the subject. It w^d. not be an accumulation of power in the Crown operative against the liberty of the subject; it w^d be an enlargement of the circle of regal dominion, in the place of provincial dominion. Every other member and faculty of the Constitution within this enlarged pale of regal dominion would receive a corresponding encrease which would therefore preserve the ballance of the Constitution as a mixt monarchy. The nobility and gentry and people of Ireland would acquire importance equal to the splendor of the Crown; the dignity of the Crown and the prosperity of the people would go hand in hand together.

A new creation of an independent kingdom, displayed in all its parts, and claiming its rank among the Crowns of Europe, w^d add a most decided importance to the united Empire among all foreign nations as well as to the family of the Sovereign under whom they are united.

The transfer of domestic dominion to Ireland would draw off its subjects from looking to foreign spiritual powers or entering into the military service of foreign princes. Free liberty of conscience in matters of religion under a domestic prince requiring no other tests but those of civil fidelity, w^d reunite all the divided parts in one national cause and restore all the sons of Ireland to her own bosom.

The residence of a Prince's Court w^d. recall the wandering absentee to his native home. It would repeople the country with nobility, gentry and yeomanry; it w^d. inspire new life into the peasantry, now most dejected and oppressed; hospitality would smile upon the land and industry would lay open all its hidden treasures: manufacturers and commerce w^d carry the glad tidings to the extremities of the earth. All these blessings may happen to Ireland if a prosperous issue should attend what has been called their emancipation. That lot is now cast. It will require much temper and moderation to steer successfully towards that prosperous issue. The world is crouded with rival nations who may not wish to see any prosperous end to these things. This maxim is therefore most infallible, that the most distant tendency to any rupture between England and Ireland would be serving the envious views of foreign rival States, and sacrificing all salutary purposes of our own.

With a domestic prince reigning in Ireland, thereby completing the circle of domestic empire, every possible jealousy arising from the apprehension of external influence w^d be removed. The volunteers of Ireland would then become the national and constitutional militia under the sanction of their own legislature, and under the command of the domestic executive power.

Edward the first gave to the Welch a native prince to reign over them. This indeed was but the favour of a name. The substantial boon which attached Wales to England being both upon one soil, was their incorporation into one Legislature. Nature does not equally favour a legislative incorporation of Ireland. Ireland, by the immutable laws of nature is, and always must remain a distinct and separate island, circumscribed by its own ocean beyond which nothing can be called domestic; but that which cannot be incorporated may still be united. The Sovereign may be the bond of union. Ireland has hitherto been a royal farm, unimproved because unoccupied. It has moved in an eccentric orb, straining heavily upon the distant hand of government. The occupancy of the throne of that kingdom by the Sovereign's eldest son, if approved by the Sovereign, w^d relieve the distant pressure. It w^d restore the equipoize of government and connect the two islands by the two hands of common sovereignty instead of one, and in future times even native princes may reign over Ireland.

The delegation of the kingdom of Ireland to the heir apparent, the inheritance being indivisible, w^d enlarge the scope of action without dividing the unity of interests. It w$^{d.}$ be a bond of affection and of unity of action within the Royal family; it w$^{d.}$ consolidate the interests of two generations. A royal settlement for the heir apparent would anticipate a new and splendid sphere of action for the successor, w$^{ch.}$ would reflect its lustre with equal dignity upon the parent Sovereign. It w$^{d.}$ prevent foreign emigrations by multiplying the objects and the means of domestic affluence; it w$^{d.}$ invigorate and protect the distant parts of the united Empire and fortify its extreme barrier where the hand of government cannot be in full strength and where the ties of common interest are feeble in proportion.

The decline of Empires commences from extreme parts; there are in all the political establishments in the world latent imperfections coeval with their original constitutions. The superintending eye of domestic government may watch over the first tokens of such defects and still keep them in a quiescent state. But if they once break out into tumult and contention, various other latent discontents are ever ready to seize the occasion and to raise their heads. The evils which are first seen are the least part, those w$^{ch.}$ are behind the curtain form the secret and desperate ambush to encompass national destruction. In such cases the only prudence of government consists in prevention or early and pacific remedy.

The infirmities of the Constitution of Ireland are too obvious to be mistaken or to be glossed over by fallacious confidence. They extend no less than to the very elements of civil and religious union. The national settlements of landed property have shallow and therefore precarious roots. In spirituals a foreign hierarchy hangs over their heads like a two-edged sword, in temporals as well as spirituals, suspended by a single thread; these are the rocks of danger to Ireland.

The new Constitution w$^{ch.}$ they have so earnestly sought for may be preferable to provincial dependence; it may be a laudable object of ambition and pursuit: but on the part of a nation which has two feeble internal parts, the meditated change should be courted not compelled. The completion of that change by a fundamental system of political establishment, compact and uniform in all its parts, may afford arguments for its adoption which the unconnected claims of single and separate parts might not be entitled to; that Constitution, if it is to lead to tranquility and permanence, sh^d arise from a general combination of congenial interests and become the basis of greatness to those who are to give and to those who are to receive. (38099–105)

VI   1786

During this year the Prince received more letters than usual from his brother William who, impressionable as ever, had lost his heart at Plymouth to another girl, the adorable Sarah (or Sally) Martin, but the romance was short-lived, for, to his dismay, 'the old gentleman' who 'kept him under like a slave' ordered him to North America: three years of banishment, he grumblingly described it. 'During the bloom of youth,' he complained, 'I am not allowed to enjoy myself like other people of my age.'

Meanwhile the Prince of Wales was enjoying life at his 'Marine Pavilion' at Brighton with his dearest Maria, on whose establishment he lavished £50,000. But a 'very unpleasant business', his mounting debts, cast a shadow over his life too. In fact, he felt that he had reached the edge of a precipice, for he owed over a quarter of a million, nearly twice the amount of his debt two years earlier; and in July he felt obliged to dismiss his Household, to announce the sale of his stud and to live like a private gentleman. The King refused to entertain the idea of relief until he had furnished a 'sufficient explanation of his past expenses' and afforded a prospect of 'reasonable security against a continuation of his extravagance'. We do not know how he reacted to the very unusual Will of his aunt, Princess Amelia, who died in November, but people thought that she would have done better to leave her money to the Prince rather than to relatives in Germany, though, as Pitt's brother remarked, 'I ... thought it a very immense sum, whereas it does not turn out to be more than £50,000 stock, which would have been a mere breakfast, and no solution of the present unpleasant state of things.'

Portsmouth, 2 Jan. 1786

Upon my arrival I received your most affectionate letter. I want words to express my gratitude, for God knows I stand in great need of a firm friend at present. It is not money matters which give me uneasiness; it is something else, which you shall soon hear by the first opportunity I can send a letter that I am sure will not be opened. I enjoin secrecy, not to open your mouth upon this subject to Lord Hood on any account, as you regard my future happiness. I must again repeat do not mention it to Lord Hood.

With respect to our business together. I am thoroughly convinced you will soon send me what I want.[1] I return you sincere thanks for all your unmerited kindness & only hope by my future conduct to prove myself worthy of your affection.

P.S. We sail Thursday morning.   (44696)

Portsmouth, 20 Jan. 1786

My last informed you of my having something on my mind which I would take the first opportunity of communicating. I think I [had] better not do it by paper but deferr till I have the pleasure of meeting you next. I have many reasons for so doing which you will approve when we talk the matter over. Nothing has occurred since I last wrote about any plan concerning my future destination. I believe it cannot now be long before something must happen, as I am of age next August. The King will in the course of the winter determine in what situation I am to appear after that period. I could wish to be employed till I was four or five & twenty years of age; in short, till my wildness was a little gone off. You will agree with me, I hope, my dear friend. Answer this letter & let me know where we differ, as I consider you as the person to direct & advise me. I must not trouble you any more with these concerns of mine, otherwise I am afraid you will consider me as a sedate Presbyterian. Do not believe me to be that: indeed the amusement I take when on shore would give me the lie. Everything goes on here in the old way. Your thoughts are engrossed by the fine dissipated scenes that are

1. Money.

215

coming on in London; much higher ones than I at present aspire at. What surprizes me is that such a generous openhearted fellow as Frederick should preferr the dull, lowminded Germans to our countrymen; there is no answering for mankind & it is lucky that the same maggot does not bite us all. In this part of the world there is nothing now stirring, so that I do not really know what to write about. There is a great deal of scandal here but it is not worth mentioning. We hear every day of some fresh accidents that happened in the last heavy gales. I think it will be happy if we escape with whole bones this winter.

I am afraid this letter will be but a dull one to you; my excuses I have already made, therefore I beg forgiveness as in your last you desired me to write often. That is a very sufficient reason for me to do so, so it will ever be my utmost wish to comply always with your requests. (44698–9)

Godalming, 30 Jan. 1786
I have this moment received your letter with the buckles & pin, for which I thank you with all my heart, as well as for your particular affection in the last unhappy business. I received 50£ note from the King who has likewise agreed that I should not return to London before I go to America.[1]

My best compliments to M.[2] & tell her she may rely in my secrecy. (44700)

155 THE DUKE OF YORK TO THE PRINCE OF WALES

Hanover, 31 Jan. 1786
I should have answered sooner your kind letter by Whitworth if I had not been acquainted by Colman that I was to expect another letter from you, which I have never received. I therefore did not chuse to delay

1. The King had continued to complain of William's 'love of low company' whilst in England, and though William believed American manners to be 'very vicious', the King decided to send him to Canada. When William raised objections he was told by the Queen that 'were the whole Board of Admiralty and the whole Navy to propose' that he should go to the Mediterranean instead, 'he would not be moved'. She added: 'Your very imprudent behaviour when abroad in not loving good company . . . and the dislike of attending to the advice of those who might have guided you, has been a means of strengthening the King in this opinion.' (*The Later Correspondence of George III*, i.211)

2. Mrs. Fitzherbert. William probably meant that his brother had informed him of the secret marriage.

216

longer writing to you to tell you how happy your letter made me as it was very long since I had heard from you. Ever since William left this place I have not received a line from him, though he promised to be a very exact correspondent. I shall therefore be very much obliged to you if you will inform me where he is and how he goes on. I am most sincerely grieved for poor Merrick's death; a better or a more estimable man never breathed.[1]

During my last journey I was shewn a very fine pelisse of sable which a gentleman wished to part with; it was given to him by the Empress of Russia and has never been made up; it is reckoned astonishingly fine of the kind. He asks two hundred and forty £ for it. It is much too fine to be made up into a common surtout which is the only way that I can wear it, but you might like it for a dressed coat; I therefore wish to know if you would chuse to have it.

I will not trouble you with a longer letter this time; I shall therefore conclude by repeating to you how happy I should be to see you and how sincerely I am ever, dear brother [etc.].   (43768-9)

156   THE DUKE OF CUMBERLAND TO THE PRINCE OF WALES

Naples, 8 Feb. 1786

I take the opportunity of Jack Payne[2] going to England to write a 2d. time to you; the first I hope you have received as it was dated the 10th of Jan., under cover to Js. Luttrell.

The climate here is mild but often changes. The Operas are the only amusements going on, for the natives themselves do not open their houses. We have seen the King three times, he is very civil indeed, but as the Queen is with child lives totally at Caserta.[3] Payne will give you the description of their boar hunt which indeed is buchery. In about three weeks more the English will go to Rome for the Holy Week to see the Church functions.

I hope by this time Princess Elizabeth is better. I feel very much for you knowing your kindness to all that you love.

This place will be shockingly dull when the English leave us, & the

1. Captain Merrick died at Naples on 18 December 1785.

2. John Willett Payne (*c.* 1752-1803), one of the Prince's intimates. Captain, 1780; Rear-Admiral, 1799; M.P. for Huntingdon, 1787-96. He was appointed Auditor and Secretary of the Duchy of Cornwall in 1791.

3. Ferdinand IV, King of Naples and Sicily (1751-1825), a son of Charles III of Spain, married (1768) Caroline, daughter of the Emperor Francis I and of Maria Theresa (1752-1814). On 18 February she gave birth to a daughter (Clotilde, 1786-92). She had seventeen children.

weather by the end of May will get so hot, as indeed all thro' Italy, that the whole day one must stay at home & only be out after seven of a night or very early of a morning. Letters are above three weeks coming here from England, & as it has happened twice, we have, from the falls of snow in Germany & the Alps, & also great rains in Tuscany, been four posts in arrear; we have now two behindhand.

I do not at present see any happy prospect in returning home to see you, for I must keep up strictly to what I told you at parting, that untill I am clear England must be the most improper place in the world for me. I have from different people that correspond with me heard you were in health; that at least is a great satisfaction to me. This letter I suppose you will hardly receive before a month or five weeks as Payne sails with Capt. O'Hara [1] of the Andromeda that brought me here this day for Leghorn where he wants some things for his ship's crew; that is three days' sail if the wind is fair. There the ship will stay for two days more, then sail for Nice, that is about three days more. There Payne disembarks & proceeds streight thro' Lyons for Paris: he talks of stopping four or five days there, therefore I fear you will not receive mine sooner than the time I mention. I do not trouble you with letters, knowing your time must be pretty much occupied. I suppose Ld. Maccartney's [2] arrival in England & the India Bill not approved in that country [3] will chagrine Administration & probably bring about some change, but you on the spot must be a much better judge than myself.

I do not see any time fixed for your Operas. Giardini is still here, I hear talks of going in Spring to the Duke of Dorset [4] at Paris; he has not vouchsafed to call upon me. I believe when he comes to England, if ever he goes, he will not find those friends there that he now expects. Here he abuses the people of this country very much indeed. Musick, I mean instrumental, are very bad indeed. Pray tell Cramer we have

1. Captain James O'Hara (d. 1789). Lieutenant, R.N., 1748; Captain, 1765.

2. George, Earl Macartney (1737–1806). M.P. for Cockermouth, 1768–9; for Armagh [I.], 1768–76; for the Ayr Boroughs, 1774–6, and for Beeralston, 1780–1; Chief Secretary for Ireland, 1769–72. Envoy to Russia, 1764, and Ambassador, 1767; Governor of Madras, 1781–5; declined Governor-Generalship of Bengal, 1785. Created Baron Macartney [I.], 1776; Viscount [I.], 1792, and Earl [I.], 1794; Barony [G.B.], 1796. Governor of the Cape of Good Hope, 1796–8.

3. Cornwallis, who became Governor-General in 1786, disliked Pitt's India Act on the ground that it conferred excessively limited powers on the Governor-General. In 1786, to meet his wishes, Pitt's Government carried a Bill amending that of 1784 and enabling the Governor-General and the Presidency Governors to act without the consent of their respective Councils, and even contrary to their opinion, in cases of emergency.

4. John Frederick, 3rd Duke of Dorset (1745–99). Captain of the Yeomen of the Guard, 1782–3; Ambassador to Paris, 1783–9; Lord Steward of the Household, 1789–99. K.G., April 1788.

just now a lad of 9 years of age, a son of Cavendish, who plays well, & I make no doubt, with study, will make a capital performer. He has played with me.

I own I am much tyred of this country, finding nothing so comfortable as my friends in England, but if I have no *good news*, must bear things quietly & remain here certainly till I am able to set off streight for home again. (54471–2)

I57 LETTERS FROM PRINCE WILLIAM TO THE PRINCE OF WALES [1]

10 Feb. 1786

I arrived at Martin's house at ten in the morning: immediately after breakfast I retired with the girl & her mother. Everything that happened during my absence proves her affection for me. Neither of us could speak when I took leave of her. I embarked at twelve & sailed immediately. We had a severe gale of wind on the Wednesday, which made it necessary to take shelter in Guernsey roads: here we remained four & twenty hours. The Governor [2] asked me to dine with him. We sat down thirty people: few got up sober, for we were at the table & bottle seven hours & a half. I am surprized I was not drunk. There is no wonder that the people in this island drink, for their wine is remarkably good & they do not pay duty for it. They are remarkably loyal & sung a vast number of very good songs in English & French. As for their women I had not time to see any of them. I am told they are pretty.

We are at this moment arrived in Plymouth Sound, so that I cannot give you any account of this place. America is my destination. In what character I do not know, I am afraid tho', still as a Lieutenant. Lord Howe does not approve of my being promoted. God only knows his reason. I have almost a mind to quit the service. My only inducement to remain is money matters: they allow me so little that I do not know how to make both ends meet. The fifty pound I got is a mere trifle. Was I to resign my commission, where could I live? You are as much distressed as I am; & what is to become of a young man of one & twenty years old, who has neither a profession nor money? A pretty situation indeed: add to all this a King's son. What shall I do? Quit the service is a hard thing after having laboured seven long years. Yet to go for three years on a foreign station with a man I have never seen is by no means an agreeable situation. Give me your advice. I will try the Army line. I have a letter prepared to Lord Howe with my resignation.

I beg to be remembered to M. [3] & ever believe me [etc.].

1. This letter has no formal beginning, and a sheet may be missing.

2. Lord Amherst, Governor from 1770 to his death in 1797.

3. Mrs. Fitzherbert.

P.S. Bad weather & contrary winds having detained us in Torbay, I take this opportunity of filling up this sheet. I have wrote a strong letter to the King in which I have expressed my wish for promotion & represented that I believed Lord Howe had given him false accounts about my conduct, & that it was his Lordship's plan to keep me back as long as he could. I am really unhappy; everything goes against me. I have been obliged to leave the girl I adore; my father will not allow me to live with the brother I am in intimate friendship with, & he does not even shew me common justice. Frederick, who is only two years older than I am, has a Regiment of Guards & is a Lieutenant-General; besides this he has been allowed £5000 ever since he has been in Germany. The difference you are so well acquainted with; I will not mention it, but I feel it most sensibly. Your situation as well as mine are both very unpleasant: & I do not even see where, how, & when the case will alter. You are as ill with our father as possible, & I shall soon be upon the same footing, if not worse. The only consolation I have is in your friendship. If I am denied my father's house or find it necessary to leave it, I am sure your doors will always be opened to receive me. I see there is a storm brewing over my head which must soon burst. S.[1] is all I regret: taking leave of her was a cruel thing; perhaps for ever. I may never see her again. Oh had I been in somebody's situation, I would have done as he has done: then I should have been happy. To be banished to America is not what I wish. My friends & connections are torn from me. During the bloom of youth I am not allowed to enjoy myself like any other person of my age. I will not at present say anything more about it. Believe me to be sincerely attached to you & to all your connections for ever. God bless you & may He let us meet again both in a happier state of mind than we were in when last parted. (44701–2)

Hebe, In Falmouth Harbour, 22 Feb. 1786
According to your desire, dear brother, I again take up my pen to let you know how things go on in our part of the world. Admiral Milbanke[2] had the civility to carry you a letter from me: since then we have been & are still at sea. I have not heard either from my father or mother; nothing is as yet determined to my knowledge. It appears to me strange that tho' I have written to both letters that require answers, I have not as yet heard from either. You have plenty of good reasons for not writing. But I am sure they cannot plead many. The Queen has I hope by this time wrote: the conversation I had with her, the last time I saw

1. Sarah (or Sally) Martin.

2. Mark Milbanke (1725?–1805). Rear-Admiral, 1779; Vice-Admiral, 1780: Admiral, 1793. At this time he was Port-Admiral at Plymouth.

you, convinces me she is a tender mother & wishes to keep peace among the chosen ones of Israel. I wish I could say as much for our worthy friend our near relation. What can be the use of his keeping us so close? Does he imagine he will make his sons his friends by this mode of conduct? If he does, he is sadly mistaken. He certainly wishes us all well & thinks he is doing the best. I am convinced he loves me by his way of receiving me last. I cannot but regard him & would do everything to please him, but he is so difficult to satisfy. In short, you know him as well as I do. The less therefore I am at home the better: but why then should I be banished to America? let me at least choose my station, now it is peace. This however is a plan of Black Dick's[1]. It would have done your heart good to have seen his black looks the other morning.

Do not forget the money matters. You know well enough that it is not for myself, but for a very particular friend of mine. You mistake him entirely if you think he has acted dishonourably by me. I know what he has done: everything has been managed with my entire approbation. Was you to know him you would think widely otherwise of him. Pray answer me this question honestly, does Sheldon know all the circumstances of the late transaction of yours? I think he does by your answer. Caution is highly necessary, & he ought to be made sensible of it. I hope you depend upon my secrecy: unless authorized by you, no one shall ever know it from my lips. Give my best compliment to M.[2] & tell her I hope she will not forget me. A favour I have to ask, which is that when certain a family go to town, you will sometimes visit them for my sake. I will not detain you any longer but will subscribe myself [etc.].
(44703–4)

Hebe, In Plymouth Sound, 1 Mar. 1786
I once more take up the pen in compliance with your request to let you know I am still in the land of the living. We arrived here last night. My hopes were disappointed: no letters from my parents, but what is worse, nothing from the best of brothers. Anxiety wears the mind down soon. What is to become of your unfortunate William? Does my father neglect me entirely, or is this his behaviour after my late openness on my unfortunate situation? A month has elapsed & no letter from him; not even a line from my mother. They are, I believe, at a loss to know what to do with me. In short, their plans have not hitherto been agreeable to me & I am afraid this one will be less so than any. I hope I ever have acted the part of an honourable man. They cannot accuse me of that: why not then give me the liberty every other young man enjoys,

1. Lord Howe.

2. Mrs. Fitzherbert.

but keep me under like a slave? My spirit they shall not nor cannot break. Live I will like a gentleman at all times. However, I must have done, as this dry stuff cannot amuse you.

Do for God's sake I beg contrive something or other about the money business for my friend: he richly deserves it. Could I give him relief, it should be done immediately. But want of power, not of inclination prevents me. Send me down any part of the sum; that will in some measure help him, he is so wretchedly ruined. Poor fellow, he is a worthy man & my most intimate friend. The worthy family are in town: do see them; speak kindly to them, consider my dearest S.[1] is a shy girl: do not be surprised if she is at first reserved. Remember who loved her, who does still with all his heart: that person, that subscribes himself [etc.]. (44705-6)

Plymouth, 11 Mar. 1786
Excuse my writing a short letter as Hanger will tell you my sentiments fully, having discoursed with him on that subject. He likewise will inform Elphinstone of the impossibility of our sailing together as the Queen's letter mentions. My finances are as low as possible, so bad that the least sum will be of use. I wish you would give Hanger in my name the single barrel gunn that I had made at Hanover by Hundorf [?]. (44707)

---

18 Mar. [?1786]
I, according to promise, reassume my pen to inform you of my wants and of different circumstances relative to myself. You are of course acquainted with the old gentleman's intention of paying my bills and of his having ordered me a set of plate. It is not yet determined whether he is to give me an outfit, but should he not, and likewise not increase my allowance, I shall be in the old way in a short time. Nothing final have I heard respecting my destination, the Mediterranean or the Plymouth station, nor has anything been settled about Hargood[2] or Mainwaring[3]. I must beg leave to recommend to your notice and protection Captain Richard Goodwin Keats[4], Master and Commander. I

1. Sarah Martin.

2. ?Sir William Hargood (d. 1839). Lieutenant, 1780; Captain, 1790; Rear-Admiral, 1810; Vice-Admiral 1814, K.C.B., 1815.

3. Jemmett Mainwaring. Lieutenant, 1789; Commander, April 1795; Captain, July 1795.

4. Sir Richard Goodwin Keats (1757–1834). Lieutenant, 1777; Commander, 1782; Captain, 1789; Rear-Admiral, 1807; Vice-Admiral, 1811. K.B., 1808. Governor of Newfoundland, 1813-15.

222

was a midshipman in his watch from the 14th June 1779 to 8th November 1781, and he is the person from whom I first learnt the rudiments of my profession. He is a very sensible man and a good officer. I referr you for his character to Elphinstone. Another recommendation I must make is Mr. Waddington who was Chaplain to the Prince George. Should any church preferment fall vacant, recommend him to the Chancellor[1]. Waddington is an acquaintance of Jack Payne. In the same honourable black corps stands parson Lloyd, Chaplain with Keith in the Warwick; he would have no objection to a good living and in so doing you would oblige me.

I received last Sunday by Molloy[2] your hair in a ring for which, together with the sword, accept my sincere thanks and ever believe me, dear brother [etc.]. (44707a)

Pegasus, In Hamoaze, 12 Apr. 1786
At last the ship is compleatly ready for sea. I must now beg you will hurry Lord Howe to send me down my commission. Till next winter the plan is settled; endeavour, pray do, to find out what is to be my lot: whether I am to keep this ship for three years or not. Whatever you think proper, I shall follow. It appears to me advisable to be continued in employment as long as possible. If after the three years I am to have another ship, it would give me vast pleasure to command a Guardship at Chatham. Let me know what you think of this plan. In this case, if I am not happily situated in London, I can always retire to that place which is no more than a morning's ride from town, so that I should hope to see you frequently. Permit me, dear brother, to return you my most sincere thanks for your kind attention to my concerns. Believe me, when I assure you I shall be happy if ever an opportunity should offer to enable me to serve the best & tenderest of brothers. You have only to command & I shall ever be happy to obey. My compliments & best wishes to our friend, & ever believe me [etc.]. (44708)

158 THE DUKE OF CUMBERLAND TO THE PRINCE OF WALES

Rome, 15 Apr. 1786
The Duchess being affraid that the summer would be too hot at Naples made her determine to quit it; we left it last Friday, the 7th of the

1. Edward, Lord Thurlow (1731–1806). Solicitor-General, 1770–1; Attorney-General, 1771–8; Lord Chancellor, 1778–April 1783, and December 1783–June 1792. Peerage, 1778.
2. Anthony James Pye Molloy. Lieutenant, 1768; Commander, 1776; Captain, 1778.

month; we shall stay here about three weeks more, then to Florence, there for about a week & then the Ds., Brathwaite[1] & Ly. Elizabeth[2] will go thro' Turin over the Mont Cona. Ly. Ferrers[3] & I & part of the servants shall embark at Leghorn for Marseilles & join the Ds. at Besançon on our way to Spa where we mean to be about the 15 or 20 of June to stay there three month, but what part of France we shall winter in is not yet determin'd.

I shall be much obliged to you if you would use your interest with Ld. Cornwallis for him to appoint Capt. Brathwaite of the 95 Foot my Equerry, who, having some business of consequence with his father, who is second in command at Madras, wishes to go to India, but there being no possibility of going to that country without an appointment, he is extremely desirous of being appointed his Aid de Camp, not only from the opportunity it will give him of seeing his father but also from the great advantage it will procure him in his military line. With respect to the going out to India, he will be ready to attend Ld. Cornwallis or to follow him by the first opportunity.

If you will be so good either to write to me yourself or order Garth[4] to do it by the 12, 16th or 19 of May à Monsieur Le Conte de Dublin, Poste Restante à Lyon; if after that Poste Restante à Metz.

A person very well versed in India affairs is actually here & informs me that Ld. Cornwallis has no controul as to the number of his family; therefore tho' my request is late I trust thro' your kind interference it will be complied with.

Think not, my dear friend, that absence can for one single moment alter that affection I have ever professed to you; *blow high, blow low* I hope at some future period we shall meet & be happy. The Duchess [sends] her kindest love to you.   (54473–4)

1. Major-General Sir John Brathwaite (1739–1803). Baronetcy, 1802.

2. The Duchess's sister, Lady Elizabeth Luttrell (*d.* 1799). She 'resided with her sister . . . played high and cheated much. She was commonly called the Princess Elizabeth. On the death of her sister she was thrown into gaol. There she gave a hairdresser £50 to marry her. Her debts then becoming his, she was discharged. She went abroad, where she descended lower and lower, till, being convicted of picking pockets at Augsburg, she was condemned to clean the streets, chained to a wheelbarrow. In that miserable situation she terminated her existence by poison!' (Sir Robert Heron's *Notes*, p. 293.)

3. The 5th Earl Ferrers (1722–78) married Anne (*c.* 1722–91), daughter of John Elliot. She died at Hampton Court.

4. George Garth, Treasurer of the Duke's Household, and his Equerry (*d.* ?1819).

Carlton House, 26 Apr. 1786

Nothing but the very difficult situation I feel myself in at the present moment should have made me presume again to trouble your Majesty upon the subject of my own private affairs, as I am conscious that your time is already but too much taken up with the multiplicity of publick business that comes under your inspection. The very disagreable consequences that must infallibly insue to me, should I not meet with your Majesty's gracious assistance, will be much better, & indeed much more amply explained to you, Sir, by Lord Southampton, than either I can or could do by any litterary correspondence, as the particulars of my situation are so numerous & require so much explanation that I do not think they could any how be reduced within the compass of a letter. I have therefore ordered Lord Southampton to wait your Majesty's commands for attending you whenever it should best suit your Majesty's convenience, & then to lay the whole state of my affairs before you in the fairest & most impartial manner. I cannot conclude without expressing how truly grateful I shall ever feel to your Majesty, should my request meet with that reception which the urgency of the present moment makes me so ardently wish.   (41849 and 16382)

THE KING'S REPLY [copy]

Windsor, 9 May 1786

Though it would certainly be my inclination to co-operate as far as depends on me in any practicable plan which can relieve the Prince of Wales from his present embarrassments and prevent their recurring hereafter, he must be sensible that I can as yet form no judgment what steps can be taken for this purpose, as I neither know the amount to which his debts have now arisen, nor what security there will be that his future expenses shall be confined within his income. Both these points must be cleared up if the Prince of Wales wishes me to consider this subject further. Till they are so, it is vain even to enquire how far any way can be found of assisting him, consistent with what I think due to my subjects and with my constant wish to avoid increasing the public burthens.   (16383, 31894 and 41850)

THE PRINCE'S REPLY

Carlton House, 14 May 1786

In obedience to your Majesty's commands which I received in the letter you did me the honor of sending me by Lord Southampton, I have order'd Colonel Hotham to make out the estimates of my debts for your inspection, & which I will take care to transmit to your Majesty, as soon as I have received. I must take the liberty, Sir, with all possible submission of recalling to your recollection that it is now two years since I first did myself the honor of applying to your Majesty for your gracious assistance in freeing me from the load of debts with which I was then incumbered, & which I fear, what with the being so unfortunate as not to prove successful in the request I then made to your Majesty, & what with the common events which will always occurr in the transaction of money matters when the settlement of them is delay'd, they have unavoidably increased to nearly the double of what the principal was at that time. This, Sir, being the case, I fear it will not be in Colonel Hotham's power to collect the whole statement of my affairs at a minute's warning, but I flatter myself that with all the diligence he can possibly employ, a few days will be the utmost extent of time that will pass, before I shall have the honor of laying them before your Majesty. You will then, Sir, have it in your power to see how truly desperate my case is, & that if it is your gracious pleasure to releive me, my situation will not admit of any delay in carrying any such plan into execution. I can only say before I conclude, that if I am to be saved from falling into the precipice which now surrounds me on all sides, nothing can encrease the pleasure I shall feel on yt. occasion, so much, as knowing that I owe it to your Majesty.   (41851–2, 16383 and 31898)

160   PRINCE WILLIAM TO THE PRINCE OF WALES

Pegasus, In the Sound, 20 May 1786
I have just received information of the plan proposed for me. I am to spend this summer on the Newfoundland station, the winter in the West Indies, to windward: the following summer in Nova Scotia & Canada, & then proceed to Jamaica for the next winter, & the remainder of the three years is to be spent on the different West Indian stations. I am very much pleased with this mode of my serving abroad till I get steadier, which I hope I shall be when I return. Whether abroad or at home you will do me the justice, I hope, to believe that I am from the bottom of my heart most sincerely attached to you & all your concerns & shall ever be happy to do you at all times any service.

I have a favour to ask of you, to give the enclosed to Erskine [1], your Attorney General, & that you will use your interest to make him defend

1. Thomas, Lord Erskine (1750–1823), the Whig lawyer. M.P. for Portsmouth, 1783–4 and 1790–1806. K.C., May 1783; Attorney-General to the Prince of Wales, 1783–92; Chancellor of the Duchy of Cornwall, 1802–6; Lord Chancellor, 1806–7.

an unfortunate seaman of my ship who will be tried for his life at the Old Bayley for obstructing a Custom House Officer in the execution of his office. The man is as innocent of the fact as I am, & will, I am afraid, be condemned to death unless I support him, as the poor fellow has no friends. Pray do speak to Erskine. I shall take it as a great favour, for I would sooner give every farthing I am worth than that this honest man should suffer. His name is Thomas Gray: ask Admiral Barrington [1] for his character. He served under him in the Prince of Wales & Barfleur, on which ship I first knew him. He was entered as a volunteer with me when I was first appointed to the Pegasus & was one of my bargemen; he has ever behaved remarkably well.

As I expect to sail in a few days, I must now take leave of you, till I return. Believe me, I feel your kindness & affection & wish only to prove by my conduct that I am [etc.].   (44711-2)

161   QUEEN CHARLOTTE TO THE PRINCE OF WALES

Thursday, 1 June 1786

My dearest son, the King orderes me to acquaint you of his having altered the Statutes of the Order of the Garter which will be declared tomorrow at the Chapter. Your four younger brothers will be made Knights, exclusive of the 26, as sons of the Soveraingn. The four vacancies will be filled up by the Landgrave of Hesse Cassel [2], Duke of Beaufort [3], Marquis of Buckingham [4] and Earl Cornwallis. The King is also desirous of having your *Gold George*, being in wont of one upon the occasion, which I beg you will send by tomorrow morning at eight a clock at latest, but if possible tonight. I beg an answer to this as soon as you can, for the not getting the George will distress very much. Adieu tout a vous jusqu'à la mort.   (38108)

1. Samuel Barrington (1729–1800). Rear-Admiral, 1778; Vice-Admiral, 1779; Admiral, 1787. He was a brother of William, 2nd Viscount Barrington (1717–93).

2. See page 94, *n* 2. He had succeeded his father on 31 October 1785 as Landgrave.

3. Henry, 5th Duke of Beaufort (1744–1803); succeeded his father, 1 56; Master of the Horse to the Queen, 1768–70; K.G., 2 June 1786 (installed by dispensation, 29 May1801).

4. George, 1st Marquess of Buckingham (1753–1813), second son of George Grenville, the Prime Minister. M.P. for Buckinghamshire, 1774–9; succeeded his uncle as Earl Temple 1779; Lord-Lieutenant of Ireland, July 1782–June 1783, and again, November 1787– October 1789; Secretary of State for four days, December 1783 (on the formation of Pitt's Ministry). K.G., 2 June 1786 (installed, 29 May 1801); created Marquess, December 1784. Held the rich sinecure office of Teller of the Exchequer, 1764–1813.

Carlton House, 10 June 1786

My dear Aunt, I had the pleasure of receiving a very kind letter from you yesterday, which did not however come to my hands till very late last night, & indeed too late to be answer'd at all events till this morning, owing entirely to my having gone out very early in the morning & not having return'd home till very late at night, & I was this moment setting out to answer it when I receiv'd another letter from you, appointing Friday as the day for our attending you in the country instead of Wednesday, which was the very thing I was going to entreat of you, myself to do, as I had also a very particular engagement on Wednesday. Prince Charles of Mecklenburgh [2] is now in London & dines with me on Monday. If therefore you chuse it, my dear aunt, I will save you the trouble of sending to him & will ask him myself in your name. However, I shall wait for your commands for the doing this, if you will have the goodness to send me a few lines by the return of the messenger who carries this to your house. I cannot conclude this letter, my dear Madam, without endeavouring, however faintly, to express my sentiments on this day by saying how sincerely I wish you may meet with many returns of it in the perfect enjoyment of health & spirits you now do, long to continue the life & spirit of every society you honor with your protection.   (Add. MSS. 33132, f.72)

163 THE PRINCE OF WALES TO THE KING

Carlton House, 15 June 1786

I now have the honor of laying before your Majesty through Lord Southampton the amount of my debts, which I am concerned at not having had in my power to do sooner, but I wish'd to be as minute as possible. In the account I here enclose, however, there are some particulars which I have not been able to collect with as much accuracy as I desir'd, as it is my wish that nothing respecting my present situation should be concealed from your Majesty's knowledge.

You will not, Sir, be able to see how dreadfully involved I am. I confess the sum is large, but what adds more to my distress is, that the longer it continues unpaid, so much the more it will continue to augment. I therefore have nothing to do but to throw myself upon your Majesty's benevolence, hoping for your gracious assistance, which if I

1. His great-aunt; a sister of Frederick, Prince of Wales. The 10th was her birthday. She died on 31 October following, at the age of seventy-six.

2. The Queen's brother.

am so unfortunate as not to meet with, will throw me into a situation below that of the lowest individual in the country. I therefore flatter myself your Majesty will be pleased, whenever it suits your convenience, to favor me with a speedy and a final answer respecting your intentions, as, circumstanced as I am, my affairs are too pressing to admit of much delay. (41853 and 31900 [wrongly dated on the back, 15 July])

ENCLOSURE

Statement of arrears due to sundry persons under the several Departments of his Royal Highness the Prince of Wales to Lady Day 1786.

	£	s.	d.
His Royal Highnesses private debts	8,000	0	0
Arrears in the Department of Privy Purse	46,900	2	6½
—do.— Compr. of the Household	12,800	14	11
—do.— Mr. Weltze in aid of Privy Purse	5,601	2	0½
—do.— Commr. of the Stables	32,399	10	2¾
—do.— Building and furnishing	52,637	14	7½
—do.— The Treasurer	1,050	17	6½
—do.— The Housekeeper	765	5	2½
Debts [sic]	160,178	6	7¼
For compleating, finishing and furnishing the works and designs now in hand at Carlton House	79,700	0	0
For incidental charges not yet come in, or to be ascertained exactly	30,000	0	0
Total	£269,878	6	7¼

(41854)

164 THE MARQUESS OF CARMARTHEN TO THE PRINCE OF WALES

Grosvenor Square, 22 June 1786

Your Royal Highness having some time ago expressed an intention of looking at Hogmagog, I of course ordered my agents to give no answers to any application which might be made respecting the renting of that place until I had the honour of knowing whether it might suit your Royal Highness on account of its situation being so near Newmarket.

I have of late received information that a gentleman is extremely desirous of taking it for a term of years. It is in consequence of this application that I now presume to trouble your Royal Highness in order to receive your commands, Sir, whether I may look upon myself as at liberty to treat for the rent of Hogmagog. Trusting to your Royal Highness's goodness to forgive this trouble, I have the honour [etc.]. (Add. MSS. 28061, f.156.)

165 THE DUKE OF CUMBERLAND TO THE PRINCE OF WALES

Spa, 26 June 1786

As I find I have been in a great mistake relative to the Installation & that on acct. of the window there is to be none this year, I do not propose doing myself the pleasure of coming over now to England; therefore the letter you was to have wrote to me to Dover will be of no service. If you have any answer to give me to what I wrote you will direct it to me at Spa.

As yet there is no company at all; the weather has been rainy this last week but now begins to take up & get hot.

I will not trespass more upon your time.

P.S. The Duchess desires her best respects to you. (54475)

166 PRINCE WILLIAM TO THE PRINCE OF WALES

Pegasus, In Trepassey Harbour, 2 July 1786

After a three & twenty days passage we arrived here last week, & as opportunities are scarce of sending letters home I shall use every occasion to write to you, as I was latterly very remiss. By the orders I have received, a copy of which I have enclosed in this, I shall be prevented seeing you these three years & more to come. You will I hope either write yourself or desire Elphinstone to write, as you will always know where I am to be found. Give Keith my best compliments & desire him to write often, as I certainly shall but am now prevented by the number of people I have been obliged to correspond with; shew him my orders that he may be able to find me out on the different stations.

Pleasuring in England as you do, my dear friend, is by far a more preferable life to what a soldier or sailor is obliged to go through. Since I have been here a most violent rheumatic complaint has prevented my going on shore, but the report of the gentlemen is very infavourable. Such a constant thick fogs that there is no seeing a mile, no inhabitants to associate with; all Irish drunken fishermen; the English bathing-places, how elegant they are with the first company in the kingdom. I hope when I return to have it in my power to go a little in the great

230

world. There is so great a want of anything stirring that I do not know what to write about, so [you] will I hope excuse me if I now subscribe myself [etc.]. (44719-20)

167 THE KING TO THE PRINCE OF WALES

Windsor, 3 July 1786

From everything which has passed between me and the Prince of Wales during these last two years, relative to his embarrassed situation, he must have seen that I hold it impossible even to enter on the consideration of any means to relieve him untill I should receive a sufficient explanation of his past expences, and see a prospect of reasonable security against a continuation of his extravagance.

On his renewing his application this year I repeated the same sentiments as formerly, and at the end of several weeks, I have received a paper called a statement of arrears due to sundry persons, making a sum total of near £270,000. Of this sum £160,000 is stated as actual debt, and is made up of private expences wholly unexplained to the amount of about £60,000. Of above £52,000 for building, &c. above £32,000 for the stables, and some comparatively small sums of household expences.

The remaining sum of £110,000 consists of a specifick charge of above £79,000 for carrying on works at Carlton House and a general demand in addition to all the rest for un-ascertained expences. A moment's reflection ought to have made the Prince of Wales sensible of the impropriety of offering such a paper to my consideration; without some examination of the expences which have led him into his present situation, it is scarcely possible to conceive a sufficient security that the same abuses will not recur. But then instead of proposing or expressing a readiness to conform to any future regulations for this purpose, this unsatisfactory account is followed by a demand of above £100,000 more to support farther extravagance, assistance from me, is, under such circumstances, out of the question.

The Prince of Wales has nothing to expect from me till I see reason to expect that the attempt to releive him may be effectual, instead of probably serving only to involve him still deeper.

For this purpose it would be necessary to have as clear an explanation as the nature of the thing will admit, of his past expenditure, and above all to ascertain that it shall be confined within proper limits in future.

It is then, and then only, that it can become a subject of consideration by what means I can cooperate in extricating him from the embarassment to which his own imprudence has subjected him.

(16386, 16535, 31875)

168 THE PRINCE OF WALES TO THE DUKE OF CUMBERLAND

Carlton House, 4 July 1786

I really do not know whether I am hurt or pleased most with the contents of your letter; hurt yt. you cd. conceive even for a single moment yt. I cd. feel anything but the sincerest affection & regard for you & ye Duchess, or pleas'd at the idea of so soon & so unexpectedly embracing my friend again. The whole reason for my silence has been the unsatisfactory accounts I cd. have sent you of the business we were both concern'd in. If I had written I must have said something on yt. score, & therefore I did not wish to trouble yr. repose & quiet with my foolish complaints. I have deferr'd my journey to Brighton on purpose to wait yr. arrival in London. I need not I hope say yt. my house, servants &c. are entirely yours. I will not tresspass long upon you at present, but merely say yt. I have much to talk over with you when I see you, & conclude with assuring you, my dear Duke, how sincerely I remain [etc.]. (41859)

169 THE PRINCE OF WALES TO THE KING

Carlton House, 5 July 1786

I yesterday had the honor of receiving your Majesty's letter from Lord Southampton, and feel myself particularly unfortunate at not meeting with that relief which I flattered myself I had some reason to expect from an application for three years successively, & trusting to your Majesty's great munificence. I feel myself greatly concerned for the trouble I hitherto have given your Majesty thro' the course of this most unpleasant business, & can only assure you, Sir, that you shall receive no farther disturbance upon that score from me, as you have now convinc'd me that I have no reason to expect either at present or in future the smallest assistance from your Majesty. (41860, 16387 and 38111)

170 HUGH ELLIOT TO THE PRINCE OF WALES[1]

6 July 1786

In consequence of the very flattering marks of confidence with which I was honoured last night at Ranelagh I presume to entreat the perusal of these lines. I shall not attempt by any reasoning to influence your Royal Highness's decisions, guided by your own judgement & sense of the most elevated of human situations, there can be no doubt, that

1. Endorsed by the Prince: 'Mr. Elliott's letter on the reduction of my Household.'

232

whatever part is finally embraced, it will be such as may impress upon your country, upon Europe & mankind the conviction that your Royal Highness has no less followed the impulse of the most distinguished sense of honour than the coolest dictates of wisdom, and unavoidable necessity. May I also, in this crisis, once more presume to make offer of my poor services, & to assert that no *consideration* shall prevent me from dedicating myself with zeal & fidelity to the accomplishment of any object which may contribute to the ease & satisfaction of a Prince whose indulgence admits of my avowing the most unbounded attachment to his person. Dare I venture to add that there are certain moments in every rank of life, which throw an irresistible bias upon its future course, & that the present therefore appears to me to be one of those critical periods in which your Royal Highness is exposed to some dilemna of choice? I am far from either knowing at present or foreseeing by what other means in future the embarrassments which have occurred can be removed, than by the decisive arrangement I was last night made acquainted with. But as it will be an event as delicate in its consequences as any that appears upon the page of history, & will be no less subject to the observation of cotemporaries than to the discussion of posterity, I do not scruple to avow that it would make me infinitely happy if any more gentle measure could be devised.

To preserve your Royal Highness to your country & splendor in it must be the wish of every loyal subject & good citizen. I am certain I need make no other apology for having ventured to express that wish with so little reserve & to renew the offers of the utmost zeal & discretion in endeavouring to contribute to the accomplishment of so desirable an event.[1] (38112-3)

171 THE PRINCE OF WALES TO LORD SOUTHAMPTON [copy, in his own hand]

7 July 1786

I am sorry yt. I am obliged to communicate to you by this letter ye last orders that I am afraid I shall trouble you with for some time, owing to the reduced state of my circumstances, wh. I am afraid you are but too

1. Sir Gilbert Elliot wrote on the 8th: 'You will see an account of the reduction of the Prince of Wales's Household today in the papers, which is so like the truth that I imagine it is put in by somebody about him. He told Hugh of his intention two or three days ago, which is to go abroad quite as a private man, and stay till something is done for him, or till he can pay his debts by saving. He wants £250,000. Hugh went to Pitt about it, who was disposed to undertake the payment of his debt, provided the rest of the money he asks might be appropriated to some specific purposes; but the Prince would not consent to that.' (*Minto*, i.112)

well acquainted with, & from wh. I had flatter'd myself & I think not without [the] best reasons, yt. I shd. have been releived by ye King. I am compell'd to dismiss (with the greatest regret on my part I assure you) all ye Gentlemen belonging to my family who have served me with zeal, attachment & fidelity ever since I appointed ym. to their respective posts. I must desire you to return ym. ye. sincerest & warmest thanks from me for their past services, & assure ym. yt. nothing shd. have separated ym. & me, but being driven to the distress I at present suffer, & without ye smallest prospect too of relief from those from whom I think I had ye greatest reason to expect it, I must therefore desire you to have proper letters made out for each individual expressive of those feelings I have mentioned in the foregoing lines & assuring ym. yt. whenever it is in my power to reassume yt. splendid situation my birth has placed me in, I shall be happy to receive ym. again with open arms into the places they now hold. With respect to yourself my dear Lord, I can only say yt. I ever shall feel most truly grateful for yt. attachment & regard wh. I beleive ever were the motives of your conduct thro'out to me. I remain ever most sincerely yr. friend.

P.S. I forgot to tell you, yt. I mean to keep Hotham, Lyte, Lake & Hulse [1], as Inspectors of my accounts and I must desire you either to bring me, or send me yr. key by ten o'clock in ye morning, as I am obliged to go out of town at yt. hour.   (38114–5 and 38116)

172   VISCOUNT MELBOURNE [2] TO THE PRINCE OF WALES

7 July 1786

I am honoured with your Royal Highness' commands, communicated to me by Lord Southampton's letter, but as I was particularly brought into your family by your Royal Highness's own bounty & friendship to me, I humbly beg myself to return your Royal Highness my dutyfull &

1. Sir Samuel Hulse (1747–1837). Knighted 1821. Equerry to the Prince of Wales, 1780; Treasurer of the Prince's Household, 1791; Master of the King's Household, 1812; Vice-Chamberlain of the Household, 1827–30. General, 1803; Field-Marshal, 1830.

2. Peniston Lamb, 1st Viscount Melbourne (1745–1828); succeeded his father, Sir Matthew Lamb, as 2nd Baronet, 1768. M.P. for Ludgershall, 1768–84; for Malmesbury, 1784–90; for Newport (Isle of Wight), 1790–3; created Lord Melbourne [I.], 1770, Viscount Melbourne [I], 1781, and Baron Melbourne [U.K.], 1815. A Gentleman of the Bedchamber to the Prince of Wales, 1783–96, and a Lord of the Bedchamber, 1812–28. Lady Melbourne's son was William Lamb, afterwards Prime Minister. Lord Melbourne was 'principally known by the distinguished place that he occupies in the annals of meretricious pleasure, the memoirs of Mrs. Bellamy or Mrs. Baddeley, the syrens and courtesans of a former age' (*Wraxall,* v.371). At one time, Lady Melbourne was the object of the Prince's admiration, and then he became attached to the Duchess of Devonshire.

sincere thanks for the many marks of favor & attention you honoured me with during the very pleasant situation I have held in your Establishment; & I must ever feel your kindness with the utmost gratitude. Allow me to assure your Royal Highness that I shall ever consider myself bound by all possible duty to your Royal Highness & your interest & shall be extreamly happy at any future day to be honoured with your commands again.

I humbly hope to be permitted to have the honour of paying my respects to you occasionally at Carlton House & I remain [etc.].   (38117)

173   LORD PARKER[1] TO THE PRINCE OF WALES, AND THE REPLY

Shirburn Castle, 9 July 1786
I have this morning been honored, pursuant to your Royal Highness's commands, with a letter from Lord Southampton informing me of the resolution your Royal Highness's situation had compelled you to take, &, in consequence, of my dismission from your service.

As an Englishman I cannot but exceedingly lament that the Prince of Wales should be permitted to be in a situation to render that resolution necessary, but having had the honor to have been for some time in a situation which necessarily gave me opportunities of a much closer acquaintance than the generality of my countrymen possess, I have the additional concern which naturally arises from any embarrassments of a person with whom we are much connected, & whom we esteem, as give me leave to say I do your Royal Highness, a friend.

I hope, Sir, this dismission precludes me only from the receipt of my salary, & that I shall notwithstanding continue in the enjoyment of access to your person & the honor of attending you in public whenever there may be an opportunity of doing so. Permit me to assure you that should an occasion offer of my appearing in attendance on your Royal Highness I shall receive more pleasure in doing so now than on any occasion where I have before had the honor of attending you.

I must entreat as a favour that your Royal Highness will give directions that, should such an opportunity offer, I may be sent to, and I think I have some right to ask, as my name stood, or rather I hope now stands, first in that line of attendants in which I have the honor to be [etc.].   (38119-20)

1. George, 4th Earl of Macclesfield (1755–1842), styled Viscount Parker, 1764–95; succeeded his father as Earl, 1795. M.P. for Woodstock, 1777–84, for Minehead, 1790–5; Lord of the Bedchamber to the Prince of Wales, 1780–6, 1787–9; Comptroller of the Household, 1791–7; Lord of the Bedchamber, 1797–1804; Captain of the Yeomen of the Guard, 1804–30.

235

THE PRINCE OF WALES'S REPLY [copy]

Carlton House, 9 July 1786

I have this instant receiv'd your kind letter & cannot help immediately answering it to return you my sincere thanks for the kind offer of your services, which I am afraid it will not be in my power to accept of, as I have taken a firm determination not to appear again in public till I can do it again with that dignity and splendour which my rank in life entitles me to & which is infinitely more than I have any private wishes for. Some advantages generally do accrue or testify themselves even in the worst of situations, tho' indeed I cannot call mine such, having the consciousness of acting right and justly to support me in my retirement, but which will always be render'd pleasant in the recollection of those friends who have so disinterestedly testified their regard and attachment to me as you have done & in whose society I flatter myself still to pass many of my leisure hours. (38118)

174   THE HON. G. F. FITZROY[1] TO THE PRINCE OF WALES

Dowl's Lodge, 9 July 1786

I yesterday received a letter from my father with your Royal Highness's orders for dismissing me with the rest of your R.H.'s servants. Permit me, Sir, to return you my thanks for all your goodness & repeated kindness to me, & to assure you of my gratitude, sincere & unalterable attachment, & how happy I shall be to obey your Royal Highness's commands whenever you think fit to honor me with them. (38121)

175   MAJOR GEORGE CHURCHILL[2] TO LORD SOUTHAMPTON

Lichfield, 9 July 1786

I was this day honoured with your Lordship's letter of dismission from the service of H.R.H., accompanied with a copy of his gracious letter to your Lordship. I cannot but lament the occasion that has forced his R.H. to this step—which though severe on us all, we must yet applaud. Nor can I have anything further to say—but to beg, should an opportunity offer, and your Lordship not think it improper—you would lay

1. George Ferdinand Fitzroy, 2nd Lord Southampton (1761–1810); succeeded his father, 1797. Groom of the Bedchamber to the Prince of Wales, 1783; M.P. for Bury St. Edmunds, 1784–7; Captain in the Army, 1780; Major, 1792; Lieutenant-Colonel, 1793; Colonel, 1796.

2. One of the Prince's Equerries.

236

me at his R.H.'s feet, & beg that I may still be permitted to approach his person to testify my most grateful sence for all his goodness & condesention towards me during the time I had the honour of belonging to him; and may I add, shall still esteem myself honoured, flattered, and happy by his commands. (38122)

176 COLONEL EDMOND STEVENS[1] TO LORD SOUTHAMPTON

Grantham, Sunday, 9 July 1786

I am this moment honoured with your letter, accompanied with a copy of a most gracious one from the Prince of Wales to your Lordship. However acute the pain may be that I feel upon this occasion on being no longer in a situation to serve so good and indulgent a master, I can assure your Lordship that I am equally sensible of the goodness I have always experienced from him; and permit me now to request of your Lordship, in addition to those marks of friendship you have always shewn me, most humbly, and with the greatest deference and respect, to present my duty to the Prince of Wales, accompanied with the only request I can make upon this occasion to his Royal Highness, that he will do me the justice to believe that the obliging favours with which he has been graciously pleased to honor me have always afforded me the greatest pleasure and shall be acknowledged with the utmost gratitude. Permit me now, my dear Lord, to thank you for your goodness to me since I have had the honor of being known to you, & believe me to be [etc.]. (38123)

177 THE REV. JOHN LOCKMAN[2] TO LORD SOUTHAMPTON

Windsor, 9 July 1786

I receiv'd the honor of your letter this morning & am very sorry for the occasion of it. In H.R.H.'s present situation I own that the resolution he has taken appears to me to have been dictated by those principles of honor & justice wch. I never had the least doubt woud always direct his actions. As for me, my Lord, I shall always think myself highly oblig'd to H.R.H. & wth. pleasure resign every lucrative idea for his

1. A Groom of the Prince's Bedchamber since February 1784, re-appointed, May 1787. In November 1786 he declined the post of Equerry to the King; having done so, he asked the Duke of Rutland, the Lord-Lieutenant of Ireland, to obtain for him a more suitable appointment (Rutland MSS. [H.M.C.], iii.360).

2. Rector of Dunstable, 1753; of Drayton Beauchamp, Oxon., 1786; Master of St. Cross Hospital, Hants.; Canon of Windsor, 1759–1807 (*c.* 1722–1807).

service. Give me leave to sollicit from your Lordship a continuance of that kind attention wth. which you have always honor'd your most respectful and obliged humble servant. (38124)

178 SIR JOHN S. DYER [1] TO LORD SOUTHAMPTON

St. James's Street, 10 July 1786
I was yesterday evening favored with yours of the 6th ins^t, with a copy of a letter from the Prince of Wales in which H.R.H. is pleased to signify, with the kindest expressions, his commands for the dismission of his family. I will not trouble your Lordship with my feelings on the occasion, as I am very sensible how much your own must be distress'd; but permit me to assure you with real truth & sincerity, I should have been happy in having the honor of serving his Royal Highness without any emolument. (38125)

179 LIEUTENANT WILLIAM BIRCH [2] TO LORD SOUTHAMPTON

Writtle [near Chelmsford], 11 July 1786
I am to acknowledge the receipt of your Lordship's favor of the 7th ins^t & to testify my concern at its cause.

I shall esteem myself sensibly obliged to your Lordship if at a proper period you would lay my humble duty at his Highness's feet with the assurance that, independent of any self-interested motive other than the opportunity it will procure me of proving my zealous attachment to his royal person—I shall ever think myself honored with H.R.H.'s commands. (30216)

180 WILLIAM WILSON [3] TO LORD SOUTHAMPTON

Palace, Kensington, 11 July 1786
In consequence of the letter I had the honour of receiving from your Lordship, I must request the favour of your Lordship to present my

---

1. Sir John Swinnerton Dyer (1738–1801) succeeded his father as 6th Baronet, 1780. He was a Groom of the Bedchamber. He committed suicide.

2. One of the Gentlemen Ushers of the Privy Chamber.

3. One of the Gentlemen Ushers of the Privy Chamber.

most respectful duty to H.R.H. the Prince of Wales, and assure him that the letter H.R.H^{ss} so condescendingly directed to be communicated to me gave me the greatest concern; that I shall always retain the most grateful sense of the obligations I am under to H.R.H^{ss}; and that it will ever be the height of my ambition to have the honour of serving H.R.H^{ss} without the least regard to salary or any emolument whatever.

I must beg leave to add that I want words to express how much I feel myself indebted to your Lordship for your goodness to me on every occasion, and that I have the honour to remain [etc.]. (38127)

181   THE BISHOP OF ST. ASAPH [1] TO LORD SOUTHAMPTON

Ashburnham Place, 11 July 1786

I trouble you with this letter to acknowledge the honor of yours by the last post, together with a copy of that in which H.R.H. the Prince of Wales in so gracious and kind a manner declares the resolution which he has form'd, and which for the honor of the country, independant of all other considerations, I trust he will not be suffered to practice but for a short time.

Permit me to assure your Lordship that I esteem as one of the most fortunate circumstances attending the honor which his Royal Highness conferr'd on me, to profess myself to be at all times with truest regard [etc.]. (38128)

182   THE PRINCE OF WALES TO THE KING

Carlton House, 11 July 1786

I have had the honor of receiving your Majesty's written message transmitted to me by Lord Southampton and am greatly concerned that my poor sentiments cannot coincide with those of your Majesty in thinking that the former message which I had the honor of receiving, pen'd in your Majesty's own hand, was not a refusal. After having repeatedly sent in various applications to your Majesty for two years successively, representing that a partial reduction out of so incompetent an income as mine, was to no purpose towards the liquidation of a debt, where the principal and interest were so considerable, I this year humbly requested your Majesty that you would be graciously pleased (having previously laid my affairs before you, Sir, for your inspection

1. Jonathan Shipley (1714–88), Bishop of Llandaff, February 1769; Bishop of St. Asaph, September 1769–1788.

and painted them in the distress'd colors which they so justly merited) that whenever it suited your convenience you would favour me with a decisive answer, as the various delays which have occurred thro' the course of this business have in reality proved more pernicious to the situation in which I have been for some time past involved than the original embarrassment of the debt. To not only these, but any future delays would I most willingly have submitted had they rested meerly upon my own patience, but the pressing importunities of many indigent and deserving creditors (some of whose very existence depends upon a speedy discharge of their accounts) made too forcible an appeal to the justice becoming my own honour and the feelings of my heart, to be any longer delayed. Another consideration is that any further procrastination might have exposed me to legal insults as humiliating to me as I am persuaded that they would have been offensive to your Majesty. I therefore, previously to my having the honour of receiving that message to which your Majesty had refer'd me, had determined that (should I not be so fortunate as to meet with that relief from you, Sir, with which I had flattered myself, and which indeed I thought that I had the greatest reason to expect) I would exert every nerve to render that just redress and assistance to my creditors which I cannot help thinking is denied to me. These are the motives, Sir, that have actuated my conduct in the step I have taken of reducing every expence in my family, even those to which my birth and rank entitle me, and which I trust will ever continue to be the principle and guide of my conduct till I have totally liberated myself from the embarrassments which now oppress me, and the more so as I am persuaded that such a line when pursued with consistency will meet with the approbation of every candid and dispassionate mind.

I shall not trespass any further upon your Majesty's leisure, but have the honour to subscribe myself [etc.].   (16388 and 31877)

183   THE DUKE OF YORK TO THE PRINCE OF WALES

Hanover, 11 July 1786

I cannot refuse myself the pleasure of troubling you with a few lines to return you many thanks for the two beautiful horses you have been so good as to send me over. It is a very great pity that Foxhunterebus's knees are broke, as I never saw a finer mover. As for Hermit I mean that he should carry me many a good day's sport this autumn.

Grenville has delivered me your kind message and Lennon has written me word that you meant to write to me soon. It is not necessary for me to say how happy your letters make me, though of late I have not had the pleasure of receiving many. I suppose that by this time all the amusements of London are over and that you are gone down to Bright-helmston. You cannot expect any news from hence which can in the least interest you; I shall therefore not tresspass longer upon your patience but shall conclude by assuring you how sincerely I am ever, dear brother [etc.].   (43802)

184   LORD SOUTHAMPTON TO THE PRINCE OF WALES

Wednesday, 12 July 1786

I obey'd your Royal Highnesses commands & deliver'd the letter to his Majesty. Nothing particular past, except enquirys about the method of the dismission of your R.H^s family, & the extent to which it has gone. I took the opportunity of shewing your letter to me of the 6th instant, which his M. read. The K— as usual did not open your R.H. letter to him. It was late before I could go into the Closet, & I was not kept long. (38129)

185   THE HON. G. J. LUDLOW ^{1} TO LORD SOUTHAMPTON

Apethorpe, 13 July [1786]

I have the honor to acknowledge the receipt of your Lordship's letter containing his Royal Highness's commands for the dismission of the Gentlemen of his family—and sincerely hope that, altho' the present situation of H.R.H.'s affairs do's not admit of his keeping up his former Establishment, he will be graciously pleased to accept of my voluntary services whenever he may find them necessary, and it will ever be considered as the highest honor, by, my Lord [etc.].   (38130)

1. Captain George James Ludlow (1758–1842), succeeded his brother as 3rd Earl Ludlow [I.], 1811. General, 1814; G.C.B., 1815; created Baron Ludlow [U.K.], 1831. He fought in America, and, with Cornwallis's army, was made prisoner at Yorktown, when he narrowly escaped being hanged by the Americans. 'An American having been some time previously seized in the British lines and hung as a spy, the troops of the United States called aloud for retaliation, and when the British army surrendered, Washington was beset by clamour and importunity to sanction the execution of an English Officer. Yielding apparently to this out-cry, Sir Charles Asgill, Captain Ludlow and others of the Guards Officers were made to draw lots. Asgill and Ludlow, great friends as well as brother-officers, were the two last for the risk. The lot fell upon Asgill. Washington delayed the execution, and Lady Asgill, the mother of the British Officer, had time to make interest with the Court of France, where she was personally and intimately known. The King of France interfered and Asgill was saved. Had the lot fallen upon Ludlow, the influence of his family might not have been able to save him' (*Gent. Mag.* 1842, ii.92).

186 J. KEMEYS TYNTE [1] TO LORD SOUTHAMPTON

Kevenmably[2], *13 July 1786*

Last night only, I had the honor of your Lordship's letter of y[e] 7th with dismission from the Prince of Wales's service.

I must beg of your Lordship to present my humble duty to the Prince of Wales, & to assure H.R.H. how sensible I have ever been of his kindness & protection whilst I had the honor of being in his service; that my attatchment & duty to H.R.H. will ever be the first object of my life, & that I shall allways be proud to have the honor of serving so good & gracious a master. All the world must approve this present measure, & none, I am sure, more than us, H.R.H.'s servants, who will (as I am) be much flatter'd by his gracious approbation of our services.

P.S. I shall leave this place tomorrow, & shall be in town on Monday, when I will have the honor of waiting on you. (38131)

187 MAJOR JOHN MACKAY [3] TO LORD SOUTHAMPTON

Bruton Street, 13 July 1786

I only came to town last night, when I found your Lordship's letter of the 7th instant, with a copy of one from his Royal Highness to yourself upon the subject of the dismission for the present of most of the Gentlemen of his family. When the Prince of Wales did me the honour to give me an appointment in his family, I considered it then as I do now the greatest that could be conferd upon me. I hope I may therefore be permitted through your Lordship to lay my duty at H.R.H.'ss feet and to express my regret and concern for the occasion which obliges him to make the present reduction in his family, and at the same time my most sincere prayer that H.R.Hss may soon be enabled to reassume that splendour and dignity to which his birth and situation so justly intitule him.

Before I conclude this letter I beg leave to return your Lordship my gratefull and unfeigned thanks for your goodness and kind attention to me ever since I had the honour of being in H.R.Hss' family. (38132–3)

1. A Groom of the Prince's Bedchamber; appointed Comptroller of the Prince's Household, November 1791.

2. Cefn Mably, near Cardiff.

3. One of the Gentlemen Ushers Daily Waiters.

Grafton Street, Sunday morning, 16 July 1786

I trust that your Royal Highness's persuasion of my respectful attachment to your person and of my sincere devotion to your service will prevail on your goodness to forgive the liberty which I take in troubling your Royal Highness with these lines.

The subject of them is to apprize your Royal Highness of a visit which I have just receiv'd from a gentleman of considerable note in the City of London, who was pleas'd to say that I ow'd it to the great goodness and condescension with which it was suppos'd that your Royal Highness was pleas'd to honour me, & which had induc'd him & some others of his friends to put into my hands a communication to your Royal Highness of certain steps which were actually at this moment in agitation by a body of most respectable persons in the City, whom he was not yet at liberty to declare & which when laid in form before your Royal Highness would bear the most unequivocal testimony of their unbounded affection for your Royal Highness's person, & of their zeal & sollicitude to remove from your mind every possible circumstance that could in the slightest degree contribute to embitter the peace of it. Conjectures, he said, had prevail'd in the City that the humanity & excellence of your Royal Highness's heart might have induc'd you to take under your consideration the means of raising money for the purpose of discharging your Royal Highness's debts, independantly of the generous sacrifices which your Royal Highness had already publickly made in the voluntary resignation even of your most reasonable pleasures & comforts, as well as of all those circumstances of splendour & magnificence which are due to your high birth and exalted rank. He was unable, he said, to express the admiration which the City as well as the rest of the world entertain'd of your Royal Highness's virtue and magnanimity upon this occasion; but that the body of gentlemen, to whom he had before alluded, were in particular most anxious that your Royal

1. Ralph, Lord Lavington (1739–1807), son of Ralph Payne, of St. Christopher, who was Chief Judge there. M.P. for Shaftesbury, 1768–71; for Camelford, 1776–80; for Plympton, 1780–4; for Fowey, 1790–1, for Woodstock, 1795–9. K.B., 1771; Governor of the Leeward Islands, 1771–5, and again, 1799–1807. Irish Peerage, October 1795. He married (1767) Frances Lambertina Christiana Charlotte Harriet Theresa (*d.* 1830), daughter of Henry, Baron Kolbel, of the Holy Roman Empire, a General in the Imperial Service. The Whig Government in the summer of 1783 had referred to him as 'very well inclined, but should be attended to'. The Opposition leaders, said Wraxall (iii.411), frequently met at Payne's house in Grafton Street. 'Erskine,' he added, 'having one day dined there, found himself so indisposed as to be obliged to retire after dinner to another apartment. Lady Payne, who was incessant in her attentions to him, inquired, when he returned to the company, how he found himself. Erskine took out a bit of paper and wrote on it

'Tis true I am ill, but I cannot complain,
For he never knew Pleasure who never knew Payne.

Highness would be pleas'd to take no step, at least for a few days, which might eventually embarrass your Royal Highness, or think of immediately releiving the wants of your creditors at the expence of any part of your future ease & comfort. These gentlemen & himself, he said, were at this time concerting a plan which, when brought to perfection, would enable them to lay at your Royal Highness's feet a sum not only competent to the liquidation of every incumbrance which oppress'd your Royal Highness's finances, but likewise to the completion of the noble design which your Royal Highness had laid for rendering Carlton House a Palace deserving of your royal residence, and of course an object of national credit & magnificence. The scheme, he added, was not yet quite sufficiently advanc'd to qualify or aut[h]orize him to impart to me the particulars of it; but he beg'd that I would endeavour to devise some means of making known to your Royal Highness the substance of this mark of the affectionate attachment of the City to your Royal Highness, and of their high admiration and applause of your Royal Highness's conduct, as well as their humble wishes that you would be pleas'd to condescend, for the space of a few days, to suspend any project or resolution which your Royal Highness might meditate for a purpose which they had themselves most sollicitously at heart. Before I engag'd to venture on the liberty for which I must now rely on your Royal Highness's indulgence, I stated to my visitor my opinion of the impossibility that your Royal Highness, though feeling the warmest gratitude for so mark'd a proof of the love & attachment of any respectable body of men, could express your sense of it in reply to any indirect information or proposal short of a clear and decided offer made with proper respect & formality; and on his expressing himself aware of this circumstance, & actuated only by the anxiety which he & his friends felt that your Royal Highness should determine on no measure for a few days, before they had an opportunity of submitting to your Royal Highness the testimony which they had in contemplation of their duty & affection for you in a due & becoming form, I consented to convey his intelligence to your Royal Highness's private ear, for your forgiveness of which I depended, Sir!, on your experienc'd goodness & indulgence.

But, Sir! after having thus laid before you the purport of this conference, I trust that I shall stand acquitted in your Royal Highness's opinion of any presumptuous meaning to suggest to you the degree in which my visitor's intelligence ought to convey pleasure & satisfaction to your Royal Highness, & to merit your countenance & approbation. Your Royal Highness views your present situation in a light so perfectly true & clear, and entertains so just a conception of the sy[s]tem necessary for your future conduct, that, on my conscience, Sir! I beleive & am persuaded that it is beyond the power of the wisest & most considerate heads among your many friends to assist your Royal Highness with any discreeter advice or more useful counsel than what arises from your own judgment. I cannot at the same time restrain the vanity which I feel in finding my own sentiments upon this business corroborated by the opinion of Lord Loughborough, who drop'd in upon me immediately on the departure of my visitor. Feeling the most sollicitous interest for the promotion of every circumstance & event which can contribute to your Royal Highness's honour & happiness, we could not but derive a sensible pleasure from the idea which had just been suggested to me; but our satisfaction arose rather from the proof which such an offer would exhibit in the eyes of all Europe, how highly your Royal Highness's amiable character stands in the public opinion, & how precious your peace & happiness are already become in the hearts of a people over whom you are one day to reign, than from any opinion that the proposal, when submitted to your Royal Highness in due form, is seriously deserving of acceptance, or at all events, of too precipitate an adoption. Lord Loughborough, unappriz'd that any part of our conversation would ever reach your Royal Highness's ear, appear'd confident that though your Royal Highness would receive & reply to the offer when made to you, with the kindest countenance & in the most flattering terms, you would nevertheless indicate no small proportion of reserve upon the occasion, & would express the firmest & most invariable determination to persevere in that independant plan which your Royal Highness has already digested & declar'd for the discharge of your incumbrances, & which has excited a degree of admiration through the nation, amounting to enthusiasm: and under this persuasion he foresaw numberless political as well as personal advantages resulting to your Royal Highness & the public, of a magnitude which reduc'd the meer liquidation of your debt to an object of very inconsiderable size indeed. He added likewise that the years which he had pass'd, & the experience which he had acquir'd in the world, had taught him to view with caution ideas which bore the fairest appearance of liberality, and to consider it possible (as human nature is constructed) that the sincerest sentiments of affection & attachment might be liable to a certain proportion & mixture of self-interest which your Royal Highness's wisdom & discernment might be very warrantably led to suspect, however kindly & graciously your goodness & affability might induce you to acknowledge the ostensible motives. I cannot, I own, suppress the effusion of joy which I myself feel at the step which is in the contemplation of the City whatever may be your Royal Highness's resolution upon it. So voluntary & zealous an offer will convince every branch of Government of the abundance of your ressources in the hearts of the people, & that you were induc'd to prefer your application for the payment of your debts to the most sacred of characters, not because your royal Highness was destitute of friends to your cause, but because it was unquestionably the fountain through which you might, on every principle of honour, delicacy, & propriety, expect to draw a supply from the treasure of a nation which evinces its approbation of your conduct by its ready zeal to support it. My heart glows with pleasure at the prospect of that admiration which cannot but attend your Royal Highness's noble & generous conduct upon this occasion, & of the contention which must prevail among all ranks of people in this Kingdom (& not improbably in its sister one) who shall be forwardest in testifying their resolution to support a Prince who has display'd a judgment & magnanimity without example in the annals of Great Britain. But I fear, Sir!, that my feelings are leading me into tediousness & impertinence and I will only beseech your Royal Highness to forgive my zeal if it betrays me into presumption, & to condescend to receive these lines, which I have the honour of conveying express to your Royal Highness by a private hand, as a testimony of that profound respect, & attachment, with which I am Sir! [etc.].

The above was began last night, & finish'd this morning, when I recᵈ the letter from Lord Carlisle[1] which, by advice of Lord Loughborough who has just call'd upon me, I take the liberty to inclose to your Royal Highness. (38134–8)

189 LORD CARLISLE TO SIR RALPH PAYNE

Grosvenor Place, Sunday Morn. [*?16 July 1786*]
In regard to the proposition mentioned last night of an intended contribution in the City towards the discharge of his Rˡ Highness the P. of Wales debt, I can entertain but one opinion; and I heartily wish those persons in whom it would not be impertinence or presumption to expose their sentiments freely to him would agree with me in thinking he ought to reject the offer. The manly perseverance in the plan he has adopted lays a wide foundation of the public esteem. The adhering to it in spite of the present temptation would determine its solidity, and the admiration that would arise from ye forebearance wᵈ amply repay him for the immediate inconvenience he seems prepared to submit to. The general motive that actuates the numbers thus to testify their zeal & affection for him is & ought to be, most flattering. The individuals who will separate themselves from the crowd, & press their pretensions for future favour as the first or most active promoters of this scheme, will embarras him in various ways. If his resolution of liquidating his debt by the efforts

1. Frederick, 5th Earl of Carlisle (1748–1825), succeeded his father as Earl, 1758. Treasurer of the Household, 1777–9; First Lord of Trade, 1779–80; Lord-Lieutenant of Ireland, 1780–2; Lord Steward of the Household, 1782–3; Lord Privy Seal, April–December 1783; K.G., June 1793. Except during the war years, 1793–1801, he voted with the Whigs.

of his own firmness, & by the generous self denial of many things a P. of Wales ought to enjoy is to be shaken, it ought alone to be effected by the interposition of the King or by the feelings of the country at large, which sooner or later cannot fail to operate in a manner to satisfy the expectations of those who love & respect him most. . . .   (38109)

190   SIR CHARLES BARROW[1] TO THE PRINCE OF WALES

Gloucester, 16 July 1786

I have often attempted to be introduced to your Royal Highness to have the honour of kissing your R. Highnesses hand, and flattered myself about six weeks with the hopes of seeing you at Windsor & there to have requested that honour.

I am sorry to hear Parliament has not augmented your income to what your rank entitles you to, and what you justly merit. I have the sum of two thousand pounds at present by me, much at your Royal Highnesses service, and if you will condescend to accept of it, I will immediately forward to you a draft on my Banker (Child & Co.) for that sum.   (38139)

191   CHARLES JAMES FOX TO THE PRINCE OF WALES

St Anne's Hill, 16 July 1786

When I had the honour of seeing your Royal Highness last, I had had no opportunity of hearing any conversation upon the step you had taken, and consequently could only guess that the judgment of the public would coincide with my own in the warmest approbation of your Royal Highness's plan. I have been since very happy to find that my conjecture was well founded, and I may without flattery as truly as cordially congratulate your Royal Highness upon having by this manly & judicious step united the universal opinion of all descriptions of men in your favour. Praise comes from some more willingly, from others with more reserve, but it comes from all, and there cannot be a more convincing proof of the wisdom of your Royal Highness's measure than this; that those who are least willing to express favourable sentiments dare not blame it, but only doubt or affect to doubt your perseverance in it. Will your Royal Highness pardon me for suggesting my opinion

1. Sir Charles Barrow (1708–89), M.P. for Gloucester, 1751–89, and a supporter of Fox. Created Baronet, January 1784 (though he had voted for Fox's India Bill). He was evidently too ill to attend on the Regency question in December 1788, and he died on 10 January 1789.

that even this doubt might & ought to be done away? It is founded as I understand upon this circumstance only, viz! that the money to be set apart for the creditors will still be in the hands of those from whom your Royal Highness has a legal right to demand it, and consequently that it will still be in your power to break the resolution which you have taken. That your Royal Highness is incapable of this, those who know your Royal Highness know. That no man of sense would break a resolution the very announcing of which has gained him such general, nay universal applause is what everyone must feel; but yet the bare possibility of such a thing is a twig to catch at for those who wish at any event to prevent your Royal Highness being thought of as you deserve. Now this possibility might I conceive be easily removed by a measure which has (I understand) been already suggested to your Royal Highness and met with your approbation, I mean by assignment of £35,000 or £40,000 per annum out of your allowances from the King to trustees for the express purpose of paying it to your creditors by such instalments as shall be agreed on. These trustees should be men of known reputation and not *now* in your Royal Highness's service, I think Lord Southampton should be one. I am sure your Royal Highness will forgive me for offering my advice even if you should not follow [it], but I really think it is a pity that so glorious an act as your Royal Highness's should not be complete and perfect. Add to this that the greater the probability of the whole business being *soon* settled, the greater the necessity of adopting the scheme of Trustees, because otherwise it may be said (and everything that can be said to lessen you will be said) that if your plan had not produced an early effect, you would not have had the resolution to persist in it, whereas, if you put it out of your own power, your greatest enemy cannot dispute your intention. With respect to the probability of an *early* effect being produced I will fairly confess that I am less sanguine than the generality of those with whom I have conversed, nay, I am not quite convinced that a *very* early effect is the thing most to be wished. I am certain that if the public see your Royal Highness living for any time upon a confined system of expence and actually converting the greater part of your income to the payment of your creditors, that they will conceive so just an opinion of your Royal Highness's character as to render you not only popular in the extreme, but (what perhaps is of more consequence) to make you considered by thinking men as a man that can be depended upon in the most difficult tryals, and such a character (excuse my freedom) is cheaply bought, especially by a Prince, by being confined in expence for one year, for more than one it is impossible to last. Most people think the next Session must settle the business. I doubt, but should not be afraid to be responsible with my life for the Session following it if (which I doubt as little) your Royal Highness perseveres in your plan. If I write too freely to your Royal

Highness it is your own fault since it is your goodness which has encouraged me to do upon the most delicate occasions, and I do so now the more readily because the sincere joy I feel at the credit & glory you are gaining by this manly step gives me unusual spirits. It is an epoch in your Royal Highness's life, and if I am not deceived, a most fortunate one. It will give the public an insight to your character which belonged before only to us who had the honour of knowing you; it will do away with those millions of calumnies which have been so industriously spread and which could only be received from a total ignorance of your Royal Highness's true character. There would be no end if I were to enumerate all the good effects which I foresee from this business; it is better a thousand times better than if you never had been in debt.

Before I conclude this long letter I would take the liberty of suggesting to your Royal Highness whether there might not be some propriety in acquainting by letter the Duke of York, the Dutchess of Brunswick and possibly Prince William too (who I understand is near of age) with the step you have taken and your motives. Possibly too the Duke of Gloucester and the Duke of Cumberland ought to be apprized of it. I suggest all this from an apprehension that your Royal Highness may not have considered the extreme importance of the step you have taken in the same light that I do. But surely it is a matter of moment enough to make it a subject of communication to the persons I have mentioned.

I beg your Royal Highness's pardon for having troubled you with so very long a letter, but I feel so sincere an admiration for your conduct that I cannot help thinking of every little circumstance that may tend to make it more perfect and troubling your royal Highness with my thoughts as they occur to me.

I am with every sentiment of gratitude & respect[1] [etc.].   (38140–3)

192 THE DUKE OF ORLEANS TO THE PRINCE OF WALES

Paris, 17 July 1786

Recevez mon compliment, je vous en prie, mon cher Prince, sur le party que vous venez de prendre on ne parle pas d'autre chose dans ce pays ci, d'apres tout ce que j'en entends dire tant aux Francois qu' aux Anglois qui sont ici j'espere qu'outre l'honneur qu'il vous fait à present, il vous fera beaucoup de profit par la Suite, je suis au desespoir d'être retenu à Paris par des affaires auxquelles ma presence est absolument nécessaire et de ne pouvoir au moyen de cela aller vous temoigner moi meme toute la part que j'y prends, comme d'apres tout ce que j'intends il est bien interessant que vous ne voyagiez pas hors d'Angleterre dans

1. The Prince's reply, dated the 19th, is in Fitzgerald's *George IV*, i. 91.

ce moment ci j' emploierai la 1er semaine que j'aurai de libre a aller vous trouver, mon cher Prince, ce sera j'espere dans le commencement du mois prochain. Si vous voulez bien me faire savoir dans quelle partie de l'Angleterre je pourrai vous joindre, ce sera un grand plaisir pour moi dont vous connoissez et ne doutirez jamais, mon cher Prince, de l'amitié pour vous. (38144)

193   JOHN LETHBRIDGE[1] TO LORD SOUTHAMPTON

Hill House, near Taunton, Somerset, 18 July 1786
I do not assume too much by calling myself an independent country gentleman, for such I have always lived & such I hope to die. A proper spirit & an easy fortune co-operate to give me a title to that character, & I reside upon a handsome estate in the county of Somerset. My breast hath ever glowed with a warm attachment for my Sovereign, the Prince of Wales & the other branches of his Royal Family, & teems also with a sincere love & regard for the honor, welfare & good of my country. Possessing such sentiments, I am struck with the deepest concern on reading certain paragraphs in the late public prints (& whether they are founded in truth or error must be well known to your Lordship) setting forth that his Royal Highness the Prince of Wales hath formed the resolution of disbanding his Household, & of abridging himself of those other marks of royalty & state; which surely are the birthright of the eldest son of the King of Great Britain; & I cannot reflect but with the severest mortification, as our national honor, I think, must be greatly tarnished, that such resolution should originate in the want of those supplies which are so absolutely necessary to be granted, & without which it is impossible the birth & high rank of the heir to the Crown of these Imperial Kingdoms can be maintained & supported with becoming dignity & splendor. I should not then in my opinion act consistently with the principles of loyalty I profess, nor the part of a good subject, if I withheld my purse or personal exertions at this particular juncture. I therefore intreat through the medium of your Lordship to make a humble tender of my most dutiful & affectionate respect & regard for his Royal Highness's person, & an offer of some few thousands for his present use, service & accommodation. I am sensible it is not more than a mite I can cast into his royal treasury, but I hope the purity of the intention will compensate in some degree for the want of ability. I do assure your Lordship I am not stimulated to this act of duty by an

1. Sir John Lethbridge (*c.* 1746–1815), created Baronet, 1804. M.P. for Minehead, 1806–7. In 1811 his son asked for a peerage for him. 'For many years' he had desired this mark of favour from the Crown.

impertinent vanity, or by views of ambition & self interest, nor is my mind actuated by any other impulse than a regard for the person, honor, & dignity of the King's immediate successor & our national character & reputation, which, I fear, will suffer much on the present occasion.

Prompted by these motives & prefering sincerity to empty compliments I shall rely upon your Lordship's goodness to excuse a formal apology for troubling you with this letter, & to make an allowance if I am deficient in those points of ceremony & etiquette of approaching you, which from a stranger as I am you may justly expect. It is my wish also to vest a discretionary power in your Lordship over this letter, & if you should judge the language & contents improper for the Prince's ear, you will be pleased to stop its further progress by committing it to the flames. On the other hand if you should not perceive any impropriety in laying it at his royal feet, & his Highness should condescend to bestow any notice on the matter contained in it, your Lordship will have the goodness to signify what his royal will & pleasure may be & it shall be obeyed with the greatest cheerfulness, punctuality & dispatch.

I shall conclude with my most fervent wishes that his Royal Highness may in due course of time equal, if not surpass his predecessors in goodness, greatness & glory, & with due respect for your Lordship's high & distinguished character, I have the honor [etc.].   (38145–6)

194   THE PRINCE OF WALES TO SIR CHARLES BARROW

19 July 1786
I this day had the pleasure of being acquainted with your very noble offer, wh. ye letter I received from you contain'd, & I cd. not delay one moment returning my thanks to you for it, tho' it is not in my power to avail myself of yr. generosity. Any one yt. has the good fortune of being acquainted with yr. character (tho' they may not with yr. person) cannot be surpriz'd when they know such an offer comes from you. I can only say yt. you have laid me under an obligation wh. I shall not easily be able to forget, & yt. I am happy in ye. assurances of yr. friendship, being with great truth [etc.].   (41865–6)

195   THE PRINCE OF WALES TO THE HON. HUGH SEYMOUR CONWAY

Brighton, 20 July 1786
My dearest Hugh, I shd. not have so long delay'd acquainting you with the situation of my affairs had not I really been pester'd to death for the

251

last fortnight with letters wh. requir'd immediate answer; in short, I have not had a single moment to myself till the present one, wh. I dedicate to you. I need not say, at least I flatter myself so, yt had you been in town you wd. not have *been the last person* I shd. have communicated my intentions to respecting ye schemes I was reduced to take; indeed I hope, & I do beleive, yt my conduct on this occasion has met with ye approbation of my dear friend, especially when I recollect what past between us upon this very business now above a year ago in ye dining room at Weltjie's. There remains now, my dearest Hugh, but one part of the scheme we then laid wh. I have not put in practice as yet, wh. I am afraid, & indeed I may say I beleive I am pretty certain I shall be obliged to put in practice before the commencement of the winter. This is ye only occasion in wh. I cd. regret ye present situation. I am now speaking very selfishly as I am afraid it will debarr me from enjoying the society of a man concerning whom my sentiments are too well known for me to attempt to say anything. Jacko has in the most friendly manner possible, as he does every thing, desir'd to be my companion, wh. is no small consolation to me for not having your society also, but do not think, my dearest Hugh, yt I shall think of stirring without first taking my leave of you & Lady Racy[1]. I have talk'd this plan over with one or two people of whom I have ye highest opinion & in whom I place ye utmost confidence, & I find yt it has met with their approbation much. They all have said yt I have acted so properly hitherto yt I cannot judge wrong in this business, do what I will, & indeed they do not see how I can take any other part than that I am alluding to, for to speak fairly, how can I, situated as I am at the present moment, go into society, go into the world, without a family, without attendants, in short, without any one single thing wh. my rank & situation in life entitle me to? As a private man I may travel, but I never can remain with any sort of propriety as an individual in the country ou je suis né pour être le premier. Only rest assured of one thing, my dearest Hugh, & yt is yt in whatever quarter of the globe, whatever country I may be in, you will nowhere have anyone yt is more sincerely [attached] to you & everything that is yrs than I am. I will not now tresspass any longer upon yr. patience but conclude with desiring you to present my best compliments to Lady Racy & to believe me [etc.].

P.S. Pray do not think me prizing or vaunting myself too much when I mention'd to you in this letter what some persons had deliver'd as their opinions relative to my conduct in this business. I assure you I did it

1. Presumably a pet name; possibly Lady Anne Horatia Waldegrave (1762–1801), daughter of the 2nd Earl Waldegrave, who married Hugh Seymour-Conway on 2 April 1786.

merely by way of putting you au fait of what their ideas were on yt subject.

My dearest Mrs. Fitz desires her best love to Lady Racy & you. I have pester'd Jacko ever since we arriv'd here to write to you, as it was impossible for me to have yt pleasure owing to ye business with wh. I was plagu'd; he has promis'd to do it every day & has compleatly neglected it, comme a l'ordinaire. (Ragley MSS.)

196 THE PRINCE OF WALES TO THE DUKE OF CUMBERLAND

Brighton, 21 July 1786

Inclos'd you will receive the letter I sent to Dover by my courier to wait yr. arrival, wh. I assure you I did most anxiously at London, as there is no one in the world I had more willingly see than you. The newpapers will already have inform'd you sufficiently of my situation for me to say nothing concerning it, except yt. I am now upon the footing of any individual, even the most private in ye. country. My father has written me a positive & firm denial. I therefore have acted upon what I thought honorable & right principles in justice to others as well as myself, & I flatter myself from what you yourself knew from me when you was last here of the antecedent transactions in the course of this business for the two preceeding years, you will not blame either my conduct or my motives. When a man, my dear friend, has a clear conscience, I think he has but little to fear.

With regard to the rest of my plan I hope in a very few weeks to embrace both you, my dear Duke, & the Duchess, as the remaining in this country a simple particulier is impossible, as Ministry have set their face against the whole of the King's family excepting himself, & as the more I am endeavoured to be crush'd, the higher my spirit rises. None of our family hitherto have been deficient in spirit, or have been apt to do shabby things, & I will not be the first to disgrace it, however the conduct *of some others* who shall be nameless seem to tend towards it.

I sh. have written to you sooner, my dear friend, but I have been so pester'd with ye. business wh. ye. necessary arrangements this unpleasant business has drawn upon me, yt. I have not had a single moment to myself till ye. present one, wh. I dedicate to you, only rest assured of one thing, my dearest Duke, yt. ingratitude never was a vice inherent in my heart, & yt. therefore thro' life I never can be mean to be guilty of any disrespect or inattention either to yourself or ye dear Duchess, but yt. I shall glory in being accused of such intentions if loving you both as much as a man can his friends & relations can be

253

deem'd such. I am again call'd off by business, I will therefore conclude with desiring you to lay me at the Duchess's feet, & to believe yt. you ever shall find me thro' life [etc.].

P.S. You shall hear from me again in a few weeks, only rest assur'd yt. when I stir I certainly will endeavour to come & see you before I go anywhere else.   (41867–8)

197   THE PRINCE OF WALES TO THE DUKE OF YORK

Carlton House, 24 July 1786

I send you this by way of recommending to your particular attention Lord Belgrave[1], an intimate acquaintance of mine, & who I am sure you will like as he is really a very charming young man; he is son to Lord Grosvenor[2].

I shall write to you everything yt. has past concerning my umpleasant [situation] & quite at length, as I now think I am perfectly at liberty to speak out to you the true feelings of my heart. Adieu my dearest brother [etc.].   (43805)

198   THE DUKE OF CUMBERLAND TO THE PRINCE OF WALES

Spa, 31 July 1786

Last Sat. post brought me two letters from you, the one of the 4 of July intended for me at Dover, the other of the 21 from Brighton.[3] I cannot say how happy you have made me in convincing me of the steadyness of your friendship towards me. I lament most heartily the situation you have been drove to but yet I have the happyness of assuring you that your manly conduct is universally approved of: this conduct proceeds from your own judgement & goodness of heart & will make you rise superior against the cruel calumny of the world that have been tryed to

1. Robert, 1st Marquess of Westminster (1767–1845), second but only surviving son of Richard, 1st Earl Grosvenor. Styled Viscount Belgrave, 1784–1802. M.P. for East Looe, 1788–90; for Chester, 1790–1802. A Lord of the Admiralty, 1789–91; Commissioner for the Affairs of India, 1793–1801; succeeded his father as 2nd Earl Grosvenor, 1802; created Marquess of Westminster, 1831. He supported Pitt, but after his death, joined the Whigs.

2. Richard, Earl Grosvenor (1731–1802). Created Baron Grosvenor, 1761; Earl Grosvenor, July 1784. His wife Henrietta, daughter of Henry Vernon, was seduced by the King's brother the Duke of Cumberland in 1769, against whom £10,000 damages were subsequently awarded. The Earl obtained a separation from her.

3. Nos. 168 and 196.

be impressed with a false idea of you by those who have not your interest at heart. The Ds. desires her kind love to you.

With regard to any future schemes you may have I shall be very glad when you acquaint me with them, but at this time if you have anything of consequence to say you [had] better send your courier to me as I shall stay here all the month of August, no determination being taken where we pass this next winter. The weather here has been remarkably bad, rainy & cold. The Milbanks are here, Ld. Leitrim's[1] family, the Camelfords[2] & some Members of Parlt., some Irish, the Archduke & Ds. of Milan[3], the Elector of Cologne who is [a] jolly fellow & much like an English farmer; Mad. Simian, the beauty of Paris, has stayed here four days from Aix-la-Chapelle with her brother, Comte Charles d'Ama [sic] & Monsr. de Chanceaux that you remember in England; some Germans & Poles but, to speak the truth, a dull society enough, but all that would be of little consequence to me if I were certain you were happy. I hope the time will come. Pray let me hear from you how you do & how you pass your time at Brighton.

I will not trespass more on your time. . . .

P.S. I have wrote by this post to Parkyns who is at Margate that you will write him your orders when he shall meet you either in London or Brighton & he will enter fully into a conversation I had with him before his departure from hence, which was last Thursday.   (54476–7)

1. Robert Clements (1732–1804) was created Baron Leitrim [I.] in October 1783, Viscount Leitrim [I.] in December 1793, and Earl of Leitrim [I.] in October 1795. He was M.P. for Co. Donegal, 1765–8; for Carrick, 1768–76, and for Co. Donegal, 1776–83. He was an Irish Representative Peer, 1801–4, one of the original twenty-eight elected in 1800. In 1765 he married Elizabeth, daughter of the 1st Earl of Massereene; she died in 1817, aged 79.

2. Thomas Pitt (1737–93), M.P. for Old Sarum, 1761–3, and 1774–83, and for Okehampton, 1768–74, and who was created Lord Camelford in January 1784, married (1771) Anne (1738–1803), daughter of Pinckney Wilkinson. His father, Thomas Pitt, and the 1st Earl of Chatham were brothers.

3. The Queen wrote to Prince Augustus on 12 October: 'We have had a visit of the Duke & Dutchess of Milan; they breakfasted with us at Kew, spent one evening with us in town, & finished with giving us one entire day at Windsor. We dined at the lower apartments in the Castle, & went to the Lodge after dinner; by seven we returned to the Castle where we met the company which was invited upon the occasion, had the Concert at the Great Guard room, & supp'd in St. George's Hall. The day unluckily for the prospect was very rayny but if you would not say I was selfish, I would almost say I was glad of it, for by that means I saw much more of the Arch Dutchess who is one of the most amiable & sensible women I know; she possesses great knowledge without making any parade of it, she speaks all modern languages well, & the Imperial Ambassador tells me that she reads both Greek & Latin with great ease, but her modesty is so great that when she was at Oxford no body could find it out. She is very affable & easy in her manner without being ever being familiar [sic]. She is not handsome but pleasing which latter *entre nous soit dit* is more lasting & consequently happier to have. I do regret her departure very much.'

12 Aug. 1786

The honors as well as favors that yr. Royal Highness has conferr'd upon me will never be forgot, & if my zeal (in congratulating yr. Royal Highness on the return of this day) shou'd have lead me to take too great a liberty, I must entreat yr. Royal Highness to add one favor more by excusing my presumption. I am, with the most profound respect [etc.].
(38147)

200   THE DUKE AND DUCHESS OF CUMBERLAND TO THE PRINCE OF WALES

Spa, 11 Sept. 1786

I own I can hardly find words to express my feelings upon your tenderness & kindness on this occasion, nor did I want this to confirm me in what I was always truly sensible of, the sincerity of your regard & affection for me. The only awkward thing in the present moment is my being obliged on account of the weakness of my left eye, to the kind assistance of Dr. Blane to commit my thoughts upon paper, but be assured that the very moment he permits me to write I shall at least have the satisfaction of opening my heart to you, as well as giving you my opinion of the doctor, whose delicacy I will not put to the blush by writing himself my opinion concerning him even upon so short an acquaintance.

The doctor has acted till Friday last at half-past eleven at night when he arrived here, the part of your courier. I will not enter into the conversation that I had with him shortly about yourself & next about my own state of health, but refer you to the letter which he has the honor of writing to you.

I think it a justice I owe to Mr. John Adair to acquaint you of his great care and assiduity, which lasted about a month before the doctor's arrival, and I have still farther the pleasure of acquainting you that Dr. Blane approved of all that had been done.

My old servant, Jackson, has been my nurse totally, and I cannot speak in too high terms of his attention as well as of his affection. The doctor called upon Atkinson, the apothecary, in order to bring some medecines with him which he has been so obliging as to weigh out himself, & of these bark is one, which he has very prudently put under Jackson's care to boil & prepare for fear of mistakes. Rest assured that whatever the doctor says shall be a law with me.

The Dutchess desires her kindest love to you.   (54478–9)

1. Brother of the 6th Duke of Hamilton, and a Lieutenant-Colonel in the Guards. He was re-appointed a Gentleman of the Prince's Bedchamber in May 1787. (1742–91)

This fresh proof of your Royal Highness's affection for the Duke by sending your own physician, Docr. Blane, has awakened my mind to a sence of pleasure five week's contemplation of the Duke's painful illness had seem'd to render it incapable of. The Duke never was in danger of death, & before the docr. arrived was recovered beyond expectation, but I wish'd to prevent the disorder taking root & producing a series of complaints similar to the Duke of Glos'ter's. Your Royal Highness's good opinion of Docr. Blane is sufficient to impress me with an idea of his infallibility, & I hope the Duke will be persuaded to choose that winter residence best calculated to prevent a relapse. We cannot remain much longer at Spa; it has been & still is uncommonly damp & cold, yet, but for the Duke's illness, I should have passed my summer very agreably. Ld. & Ly. Beauchamp & Mr. Lampton leave us tomorrow; they go by slow marches to Francfort, see everything in their way & arrive time enough for the last ten days of the Fair. Col. Sheldon only accompany's them as far as Aix-la-Chapl. & then I believe will join his Regiment at Nancy. The Milbanks are still here but set out in two or three days on their return to England. George Conway[2] remains at Spa ten days longer to take care of a little Countess in the absence of her husband. I believe I have named all that have the honor to be known to your Royal Highness excepting Mr. Pechell, who will speak for himself. The Archduke & Duchess were very desirous of making yr. Royal Highness's acquaintance & I wish them that satisfaction in return for the politeness with which we were received by them & indeed all the Imperial Family in the various countrys they govern.

My good friend Lady Ferrers is by this time in London; her accident obliged her to leave me, to her & my great regret. I hope yr. Royal Highness will be so gracious as to call on her for my sake. (54480–1)

201   MINUTE OF SIR JOHN MACPHERSON [3] [copy]

Fort William, Calcutta, 12 Sept. 1786

This being the first meeting of the Board[4] since the change which has taken place in the Government, I beg leave to offer to my noble and very illustrious successor my most sincere congratulations upon the

---

1. These last two paragraphs were added by the Duchess.

2. Perhaps Lord Hertford's son.

3. He had just been made a Baronet, and, since February 1785, had been Governor-General of Bengal, pending the arrival of Cornwallis (on 11 September 1786).

4. The Governor-General's Council.

occasion. It is not in the common and formal language of compliment used upon similar occasions that I tender these congratulations to Earl Cornwallis. His Lordship will feel in the principles on which he has undertaken his present office from his country the best explanation of my sentiments. The cheerfulness of my future co-operation in the station which I still occupy in the Administration will convince the India Company that the compliment which I have addressed to my successor is the language of my real feelings.

It has been my peculiar fortune to have served as a Member of the Administration of Bengal and to have risen from the junior to the highest seat in the Supreme Council during a period of extraordinary service and great public difficulty. To compare the situation of the British possessions in India on the present day with the position of public affairs in August 1781, and to reflect upon the part which I endeavoured to act in the intermediate most eventful period, is to me enough, nor until I had the power of making the comparison conclusively and of enjoying the satisfaction arising from it, could I have conceived the happiness which may be found in the duties of the public service. To this happiness is added that of seeing my plans for the relief and improvement of the Company's affairs in India committed to the protection of a ruler who possesses the powers as well as the disposition to render them permanently useful to India and to Great Britain.

I will not on the present occasion enter on any laboured detail of the measures which were adopted by this Government while I presided in Council. I know that Earl Cornwallis is fully informed upon the subject in all its parts, and that he has perused our dispatches to the India Company to the latest period.

In these dispatches every care has been taken to give the most faithful and minute detail of public affairs in their various branches; our political situation with the native powers and the Governments of European nations, has been amply and progressively explained. The various orders of the Company received during the late Administration have been fully kept in view and the point to which they have been executed is likewise stated. The Regulations that were adopted for ascertaining, checking and retrenching the expenditures of this Government are kept in a separate Department, entitled that of Secret Inspection and Reform, and the letters to the Company in that Department, with official statements, exhibit all that has been yet performed in this line. The administration of the public revenue has been unusually successful, and the improvements which have been adopted in that important branch are the more interesting as they have anticipated the wishes of the Company. This will appear from a perusal of the last General Letters to the Company in the Revenue Department.

On the subject of the Commercial Department, that which comprehends the chief value of these colonies to the parent State, it will be found that much has been performed in favour of the Company by the late Administration. The first and of course the most difficult steps have been taken to provide goods[1] by sealed proposals at the lowest prices, and according to fixed specimens of quality; much is still to be done and in this branch as well as in that of the revenue, I trust the progress which has been made in surmounting local and original embarrassments has opened the road to the greatest public benefits. The labours of the late Administration to reduce and regulate the military expenses of this Government and to adopt plain and uniform Regulations in the Military Department appear with much credit on record. The absence of the Honble. Member who took the lead in these labours affords me an opportunity of paying a just tribute to his merits of General Sloper[2]; I can truly say that I never met with a more cheerful or a more active associate in public business, and I am certain his noble successor in the military command will find many testimonies of his professional abilities in the method of the general arrangements and the precision of the details which he recommended. In regard to my other associates in the Administration, I may justly observe that a difference with them in any public opinion was not a diminution of private regard, or any interruption to that mutual goodwill without which the operations of Government are frustrated, if its members differ in disposition to each other as they must sometimes in opinions on public business.

We have all and mutually the satisfaction of having received unanimous approbation from our employers for our exertions in their service, an approbation which cannot but bind our future unanimity in supporting the new Administration.

Tho' I might with justice claim extensive credit to the combined efforts of the late Administration from their unwearied endeavours to ascertain with accuracy the state of the Company's debts and incumbrances in all their Presidencies and from their efforts to lessen the public expense and apply the existing resources to the most necessary purposes with an impartiality that has removed distress from the other Presidencies and raised the credit of the Bengal Treasury; tho' the goods that have been provided for the Company's markets in Europe without any extra drafts on their credit at home cannot but meet their approbation; and tho' all the proceedings of this Government in external and

1. For the Company's 'Investment'—i.e. its imports into Europe from India and the Far East.

2. General, afterwards Sir Robert Sloper (d. 1802). Commander-in-Chief at Madras, June–July 1785, and subsequently in Bengal, from July 1785 to September 1786, when he was superseded by Cornwallis. Sloper was prevented by illness from attending the meeting of the Supreme Council that day.

internal management have been remarkably fortunate for these nineteen months past, still I must confess that only the great lines are adopted of that general system which promises happiness and security to our possessions in India with a suitable return of advantage to Great Britain. The Administration at home has made great exertions, and I observe with infinite satisfaction that they have felt and answered our call upon them to co-operate in the public service.[1] Many and very important objects of that service remain yet to be regulated and improved from home and upon the spot, I mean particularly a mode of funding or providing for the Company's debts, a general comprehensive plan for making their expenses in all their settlements subordinate to their regular resources, and Regulations to make the movements of their troops less expensive and more rapid.

The completion of a system connected in all its parts and firm on the principle of reducing the expenses of all the Presidencies and establishments of India within the limits of our income is a most arduous undertaking, and constantly subject to new obstacles and successive interruptions. Yet until India is administered within the line of this system (while the profits of its commerce are secured to the parent State) India cannot be said to be well regulated or firmly held. And one of the cruel discouragements which I have always felt while at the head of the Company's affairs will press continually against my successor; I mean the indefinite demands of the subordinate Presidencies and the delay and irregularity which are experienced in the transmission of the accounts of their expenditure as well as of those services for which they make general demands. The present Governor of Fort St. George[2] will execute, I am confident, all that zeal and ability can arrange in his Government. Relative to Bombay, it is sufficient to observe that notwithstanding the continuance of their representations of their distresses and of fresh applications for supplies, the account of the amount of the military arrears of their army for the service of the late war has not been hitherto transmitted to Bengal, tho' the funds for discharging those arrears have been amply furnished without the introduction of a rigid system limiting the expenses of the other Presidencies within fixed bounds, and these formed in some proportion to their resources. The labours of the Bengal Administration to lessen the expenses of the Bengal Government and to improve its resources are insufficient to the great object of maintaining India on the footing of a great, general and secure Government. I am equally apprehensive that there is an error at home in limiting our expectations of aid from the Provinces of Oude, while the diminution of our demands does not lessen the severity with

1. 'See Revenue letter 12th April, paragraph' [a marginal note].

2. Sir Archibald Campbell (1739–91), Governor of Madras, April 1786–9. Major-General, 1782; K.B., 1785.

which the revenues will ever be collected from the subjects of the Vizier's Government.

After these general observations I have only to add that I will, with pleasure, communicate to our Governor-General the great points of view in which the interests of Great Britain in India have occasionally struck me, as they appeared to check and to influence the designs of rival and other nations in Europe. Upon this subject my hopes and my wishes for the prosperity of the British Empire may have made me sanguine and perhaps speculative, yet the more I have examined the subject the more I am convinced that a firm hold of our possessions in India must operate in the end to produce a good understanding with the new Powers that have arisen in the western world, and that the union of France, of Spain and of Holland is to be chiefly counteracted and dissolved in and from India.

The detailed and more minute information which I have endeavoured to acquire and arrange; in the revenue the Phousdary or native magistracy, the Investment, the arrangement of offices and the intelligence of the native Courts I shall communicate to the Governor-General progressively and as his time will admit of discussion and explanation on each different head. I am happy to remark that he will find the public business completely brought up, in every Department except that of the appeals in the Sudder Dewanny Adawlut[1] where there are about sixty principal causes to be decided. Measures have been taken for ordering the different vaqueels[2] to attend, and it will be found I believe necessary to change one part of the Addaulut regulations, that which encourages parties to appeal and of which they avail themselves merely to delay the decision of justice.

I had proposed to record upon this occasion a solemn declaration relative to the principles upon which I had endeavoured to discharge my duty as a member of this Government from the time I took my seat in the Council, and especially while I held the office of Governor-General. Another time will be more proper for such a declaration, I mean that in which I can make it fully and conclusively.[3] (38148–54)

1. The Sadr Diwani Adalat (the Supreme Civil Court).

2. Vakils (pleaders).

3. Macpherson was almost alone in believing himself a great reforming Governor-General. Most informed people in India had the greatest contempt for him. John Shore, his colleague on the Supreme Council, declared, 'Lord Cornwallis upon his arrival found a Government rendered contemptible from its imbecility; all confidence in its measures or abilities destroyed, and private and public credit depreciated. . . . Never was any Administration so thoroughly despicable as his [Macpherson's]: a total want of energy, dignity and common sense distinguish it.' Macpherson, who could not understand why he had been superseded, sailed for home in December and landed at Southampton on 10 August 1787. (A. Aspinall, *Cornwallis in Bengal*, pp. 8–10, 21.)

Spa, 18 Sept. 1786

I can hardly find words to express my thanks to you for this fresh mark of your kindness to the Ds. & myself. Doctor Blane has taken great care of me & you see he has kept his promise in permitting me the satisfaction of writing to you. After mature deliberation he has determined to carry me back to you as he knows I have no opinion of the foreign physicians & that if I have a relapse I can there have immediate relief. The Ds., who agrees in everything that is either conducive to my health or wishes, altho' she fears the climate of England for me, yet gives up her opinion. The agitation of mind the Ds. has had during my long & painful illness has given her a pain in her side for which next Wednesday she & Ly. Elizabeth [1] set out for Aix-la-Chappelle to drink the waters. The doctor hopes to carry me to her next Sunday & we mean to leave that place for dear England on Sunday the 15 of Octr.; therefore five or six days will land us safely at Cumberland House where I shall stay for five or six days & then go to the Lodge. I shall bring Doctor Blane with me to England & I only hope you will not have occasion for his skill but I do in the strongest terms recommend him to your protection, for I have the strongest proofs of his ability & steadyness. I must not yet use my eyes too much, therefore believe me [etc.].   (54482)

Hanover, 26 Sept. 1786

I have many thanks to return you for last kind letter by Lord Belgrave who arrived here on Thursday. I think him a very agreable young man, and have done everything in my power according to your desire to render the place as agreable to him as possible.

I hope you will do me the justice to believe that it is not through any want of affection towards you that I have hitherto remained silent upon a subject which must for every reason be very distressing to both of us to touch upon. As I am at so very great a distance it is impossible for me to form any exact judgement about it. I cannot however help saying that I am most sincerely sorry that things are gone so far and that you have thought that the situation of your affairs obliged you to take so very publick a step.

I suppose that by this time your hunting is begun. We have already

1. The Duchess's sister, Lady Elizabeth Luttrell. See page 224, *n* 2.
2. The draft of this letter is dated 25 September (43814).

had some very good runs; the hounds which our friend Lake has sent me over are most excellent, and Hermit goes incompatably well.

As I have nothing in particular to add I will not trouble you with a longer letter at present. I shall therefore only beg you to write often and to believe me [etc.]. (43815)

204 THE DUKE OF ORLEANS TO THE PRINCE OF WALES

Paris, 8 Oct. 1786

Ce n'est qu hier que j'ai reçue, mon cher Prince, la lettre que vous avec bien voulu m'écrire par Smith, parceque les vents l'ont retenu 15 jours a Brighton; elle m'a fait bien grand plaisir ainsi que toutes les marques d'amitie que vous me donnez, j'accepte bien volontiers l'offre que vous me faites de vos neuf chevaux de Carosse quand au phaeton, je ne m'en soucie pas parceque dans ce pays ci je n'ourois me servir d'une voiture aussi haute; je vais dire a Mr. Hammerstley [1] [*sic*] qui est ici de prendre vos ordres pour remettre a qui vous voudrez la Somme de 720 pour le prix de ces 9 chevaux et j'envoyerai un homme expres les chercher. Je vous prierai, mon cher Prince, de donner ordre qu'on les guarde dans vos ecuries jusques a ce qu'il vienne quelqu'un les chercher de ma part c'est a dire avec un ordre signé de moi. Je me suis acquitté de toutes vos commissions. Lauzun et moi nous vous ferons certainement notre Cour a la fin de l'hiver ou au commencement du printemps. Croyer moi toujours, je vous prie mon cher Prince, un de vos plus fideles ami et serviteurs. (38155)

205 THE PRINCE OF WALES TO CHARLES JAMES FOX

Carlton House, 4.30 p.m., 27 Nov. 1786

I was just going to write to you when I received your letter this morning & will endeavour to take those measures you wish respecting Mr. Stephens, by laying his situation before the Counsel of the Duchy. I have already said I was just going to write to you when I receiv'd your letter, to ask you whether it wd. be very inconvenient to you to come to London to me for an hour tomorrow morning, or whether I shd. come down to St. Anne's[2], as I wish to consult you about some business (& shew you some papers) wh. will not admit of delay & therefore I name tomorrow particularly. Pray send back the boy who will carry this to

1. Thomas Hammersley, the banker (1747?–1812).

2. St. Anne's Hill, Fox's country home near Windsor.

St. Ann's as soon as you possibly can, & in answer name what hour wd. be most convenient *to you* for me to expect *you*, or for me to come down to you at St. Anne's. I have kept myself totally disengag'd all day on purpose. I beg you will remember me in the kindest manner possible to Mrs. Armistead[1], & beleive me [etc.].

P.S. Pray excuse haste.　(Add. MSS. 47560, f.21)

206　THE PRINCE OF WALES TO THE HONOURABLE HUGH SEYMOUR-CONWAY

Park Street, 30 Nov. 1786

We have had a report in London that Lady Racy has been much indisposed. I therefore cannot help troubling you with these few lines as I hope you are too well acquainted with the sincere affection I entertain for you, my dearest friend, not to think yt everything yt concerns yourself & Lady Racy must interest me most particularly. My dear Mrs. Fitz had already ye pen in her hand & was just a going to put it to the paper in order to make the same enquiries yt I am making at present, when a little fit of jealousy came across *me*, not such I beleive as you & I have already experienced in the course of our lives, but of *priority of friendship, a title* I assure you, my dear Hugh, when it regards yourself I will resign to no person existing in this world. It is so seldom yt. I can have the pleasure of seeing you yt. I cannot help rejoicing in & seizing every opportunity yt. offers itself of recalling to yr. mind one who so sincerely loves & esteems you as I do. We both of us therefore desire you will present our best & most affectionate respects to dear Lady Racy & tell her yt. we join most sincerely in hoping yt. ye report we have heard *is false* & shall be as much offended with you *as we possibly can be* if you do not give us the earliest intelligence possible of the state of her health. I remain, my dearest friend, ever most sincerely & affectionately yours. George Augustus Frederick[2] P. (Ragley MSS.)

207　PRINCE WILLIAM TO THE PRINCE OF WALES

Dominique, 1 Dec. 1786

It is neither owing to idleness nor forgetfulness, my dear brother and friend, that neither from St John's nor Halifax I did not write; but from that total want of subject which makes all letters dry. You may well say at this present time that I must have less to converse upon as I am in

---

1. Mrs. Armistead (*c.* 1750–1842) was Fox's mistress. He married her in September 1795 at Wyton, near Huntingdon, but the marriage was not publicly revealed until 1802.

2. For the Prince to give his full name was most unusual, if not unprecedented.

the open sea above two hundred leagues from any land. I will allow it: however, man is a man, by which I mean he has his sociable and unsociable hours. My humour is at present conversible, & makes me write: this to you must appear inexplicable, who enjoy all the pleasures & luxuries of life, but those that are obliged in certain situations to find their own amusement, are on that account more inclined to think than their neighbours who find everything cut and dryed.

Since I have left England I have been in Newfoundland, a country of no amusements, but there I was happy: at Halifax, a very gay and lively place full of women and those of the most obliging kind, I wished myself back to the inhospitable shores, foggy atmosphere and rugged barren cliffs of Newfoundland: and yet I mixed in the assemblies and balls in America: but the reason was that at Plymouth I was fond of a most lovely girl[1]; with whom I constantly danced, & ever since every woman appears to me insipid. I was more really in love at Portsmouth, but at Plymouth I enjoyed a higher gratification: do not imagine that I debauched the girl: such a thought did not once enter my head: the highest crime under Heaven next to murder is that of debauching innocent women; and is a crime I can with a safe conscience declare I never committed.

The newspapers have informed me that you have found it necessary to retrench your expences, in which I commend you extreamly, as do the British nation. How I am to keep my head above water is beyond my comprehension, for provisions are so excessively dear abroad in America and the West Indies that it is almost impossible to purchase them. You will I suppose still live in London in the winter; by this management and a frugal œconomy you will I suppose soon set everything in its proper way again.

Pray write often and let me know what footing we both are on with a near relation of ours: the longer I remain abroad the more likely in my opinion we are to agree with him. If I have my health in the West Indies, I shall wish to remain out, for my time is really spent in the most agreeable manner.

Remember me to all my friends in England and believe me [etc.]. (44713-4)

1. Sally Martin. Sally Winne was equally adorable, but a later attraction (December 1787).

Chatsworth, 11 Dec. 1786

I am this moment arrived from Hardwick, my dearest, dearest brother, and found your delightful letter here. Tho' no post goes out till tomorrow evening I cannot delay for a moment thanking you over and over again. If you had seen how much I felt at receiving your letter you would never doubt for a minute the affectionate, tender and sincere friendship I have ever had and shall have for you. Circumstances may sometimes have made you feel discontented with me and in the same manner I may have felt hurt, mais les veritables sentiments d'une amitié constante et parfaite n'ont jamais perdus leurs droits dans mon coeur. I don't know how to thank you enough for your goodness about Mr. Phillips[1], vous etes la bonté même, pour moi, cher, cher, cher frère.

I accept with great pleasure the office you assign me, and shall wear the beautiful key with great pleasure and pride; it is really the prettiest ornament I ever saw. Je harderai bien les secrets de votre coeur, mon cher frère, et je me flatte que vous me trouverai toujours digne de l'amitié que vous me temoigne—indeed I am worthy of it by the truth of my affection and sincere good wishes for you.

We have many, many enemies, my dearest brother, but I flatter myself you never will believe any report to my disadvantage without first asking me.

I have just heard that my sister[2] is not well. I was very much hurried at seeing Lord Duncannon's handwriting; I hope it is nothing that signifies.

Bon soir, mon cher frère, j'ajouterai un petit mot demain pour vous parler de nos projets qui ne sents pas encore décidé; avant de me coucher il faut encore vous remercier pour toutes vos bontés et surtout la jolie petite clef. (Add. Georgian 21/71)

Tuesday [12 Dec. 1786]

I believe we shall go to Buxton on Thursday for a fortnight or three weeks. I send my little girls[3] to town tomorrow and I hope to follow

---

1. J. Philips (variously spelt) was one of the Prince's surgeons, but the reference may well be to someone else.

2. Henrietta Frances (1761–1821), second daughter of John, 1st Earl Spencer. In November 1780 she married Frederick, Viscount Duncannon (1758–1844), who succeeded his father as 3rd Earl of Bessborough on 11 March 1793. He was M.P. for Knaresborough, 1780–93, and a Lord of the Admiralty, March–July 1782, and April–December 1783.

3. Georgiana Dorothy (1783–1858), who married Lord Morpeth, later 6th Earl of Carlisle (1773–1848), on 21 March 1801; and Henrietta Elizabeth (1785–1862), who married Lord Granville Leveson-Gower, later 1st Earl Granville, on 24 December 1809.

them soon. Indeed I shall be very, very happy to see you and to thank you a thousand times. Perhaps if you have leisure you will write to me again and if you do pray tell me that you will never again think it possible that I should have changed the sentiments of affection and friendship I ever have had and ever shall have for you. You know that treating you really as my brother I have always told you when I had anything sur le coeur about you; do the same by me, my dearest brother.

Lady Elizabeth[1] and the Duke desire me to give their best respects to you. I should never have done if I was to tell you all I think about your goodness and how very, very much I am obliged to you, et combien je vous aime, mon cher frere. Adieu, je porterai toujours la charmente petite clef, quoique elle n'est pas necessaire pour me faire penser a vous, elle m'est bien chere parceque elle vient de vous.   (Add. Georgian 21/71)

209   THE PRINCE OF WALES TO COLONEL G. HOTHAM, AND A REPLY

Carlton House, 26 Dec. 1786

I think proper to acquaint you that I am by no means satisfied on finding the directions I gave you by Lord Southampton respecting Mr. Hammersley have not been punctually complied with, particularly as I expressed to his Lordship my disinclination to receive any reply or argument against the regulation I proposed. But to obviate every objection I have determined to revoke the power for the receipt of my allowance now in force at the Treasury or Exchequer, & to appoint you, together with the three other gentlemen engaged for the execution of the Deed of Trust, to transact the business at those offices; continuing to you yr. several respective salaries and leaving to your joint directions & management the mode of lodging my money with Hammersley & giving orders on him for the necessary payments to my Household & pensions. I shall of course therefore take it for granted that the measures I propose will be immediately carried into execution.   (41869)

COLONEL HOTHAM'S REPLY

Stanhope Street, 28 Dec. 1786

The honour of your Royal Highness's letter of the 26th reached me yesterday afternoon. I take the very earliest opportunity of acknowledging its receipt, consistently with the mature attention I ought to pay to any command of your Royal Highness's in any point where most certainly my own character, & eventually, perhaps, your Royal Highness's interest, may be materially concerned.

1. Lady Elizabeth Foster.

It gave me, Sir, as your servant, much uneasiness to find that your Royal Highness was by no means satisfied in consequence of the directions you were pleased to give me by Lord Southampton respecting Mr. Hammersley having not been punctually complied with.

Your Royal Highness's commands on that subject were delivered to me by Lord Southampton on the 24th of July verbally, nor did his Lordship at all suggest to me that your Royal Highness would admit of no answer; on the contrary, he demanded to know what answer he should return; received it, & appeared happy when he did so. Mr. Lyte was present when the order was deliver'd me, & when my dutiful answer was given to that order; & that gentleman will I am sure, do me the justice to say, the answer was couched in the most respectful terms, implying my readiness to do my duty under any defalcation of emolument whatever, but that it was impossible for me at any time or in any circumstances to do any business with Mr. Hammersley, from personal ill treatment which I apprehended I had received from him as a banker, but suggesting the means whereby everything would be made smooth.

To this my humble reply I never received the least answer; & tho' I had the honour of waiting on your Royal Highness personally on the 18th of October, (with the other Trustees of your Royal Highness's Deed of Trust) I heard no one single expression of dissatisfaction at the mode I had, by Lord Southampton, proposed, as was my duty to your Royal Highness, for the making of all matters easy.

Your Royal Highness is pleased to communicate to me your determination to revoke the power for the receipt of your allowance, now in force at the Treasury or Exchequer. I can only observe upon it that the moment you are pleased to do so, such act, of itself, dispossesses me from the office of your Treasurer.

The subsequent power your Royal Highness means to execute in favour of the other three gentlemen engaged in the Deed of Trust, & myself, (whatever my opinion may be of their honour & integrity, & however I have lived with them in habits of intimacy & friendship) appears to me to be an harsh, humiliating, & degrading measure towards me, who have been an old servant, & I am sure a faithful one, to your Royal Highness. Humiliating it must be, if, without any cause, gentlemen inferior to me in your Household, are raised, in that Household, to be my equals; degrading if, without a cause, I am lower'd to an inferior rank in order merely to be levelled with them; & harsh, because the terms & style of your Royal Highness's letter is very different from any I have had the honour to receive from you at any time.

It may perhaps be disagreable to your Royal Highness to reflect on my past services in another part of your life; but as far as relates to my proper attachment to your welfare, & my fidelity to you in the situation I then held, as far as I had power to guide, my conscience is perfectly at

268

ease; & I flatter'd myself the gracious condescension you then shewed me would not have been so very easily withdrawn.

The cancelling my present powers I naturally look upon as the prelude to my dismission; for it is impossible I can submit (in conformity to my ideas of my own honour) to allow any coadjutor with me in an office which never yet had any, & which I know can be more easily managed by one person than by more. To be accountable alone to my master is what I can very easily manage, but to be one of four, & to be responsible for what the rest of those gentlemen, or their successors, may do, in an office where I have been accustomed to be single, & in which all my predecessors have been single before me, is (however it may be meant or intended) what I cannot, & what I think I ought not, to subject myself to.

If I, in the execution of my duty as your Treasurer, have misbehaved even in the most trifling instances, my immediate dissmission with ignominy is perfectly just. If I have not, your Royal Highness's new arrangement is a degradation to me, perfectly unmerited, & therefore, what no gentleman, worthy of being in your service, can, or ought to submit to, be the consequence what it may!

These, Sir, are no new sentiments; they are what you have often heard me hold in former times; & I should be sorry indeed, in points like this, not to practice myself what I had then the honour of endeavouring to inculcate into your Royal Highness's breast.

The next receipt of your Royal Highness's money from the Exchequer will scarce be before the 15th of Jany. next, if then; though the particular days of receipt are very precarious; I mention this merely for information to your Royal Highness, that any new appointment you may be pleased to make in my room (if that is your pleasure) will have full time to be perfected before any money from thence is likely to be issued.

Whatever may be your Royal Highness's commands to me in consequence of what I now take the liberty of addressing to you, I will endeavour to obey them with the diligence & attention that becomes me; & if my dismission is thought necessary to your Royal Highness's service, it is proper I should remind your Royal Highness of the necessity there must be to constitute some other person a Trustee, in my room, for the management of the sums you have been pleased to appropriate for your creditors.

Some few accounts, which I intended to present to you for your signature in Jany. next, are yet unpassed; the passing these, & my restitution of your Seals, which I apprehend I can only make on your Royal Highness's special command, it likewise becomes my duty to mention, should your Royal Highness be pleased to determine on such my unmerited dismission from your service. (41870–1)

269

FROM THE PRINCE OF WALES

Carlton House, 31 Dec. 1786
In my letter of the 26th inst. I do not conceive that I expressed myself in any manner that could induce you to think I either meant to degrade you or dismiss you from my service. I must therefore freely confess to you, that I did not expect to have received an answer from you couched in such terms that must, I am persuaded, upon *cool reflection*, appear to you as improper for you to have written as for me to have received: nor could I have imagined it possible for you to have taken offence at the plan I proposed of continuing you at the head of those gentlemen with whom you are already connected in my general Trust. My intention was by that means to fufill my promise to Hammersley, *from which I will not depart*, at the same time consulting *the delicacy of your feelings* in wishing to avoid a personal transaction of business with him. If you can suggest any method more agreable to yourself for answering the above purpose, I will not object, provided my engagement with Hammersley is strictly adhered to. At the same time I must call your attention to the letter which with the greatest concern I wrote to Lord Southampton to dismiss *all the gentlemen of my family*, in which I did not except any individual, but in the postscript to his Lordship I mentioned my intention of keeping you, Lyte, Hulse & Lake, *merely as Inspectors of my Accounts with equal powers*, & the same salaries annexed to the places you respectively held *in my late Establishment*, & which from that moment, I conceived to be dissolved. Having now so fully explained to you my sentiments upon this business, I trust no farther difficulty can occurr to prevent my orders being carried into *immediate execution.*   (41872)

VII 1787

The Prince's financial situation was becoming even more desperate and he was driven to the expedient of borrowing money abroad. His advisers thought it imperative that the assistance of Parliament should be secured, and his barefaced denial of his marriage through the mouth of Charles Fox at the end of April caused some of the independent members of the House of Commons to view rather more favourably his claims to financial relief, and Ministers were at last reluctantly prepared to do something for him. After lengthy exchanges matters were finally settled on 21 May, the Prince undertaking 'never to incur future debts, which must undoubtedly be as disagreeable to the King as painful to himself'. The precise value of this promise was made clear to all the world before many years had passed, and the reconciliation with the King which followed the settlement of that 'unpleasant business', proved to be of short duration. But for the moment everyone was delighted. The Commons voted £161,000 for the payment of his debts, and a further sum of £60,000 for the completion of Carlton House.

His brother William too had got into debt (he found it utterly impossible to live on £3,000 a year), but in 1787, as captain of *Pegasus*, in the West Indies, he was pre-occupied with disciplinary matters. The Admiralty, unfortunately, sided with the two Lieutenants, Schomberg and Hope, and disapproved of the Prince's conduct in threatening them with a court martial. His younger brothers Ernest and Adolphus were now being educated at Göttingen University, and found life there very agreeable. Edward, after a short spell at the Academy at Lüneburg, was in the Hanoverian army. The Duke of York was allowed to return home after an absence of six and a half years, and the King's anxiety to keep his younger sons away from the undesirable influence of the Carlton House ménage is all the more understandable when one remembers what happened after Frederick got back from Hanover in August. His friend Grenville, who accompanied him, wrote (20 December): 'We are totally guided by [the Prince of Wales] . . . and thoroughly initiated into all the extravagances and debaucheries of this most *virtuous* metropolis.' He added: 'Our visits to Windsor are less frequent, and I am afraid will at last be totally given up. I flatter myself still, however, with the hopes that when the first burst is passed, some little reflection will come to our assistance, and we shall perceive before *it is too late* that we are losing ourselves in the eyes of the world, and throwing away the finest game that ever man had presented to him.'[1] And on 6 April 1788 General Grant, another of Cornwallis's correspondents, continued the depressing story: 'The Prince has taught the Duke to *drink* in the most liberal and copious way, and the Duke in return has been equally successful in teaching his brother to lose his money at all sorts of play—quinze, hazard &c. to the amount, as we are told, of very large sums in favour of India General Smith and Admiral Pigot who both wanted it very much. These play parties have chiefly taken place at a new Club, formed this winter by the Prince of Wales in opposition to Brooks's, because Tarleton and Jack Payne, proposed by his Royal Highness, were blackballed.'[2]

210 COLONEL HOTHAM TO THE PRINCE OF WALES

Stanhope Street, 1 Jan. 1787

It was an heavy aggravation to the uneasiness I have long suffer'd to find, by the honour of your Royal Highness's letter of yesterday, that you could think me guilty of using any terms or insinuations of disrespect, which not only to yourself, Sir, but to every branch of the Royal Family, I utterly disclaim. It is in vain I have endeavoured to recollect what passages in mine could have called for your Royal Highness's reproach; and can only offer my humble assurances that no impropriety can ever be intended by me, in any letter I can have the honour of addressing to your Royal Highness.

I can with truth declare that, till your Royal Highness's letter reached me yesterday, I had no imagination whatever that I have not had the honour of being your Treasurer since the 7th of July last. My exercising

1. *Cornwallis Correspondence*, ed. Ross, i.360.

2. *Ibid.*, i.374–5.

273

that office so many months after it was your pleasure it should cease, (which, for want of a proper explanation of your orders, I most certainly have done) has proceeded from ignorance alone. I am to ask your Royal Highness's pardon on this occasion, flattering myself your justice will not attribute to any arrogance or presumption what was clearly owing to a misunderstanding only.

I esteem myself much obliged to your Royal Highness for your indulgence in allowing me to suggest anything that can remove the present difficulties. I own I think it a degradation to me that three gentlemen inferior to me in your Household should be raised, with equal powers to myself, to the execution of an office jointly with me, which I had long executed alone, without impeachment of blame, particularly as that office was a trust and direction of money. I apprehend a great part of the world may think so too, and may be more severe in undeserved censure of me than I might chuse they should be in consequence.

My differing so totally as I do in opinion, sentiments, and conduct with Mr. Hammersley is my other unhappiness; the matter between that gentleman and myself appears to be briefly this. He is pleased to insist on having the whole of about £62 or £63,000, which was in *my* possession, in *his* possession. I beg leave to retain only about £14,000 of it, and hope he may be contented with the remainder. He says, no; he will have the *whole*. The world may judge who is the most reasonable man of the two.

This is the exact state of the case; but, encouraged by the kindness of the expressions contained in your Royal Highness's letter of yesterday, I beg leave most humbly to repeat my suggestions transmitted by Lord Southampton. They seem to me to obviate every difficulty whatever and to give into Mr. Hammersley's instant possession the whole of your Royal Highness's revenue, except the sum allotted for your salaries, wages and pensions, the possession and disposition of which I entreat as a favour to have under my own care, alone, as formerly; a circumstance I am the more urgent about as, after what has passed, it is absolutely impossible for me, on this account as well as my own, to have the very smallest intercourse of business with Mr. Hammersley.   (16541)

211 MESSAGE FROM THE PRINCE OF WALES TO COLONEL HOTHAM,
AND THE REPLY

4 Jan. 1787
On the 4th January 1787, Mr. Lyte brought Colonel Hotham a verbal message from his Royal Highness the Prince of Wales, importing that his appointment of Mr. Hammersley as his banker was subsequent to

the dissolution of his establishment on the 7th July last. That his Royal Highness did not wish Colonel Hotham should quit his service; but that if his feelings did not permit him to comply with the Prince's plan, already mentioned, in consideration of his long and faithful services, his Royal Highness desired Colonel Hotham to accept of £1,000 per annum upon his quitting his Royal Highness's service. (16544)

COLONEL HOTHAM'S REPLY
5 Jan. 1787

I am truly sensible of your Royal Highness's indulgence in allowing me time in the giving my answer to the verbal message I had the honour of receiving from your Royal Highness by Mr. Lyte yesterday; but it is my duty to create as little delay as possible, more particularly as I know inconveniencies to your affairs may happen from there being any.

It is with the utmost concern that I lament my inability to bring my own sense of honour to submit to the two points objected to by me, and insisted on by your Royal Highness. The ideas of many, perhaps, would approve of my doing so; but that consciousness of having done only what I truly thought to be right (which is now likely to be my chief solid comfort) would then be wanting.

I am infinitely grateful to your Royal Highness for the noble offer you are pleased to make me on retiring from your service; an offer greatly exceeding the expectations of a man who undoubtedly had no idea of any at all being made; and my opinion that your Royal Highness thereby not only consulted my own distresses, but those of my family, who must depend on me for their support, greatly enhances the obligation. But I am persuaded your Royal Highness will not be offended if I take the liberty of saying that, as from the moment your Royal Highness has read the preceding paragraph, I can no longer look upon myself in your service. I esteem it my duty to receive the King's commands what I ought to do on that subject; as I should by no means think myself justifiable in receiving any stipend for an office I no longer executed, or as a reward for my past services, without *them*; the rather, as his Majesty placed me himself in both the situations I have enjoyed; and in my present one, I can now esteem myself as a servant of his Majesty only.

Should the King, on my dutiful application, which I will make as soon as possible, send me his commands to accept your Royal Highness's very kind offer, I shall do so with the gratitude which becomes me, not in the least doubting but that your Royal Highness will not wonder that I should be careful on the present occasion, of doing anything that my enemies might interpret as having a greater regard to my own interest than desire of exerting myself in your Royal Highness's service.

Should your Royal Highness hereafter think of anything in which, either by assistance to those gentlemen with whom I have been lately a colleague in your Deed of Trust, or in any other point, I can be conducive to your Royal Highness's service, no pains, diligence or attention shall be wanting, on my part, to prove myself at all times [etc.].[1]

(16545)

212 LETTERS FROM PRINCE WILLIAM TO THE PRINCE OF WALES

Pegasus, English Harbour, 8 Feb. 1787

The West Indies are likely to prove a disagreeable scene to me from an affair that has happened on board my ship. I have to request the utmost secrecy on your side in this business, as it is of consequence to the Naval service in general, and must stamp my character as an officer. Elphinstone you may communicate the matter to, and I shall send you a narrative of the business which he will explain to you. Do not shew this to any other officer but him, as the correspondence and the particulars must first be made known to the Commander-in-Chief in these seas, so that I may know whether the affair can be settled by a court martial in the West Indies or be referred home to the Admiralty. You must therefore see the necessity of secrecy, and more particularly the propriety of not informing the King and Lord Howe, till his Lordship receives it officially. By the enclosed narrative[2] you will be surprized to find Mr Schomberg to be the man who of all others ought most particularly to have been careful in his conduct; after my having released him from confinement, so immediately to fly in my face I cannot but consider as downright mutiny. I will not enter into the detail of the circumstances, nor explain the Article of War; as Elphinstone from his experience and

1. Daniel Pulteney, M.P., wrote to the Duke of Rutland (18 January), 'Hotham's resignation was, I hear from pretty good authority, occasioned by a suspicion of the Prince's connexions with Hammersley not being quite consistent with his trust deed. The Prince offered him £1,000 a year, and he accepted the same sum from the King as a pension of more propriety' (Rutland MSS. [H.M.C.], iii.366).

2. Folios 44738–51. '...I had frequently had occasion to be dissatisfied with Lieutenant Schomberg's conduct, for want of respect to me as his commanding officer....' On 13 January the Prince informed him that he would be court martialled. Two days later the First Lieutenant, in the presence of his brother officers made 'a full and ample apology for his past misconduct'. Subsequently the Prince again charged him with neglect of duty. Schomberg then applied to Captain Nelson, the senior officer upon the West India station, to be tried by a court martial. This being done without the Prince's permission he considered it as a great mark of disrespect and calculated to put an end to discipline in the naval service. On 23 January, Nelson informed the Prince that he had ordered Schomberg's arrest. Schomberg had been a Lieutenant since 1777. In November 1790 he became a Captain.

knowledge of our service will point them out. Sufficient to say, I feel, brother, within myself I am right: the officers in this station approve of my conduct, particularly the Commanding Officer for the time being, Captain Nelson, who, though a young man, has a sound judgment. I am sure Elphinstone will likewise find my behaviour on this disagreeable affair was officer-like, and free from all private pique.

My letter by the last packet to Elphinstone you have no doubt seen. I am obliged to live in a certain decent way, and the necessary articles are so dear in the West Indies and America that upon my present allowance I cannot continue abroad without running in debt, and therefore I must resign the command of my ship and plant cabbages for my subsistence.

Whatever turns up, I shall let you know as soon as possible. I have reason to expect that Schomberg means to prosecute me; in this case I must have recourse again to our inginious [sic] friend and pleader Mr. Erskine. (44736-7)

Nevis, 15 Mar. 1787

Since I last wrote Schomberg wrote to me endeavouring to beg my pardon and to have his letter requesting the court martial recalled. I answered him the matter had now gone so far that I was determined to convince the officers in the Navy that disrespect from a Lieutenant to his Captain would be severely punished. I had another strong motive, which is the strong suspicion Mr. Hope[1], the Third Lieutenant, labours under, in my opinion, of encouraging Schomberg to take the improper steps he has. I have almost positive proof of Hope's guilt. However, so much will come out in Schomberg's Court Martial as to enable me to form my judgment on Hope whether a Court Martial can investigage the matter or I shall be obliged to refer [it] to the Admiralty. At all events when the business is concluded it will be proper for me to enclose the particulars which I have and shall collect into a narrative for their Lordships' information. Whatever steps I may take you shall be the first person informed, for which purpose I have enclosed the continuation of the narration. The more I consider the matter the more I am in my own mind convinced my conduct has been throughout officerlike.

By the last packet I received a letter from Hotham in which he complains most sadly of my drawing on him before my allowance is due, and likewise that as I drew for the whole the tradesmen cannot be

1. Sir William Johnstone Hope (1766–1831). Lieutenant, 1782; Captain, 1794; Rear-Admiral, 1812. M.P. for Dumfries Burghs, 1800–2; for Dumfriesshire, 1804–30. A Lord of the Admiralty, April 1807–November 1809, and 1820–7; and a Member of the Lord High Admiral's Council, 1827–8. K.C.B., 1815; G.C.B., 1825.

payed. I answered him I would no more draw before it should be due and that tho' at first sight £3,000 seemed a large sum, it was by experience utterly impossible for me to live on that stipend. I well know the difficulty of persuading the King that my allowance is too small, yet to have my bills protested is to a man of honour, as I hope I am, a most cutting and disgraceful thing, and how ridiculous it is, for at the end he must pay these debts or else they must remain unpayed.

Elphinstone wrote to me by the last packet from Scotland. If I have not time to answer him tell him his letter is safe arrived and I will answer him whenever it is my power. As for news, we have none in this part of the world except that the Maidstone frigate arrived last month from England and that we are anxiously looking out for another man of war to begin on these Court Martials, where I have so much at stake. I am afraid you have forgot to send me the sword you promised, which I beg you will forward. By this packet I have taken the liberty of committing to the care of the Captain six dozen of kegs [?] purchased at Martinique which I beg you will accept as I have every reason to believe it to be very fine and genuine. When the wheather becomes fine I shall send you a couple of fat turtle.   (44752–3)

213   CAPTAIN GEORGE KEITH ELPHINSTONE TO THE PRINCE OF WALES

Edin^t, 31 Mar. 1787

I am this instant honored with your commands signified to me by Coll. Lake at the same time enclosing a letter from Prince William on the subject of a dispute with L^{tts} Schomberg and Hope of the Pegasus. I am extreamly sorry for this on every account but particularly because (from the Prince's letter) it gives him deep concern, and which, as he feels himself perfectly right, it ought not to do, by reason that H.R.H. will in time be convinced that he who has charge and command over many must at times give offence to some.

With respect to the present instance I have no difficulty in advising his R.H. to avoid trying his officers if their offence is of such a nature as will admit of forgiveness, and they, being sensible of their errors, solicit indulgence: at the same time as his R.H. imagines L^{tt} Hope to be the cause or promoter of this discord I would advise the Prince to get rid of him at least, if not both, which can be done by applying to the Commanding Officer on the Station to exchange those officers for any other two in the Squadron unless when your Royal Highness may mention this affair to Lord Howe, the Admiralty may think proper to send two officers from home of the Prince's election to serve in his ship.

My reasons for the above advice are, with due submission as follows. First, courts martial, altho' absolutely necessary, are at all times dis-

278

agreeable, and admiting a sentance against the officers, many there are in a country like this, and at this time, who would pretend that such sentance was in compliment to the high rank of the prosecutor. Secondly, it would be very mortifying to Prince William if they should be acquited, or perhaps slightly reprimanded. Thirdly, his R.H. should recollect that being moved from his ship and protection is a very severe punishment of itself; besides, one of that great consideration should rarly lose an opportunity of doing a gracious thing towards men who are ready to acknowledge their faults. But, Sir, should these things have gone so far as to render a court martial unavoidable, let the Prince prosecute with firmness, without heat, upon as few articles as possible, so that the Court and the world may be convinced that he is not influenced by rancour or ill humour but does it meerly as a duty for the sole purpose of preserving good order and supporting proper discipline.

With respect to the last letter I had the honor to send your Royal Highness on the subject of Prince William's finances, I am most ready, as is my duty, to take any step your R.H. may approve of or consider for his advantage. I wrote to Coll. Hotham by Prince William's directions beging to know an exact state of the allowance and telling what I thought it should be. In answer I received a stiff letter saying the whole sum was 3000 a year; that he had a letter from the Prince before him which did not mention any intended application to the King and therefore he could not presume to offer any advice but naturally supposed I would be guided by your Royal Highness directions.

Upon the whole wretched system that has been persued all along with regard to [the] Prince is astonishing! That he to whom this nation looks up to in his line should be suffered to tumble up and down the sea from station to station upon three thousd. pounds a year without any establishment, or even a person of rank and experience about him with whom he might advise or communicate his sentiments to when at a lose, it is really surprising at his time of life that his conduct has been so well as it is.

I have only to add that whenever your Royal Highness or Prince William's affairs require my attendance I am ready to set out on a moment's warning to attend my duty and to return sincere thanks for the indulgence that has already been shown to your Royal Highness's [etc.].

P.S. Your R. Highness vote in favor of Lord Kinaird[1] had the effect of making a *Peer* in the King's life.   (44754–6)

1. George, 7th Lord Kinnaird (1754?–1805), succeeded his father in 1767. He was a Representative Scottish Peer, 1787–90, having failed to secure election in 1784 by three votes. In 1787 he and Lord Selkirk received 26 and 41 votes respectively, the two unsuccessful candidates, Lords Cathcart and Dumfries, polling 25 and 7 respectively. He was said to be a member of the 'Armed Neutrality' in December 1788, and he voted with the Prince's party on the Regency question.

Carlton House, 1 Apr. 1787

In consequence of the conversation I had yesterday with your Lordship, and the wish that you then signified that I would furnish you in writing with the purport of the message to be deliver'd to his Majesty from me, and for which purpose I had made choice of your Lordship not more from the former situation you held in my family & in which you were the necessary instrument of communication between his Majesty & myself, than it is that I am persuaded such an election in the present instance would be most agreeable to him, I am therefore to desire your Ldship will wait upon the King and in the most dutiful and respectful manner possible on my part, acquaint his Majesty that the first payment to be made from the appropriated part of my income towards the liquidation of my debts will be on or about the tenth day of the present month. At the same time I beg you to observe to his Majesty the very incompetent fund this is for the purpose of accomplishing the propos'd end, by the large proportion of it that is necessarily deducted for the payment of the interest of the original incumberance, and the impossibility of effecting this object by such small installments. I am therefore now call'd upon to remind his Majesty of his most gracious promise, convey'd in several parts of his former messages, of exonerating me from the present embarrassments & distress in which, I am involv'd, when I should have adopted the measures (which your Lordship's information on the subject will enable you more fully to confirm) which his Majesty prescrib'd, in the reduction of every possible expenditure both in my family & establishment out of an income originally too narrow & confin'd for the rank & situation of my birth. But in spite of all that has been done I find with concern the total inefficiency of the measures that have been adopted. Tis thro your Lordship I wish to have this information convey'd to his Majesty, & to express at the same time how grateful I shall feel in having it in my power to acquaint my creditors of so satisfactory a piece of information as his Majesty's compliance with the request I have desir'd your Ldship. to make in my name would enable me to do.   (31903 and 41873-4)

215 THE PRINCE OF WALES TO THE EARL OF HERTFORD

Carlton House, Sunday night, 22 Apr. 1787

I hope you will forgive my troubling you with these few lines, but trusting to yr. known goodness to me upon every occasion, I cannot help mentioning to you yt. ye question relative to my affairs comes on in ye. House of Commons on Friday sennight ye fourth of May. May I depend *upon ye. attendance of my four friends, yr. sons*? [1] How happy shd. I have been not to have omitted ye fifth [2] *on this occasion*, who, tho' named ye. last, yet I assure you is not ye least in love. My reason for troubling you with these particulars is, yt. I understand my friend Robert is going ye beginning of the week to settle his family for the rest of the year in Wales, & yt. Ld. Beauchamp, William & George are all out of town & not known when they are expected again in London, & as their attendance at this moment is of too much consequence to me to be omitted, I cd. not help mentioning it to you, being already too well acquainted with yr. good wishes to me, to doubt ye continuation of ym. on this occasion. [3] (Egerton MSS. 3262, f.4)

216 PRINCE WILLIAM TO THE PRINCE OF WALES

Pegasus, Rozeau, 23 Apr. 1787

In my last letter to Elphinstone you will have seen the reason of my not then writing to you at that time, and the continuation of this unaccountable and extraordinary conduct of Schomberg, I have now more to relate. The evening before I sailed from English Harbour he wrote to Captain

1. Lord Beauchamp, M.P. for Orford; Robert Seymour-Conway, M.P. for Wootton Bassett; William Seymour-Conway, M.P. for Downton; and George Seymour-Conway (1763–1848), M.P. for Orford, 1784–90, and for Totnes, 1796–1801.

2. Hugh Seymour-Conway (1759–1801), M.P. for Newport, Isle of Wight, 1784–6, for Tregony, 1788–90; for Wendover, 1790–6, and for Portsmouth, 1796–1801. Captain, 1779; Rear-Admiral, 1795; Vice-Admiral, 1799; a Lord of the Admiralty, 1795–8.

3. Alderman Newnham had given notice of a Motion on the Prince's financial situation for 5 May, but on the 4th he announced that, as it was no longer necessary (Ministers having agreed to take the subject into consideration), he should not bring it forward. See the following correspondence. Lord Beauchamp, then, was justified in declaring that 'the Prince begins a most active canvass of the House; applies by letter or personally to every little knot o members, and indirectly to almost every individual, offering to submit his plans and his interests to the country gentlemen, producing his accounts, showing every letter, and, by the specimen I have seen, he has been guarded to an extreme degree. In short, Marsham, Powis, Hussey, Pulteney, Astley, and others of that calibre, became converts to his cause, in spite of their original dislike to it. On this footing the business rested, when, the night before the motion was to be made, Mr. Pitt acquaints the Prince, by letter, with his Majesty's gracious intention to comply with his wishes, and only hints at previous explanations being made by the Prince, by which it was understood that in future he was to be no party man; but, whatever interpretation was intended to be put upon them, the Prince instantly communicated his readiness to acquiesce, and personally to assure the King of his resolution to act in future as he would wish.'

Sir William Lowther received instructions from his cousin Lord Lonsdale to attend the House on the 4th. On his arrival he was 'happy to find matters in a train of accommodation. ... The Duke of Portland, the Cavendishes and many others were against the Prince' (Lonsdale MSS.).

Nelson saying that as the preparations indicated the Pegasus's not returning to Antigua, and from his seeing daily reports being made to me of his being under confinement by Captain Nelson, the Commanding Officer of the King's Squadron, and from his long and close confinement, he could wish to be furnished either with the charge or charges Captain Nelson meant to exhibit against him; besides Schomberg in his letter mentioned that he could not conceive himself under arrest from the letter he had wrote applying for a court martial, as it was the only way prescribed by the Articles of War and general printed instructions for an officer accused unjustly to clear his character. Captain Nelson in my humble opinion answered this extraordinary letter in a very proper style: he assured Mr Schomberg that he complied with his request that Captain Nelson might not be afterwards taxed by him for not having granted him a court martial: that the order he had given out on the 28th January, a copy of which I sent you, respecting officers writing to the Commander-in-Chief for a court martial on frivolous pretences at a time there were not ships enough to bring them to immediate trial thereby depriving his Majesty of their services at a time they were wanted, was issued on account of his letter requesting a court martial, and to prevent the like abuses. In the evening after I had taken leave of Captain Nelson, to my utter surprize and astonishment an officer came on board with a message from Captain Nelson: that upon his return to the Boreas he found another letter from Mr Schomberg which appeared to me more ridiculous than the first. Listen to the contents, that he, Schomberg, tho' positively informed that very evening by Nelson of his motives for issuing that order on the 28th January, could not conceive it possible, as five days intervened between Schomberg's writing and Nelson giving out this order: that had he had any reason even of so much importance for the service to write for a court martial, and although the twenty first Article of War and the fourth article concerning courts martial authorized officers in certain situations to apply in this manner, this order totally prevented any such application. Schomberg in his letter said a vast number of things so absurd that they are really not worth the trouble of your reading and my writing. Nelson's answer, which he sent open for me to see, was proper and officer-like. He began by saying that he thought he had complied with Mr. Schomberg's request, as Mr. Schomberg, had he not wished to be from under my command, would not have wrote for a court martial till there were ships enough for him to be tried at once. Captain Nelson's officer told me he was likewise charged with a message to Schomberg, which was to be previously delivered to me, that Captain Nelson had put him under arrest as he conceived by the tenor of his letter requesting the court martial that he considered himself hurt by my conduct as his Captain. After the officer had delivered the letter and this message, he returned to me to inform me of Schomberg's answer: that when he wrote this letter concerning his application to be tried, he had been in hopes that Captain Nelson, from his former acquaintance, would not have complied with his request till Nelson had seen and conversed with him: that as matters now stood that he, Schomberg, was confident he would and could clear his character and honour before a court martial, as he would do the first opportunity when Captain Nelson and himself were on half pay. What can be Schomberg's motives for making this extraordinary assertion is to me inexplicable after I positively told him when he was put under arrest the last time that as I must necessarily be a witness on his court martial, that I would and should swear that he had disobeyed my orders, deny it he may: but I fancy Mr. Schomberg will find very great difficulty to prove he did comply with my commands. I at first pitied him: at present from his late impropriety and folly I despise him.

We sailed from English Harbour the 19th, and arrived the same evening at Prince Rupert's Bay, Dominique, and sailed again from thence on the 22d and arrived at Roseau the 23d: upon my anchoring I was informed that Captain Collinwood [1], who commanded the Rattler was dead: upon that Mᵣ Hope has applied to me to be appointed Second Lieutenant of the Boreas in the room of Mᵣ Wallace promoted to the command of the sloop: I have accordingly wrote to Captain Nelson to request this wish of Mᵣ Hope may be complied with. I cannot but express my satisfaction at Hope's leaving the ship: we are to sail tomorrow for Grenada: adieu, dear brother, give my best compliments to Keith, and ever believe me [etc.].   (44757-8)

217   THE DUKE OF YORK TO THE PRINCE OF WALES

Hanover, 27 Apr. 1787

As I am thoroughly convinced of your affection and how glad you will be at our meeting again I cannot help taking the first opportunity to acquaint you myself that the King has consented to my returning home and has ordered me to be in England towards the beginning of August. It is not necessary I trust to express to you the joy which I feel at this permission, and the impatience with which I wait for the time of se[e]ing all my friends and relations again after so very long an absence, and particularly you, brother, with whom I was from my childhood brought up and who always gave me such proofs of your affection.

I shall set out about the middle of May for Berlin and Potsdam in

1. Wilfred Collingwood, who, however, was apparently only a Commander (from January 1783), not a Captain.

order to take leave of the King of Prussia, and shall employ most of the time which I have still to remain in Germany, in taking leave of the different Princes who have been particularly civil to me.

News you cannot expect from us here. The pretty expedition of his Highness the Landgrave of Cassel has turned out as it ought to do to his own disgrace. He spoke very big to the very last, but however when he saw that everybody was in earnest against him, he thought it most prudent to retreat.[1] Adieu, dear brother, believe me [etc.]. (43819)

218 HENRY DUNDAS[2] TO THE PRINCE OF WALES

Sackville Street, 2 May 1787

Mr Dundas has been honoured with the Prince of Wales' commands, conveyed to him by his Royal Highness the Duke of Cumberland, and will in obedience thereto attend at Carleton House this evening at 11 o clock. (38159)

1. In February the Landgrave of Hesse-Cassel put forward a bogus claim to the territories of Lippe-Schaumburg and attempted to seize them by force, but a few weeks later he thought it expedient to obey an Imperial decree and to withdraw his troops. See *The Later Correspondence of George III* (ed. A. Aspinall), Nos. 334, 344, 349, 351 and 355.

2. Henry Dundas, 1st Viscount Melville (1742–1811), M.P. for Midlothian, 1774–82 and 1783–90; for Newtown, Isle of Wight, 1782; for Edinburgh, 1790–1802. Solicitor-General [S.], 1776–75; Lord Advocate of Scotland, 1775–83; Commissioner for India, 1784–93; Treasurer of the Navy, 1782–April 1783, and December 1783–1800; Home Secretary 1791–4; President of the Board of Control, 1793–1801; Secretary for War, July 1794–March 1801; First Lord of the Admiralty, May 1804–April 1805. Peerage, December 1802.

'There existed', wrote Wraxall, 'a disposition to accommodate matters, without making disclosures in the House of Commons, equally painful to the King and to the Prince.... A respectful intimation being conveyed to his Royal Highness requesting permission on the part of Dundas to attend him at Carlton House, an interview took place between them on Wednesday the 2nd of May.... Dundas experienced the most gracious reception. After ascertaining from the Prince's own lips the extent of his pecuniary encumbrances, which amounted to full £200,000, Dundas gave him an assurance that prompt as well as liberal assistance should be extended to him. This amicable conference was subsequently moistened with no ordinary quantity of wine.... The ground being now prepared, and the preliminaries adjusted on the following day, Thursday, Pitt was admitted to an audience at Carlton House. Every article of the accommodation was finally concluded' (*Wraxall*, iv.463).

Sir Gilbert Elliot had to admit that there was 'a considerable division of opinion even amongst those who might most naturally have been expected to take a decided part for the Prince—I mean those who generally vote with Opposition.' He added, 'I understand that several *of our country gentlemen* are against him, and I doubt the extremely delicate subject of his connection with Mrs. Fitzherbert, and the constitutional dangers and doubts belonging to this most equivocal condition of things will force itself into the discussion' (*Minto*, i.155). A few days later he remarked that the Prince's business had been brought on 'against the advice of the Duke of Portland, Fox, and the principal people of the party' (*Ibid.*, i.159).

Downing Street, 11.50 p.m., 3 May 1787

In obedience to the commands with which your Royal Highness was this day pleased to honor me, I took the earliest opportunity of waiting upon the King with your Royal Highness's message.[1] I am directed by his Majesty to acquaint your Royal Highness that he receives with great satisfaction the expressions of your Royal Highness's personal sentiments towards his Majesty. The King considers himself as having conveyed thro the whole of his correspondence his readiness to assist in relieving your Royal Highness from the embarrassments of your present situation, whenever he is enabled by sufficient explanation to take any steps with propriety for that purpose[2]; and his Majesty thinks this confirmation of the uniform tenor of his sentiments cannot fail to remove any doubts on the point which it was the object of your Royal Highness's message to ascertain. (16569 and 38160–1)

220   THE PRINCE OF WALES TO THE QUEEN, AND THE REPLY

Carlton House, 4 May 1787

I cannot help seizing the earliest opportunity after the gracious message I receiv'd from the King last night, to express my eagerness to be again admitted to yr. presence. I therefore take the liberty thro' yr. means, which ever must be the most pleasing to my feelings, of soliciting to know when my attendance will be agreable both to the King & you. I remain, my dearest mother [etc.]. (41876, 41877, and, in the King's hand, 41878–9)

1. Alderman Newnham had given notice of a Motion on the subject of the Prince's debts: 'That an humble Address be presented to his Majesty, praying that an enquiry might be made into the situation of H.R.H. the Prince of Wales, and that such measures might be adopted as should, in his royal wisdom, appear most expedient to rescue him from his present embarrassments; and that this House would make good the same to his Majesty.' John Robinson thus referred to the great efforts made by the Prince's friends to secure a good attendance on that occasion: 'The Duke of Portland, who was averse, is now satisfied, and his friends will vote for the motion. I suppose all the Cavendishes, Walpoles, &c. &c. Lord Sandwich has been active in canvassing, making out lists, &c., and they reckon on having 181 certain. They say all the Lonsdale party will be with them, and most of the Navy; that they fully expect to carry the question, and it is determined that it shall be brought on, but if perchance not successful, to have debts paid, to go abroad. . . . The Duke of Bedford is eager. Rigby will vote for. . . . Every man in opposition has been warmly solicited, and much canvassing is going forward on that side' (Add. MSS. 38567, f.203).

2. This was interpreted to mean that in future the Prince was to be no party man. 'Whatever interpretation was intended to be put upon them, the Prince instantly communicated his readiness to acquiesce, and personally to assure the King of his resolution to act in future as he would wish' (Auckland, *Journal and Correspondence*, i.416).

THE QUEEN'S REPLY

Queen's House, 4 May 1787

I have this instant received your letter & shall with pleasure acquaint the King at his return from St. James's with your desire of waiting upon him. The moment I receive his answer I shall inform you of it & not feel a little happy to assure you again by word of mouth how sincerely I am, my dearest son [etc.]. (36368)

221 THE PRINCE OF WALES TO WILLIAM PITT, AND THE REPLY

Carlton House, 4 May 1787

When I recollect the conversation that passed between you and me yesterday, I cannot but be very much surprised at some expressions that I understand have dropt from several of *your friends*, not that I harbour the smallest doubts of *your honor*, but I think that some sort of an explanation upon that is absolutely necessary. With regard to the explanations that are hinted at in his Majesty's message I am exceedingly impatient to know what they are, and am ready to give him every satisfaction in my power. I have desired Mr. Sheridan [1] to call upon you, as such an interview may most likely prevent a more formal discussion. (41875, copy, in the King's hand)

PITT'S REPLY

Downing Street, 11.30 p.m., 4 May 1787

I have been honored with a letter from your Royal Highness delivered by Mr Sheridan, and regret that I do not sufficiently understand on what points your Royal Highness has been induced to suppose that

1. Richard Brinsley Sheridan, dramatist, Whig politician, and friend of the Prince of Wales (1751–1816). Whig M.P. for Stafford, 1780–1806; for Westminster, 1806–7; for Ilchester, 1807–12. Treasurer of the Navy, 1806–7. Sheridan rather than Fox was chosen to have this conference with Pitt, partly, at any rate, because Fox, like Burke and Portland, had disapproved the bringing the business of the Prince's debts before Parliament at that time. 'I find', wrote Sir Gilbert Elliot (5 May), 'there was a strong disinclination to the business in many persons of the greatest weight among his friends, or those at least lately accounted so. The Duke of Portland in particular had strongly dissuaded the Prince from bringing it on, principally on the knowledge he had of the very general dislike to it amongst the principal men in the party, but also ... from a disapprobation of the measure in his own mind. Fox had been of the same opinion, and the Prince had determined of his own head or on the advice of nobody knows who, to force it on contrary to the sentiments and wishes of his principal friends. I am sorry to find that there had been rather an angry conference between the Prince and the Duke of Portland on the subject, and that the Prince considers the Duke as no longer on terms of friendship with him' (*Minto*, i.161).

286

some explanation from me is necessary. At the same time I humbly hope that your Royal Higness will allow for the impossibility of my entering into a discussion with any third person on the subject of the conversation with which your Royal Highness thought proper to honor me. Conceiving that the message which I had the honor of transmitting by his Majesty's commands last night fully confirmed what I had had the honor to state as his Majesty's sentiments on the only object of the communication which your Royal Highness directed me to make in your name to his Majesty, I cannot presume to take any step for obtaining further explanation without your Royal Highness's express orders. (38162–3)

222 THE QUEEN TO THE PRINCE OF WALES

Queen's House, 5 May 1787

I have taken an opportunity of communicating your letter of yesterday to the King, who has directed me to express how much he is pleased with your wish of being again received by him. But as your long absence has alone arisen from your own choice, not his commands, he thinks it must mutually be more agreable to defer fixing the time of the interview till the whole of the unhappy affair be settled, and consequently no room left for further misapprehensions. (36371)

223 MESSAGE FROM THE PRINCE OF WALES

Carlton House, 5 May 1787

His Royal Highness is desirous to give every explanation in his power of his past expences, and that the accounts themselves will furnish, as well of all debts. His Royal Highness will also engage not to apply hereafter for the payment of any farther debts if his Majesty affords his Royal Highness such relief as his Royal Highness shall think sufficient in any of the modes hereinafter stated. What his Royal Highness most wishes is an encrease of £40,000 p^r annum to his income, and that his Majesty should pay what Carlton House has hitherto cost his Royal Highness, and what will be necessary to compleat it. The rest of the debts his Royal Highness will take upon himself, and would in this case resume his Establishment. As to the other two modes that his Royal Highness might insinuate to his Majesty, he should prefer the encrease of income of £40,000 p^r annum without the payment of debts to that of payments of debts without encrease of income, as the former mode of these two tends after a course of years to his Royal Highness having a proper Establishment, and being able to pay his respects again at Court. (41881–2)

224 LETTERS FROM THE PRINCE OF WALES TO WILLIAM PITT,
AND THE REPLIES

Carlton House, 9.30 a.m., 5 May 1787
The Prince of Wales desires Mr. Pitt will come to Carlton House at two o'clock this day, and desires he will bring with him any other person whom he thinks he can depend upon as a confidential friend. (41880)

PITT'S REPLY
Downing Street, 10 a.m., 5 May 1787
Mr Pitt will have the honor of attending his Royal Highness the Prince of Wales at two this day, in obedience to his Royal Highness's commands, and intends to beg the favor of Mr Dundas to accompany him. (38164)

THE PRINCE OF WALES'S REPLY

Carlton House, 5 May 1787
The Prince of Wales is very sorry to give Mr. Pitt any further trouble in this business, but in reconsidering the first proposal he wishes merely to say respecting Carlton House that his intentions are that not only the sum which it has *hitherto* cost him should be paid, but likewise that which will be necessary to compleat it. Upon the proposals being returned with this addition to the Prince of Wales, he will sign them and send them back to Mr. Pitt. (38166)

PITT'S REPLY

Downing Street, 5.05 p.m., 5 May 1787
In obedience to the commands of his Royal Highness the Prince of Wales Mr Pitt has the honor of enclosing two copies of the memorandum taken this day at Carlton House according to his Royal Highness's order, and Mr Pitt will lose no time in transmitting one of them to his Majesty as soon as he receives it back from his Royal Highness. (38165)

The Prince of Wales
by Cosway

Frederick, Duke of York
by Reynolds

THE PRINCE OF WALES'S REPLY

Carlton House, 5 May 1787

The Prince of Wales returns Mr. Pitt the paper with the alteration in it, which he now perfectly approves of; he flatters himself that Mr. Pitt will endeavour to obtain for him from the King as decisive and speedy an answer as possible. (38168)

PITT'S REPLY

Lower Grosvenor Street, 7.30 p.m., 5 May 1787

Mr. Pitt has the honor of returning the papers which he has just received from his Royal Highness the Prince of Wales, with the addition of the words which his Royal Highness proposes in his note to insert. Mr. Pitt trusts his Royal Highness will approve of his having interlined them in order to save the time of copying. (38167)

FROM PITT

Hollwood, 10 p.m., 6 May 1787

Mr Pitt has the honor to inform his Royal Highness the Prince of Wales that he has his Majesty's commands to communicate to his Royal Highness an answer to his Royal Highness's message. Mr Pitt begs to know at what time it will be most convenient to his Royal Highness to permit him to have the honor of waiting upon his Royal Highness for that purpose. (38169)

225   THE KING TO THE PRINCE OF WALES

6 May 1787

The King learns with great satisfaction that the Prince of Wales is disposed to give such explanations respecting his expences and debts as his Majesty has judged necessary to enable him to take any steps for relieving the Prince from the embarrassment of his present situation. His Majesty wishes an examination into particulars to be entered upon immediately, as the nature and mode of relief as well as the measures necessary to prevent debts in future, must in a great degree depend upon the result of such an examination. But his Majesty thinks proper to add that while the Prince of Wales continues unmarried, he does not conceive any encrease of income can be necessary to enable him to support an establishment suited to his rank and station. (16583-4)

Carlton House, 7 May 1787

The Prince of Wales having received with all dutiful respect his Majesty's answer to the proposals he had the honor of laying before him, the Prince begs leave to represent that, in conformity with what he has always express'd thro' the whole progress of this business, he is very willing to give such explanations respecting his expences & debts as his Majesty may judge necessary, & so far from objecting to have any examination of particulars entered upon *immediately*, the necessity of his Royal Highness's situation is such that he would on his part have made it the object of a peculiar supplication to his Majesty that there should *not even be the delay of an hour*.

His Royal Highness will accept with thankfulness the payment of debts *even without* the encrease of income, but in that event he must with great submission express to the King the *total impossibility* of resuming his family & establishment without incurring the risk of defeating those measures which his Royal Highness will be most happy to take in order to prevent his contracting any fresh debt.

As his Majesty seems to have rejected the Prince's first two proposals, his Royal Highness would not willingly recur to them, tho' were a comparison to be drawn between the times in which the present Prince of Wales lives & those in which his Majesty's father's establishment was settled (an establishment which *even then proved itself totally insufficient*), his Royal Highness cannot but think himself justified in proposing, *tho unmarried*, such an increase of income as he had the honor of stating to his Majesty in his *first proposal*, & which *alone* can enable him to support that *rank & situation which his birth has entitled him to*.   (38183)

227   THE PRINCE OF WALES TO WILLIAM PITT [copy [1]], AND THE REPLY

Carlton House, 12 midnight, Monday, 7 May 1787

The Prince of Wales encloses to Mr. Pitt his observations on the answer he had the honor of receiving by him from the King, by which Mr. Pitt will perceive the anxiety the Prince feels for a speedy termination of this business, which as far as it depends on the execution of accounts, may undoubtedly be obtained in a few hours as well as in as many days. For this purpose his Royal Highness has ordered the three Commissioners of his Accounts, Mr. Lyte, and Colonels Lake and Hulse to wait upon Mr. Pitt tomorrow at any hour Mr. Pitt shall appoint.   (41883)

1. In the King's hand.

Downing Street, 9.15 a.m., Tuesday, 8 May 1787
Mr Pitt begs leave most respectfully to acquaint his Royal Highness the
Prince of Wales that he has had the honor to transmit to the King the
paper received this morning from his Royal Highness. In consequence
of his Royal Highness's commands, Mr Pitt has desired to see Mr Lyte,
and Colonels Lake & Hulse at half past eleven this morning.   (38170)

228   THE PRINCE OF WALES TO CHARLES JAMES FOX

Carlton House, 10 May 1787
No answer is come as yet from Pitt excepting yt. he was to see ye King
tonight & wd. endeavour to get everything settled if he cd.; some sort
of an answer I shall certainly have this evening when he quits the
Queen's House, wh. I will communicate to you as soon as possible after
I have receiv'd it. His own statement yt. he has made out, as expenses
for every year from the time I came of age, is thirty thousand pounds a
quarter, consequently annually an hundred & twenty thousand pounds;
ye moment I get a copy of ym. I will transmit it to you for yr. inspection.
In ye meantime, I beg you will not think of going to Newmarket till
you have heard again from me; how late it may be I cannot answer for.
Adieu, my dear friend. Pray excuse haste.   (Add. MSS. 47560, f.27)

229   LETTERS FROM THE PRINCE OF WALES TO WILLIAM PITT,
AND THE REPLIES

Carlton House, 1 p.m., 10 May 1787 [copy]
Mr. Pitt having [now] had two whole days for the examination of the
Prince of Wales's accounts, and *every satisfaction* respecting these
accounts which either the Prince himself, his servants, or the accounts
themselves can afford him, the Prince cannot help saying that he thinks
that any further procrastination in this business will be not only very
unpleasant, but perfectly unnecessary, and therefore must hope that
Mr. Pitt will obtain for him from the King a decisive answer during
the course of this day.   (41884 and 38183)

PITT'S REPLY

Downing Street, 1.20 p.m., 10 May 1787
I am honored with your Royal Highness's commands, and beg leave in
the most respectful manner to assure your Royal Highness that I have

endeavored to obey the King's orders in the examination of the accounts furnished by your Royal Highness's officers with all the dispatch which the time required by them for making out the necessary abstracts would admit. Previous to laying these papers before the King, which I hope to have an opportunity of doing in the course of a few hours, it is my wish to have the result of them, as it appears to me, checked by your Royal Highness's officers in order to prevent any mistake; and I should also think it my duty to submit it to your Royal Highness's own inspection in any manner which your Royal Highness may be pleased to direct. (38171-2)

THE PRINCE OF WALES'S REPLY

Carlton House, 5 p.m., 10 May 1787
The Prince of Wales has desir'd Mr Robinson to wait in person upon Mr Pitt with the statement wh. the Prince now perfectly approves of. However, the Prince cannot help wishing, as time presses very much, yt. Mr Pitt will if possible draw everything to a final conclusion this evening.

P.S. The Prince wd. be very glad to have a copy of ye abstract Mr Pitt made out in his own hand, as soon as he conveniently can.   (38174)

PITT'S REPLY

Downing Street, 11.55 p.m., 10 May 1787
I take the earliest opportunity to transmit to your Royal Highness the enclosed message from the King, conceiving this mode of communicating it to be more expeditious and more convenient to your Royal Highness than presuming personally to tresspass on your Royal Highness at this hour.   (38173 and 38190)

[Enclosure] THE KING TO THE PRINCE OF WALES

Thursday night, 10 May 1787
From the abstract deliver'd by the Prince of Wales' Officers it appears that the salaries & allowances of his Establishment have amounted to a sum of from £15,000 to £20,000 pr annum, & that his Household expences (including arrears) have been annually about £16,000.

These sums would leave out of his ordinary income at least £26,000 for the remaining heads of Stables, Privy Purse & Extraordinaries, but the expences of the Stables alone (including arrears) have been no less than £21,000 pr. annum, a sum much exceeding what can be supposed to be necessary in that department. Under the head of Privy Purse there has been paid during three years £16,000, & an arrear contracted of £44,000, besides which there has been paid to the Prince's particular orders £37,000, and a debt is due on bond of £13,000. Of the application of these sums, making in the whole about £110,000, the accounts furnish no explanation. Anxious as his Majesty is to deliver the Prince of Wales from the embarrassment of his present situation, he would not be disposed to consider strictly articles of past excess if there were a reasonable security that it would be avoided in future, nor does his Majesty require the disclosure of particulars which the Prince may think himself engaged in honour to conceal, but this consideration cannot apply to a sum of such an amount, & his Majesty cannot reconcile it to what he feels due to his people to make any application to Parliament on the subject without previously receiving every explanation which the nature of it will properly admit, & which must be expected on such an occasion. If his Majesty receives a satisfactory answer on this point, & the Prince will engage to avoid debts in future, and establish proper regulations for that purpose, his Majesty will in that case desire the assistance of Parliament to relieve the Prince from his debts & to provide a reasonable sum for compleating Carlton House. But his Majesty cannot approve of any encrease of income while the Prince continues unmarried, as the accounts hitherto produced confirm his Majesty in the opinion that the Prince's present income is sufficient, under proper management, for every expence suited to his rank & station.   (38190)

230 LETTERS FROM THE PRINCE OF WALES [copies] TO WILLIAM PITT, AND A REPLY

Carlton House, 11 May 1787
The Prince of Wales begs to observe to Mr. Pitt that there must have been some very great misunderstanding respecting the accounts if it is supposed that there is one hundred & ten thousand pounds of which there is no explanation. In the first place the sum is but one hundred thousand pounds, instead of one hundred & ten thousand pounds, which is a mistake in the addition, & in that sum are included a variety of articles which would have been submitted to Mr. Pitt if he had wish'd to see them, & which the Prince now encloses, consisting of bills to various tradesmen, & which if he chuses now to examine he will be further convinced of. These articles appear to amount to half of the above-mentioned hundred thousand pounds, & in the remaining half are included all Newmarket expences & losses (amounting as far as the Prince can ascertain to little short of twenty thousand pounds), post

horses & travelling expences of all sorts, besides all pocket & other disbursements since the time the Prince's establishment was first form'd, & into which it is professed there is no intention to enquire.

The Prince of Wales flatters himself that this explanation will now appear perfectly satisfactory to the King. It is also undoubtedly the Prince's intention to establish proper regulations to avoid debts in future, but in order to adhere to this resolution, his Royal Highness cannot forbear repeating *the total impossibility* he feels himself under of resuming his establishment upon *his present income*, however natural it must be to his feelings to be desirous of living *in a manner suited to his rank & station*, as well as to restore those servants whom his late arrangement obliged him, with great reluctance, to dismiss & who have ever served him with the utmost fidelity & attachment.

ARREARS DUE ON ACCOUNT OF ROBES & PRIVY PURSE

Jeffries—Jeweller	£1,203
Martin—do.	1,312
Gordon—Lace Draper	2,180
Mr. Broadhurst	2,200
Kings—Mercer	2,588
Davies—do.	2,683
Gray—Jeweller	12,849
Bazalgetti—Taylor	16,774
Duvall—Jeweller	939
Shrapnell—do.	380
Bunnell—Laceman	384
Newcomb—Bootmaker	348
Fermin—Button Maker	309
White—Breeches Maker	380
Egg—Gun Maker	548
Cater—Hatter	523
Vulliamy—Watchmaker	392
Lawer—Jeweller	439
Bland—Sword Cutler	222
Rymer—Shoemaker	236
Derrit—Perfumer	250
Embroyderers	310
Painters, &c., &c.	1,018
Bicknell—Hosiers	590
Hodgson—Draper	350
Beckett—Bookseller	289
Grigson—Watchmaker	205
Le Brun—Perfumer	268 : 19 : —
Sundry Small bills	822
	£50,991 : 19 : —

AREARS DUE FOR STABLE ACCOUNT

	£	s	d	£	s	d
For purchase of horses from different dealers	5,302 :	13 :	6			
For purveyance & other exp^{ces}. for horses keep	5,905 :	7 :	8			
Coachmakers, Sadlers, Taylors, Lacemen & other tradesmen's bills sent in on account of the stables to Mr. Robinson	17,366 :	4 :	10	28,574 :	6 :	—

[sic] £79,566 : 3 : —

(38191–2)

FROM PITT

Downing Street, 11.45 p.m., Saturday, 12 May 1787
Mr Pitt begs leave to acquaint his Royal Highness the Prince of Wales
that he has just received the King's commands to deliver a message to
his Royal Highness and requests his Royal Highness's orders at what
hour tomorrow he may be permitted to wait on his Royal Highness for
that purpose. (38175)

THE PRINCE OF WALES'S REPLY

Carlton House, Saturday Night, 12 May 1787
The Prince of Wales has receiv'd Mr Pitt's note & will be glad to see
him at one o'clock tomorrow. The Prince desires Mr Pitt will come
either dress'd or undress'd whichever suits his convenience best.

(38176)

231 MESSAGE FROM THE KING TO THE PRINCE OF WALES

12 May 1787
The King has taken into consideration the explanations transmitted
yesterday by the Prince of Wales to Mr. Pitt for his Majesty's information, and altho' many of the articles of expence accounting for such parts
of the sum of £100,000 as are explained in these papers cannot be
consider'd as having been either necessary or proper, yet from his

paternal affection to the Prince & his earnest desire to take every practicable measure for restoring him to the situation which he ought to fill in this country, his Majesty is disposed to content himself with this explanation of the past, provided a proper arrangement is made for the future, and the regulations establish'd which the Prince expresses himself ready to form for preventing farther debts. His Majesty therefore wishes a plan to be immediately prepared by the Prince's Officers under his inspection, arranging his expences in the several departments, & settling a regular order of payment for each under such checks as will effectually avoid any arrear.

And his Majesty has no doubt that when the Prince examines attentively the particulars of such a plan, he will find that his present income is sufficient to enable him to restore the servants he has dismiss'd & to support an establishment suited to his rank & station. When this plan is arranged & an estimate prepared for compleating Carlton House in a reasonable & proper manner, his Majesty will immediately apply to Parliament for their assistance, & for this purpose an account of the Prince's debts and expenditure should be prepared, with the Prince's concurrence, in a proper form to be laid before Parliament as the ground of his Majesty's application. (38192–3)

232 ABSTRACT OF THE QUARTERLY EXPENDITURE OF HIS ROYAL HIGHNESS
THE PRINCE OF WALES FROM 10 OCTOBER 1783

		£	s	d	£	s	d	£	s	d
1783 Octr. 10th	Salaries & allowances	3,374	12	9						
	Stable expences	2,497	16	0						
	Mr. Robinson's disbursements	243	13	2						
	Disbursed by Col. Hotham for Privy Purse, &c.	5,391	18	11	11,508	0	10			
1784 Jany. 5	Salaries & allowances	3,717	10	5						
	Stable expences	3,075	1	9						
	Extras Mr. Robinson as above	318	16	10						
	do. Col. Hotham do.	9,049	12	4	16,161	1	4			
April 5	Salaries & allowances	4,267	2	11						
	Stable expences	7,283	7	9						
	Extras Mr. Robinson	268	17	5						
	do. Col. Hotham	5,795	19	8	17,615	7	9			
July 5	Salaries & allowances	4,461	19	7						
	Stable expences	3,956	6	4						
	Extras Mr. Robinson	260	2	10						
	do. Col. Hotham	9,637	16	1	18,316	4	10			
Ann¹ expenditure from 10th October 1783 to 5 July 1784								£63,600	14	9

Date	Description	£	s	d	£	s	d
1784 Octr. 10th	Salaries & allowances	4,787	19	10			
	Stable expences	1,625	14	4			
	Extras Mr. Robinson	616	19	2			
	do. Col. Hotham	5,605	5	10	12,635	19	2
1785 Jany. 5	Salaries & allowances	4,692	13	10			
	Stable expences	6,765	8	4			
	Extras Mr. Robinson	896	14	8			
	do. Col. Hotham	8,203	19	8	20,558	16	6
April 5	Salaries & allowances	4,877	9	3			
	Stable expences	1,479	13	6			
	Extras Mr. Robinson	297	9	6			
	do. Col. Hotham	6,966	–	6	13,620	12	9
July 5	Salaries & allowances	4,875	–	9			
	Stable expences	2,599	2	10			
	Extras Mr. Robinson	342	15	1			
	do. Col. Hotham	10,331	14	4	18,148	13	–

Annual expenditure from 10th Octr. 1784 to 5 July 1785 — £64,964 1 5

Date	Description	£	s	d	£	s	d
1785 Octr. 10	Salaries & allowances	4,875	1	9			
	Stable expences	991	9	6			
	Mr. Robinson's dis-bursements	838	16	–			
	Disbursed by Col. Hotham	9,286	13	–	15,992	–	3
1786 Jany. 5	Salaries & allowances	4,885	1	9			
	Stable expences	5,562	16	8			
	Extras Mr. Robinson	1,297	11	11			
	do. Col. Hotham	6,803	2	–	18,548	12	4
April 5	Salaries & allowances	4,915	4	3			
	Stable expences	1,250	13	11			
	Extras Mr. Robinson	882	–	4			
	do. Col. Hotham	5,450	10	–	12,498	8	6
July 5	Salaries & allowances	5,004	9	3			
	Stable expenses, ex-tras & gratuities on dismission	13,073	4	5	18,073	13	8	[sic]

Annual expenditure from 10 Oct. 1785 to July 5 1786 — £65,112 14 9

Date	Description	£	s	d	£	s	d
1786 Octr. 10	Salaries & allowances	2,784	16	6			
	Extras Mr. Robinson	852	9	–			
	do. Col. Hotham	9,121	6	3	12,758	11	9
1787 Jany. 5	Salaries & allowances	2,768	8	10			
	Extras Mr. Robinson	1,013	12	7	3,782	1	5

Note the above quarter's account passed & signed by the Commrs, Messrs. Lyte, &c.

(Signed) A. Robinson, Acct

(38184/5)

297

	£	s	d	£	s	d
Ballances upon bills delivered, &c.				143,077	8	9
No. 1. All sums under £40 paid in full; and under £100, one half the amount is	2,146	6	10			
No. 2. Sums under £1,000—9 pr. ct. upon the amount	2,774	13	–			
No. 3. All larger bills at 9 pr. cent	9,807	9	11	14,728	9	9
Ballance remaining due				128,348	19	–
Bills found to have been omitted near	1,000	–	–			
Purchase of houses in Stone Cutter Court	4,000	–	–			
Bond debts, &c.	13,000	–	–	18,000	–	–
				£146,348	19	–
Say, two years interest on £162,077				16,206	–	–
				£162,554	19	–

(Signed) A. Robinson, Accompt.

(38185)

NO. 3

Arrears appearing due from his Royal Highness the Prince of Wales to sundry trades people under the respective departments conducted by Mr. Lyte, Col. Lake, Col. Hulse, Mr. Holland the builder, & Mr. Gaubert, exclusive of the accumulation of debts since the 5 July 1786

Mr. Lyte for Robes & Privy Purse	£44,000
Carlton House expence of building & furniture	55,000
Col. Lake for arrears of stables	26,095
Col. Hulse for arrears of house expences, including Bagshot, Col. Hulse apprehends must be	18,000
	£143,095

(38186)

NO. 4

A. ROBINSON TO [?]

Pall Mall, 9 May 1787

I have the honor to enclose to you a computed state of his Royal Highness' debts as they appear severally due under the different departments. Mr. Lyte's account of Robes and Privy Purse, deliver'd to me this morning, you will please to observe amounts to £4,000 more than our hasty calculation made last night; a very considerable error was also made in the casting up the Stable account last night. Col. Lake's department is drawn up, as well as that of Col. Hulse with as much exactness now as I have found practicable, & you, I dare say, Sir, will be so candid as to admit that from the method I have been obliged to adopt in the division of the accounts, if any errors have taken place I am greatly entitled to indulgence.

The amount of the Com^rs account of payments from Octr. 1783, which you, Sir, was pleased to desire information of, I find to be £29,277. (38186)

NO. 5

					Mr. Lyte
Octr. 1783	The P. by Col. Hotham	2,000 : – : –	Oct. 1783	1,000 : – : –
Janry. '84	do.	1,000 : – : –		500 : – : –
				200
Octr. '84	Hammersley	4,000 : – : –		2,000 : – :
April '85	Mr. Birch	1,518 : 15 : –	April 1784	1,000 : – : –
	Hammersley	4,000 : – : –	July 5th	1,800 : – : –
July 5, '85	ditto	5,000 : – : –		1,000 : – : –
	Birch	1,537 : 10 : –		200 : – : –
			Jany. '84	3,000 : – : –
Octr. 10 '85	Hammersley	5,000 : – : –		1,000 : – : –
	Birch	1,556 : 5 : –		200 : – : –
Jany. '86	do.	1,591 : 4 : 6	July	350 : – : –
			Octr.	600 : – : –
April	Hammersley	3,000 : – : –	Jany. 1786	1,700 : – : –
July	ditto	5,000 : – : –	April	500 : – : –
	Thompson	2,000 : – : –	July	1,000 : – : –
		£37,203 : 14 : 6		£16,050 : – : –

Extract from the books.
(Signed) A. Robinson, Acct. 8th May 1787.

Arrear supposed due from the different departments as near as can be from recollection

Privy Purse	£40,000 : – : –
Carlton House	55,000 : – : –
Compt^rs. Acc^t	16,000 : – : –
	£111,000 : – : –
Arrears of Stable	33,346 : – : –
	£144,346 : – : –

(38187)

299

It appears from the abstracts Nos. 1, 2, 3 that the sums actually
  paid in the year ending 5th July 1784 amounted to   £63,600
In the year ending 5th July 1785 to   64,964
In the year ending 5 July 1786 to   65,112
That the arrears incurr'd during those three years amounted to   143,095
And that debts are owing by his Royal Highness on Bond   13,000
For purchase of houses   4,000
And for interest calculated on two years   16,206
Making the whole of his Royal Highness' expenditure for these three
  years   369,977

The particulars of this expenditure as far as appears from the
  accounts furnish'd by his R. Highness's officers were as follows

1st. Salaries & allowances to his Royal Highness's officers & ser-
    vants (as pr. abstract No. 1), the particulars of which appear'd
    in the books produced

                 In the 1st year   15,819
                 In the 2nd year   19,231
                 In the 3rd year   19,679
                       Making together   54,729
which sum includes the whole expended on this account, there
being no arrears under this head.

2d. Stable expences (as pr. abstract No. 1) the particulars
    of which also appear in the books produced
                 In the 1st year   £16,811
                 In the 2d. year   12,468
                 In the 3d. year   8,664

                     making together   37,943
To which sum is to be added the amount of arrears under
this head, which appear from the abstract No. 2 to be   26,095
         Making ye whole expenditure on this account   64,038

3d. Mr. Robinson's disbursement (as pr. abstract No. 1)
    the particulars of which also appear in the books
    produced
                 In the 1st year   1,089
                 In the 2d. year   2,151
                 In the 3d. year   3,733
                     making together   6,973
which sum includes the whole expenditure on this account,
there being no arrears under this head.

4th. Col. Hotham's disbursements (as pr. abstract No. 1)
including issues on account of household expences,
on account of Privy Purse, on account of sums paid
by his Royal Highness's particular order which
issues severally appear in the books produced but
without any more particular account of their application.

The total of these disbursements is stated separately for
each of the three years, but the amount falling under
each of the different heads specified above is not distinguished in the same manner.

The totals of these are:

Household expences for ye three years as stated by Mr. Robinson, No. 4, amounted to	29,277	
To which is to be added (as pr. abstract No. 2) arrears under this head	18,000	
making together		
which sum includes the whole expenditure on this account.		47,277
Privy Purse for the three years as pr. abstract No. 5	16,050	
To which is to be added (as pr. abstract No. 2) arrears under this head	44,000	
making together		
which sum includes the whole expenditure on this account.		60,050
Sums paid by his Royal Highness' particular orders for the three years (as pr. abstract No. 5)		37,203
which sum includes the whole expenditure on this account.		
Other extraordinary expences for the three years, about		11,406
Nothing appears in the abstract as having been hitherto paid on account of buildings at Carlton House, but the arrear incurr'd under this head (the particulars of which appear'd in the books produced) are stated (as pr. abstract No. 3) to amount to		55,000
To these sums are to be added his Royal Highness's debts (as above stated) on Bond	13,000	
For purchase of houses	4,000	
And for interest	16,206	
making together		33,206
Total of the particulars of his Royal Highness's expenditure (as far as appears from the accounts) in the three years		£369,882
It appears (pr. abstract No. 1) that the sums paid in the two quarters ending 10th Octr. 1786 & 5th Jany. 1787 amounted to	16,540	

And it is stated by H.R. Highness's officers that some arrear has
been incurred since that time but the amount of that arrear &
of the sums paid in the quarter ending 5th April 1787 has not
yet been ascertained.

233 THE PRINCE OF WALES TO WILLIAM PITT [copy]

Carlton House, 14 May 1787

The Prince of Wales now sends by the three Comm^{rs} of his accounts to Mr. Pitt the answer to his Majesty's message as well as *the only estimate upon which he can resume* his Establishment. The Prince now having complied with every intimation that he has receiv'd of his Majesty's wishes upon this subject, cannot but be confident that there will be no farther delay in the final arrangement. His Royal Highness's officers have orders to consult with Mr. Pitt upon the form of the statement proposed to be laid before Parliament, which the Prince takes for granted cannot be meant to be made a matter of detail. (38193)

234 MESSAGE FROM THE PRINCE OF WALES TO THE KING

14 May 1787

The Prince of Wales has receiv'd with the utmost gratitude the King's most gracious message communicated to him the day before yesterday by Mr. Pitt. His Majesty's expressions of paternal affection to the Prince have given him the most heartfelt satisfaction.

In conformity to the King's wishes, the Prince immediately directed a plan to be drawn out under his own inspection arranging his expences in the several departments, & settling a regular order for the payment of each: his Royal Highness encloses this plan but he is sorry to observe that the result of it only confirms him in his former opinion of the *utter impossibility of resuming* his establishment without the risk of incurring new debts, which it is his Majesty's wish as well as his Royal Highness's *sincere & firm determination at all events* to avoid. The Prince therefore humbly begs leave to state to his Majesty that if he will be graciously pleased to permit the application to Parliament to include the small difference between his Royal Highness's present income & the amount of the plan for restoring *the whole* of his establishment, his Royal Highness will receive such a mark of his Majesty's paternal goodness with the utmost gratitude, & will be happy to find himself enabled to restore the servants he was obliged to dismiss as well as to feel himself restored to the situation which his Majesty is graciously pleased to say he might fill in this country. (38193)

Carlton House, 14 May 1787

For compleating the stone work to the front & portico next Pall Mall agreable to the elevations made & approved of, in which it is designed the front & return of Malcombe House should be new faced & the roof alter'd, putting up the iron work to the areas, making & fixing the steps & pavement under the portico, also the ceiling on soffite, compleating the purchase of & taking down more of the old houses & paving the courts, building the screen wall next the street, making the entrance gates, decorating the end walls of the court, finishing the hall, octagon & staircase. In the hall, the paving, marble pillars, doors & windows, part of the ornamental & plain stuce work, some steps, the stone grates & painting the whole. In the octagon vestibule laying down the pavement, finishing the joiners work & painting it. In the under octagon laying down the pavement & finishing it, & making an opening into the apartment next the gallery.

In the staircase putting up the iron work, compleating the joiners work, finishing the plain & ornamental plaistering of the lower parts, glazing the skylight with circular plate glass, putting up the iron work & thermes in the arcades, making the figures for the wind dial & clock, & painting the whole. In the upper octagon glazing the skylight with ornamental glass, putting up the therm figures & ironworks in the arcades, putting on a handrail, party gilding the ironwork & painting the whole.

The porter's room, the lobby, & chair passage to fit up & finish, carrying up & finishing two small staircases. Finish the stewards room, the larder; under it & two stories of rooms above. In the kitchen, pantry & dry larder some of the timber work of the carcase to compleat. Some vaults to make for coals under the court, some of the passages & cellars under the hall to finish, altering the window & chimney in the Beaufett room & new fitting it up.

The Great Drawing Room to compleat the finishings to the windows, floors, doors, ceiling, chimney piece, carving, gilding & painting; making some alterations in the Throne Room.

The baths to fit up with marble & finish; the supply of water to provide for & to put up boilers for the hot bath.

The State apartments on the principal floor to compleat, the finishing, painting & gilding.

Building a circular music room, forty feet diameter & finishing, painting, carving & gilding the same, this room being necessary to give a communication between the Drawing Room & the eating room, but the adjoining house must be purchased, the expence of which is estimated. Forming & finishing the anti-room between the hall & the eating rooms which are intended to be laid together.

To the south front of the palace to make a stone gallery ten feet wide & the whole length of the front level with the principal floor supported on stone pillars.

To build the stables, coach houses, riding houses, lodging rooms for the coachmen & grooms, haylofts, & granary & to form a mewse at the end of the garden, the whole fitted up & finish'd, the yard paved, the water laid on and a communication made with the park.

Estimate of these works amounts to the sum of £49,700 : o : o.

To build four wings to the palace, intended for the following purposes:
The first at the south east angle adjoining the State apartments intended to compleat it by making sufficient accommodation for ladies.

The wing at the south west angle intended as a library, mathematical instruments, pictures & private theater.

The wing to the north west, next Pall Mall intended for the accomodation of the great officers, as the Treasurer, Council, Audits, Accounts, &c., &c.

The wing to the north east intended for the kitchen, offices, and a chapel.

To erect these wings it will be necessary to purchase more of the adjoining houses which are leasehold, held under the Crown. These wings are necessary to render the palace compleat, & will cost about twenty five thousand pounds to build them; they have been included in former estimates, but as they are not immediately necessary for the accommodation of his Royal Highness the estimate of them has now been seperated.

Made out & calculated by me, (Signed), Hy Holland.

Estimate for the furnishing Carlton House
For all the hangings, glasses & furniture necessary in the hall, vestibule, staircase, octagon, anti-room or the basement story, the music room, the great eating room, as intended to be altered, the new lodging rooms over the kitchen & at the stables.

For compleating the hangings & furniture in all the other apartments & rooms which are very far advanced.

As several of these apartments & rooms are not built, form'd or finish'd & as a great part of the furniture is in an unfinish'd state, it is impossible to ascertain or describe exactly what will be wanted, but from as exact an account as can be ascertain'd the sum of five thousand five hundred pounds will be necessary.

Made out & calculated by me, (Signed) Hy. Holland, 14 May 1787.

Captain J. W. Payne, R.N.
by Hoppner

Colonel George Hotham
by Gilbert Stuart 1786

Pensions & annual donations

Sir Richard Jeb [1]	£200 : — : —
Mr. T. Dunkerley [2]	100 : — : —
Mrs. M. Robinson [3]	500 : — : —
Donation to the Welch Society	105 : — : —
Mr. Pellett	100 : — : —
Mr. Montagu	121 : — : —
Randel & Towers (late coachman & groom)	100 : 10 : —
Mr. Robinson for care of Carlton Garden	90 : — : —
Musicians	300 : — : —
Mrs. King—Windsor	30 : — : —
Humphreys, Rat catcher	31 : 10 : —
Weltjie, confectioner	40 : — : —
Drew, Porter	50 : — : —
Humane Society	20 : — : —
St. George's Hospital	20 : — : —
Widow Sharpe	30 : — : —
Widow Jones	20 : — : —
Widow Watson, for lodgings	10 : — : —
Brown, Botanic painter	10 : — : —
Mrs. Duck for coals & necessaries	25 : 4 : —
Mrs. Smith	21 : — : —
Wheeler, watchman	25 : 4 : —
Treasury gifts	5 : 15 : 6
Blackstock & Croft	15 : 15 : —
	£1,970 : 18 : 6

(38193–5)

1. Jebb did not enjoy his pension for long: he died in July 1787, having 'fallen a sacrifice to exertions beyond his strength during the late illness of the Princesses' (Rutland MSS. [H.M.C.], iii.397).

2. Thomas Dunkerley, believed to be one of George II's sons. Before 1782 he had a secret service pension of £200 a year, and he 'pleads disappointment and distress' (P.R.O., Chatham Papers, 229). His daughter, who 'had the misfortune to have her right leg cut off above the knee', was also on the pension list.

3. 'Perdita'. 'The Prince's attachment to her, which was fugitive, served only by its speedy extinction to embitter the remainder of her life, without much augmenting her fortune. Her health and her beauty became victims to acute rheumatic disorders, under which, aggravated by pecuniary distress, she finally sank, after surviving all her attractions' (*Wraxall*, v,369).

A PLAN OF THE PRINCE OF WALES'S ANNUAL EXPENCE UPON THE SUPPOSITION OF THE WHOLE OF HIS ROYAL HIGHNESSES LATE ESTABLISHMENT BEING RESTORED, ARRANGING HIS EXPENCES IN THE SEVERAL DEPARTMENTS & ASCERTAINING A REGULAR ORDER OF PAYMENT FOR EACH, AS THE MOST EFFECTUAL CHECK TO AVOID ARREARS IN FUTURE

Establishment salaries	£	s	d	£	s	d	Remarks
Groom of the Stole	1,200	–	–				
4 Gentlemen of ye Bed-chamber	2,000	–	–				
Treasurer	1,000	–	–				
Master of ye Robes & Privy Purse	500	–	–				
Comptroller of the Household	500	–	–				The amount of the
7 Grooms of the Bedchamber	2,800	–	–				Establishment here
Commr. of the Stables	500	–	–				stated is formed as
5 Equeries	1,500	–	–				it stood at the per-
2 Pages of Honor	400	–	–				iod when his Royal
2 Gentlemen Ushers Privy Chamber	400	–	–				Highness made the
2 do. Daily Waiters	300	–	–				reduction, the ab-
Private Secretary	300	–	–				stract of which was
Sub. Treasurer & Accomptant	500	–	–				transmitted to Mr.
Physicians	330	–	–				Pitt ye 10th inst.
Surgeons	250	–	–				
Clerk of the Closet	200	–	–				
2 Librarians	348	–	–	13,028	–	–	
Lower Establishments							
Housekeeper	400	–	–				
Sempstress	200	–	–				
Laundress	170	–	–				
5 Pages of the Back Stairs	1,105	–	–				
5 do. of the Presence	450	–	–				
Messenger to the Treasurer	80	–	–				
Pagesmen	90	–	–				
3 Porters	143	10	–				
8 Footmen	408	8	–				
1 Chasseur	51	1	–				
1 Watchman at Kew	25	–	–				do.
Dentist	105	–	–				
Hairdresser	150	–	–				
Comptroller of the Kitchen	500	–	–				
Kitchen servants	922	–	–				
Mr. Gaubert	50	–	–				
2 Coachmen	100	–	–				
1 Postillion	25	–	–				
Servants, Coach House, Stable, Hunting Stable	107	–	–				
1st Groom	87	6	–				
2d. ditto	[sic]						
2 Hack Grooms	111	–	–				
2 Hobby ditto	111	–	–				
4 Senior Stable Boys	82	–	–				
7 Additional helpers	88	4	–				
Clerk of the Stables	121	–	–	5,737	19	–	
Allowances to Preceptors & late Masters				1,390	2	–	Continued as origin-ally settled by his Majesty.
Salaries & allowances				20,156	1	–	
Pensions & annual donations				1,970	18	6	The particulars of this head are transmit-ted in Paper No. 1.

	£	s	d	£	s	d	Remarks
Household exp^{ces} under ye Comptroller	15,600	–	–				It is evident that the restoring H.R.H.'s Court & Establishment must considerably augment this head of expenditure tho' little regard has been paid to that consideration.
Wear of linnen, table furniture, &c.	800	–	–				
Coals	900	–	–	17,300	–	–	
Various other tradesmen's bills not included under the head of Housekeeping				2,700	–	–	This article is estimated upon an inspection of past bills & relate to repairs of all sorts in furniture & decorations, lamps, pictures, books, &c.
Taxes & Rent							
Rent of houses in Stone Cutter Court, Sr Wm Ashurst's House & Office	410	–	–				
Taxes on Carlton House, &c.	704	7	6	1,114	7	6	
Board Wages & Gratuities							
Pages of the Back							
Stairs p^rq^r 62 :10:–							
do. of the Presence 30 :–:–							
Pagesmen & Porter 15 :–:–							
Hunter 7 :10:–	460 [*sic*]	–	–				
Ditto to inferior servants							
4 maid servants & board wages p^rq^r at £6 :16 :6 each is £27 :6:–	109	4	–				
Ditto to other inferior servants at £113 :5:– p^rquarter	453	–	–				
Gratuities to 5 Pages &c. & allowances for mourning	130	–	–				
To 4 Pages of the Presence	40	–	–				
Bidgood & Troop	30	–	–				
Porters	10	–	–				
Housekeeper's allow^{ce} for mourning	25	–	–				
Allowance to Footmen for Crosses & Wardrobe	24	3	0	1,281	7	–	
Disbursements at the office of Treasury for the payment of Sundry small bills not comprised within the other departments	600	–	–				
Apothecaries Bills	300	–	–	900	–	–	
Robes & Wardrobe							
Taylor	4,000	–	–				This estimate is calculated more upon the amount of H. R. Highness' expenditure in those articles before he left the Queen's House than upon the annual amount of the bills since, which have very considerably exceeded the sum here stated.
Embroiderers	900	–	–				
Lacemen	500	–	–				
Silk mercers	200	–	–				
Hosier	250	–	–				
Hatter	120	–	–				
Shoe & Bootmakers	150	–	–				
Lace Draper	400	–	–				
Linnen Draper	300	–	–				
Sword Cutler & Jeweller, & various other articles	500	–	–				
Breeches Maker, Glover & Perfumer	100	–	–	7,420	–	–	

	£	s	d	£	s	d	Remarks
Stables							The utmost attention has been paid in estimating the probable amount in this department & the Comm^r. of the Stables has reduced it as low as possible. But is apprehensive that the sum proposed will by no means be found sufficient for the purpose, as the adhering to any estimate must always depend upon a great variety of accidents and contingencies, which it is impossible to foresee or provide for in this Branch of H.R.H. expenditure. It is also to be observed that under the head of Stables are included various articles, such as Board Wages & Liveries to Footmen, &c., &c., in the same manner as in his Majesty's Stables, which does not properly seem to belong to that department.
Carriages, Harness, & Coach-makers Bills	1,600	–	–				
Carriage Horses, 2 sets Phaeton do.	1,500	–	–				
Hacks & Hunters for H.R.H.	2,200	–	–				
Servants Horses	600	–	–				
Purchase of Horses	900	–	–				
Sadlers Bills, Horse Cloathing	600	–	–				
Bittmakers	100	–	–				
Smith & Farriers	650	–	–				
Sundry necessaries for the Stable	400	–	–				
Tradesmen's Bills for Liveries							
Taylor	400	–	–				
Lacemen	1,600	–	–				
Woolen Draper	1,100	–	–				
Hatter & Capmaker	220	–	–				
Boot maker	120	–	–				
Breeches maker	80	–	–	12,070	–	–	
Board wages to Stable Servants & Rent of Stables				771	6	–	
Travelling charges				1,900	–	–	This, tho' usually charged under the head of Stables is in fact a seperate article & has hitherto amounted to a much greater sum.
Expences Bagshot				750	–	–	
Expences at Brighthelmstone				1,000	–	–	
Privy Purse				10,000	–	–	
Total				£79,334	–	–	

ORDER IN WHICH THE SEVERAL PAYMENTS ARE PROPOSED TO BE MADE

Rent & Taxes
Tradesmen's Bills
Menial Servants
Pages &c.
Pensions & Donations
Establishment
Board Wages & Gratuities
Household
Stables
Official Disbursements
Travelling Charges
Expences at Bagshot & Brighton
Privy Purse

By this order of payment no exceeding in any department can happen without its falling as a charge upon the Privy Purse, & of consequence coming quarterly to the notice & inspection of H.R. Highness.

The Comm^{rs} humbly beg leave to observe that in forming their estimates in the preceding several departments they have proceded upon the supposition of a considerable reduction in many of the most material articles of H.R. Highnesses expenditure, otherwise they should not conceive themselves justified in supposing that the amount here stated would answer the whole of H.R. Highness Establishment & expences, or that they could accomplish the earnest desire H.R. Highness has expressed that every part of his Household should be managed with such attention & oeconomy as shall prevent the risque of incurring debts in future. At the same time they conceive it their duty to observe that there must probably be some articles of unforeseen & precarious expence which it is not in their power to class under any particular head or in any distinct manner to advert to.

(Signed) H^{y}. Lyte; G. Lake; S. Hulse. (38196–8)

237 WILLIAM PITT TO THE PRINCE OF WALES

Downing Street, 9.40 p.m., 15 May 1787
Mr Pitt has been honored with the commands of his Royal Highness the Prince of Wales, and will lose no time in transmitting to his Majesty his Royal Highness's message and the papers accompanying it. (38177)

309

20 May 1787

On examining the plan prepar'd under the inspection of the Prince of Wales, arranging his expences in the several departments, the King observed many articles in which his Majesty thought there was room for considerable reduction, but in order to avoid as far as possible entering into detail on the particulars of the estimate, his Majesty directed Mr. Pitt to express thro' the Prince's Officers his Majesty's wish that it should be revised by the Prince's direction.

His Majesty is sorry to find that this has been declined & that at a time when the Prince is so strongly called upon to shew his disposition to confine his expences within the most reasonable bounds he adheres to an estimate in which most of the articles are stated at a higher rate than can appear to his Majesty on any calculation to be necessary. This observation applied particularly to the Household expences under the Comptroller, the Robes & Wardrobes, the Stables & the Privy Purse. A proper regulation under these heads might, as his Majesty is persuaded, enable the Prince to reduce his expences within his income & also to support an Establishment of officers & servants such as is stated in his plan. Under these circumstances & at the time of calling upon Parliament for their assistance to discharge so heavy a debt, it is impossible for his Majesty to propose any augmentation of income which shall bring a further expence on his subjects. But as a proof of his Majesty's paternal affection & in order to remove any possible doubt respecting the sufficiency of the Prince's income to support amply the dignity of his situation, his Majesty is ready whenever the plan is settled for preventing arrears in future to allow £10,000 pr. annum in addition to the sum now paid to the Prince out of his Majesty's Civil List, a sum which exceeds the difference between the salaries & allowances of the Prince's family at present & his proposed establishment. His Majesty approves of the order of payment which the Prince proposes to establish, but as his Majesty must in this application to Parliament pledge himself for every possible security that new debts will not be contracted, his Majesty desires that the Prince will give a general order for the officers at the head of each department to receive immediately at the end of each quarter the sums respectively allotted to them, & that he will direct an abstract of the total sums paid authenticated by the proper officers & certifying what arrear[s] if any, are outstanding to be laid before his Majesty within one month after the expiration of every quarter. His Majesty is also willing to recommend it to Parliament to make a proper provision for compleating Carlton House, but the charge on this account may probably be much reduced, & it must be more explained than in the paper sent by the Prince of Wales before any specifick sum can be named. (38198-9)

Nevis, 20 May 1787

My last letter from Dominique I hope arrived safe, by which you was informed of Mr. Hope's request to quit the ship; and though it is not quite a month since I wrote last, various and many things have happened. . . .

From the time Mr. Hope applied to quit the ship, till he left her, he was quiet, but upon my refusing to sign in the certificate his having complied with the general printed instructions, he refused to take the certificate, which I conceived to be a piece of impertinence, for if the Captain is to sign the certificate he has certainly the power of certifying what in his opinion is truth. I have therefore enclosed to you a copy of my letter to the Admiralty. I am now delivered from Mr Hope, an officer of a very troublesome, disrespectful and violent disposition.

And now for Schomberg. He has been ever since the 23ᵈ January under arrest. Justice therefore demands that he should be delivered as soon as possible from this miserable situation. It has struck Captain Nelson in the same light, who has in his usual officer-like and proper manner suggested to me going down in the Pegasus and taking with me the Rattler in case there should not be ships enough to try Schomberg at once at Jamaica. You may easily conceive I embraced this offer with pleasure, for I am now going to Commodore Gardner[1], an officer universally respected in our corps for his honour, experience and knowledge; besides Captains Ranier[2], Brown and Vashon[3], officers of some standing in the service are there: besides, should Commodore Parker[4] arrive unless he brings a ship with him, Schomberg could not be tried, for Captain Newcome is gone down after a pirate to the Bahamah Islands, and by the Admiralty orders I must be on the coast of North America by the middle of June, so that I have at last a prospect of bringing matters to an issue. I should be happy if every officer had behaved in the respectful manner Mr Hargood, the Second Lieutenant, has ever done. From affairs being in this situation I have by this opportunity thought proper to relate the business to his Majesty, to enclose my narrative and all other papers requisite to explain the business. By my

1. Alan, Lord Gardner (1742–1809). Lieutenant, 1760; Captain, 1766; Rear-Admiral, 1793; Vice-Admiral, 1794; Admiral, 1799. Baronetcy, 1794; Irish peerage, 1800; British peerage, 1806. M.P. for Plymouth, 1790–6; for Westminster, 1796–1806; a Lord of the Admiralty, 1790–5.

2. Peter Rainier (1741 ?–1808). Lieutenant, 1768; Captain, 1778; Rear-Admiral, 1795; Vice-Admiral, 1799; Admiral, 1805.

3. James Vashon (1742–1827). Lieutenant, 1774; Captain, 1782; Rear-Admiral, 1804; Vice-Admiral, 1808; Admiral, 1814.

4. Sir Hyde Parker (1739–1807). Lieutenant, 1758; Captain, 1763; Rear-Admiral, 1793; Vice-Admiral, 1794; Admiral, 1799; knighted, 1779.

311

next I hope to have brought everything to a conclusion, and to send you the proceedings. My best compliments to Elphinstone, and show him this and the enclosed. He must easily conceive that my illness and present occupation have prevented my writing. However, whether I direct to you or him, it is all one.[1]

God bless you and grant me success for I am this instant going to Jamaica. (44769–70)

Carlton House, 20 May 1787

The Prince receives with the truest gratitude the gracious proof of paternal affection which his Majesty has been pleased to give in offering to allow the sum of £10,000 from the Civil List in support of R.H.'s Establishment. The Prince humbly begs leave to assure his Majesty that he did not decline to revise the estimate formed in obedience to his Majesty's commands from any indisposition to confine his expences within the most reasonable bounds, but from a sincere apprehension that as the estimate had been formed upon distinct & minute enquiry made by the Prince himself, he might incur the risque of again exceeding his income had he ventured to state the various heads of expenditure alluded to by his Majesty in a way which the information & calculation before him did not warrant.

The Prince is happy that his Majesty is graciously pleased to approve the order of payment which he proposes to establish, & in obedience to his Majesty's requisition, founded as his Majesty is pleased to declare on the necessity previous to an application to Parliament of having every possible security that new debts shall not be contracted, the Prince will establish an invariable rule that the officers at the head of the respective departments shall immediately at the end of each quarter receive the sums respectively allotted to them, & that an abstract of the total sums paid, authenticated by the proper officers & certifying what arrears, if any, are outstanding, shall be laid before his Majesty within one month after the expiration of every quarter, and the Prince begs leave further to assure his Majesty that feeling with his Majesty a sincere regret in whatever tends to diminish the public resources, however equitable he may conceive his claim to public assistance, & grateful for his Majesty's paternal attention to the circumstances of his situation, his R.H. has no object more at heart than steadily to adopt such a plan & system of management as may fulfil his Majesty's expectation upon this subject &

1. Schomberg was discharged from the ship on 10 June 1787 by order of Commodore Gardner (P.R.O., Adm. 36/10705).

preclude the chance of the Prince's again experiencing embarrassments equally repugnant to his own feelings & unsuited to his rank & station. (38199–200)

Carlton House, 21 May 1787
As his Majesty did not appear to be entirely satisfied with the last sentence in the message H.R.H. had the honor of sending to his Majesty on the 20th inst. relative to the assurances of H.R.H. not involving himself again in future, the Prince begs leave to explain to the King that his wish was to convey in that last sentence to his Majesty assurances that as far as it is in human power to foresee events he does most sincerely mean never to incur any future debts, which must undoubtedly be as disagreable to the King as painful to himself.   (38200)

241   THE PRINCE OF WALES TO THE QUEEN

Carlton House, 21 May 1787
As you was so good as to say that you would inform me when it would be agreable both to the King & you for me to pay my respects at the Queen's House, this unpleasant business being now entirely concluded, I wish to know whether you would allow me to pay my duty between six & seven oclock this evening.   (41891)

242   WILLIAM PITT TO THE PRINCE OF WALES

Downing Street, 23 May 1787
I beg leave most respectfully to acquaint your Royal Highness that from the circumstances of the accounts prepared by your Royal Highness's officers being to be laid before Parliament only today, it will be impossible to proceed immediately to the consideration of his Majesty's Message, and it is therefore proposed to defer the Motion for an Address till tomorrow.[1]   (38178)

1. This is the last of the series of letters on the subject of the Prince's debts. The discussion in Parliament, remarked Wraxall, 'terminated with an expression of general consent amidst testimonies of universal satisfaction. Not an allusion was made either by Rolle or from any other quarter to the lady who formed the object of his attachment. . . . The relief extended to the Prince on the present occasion produced in fact no permanent benefit. H.R.H. resumed indeed for a time his Household and Officers of State, but as no system or principles of economy pervaded his general mode of life, while his embarrassments rapidly accumulated, in the course of a few years the interposition and aid of Parliament became again necessary (notwithstanding the Minister's assurances to the contrary) for his extrication' (v. 24–5).

243 THOMAS COUTTS [1] TO THE PRINCE OF WALES

Strand, 24 May 1787

I hope there is not any impropriety on the present occasion in my once more submitting my case to your Royal Highness's goodness & justice.

As to the *emolument* of being Banker to any appointment, I am perfectly indifferent—but I suffer severely in the point of *honour*, having been for so many years Banker to three Royal generations. To be deprived of such a distinguish'd situation, without a fault being imputed, I think must be consider'd as very hard—and I flatter myself your Royal Highness in your great goodness will at the proper time, & in your own way, remove from me the disgrace that at present so cruelly covers & afflicts me. (41892)

244 RALPH WILLETT [2] TO CAPT. J. W. PAYNE

Merly, 31 May 1787

Dear Payne, I thank you for yr. friendly enquiries abt. my present health. It hath continued to mend ever since I left the cursed town of London; indeed, I was better before I left it, & am surprized the maid should give that acct. of it to you & others that alarmed you. I was particularly better the morning I set out than I had been for some time before, or I should not have come away. But if I am better in my bodily health, my mind is suffering very much. Mrs. Willett hath been very ill ever since our arrival, with a bilious fever; sometimes it is a little better & then returns with violence; & what aggravates my feelings very much, our correspondence with Wimborn is entirely cut off by the smallpox prevailing so much there at this time, so we can get no medical assistance, & I am forced to be physician, apothecary & nurse myself.

I am heartily glad that ye Royal master hath settled his affairs to his satisfaction and with credit; it is the first instance of a Prince of Wales's debts being paid by the publick, & I hope will never occur again. The

1. The founder of the banking house, Coutts & Co. (1735–1822).

2. A wealthy West India proprietor (*d.* 1795) who had purchased a fine Dorset estate in 1751. Farington thus referred to him: 'Willett ... at an early period of his life formed a connexion with a young woman with whom he cohabited many years. On her deathbed she solicited him to marry her, which he did while she was in that situation. After her death he employed the late Mr. Penny to paint a picture representing the ceremony as it took place. He also engaged John Hunter to open her body, had her heart taken out and preserved it in a glass case which stood in his bedroom. Mr. Willett left his great fortune, said to be £10,000 a year, to Mr. Adye [his maternal cousin], who has taken the name of Willett. To Sir Ralph Payne (now Lord Lavington) who was his relation in an equal degree, he left only £1,500, and to the brothers and sisters of Lord Lavington only £1,000 each'.

314

republicans will rejoice, but the sincere friends of the family will be sorry that the necessity ever took place. I look on the expence for furnishing Carlton House with a more favourable eye, & consider it as the permanent residence of the second character in the kingdom & therefore properly a publick expence. I could wish to see £50,000 pr. ann voted for building a palace more suitable to the dignity of a King of England: these are expences that do honor to a country, are permanent & descend to posterity, while the payment of debts incurred by frivolous expences do it no credit. I am only sorry that such an excellent spot of ground as that on which Carlton House stands had not had an entirely new edifice erected on it; the back part next to the gardens will never do it honor.

I am heartily sorry that any new event should lessen the satisfaction we began to feel on the recovery of Lady Payne's health; I hope our next acct. will be more favourable. My own health & the present state of Mrs. Willett's make it impossible to compose my mind sufficiently for writeing to yr. brother Ralph. As soon as I feel myself collected enough to write to him I will inclose the letter to you & desire yr care of it.

I am glad that Short's amour will end so favourably, tho' I rather wonder that a lady who was not to bring a penny of fortune should be so delicate abt. a settlement that might be made in a twelvemonth, more especially as her charmer had been so much overlooked to the age of 27 *at least*.

If William[1] is in town give my love to him & the rest of the family; Mrs. Willett & Mrs. Hopkins desire their complimts.   (38201–2)

245   THE DUKE OF YORK TO THE PRINCE OF WALES

Hanover, 1 June 1787

I cannot let the post set off without sending you a few lines to express to you the joy which I feel at the reconciliation which has taken place between the King and you. Be assured that though, as you have never mentioned this unhappy difference to me, I did not think it right to touch upon it to you, yet that it has made me pass many very unpleasant moments. The attachment which I bear to the King and the real affection which I have for you, with whom I was always brought up, make me rejoice in this happy event more than I can describe. This will be an additional reason for me to rejoice on my at last returning back to my native country when I shall have the pleasure of finding all those who are most dear to me again united together.

1. ? William Payne, who became a Lieutenant in the Navy in October 1795.

I only returned on Tuesday from a small tour which I have made to the Prussian Manoeuvres at Potsdam, Berlin and Magdeburg. I never saw the troops finer or in better order, and certainly there is no reason whatsoever to think that the present King of Prussia will allow the work of that wonderful machine to go down.

I am affraid I shall miss the post if I add more. I shall therefore only assure you how sincerely I long for the beginning of August, when I trust that I shall see you again and shall be able to assure you myself how truly I am [etc.].   (43853-4)

246   RALPH WILLETT TO CAPTAIN J. W. PAYNE

Merley, 8 June 1787

Dear Payne, Some company have broken in upon me so that I have only time to desire yr. care of the inclosed & to supply the rest of the direction. I am not certain if the foreign postage must be paid here; if tis payable here pray take care of that article & I'll reimburse you.

I am heartily glad the Prince is on the recovery. I have almost lost poor Mrs. Willett; for three daies she was in the greatest danger. She is better now, tho' very weak fm. her fever. My own health is very poor, but no matter while hers is improving.

P.S. I have just had a letter fm. Captain William, who sets off, he says, to join Sr. Ralph[1] ye 15th inst. Will this not be the best opportunity of conveying the letter?   (38203)

247   LETTERS FROM PRINCE WILLIAM TO [THE PRINCE OF WALES]

Port Royal, 10 June 1787

Everything is now settled. Schomberg has left the ship; and now for the particulars. Upon my arrival at Jamaica I immediately waited upon Commodore Gardner with Nelson's letters and my narrative. He at once was sensible of my peculiar situation in being the only witness to support the charges. On that account you will observe I never wrote for a court martial, but left it to the Commander-in-Chief to do as he judged best. The Commodore told me it was a matter of too much consequence for him to decide on till the ships should return from sea; that he entirely approved of my conduct. The Europa came in shortly after my arrival, so that the Commodore had two officers of judgment and

1. Sir Ralph Payne.

experience to consult, Captain Brown of the Amphion and Captain Vashon of the Europa. As I have enclosed the letters that passed, and as I really have a great deal to do you will excuse my giving you a long detail. I accepted his apology before Brown and Vashon. He is gone home, & I have by the Commodore's desire appointed one of the Gentlemen to act as Lieutenant. On Monday next I sail for America from hence. I shall write by every opportunity.

As the Rattler sloop of war carries my letters home, I have put under Wallis's care two turtles to send to Carleton House. I hope they will be good. (44786)

Halifax, 4 July 1787
My last from Jamaica was very short owing to that business which I gave a very full account of to the King. . . .

I remained a fortnight at Jamaica, during which time the prickly heat troubled me so much as to prevent my sleeping. This complaint is peculiar to the West Indies, owing its rise entirely to the heat, and is always reckoned wholesome for so long as it remains on the skin it keeps off all fevers. It appears upon the skin as a very small eruption, indeed the smallest to be seen. When I was at Jamaica last war I never had it, and in the Windward Islands it was sometimes to be perceived upon my skin; but during this time I remained at Port Royal it encreased every day and particularly in the head so that I had large blotches almost as big as a shilling instead of being scarce perceptible, attended with such violent heat and itching as to prevent most effectually my sleeping. Upon my going to sea I was in hopes that the virulency of the complaint would go off as I went to the northward, instead of which the prickly heat went off, and a great number of inflamed and large boils came on my head and neck, attended with a smart fever and rheumatic pains and a total loss of sleep and appetite. My surgeon gave me for three days antimonial medicines, but no no purpose. The symptoms increased, all except the fever, which gave way; these boils broke, from whence came away a very great discharge: strong purgatives did a great deal of good and I am now quite recovered.

My reasons for being so minute are for to convince you how much I have suffered and that you should not be alarmed at any idle reports. It is not any fear I have at present, but for my being in the same way when in the autumn I return to Jamaica. The symptoms I have had were so violent that had this complaint attacked me at Fort Royal I do really believe they would have proved fatal. With these sentiments you may easily conceive I do not look forward with any pleasure on my return to the West Indies. However, there are many things to be considered.

Suppose I was to write to go home, there are two very strong objections I have: the one, because I think it to be the duty of every officer to remain abroad so long as his ship is kept on a foreign station: the other, from the uncertainty of the situation I am now in; nothing to depend on but what my father chooses to allow except my half pay, which is a hundred a year: no house to go to, for I cannot at present live with the King. When I was at last at home [*sic*], he told me he had no place to put me in. Was I in your situation to live with you, we both well know how little that would be relished. Another singular circumstance, I never receive an answer or letter from the King. It is now eighteen months since I last saw him. I have had one letter dated the 4th March 1786. I am totally in the dark whether my conduct is approved of or not. Many bills I know are unpayed. How to proceed I do not know. In this situation it would be improper for me to wish to return. I mean to pay the strictest attention to my health next winter in the West Indies. How different the two brothers, Frederick and myself: he is the favourite, and in a situation not to require advice, receives three times a week letters: myself in a professional character, liable to the censure of all the world in a free country like England, and even acknowledged by the King not able to govern myself, never receiving so much as an answer. My unpleasant situation makes me really quite melancholy.

You will receive this letter from Fidge my surgeon, who, poor fellow, is quite wore out in the King's service and has been invalided, and to whom I have given this letter as an introduction to you. Pray be kind to the old man for I really have a sincere regard for him. I have now nothing more to add than that I received a letter from Elphinstone in Scotland who says he is by this time a Benedict. Who would have thought it? Tomorrow we sail for Quebec whenever the wind is fair; from whence I shall write. Adieu. (44789–91)

248 THE PRINCE OF WALES TO THE QUEEN

Kew, 10 July 1787
Nobody ever doubted *your prudence* & I think you have shewed *a prodigious proof* of it in your declining accepting ye cadeau I wish'd to make you. In short, c'est déterminé que vous les aurez ces six petits rats blancs. The moment you left Kew, I took my measures for fear your *excessive prudence* should make you decline giving yourself this innocent & trifling satisfaction. As to ye idea of it not suiting your finances I hope you cd. not for a moment encourage an idea yt. I would suffer such a reason to be even for an instant a bar to any sort of satisfaction or pleasure it was within ye. narrow compass of my poor means to afford

you. I sent to Lord William immediately (who is flatté et charmé au dernier dégré). I repeat, as I knew your *excessive prudence*. In short the ponies are mine, they will be attended by two little boys in your livery; they will stand in my stables, & whenever you chuse to honor ym. by making use of them they will be at your immediate command, & unless you make use of them (they shall be perfectly well fed) they will die of an apoplexy, for good living without exercise you know will not very well do. But to speak seriously, I cannot send them back to Lord William without offending him, & he really is such a pleasant good natured creature yt. I cannot bear to do anything to displease him, & the ponies are so pretty that I think they will suit you excessively well. I am determined that you shall have ym. so there is enough upon this very important subject. Only think what a horrid wicked light I shall appear in in the world in having been able to debauch my own mother & in keeping her a carriage. Vous savez ma façon de plaisanter & j'éspére que vous me le pardonnerez, car vous savez que je ne fais rien au monde sans plaisanter.

I am afraid I must have tired you to death by this long epistle. I will therefore conclude with entreating that whenever you wish to employ anyone upon any business whatever in wh. you wish ym. to exert themselves to ye utmost of their might & main, you will think on such an occasion of Your [etc.].

P.S. I forgot to tell you yt. ye intelligent creatures will be at Kew for you to see on Wednesday. Love to ye girls. (41893–4)

249 LETTERS FROM THE DUKE OF YORK TO THE PRINCE OF WALES

London, 2 Aug. 1787
I have but a moment's time to acquaint you that I am this very instant arrived here and shall set out as soon as possible for Windsor. It is not necessary to express the joy which I feel at being at last returned, and how glad I shall be to see you. (43863)

Stable Yard, 10 Aug. 1787
As I was by no means in a condition yesterday evening to take leave of you I cannot help sending you these few lines to express to you my hopes that I did not say anything in my cups which may have been disagreable to you. I believe nobody ever was more shockingly drunk than I was. I have mentioned to you already the Gentlemen whom I

have appointed to form my Establishment.[1] You will be surprised to see Hotham's name as Treasurer. As you know that he was recommended to me so strongly by certain persons[2] that I could not any ways refuse to nominate him. (43865)

250 PRINCE WILLIAM TO THE PRINCE OF WALES

Pegasus, Off Quebec, 19 Aug. 1787

Since I last wrote, I have again been ill, so ill indeed as to make it requisite for my leaving the Fleet, going to Quebec, and to proceed to Louisburg to recruit my health, where I remained a fortnight, and in which time, being recovered, I sailed to join Commodore Sawyer[3]: my disease was from the same cause as my former one, checked perspiration and the violent and sudden change from excessive heat to damp cold. . . . Since I last wrote, it has been totally out of my power to learn any news, for I have not seen a creature these five weeks except those on board. When I was taken ill, the Commodore was on his passage to Quebec, and for the last ten days before we sailed he would allow no person to go on shore. Early in November I shall sail for Jamaica and mean to call in at Antigua in my way. Captain Osborne[4] being ordered home in the Ariadne, I have taken this opportunity of writing. I arrived on the 14th of August at Quebec and received here a letter from Elphinstone informing me of your wishes concerning my writing to his Majesty for a proper allowance. You may rely on my doing nothing precipitately or with too much heat, and that I have not in the least any idea of resigning; on the contrary, I glory in the service and it ever will be the height of my ambition and always my wish to be employed. I must once more repeat the real happiness I felt at receiving certain accounts of your affairs being settled to your satisfaction. Excuse me if I now conclude, for various engagements call me away. (44795)

1. Comptroller and Master of the Household: Major-General R. Grenville.
   Treasurer and Secretary: Colonel G. Hotham.
   Grooms of the Bedchamber: Lieutenant-Colonel Morshead, H. Bunbury, Captain C. Craufurd.
   Equerries: Captain W. Wynyard, Captain C. Asgill, Captain C. Fitzroy.
   Accountant and Sub-treasurer: Mr. Robinson.
   Surgeon: T. Keate.
   Dentist: Mr. Fowler.
   Comptroller of the Kitchen and Cellars: C. Weltje.
   Secretary for Foreign Affairs: Major-General De Budé.

2. Especially, no doubt, the King.

3. Herbert Sawyer (1731–98). Lieutenant, 1756; Captain, 1758; Rear-Admiral, 1787; Vice-Admiral, 1793; Admiral, 1795.

4. Samuel Osborn. Captain, 1782; Rear-Admiral, 1804; Vice-Admiral, 1808; Admiral, 1814.

Brighton, 2 Sept. 1787

I have just dispatch'd my servant off to acquaint you yt. it will not be in my power to have ye. pleasure of shooting with you tomorrow, but if my dogs & my Jager & gamekeeper, Schwertzel & child can be of any service to you, I beg you will order ym. over from Bagshot to attend you. As for me you may depend upon seeing me at Windsor on Tuesday afternoon at latest. I shall then go to the Course on Wednesday & Thursday mornings & after ye. Race on Thursday again set off for Brighton where I hope our party will hold good, & where you will find everything prepar'd & I hope commodiously for yr. arrival. Pray write to Lothian[1] & remind him of his promise of coming to meet you at my house. If you wish to send any horses of yr. own I will take care & prepare stabling for ym. but in case you shd. not, I wish you wd. order Tinker to bring my little grey horse down from London on Wednesday or Thursday morning. However, I think at all events whether you send any horses or not, you had better send my little horse down. Pray forgive my giving you so much trouble but it proceeds entirely from ye. anxiety I feel yt. you shd. not find ye. want of one single thing whilst you are with me.[2]

1. William John, 5th Marquess of Lothian [S.] (1737–1815). Major-General, 1777; Lieutenant-General, 1782; General, 1796. K.T., 1776; Gold Stick, 1777; Representative Peer [S.], 1778–90. He had voted against the India Bill in December 1783, but he voted against Pitt's Regency Bill in 1788, and for so doing he was deprived of his command of the 1st Life Guards (1789).

2. It is well known that the passion of both of them for horse racing and gambling cost them dearly. 'His Grace of York has not, I believe, lost his Yorkshire estate, but near £40,000' (T. F. Fremantle to W. H. Fremantle, 31 March 1788). 'To the attractions of the other sex he [the Duke of York] was not insensible,' wrote Wraxall, 'but a rage for play absorbed every other passion in his bosom; Charles Fox scarcely exceeded him in his devotion to faro.... The sums reserved from the revenues of the Bishopric of Osnaburg having accumulated to a large amount, were, by his Majesty's direction, applied towards the purchase of Allerton Mauleverer, a valuable landed property situated in the West Riding of Yorkshire, not far from Knaresborough. This fine estate the Duke lost at play within a few weeks after he came into its possession. The same ruinous propensity has accompanied him through life, and has never ceased to exercise a dominion over him' (v. 394–95). Wraxall's version may not be quite accurate. As late as December 1788 the newspapers were informing their readers that Thellusson was offering £105,000, with the furniture and stock, for the Duke's Allerton estate, whilst the Duke's agent was asking about £10,000 more.

The Princess Royal wrote to Prince Augustus on 20 November:
'. . . On the first of October my birthday was kept and Papa gave us a very fine ball which lasted from half past seven till six in the morning all the gentlemen wore the Windsor Uniform and the ladies white gowns with Garter Blue petticoats and belts my brother set out from the Ball for Newmarket and Frederick after spending three or four days three [*sic*] went to his own estate in Yorkshire, Allerton, with which he is very much pleased. This expedition took up about three weeks and I was not a little happy to see him again after this separation.'

Allow me, my dearest Frederick, before I conclude to seize this opportunity of expressing how happy I feel at ye. idea, yt. yt. affection, wh. ever has subsisted between us from ye. earliest period of our lives, still exists in a livelier sense if possible than it ever yet did, & I hope you will not think I am advancing more than what are ye. real sentiments of my heart, when I say yt. it ever shall be ye. study of my life to preserve yt. affection not only in its present state, but in an increasing one to the latest hour of our existance. Adieu my dearest Frederick, I will not tresspass any further upon yr. patience, but will conclude with desiring you to believe me [etc.]. (43867–8)

252 THE DUKE OF YORK TO THE PRINCE OF WALES

London, 15 Sept. 1787

I cannot let Welsher [1] return to Brighthelmston without sending you a few lines by him to return you many thanks for all the kindness and affection which you was so good as to shew towards me during the few days which I passed with you at your own house. Indeed I never passed so pleasant a time in my life. I shall most certainly not fail to be with you according to your kind invitation at latest on Saturday at breakfast. Give my best respects to Mrs. Fitzherbert and tell her that I have just been to look at her house, which is not as yet begun to be altered, but on Monday the workmen mean to begin. I think it will be the prettiest house of its kind that can be seen. [2] Crawford [3] has desired me to present his duty to you, and to beg leave to present his book to you. As I do not suppose that you mean to read it I shall not send it to Brighton, but leave it at Carlton House. Adieu. (43870)

253 LORD RAWDON [4] TO THE PRINCE OF WALES

Newmarket, 7 Oct. [?1787]

Just as I was setting out from London yesterday, Lord Thurlow called & showed to me his Majesty's answer. As Lord Thurlow said that he

1. C. Weltje. *The Times* reported on 7 November 1788 that the Duke had dismissed Weltje from his service as Steward to his Household.

2. Until the house which the Prince took for her in Pall Mall was ready (in 1788), Mrs. Fitzherbert was at Brighton.

3. Sir Charles Gregan-Craufurd (1761–1821). Major-General, 1803; Lieutenant-General, 1810. M.P. for East Retford, 1806–12. G.C.B., 1820. 'A very handsome young man,' said Fanny Burney.

4. Francis Rawdon-Hastings, 1st Marquess of Hastings (1754–1826), one of the Prince's closest friends. Styled Lord Rawdon from 1762 (being the son of John, 1st Earl of Moira [I.]). Major-General, 1793; Lieutenant-General, 1798; General, 1803; A.D.C. to the King,

should immediately write to your Royal Highness, & with your permission wait upon you, I did not think it necessary either to write or to stop my journey.

The Duke of York being here, I conceived it right to mention the result to him. He was much distressed at it, and expressed himself with the most affectionate warmth towards your Royal Highness. Expecting to meet you according to appointment in town on Wednesday, he entreats that you will not make any final arrangements till he shall have conversed with you. The more I consider the business the more I am satisfied that, by the firmness & magnanimity with which your Royal Highness will prosecute your plan, more ultimate advantage will accrue to your Royal Highness than could have flowed from a more gracious determination on the part of the King. (38204–5)

254 PRINCE WILLIAM TO THE PRINCE OF WALES

Quebec, 8 Oct. 1787

Since my arrival at Quebec, my dear brother, I have received from Elphinstone three letters of 2d April, 15th & 29th May, which it is now my intention to answer. Permit me once more to express my satisfaction that all is set right between a certain great personage & yourself, & from what I learnt passed on that occasion to inform you of my ideas concerning my own affairs. Pitt we both are aware is very much averse to increasing the burdens of the nation & there indeed he is right, but his shameful hanging back & wishing to put off your business & then wanting an account of the manner in which the debts were contracted must plainly show his wish to be uncivil. If he is so rude to the Heir Apparent, how much more so will he of course be to me who am only the third son, known to nobody in England & so far removed from the place of action as not to be informed of what is going on till all is over: an additional reason besides: the very particular regard & affection with which you, my dear brother, have ever honoured me, cannot have escaped him unnoticed. I have therefore no reason to expect anything from Pitt but opposition. Another particular friend of ours is Hotham. We both are well acquainted with his Jesuitical temper. He told Elphinstone I was allowed £3800 yearly & he informs me only £3000. Why should not Hotham let me know what is the extent of my income? For your satisfaction I have enclosed a copy of that part of his letter that relates to my finances. He likewise does not choose to make any sort of application

1782–93. Created Baron Rawdon, 1783; succeeded his father as Earl of Moira [I.], 1793. Commander of the Forces in Scotland, 1802–6; Master-General of the Ordnance, 1806–7; Constable of the Tower, 1806–26; Governor-General of Bengal, 1813–22. Marquessate, 1817.

till desired by me. He may, I can assure him, wait long enough till I ever apply to him for a mediation. Hotham in my opinion takes too much on himself. He has no more business to regulate my expences than the Pope at Rome. His duty is to give me the money as it comes due & nothing more shall he do. In short, Pitt & Hotham are both against any increase & we are well aware somebody else is.

My father's conduct towards me is inexplicable. It is near two years since I last saw him & I have on certain points asked his advice, but he never honours me with an answer. I can by no means find out whether my conduct is satisfactory or not. My applying to him though it is your wish, I am afraid will not avail. However, I shall certainly apply when I arrive at Jamaica whether I find a letter from him or not, but as there is every reason for me to suppose he will write his sentiments about Schomberg & at the same time speak also on the rest of my conduct, I could wish to know something about the carte du pays, before I enter on a subject of so much importance for myself. Could I imagine what are his intentions to do with me when I return, then indeed I might adopt some plan: but between ourselves a certain affair is likely to [take] place that will spoil the whole. Those damned women cause me more uneasiness than enough. For fear of the letter being opened I shall not at present say any more, but on another occasion you shall hear the particulars.

I have to request a favour of you, which is to recommend to Lord Carmarthen M.r William Hanbury, the King's Consul at Hamburgh, to be promoted on Matthias's[1] death to be the Minister in that part of Germany. I have given Hanbury a letter of recommendation for that purpose to you. He is a very worthy young man & I can safely recommend him to your notice. The greatest part of this summer I have spent in Canada at Quebec & Montreal & am vastly pleased with the country & inhabitants & particularly with the civilities I received from Lord & Lady Dorchester[2] so much as for me certainly to return to this part of the world next summer if no disturbances arise in Europe. I have now nothing more to add except subscribing myself [etc.].   (44796–7)

1. Emanuel Matthias (d. 1790). Resident at Hamburg, 1772–90; Minister Plenipotentiary to the Circle of Lower Saxony, 1784–90.

2. Sir Guy Carleton, Lord Dorchester (1724–1808). Lieutenant-General, 1777; General, 1793; Lieutenant-Governor of Quebec, 1766–8, and Governor, 1768–78; Commander-in-Chief in North America, 1782–96; Governor-General of Canada, 1786–96. K.B., 1776; peerage, 1786. In 1772 he married Maria (1753–1836), daughter of Thomas, 2nd Earl of Effingham.

Göttingen, 10 Oct. 1787

Dear George, I believe you are a little surprised at the long silence I have kept. Indeed, I have no excuse but my studies in which I am at present very busy, for you know, dear brother, the more I learn now the less hereafter. The bearer of this letter, Brawn[2], will bring you a shade with it which, when you see [*sic*], think there is a being who thinks often of you and those kindnesses you have so often shewed him. The little trinket, dear George, you was so kind as to give me before my departure I always have upon me.

Now since I have once broak this long silence I hope, dear brother, to continue this correspondence with vigour on my part, I promise it. Were you so kind now and then when it suits you to write a line it would give an infinite pleasure to your ever affect. brother. (47826)

256 R. WILLETT TO [CAPTAIN J. W. PAYNE]

Merly, 14 Oct. 1787

Dr. Sir, You have done a handsome thing in the handsomest manner in the choice you have made of young Miller for yr second Lieutenant. As I have vanity enough to think that I have some share in yr appointment of him, accept my thanks for yr. early attention to him. I am in hopes that I shall have yr. thanks likewise when you know him, as I look on him to be not only a gallant young fellow but a sensible & good officer.

If a favourable opportunity offers I wish you to make him known to Admiral Barrington, with whom I am well acquainted, & who may possibly be able to serve him if this bustle should continue long enough. If you find the Admiral at all disposed to be of use to him I will write to him hereafter myself, but if you find him very much engaged, you know me well enough to know that I wish not to be troublesome. A bare mention therefore of young Miller to him is all I desire of you until he is pleased to take further notice of him himself, but so long as he continues in the subaltern state, it will be his desire & my injunction that he remains Lieutenant of the Phoenix while she is commanded by Capt. Payne.

I can't close this letter without thanking you for yr. attention to

1. The King's sixth son (1773–1843), created Duke of Sussex, November 1801. K.G., 1786. In defiance of the Royal Marriage Act of 1772 he secretly married at Rome (4 April 1793) and again, privately, at St. George's, Hanover Square, 5 December 1793, Lady Augusta Murray, second daughter of John, 4th Earl of Dunmore, and had two children by her.
2. Braund in No. 259. A person named Brawn was one of the King's pages until 1804, when he was dismissed.

yrself. You know how deeply I am interested in every step that may promote either yr. reputation or yr. fortune. You have certainly consulted the first by thus stepping forward where yr. inducements to idleness under the wing of yr. Royal master were so strong, & I hope the latter will be benefitted if there should really be a war; it is only fm. that view that I can submit to see my old age harrassed again by the doubtful state of West India possessions.

I had a letter fm. Captain William abt. ten daies ago that makes a favourable mention of Lady Payne & yr bro. Mrs. Willett desires her love to you. (38207)

257   THE PRINCE OF WALES TO SIR JOHN LADE[1]

Windsor Lodge, Sunday Evening, 28 Oct. 1787
The Prince of Wales presents his compliments to Sir John Lade, & understanding from young Mr. Leigh, yt. Sir John had five white or grey ponies yt. he was inclined to dispose of, & yt. twelve guineas a peice was their price, if yt. price is agreable to Sir John, ye Prince will be very glad to take ym. on those terms, & the Prince has therefore order'd a lad over to fetch ye ponies if agreable to Sir John. (41895-6)

258   PRINCE WILLIAM TO THE PRINCE OF WALES

Halifax, 11 Nov. 1787
Since I last wrote from Quebec I have been in various situations which it is now my design to make known to you: on the 10th October we sailed with the fleet from Quebec to Halifax & got out of the river St. Laurence the 16th at night. In the morning of the 17th it blew hard & the Commodore endeavoured to get into anchorage in Chaleur Bay, in doing which he struck the ground. I was not in my ship twice her length from the Leander when she got aground. At first I thought some man was fallen overboard but immediately perceiving my mistake I wore my

1. The son of Sir John Lade, 1st Baronet (*d.* 1759) and of Anna Thrale, Henry Thrale's sister (1759–1838). Thrale seemed to think that Fanny Burney would make Sir John Lade a good wife (Fanny Burney's *Diary*, i. 81 [1876 edn]). What is more certain is that he would have made her a very poor husband. In 1787 he married Letitia Darby (*d.* 1825), an adventuress who had been under the protection of the Duke of York. Before her marriage with Lade she went by the name of Mrs. Smith, and, it was said, she had been the mistress of Rann, the highwayman. Sir John received, jointly with his wife, an annual pension of £300 from the Prince, when Regent (Boswell's *Johnson*, ed. L. F. Powell [1950], iii.477; iv.552). There are portraits of Lady Lade by Reynolds and Stubbs.

ship clear of all danger. The Commodore remained about ten minutes in that situation when he luckily forced the ship off with a press of sail. We then immediately proceeded into Chaleur Bay. The Commodore carried his family round to Quebec & was now returning with them to Halifax. You may therefore easily conceive the terror of these young ladies when the ship made five feet water in an hour. I proposed to the Commodore to give up my cabin to his family, which he did not accept without much persuasion of my side; however, on the 19th he hoisted his broad pendant on board my ship & brought his family with him. My endeavour was to make everything as pleasant & convenient as possible for the ladies. They seemed satisfyed & I am sorry the shortness of the notice would not allow my accommodating them better. The 26th we arrived at Halifax after a remarkable fine passage. I found here a letter from my agents, Messrs. T. & W. Maude, Downing Street, Westminster, with a long state of accounts & desiring the sum of £495 : 11 : 6d to be paid them. You, my dear brother, will know my inability to furnish the money. All my other bills of my tradesmen are likewise unpaid. In short, I am most perfectly at a stand, for even at Quebec I have drawn on Hotham for money before it is due & I can expect nothing of him but his not accepting my draft. Enclosed you will find my agents' account & I must request you will desire Elphinstone to call on my tradesmen & collect their bills in order that I may be aware of my debts. Since I last parted from you till now nothing to my knowledge has been paid. Neild I believe is my principal creditor & the one I would soonest settle with because he is not troublesome for the money. The hatter and perfumer and taylor, as indeed they all are, stand in the same predicament. I am in hourly expectation of a packet before I sail for the West Indies, which is to be next Thursday; by her I hope to have letters that will instruct me how to proceed.

From the convulsed situation of Europe[1] & our naval preparations I have offered my services to his Majesty & Lord Harvey[2] & have taken the liberty of applying for the Foudroyant of 84 guns on two decks. You will I trust believe me when I assure you my ambition is beset on obtaining that fine ship that I may distinguish myself & afterwards merit a flag. Make interest with the King for me to have the Foudroyant. You must do something about this account with my agents; perhaps a certain person will relent & give me more money.   (44800–1)

1. There were troubles both in western and eastern Europe. In the west Prussian troops invaded Holland and ended what amounted almost to civil war between the republican faction and the Orange party by restoring William V, Frederick William II's brother-in-law, as Stadholder. In the east war broke out between Russia and Turkey, in August, and Catherine II was soon supported by the Emperor Joseph II.

2. John Augustus Hervey (1757–96), second but first surviving son of the 4th Earl of Bristol (1730–1803), and styled Lord Hervey. Captain, R.N., 1780. Envoy to Florence, 1787–91.

THE PRINCE OF WALES TO PRINCE AUGUSTUS

Carlton House, 30 Nov. 1787

I assure you that no one could be more happy than I was at receiving (after so long a silence) so kind a letter as you sent me by Braund [*sic*], & I hope now yt. you have once broke thro' the ice you will not think yourself troublesome, when you have nothing better to do, if you will now & then write me a line, as I assure you no one can love you more sincerely than I do, & consequently can wish to hear that you are well & happy. Braund tells me yt. you are very happy & are grown very tall. I confess I shd. be very glad to see you, as you know I always lov'd you very much, & shd. be much delighted to hear the good accounts he brought me confirmed by yr. own lips. I have sent you some little trifling presents by ye. messenger, what I cd. guess wd. be most agreable to you. In short, to acknowledge the truth, I was oblig'd to call in the aid of Braund to know what he thought you wd. like best, & only hope yt. any little trifling things you may want from this part of the world you will write to me & let me be yr. purveyor. I have also taken *the liberty* of sending Ernest & Adolphus[1] some few little things, *if they should be alive*, but as I suppose by their silence they are no longer in this world, I have already bespoke my weepers to be ready to put upon my coat in case such disagreable tidings shd. be confirm'd by yr. next letter. God bless you, my dear Augustus, I hope most sincerely yt. you will long continue to be as happy as I understand you now are, & remain [etc.].   (Add. Georgian 9/41)

THE PRINCE OF WALES TO SIR JOHN LADE[2]

Windsor Castle, Thursday night, twelve o'clock[3] [*Nov. 1787*]

I am just arrived here & hope to have the pleasure of meeting you at Bagshot tomorrow morning to shoot between nine & ten o'clock. Pray excuse my saying no more at present as I am excessively tir'd, except yt. I am, most sincerely yrs.   (41897–8)

1. Adolphus Frederick, Duke of Cambridge (1774–1850), the King's seventh son. Colonel in the Hanoverian Army, 1793; Lieutenant-General, 1798; transferred to the British service, June, 1803; General 1808; Field-Marshal, 1813. Dukedom, November 1801; the King's resident representative, from December 1813, and Viceroy of Hanover, from November 1816 to 1837. In 1818 he married Augusta Wilhelmina Louisa, daughter of Frederick, Landgrave of Hesse-Cassel (1797–1889).

2. Addressed: Taplow, Bucks.

3. Endorsement.

Göttingen, 15 Dec. 1787

Forgive me for not having wrote to you before, but I feared you should find my correspondence tiresome, but for the future I will write very regularly to you, as Augustus told me that in your letter to him you accused me of having forgot you, an ingratitude which I hope you will never think me capable of.

Here do I lead a very happy life, being in company with a number of young noblemen of all countries from the age of 17 to 21. Every week have we public concerts, assemblies and balls where nothing but joy reigns. I must make my letter much shorter as [*sic*] first intended, for the post is ready to go off. Permit me therefore to leave off by returning you a thousand thanks for the very handsome buckles and spurs you was so obliging to send him who remains for ever and ever, your most affectionate and devoted brother.

[*P.S.*] A line from you will be looked on as a great favour.   (46993)

27 Dec. 1787

The day after I received Keith's letter, a messenger brought me my orders to proceed to Plymouth and there refit for foreign service, and likewise a letter from Lord Howe signifying that I was to return abroad and explore our colonies. I have applied to the King through his Lordship for a larger ship, which I sincerely hope to get as the one I now command is really too small for my purpose. In a few days I shall write myself and enter upon my money matters, and shall enforce the business by a strong and real argument, which is, that if my allowance is not more extended it will be utterly impossible for me to return abroad. Had I continued on foreign service I should not have disliked it, but I do not much relish the going out again. However, I am determined never to refuse to serve and therefore was it offered to me to remain at home I would still go abroad. I shall send you a copy of my letter to the King, and shall inform you of every step before I take them. With respect to my asking for leave of absence I shall be guided by what I hear from the King and your determination on the subject. As for myself I shall embrace the earliest opportunity of visiting you, but we both well know that I never yet have been permitted to visit you. There can be no great pleasure in going, with a certainty that my Christmas box or New Year's gift will be a family lecture for immorality, vice, dissipation, and expence, and that I shall meet with the appellation of the prodigal son.

The conduct of late years I have met with from a certain quarter[1] has been so different from what I observe in other families that those tender sensations have been considerably worn out. I never have been able to find out the motives that have actuated him: our two other brothers have been distinguished by very particular marks of favour and I fancy no recapitulation respecting ourselves is necessary.

The few days I have passed in Ireland make me regret my departure. The treatment I have met with has been such as I should be ungrateful to the highest degree were I to forget it. Lords Shannon[2], Tyronne[3], and Grandison[4] were particular in their attention to me. In short, all ranks and sexes were equally desirous of being polite.

I have received a letter from Lord Hood, in which he informs me that Schomberg is with him as his First Lieutenant. I must confess, considering the intimacy that has subsisted between his Lordship and myself, I am not a little hurt at his thus publickly supporting Schomberg. I knew from the beginning of the business that Lord Hood had disapproved of my conduct throughout this unpleasant affair, but I never could have suspected that his Lordship would have so soon and in so publick a manner have marked his disapprobation.

I am this instant arrived, and in the course of very few days either you or Keith shall hear from me. Rest assured I shall consult you before I take any step, and ever believe me [etc.].   (44806-7)

Plymouth, 31 Dec. 1787
Admiral Graves[5] having heard that you mean to pay me a visit, has requested me to signify his wishes and those of my brother officers that you would give him eight and forty hours notice, as it is the wish of us all to give you a dinner on board the Flagship: except on that occasion, no ceremony will be observed. Mackbride[6] and myself will endeavour to do everything to your satisfaction. I have got you a town and country house. (44810)

1. From the King.

2. Richard, 2nd Earl of Shannon (1728-1807), succeeded his father, 1764. Vice-Treasurer of Ireland, 1781-9, being dismissed for his opposition on the Regency question. A Lord of the Treasury [I.], 1793-1804; supported the Union.

3. George, 2nd Earl of Tyrone and (1789) Marquess of Waterford [I.] (1735-1800). Succeeded his father as Earl, 1763; created Baron Tyrone [G.B.], 1786, and Marquess, in the Irish peerage, 1789.

4. George, 2nd Earl Grandison [I.] (1751-1800), succeeded to his mother's Earldom, 1782.

5. Thomas, Lord Graves (1725-1802). Rear-Admiral, 1779; Vice-Admiral, 1787, Admiral, 1794; Commander-in-Chief at Plymouth, 1786-9. Irish peerage, 1794.

6. John Macbride (*d.* 1800). Lieutenant, 1758; Captain, 1765; Rear-Admiral, 1793; Vice-Admiral, 1794; Admiral, 1799; M.P. for Plymouth, 1784-90. He was said to be a member of the 'Armed Neutrality' in 1788, and he voted with the Prince's friends on the Regency question.

VIII   1788 (to October)

The Prince's brothers were his chief correspondents during the first nine months of 1788. William had been recalled to England rather unexpectedly at the end of 1787 because of the threat of war in Europe, but his father had no intention of allowing him to remain indefinitely: he must be kept away from the undesirable influence of Carlton House. He would have liked to go to the Mediterranean, or, better still, remain on the Plymouth station so that he could have frequent opportunities of seing the very charming Sally Winne, with whom he had fallen violently in love. Both requests were refused, and in July, much to his disgust, he was ordered to return to North America. Had he been financially independent he would have abandoned the sea altogether.

Augustus was 'perfectly happy' at Göttingen, enjoying 'very good company of both sexes', but he fell ill in the late summer with a chest complaint, and the King, just before the onset of his own illness, ordered him to winter in the milder climate of Hieres.

Edward, who had chosen to enter the army, was now a Colonel in one of the Hanoverian regiments of foot guards, but, having followed the example of his other brothers in getting into debt whilst at Hanover, he had fallen into disgrace. He admitted that he had been shamefully disobedient, and his father complained of his 'absurd singularities'. About the end of 1787 or the beginning of 1788, having been ordered to leave Hanover, he arrived at Geneva with his military tutor, Colonel

Wangenheim. There he soon fell in love with a Mrs. Rainsford, but she returned to England in June, and Edward was anxious to follow her. 'Never sailor wished more for harbour than I do to see my country again,' he told his eldest brother.

The Duke of York, who had bought Lord Galway's estate at Allerton in Yorkshire just before his return to England, out of the accumulated revenues of his bishopric of Osnaburg, was soon compelled to sell it to pay off gambling debts. His friend Grenville thus referred to him in April 1788: 'That very strong passion for gaming which I always foresaw would be the rock which we should most likely split upon, has broke out with all the violence I apprehended, and the too frequent opportunities which offer for indulging it fill me with the most serious apprehensions.'[1] In the summer the Duke took up residence at Oatlands, near Weybridge.

263 PRINCE AUGUSTUS FREDERICK TO THE PRINCE OF WALES

Göttingen, 2 Jan. 1788

I return you many thanks for your kind letter & present & esteem it a great kindness in you to express a wish to hear of my welfare & the poor news I can write you, hoping at the same time, dear brother, that when time hangs heavy on your hands you would dispell it for a few minutes in writing to me. Permit me, dear George, to send you this shade, which, tho' badly executed, may serve as a remembrance & think always in looking upon it that there is a being who desires your friendship & is then happy. To tell you the truth I am as happy here as anyone can be at a distance from his relations, especially as everyone seems so affectionate & desirous to shew their zeal to us. In short, it is always pleasant to be with young men, with which sort of *merchandize* this town is pretty well stocked, there being near a thousand. (47829)

264 LETTERS FROM PRINCE WILLIAM TO THE PRINCE OF WALES

Plymouth, 19 Jan. 1788

Yesterday I received Keith's letter, and now take up my pen to answer your wishes. I hope everything at the Queen's House has gone on well, but for God's sake prevent my going to London & send Doctor Warren to Plymouth. My situation at home would not be pleasant and you know I have other motives to continue here. My health was never better; but what you conceived to be alarming was nothing more than a cold caught

1. *Cornwallis Correspondence*, i.379.

in consequence of my having been irregular as to the hours of my meals.[1]

Since I saw you last, I have received an extraordinary letter from Lord Howe respecting Lieutenant Vinter[2] of Marines and my gunner, and am to request you will desire an explanation from his Lordship, for which purpose I have enclosed it. You will likewise receive an account of things from my steward. I believe the birthday was spent in a more agreeable way by me than by you two. Give my best compliments to Frederick and tell him I will write shortly. Was I permitted to choose my station it would be that of the Druid, who cruizes from Torbay to the Land's End. However, at all events I am glad to find I am not to return to the West Indies. You will receive my hair in a piece of paper; let it be set in diamonds and send it down immediately. I again repeat, do not desire me to go to town; you are sufficiently acquainted with my motives for not wishing it.

As for news I have none, and am hourly in expectation of receiving something relative to the Pegasus and Andromeda, which you shall immediately be informed of. (44813–4)

Plymouth, 30 Jan. 1788
I have this instant heard a rumour that a squadron of ships is to go to the East Indies. Tomorrow I shall by letter offer my services to Lord Howe. With respect to the size of the ship I do not stand, provided he will send me there: the Crown, Captain Pool[3], say something about; you know the esteem I have for my friend Charles Pool, and it would give me real satisfaction that he should be one of the squadron. Mackbride is going to town, and will attend you at Carleton House about Winne's being made Agent Victualler at Plymouth: but I beg, my dear brother, you will not mention his daughter's name to Mackbride, or should Mackbride enter upon the subject of Sally Winne, wave talking on the business to anybody, but particularly to Mackbride as it is utterly impossible for him to keep a secret: I am as yet totally in the dark whether the Pegasus or Andromeda is to be the ship. Hurry the man with

1. In November 1787 the Prince had received unexpected orders to return home, and he arrived at Cork on 3 December. Soon afterwards, whilst at Plymouth, he fell violently in love with Sally Winne, the daughter of a merchant there. When the King heard about the affair he gave William command of the frigate *Andromeda* and ordered him to return to America. By the summer he was back in Halifax Harbour. He tried hard but without success to secure for Sally Winne's father the office of Agent Victualler at Plymouth. See page 338*n*.

2. George Vintner, 1st Lieutenant of Marines.

3. Sir Charles Morice Pole (1757–1830). Lieutenant, 1777; Captain, 1779; Rear-Admiral, 1795; Vice-Admiral, 1801; Admiral, 1805. G.C.B., 1818.

the hair and send it down as soon as finished. You may easily guess who it is for. I have nothing more to add than that I am [etc.].   (44816)

1 Feb. 1788

I have, dear brother, had a long conversation with Oakes relative to the money business we talked over at Plymouth[1], the result of which is that I upon recollection certainly did authorize him to use my name as I promised him to stand security for a thousand pound. He is ready to bring the man before you and relate the circumstances. He seems sensible of the impropriety of his former conduct and has wished me to apply for his employment, which I have done through the Duke of Cumberland. (44817)

265   THE KING'S MESSAGE TO THE PRINCE OF WALES[2], AND THE REPLY

2 Feb. 1788

His Majesty cannot help expressing his astonishment at the message the Prince of Wales has been so ill advised as to send him, and should have required its being stated on paper, if he was not so thoroughly convinced of the correctness of Lord Southampton, who he is certain would take care to convey it in the least objectionable manner. But as the King wishes that his answer may be clearly understood, he has as nearly as he could put down the Prince of Wales's message in the very words as delivered by Lord Southampton, viz.

'That the Prince of Wales has commanded Lord Southampton to go to Gloucester and Cumberland Houses, that Lord Southampton demurred going to the Dutchesses the King having many years ago forbid him; his Royal Highness hopes his Majesty will not consider his persisting in this command as any mark or want of duty or want of respect to his Majesty.'

The Prince of Wales must recollect the direction the King has uniformly given concerning the Dukes of Gloucester and Cumberland, that if they have Levées, any of his Majesty's servants may appear on those occasions, but are excluded going there at other times. The King is certain the Duke of Gloucester has too thorough an idea of the duty owing from a son to a father, to be desirous of the Prince of Wales's giving any injunction to his servants, which his Majesty could only view as personally disrespectful to him.   (41901)

1. Doubtless to the King's annoyance, the Prince of Wales and his brother the Duke of York went to see William at Plymouth before he returned to the North American station.

2. Sent through Lord Southampton.

335

THE PRINCE OF WALES'S REPLY

7 Feb. 1788

The Prince of Wales has received the King's message communicated to him by Lord Southampton, & must in future consider Lord Southampton as a *privileged person*, & at liberty to act in every *respect for himself*, tho' perfectly contrary to ev'ry principle & ground upon which the Prince of Wales deems it absolutely necessary for him to preserve a proper authority & power over the other individuals that constitute his Family. (41902 and 31901)

266 PRINCE WILLIAM TO THE PRINCE OF WALES

16 Feb. 1788

Sr Hyde Parker being paid off in the Orion will deliver you this letter. At Plymouth I informed you of his character and requested you would shew him politeness and attention. I now therefore take the liberty of putting you in mind of him as he is an excellent officer, a well bred man and a gentleman.

With respect to myself I have heard nothing final except that through your kind offices I am for certain to have the Andromeda. Should my destination be altered, I do not well conceive where they will send me.[1] The Mediterranean is certainly my wish, but we are both sure old square toes will not approve of my going there. My mother has just now wrote me she is persuaded my affairs will be settled. She made use of the most affectionate terms towards your humble servant: indeed at all times her conduct has been most friendly. I was therefore surprized when you told me she had lately altered with respect to yourself. I understand the old boy is exceedingly out of humour and I am in hourly expectation of a thunderstorm from that quarter. Fatherly admonitions at our time of life are very unpleasant and of no use; it is a pity he should expend his breath or his time in such fruitless labour. I wonder which of us two he looks upon with least eyes of affection.

Your time I fancy goes quicker than mine: amusements are very scarce here. Was it not for a certain person I would have gone to Bath, but in my present situation Plymouth I prefer. This matter must be a secret. The hair will I hope be soon finished and sent down. Frederick is in the trade winds from one pleasure to the other. How goes on our young cousin?[2] Is she fond of the Bishop? I suppose she wants holy

1. The ship's doctors (Fidge and Wright) advised against the Prince being again sent to the West Indies (44822). Dr. Fidge's letter to Captain the Hon. George Keith Elphinstone (44818–9) is dated 13 February. A joint report by the two doctors (44823–4) is dated 2 March.

2. The reference, presumably, is to the Duke of Gloucester's only surviving daughter, Sophia Matilda (1773–1844).

water to make her deeds pure. By the by, our left-handed relation, my Lieutenant[1], has drawn for twenty pounds, for which sum I shall be troublesome to you. (44820–1)

2 Mar. [*1788*]
By Captain Pole you will receive this and the enclosed state of my health, adjusted and signed by both Fidge and Wright[2] according to your desire. You will observe in their opinion they think it prejudicial for me to return to the West Indies. The use you will make of this as you judge best. As for news here we have none, therefore do not expect any. I yesterday wrote to Elphinstone to signify that if it was your wish for me to apply to the King for the Mediterranean I shall by all means do so. (44822)

267 LORD SOUTHAMPTON TO A. ROBINSON

8 Mar. 1788
Mr. Robinson knows that there have been several objections made to the form of the warrants. The inclosed[3] will shew more fully where the point rests by the allusion to *noblemen's chaplains*. The Prince of Wales makes an unlimited number of chap[s], as the King does, by warrant, *not* under his *Sign Manual*. If this is not allow'd he can only nominate by Sign Manual as a Peer & gives up all right as Prince of Wales. Look to the King's warrants, get a copy from the Cham'.[s] Office & get Doc[r] Scot. to produce an appointment of the late Prince of Wales. I would attend you to the Faculty Office myself but have been confined by a most obstinate cough attended with fever. (38223)

1. William Hargood was 1st Lieutenant, Stephen George Church 2nd Lieutenant (his commission dated 30 June 1787, and he became a Captain in October 1794); and Jemmett Mainwaring, who was born in Staffordshire, was Acting Lieutenant.

2. Robert Wright. He is described in the muster book as 'Surgeon's Mate' (P.R.O., Adm. 36/10705).

3. '21st Henry 8 Sect. 22.
   Provided always that the said Chaplains so purchasing, taking, receiving and keeping benefices as is aforesaid shall be bound to have and exhibit where need shall be letters under the sign and seal of the King or other their Lord and Master testifying whose Chaplains they be and else not to enjoy such plurality of benefices by being Chaplain anything in this Act notwithstanding.' (38224)

10 Mar. [1788]

I hope Captain Pole delivered into your hands the letter and the enclosed state of my health. Another request I have to make, which is that if you could procure me the channel service from Torbay to the Land's End I should be infinitely obliged to you. I have a particular reason for it. If it is absolutely determined that I must go abroad you will I trust send me down two mourning frocks and three pair of mourning buckles, but this must be kept a profound secret. One of these days you shall, my dearest brother, know my motives; from the friendship and intimacy that subsists between Mr. Winne and myself you will I hope stand his friend concerning the appointment of Agent Victualler at Plymouth.[1]

Tomorrow or next day the Andromeda is to be commissioned. The determination of the business relative to Hargood and Mainwaring you will send me as soon as you can because I must arrange accordingly. Let me recommend in the strongest terms my friend Whitehead for promotion whenever it offers; the things for him are Clerk of the Checque in one of the Yards either at Portsmouth or Plymouth, or Commissioner of the Victualling or Agent Victualler.

I return you my thanks for the furniture and am to request you will send me a dressing box with a set of good razors.

In the course of a few days I shall write again; till then adieu and ever believe me [etc.].   (44825)

7 Apr. [1788]

From the friendship and regard you well know subsists between my friend Winne and myself, you will I hope excuse me that I now trouble you again on the subject of his appointment to get the Agent Victuallership at Plymouth. The time now draws near for a vacancy. The present possessor of that post is exceedingly ill and on his way to Bath, from

1. Though he hardly knew him, the Prince wrote from Plymouth to John Rolle, M.P. for Devonshire, on behalf of his 'worthy friend Winne', on 29 June, and Rolle sent a copy of the letter to Pitt five days later, with a suggestion that the request might properly be complied with. 'Two years since,' wrote William, 'I promised Mr. Winne to use my influence in procuring him the Agent Victuallership at this port. Mr. Tonkin, the present Agent, is at the point of death. It is now therefore time for me to request you will apply to Mr. Pitt and your other ministerial connections for the appointment of Mr. George Winne. . . . His character, I may safely say, will bear the strictest enquiry, and he is a very fit person for the place, being well versed in business and accounts' (P.R.O., Chatham Papers, 173). The salary was £200 a year.

Incidentally, the muster book shows that John Winne joined *Pegasus* as Master's Mate on 4 February 1788. He is described as nineteen years of age, and born at Plymouth (P.R.O., Adm. 36/10705).

whence, like poor Le Fêvre, it is supposed he will never march. Now, my dear brother, exert your interest for the sake of my friend Winne: he is really an honest respectable man and from whom as well as from his family I have received the greatest civility and friendship. At this present moment I am with them in the country at their house and mean to return next Thursday to Plymouth. I must once more repeat do all you can for him. I hope you will succeed in getting me the Channel Station: there is a very good argument in representing the unsettled state of Europe. (44831)

Plymouth, 2 May 1788

I have hitherto delayed writing in hopes of hearing from you in answer to the letter Ingram sent you at my request. I now therefore take up my pen to give you my ideas on the subject of resigning my ship. Everything I have asked has been refused either by Lord Howe or by the King through his Lordship's instigation. And now to enumerate them: the *Melampus I applied for, my First Lieutenant to be made a Captain, the Acting Lieutenant to be confirmed, the Channel Station or the Mediterranean*; all of which have uniformly been refused: *the gunner belonging to my ship, who came out of a third rate, I desired might be appointed to a first rate*: likewise not granted: *Mr. Vinter, the Marine Officer, applied to me to be appointed either Adjutant, Quarter Master or Pay Master*; Lord Howe's answer was, there were more eligible candidates. But to crown all, after my having received my orders and the most positive assurance that I was to return next May, I, out of a sincere wish to serve, offered to go with this fleet for the summer: am informed that after that *I am still to be a twelvemonth abroad*. I must confess this is too much.[1] My only motive for not giving up is the miserable state of dependance I am kept in: where to go if I give up. Your doors I know are always open, but ill blood would arise in a certain quarter which can do you no good. The more I am afraid we have to do with Lord Howe, the worse it will be. Let me request your opinion whether I am to go abroad or give up. I shall be totally guided by you. Write or make Elphinstone answer me immediately.

I have lately received a most impudent letter from Hotham, a copy of

1. Prince William received another communication from Lord Howe on the 20th: 'Having had the honor to submit your Royal Highnesses request to attend the Squadron of Guardships assembled for the purpose of exercising the officers & men, I have received the King's commands for that change to be made in your present destination: his Majesty's further intentions being that your Royal Highness should afterwards remain abroad on the service expressed in your former instructions, for such longer time as the opportunity to extend your local knowledge on the foreign Stations might have been otherwise limited on that account. (44838)

339

which I have enclosed, and in consequence of which I have wrote to
him to pay quarterly my allowance into the Agents' hands. Give to him
when you see him [*sic*]. The only news I have to give is that my
outfit has cost £2000 instead of £400.[1]

Andromeda, 14 June 1788
I have felt very much that you did not write yourself or make Elphinstone answer me. The situation I am at present in I like and is a proper
one for me to gain a perfect knowledge of naval manoeuvres, but the
going abroad if it can be avoided is what I wish. There is no frigate
commissioned to relieve the Lowestoff whose station was off Plymouth.
This is what I should like to have till next summer when the general
relief of guardship is to take place, and I cannot see any reason why you
should not apply or they should refuse you and me. Has not Frederick,
without asking, a regiment of Guards, and so why refuse me so small a
favour as a guardship? If the idea of my wishing to be in London is the
obstacle to my being employed in England I will pledge my honour to
remain with my ship. My principal wish is to keep away from home,
and my time is spent so agreeably at Plymouth that I have nothing to
regret but the not living with you. Let me beseech you, my dear brother,
to try all you can. I have it very much at heart not to go abroad but to
remain in England.

I sailed from Plymouth and joined the Admiral the same day off the
Start, since which time we have had the finest weather possible, con-
stantly manoeuvring between 70 and 40 leagues to the westward of
Scilly where we are to remain till the 24th, when we are to proceed to
Plymouth, so that by the 27 we shall be in to port. Try all you can to get
me the Plymouth station.   (44839)

269 THE QUEEN TO THE PRINCE OF WALES

Kew, 20 June 1788
To give you a proof of my sincerity I think it right to mention that since
our conversation on the King's birthday about the unfortunate Mrs.
Hesse[2] I have lookd & find that the promise was not made to the now

1. The King had recently paid his debts (Colonel Hotham to Prince William, 10 March 1788
[44827]).

2. The daughter of a West India merchant in the City named Gunthorp. She married George
Hesse, a civil servant, in 1780: 'a lady of exquisite beauty, refined manners and liberal
fortune.' During the American War he was Agent to some of the German auxiliaries in the
British forces, and subsequently he had the agencies of several infantry regiments. He shot

living sister of Mrs. Chetwin[1], but to her that is dead. That being the case she can surely not be in the way of anybody, but the King from the beginning of my coming to England having desired me to keep every place in my Family as near to the rank in which I found it, must of course preclude the person in question. I hope my sincerity will meet with your approbation & not be imputed to any dislike of mine towards the unfortunate widow whose distress nobody pities more sincerely than I do.

I hope your return to town on Tuesday was not attended with any bad accident or gre[a]t fatigue: the latter I feared much on account of the violence of the heat. (36372)

270 PRINCE EDWARD TO THE PRINCE OF WALES

Geneva, 21 June 1788

No words can express the joy I feel in being once able to tell you how truly and sincerely I am attached to you. A thousand times have I anxiously wished to write to you, and as often been prevented from doing it by reasons which you will easily guess, as I can tell you. But believe me, my heart has never been in fault, and my only intention in writing now is to obtain what I most anxiously wish to acquire, your friendship and love. Had I written this by any common occasion I might fear you would cast a careless eye upon these lines, and think no more of a brother who, for so many years, you have not heard of: but I know you are a man of too much gallantry to refuse that to the fair hand who will deliver you this letter, which you might perhaps refuse me: at least, were you actuated by those sentiments which I feel for her, I am certain there is no one thing upon the face of the earth which, if Mrs Rainsford deigned to ask of me, that I ever should have the heart to refuse her. You will certainly look upon me as a very old fashioned fellow, and as very ridiculous, for thinking of making my confessions to you; but as you are the only man I can speak to openly you must hear me out with patience when I tell you that amongst the whole number of women whom I ever have seen, though many have fixed my attention

himself at the beginning of June 1788. 'He made last year an acquaintance with the Prince of Wales at Brighthelmstone, was introduced into everything that was fine; this winter played, lost, could not pay, and has killed himself' (Auckland, *Journal and Correspondence*, ii.211). The name reminds one of Captain Hesse, the dashing young cavalry officer and the reputed son of the Duke of York, with whom Princess Charlotte fell in love and acted indiscreetly when she was about sixteen. See *The Letters of George IV*, i.321n.

1. 'Mrs. Chetwyn ... though a nobleman's daughter, is the Queen's laundress.' (Fanny Burney's *Diary*, ii.289)

for a moment, I may with confidence and truth assert it, my heart was still in my possession till I saw her. It is with sorrow and concern that I reflect, when you will receive this letter, how many hundred miles I shall be from her; and you can easily conceive, if, now that I still have the blessing of seeing her, those ideas agitate me, those sentiments that I feel for her are either light or superficial. She promised me to tell you how happy you would make me by writing a few lines *en frère et ami*, and I think if I have such an advocate in my cause, whatever I can say myself will be *de trop*. I am very backward the first time I write to make a request, but if you can, I am vain enough to think you will effect the success of it, and that is to prevail upon the King to recall me to England, for never sailor wished more for harbour than I do for to see my country again. Now I am afraid of trespassing any longer upon your patience, therefore I will here conclude by signing myself from the bottom of my heart your [etc.]. (45760–1)

271 LETTERS FROM THE DUKE OF YORK TO THE PRINCE OF WALES

Oatlands[1], *14 July 1788*
Latimer has just delivered me a message from you which I do not in the least comprehend, as Payne told me that you did not intend to set out for Brighton till Wednesday. Tomorrow I am very particularly engaged, but if you have anything of consequence to say to me pray write it to me. On Wednesday morning very early I shall be in town and if I do not hear from you I shall not fail to call upon you. God bless you. (43891)

Oatlands, 20 July 1788
I am exceedingly sorry it is not in my power to go to Cheltenham[2] this week as I have some very particular business which requires my being in town on Friday next. As, however, I should not chuse to delay my visit there any longer I intend to go there next Monday. I understand from Jack Payne, who was so good as to call upon me the day before yesterday, that you are now quite settled at Brighton. He brought me

1. The Duke, who was negotiating the sale of his Yorkshire estate at Allerton, was on the point of taking up residence at Oatlands, near Weybridge, as his country house. Incidentally, he wrote to the King on the 14th from St. James's (*Later Correspondence of George III*, ed. A. Aspinall, i.381).

2. See No. 274.

back Mr. Pitt's letter.[1] You can well but be of my opinion that it is the strangest epistle you ever read. I mean to write to him today that I am rather astonished that there should now be difficulties when from his last letter I had had every reason to suppose that everything was settled, that I therefore wished Articles might be directly drawn up according to what had been settled between him and me, in the form of a bond, in order not to lose the time which a Patent under the Great Seal would take in making out. God bless you, believe me [etc.].   (43892)

272   PRINCE WILLIAM TO THE PRINCE OF WALES

Edgar, off the Lizard, 20 July 1788

This instant I have received an order to proceed to America without anchoring. The sensations I feel you may more easily guess than Frederick. I all along was afraid of it. Excuse me if I write but a few words, my time being so short. Conway will give you this. Write by the August and September packets to Halifax and after that to Jamaica. Gob bless you and ever believe me [etc.].   (44844)

273   PRINCE AUGUSTUS TO THE PRINCE OF WALES

Göttingen, 21 July 1788

Forgive me my long silence. It has been occasion'd by an illness I have had. I take the liberty of writing to you as you was so kind as to mention to me that our welfare here interested you. I can assure you I am perfectly happy, having here very good company of both sexes. Riding and dancing are at present our principal amusements. About 3 weeks ago we had a Ball in a wood which was very splendid. It consisted of about two hundred persons, almost all in carriages, some few on horseback. We returned all together about 40 carriages. Such a sight you never saw as many of the coachmen were drunk; 2 or three carriages were overturned

1. There is a considerable correspondence in the Chatham Papers in the Public Record Office on this subject of the proposed grant to the Duke of the revenues of the Nova Scotia mines. Pitt's letter to the Duke is dated the 10th: 'Mr Pitt is extremely concerned to be under the necessity of begging permission of his Royal Highness the Duke of York, humbly to acquaint his Royal Highness that it has not yet been in his power to ascertain the necessary particulars respecting the form and terms of the proposed grant of the mines in Nova Scotia. He hopes however in a very short time to be able to give his Royal Highness a more satisfactory account, and he trusts the delay will be attended with the less inconvenience, as he apprehends the season for sailing to North America will last some time longer, and a packet is dispatched to New York once in every fortnight.' (43889)

343

in the ditch that in this country seperates the high road from the fields. Some broke down (we also suffered in this way three times) and some riders were thrown from their horses. It would serve really for a subject for Bunbury[1]. I wish you only for one day here (longer not because I believe you could not *quit old England* for a longer time). You would amuse yourself very well. Blanchard[2] passed through here yesterday with his little mistress for Bru[n]swick where he intends to take a flight in the air. I believe he had better have left her behind as she does not intend to go up with him but will serve rather to make *him uneasy* on his journey.

Dear brother, you would do me a great favour if you would send me by the messenger a ring of your hair and a jockey w[h]ip, the first for your sake, the other because such a thing is not to be got here.   (47839)

274   THE QUEEN TO THE PRINCE OF WALES, AND THE REPLY

Cheltenham[3], *10 Aug. 1788*

To convince you that amongst all the hurry & bustle in which I live at present you are not forgot, I seize this moment to congratulate you upon the return of the 12th as the only way left me to convey unto you my sincerest wishes upon the occasion. That every return of this day may bring with it new prosperity & blessings is not only what I wish, but that you may also enjoy it without interrupted felicity, & tho multitudes will agree in this none can have it more truely at heart than [etc.].

P.S. I hope to see you well on the 19th[4] when we shall rejoice in celebrating your birthday with a Ball as you desired.   (36373)

1. Bunbury was one of the Duke of York's Grooms of the Bedchamber.

2. The celebrated aeronaut (1753–1809). He made his 56th ascent in a balloon in 1804, when four young couples went up with him and danced a quadrille 1,500 feet above ground. Madame Blanchard, 'the intrepid female aeronaut', ascended once too often in 1811, whilst in Rome, and crashed. Horace Walpole wrote, 2 December 1784: 'Lunardi, the Neapolitan Secretary, is said to have bought three or four thousand pounds in the Stocks by exhibiting his person, his balloon, and his dog and cat, at the Pantheon for a shilling each visitor. Blanchard, a Frenchman, is his rival, and I expec that they will soon have an air-fight in the clouds, like a stork and a kite.' Blanchard crossed the Channel from Dover on 7 January 1785.

3. On medical advice the King had gone to Cheltenham on 12 July to drink the waters 'which are particularly good for all bilious complaints.' He was there for about five weeks.

4. The date is wrongly given (29th) in Lady Harcourt's Memoirs (*Harcourt Papers*, iv.8).

344

Brighton, 13 Aug. 1788

The unexpected arrival of one of my servants from London with your delightful & kind letter just before I was sitting down with a large company to dinner, occasion'd me, I assure you, more real heartfelt satisfaction than any other circumstance that cd. possibly have happen'd. I flatter myself I need not say that had those sentiments wh. I have ever not only profess'd for you but felt from the bottom [of my] heart not been such as I have in every instance thro' life testified towards you, I should deem myself perfectly unworthy of those kind sentiments you are so good, my dearest mother, as to profess for me in yr. charming letter, but feeling conscious yt. I ever have to the best of my poor abilities, endeavour'd thro' life to testify to the world & to yourself, what my heart not only delights but glories in, my respectful dutiful & unbounded attachment to you, I think I may rest myself contented in the pleasing thought of not being entirely unworthy of yr. goodness.

I shall not tresspass upon yr. patience long, with a tedious account of how some of my friends were so good as to celebrate the day with me. I gave a large dinner to between thirty & forty persons of fashion, some resident here, others of the neighbourhood & county, among whom were the Duchess of Ancaster[1] & Lady Charlotte[2], Sir Peter Burrell & Lady Willoughby[3], Lord & Lady Clermont, the Duke of Queensberry[4] &c. &c. &c. & many other people besides whose names I fancy, my dear mother, never came to yr. notice; & in the evening the gentle-

1. There were two Duchesses of Ancaster at this time. The 3rd Duke (1714–78) married (1750) as his second wife, Mary, daughter of Thomas Panton. She, the Dowager (*d.* 1793), was Mistress of the Robes to the Queen, 1761–93. The 4th Duke (1756–79) died unmarried. His uncle, the 5th Duke (1729–1809), married (1769) as his second wife, Mary Anne, daughter of Peter Layard (1743–1804). One may assume that the reference is to the Duchess Dowager.

2. Lady Charlotte Bertie (1764–1838), second daughter of the 3rd Duke of Ancaster, married (1791) George James, 4th Earl of Cholmondeley (1749–1827), who, in 1815, was created Marquess of Cholmondeley.

3. Lady Priscilla Barbara Elizabeth Bertie (1761–1828), first daughter of the 3rd Duke of Ancaster, married (1779) Peter Burrell (1754–1820), who was created Baron Gwydir in 1796. A few months later (July 1779) by the death of her brother, the 4th Duke of Ancaster, she became, with her younger sister, his co-heir, and in March 1780 she was declared by patent *suo jure* Baroness Willoughby of Eresby. Burrell, who was knighted in July 1781, was M.P. for Haslemere, 1776–80, and for Boston, 1782–96. In August 1781 he was appointed Deputy Lord Great Chamberlain, that hereditary office having devolved on his wife and her sister as co-heirs of their brother. In April 1787 he succeeded his great-uncle, Sir Merrick Burrell, as 2nd Baronet.

4. William, 4th Duke of Queensberry [S.] (1724–1810), succeeded his cousin in the Dukedom in 1778. He was a Lord of the Bedchamber, 1760–89, and a Representative Scottish Peer, 1761–86, when he was created a Peer of Great Britain as Baron Douglas. 'Old Q.' was a notorious rake. See *Wraxall*, iv.356–8. He ratted on the Regency question and was consequently dismissed.

men of the county, with my old friend Tom Pelham[1] at their head, gave an excessive fine Ball & Supper, where we remain'd till near six this morning, & indeed I must say we spent the evening with as much hilarity & good humour as ever I spent any evening in my life. As to chit chat or news I have none to tell you as this place affords none. I will therefore conclude with desiring you, my dearest mother, to believe yt. no one can love you more sincerely than [etc.].

P.S. May I beg my dutiful respects to the King & my love to my sisters, & particularly, my dear mother, do not forget me to my dearest Augusta. I say nothing to you in this letter of my not having been to pay my respects to you at Cheltenham. I will explain yt. to you when we meet on the 17th. I assure you 'tis not my fault I have not spent some days with you. Once more adieu my dearest mother. (41903-4)

275 LORD RAWDON TO THE PRINCE OF WALES

Shrewsbury, 7 Sept. [*?1788*]

Your Royal Highness's servant overtook me last night, thus far advanced on my way towards Ireland. I have only to regret in my departure from home that it has given him so much additional trouble. I shall not fail to attend your Royal Highness in town at the time fixed, as I hope you considered certain when you expressed the wish to see me. The unwearied kindness with which you have been pleased to honor me would be most undeservedly placed did I not feel the highest gratification in setting aside for your convenience any plan of my own. With the justest sense of your Royal Highness's goodness towards me, & of the kind language you have deigned to use in your letter, I have the honor to remain [etc.]. (38226)

276 LORD RAWDON TO CAPTAIN J. W. PAYNE

London, 12 Sept. [*?1788*]

I have received yours of yesterday. Present my duty to the Prince and entreat that his Royal Highness will regulate his coming to town on

1. Thomas Pelham (1756-1826) succeeded his father as 2nd Earl of Chichester in 1805. M.P. for Sussex, 1780-1801; Surveyor-General of the Ordnance, 1782-3; Chief Secretary to the Lord-Lieutenant of Ireland, 1783-4, and 1795-8. Secretary of State for Ireland, 1796-7. Peerage (during his father's lifetime), as Lord Pelham, June 1801; Commissioner of the India Board of Control, 1801; Home Secretary, 1801-3; Chancellor of the Duchy of Lancaster, 1803-4; Joint Postmaster-General, 1807-23; Postmaster-General, 1823-6. Had the Whigs come in in 1789 Pelham would have gone to Ireland as Chief Secretary.

Saturday, or not, just according to any motives of convenience which may in the interval occur to him. I beg him to consider my time as entirely at his disposal; and hope he will believe I cannot have a higher satisfaction than what I must feel from any proof of his reliance upon my respectful attachment. (38227)

277 LORD RAWDON TO THE PRINCE OF WALES

London, 20 Sept. [*?1788*]

I have this morning been honored by your Royal Highness's letter. My answer to which must begin with very grateful assurances of my sensibility to your invariable kindness. You estimate my trifling services much too generously when you think them fit to be repaid by such expressions of condescending friendship. Once again let me say, Sir, that my time shall be disposed entirely according to your convenience, and that I cannot think of absenting myself at a moment when your Royal Highness may find any satisfaction in employing me. That you may have no difficulty about honoring me with your commands, I will mention that I have this day had a letter from Ireland which removes any positive necessity for my going thither at present. With a lucky foresight, I wrote a letter from Shrewsbury, grounded on the presumption that your Royal Highness might find more reason to detain me than at the moment seemed to occur; and the arrangements which I proposed in it have settled some material business without my presence. I therefore not only await your Royal Highness's orders on Saturday, but any further or eventual plan you may see cause to prescribe. I have dispatched a letter to Lord Thurlow, appointing him, according to your directions, on Saturday.

Allow me now, Sir, to make excuses for an omission in my letter of Tuesday, which fatigue of eyes may extenuate, tho' I was uneasy in the recollection of it. I ought to have apologized to your Royal Highness for the censorious expressions respecting your want of economy which I proposed for your adoption; & for a cursory allusion to the same purpose in my letter. But in truth, Sir, you feel that there has been indiscretion in your expenditure; & it cannot be disguised to the public. It is therefore policy as well as magnanimity to make the confession distinctly, for when you yourself have once condemned the profusion, you have disarmed others of the strongest weapon with which they could have attacked it. (38228–9)

278

25 Sept. [*?1788*]

I write you these few lines by the Queen's desire to beg you will acquaint your gentlemen that there is to be a ball at Windsor on the Princess Royal's birthday[1], or rather on the 1st October, and that their Majesties wish to see them all there. Lord Ailesbury has orders to send invitations to every one of them but as he does not know where each of them are at present the Queen thought it the shortest way to make me beg you to let them know.

Louis has brought me this morning my uniform according to your direction, which I think exceedingly pretty.

Adieu till Saturday when I mean without fail to have the pleasure of being with you according to your kind invitation. My best respects to Mrs. Fitzherbert.   (43898)

279

London, 26 Sept. [*?1788*]

As the delay of a day or two did not signify, I thought it most respectful to solicit the Duke of York's permission to wait upon him at Elden[2]; & for that purpose wrote on Monday, proposing to attend his Royal Highness tomorrow. Lord Thurlow has but just now brought back to me the draft of the letter which I sent to him on Monday. He approves it entirely; and desired me to return his thanks for your Royal Highness's condescension in imparting it to him. For myself it would be fruitless to attempt expressing how much I feel the unremitting goodness with which you treat me; therefore I must confessing myself [*sic*] with professing in ordinary terms the true & respectful attachment with which I have the honor to remain [etc.].   (38230)

280

Brighton, 27 Sept. 1788

I have receiv'd yr. kind letter & shall most certainly obey with the greatest pleasure the Queen's commands. Indeed it was always my intention to have been at Windsor tomorrow evening & I should have been there the beginning of this week owing to the reports concerning

---

1. 29 September. In 1788 the Ball *was* on the 29th, a Monday, so the date suggested may not be correct. The letter is preserved with the 1788 correspondence.

2. In Suffolk, near Thetford.

poor dear Elizabeth wh. have alarmed me very much[1], had I not been prevented by a violent billious attack wh. confin'd me to my bed for eight & forty hours. Thank God I am better now, tho' still very weak & nervous. Eley will be in town by the coach time enough for any orders you may have for him, & now God bless you I really am so weak I can hardly write.   (43899)

281   PRINCE WILLIAM TO THE PRINCE OF WALES

Halifax, 30 Sept. 1788

The whole month of September being elapsed and no packet being yet arrived from England, I think I cannot with any propriety remain here any longer, particularly as I am at present second in command on this station, and as the Commodore has sent me out with the ships under my command. Accordingly, tomorrow at daylight we sail and I trust to be back here again in three weeks time so as to write by a confidential person who leaves this place between the 1st and 5th of November. I was in hopes of having heard from you, but my duty obliges me to sail. My reason for not writing by the last packet was my not having anything to say. I am still in that situation and so must remain till I hear from you. Everything goes on with me as usual. I am still very nervous, and am afraid the West Indies will do me no good. I wish most heartily I was in England. My friend Charles Pole you have seen and I make no doubt you will be civil to him. I am sorry to say my expences have been very great: between four and five hundred pounds. God knows how things go in a certain quarter: very far from right; some day or other I must expect a winding up. I am ashamed of troubling you with this nonsense, but upon my honour I have nothing else to say, so adieu till I write again. God bless you and ever believe me [etc.].   (44849)

1. The Princess Royal wrote to her brother Augustus on the 26th: '. . . Elizabeth has been ill but is recovering and hopes to be well enough to go to the Castle on my birthday where there is to be a great Concert which it is rather unfortunate should be the only amusement that we can have, as I am not more partial to music than when you left us. We were to have had a great entertainment, as Mrs. Siddons was to have read a comedy, but alas she has leave of absence from the Managers and is some hundered miles from London for a month, therefore it would have been quite cruel to have sent for her; *ainsi il faut faire bonne mine a mauvais jeu* and at least try to keep awake during that evening which will indeed be some thing new for me to do at Harmony. I am afraid that you will not have a very great opinion of me from this confession as in general a love of music to distraction runs through our family of which I alone am deprived. Pray my dear Augustus do not love me less for my want of ear and consider that music is almost the only thing that we differ about. In drawing we are both artists and I hope by the next messenger to send you a proof that I have not lost my time since my return from Cheltenham . . .' (Add. MSS., Georgian).

Newmarket, 16 Oct. 1788

I am oblig'd upon many accounts to trouble you with this letter, as I wish to beg of you to undertake two or three commissions for me. Knowing how deep I am upon the Turf & having read of yr. neighbour's Mr. Popham's death, I wish you wd. secure for me the refusal of Erasmus, & indeed ye. refusal of the whole of his stud, but I am very particular about Erasmus as I have a very deep laid scheme about him. I mean to be at Oatlands about or before eleven o clock on Sunday morning, unless you are oblig'd to be in town, & then I will beg of you to send a few lines to Carlton House on Saturday, to know whether or not I am to come to Oatlands, & wh. I shall find on my arrival from Newmarket. There is a horse of mine now at Layton's at Walham Green[1], wh. if you remember I meant to have offer'd to the King as a stallion, thinking that he wd. never stand sound, but now I find he is not only sound but likely to continue so. I therefore beg you will accept of him as I think he will make you a very pretty riding horse. After all this preamble I will tell you yt. the horse is *Soldier*, yt. I gave 450 guineas for at Kelly's sale, & if you like him I shall be excessively happy. I write to Layton by this same post in order to deliver him to any lad you may chuse to send for him. If you go to the Review on Monday, I will also be there as I have had an excessive civil letter from Grenville to acquaint me yt. the Regiment was to be review'd on that day. I will not plague you my dear brother with a longer letter at present but will therefore conclude with entreating you not to forget to write a few lines on Saturday to Carlton House to let me know what I am to do, about Sunday morning. (43901–2)

1. Near Putney.

ix   The Regency, 1788-1789

The King had been ill throughout the summer, and a neglected cold in October threw him into a violent fever, and, for the second time during the reign, upset the balance of his mind. For some days his very life was in danger, and Parliament had to meet without the customary Speech from the Throne. The doctors declared him to be incapable of performing his official duties and that the time of his recovery was extremely uncertain. It therefore fell to Parliament to provide for the government of the country. One the one hand, the Prince's friends maintained that he had an indefeasible right to the Regency during the continuance of his father's incapacity. The Ministers, on the other hand, maintained that it was for Parliament to determine who should be installed as Regent, and on what conditions. Whilst Fox and his friends claimed to be safeguarding the sovereign rights of the Crown in repudiating limitations or restrictions (a seemingly unnatural position for Revolution Whigs to take up), Pitt and his colleagues held that, whilst the Prince should be appointed Regent, he should not be given powers which might be used to embarrass the exercize of the King's authority in the event of his recovery. The proposed restrictions, which were based on the supposition that the King's illness was not likely to be prolonged, and designed to prevent any other set of Ministers from governing the country except under a load of disadvantages, were agreed to by the two Houses of Parliament on 23 January.

1. The Regent should have no power to bestow any peerage except upon his Majesty's issue, having attained the age of 21.

2. He should have no power to grant any office in reversion, or any office or pension, otherwise than during pleasure, except those (such as the Judges') which were required by law to be granted for life or during good behaviour.

3. He should not be empowered to dispose of either the real or the personal property of the King, except so far as related to the renewal of leases.

4. The care of the King's person and of the Household, and the appointment and dismissal of all Household officers, should be reserved to the Queen.[1]

In December 1783 the King had shown in convincing fashion how far from becoming obsolete his right to choose the Ministers then was. In 1789, if the King had not quickly recovered his senses—if, in other words, the Prince had become Regent—Pitt would at once have been dismissed, and the Whigs would have been called upon to form a Government with Portland as First Lord of the Treasury. Whilst the Regency Bill was being discussed in Parliament—and even before it was actually introduced—the Prince and Sheridan, much to the embarrassment and even annoyance of Fox, who did not get back from Italy until 24 November, were busy Cabinet making, and most of the principal and many of the subordinate offices were provisionally apportioned. The Sovereign's right to choose his Ministers was indeed limited in some measure by Parliament's negative voice, but, in the conditions prevailing before the Reform Act of 1832 which swept away nearly all the rotten and nomination boroughs, the Ministers of the Sovereign's own choice could, in practice, gain the support of a majority in the House of Commons by dissolving Parliament when the existing majority was hostile (as the King had done in March 1784 in support of Pitt, and as he was to do again in March 1807 in support of the anti-Catholic Ministry of the Duke of Portland). Always provided that a substantial proportion of the independent Members—those, that is, unconnected with party—supported Ministers, the electoral influence of the Crown, though already diminishing, was still strong enough to secure for Ministers a majority in a new House of Commons. The attitude of the independent country gentlemen, who represented in a substantial measure what public opinion there was in the days of the unreformed House of Commons, was, then, likely to be of great if not decisive importance. Fox and his friends were not so sure of their popularity that they could venture without hesitation to recommend a dissolution when the Prince

1. Another restriction was thought of but abandoned as either impracticable or indefensible —that the Regent should be debarred from dissolving Parliament.

became Regent. Lord Spencer, for one, admitted that they were not particularly strong in the country, and believed that an immediate dissolution might not be practicable. The Duke of Bedford even thought that a new Parliament would be a worse one from their point of view, but Sheridan disagreed with him. Fox was not at all hopeful that a meeting of his own Westminster constituents would have beneficial results, and he decided, reluctantly, to drop the idea. 'I am very much afraid,' he said, 'of the same timid disposition which was the occasion of our doing perhaps right in this instance, causing us much mischief in future'. He added, 'I am very much pleased with what they have done at Warwick, and I cannot help thinking that unless we can get from various places declarations something similar to that contained in their Resolution of thanks, we shall have done little good towards a general election.' He was very uneasy at the prospect of another contested Westminster election which would necessarily follow his acceptance of office.

Pitt on the other hand, was undoubtedly the popular idol. The counties began sending him Addresses thanking him for supporting the rights of Parliament. Sir Gilbert Elliot had to admit that Pitt was 'the only object the nation can perceive, and the only thing they think valuable in the world'; and he went so far as to say, 'I rather think they would be content and pleased to set aside the whole Royal family, with the Crown and both Houses of Parliament, if they could keep him by it.' And the London bankers, appalled at the mere suggestion that Sheridan might be Chancellor of the Exchequer in the Prince's Ministry, were ready to subscribe large sums to give Pitt, if forced out of office, an annuity of £3,000 for life. In striking contrast to his enormous popularity in the country was his weakness in the House of Commons bereft of the King's support. His following of personal friends there was said to number only 52, and, in the event of a general election, it was believed that he would lose all but about twenty if he were no longer Minister. And, with his opponents in power, he would lose the support of 'the party of the Crown' which included all those who habitually voted with 'any Minister not peculiarly unpopular'. Anticipating victory in this bitter struggle, the Prince and his friends made great efforts to strengthen their position even in the existing Parliament, and to counteract the effects of the proposed restrictions, by using the 'reversionary' influence of the Crown. Lord Palmerston was optimistic enough to think that a dissolution would prove unnecessary. 'A Government once established would, I doubt not, have had a very decent majority in this House of Commons.' Members could be seduced by promises—promises of offices, civil, military and ecclesiastical, of pensions, of peerages, of ribbands, and even little acts of attention such as invitations to dine at Carlton House on Saturdays and Sundays: promises to be

354

redeemed when the Regency was established, or as soon as the restrictions which Pitt, in self-defence, was determined to embody in the Regency Bill, expired.[1] It was alleged that these weapons were extensively used to win over Members of both Houses of the Irish Parliament too. Powerful borough proprietors like the Earl of Lonsdale, who nominated eight Members of the House of Commons, were approached, not without success. Nineteen new peerages, it was said, were promised. About thirty Household officials who had seats in either House of Parliament, and who were now, for the most part, the recognized servants of the Crown, could be dismissed and replaced by the Prince's friends, when once the restrictions came to an end. And a few even of the existing placemen, evidently counting either on the King's demise or on the permanence of his affliction, made a fatal miscalculation and went over to the Whigs. When someone remarked that Fox, in raising the question of the Prince's *right* to the Regency, had let the cat out of the bag, Lord Carmarthen wittily commented, 'So much the better— the rats are grown very troublesome.' Thurlow, the Lord Chancellor, gave every indication of a willingness to rat, and his colleagues thought him guilty of the blackest treachery, but he was too clever to commit himself decisively in his intercourse with the Prince and the Opposition, and in the end he drew back in time when he saw that the King was likely to recover.

The situation made the support of the Press a matter of paramount importance to both political parties, and *The Times* declared that 'no money was spared [by the Whigs] to corrupt the Press and purchase its assistance against the King and his friends'.[2]

The belief, then, was that the 'reversionary' interest would be strong enough to counteract the effect of the limitations which the Regency

1. Intimidation as well as cajolery was resorted to. Lord Harcourt wrote (28 December 1788): 'Lord Parker has been sent for and threats thrown out unless his father would vote against the present measures, to which the latter answered he was an independent Peer and as such he should vote' (*Harcourt Papers*, iv.95).

2. See A. Aspinall, *Politics and the Press, c. 1780–1850*, pp.270–4. Sheridan sent paragraphs to the *Morning Herald*, and even the Prince's cook and major domo, Weltje, was alleged to be active in seducing the newspaper proprietors. 'Would it not . . . perfectly become you', *The Times* addressed him (30 January 1789), 'to confine your studies to your stew pans and your influence to your patron's closet? Are you a fit person to influence the Press or to assist its prostitution in favour of a factious party? Have you not within these few days purchased a leading share of a morning print, with the express view of making it subservient to the Prince's friends?' Stung by attacks of this kind, Weltje threatened to bring an action against John Walter, the proprietor, who, undaunted, proceeded to refer to him as 'an itinerant German music-grinder, raised from earning halfpence by the discordance of a street-walking concert, to the regular perquisites of Lord of the Kitchen to a Prince, and naturalised a few years ago in order to give him the benefits of a British subject' (31 January 1789). And, on 4 February: 'An English Prince who shews a predilection for foreigners as

Bill was to embody. 'There seems to be an idea', wrote Fawkener, the Clerk of the Privy Council, 'that the limitations will be carried in the House of Lords but not in the House of Commons, from the many promises made of peerages, &c.' No doubt he was wrong, but, as we have said, Pitt would certainly have been dismissed had the Bill passed (and it would have done but for the King's recovery towards the end of February). Parliament would probably have been dissolved at the end of the Session, and the new one, 'chosen' by the Whig Ministers, might conceivably have amended the Regency Act by repealing the restrictions which, in any case, were to be merely temporary. This was certainly the plan which the Whigs had in mind. This, said Sheridan, was their great secret.

Pitt played for time, and the Opposition played into his hands. They saved him. In claiming the Regency for the Prince as a matter of right, Fox blundered badly, for his tactics produced delays which proved fatal to the Opposition's prospects of office. As Wraxall, one of Pitt's supporters, remarked, 'If, instead of preferring a claim which he had not the means to enforce, Fox had professed the Prince's readiness to accept the Regency on any terms, under any conditions, and with any limitations or restrictions which Parliament might think proper to impose, the Minister would have been disarmed. His only efficient weapon, delay, would have been broken in his hand. The Prince must have been declared Regent before the middle of the approaching month of January.' He added, 'If Fox had displayed at that time as much ability in getting possession of power as Pitt exhibited in keeping possession of it, the latter never could have held out till the King's recovery.'

Ironically enough, the King was far more popular now that he was out of his mind than when he had been in full possession of his senses. As Pitt said, his lamentable situation excited in his subjects something more than the loyalty they had always shown him; it had aroused in their hearts a greater degree of affection, blended with grief and compassion, that partook of veneration and respect. The doctors attending him told Fanny Burney that their own lives would be in danger if he did not recover, so high ran the tide of affection and loyalty.

There was a clause in the Regency Bill which would deprive the Prince of all authority if he married a Catholic. The egregious Mr. Rolle proposed an amendment to extend the deprivation in the event of the Prince's having already married a papist, 'in fact or in law'. But he was

his domestics, cannot be said to love his countrymen. Many a British subject of infinite merit is out of bread at this moment, whilst a great German toad-eater has amassed an enormous fortune in the Prince of Wales's service.' 'The great Weltje has forgot his humility when he used to keep a gingerbread stall in the neighbourhood of Leicester Fields. A little now might be of service to him and bring down that corpulence now puffed up with pride and ignorance.'

unsupported, Members evidently thinking that the Protestant Constitution in Church and State was already adequately safeguarded by the Act of Succession and the Royal Marriage Act of 1772, and that a new Parliament 'chosen' by the Prince's Whig Ministers would not venture to repeal these laws. Towards the end of December Sheridan heard rumours that the Ministers were planning to embarrass the Prince by obliging him to declare that he had not contracted a Catholic marriage. At the beginning of January Mrs. Fitzherbert received a handbill announcing the publication of a pamphlet to prove that the Prince had actually forfeited his right to the succession to the Crown by marrying her. Sheridan succeeded in suppressing it. (Whether this was the pamphlet in which she was said to have had a child by the Prince we have no means of knowing.) Had it come to the point the Prince would doubtless have lied about it, as he had done in 1787 to Fox; nevertheless the mere rumour that Rolle meant to raise the matter in the Commons and Abingdon in the Lords threw the Prince into a panic, and Sheridan said that he had 'the most womanish mind' he had ever known. The newspapers too hinted that things could be done which were forbidden by Act of Parliament, and that with a 'bad' Ministry and a 'bad' Parliament almost anything might be possible. The Act of Succession and the Royal Marriage Act were Statutes which, like any other, could be repealed. Anti-Catholic feeling, in fact, was being stirred up, and the civil war which some people professed to be fearing was in the offing, would have had a religious aspect. 'The Jockey'—the Duke of Norfolk—was alleged to be making great electioneering strides (at Horsham, at Arundel, at Gloucester, at Carlisle and in Cumberland). True, he was a Protestant, but he *had been* a Catholic. 'Remember, once a good Catholic, always one. A turn-coat can have absolution!' declared *The Times*. Sheridan seemed perfectly prepared to face with equanimity the terrifying prospect of civil war, but Grey, for one, told him that they would be on different sides. 'Not for us!' cried Sheridan. 'No!' replied Grey, 'I should be in the Parliamentary Army!'[1]

The Prince of Wales, then, found it expedient to play down his connexion with Mrs. Fitzherbert and to declare that, although, from his amiable character, he retained his friendship for her, she had no influence with him; that he was quite tired of her, that he loved somebody else, and that the public therefore need be in no alarm on her account.

Far more seriously than in 1783 the Royal Family was now a House divided against itself. The Duke of Cumberland, as was to be expected,

1. 'The Chancellor', wrote Carmarthen on 8 December, 'agreed with me in thinking there was no probability of the K.'s recovery, and that for the quiet of the country the melancholy circumstance of his death might not be a very unfortunate event' (*Political Memoranda of Duke of Leeds*, p. 133).

sided with his nephew, though Gloucester rejected Opposition overtures. The Duke of York, the King's favourite son, turned against the
King's Ministers and against his mother, and threw himself without
restraint into the arms of the Prince of Wales. And, had he not been
nearly five thousand miles away, they would have been joined by Prince
William, who would have been decisively alienated by the Government's
proposal to debar the Regent from creating a younger brother a Peer
whilst out of the Kingdom.

Finally, the international repercussions of the crisis deserve a brief
mention. Much more important than the tears shed both by Louis XVI
and Marie Antoinette in the presence of the British Ambassador when
they were told of the dreadful sufferings of his Sovereign, was the consternation of the French Government on hearing that a change of
Ministers in England was apparently the inevitable consequence. They
were seriously apprehensive that the Whigs would try to find a pretext
for going to war with France: Fox, it will be remembered, had recently
opposed the 'Eden' Treaty on the antiquated ground that the two
countries were traditional enemies.

Much anxiety was felt, too, in Berlin, on account of Britain's uncertain
attitude to the crisis that had arisen in eastern and northern Europe
following the outbreak of war between Russia and Turkey, and the
probability of its being dangerously extended by the intervention of the
Emperor Joseph II on the side of Catherine II, and of Prussia on
behalf of the Sultan. The Prince of Wales, indeed, declared that he
meant to pursue his father's system of policy, and his declaration was
passed on to the Prussian Court, but he declined committing himself by
enlarging on that theme. If tears of sorrow were shed at Versailles on
account of George III's illness, tears of happiness were shed in Berlin
(by Count Hertzberg, the Prussian Minister) when he received the joyful intelligence of the King's complete recovery. 'It would be impossible
for me', wrote Joseph Ewart from Berlin, to the Duke of Leeds, the
Foreign Secretary, 'to do justice to the universal joy testified here at this
happy event'.

283 THE DUKE OF YORK TO THE PRINCE OF WALES

Oatlands, 24 Oct. 1788
I am exceedingly happy to have the pleasure of acquainting you that I
saw the King this morning and that I think him getting well very fast.
Dr. Baker [1] has confessed to him that this was no return of the spasms

1. Sir George Baker (1722-1809). Physician to the King and Queen. Knighted, 1776.

which he had in the beginning of the summer, but a rheumatic attack in his stomach owing to his having remained the whole day with his feet wet, and that with a common degree of precaution he will not be liable to it again. As I do not mean to come to town before the middle or end of the next week I shall not, I am affraid, have the pleasure to see you before Augusta's birthday[1]. Pray give my love and respects to Mrs. Fitzherbert, God bless you. (43903)

284 PRINCE WILLIAM TO THE PRINCE OF WALES

26 Oct. [*1788*]

Before I leave this station, my dear brother, I must put you in mind of myself: through Charles Pole I have received your message about returning home next Spring. Much as I wish to see England and more particularly you, my only friend, yet unless ordered I cannot with propriety return. Let them treat me ever so hard, it can be no reason for me to do wrong. Nothing but want of health can possibly bring me home without leave. Permit me to return you my sincere thanks for all your kindness and more particularly for having interested yourself for my good and worthy friend Winne: though unsuccessful, believe me, dear brother, I feel the obligation equally. He does likewise, and wishes me to express his sincere gratitude with his whole family for your kind interference. I want words to express my feelings for your attention to this business: you will I hope be able to do something for my good friend. You well know the regard I have for him and his family and when we next meet we will with your permission talk that matter over. Be civil to Charles Pole. I value him highly and you may safely trust him in all that concerns me. . . .

. . . On the 30th I sail for Jamaica from whence by every opportunity you shall hear. Say everything that is right from me to Frederick, and tell him for want of time I cannot by this occasion write, but will from the West Indies. I am sorry Elphinstone is so ill. On my present allowance it is impossible for me to live. I must inevitably be in debt and God knows who will pay them. The day will come when I am afraid my father will some [*sic*] everything up in a horrid manner. The storm is gathering and must burst over my head. (44850–1)

1. 8 November.

Windsor, 29 Oct. 1788

I think it right to inform you that having called at Kew, and been informed that the King was not well enough to come to town this week for the Levée and Drawing Room, I immediately came here. I found him with respect to his rheumatic complaint certainly better, though still very weak, but it appears now as if everything has thrown itself upon his nerves, which has given him a very violent degree of agitation which nothing but rest and quiet will remove. I cannot help adding that he spoke with tears in his eyes and with the greatest affection concerning you and said how happy you had made him by coming to see him. God bless you, I hope you have had good sport and great success.[1]   (43904)

286 RICHARD BRINSLEY SHERIDAN TO CAPTAIN J. W. PAYNE

Friday, past six [? 31 Oct. or 7 Nov. 1788]

I have the honor of the Prince's letter safely, and have detained the messenger awhile in expectation of having a note from the Chancellor— but there is none yet come and I will not stop the man's return. I beg you will present my duty to his Royal Highness, and as I perfectly comprehend the distinction his Royal Highness has suggested in conversing with the Chancellor, I will be careful to attend to it. I will immediately acquaint his Royal Highness with the result.

The town is full of consternation & strange reports—and these are encreased by the silence of the papers. I have taken measures to have the best information that can be had of the motions of certain persons, and their probable intentions. The Chancellor yesterday after parting with the Duke, wrote immediately to Pitt. I am not sure whether he saw him or not, but messengers were instantly dispatched to the Duke of Richmond, Lord Stafford &c. to bring them to town. I sent an express to you yesterday at Brighton, understanding that you were there[2], to beg you to come to town, as there are some most important considerations which can only be treated of *in conversation*, but which it is of the utmost consequence should be submitted to the Prince's early attention, and I conceived the possessing you with the circumstances would answer every

1. On the face of it, the 31st would be a more probable date for this letter. The Prince of Wales was at Brighton before the 26th; on the 26th he set off for Newmarket, was back at Carlton House on the 28th, and visited the King on the 30th.

2. If Payne was with the Prince, as one would expect him to be, the suggested date 7 November may not be correct, for the Prince was then at Windsor. (See Payne's letter to Loughborough, 7 November.) As the Prince was at Brighton on Friday, 31 October, that may be the correct date.

purpose to the Prince's service, without the indelicacy of solicitating [*sic*] his Royal Highness's direct attention to them, and if now his Royal Highness could spare you for a few hours—I think it would be of *essential advantage* that his Royal Highness should have the means of being so confidentially apprized of certain matters.

We have been anxious also about his Royal Highness's health, as we heard he was blooded & very much indisposed. I will detain the messenger no longer.   (Add. MSS. Georgian, 3, f.3)

287   THE PRINCE OF WALES TO PHILIP GOLDSWORTHY [1]

Carlton House, 6.30 p.m., [*?c. end Oct. or early Nov. 1788*]
I beg you will have the goodness to inform the Queen in private & the first opportunity you can, yt. I obey'd her commands, as expeditiously & I flatter myself as punctually, respecting both Dr. Heberden [2] & Sir George [3] as she cd. possibly wish. Dr. Heberden thinks of being at Windsor about eleven tomorrow. I am afraid the Queen has misunderstood Sir George respecting Mr. Pitt, as her Majesty told me she understood he was not to come to Windsor tomorrow, & Sir George tells me yt. he has carried him the King's express commands to attend H.My. there tomorrow, Sir George having signified to me his wish yt. the King shd. be kept as quiet as possible & consequently yt. he rather wish'd yt. Mr. Pitt's presence might be dispens'd with, notwithstanding his having carried him the King's commands, (& in wh. opinion I believe the Queen will most perfectly agree with both my brother & me) I have desir'd him to mention ye subject thro' you to her Majesty, & therefore hope as soon as you have receiv'd her Majesty's commands on this head, yt. you will write me such a note inclos'd in yr. letter to me, as I may shew Mr. Pitt, or send to Mr. Pitt, yt. will furnish him with some apparent reason for preventing his taking up those moments of the King's time, wh. I sincerely hope his Majesty will devote to rest. With respect to some other business the Queen employ'd me in, I wish you wd. inform her Majesty yt. I have hunted & sent after the principal person everywhere, but have not yet been fortunate enough to be able to meet with ym., & I therefore thought it was better not to name it to the other persons it concern'd till I had seen her Majesty again. I hope,

1. General Grant thus referred to him in April 1788: 'Goldsworthy, who neither spends or loses his money [i.e. by gambling] gets a step as Clerk Marshal and First Equerry, with a house and three hundred a year of additions, by the death of Carpenter' (Ross, *Cornwallis Correspondence*, i.375).

2. William Heberden (1710–1801). Physician.

3. Sir George Baker.

my dear Goldsworthy, you will be able to make out this scrawl, but I really write in an agitation of mind yt. is easier to be conceived than described.   (41938–9)

288   EARL CORNWALLIS TO THE PRINCE OF WALES [duplicate[1]]

Calcutta, 1 Nov. 1788

Your Royal Highness' most kind letter of the 16th of September 1787, which I received in May, gave me on every account the greatest satisfaction.

I felt the most sensible pleasure at being assured not only that I still had a place in your recollection, but that the good disposition which you had always so graciously shewn towards me was not altered. It was likewise a most agreeable circumstance to me to find that I had already anticipated your Royal Highness's wishes, for in the late arrangement of the Residency at Lucknow, I had an opportunity of placing Mr Johnstone in the best and most eligible situation that his rank and standing in the service permitted him to hold.

In July I received your commands of the 12th March in regard to Mr Treves. Col: Lake will have long since informed your Royal Highness that I had contrived that he should not be removed from Benares, which was very agreeable to him; he is I believe convinced of my desire to shew him every kindness in my power, and I can with pleasure say that he now behaves very well, and is attentive to his business, but his income must for a considerable time be very limited, and I suspect that at his first setting out he contracted incumbrances that will be long distressing to him.[2]

The times for making rapid fortunes in India are past, and it will now be only by the industry and œconomy of a course of years that a servant of the Company who conducts himself like a man of honor, will be enabled to return with a competency to his native country.

The command which your Royal Highness has been pleased to lay upon me to write to you, is very flattering, but I fear that I could not make the business of this country interesting, or indeed intelligible to

1. Because of the danger of shipwreck Cornwallis sent both his private letters and official despatches home in duplicate, by different East Indiamen.

2. The Prince's letter of 12 March 1788 to Cornwallis is in *Cornwallis Correspondence*, i.363: 'on a subject I have already mentioned to you. . . . Having understood that the India Directors have sent a species of order to have young Treves removed from his present situation, and feeling myself much interested in this young man's welfare, I cannot help first recalling to your mind that I took the liberty some time ago of recommending him particularly to your protection, and only hope that if his conduct has not been improper in his situation, you would not admit of his being an innocent sufferer. . . .'

you, without entering into so long a detail that the opening of my letters would become an object of real terror.

I will only without going into particulars request of your Royal Highness to be guarded against prejudices, and to believe that notwithstanding all you may have heard about Indian delinquency, there are amongst the Company's servants on the Bengal establishment many men of ability, strict integrity, and truly liberal sentiments. A Government therefore which has the power and inclination to select the best instruments may do a great deal, but it is by an attention to this point alone that the national honor and interest can be promoted.

I should apprehend that many of my best friends and nearest connexions would complain that I have not attended to their recommendations, if I did not feel that the example of your Royal Highness, and the goodness with which you heard and admitted my objections to a proposal which had the powerful support of your good wishes, must defend me from all attacks and silence the most unreasonable complainants.

Our finances, as I believe your Royal Highness knows, are a little deranged here as well as in other places, and the Company's European force is wretched beyond description, but the native troops are very fine, and I can with pleasure bear witness of the good appearance and discipline of the only two of his Majesty's Regiments which I have seen since I have been in India, the 71st and 73d.

Nothing in my opinion will be more likely to insure peace to us in this country than our having a respectable corps of European troops, and I really hope and believe that a few years of peace and tolerable management will restore our possessions in Bengal to their former flourishing condition. (38247–8)

289   THE DUKE OF YORK TO THE PRINCE OF WALES

[*?4 Nov. 1788* [1]]

I only received your kind letter just as we sat down to table and have not been able to get out of the room till this moment. The Queen has

1. The Prince of Wales was at Oatlands on 3 and 4 November, and visited the King at Windsor on the 4th. Dr. Heberden was called in to assist Sir George Baker about that time. According to *The Times*, the King's illness caused the Prince and Mrs. Fitzherbert to leave Brighton at least a fortnight earlier than had been intended, and on Friday the 8th his Household staff were ordered to town in such haste that they were obliged to take their linen wet from the washerwoman.

On the 1st the Duke of Gloucester wrote a brief note to the Prince of Wales: 'The Duke of York seemed to be pleased with the thoughts of your coming tomorrow or next day to him at Oatlands and may be under the present circumstances you may think it more adviseable than going to Mr. Cooke's. I shall certainly stay in town to pass to you anywhere any accounts I

insisted upon my staying here till their Majesties go to bed, so that I shall not be able to be with you till after their supper. I am greatly rejoiced that you are at Oatlands for every reason, and particularly as I have many things of the greatest consequence to the whole family and to us in particular to say to you. Heberden you will have heard is called in. With regard to the King's health I cannot give you any good intelligence. When I see you I will inform you of what the phisitians say. God bless you till we meet.

P.S. The Queen, whom I have informed of your being at Oatlands, thinks that we may very well come over here together tomorrow morning. (43897)

290 RICHARD BRINSLEY SHERIDAN TO THE PRINCE OF WALES

Thursday night [?6 Nov. 1788]
I entreat your Royal Highness to pardon my intruding for a moment on your attention at a time when your Royal Highness's mind must be so wholly engaged in the most distressful & embarrassing occupations, and I trust your Royal Highness will believe that nothing but the sincerest zeal & devotion to your service could have induced me to it. There are circumstances which I will not now presume to detain your Royal Highness's attention by relating, which made me think it an indespensible duty to endeavour at this moment to have that species of communication with the Chancellor which under your Royal Highness's sanction was before proposed, and that I should not answer the service I owe your Royal Highness if I omitted it. Your Royal Highness will perceive by the note I have the honor to enclose that this evening was fix'd for my seeing the C. but that your Royal Highness's command has call'd him to Windsor. Lord Loughborough was equally convinced of the propriety of the measure, & I thought myself bound to venture on it without further instructions from your Royal Highness at present so delicately and affectingly circumstanced, but certain considerations now induce me most humbly to request your Royal Highness would be graciously pleased to think a moment on the subject, for tho' according to my poor judgement, most sincerely directed to your Royal Highness's service, it appears a measure *most conducive* to your Royal Highness's just & worthy objects, yet I dread at such a juncture taking the smallest step that may not meet your Royal Highness's approbation. I trust I need not assure your Royal Highness that whatever commands I am

may receive from Windsor. Sr. George Baker tells me he has send you his account by Lake; indeed I am much better satisfyed than I expected with his account. He says at present there is no danger. I believe Hebberden is to be consulted. He was cupped again this morning; afterwards he went out as usual, riding.' (54412)

honour'd with will be received & executed with the most sacred confidence. Your Royal Highness will perceive that it is probable the C. will send to me immediately on his return, which has compell'd me to this abrupt intrusion. I have taken the liberty to desire Weltje to send this in the most proper manner, and perhaps your Royal Highness will be pleased to return to him whatever commands I am to be guided by.

I shall endeavour peremptorily to enforce your Royal Highness's commands respecting the public papers, or any wish on the subject signified by your Royal Highness.

I have only again to implore your Royal Highness to forgive my trespassing on your patience at such a moment, and to attribute it to the earnest zeal & attachment with which I have the honor [etc.].

(41915–6)

291 THE PRINCE OF WALES TO RICHARD BRINSLEY SHERIDAN

Windsor, 7 Nov. 1788

I have just receiv'd yr. packet & return ye two notes it enclos'd. I think the best way you can act at present is to proceed with the same overtures as if nothing had happen'd, to say yt. I was thoroughly appriz'd yt. it was probable you wd. have an interview with the C[hancellor] & what was most likely to be the subject of conversation, but not take any notice of yr. having sent to me to wish to know in what manner I was desirous you shd. act *at the present moment*. Let me know ye result of yr. meeting, & if you think proper, (wh. in my opinion will be the best & most candid way) acquaint him with yr. intentions of doing so. You may suppose yt. I write in ye utmost hurry, & therefore must conclude with assuring you *of my friendship.*[1] (41905)

1. Thurlow's tortuous politics during the Regency crisis are not unfairly summed up by the Prince's friend Lord Rawdon at the end of February: 'The Chancellor, from detestation of Pitt, and still more from love of office, for a time coquetted with the Prince of Wales, though indeed that expression is not strong enough to mark the apparent decision which he had made of taking part with us; but having taken fright and drawn back a little upon a show of amendment in the King, he received from the Prince and Duke of York (before Fox) so rough a charge of double-dealing that it is now impossible he can close with us. I believe sincerely that he hates Pitt beyond any man in England, and Pitt speaks most contumeliously of him in private, yet you see they draw together admirably, and a joint interest will now, I think, keep them from separating.' (*Cornwallis Correspondence*, i.422). 'The Chancellor highly disapproved of Hastings's impeachment, in which Pitt had concurred. . . . The Slave Regulation Bill, in adopting and forcing which measure through the House of Peers Lord Thurlow considered Pitt as having violated ministerial faith with the mercantile part of the nation, added to the preceding subjects of irritation. Arden's appointment to the office of Master of the Rolls gave him likewise deep offence. In such a frame of mind it was natural for him to consider whether, if the King's recovery appeared hopeless, he might not retain the Great

Saturday, [*?1 or 8 Nov. 1788*]

In obedience to your Royal Highness's wishes I have been with the Chancellor this morning and stay'd with him near two hours. I have taken the liberty of communicating the most material points to Payne as the shorter method of submitting the result to your Royal Highness's consideration. It is with the greatest satisfaction that I have the honor to assure your Royal Highness that the business appears to be precisely in the train your Royal Highness would wish it, and to promise under your Royal Highness's approbation an essential advantage to your Royal Highness's service.

I am to hear again from the Chancellor, and I will immediately transmit to your Royal Highness an accurate account of the result. (38373)

293 WILLIAM PITT'S MEMORANDUM RELATING TO A CONVERSATION WITH THE PRINCE OF WALES, CONCERNING HIS MAJESTY'S HEALTH

[*?c. 8 Nov. 1788*]

Began his conversation by saying that he had sent to me in consequence of the present distressing situation of the King.

The Prince of Wales then communicated a particular account of the progress and circumstances of the King's disorder, and many instances of conversation and conduct which shewed the derangement of his mind. He then sent for Drs Baker, Warren and Reynolds, who stated their opinion of the present situation; which was that his Majesty's understanding is at present so affected, that there does not appear to them

Seal under a Regency' (*Wraxall*, v.197).

Reports were in circulation before the end of November that Thurlow was intending to join Opposition. The *Morning Chronicle*, 3 December, described them as slanderous rumours.

'His situation', wrote Grenville (30 November), 'is a singular one. It is unquestionably true that he has seen *Fox*, and I believe he has also seen Sheridan repeatedly, and certainly the Prince of Wales. And of all these conversations he has never communicated one word to any other member of the Cabinet. Yet I am persuaded that he has as yet made no terms with them, and that whenever they come to that point they will differ. . . . You will be at no loss to guess where the Prince acquires his knowledge of the plans of Regency which are to be proposed, because, even supposing the Chancellor not to have directly betrayed the individual opinions of his colleagues, yet still his conversation upon these points, in all of which he has explicitly agreed with the opinions of Pitt, must lead to the communication of the plans in agitation' (Buckingham, *Courts and Cabinets of George III*, ii.23).

Lord Kenyon, the Lord Chief Justice, wrote in his Diary, 8 December: 'Dined at Lord Chancellor's. He is in very ill humour with Mr. Pitt. I endeavoured to soothe him and stated the impropriety of his thinking of private quarrels in this crisis of public business.' (Kenyon MSS.)

any interval, in which any act that he could do, could properly be considered as done with a consciousness and understanding of what it was about—that the disorder might either be one locally fixed on the brain, or be a translation of a disorder from one part to another, that if it proved to be the latter, there might be a hope of removing it, but there would then be a possibility that it might attack some part where it might be dangerous to life—that if it was the former there was more reason to think the disorder would be permanent, without affecting life; but that it was also possible it might proceed from local causes, which might come to affect the life. That on the whole there was more ground to fear than to hope, and more reason to apprehend durable insanity than death.   (Add. Georgian 2, f.2)

294   LORD LOUGHBOROUGH TO CAPTAIN J. W. PAYNE

Saturday evening [*?8 Nov. 1788*]

I can with truth assure you that my attention has never deviated to any other affair than the subject of our conversation, from the moment I received last Thursday an order to turn my thoughts to it. I should feel an equal pride & happiness if it were in my power to contribute in the smallest degree by any possible exertion of zeal to the ease & tranquillity of H.R.H. in so trying a situation as Providence has prepared for him. I consider that there are but three possible events in immediate expectation—an ambiguous state of the K's disorder, an evidently decided state, or a sudden termination, which can be looked for only in one way, for an entire & speedy recovery seems to be beyond the reach of any reasonable hope.

In the two first cases it is the result of my most deliberate judgment that the administration of the Government is as directly cast upon the Heir Apparent as the right to the Crown is in the last case; all are alike the act of God, & the law of England knows no interval in which there can be an interregnum. But holding as I do the principle of right to be as distinct & plain in the extraordinary, as it unquestionably is in the ordinary case of a demise; it must be allowed that there would be some material difference in effect. No precedent can be found except one little known, & in times where both the frame of the Government & the manners of the age were so little similar to what they now are that it could be of small authority. In a case supposed therefore to be new; men would for a moment be uncertain by what rule they were to be guided; and upon the supposition of an ambiguous state of the disorder, great industry would be used to prolong that state of suspense, every appearance of favorable intervals would be magnified, & the apprehension of a change would be studiously excited to prevent the publick opinion attaching itself to the apparent acting power. To oppose this, great spirit & steadiness would be necessary, but I have no doubt that the only measure would be to assert that authority which no other person had a right to assume, & which with an united Royal Family no opposition would be long able to thwart. Whenever an incident[1] occurs in which a declaration of the K.'s pleasure is necessary, that declaration must be made by the only person who can legally be presumed to be authorized to make it.

The case of an evidently decided disorder is attended with very little embarrassment. There would be no expectation of change to encourage & rear up an opposition to the full acknowledgment of the right to the administration of Government. It would be declared to the nation by Parlt without restriction, for any partition of authority I hold to be totally inconsistent with the frame of our Government, which has provided a sufficient controul in the Parlt, and admits of no intermediate & secondary controuls. I doubt not but some wishes might be entertained for the purposes of private ambition to create Councils, & to devise restrictions; but they would terminate (as they ought) in the confusion of those who had the presumption to propose them.

The third case is not new. There are known forms to be observed which should be carefully inspected & prepared. The most essential is a declaration to be made & entered at the first meeting of Council, the substance of which should be well considered & digested, because it would be taken for an indication of the spirit of the future Government. It should be short, general & at the same time satisfactory to the publick on the great lines of policy.

I have not the least apprehension of any mischief or even inconvenience that can arise to H.R.H. but from his own virtues. It may sound harsh, & you will with some reason impute it to the coldness of age when I say that the dutys of publick life in the highest state of human greatness may often require, not dissimulation (for I hold that unworthy maxim that it is necessary for government to be equally false & foolish) but a certain reserve & guard upon the frankness of that amiable disposition which is the ornament & delight of society.

I should be compleatly the old man [tiresome & impertinent[2]], if I were to permit myself to run on farther; you will excuse & I am sure you will not expose a[ny suggestions of[3]] too forward zeal, from [etc.].
(38237–9)

1. This letter is printed, with trifling differences, in Campbell's *Lives of the Lord Chancellors*, viii.87 (1868 ed.). There 'precedent' is to be found, instead of 'incident'.

2. Not in *Campbell*.

3. Not in *Campbell*.

295 THE PRINCE OF WALES TO THE LORD CHANCELLOR (LORD THURLOW), AND THE REPLY [draft]

8 Nov. 1778 [1788]

After the communication we have already had I wish you to be acquainted with the result of ye interview I had this day with Mr. Pitt. I introduc'd the physicians to him to express their sentiments, wh. they did in nearly ye same language they did to you. I do not proceed further *nor shall I*, without that advice I deem'd it absolutely necessary in ye first instance to consult. I am sorry to acquaint you, yt. H. My. is in infinitely a more dangerous state than he has hitherto been, having no recollection whatever. (38249)

LORD THURLOW'S REPLY

Ormond Street, 9 a.m., 9 Nov. 1788

The Chancellor begs leave to acknowledge the receit of your Royal Highness's letter, and to express the great sense he entertains of the honour conferred upon him. He holds himself in readiness to obey your Royal Highness's commands any moment he receives them.

There now appears some gleam of hope that his Majesty's unhappy disorder points to a crisis, any termination of which his most devoted friends must prefer to the total deprivation of his reason. (38250)

296 RICHARD BRINSLEY SHERIDAN TO CAPTAIN J. W. PAYNE

4.30 p.m., Monday [?3 or 10 Nov. 1788[1]]

I find there is a messenger going directly by return. I have only time to acknowledge the receipt of yours. If the state continues to be such that a *Regency* is to be thought of, the most early as well as the best formed judgements must be obtain'd—for in all the discussions we have had on the subject I perceive new reason to find the prospect full of delicacy and embarrassment. I will prepare a digested statement of the most authoritative opinions that can be collected on this point. (41918)

1. The 10th may be the more likely date, since it was not until the 6th, apparently, that Lord Loughborough's counsel was sought—by Captain Payne, on the Prince's behalf (Campbell, *Lives of the Lord Chancellors*, viii.84 [1868 ed.]). This seems clear from No. 294.

[*?10 Nov. 1788*]

It gives me infinite satisfaction that any expressions of my zeal for the service of the P. & I may truely say of the publick, for they are now the same, can seem to deserve H.R.H. attention, & I can say with perfect truth that I feel an enthusiasm for his glory that would carry me much beyond any motives of personal or what is more honourable of party interest. The latter I wish only in subservience to his advantage & happiness, & the former well understood (as I hope I do) affords me few motives of ambition.

Upon the supposition which your letter makes probable, of a state of disorder continuing for some time without hope of amendment but without the prospect of an immediate release; the principle of the Prince's conduct is perfectly clear. The administration of Government devolves to him of right; he is bound by every duty to assume it without diffidence of his title, & his character would be lessened in the publick estimation were he to accept it on any ground but right or under any sort of compromise. The authority of Parlt as the great Council of the Nation I think requisite to declare not to confer the right, for there is nothing of an elective royalty in the British Constitution.

The mode of proceeding which occurs to my mind would be this. In a very short time, the P. should signify his intention to act by directing a meeting to be called of the Privy Council where he should declare his intention under the circumstances stated to take upon himself the care of the State; the Council, after ascertaining the circumstances by examining the physicians, who should have previous notice to attend, should express their gratitude, duty & assent. He shd immediately direct a Proclamation for the meeting of Parlt as soon as it possibly can have notice. This done, the P. should direct the several Ministers to attend him with the affairs of their offices.

In the execution of this it seems infinitely material that the measure shd originate with the Prince alone & be decided in his own breast. It should not be put in open consultation, tho' it may be fit to communicate it to those who can be trusted a short time before it takes place—perhaps it might be expedient to do some act marking distinctly the assumption of Government, & it most certainly is necessary that his determination to act of himself should appear. By this conduct & by cautiously avoiding to raise strong hope or strong fear, men's minds will be kept in expectation of what may arise out of this reserve, & all will be disposed to mark their observance of his wishes. Were the state of things more decided perhaps I shd think an opposite line of conduct better, but till opinion settles on a new case some caution is necessary.

I write to you immediately on receiving your letter without the least communication with any one, & except one person I am very anxious that our correspondence should be unknown to everyone. (38240-1)

Wednesday morning [?12 Nov. 1788]
H.R.H.'s conduct gains the applause of all men, & even those who secretly wish that he should not fix himself in the hearts of the people, are oblidged to fall in with the general opinion.[1] The longer he remains in a situation which calls forth the exercise of his virtues, the more will his character be known & admired.

Nothing can be more prudent than your idea that there should not appear the least desire to attain that power which the publick anxiety will soon press him to accept, & that it is above all things necessary that before any step is taken, a general conviction of the true state of the case should precede it. S[heridan], whose judgment astonishes me as much as his extraordinary talents, was to write very fully last night, & I can add nothing to it. One observation however I think very material. I have seen a person who I know is very much connected with the Administration, & from his discourse I am sure H.R.H. is very much watched. He even mentioned that he had gone for a few hours to Bagshot in answer to an observation how constant his attendance had been at Windsor. You know very well the sort of Blifils[2] & Joseph Surfaces[3] who go about in praise of the Ministry, & who compose a good part of their corps; the shape their detraction assumes to make itself less odious is by expressing a pious hope of the P's perseverance to suggest & insinuate a doubt of it. Expressions at table I am persuaded are very often collected & sent to some people, & it is indeed extremely necessary for the P. to be very attentive before whom he speaks, for he will find that whoever has the habit of repeating has also the habit of misrepresenting. Reserve is irksome to an open generous temper, but in critical situations it is necessary to assume it. (38232-3)

1. Sir Gilbert Elliot wrote on 26 November: 'The Duke of York has been constantly with him [the Prince of Wales], and they have both conducted themselves in a most exemplary way. They have both, I believe, been indulged with a visit to their respective *Princesses* now and then; the Prince at Bagshot, and the Duke to I don't know where—and no offence in that, I hope' (*Minto*, i.240).

2. Captain Blifil—a character in *Tom Jones*.

3. Joseph Surface was a character in Sheridan's *School for Scandal*—a plausible schemer who 'lays his hand on his heart', with 'tears in his eyes and a flood of fine sentences on his lips, while he smirches his brother's good name and attempts the honour of his neighbour's wife'.

Naples, 12 Nov. 1788

Your Royal Highness will I hope pardon the great liberty I have taken in sending you a case containing a colossal head in marble of an Augustus, of true Grecian sculpture which I discovered in an old tower in this city, and which, in the building thereof, had been made use of as a common stone. When the noble owner of the tower allowed me to have it extracted, I luckily found it infinitely beyond my expectation excellent, and (except a part of the nose, part of one ear and a lock of hair, which had been broken off) in good preservation. I sent it to Rome to have those parts properly restored, and I flatter myself that now your Royal Highness will not think this monument of antiquity unworthy of a place in Carleton House. I will tell your Royal Highness truly what induced me to think of taking so great a liberty. When I was last in England I perceived with pleasure that your Royal Highness had a great love for the Arts and a desire of acquiring a knowledge of them. The only method is to examine with attention such works of art as are avowedly & undoubtedly of the first class and compare them with others that only pretend to be so. I am convinced that when this bust is placed in a good light and at its proper height, and your Royal Highness has been accustom'd to look upon it you will never bear the sight of a bust of indifferent sculpture. His Majesty, who is certainly a great lover of the Arts, and has given them great encouragement, for want of having formed his taste early on works of the first class, has never arrived at being sensible to what is properly call'd the sublime in the Arts.

This favorite subject of mine has I fear already carried me too far. May your R. Highness enjoy health and every happiness and that the Arts in Great Britain may flourish one day under the auspices of your Royal Highness to as great a degree of perfection as they did at Rome in the days of Augustus is the sincere wish of Sir [etc.]. (38251–2)

299 THE PRINCE OF WALES TO THE LORD CHANCELLOR, AND THE REPLY

Windsor Castle, 14 Nov. 1788

Having some business on wh. I wd. wish to consult your Lordship, I must request yr. attendance at my apartments at Windsor Castle at eleven o clock tomorrow morning. (38253)

1. The diplomatist and husband of Nelson's Emma (1730–1803). K.B., 1772. Envoy to Naples and Sicily, 1764–1800.

10.30 p.m., Friday, 14 Nov. [1788]

The Chancellor thinks it his duty to acquaint your your [*sic*] Royal Highness, that he has received the honour of your commands; and that, of course, he will wait upon your Royal Highness at eleven o'clock. (38254)

300   SIR GODFREY WEBSTER [1] TO THE PRINCE OF WALES

Bignor Park, Sunday evening [?16 Nov. 1788—possibly later]

On Wednesday last I ventured to address your Royal Highness & to inclose the hasty sketch of a plan, the attempting the execution of which, might, if it had failed, have involved me alone in considerable hazard; had it succeeded, the benefit might have been considerable to your Royal Highness in the present crisis.

Attachment to your Royal Highness's person & cause, and zeal for the party I have always acted with, & which is honored with your Royal Highness's confidence, alone prompted me to set down those hints, (crudely expressed, from want of time) & made me presume to offer my services.

Possibly what I suggested might have been thought of & attempted again (as in 1783), & probably, what I mentioned—your Royal Highness, & those you condescended to consult, might deem inexpedient in 1788. My zeal may have been indiscreet; it certainly was not insincere. Had not your Royal Highness done me the honor to employ me in May 1787 & at present, & not always without success—I should not have dared to obtrude myself on your notice.

I perfectly well know the very great station your Royal Highness fills. I never for a moment forgot you was born to be the Sovereign of this great Empire. I never infringed in the slighest degree on that deference & respect that was due to your Royal Highness. At the same time, I knew what, in common with every gentleman, was due to myself. Not even to a person of your most exalted rank would I have addressed a letter, I could have conjectured would have experienced such a fate, as not not [*sic*] to receive either an answer from your Royal Highness, or one commissioned by you.

1. Sir Godfrey Webster, 4th Baronet (1719–1800). M.P. for Seaford, 1786–90; for Wareham, 1796–1800. In 1797 he divorced his wife, Elizabeth, who then married her seducer, Lord Holland.

I do most humbly beg your Royal Highness's pardon for venturing to write last Wednesday.

At present I feel both called upon & justified in writing.

I am not conscious of meriting the displeasure of your Royal Highness. I therefore trust I have not incurred it. (38368–9)

301 THOMAS ERSKINE TO CAPTAIN J. W. PAYNE

Serjeants Inn, London, 17 Nov. 1788

I observe by the newspapers that many persons less bound in immediate obligation, & I am certain not before me in good wishes, have from a very proper & commendable respect to his Majesty & the Prince made *personal* enquiries at Windsor. Independently of the duty & regard which in common with others I owe to & have for the King, I feel so very much for the Prince my Master in his present affecting situation, & have besides such a debt of gratitude to his Royal Highness for the many unmerited marks of his regard which you know I have been in the course of receiving, that I should be peculiarly inexcusable if I were wanting in the least mark of form or ceremony, much less of affection which cannot be doubted.

I desire therefore to depend on you as a friend to tell me whether I ought to leave my name at the Prince's apartments at Windsor & also to say to the Prince at a proper season that I have only been withheld thro fear of officiousness from manifesting that solicitude & attachment which I must ever feel for every thing that concerns him. (38255–6)

302 LETTERS FROM RICHARD BRINSLEY SHERIDAN TO CAPTAIN J. W. PAYNE

Bagshot, past 9, Monday night [*?17 Nov. 1788*]

I think the Prince cannot avoid seeing any of the Ministers if they desire it, but I own I think the *safe line* is his Royal Highness having them there in a body, which I suppose will still be his determination. The D. of R[ichmond]'s duplicity is quite diverting. But I think Pitt's pretending to convey to the Prince any idea of what ought or ought not to be done *in Parliament* on the first day's meeting is evidently a snare, and depend on it, some advantage would be taken of any action or any opinion even, which they would draw from the Prince on such subject. We should square our conduct on that day of course to the Prince's wishes—but to do it with effect whether by silence or speaking, the Prince should stand clear of their having the least pretence to insinuate that any interference

374

or wish of his had govern'd our proceedings. Possibly the Prince will think it adviseable to speak a little more plainly to the Chancellor about Pitt, for I think it a thing much to be avoided to give the least ground to old Thurlow to imagine that the Duke of R. or P. can ever practice any successful maneuvres either with the Prince or with us. I say this because he (the C.) threw out to me a suspicion that Pitt & we should come together, which I told him I thought utterly impossible for many reasons—& the principal one the Prince's own feelings—at which he seem'd much satisfied.

I scribble this just as I am going. I will send to Windsor in the morn. with whatever news I hear in town. (41919-20)

Near 6 [18 Nov. 1788]
I was in great hopes to have heard from you before this—there will be a meeting in the morn. before which I wish to be possess'd of his sentiments—every one says Pitt is to make a prancing harangue, but I don't have to beleive it. I have been at home all day, not being well. I have really a very bad pain in my head & have had for some days. I don't know whose sins are visited upon me. Pray let me hear tonight or early in the morn. I write to the Prince, repeating my extreme desire for unconditional acquiescence[1] on Thursday *on our parts*.

Pray look at a letter today in the *M. Chronicle* sign'd *M. B. Amicus*.[2] It is written by Horne Tooke[3]. (41834)

1. In the adjournment of the House on 20 November.

2. Occupying nearly two columns, enlarging on the theme, 'the discussion of a Regency is a mere trick of party'. 'The heir-apparent . . . has no clearer *right* than the writer of this letter, to create a Regency. . . . A Regency in which either the Prince of Wales, the Queen Consort or any of the Royal Family is included, is unauthorized under any circumstances that may happen by the Constitution. . . . The Cabinet Ministers are undoubtedly the representatives of the Crown fully authorized to act for their Royal Master with the concurrence of the two other branches of the Legislature. . . . We have nothing to fear from such a devolution of the royal power under the direction of the best Administration of the present reign, and the most patriotic Parliament. . . . I contend for things remaining exactly as they are for a reasonable time. . . . At no time till the dissolution of Parliament . . . will a Regency be necessary.'

3. John Horne Tooke (1736-1812), the Radical agitator and M.P. for Old Sarum, 1801-2. As a clergyman of the Established Church he was ineligible for re-election, an Act having been passed whilst he was an M.P. (1801) declaring clergymen of the Established Churches (but not Nonconformist ministers) ineligible to sit in the House of Commons.

375

THE EARL OF SANDWICH TO CAPTAIN J. W. PAYNE

Hertford Street, 18 Nov. 1788

I have nothing to say to you worthy your notice except that the messenger that was sent to Mr Fox was detained three days at Dover, & did not leave England till last Saturday se'enight.[1]

If there are any commands for me I trust that you will convey them to me. (38257)

304   LORD RODNEY[2] TO CAPTAIN J. W. PAYNE

Bath, 18 Nov. 1788

You may easily imagine my concern when I tell you that a damn'd fit of the gout in both feet which confines me to my bed prevents my appearing in the House of Lords on Thursday, and as my vote shall ever go as may be most agreable to our Royal friend I have sent for a proxie that I may sign it, and will send it by express to you, that it may be given to Lord Southampton or any other firm friend of H.R.H. Wuther [*sic*] it may be proper to lay my humble duty at his feet, and sollicit his naming to whom my proxie should be given, I know not—but you will act, my dear Jack, in this affair as you may think will be most agreable to your and my royal friend and his dignity. Pray answer my letter that I may know how to act in this urgent affair as may be most agreable to the person I wish most to shew my attatchment & duty. Adieu and be assured that I am with real truth and sincerity [etc.].   (38258–9)

305   THE PRINCE OF WALES TO THE LORD CHANCELLOR, AND THE REPLY

Windsor Castle, 19 Nov. 1788

The day being passed on which I expected to have had the pleasure of hearing from you, I have order'd my private secretary Captain Payne to wait upon your Lordship by way of saving you a journey to Windsor, as I thought you wd. most likely be busy on the eve of the meeting of Parliament. Shd. you have any thing particular to communicate either

1. 8 November. Fox arrived back in London from Italy after a hurried journey, on the 24th.

2. The Admiral (1719–92). Rear-Admiral, 1759; Vice-Admiral, 1763; Admiral, 1778. Created a Baronet, 1764; created Baron Rodney, 1782, following his crushing defeat of the French fleet under De Grasse at the battle 'of the Saints' off the Leeward Islands. He voted against the Regency Bill, being one of the rats, like the Duke of Queensberry and the Duke of St. Albans.

by messenger or otherwise, it will by him be immediately convey'd to me, both with security and dispatch.   (38260)

LORD THURLOW'S REPLY

[?*Wednesday, 19 Nov. 1788*]

The Chancellor is extreamly mortified to find, that your Royal Highness had expected a letter from him at all events on yesterday: because he must have misunderstood your Royal Highness: it was not a thing to forget, at the same time, if any thing had occurred, which he had thought deserving of your Royal Highness's attention, he certainly would have written. The exact shape of tomorrow's business he is not yet acquainted with.[1] But he supposes, that nothing will be proposed on the part of Ministry, but an Adjournment; and that probably for a fortnight, tho' a week has been thought of. But it seems rather more convenient to give the time, which may be requisite to form a more definitive opinion on the subject of their deliberation: and it bears an analogy to the Act for sudden calling together of Parliament, which still requires a fortnight. The C. will inquire of Mr Payne, whether there be anything more particular, on which your Royal Highness requires information.   (38298)

306   THOMAS ERSKINE TO CAPTAIN J. W. PAYNE

Saturday, 22 Nov. 1788

I return you my best thanks for your very kind & friendly letter. I propose to be at Windsor tomorrow morning, having the list of Sheriffs as named by the Council to lay before his Royal Highness, which (if his Royal Highness should be busy or abroad while I am there) I shall take the liberty of leaving with you.

I shall enquire for your apartments when I stop, & shall be very happy to meet with you at home.

The public seem to be deeply impressed with the character of the Prince. His Royal Highness's conduct during the present disastrous

1. Parliament met again, after the recess, on Thursday 20 November, and the Commons agreed to Pitt's proposal that the House should adjourn to Thursday 4 December. 'The friends of the Minister only desired to gain time, in order for ascertaining whether any beneficial change might intermediately take place in the King's complaint; while the principal persons in the Opposition, deprived of their leader by Fox's absence on the Continent, impatiently anticipated his return.' (*Wraxall*, v.193)

conjuncture (whatever issue it may please God to give it) will never be forgotten by the country.[1] (38261)

307 THE EARL OF SANDWICH TO CAPTAIN J. W. PAYNE

Hertford Street, 22 Nov. 1788

I have received your letter & shall depend upon seeing you when next you come to town.

I conclude that it is wished that we should collect as much strength as we can in the House of Commons against the next meeting. I have therefore fixed one doubtfull member, who thinks he can carry another with him. The person I mean is Mr Burton[2], who has authorized me to put his profession of faith down in the following words: 'Mr B. considers himself as unequivocally bound to the Prince of Wales's measures, & has allowed Ld Sandwich in his presence to put this memorandum into writing; & if he thinks proper, to inform his Royal Highness thereof.'[3] (38262)

308 RICHARD BRINSLEY SHERIDAN TO THE PRINCE OF WALES

Sunday evening [?23 Nov. 1788]

Altho' the message I was honor'd with makes it probable that your Royal Highness's commands may give me an early opportunity of personally submitting to your Royal Highness's judgement whatever information or idea I have for your Royal Highness's service, yet I cannot refrain from entreating your Royal Highness to pardon my

1. 'The Prince', wrote Sir Gilbert Elliot (26 November), 'is, I suspect, pretty sick of his long confinement at Windsor, and it is very natural he should be so, for, besides the scene before him, he has been under greater restraint in his behaviour and way of life than he has ever known since he was his own master. His residence, however, at Windsor has been useful in several ways, for, besides placing things under his eye and preventing the attempts at imposition and concealment with respect to the King's situation which would probably have been practised if the courtiers had been left to themselves, it has given a favourable impression of the Prince's attention to his father, and has also prevented him from breaking out into any unseasonable indulgence of his spirits before the public, which might have happened if he had resided in London.' (*Minto*, i.239–40)

2. Sir Robert Burton (1738?–1810). M.P. for Wendover, 1784–90. Knighted, 1800. He owed his seat to Lord Verney, a Rockingham Whig who had brought Burke into Parliament for that borough.

3. Lord Sandwich had had a following of a dozen or fifteen in 1783, but it subsequently melted away: some members were not re-elected in 1784; others went over to Pitt.

378

intruding now for a moment on your Royal Highness's attention, convinced as I am that your Royal Highness's situation is the most arduous, the most delicate & difficult that can be conceived in the history of any country. Your Royal Highness I am confident will not doubt my sincerity and I only hope you will pardon the liberty I take, in saying that your Royal Highness can want no counsel where you have time & opportunity to turn to the suggestions of your own clear understanding. All my apprehension is that the magnitude of many of the objects which must present themselves to your R. Highness's mind, may render it impossible to advert to lesser points, which may appear of slight import, but which in the event may be of the last importance. I probably may be too precipitate in my anxiety, but the rumours of the day urge me with all humility, but with the utmost earnestness, to implore your Royal Highness to suspend giving authority or countenance either to the idea of calling in a *different medical opinion* on his Majesty's case, or to the *removal of his Majesty*, or even to the removal of any *part of the Royal Family* on the ground of amendment being despair'd of, *untill*, by your Royal Highness's command, a meeting of his Majesty's Cabinet Ministers shall have been held at Windsor, and they shall have given, upon deliberate and solemn enquiry, an opinion which may bring responsibility where it ought to rest, and prevent the misconstruction of malice in every possible event.

I have again to entreat your Royal Highness to pardon a caution which may probably be needless, but as it is with the sincerest satisfaction that I hear a universal sentiment of warm & respectful approbation of the whole of your Royal Highness's conduct during this critical & arduous trial prevail thro' all ranks & descriptions of people, I cannot help feeling a proportion'd anxiety that no possible ground should be afforded to any, whose malignity or disappointment might hereafter lead them to misrepresent the best actions.

I will not *now* venture to detain your Royal Highness by stating the particular reasons which have induced me to be so urgent on this head, nor add more than to repeat the duty & attachment with which I have the honor [etc.]. (41921-2)

309 RICHARD BRINSLEY SHERIDAN TO CAPTAIN J. W. PAYNE

7 p.m. [*?23 Nov. 1788*]

I have just got your letter, just as I had finish'd a letter to his R.H. I will not stop to tell you the reasons which have induced me [to] trouble him—but if what I heard today, & it was said on the authority of Warren, that there is any idea of calling in Dr. W[illis] or of the King or Queen moving[1], before there has been a Council at Windsor, for God's sake second my entreaties that it may be suspended, & I am sure my reasons will not be disaproved of when I explain them. The man is to wait for a line from you. I have a good deal to tell you.   (41923)

310   COLONEL WILLIAM FULLARTON[2] TO CAPTAIN J. W. PAYNE

[*24 Nov. 1788*]

I arrived from the north last night & immediately called for you at Carleton House, but finding that there is no probability of your being in town for some days, I must trouble you with this letter to assure you how much I shall be flattered if you suggest to me any means of rendering myself usefull in the present state of things & of proving my sincere zeal & attachment to the cause & interests of his Royal Highness. I need not tell you that I should consider it as the most distinguishing circumstance which could befall me in life if I had the good fortune, by deeds rather than by words, to merit the Prince's approbation. Should you have any hints to give me concerning the grounds I ought to take, in the event of a debate on Thursday s'ennight, you will be so good as to communicate them; and if you can without inconvenience give me half an hour's conversation, let me know & I will wait on you at Windsor. Indeed I should have done so this forenoon had I not been afraid of disturbing you at a time when you must unavoidably be very much engaged.

Fox arrived this morning at six o'clock, in 9 hours [*sic*] from Bologna[3]

1. The King was moved from Windsor to Kew on 29 November.

2. Of Fullarton House, Ayrshire (1754–1808). M.P. for Plympton Erle, 1779–80; for Haddington Burghs, 1787–90; for Horsham, 1793–6; for Ayrshire, 1796–1803. A Foxite Whig, he was soon (1792) to be one of the 'Friends of the People'. He was described in 1788 as 'independent. . . . Made his fortune in India. . . . Connected with the Prince and Opposition' (*Political State of Scotland in 1788*, p. 37) and according to the newspapers he was being considered for the Governorship of Madras—when the Whigs came in.

3. 'Fox arrived yesterday at six in the morning', wrote Sir Gilbert Elliot on the 25th. . . . 'The messenger whom the Duke of Portland sent in quest of him left London on the 6th of this month, but could not cross till the 8th. He came up with Fox at Bologna, 200 miles beyond Turin, in seven days from Calais. Fox had not heard from England since the month of September and had no suspicion of the King's illness. . . . He set off immediately, and the poor messenger, instead of resting at the end of such a journey, rode back again night and day . . . and they reached London together in nine days.' (*Minto*, i.236–7). See also, Buckingham, *Court and Cabinets of George III*, ii.19. And Wraxall wrote: 'His personal appearance in the House of Commons . . . excited a great and general sensation. I never saw Fox, either previously or subsequently, exhibit so broken and shattered an aspect. His body seemed to be emaciated, his countenance sallow and sickly, his eyes swollen, while his stockings hung upon his legs, and he rather dragged himself along than walked up the floor to take his seat' (v.203).

380

—as you, I suppose have heard already. Pray, where are Sir Ralph & Lady Payne?

It is a subject of no less joy than exultation to all your friends that the general applause & admiration which his Royal Highness has excited in the mind of every man by the superior manner of his acting in such trying scenes, is considered by the nation at large as affording the best grounded expectations & prognostications of his future government. (38263–4)

311   RICHARD BRINSLEY SHERIDAN TO THE PRINCE OF WALES

Deepden[1], *12 noon, Monday* [*?24 Nov 1788*]

I think it my duty to inform your Royal Highness, lest your Royal Highness should not be immediately apprized of it from town, that Mr. Fox arrived at seven o clock this morning.[2] His servant is this moment come to me at this place, where I meant to have stay'd the day —but I shall go directly to town and remain in the way to execute any commands from your Royal Highness. I also take this opportunity of submitting to your Royal Highness's perusal a letter I received from Lord Loughborough. I take the liberty of doing this from a persuasion that it was Lord Loughborough's intention that I should do so, and that he thought it of consequence that your Royal Highness should be apprized of what it contains. I confess, however, that I have not myself the slightest apprehension that any of the efforts Lord Loughborough alludes to can have the smallest success. At the same time it is undoubtedly prudent to be provided against all possible machinations, and it is with great pleasure I can venture to assure your Royal Highness, from a direct communication with many neutral & moderate people, and with some who might from connexion be supposed to be adverse, that there would *even at present* be a great deal & decided majority in favour of that plan of settlement which alone would do justice to your Royal Highness's right or suit the principles of the Constitution.[3] (41832–3)

1. Deepdene, near Dorking. The Duke of Norfolk had recently lent the Sheridans his villa there.

2. If, as seems likely, this refers to Fox's return from Italy, the date must be Monday, 24 November 1788.

3. Until Fox's return from Italy the Prince of Wales necessarily had to consult other advisers. Lord North, suffering from cataract, was now virtually blind, and the Prince had quarrelled with Portland, the nominal head of the Coalition in 1783 (see Nos. 215, *n* 3 and 323). The Prince temporarily relied on the advice of Lord Loughborough and Sheridan. 'His [Loughborough's] counsels throughout the whole period of the King's malady, were, if not unconstitutional, at least repugnant to the general sense of Parliament and of the country,

312 THE LORD CHANCELLOR (LORD THURLOW) TO CAPTAIN J. W. PAYNE

Carlton House, Monday [*?24 Nov. 1788*[1]]

Lord Rawdon informs me the Prince is to be in town tomorrow night and is to see the Queen on Wednesday. Perhaps his Royal Highness may wish to [see] the paper I have to communicate before. I shall be ready to attend his Royal Highness tomorrow on his arrival here or at any other time he pleases. (38299)

313 THE PRINCE OF WALES TO THE LORD CHANCELLOR [copy], AND THE REPLY

Windsor Castle, 24 Nov. 1788

Having some particular busines to communicate to you, I must desire yr. attendance at twelve o'clock tomorrow, if yt. hour is convenient to you. (38265)

LORD THURLOW'S REPLY

24 Nov. 1788

The Chancellor will obey your Royal Highness's commands, and attend at your Royal Highness's apartments in the Castle of Windsor at twelve o'clock tomorrow. (38266)

violent, imprudent and injurious to the cause that he espoused.' Sheridan's 'trancendent powers . . . combining with the conviviality of his disposition, and partiality to the pleasures of the table, were well calculated to establish him in H.R.H.'s favour.' (*Wraxall*, v.194–95).

'The jealousy with respect to Sheridan', wrote John Moore, the Archbishop of Canterbury (16 January 1789), 'is not lessened by his being actually an inmate at Mrs. Fitzherbert's now, with his wife. They took refuge there on being driven out of their own house by the bailiffs who are now in it. He is on all hands understood to be the prime favourite, and to be so sensible of it as modestly to pretend to a Cabinet place, which is hitherto firmly resisted by the Duke of Portland, who says they cannot both be in the same Cabinet. Sheridan would willingly submit to be Chancellor of the Exchequer, but it is thought things are not yet ripe enough for the manager of Drury Lane to be manager of the House of Commons' (Auckland, *Journal and Correspondence*, ii.267).

> 'Poor Fox from Bologna was sent for in haste,
> And forc'd to forsake Betty Armstead the chaste;
> But when he arriv'd 'twas already too late,
> For *Dick* had usurp'd the first place in the State.

> 'Our Prince, with a view to improve this dull age,
> Has sought o'er all England for Counsellors sage,
> And hopes by his choice to distinguish his reign,
> Having chosen—the Manager of Drury Lane.'

1. Not, evidently, before the 23rd.

314 THE PRINCE OF WALES TO MRS. TUNSTALL [1]

Windsor Castle, 24 Nov. 1788

Tunstall, his Majesty's physicians having judged it necessary to remove him to Kew for the benefit of air & exercise, you will take such measures after consulting Mr. Dundas [2] as will be expedient for the accomodation of the King & such attendants as will accompany him. (38267)

315 CHARLES JAMES FOX TO THE PRINCE OF WALES

St James's Street, 2 p.m., [c.25–26 Nov. 1788]

I am just returned from Lord Thurlow with whom I have had a long but a general & loose conversation. [3] The result of what passed is that, while he is in the habit of consulting with the present Ministers as he is now obliged to do, he does not think it fit for him to enter into anything like negotiation with any other persons. However, he is very open in declaring that he has no further connection with them than that which arises from the accident of the moment, and upon the whole it is my opinion that it is his present intention to treat with us as soon as that connection is dissolved. Upon the subject of the Regency I should rather gather from his conversation that he will be right; but this is all conjecture on my part, and I have often known him so governed by humour that perhaps even if we were to know for certain his present thoughts, we might still be mistaken as to his future actions. What I am quite clear of is that it is now best to let the matter rest where it is and when your Royal Highness has the power, to make such offers as may be thought adviseable.

From all I have heard as well as from [the] Lord Chancellor as others I am convinced there will be no attempt at another adjournment [4] and

1. The Housekeeper at Kew, appointed in 1786. 'She seems a good sort of woman', remarked Fanny Burney. She 'had one daughter spared to her out of sixteen, her only son also having died in infancy' (Mrs. Papendiek, *Court and Private Life in the time of Queen Charlotte*, i.48).

2. David Dundas, surgeon.

3. On the 30th Grenville said that Fox had seen Thurlow (Buckingham, *Court and Cabinets of George III*, ii. 23). On the 26th Sir Gilbert Elliot said that 'Fox is certainly better company than the Chancellor, who has lately had frequent access to him, and is indeed in favour with him' (*Minto*, i.239).

4. 'We are still under some uncertainty whether or not to propose a further adjournment', wrote Grenville on the 29th. 'In the meanwhile we have thought it absolutely necessary to summon all our friends, as without their attendance we should not even have the decision of that question in our own hands.' (Buckingham, *Court and Cabinets of George III*, ii.22) The following is a copy of the earlier 'Treasury note' which was circularized:

'Sir, From the unhappy continuance of the King's illness, it is doubtfu]whether there

that the only possible alternative besides the right measure is a temporary Regency limited in powers but not by Counsellors. Whether your Royal Highness would accept of such an offer is a mere question of dignity because either by accepting or rejecting it your Royal Highness would be equally sure of enjoying the situation that belongs to you in a few weeks. In short, Sir, everything appears to me as favourable as possible unless any physicians can be found to falsify in the grossest manner the state of his Majesty's health, and even in that case the delusion must be very short and the measures to be taken by Ministers very embarassing indeed.

I believe I need not mention that what passed between Lord Chancellor & me is in confidence, and that I said I should mention it to your Royal Highness only.   (38235–6)

316   THE DUKE OF YORK TO THE LORD CHANCELLOR [copy], AND THE REPLY

Windsor, 26 Nov. 1788
My brother being very particularly engaged[1], has desired me to request your Lordship's presence at his apartments at Windsor tomorrow at one o'clock, as her Majesty means, if it is in her power, to see you. (38268)

LORD THURLOW'S REPLY
4.20 p.m., Wednesday, 26 Nov. 1788
I am this moment honoured with your Royal Highness's commands and I will not fail to attend the Prince tomorrow at one o'clock at his Royal Highness's apartments at the Castle.   (38270)

will be a possibility of receiving his Majesty's commands for the further prorogation of Parliament; and if there should not, the two Houses must of necessity assemble on Thursday, the 20th instant. I think it my duty to apprize you of these circumstances, and earnestly request your attendance on that day.

I have the honour to be [etc.].
14 Nov. 1788'

1. 'Charles Fox went today to meet the Prince,' wrote Sir Gilbert Elliot on the 26th. 'What has passed, or what the consequence of their interview may be, I do not yet know, but as everything depends so entirely on the Prince's steadiness, Fox is certainly better company than the Chancellor' (*Minto*, i.239).

317 THE PRINCE OF WALES TO THE LORD CHANCELLOR,
AND THE REPLY

Windsor Castle, 26 Nov. 1788
Since I had ye pleasure of seeing yr. Lordship yesterday and the
physicians communicated to you their opinion respecting his Majesty's
removal, doubts have arisen in my mind of the propriety of immediately
adopting their sentiments and acting *on my own authority* without a
previous communication with all his Majesty's confidential servants. I
therefore have to desire your Lordship both from myself and on the
part of the family to fix a meeting of his Majesty's Cabinet Ministers at
Windsor tomorrow at two o'clock, in order that his Majesty's situation
may be fully & formally examined into by them previous to any new
arrangement whatever being adopted. I shall direct the physicians and
all other persons who have been in attendance on his Majesty to be in
readiness to give every information possible to the Council.¹ (38271)

LORD THURLOW'S REPLY

10 p.m., Wednesday, 26 Nov. 1788
As your Royal Highness's commands leave no room for hesitation, the
Chancellor will communicate them instantly to his Majesty's confidential
servants, and has no doubt but they will be obeyed.² (38272)

318 RICHARD BRINSLEY SHERIDAN TO [?] LORD THURLOW

[*?27 Nov. 1788*³]
The Prince wishes your Lordship to inform his Majesty's confidential
servants that it is with the deepest concern & regret that the family have
received communications from the physicians attending on his Majesty
upon which the Prince must decline giving any opinion untill the whole
of his Majesty's situation has been fully examined into by his Majesty['s]

1. 'The Prince of Wales', wrote Grenville on the 27th, 'has sent a letter to the Chancellor
desiring that all the members of the Cabinet may attend at Windsor today—but this, I
imagine (and, indeed, his letter conveys it) has no relation to any other subject, but to an
idea of moving the King to Kew, where he can take the air without being overlooked, as is the
case at Windsor' (Buckingham, *Court and Cabinets of George III*, ii.20).

2. At 10.30 p.m. Thurlow wrote to Pitt, telling him about his correspondence with the
Prince of Wales, and asking him (Pitt) to 'have the goodness to circulate this message, that
the Ministers may attend accordingly' (P.R.O., Chatham Papers, 183).

3. ? Shortly before the Cabinet meeting.

confidential servants and such persons as they shall choose to join in their deliberations, and the opinions & proceedings of the physicians have been laid for them [*sic*].   (38245)

319   LORD LOUGHBOROUGH TO RICHARD BRINSLEY SHERIDAN

Thursday night, [*?20 or 27 Nov. 1788*]
Some intelligence that Lᵈ Stormont has received coincides so exactly with the tone of the Chancellor's conversation that on comparing them we are clearly of opinion that a project is seriously entertained to deny the P.'s right & to form a Government either under his name as an elected Regent wᵗ limitations, or in the King's name by issuing Commissions & orders by an authority delegated from the two Houses to the Ministers. Such projects not perfectly digested have been broached to several individuals to try their sentiments, & applications I know have been made to several Bishops, some of whom, & those such as the P. would least doubt, have lent a very favorable ear to them.

I am satisfied that by a temperate but at the same time an active resistance it will not be difficult to defeat these schemes, but I think it will be absolutely necessary (while the P. appears to take no concern in any matter beyond his attention to the King's health), that such person or persons as he pleases should have express authority to talk to Peers & Members in his name, with a declaration that he will not submit to any encroachment of his just rights, that he fully understands & will assert them whenever the publick service makes it necessary for him to act. From vague professions of duty he can rely on no support, the questions are [in] short whe[the]r he shall be excluded from the Government? restrained by limitations so as to have merely the name without the substance of authority? or established & recognized in the free tho' temporary exercise of it. The last the Ministers do not mean, but I am certain that it is impossible for them, without the utmost imprudence & negligence on the part of the P. & his real friends, to carry either w[it]h the publick or the Parlᵗ an approbation of this Mahratta Government they wish to set up.

I am extremely anxious that you should take an early opportunity of receiving his commands & laying before him the present critical tho not dangerous state of things. The strictest canvass must immediately be made in all quarters, but without some general direction & some degree of countenance from him that canvass will be very imperfect. Before the adjournment expires[1] it will be necessary to have a large meeting, & perhaps it might be proper for the P. to step forward, but it is certainly

1. The House of Commons adjourned from 20 November to 4 December.

adviseable that he should wait to receive some proposition from the Ministers, which he sh^d take care to have in writing. I can hardly think they will avoid this step, tho if they have taken the measure they did today[1] without opening any plan to him, their disrespect already shewn makes it possible they may pursue the same conduct in their future proceeding.

I set out to look for you this evening & was told by Ld J^n Townshend[2] that you had gone home indisposed, & I have rather chosen to trouble you w[it]h this letter in the morning because I am afraid I shall be very much engaged in the course of the day, & I am very desirous that you shd. lose no time in seeing H.R.H. Ld Rawdon comes to me tomorrow morning by his own appointment. He seems very well disposed, but I am afraid of his asking questions that I have no right to answer. (38242–4)

320 THE PRINCE OF WALES'S MESSAGE TO THE CABINET [3]

Windsor Castle, 27 Nov. 1788

The P. of W.[4] has deem'd it absolutely necessary, not chusing to act upon his own authority, to convene the King's confidential servants, that they may enquire into the exact state of H.M.'s unfortunate & melancholy situation of his physicians as well as into ye propriety of removing H. My. to Kew, such a proposal having been laid before H. Rl. Hss. by the King's physicians not only as proper for H.My. but as absolutely necessary for the re-establishment of his health.[5]

(43909 [draft] and 38273)

1. If this refers to the Adjournment, the letter was written on the 20th.

2. Second son (1757–1833) of the 1st Marquess Townshend; M.P. for Cambridge University, 1780–4; for Westminster, 1788–90; for Knaresborough, 1793–1818. A Lord of the Admiralty, March–July 1782 and April–December 1783; Joint Paymaster-General, 1806–7.

3. Endorsed, 'Deliver'd by the Duke of York to ye Cabinet assembled at Wr.' 'The Prince', said Wraxall, 'exerted every endeavour to secure the cordial co-operation and support of his brother Frederick. . . . He manifested the utmost anxiety to prevent any discordance of sentiment arising in a quarter so near the throne. It might, on the other hand, have been naturally expected that a Prince whom the King had always treated with marks of great parental affection if not with decided partiality, would feel a disinclination or rather a repugnance to overturn the existing Administration. His scruples, if any such he had, were, however, speedily surmounted. A promise of being placed at the head of the Army, with all the appointments, power and patronage of a Commander-in-Chief, effectually gained him over to his elder brother's party' (v.200–1).

4. The words 'feeling the delicacy of his situation' are here scored through the draft (43909).

5. 'When the Cabinet went down to Windsor two [*sic*] days ago', wrote Grenville on the 30th, 'in consequence of the Prince of Wales's letter, he did not see them, but sent a written

At his Royal Highness the Duke of York's apartments, Windsor Castle, 27 Nov. 1788

In consequence of the wish intimated to us through the Lord Chancellor on the part of his Royal Highness the Prince of Wales and the Royal Family, we have attended at Windsor, and have received the message from his Royal Highness the Prince of Wales which his Royal Highness the Duke of York communicated to us. We have since heard the sentiments of the King's physicians on the subject of the [proposal for] removing his Majesty to Kew, and being of opinion that their advice ought to be followed in all points material for his Majesty's recovery, and having received from them the paper [herewith] annexed, we are satisfied in our judgements, that it is desireable that his Majesty should be removed to Kew whenever the physicians think it convenient.[1]

Thurlow
Stafford[2]
Richmond Lennox & Aubigny[3]
Carmarthen
Chatham[4]
Sydney[5]
(38274–5)   William Pitt

message by the Duke of York, respecting the King's removal. This message, whether accidentally or not, was couched in terms that were thought a little royal. Some caution was thought necessary in wording the answer to avoid the style of giving his Royal Highness advice, or of acknowledging any authority in him.' (Buckingham, *Court and Cabinets of George III*, ii.23. See also *Political Memoranda of Duke of Leeds*, pp.121–4; *Dropmore Papers*, i.376).

1. 'The Ministers', wrote Grenville on the 28th, 'were all sent for to Windsor yesterday by the Prince, in order to give their advice with respect to moving the King. They were detained so late that Pitt went to Salt Hill to sleep there [i.e. at the famous hotel]' (Buckingham, *Court and Cabinets of George III*, ii.20). Camden was absent, being ill.

This is probably the only Cabinet Minute (if indeed, it can properly be so described) of the period 1783–1835 which was actually signed by the Ministers present, and its entirely exceptional nature (every other being communicated to the Sovereign, or Regent with sovereign power) accounts for its unique character. The copy in Add. MSS.28059, f.176, is headed in the usual way with the list of Ministers present. Otherwise it is identical with the Windsor document, apart from a trifling difference in the second sentence, where the words enclosed within square brackets read 'propriety of', and for 'herewith' is 'hereunto'.

Pitt wrote the following letter to the King from Windsor Castle on Saturday, 29 November 1788 (the day when the King was removed to Kew): 'Mr. Pitt humbly begs leave to acquaint your Majesty that he finds the physicians think it of the greatest consequence for your Majesty's recovery to change the air; and they have informed Mr. Pitt that they think themselves obliged not to permit Mr. Pitt to pay his duty personally to your Majesty again till after your Majesty's arrival at Kew, as fatigue in the meantime ought to be avoided.' Underneath was written: 'We think it advisable that the above-written note should be sent by Mr. Pitt to the King'; signed by the physicians—R. Warren, G. Baker, L. Pepys, H. Addington, H. R. Reynolds (Add. MSS. Georgian/2, f.3). Wraxall considered that the castle in Kew

Geneva, 27 Nov. 1788

At the same time that I must condole with you upon his Majesty's most truly melancholy situation it is my duty to return you my warmest & most affectionate thanks for your kind remembrance of me at a moment when, so much agitated as you must be, I had no right whatever to imagine that your thoughts would fall upon me. Accept my sincerest acknowledgment for the information you was so good as to send me through the Duke of Gloucester[1], & though deeply affected by the most

Gardens constructed by the King in the course of half a century was a 'most singular monument of eccentricity. . . . Its position, opposite to the smoky and dusky town of Brentford, one of the most detestable places in the vicinity of London, only separated by the stream of the Thames, is very unkingly as well as incommodious' (v.378). The palace was taken down in 1828.

2. Granville Leveson-Gower, 1st Marquess of Stafford (1721–1803) succeeded his father as Earl Gower, 1754, Marquessate, 1786. President of the Council, 1783–4; Lord Privy Seal, 1784–94.

3. Charles Lennox, 3rd Duke of Richmond (1735–1806), the Master-General of the Ordnance. Major-General, 1761; Lieutenant-General, 1770; General, 1782; Field-Marshal, 1792; Colonel of the Royal Regiment of Horse Guards, 1795–1806. Secretary of State (Southern Department), 1766; Master-General of the Ordnance, March 1782–April 1783, and December 1783–January 1795.

4. John, 2nd Earl of Chatham (1756–1835), the First Lord of the Admiralty, and Pitt's elder brother. Major-General, 1795; Master-General of the Ordnance, 1801–6 and 1807–10; Lieutenant-General, 1802; General, 1812; First Lord of the Admiralty, July 1788–December 1794. Lord Privy Seal, December 1794–September 1796; Lord President of the Council, September 1796–July 1801. In 1809 he commanded the military forces in the Walcheren expedition.

5. Thomas Townshend, 1st Viscount Sydney (1733–1800), grandson of Charles, 2nd Viscount Townshend. M.P. for Whitchurch, 1754–83; a Lord of the Treasury, 1765–7; Joint Paymaster-General of the Forces, 1767–8; Secretary at War, March–July 1782; Home Secretary, July 1782–April 1783, and December 1783–June 1789. Created Baron Sydney, March 1783; Viscount, June 1789.

1. The Duke, who is not again mentioned in the Prince of Wales's correspondence during the Regency crisis, had written to him on the 19th: 'I desired the Duke of Cumberland to make my excuses to you for not having been at Windsor these last days, having had a return of the asthma from the great cold of Saturday night. I have had my carriage ready at the door today, but really find myself not well enough to come as I am not essentially called upon. If I can I will be at Windsor by ½ p. 12 o'clock tomorrow. The accounts from Windsor differ much; I think they should not. I have continued to write to my sister without giving her any flattering hopes as to the main complaint.' (54393)

The Duke, remarked Grenville on 17 December, 'has held aloof from all cabal with them [i.e. the Prince of Wales and his brothers], and even declared in the House of Lords that he had done so' (Buckingham, *Court and Cabinets of George III*, ii. 65; *Political Memoranda of Duke of Leeds*, p. 135). Mrs. Harcourt wrote (30 December): 'I hear that the Duke of Gloucester has had great offers made to him and has rejected them. He says he should find it impossible, while his brother lives, to owe an obligation to any representative of his power, and in consequence of his refusal he is in complete disgrace' (*Harcourt Papers*, iv. 102).

dreadful and alarming accounts which his letter contains, I cannot deny that I was much flattered by the kind and affectionate assurances of your friendship and remembrance. I will not trespass, dearest brother, any longer upon your present moments, as they must surely be very much occupied, and therefore shall conclude, with recommending myself to your protection and friendship, begging you to be assured that you will ever find me to be [etc.]. (45766)

323   THE PRINCE OF WALES TO [?] THE DUKE OF PORTLAND

Windsor Castle, 28 Nov. 1788

My Dear Duke, I should long since have answered your letter, but thinking that you was in no immediate hurry for the return of your servant I took the liberty of keeping him, as I did not return to Windsor till my dinner was upon table.

As to the transaction you so painfully recal to my mind, I cannot help perhaps at the present moment feeling as otherwise than fortunate [*sic*] as I should not under other circumstances have had so powerful an opportunity of proving to you the high opinion and sincere regard I ever entertain'd for you, notwithstanding I cannot but confess my feelings as a man and as your friend were greatly hurt.[1] I flatter myself this is the last time we ever shall have occasion to mention to each other a subject of so distressing as the one I allude to, and which I do assure you is from the present moment entirely obliterated from my mind. I remain, my dear Duke, most sincerely yr. affectionate friend.[2] (38276).

1. The proposal, in 1787, that Parliament should pay the Prince's debts 'was not a favourite measure of Opposition, though they all agreed to support it except the Duke of Portland and the Cavendishes, who absolutely refused' (Lieutenant-General Grant to Cornwallis, 16 April 1787. *Cornwallis Correspondence*, i.301). William Grenville wrote, 4 December 1788: 'There is a report that before the Duke of Portland would consent to have any communication with the Prince of Wales, he insisted on an apology being made to him for some very rough treatment which he received at the time of the question of the debts; and that this apology has been made' (Buckingham, *Court and Cabinets of George III*, ii. 32. See also *Minto*. i.241). In 1786 the Duke had refused to allow the Duchess to receive Mrs. Fitzherbert at Burlington House (Rutland MSS. [H.M.C.], iii. 300).

2. The following undated letter from the Duke to the Prince of Wales may possibly refer to their reconciliation at this time: 'I humbly beg leave to acknowledge the great condescension & magnanimity of your Royal Highness, in the message which Mr Fox was directed by your Royal Highness to deliver to me. The gracious, & I confess, to my feelings, the very affecting manner in which your Royal Highness has been pleased to lay your commands upon me to forget a transaction in which my zeal for your glory, though sincere, was perhaps intemperate, will, I trust, procure me your Royal Highness's forgiveness for transgressing at this moment the strict letter of your command by reflecting for once on an event which can certainly produce upon my mind no other effect than to animate those endeavours, & give energy to

Windsor, 12.30 p.m., Friday [*?28 Nov. 1788*]

I am this moment arrived here, to enquire after the health of his Royal Highness, & if proper, to pay my duty to him.

Since I saw you yesterday, I have had some conversation with two Members who, if judiciously managed, I make little doubt, would vote with us—should Ministry venture (which in spite of their boasts I don't believe) to try a question on the Regency, if proposed at the Call of the House.

I suppose you observed the Shelburne gang were down yesterday.[1]

Almon, the printer of the *General Advertiser*, is a creature of Lord S[helburne]'s & that paper speaks the language of that party, as far as you can judge of such men by language. He has inserted in the paper of this morn—a dozen reasons, for a sole Regent, seemingly above the production of a mere grub. I have brought the paper.[2] Pray give me a line. (38367)

Whitehall, [*? on or after 28 Nov. 1788*]

The Chancellor's compliments to Mr. Payne. He received his note at Lord Stafford's where he dines. If the message presses he will either expect Mr. Payne here or see him at Carlton House in his way home. Otherwise he will be happy to see Mr. Payne at any time tomorrow morning. He goes to Kew at 11 o'clock.[3] (38211)

those exertions, which the confidence your Royal Highness is graciously disposed to place in me, intitles you at all times to command. (39392)

Sheridan has an interesting reference to the reconciliation between the Prince and the Duke of Portland, in an undated letter to Lord Palmerston, written, evidently, a few days later. 'His [the Prince's] conduct to the Duke of Portland, whom he saw at Burlington House on Saturday, has been everything that's right, desiring him to shake hands, and that they would never again think of the dispute they had about the motion for paying his debts, &c.' Sheridan added: 'The King is certainly worse than ever. Pitt and Chancellor have both seen him: he abused Pitt like a dog . . .' (Broadlands MSS.).

1. 'The Marquis of Lansdowne's friends, Barré, &c., were with us [i.e. with Ministers]', wrote Sir William Young on 23 December, with reference to the two divisions on the 22nd. (Buckingham, *Court and Cabinets of George III*, ii. 72, and see No. 370.)

2. Only a few issues of the *General Advertiser* for 1788 are in the British Museum, and the only Friday issue is that for 12 December, which is not the one referred to here.

3. 28 November would therefore seem to be the earliest possible date of this letter. The King was removed from Windsor to Kew on the 29th. 'There was considerable difficulty in persuading him to agree to this removal,' wrote Grenville on the 30th, 'but it was at last accomplished without violence. Pitt saw him again at Windsor before his removal, and thought him rather less well in his manner than on the preceding day.'

Sunday, 30 Nov. 1788

Upon communicating to Lord Weymouth[1] your Royal Highness's
wish that he should be present at sealing up the King's papers at
Windsor, he answered (of course) that, if those were your Royal Highness's commands, there could be no question or hesitation about
obeying them. But he begged leave to suggest, first, whether it would not
be still more delicate and respectful to the King to bring the drawers &
other repositories unopened to Kew, and deposit them there in some
safe place; secondly, if the papers are to be in any measure sorted and
packed, that can only be done with tolerable neatness by some hands
used to the package of papers. Those are to be had only from some
publick office, and most properly from the Secretary's of State. He
therefore wished to submit to your Royal Highness how far it would
be thought convenient to draw a business into private hands, which in
several respects seemed to belong to the Secretary of State, especially if
his clerks were to be employed in it. These suggestions appeared to
deserve so much consideration that the Chancellor has thought it his
duty to lay them before your Royal Highness.   (38277)

327   MEMORANDUM BY THE LORD CHANCELLOR

[*c. Nov. 1788*]

This seems to be a case wherein the law has yet made no adequate
provision, there being no person yet authorised to assume the exercise
of the Royal functions.

It is also a case where the Legislature is, strictly speaking, incapable
of making such provision, by reason of the personal imbecility of one
constituent branch.

The defect is too great to be supplied by the authority of any private
advice or of any less than the great Councils of the Nation. Nay, if the
adhibition of the King's authority to the Parliament were made in any
manner, even by such advice, it would still be necessary to have an Act
of Parliament declaring that, under the pressure of such necessity, it
was properly done and good in substance as well as form.

It is also agreed that the only person in whom the exercise of so much
of the Royal function as the occasion requires can be properly vested
is the Prince.

These ideas seem to be provided for in the second and third Resolutions; the only question which remains is in what manner the Royal

1. Thomas, 3rd Viscount Weymouth and (August 1789) 1st Marquess of Bath (1734-96).
He had been a Secretary of State in Lord North's Ministry. He was Groom of the Stole and
First Lord of the Bedchamber, 1775, and 1782-96.

authority is to be united to the Houses so as to give them the vigour of a Parliament. This may be done by desiring the Prince to act as Regent to that end, and with a view to confer in a legal manner the requisite authority for other future purposes.

This (which is suddenly thought of) appears to me desirable in many views if there be no more solid objection than I am yet aware of. First, it goes the whole possible length, consistently with the above-mentioned principles of meeting with the ideas of others, and if it procures their concurrence, will give the proceeding an authority of which, in a new case, it will stand in much need. Secondly, it will tend to demonstrate what I should think wise to assume, that the Minister aims singly at restoring publick order without seeking to derive an advantage of a personal kind in a party conflict, at a moment so delicate and anxious as this.

I am aware that in this case also it will be equally necessary to have an Act of Parliament declaring that, under the necessity of the case, it was properly done and good in substance as well as form.

But in this case it would be easier to obtain such Act, and the whole proceeding would be much safer and more authoritative and more dignified with respect to individuals and the publick.

All adverse, irritating measures tend so directly and manifestly to publick confusion that either party running into them will have, and deserve, the publick execration, for they will unavoibly [sic] be referred to private views instead of the publick good.

(Add. MSS. Georgian/2, f. 5)

328   WILLIAM WINDHAM [1] TO CAPTAIN J. W. PAYNE

Park Street, Westminster, 7.30 p.m., Monday [? Nov. 1788]
I have seen Mr. Pitt since I parted with you, and in the course of our conversation mentioned my having been honoured with an interview with H.R.H. and of the general idea which I had of H.R.H.'s dispositions. I stated to him also the substance of the conversation which I had had with you. Mr. Pitt did not appear to me to have any ideas on the present state of affairs or of the measures that might eventually be necessary other than what H.R.H. might approve, or at least think allowable in the persons who entertained them.   (38061)

1. Windham (1750-1810) was M.P. for Norwich, 1784-1802; for St. Mawes, 1802-6; for New Romney, 1806-7; for Higham Ferrers, 1807-10; Chief Secretary to the Lord-Lieutenant of Ireland in the Coalition Ministry, 1783; Secretary at War, as one of the leading Portland Whigs, in Pitt's Ministry, 1794-1801; Secretary of State for War and the Colonies in the 'Talents' Ministry, 1806-7.

329 THE PRINCE OF WALES TO THE CABINET

[? *Nov. 1788*]

I am extreamly obliged to you for the communication of the papers you have submitted to me, although no particular observation upon them occurs to me at present.

The management of the King's person must, of course, be trusted to the discretion of the most accredited physicians in London; and it certainly belongs to his confidential Council to attend earnestly to his situation.

I feel, as you justly suppose, every degree of anxiety about His M.'s health, both on publick and private grounds, which can animate the duty of a son and a subject on this interesting occasion; and that very duty restrains me from interfering in a matter of which I cannot possibly judge. (38278)

330 THE PRINCE OF WALES TO BARON ALVENSLEBEN [copy]

[? *Nov.-Dec. 1788*]

I have sent for you, Sir, to acquaint you that the King my father having for some time past been afflicted with a severe & melancholy disorder, which renders him incapable during its continuance of attending to publick business or transacting any affairs whatever, in his own person, and the care of his interests in his Electoral dominions and the administration of the Govt. in these countries on his Majesty's behalf, having for these reasons devolved on me during the interval of his Majesty's incapacity—I feel it my duty not to neglect longer the execution of a trust so important to his Majesty & to the welfare of his Electoral subjects; I have therefore judged it proper to make to you this communication of my intention to take upon me immediately the administration of affairs in the Electorate, & to desire that you will without delay inform the Regency thereof in such a manner as may best prove my personal regard for them & my affection for the interests of Hanover.[1] (38434)

1. Sir Gilbert Elliot wrote to his wife on 27 December: '[Lord Malmesbury] is, or pretends to be, at all hours with the Prince of Wales, and has got himself consulted by him about Hanover, which I daresay he considers as a good step towards being Foreign Secretary of State, and so it is. But there are, unfortunately for him, some strong men before him for that post' (Minto MSS.).

[c. beginning of Dec. 1788]

To express to his R.H. our sincere condoleance & sympathy with him in the affliction her Majesty the Queen, the Royal Family & the whole nation suffer from the heavy visitation which has disabled the King from continuing to exercise as he has done to the benefit & comfort of his people the arduous functions belonging to his Royal authority; that by this dreadful calamity his faithful subjects are fallen into a general consternation, that all the national councils are [at] a stand, & that every act of State, legislature & revenue, the administration wh. we acknowledge to be the justly & constitutionally in the Crown are suspended. That in this exigency whilst his Majesties faithful subjects suffer under an extraordinary dispensation of Providence, they look for assistance & trust for their relief in his Royal Highness the Heir Apparent of the Crown, to whom in all unforeseen extremities wh. disable the possessor, the rights of the Crown are naturally devolved, whose high interest in the object places them in the surest custody, & whose virtues promise to the nation the most salutary & constitutional exertion of them.

That this House hopes that his Royal Highness having abundantly more than sufficiently sacrificed to the private sentiments of his filial piety & natural affection will listen to the earnest supplication of his Majesties faithful Commons & undertake the duties & cares of government until his Majesty shall be restored to the anxious prayers of his Royal Highness & that he will be persuaded that in no way can he demonstrate to the world his filial attachment & reverence to his Majesty, his royal father, than by taking upon him the charge of the welfare of his faithful subjects & by supplying the care & protection which nothing but the hand of God could prevent his royal father from continuing to be to his people.

That his Majesties faithful Commons humbly trust & presume that at this time of destitution of all the ordinary means of their safety & happiness they have, from their relation to his Majesty & his royal & their constant zeal for the rights of the Crown, & from the innate goodness & benevolence of his Rl. Highness' disposition, a just claim on his Rl. Highness for his services in this interval, assuring his Rl. H. that they will take all necessary steps to support his Rl. Highness in the full exercise of these rights which the Constitution, for wise & salutary purposes, has vested in the Crown of these kingdoms.[2] (38420)

1. Edmund Burke (1729-97) sat for Wendover, 1765-74; for Bristol, 1774-80; for Malton, 1780-94. He was Paymaster-General in the Rockingham and Coalition Ministries, March-July 1782, and April-December 1783.

2. Sir Gilbert Elliot wrote on 5 December 1788: 'Burke made a very rough crude sketch of an Address to the Prince of Wales from the House of Commons inviting him to assume the

Kew, 2 Dec. 1788

Since I saw the Chancellor & conversed with you, I have considered the painful subject over with great attention, & find the situation with regard to myself so very delicate that I am doubtful of my own powers of acting in such distressing circumstances, & still am of opinion the Chancellor might do better than myself.[1] I wish therefore that you would be so kind as to desire him to reconsider it, & let me have both yours & the Chancellor's opinion upon paper. By doing this you will greatly oblige, my dearest son [etc.]. (36374)

333 THE EARL OF SANDWICH TO CAPTAIN J. W. PAYNE, WITH AN ENCLOSURE

Hertford Street, 2 Dec. 1788

You will if you think proper communicate the enclosed letter in a certain place; it will at least shew the zeal of our friend B[urton], tho' I rather think that Mr. H.[2] was originally well disposed.

Can I have an opportunity of seeing you, or should I pay my duty to H.R.H. before the meeting of the Parlaiment [*sic*] on Thursday next?

The person alluded to in Mr. B's. letter is Mr. Hunt, Member for Bodmyn. (38300)

[Enclosure] ROBERT BURTON TO THE EARL OF SANDWICH

Gr: Pl., 2 Dec. 1788

Since I wrote my letter to your Lordship I have seen my western friend, and after a long conversation with him upon the subject he was inclined

Regency, that we might be ready with it when the proper time comes. He showed it me, and desired me to revise it, but I found the best way was to draw a new one on my own plan, adapting a few of his phrases where I could. This I did the day before yesterday. It was much approved of by Burke, the Duke of Portland and Fox.' (*Minto*, i.243)

1. 'The Chancellor told me', wrote Carmarthen on the 2nd, 'he had been to Kew in the morning, and had seen the Queen, that her Majesty had accepted our proposal of taking care of the K.'s person, tho' with evident marks of diffidence and apprehension respecting so important a charge' (*Political Memoranda of Duke of Leeds*, p. 127). Lord Kenyon, the new Lord Chief Justice, wrote, in his Diary, 1 December: 'Dined at the Marquess of Stafford's —same company as at Mr. Pitt's [i.e. Thurlow, Richmond, Stafford, Chatham, Carmarthen, Weymouth, Sydney and Hawkesbury—on 29 November], with the addition of Earl Camden. Signed a paper with the Cabinet Ministers, requesting the Queen to take upon her the management of the King's person during his illness' (Kenyon MSS.).

2. Thomas Hunt (*d.* 1789), M.P. for Bodmin, 1784-9. 'He attached himself to no party, and voted upon all occasions to the best of his judgment, for the good of his country.' (*Gentleman's Magazine*, 1789, ii. 962.) He did not support Pitt on parliamentary reform in 1785, and opposed him on the Irish Commercial Propositions in 1785 and on the Regency.

to think the *sole* Regency should be in the P. of W. I urged the matter, and obtained his permission to write down the following words and send them to your Lordship. "That he should be for the sole Regency of the P. of W. and that he hoped in any Administration under that Regency he should always vote in support of their measures." He farther authorized me to say that "my friend (meaning your Lordship) might acquaint the P. of W. with this determination."

I am flatter'd with the hopes of being able to influence two or three other friends upon this great occasion, but shall signifye nothing to your Lordship till I have an absolute certainty. (38301)

334   RICHARD BRINSLEY SHERIDAN TO CAPTAIN J. W. PAYNE

[*? Tuesday, 2 Dec. 1788*]

Tho' I have nothing material to communicate to the Prince, I am too anxious not to wish to hear from you, & the state of things tonight.[1] Here *reports* have made a total revolution both in opinions of the *future*, and even of what *has been* the *past* state of the *K's* situation. The Prince will of course govern his communication to the Council if his R.H. has call'd them, by the state of things tomorrow. I shall be happy to hear that the Prince is well himself. It is true that letters are sent to all Members of Par.^t &c. and those letters, as you will observe, even suppose a *possibility* of the K. being well enough to *prorogue Parl*^t between this & *Thursday*! a curious piece of deception truly.[2] (41911)

335   AT THE COUNCIL CHAMBER, WHITEHALL, 3 DECEMBER 1788[3]

PRESENT   The Lords of his Majesty's most Honourable Privy Council.
RESOLVED   That copies of the examinations of Dr. Richard Warren,

1. 'The contradictions in the daily prints respecting the King's health are truly ridiculous,' remarked *The Times* on 3 December.

2. 'Treasury notes', as always, were now accompanied by, or followed by, private appeals to influential people. Thus Pitt wrote to Lord Kenyon, the Lord Chief Justice, on 10 December: 'It now seems that we are likely to come to business in the House of Commons on Monday or Tuesday next. You will imagine we are anxious to summon all our strength; I understand Mr. Ambler [M.P. for Saltash] is in Berkshire near Maidenhead, and perhaps a letter from you might be the surest way of obtaining his attendance—Popham [M.P. for Taunton] I believe is a very good friend, but if you have an opportunity of speaking to him, so much the better' (Kenyon MSS.).

3. Loughborough's note to Captain Payne (? 2 December) may refer to this Privy Council meeting: 'I have just received a "summons as a Privy Counsellor to attend tomorrow at 12 when H.M. physicians are to be examined touching the state of his health". This seems a

Sir George Baker, Bart., Sir Lucas Pepys, Bart.[1], Dr. Henry Revell Reynolds[2], and Dr. Anthony Addington[3] touching the state of his Majesty's health, which were this day taken on oath before their Lordships, be laid tomorrow before both Houses of Parliament, and that the same be laid before the House of Lords by the Lord President[4] and before the House of Commons by the Chancellor of the Exchequer.

Examination of Dr. Richard Warren

Q. You are desired to acquaint the Board whether the state of his Majesty's health is such as to render him incapable of coming in person to his Parliament or of attending to any kind of publick business.

A. Certainly incapable.

Q. What are the hopes you entertain of his Majesty's recovery?

A. The probability of cure can only be determined by past experience,

prelude to some measure. Will you have the goodness to put the enclosed w[it]h your letter to go by the messenger?' (38246)

Sir Gilbert Elliot thus commented on the proceedings: 'The ministerial members of the Privy Council seem to have formed their plan for suppressing as much of the truth as possible, and indeed for disguising it, as well as for preventing its reaching the public. For this purpose they set down on paper three or four queries which were to be answered by the physicians, and they endeavoured to settle an agreement or resolution of the Council that no other questions should be asked, and no further or closer examination should be permitted. The pretence for this was to avoid what was called the indelicacy of inquiring into the particular acts committed by the King' (*Minto*, i. 242).

Wraxall wrote: 'Above fifty members . . . were present . . . but as at least one-third of the number belonged to the Opposition, it was judged proper, with a view to prevent disclosures of an unbecoming nature, to determine previously the questions which should be proposed to the physicians. The precaution formed a salutary check' (v. 204). The questions were prepared by the Lord President of the Council. Fox was too ill to attend the Privy Council meeting, and none of the Royal family was present. (Buckingham, *Court and Cabinets of George III*, ii. 30, and see *Political Memoranda of Duke of Leeds*, p. 129).

1. Sir Lucas Pepys (1742-1830), the King's physician; created Baronet, 1784; President of the College of Physicians, 1804-10.

2. M.D., Cambridge, 1773 (1745-1811). Physician-in-ordinary to the King, 1806.

3. Anthony Addington (1713-90), who practised in Reading and who had attended Pitt's father, Chatham, in his last illness. His son Henry was soon to be Speaker of the House of Commons. 'Addington told Pitt', Grenville wrote on 29 November, 'that he had himself kept a house for the reception of these unhappy people for seven years; that during that period he had hardly ever had fewer than ten or twelve with him, and that of all those one only was not cured, he having died in the house of bursting a blood vessel.' When he appeared at the bar of the House of Lords to be sworn, the doctor was dressed in a light-coloured horseman's greatcoat, and it was suggested that he looked rather to be in need of a physician than to be a physician himself.

4. Sir Charles Pratt (1714-94), 1st Baron (1765) and 1st Earl (1786) Camden. Chief Justice of the Common Pleas, 1761; Lord Chancellor, 1766-70; Lord President of the Council in the Rockingham and Shelburne Ministries, and under Pitt, December 1784-94.

by which I learn that the greater number of persons who have fallen into the same state in which his Majesty now is, including all the species of the disorder, have been cured.

Q. Can you form any judgment or probable conjecture of the duration of his Majesty's illness?

A. The time necessary for obtaining the cure cannot be ascertained.

Q. Whether in that particular species of the disorder that his Majesty has fallen into it has been found from experience that the greater number of persons so affected have been cured?

A. It is not in my power to ascertain the species because no known distemper has preceded that can account for it.

Q. Whether so far as experience enables Dr. Warren to judge of his Majesty's disorder he thinks it more probable that his Majesty will or will not recover so as to render him capable of attending to publick business?

A. I have not, and I believe it is impossible for any one to have, data sufficient for the answer to this question.

Q. What degree of experience has Dr. Warren had himself, or does he know others to have had in this particular species of disorder?

A. It has fallen to my lot to see a great number of persons in the course of twenty seven or twenty eight years practice who have had the same disorder with which his Majesty is now afflicted. I have generally attended them for a short space of time and have seen some of them get well, sometimes under my sole care, sometimes in conjunction with physicians who profess this branch of medicine only. It has frequently happened, but not always, that if the patient did not soon get well I left him under the care of the physicians who professed this particular branch of medicine only, who sometimes afterwards sent for me in consultation.

Examination of Sir George Baker, Bart.

Q. You are desired to acquaint this Board whether the state of his Majesty's health is such as to render him incapable of coming in person to his Parliament or of attending to any kind of publick business.

A. His Majesty in his present state is unfit for any publick business.

Q. What are the hopes you entertain of his Majesty's recovery?

A. The hopes that I entertain of his Majesty's recovery depend upon the experience of physicians, particularly those who attend the publick hospitals, by which we learn that the greater part of those who have been affected, as his Majesty now is, have been cured.

Q. Can you form any judgment or probable conjecture of the duration of his Majesty's illness?

A. I can form no conjecture of the duration of his Majesty's illness.

Examination of Sir Lucas Pepys, Bart.

Q. You are desired to acquaint this Board whether the state of his Majesty's health is such as to render him incapable of coming in person to his Parliament or of attending to any kind of publick business.

A. Undoubtedly the state of his Majesty's health is such.

Q. What are the hopes you entertain of his Majesty's recovery?

A. There is a probability of his Majesty's recovery.

Q. Does Sir Lucas Pepys found the opinion given in his answer to the preceeding question upon the particular symptoms of his Majesty's disorder or upon general experience in other cases of the same nature, or upon both?

A. I do not found my opinion of the probability of his Majesty's recovery on any particular symptom or circumstance peculiar to the case of his Majesty, but on the general consideration that the majority of those who are afflicted with symptoms of a similar disorder do recover.

Q. Can you form any judgment or probable conjecture of the duration of his Majesty's illness?

A. It will be impossible to form any opinion upon that.

Q. What degree of experience has Sir Lucas Pepys had himself, or does he know others to have had, of this particular species of disorder?

A. I have occasionally attended patients who have had a similar disorder but more frequently with those physicians who have made it their particular practice to attend such patients.

Examination of Dr. Henry Revell Reynolds

Q. You are desired to acquaint this Board whether the state of his Majesty's health is such as to render him incapable of coming in person to his Parliament or of attending to any kind of public business.

A. I think the state of his Majesty at present is such as will prevent him from doing that.

Q. What are the hopes you entertain of his Majesty's recovery?

A. I think that the probability is in favour of his Majesty's recovery.

Q. Does Dr. Reynolds found the opinion given in his answer to the preceeding question upon the particular symptoms of his Majesty's disorder or upon general experience in other cases of the same nature or upon both?

A. Upon general experience, upon my own experience, and upon the experience of gentlemen older in the profession than myself, with whom I have conversed upon such subjects.

Q. Can Dr. Reynolds form any judgement or probable conjecture of the duration of his Majesty's illness?

A. No, I cannot; it may be some weeks, it may be some months, but it is impossible to ascertain the time.

Q. What degree of experience has Doctor Reynolds had himself, or does he know others to have had, in this particular species of disorder?
A. I have been very near twenty years in the practice of my profession. I have seen several persons afflicted with the malady with which his Majesty is afflicted, both singly and in consultation with gentlemen who have dedicated themselves to that particular branch.

Examination of Dr. Anthony Addington

Q. You are desired to aquaint this Board whether the state of his Majesty's health is such as to render him incapable of coming in person to his parliament or of attending to any kind of publick business.
A. Most certainly it is.
Q. What are the hopes you entertain of his Majesty's recovery?
A. The same hopes that I should have of any other patient in whose family this disease is not hereditary. His Majesty has no symptom whatever that I know of but what I have seen in other patients who have recovered.
Q. Can you form any judgment or probable conjecture of the duration of his Majesty's illness?
A. I protest I cannot with any kind of certainty.
Q. Whether so far as experience enables Dr. Addington to judge of his Majesty's disorder, he thinks it more probable that his Majesty will or will not recover so as to render him capable of attending to publick business?
A. I should think it more probable that his Majesty will recover so as to be in health to enable him to attend to publick business. By which I mean in as good health as he was before he had the misfortune to labour under his present illness.
Q. What degree of experience has Dr. Addington had himself, or does he know others to have had of this particular species of disorder?
A. It is impossible to be a physician for any length of time without being concerned with patients afflicted with this disorder. They were so common in the neighbourhood of Reading that I built an house, contiguous to my own dwelling house, for the reception of such unfortunate patients.[1] In this house I had constantly patients attended by myself every day, unless I was ill, for five years. The house usually contained eight or ten such patients; of those I believe I never saw an instance of any who was not reasonably deemed to be an incurable before he or she were brought to my house but what recovered within the year, and many in much less time. I never saw but two patients of my own confined

1. *The Times*, commenting on this part of the doctor's evidence, inquired: 'Is it *the water of Reading*, or is it the air, to which the madness of the people of that part of England must be attributed? Mr. Addington should clear up this point, after making so severe a charge against its inhabitants.'

longer than one year. Perhaps it may be material to say that several of these patients had been afflicted for two or three years before they came into my house. (38305-11)

336

Burlington House, Wednesday 3 Dec. 1788

As your Royal Highness is probably anxious to be informed of the result of the Council I presume with all deference to lay before you a short state of what has passed previous to my obtaining copies of the questions agreed to be put to the physicians & their answers, which shall be transmitted to your Royal Highness the moment I receive them, which I expect in the course of this evening, & which I humbly submit to your Royal Highness may be a less exceptionable mode of your Royal Highness's being possessed of them, than by sending for them to the Council in your own name. The Council in general, influenced by motives of delicacy not perhaps quite consistent with the magnitude & importance of the case under their inquiry, were inclined to concur in abstaining from putting some of those questions to the physicians which might possibly have elucidated the real state of the King's disorder, & the real & specifick probability of his Majesty's recovery. The physicians, though on different grounds & in different degrees, concurred in the probability of the King's recovery. Dr Warren's opinion was indeed given with some reserve, as he grounded it solely on a calculation that in the *specieses* [*sic*] of the disorder under our consideration, the greater number of those afflicted with it did recover. Dr Addington went farther than any of them, declaring that he thought it probable that the King might recover as complete a sanity & as great a fitness for business, as he possessed before his malady. Dr Addington's examination closed the business, & it was then determined to lay the whole of the evidence before the two Houses tomorrow & to move to take it into consideration on next Monday, after which Mr. Pitt endeavoured to induce those of the Council who were members of either House to enter into something like an engagement not to proceed into any farther investigation of this matter in their parliamentary capacities, but this, as your royal Highness will believe, was not assented to. (38302-3)

Burlington House, 8 p.m., Wednesday 3 Dec. 1788

My concern at your Royal Highness's disappointment is in some measure alleviated by my endeavours to have prevented it. The moment I returned from Council, I attempted to give your Royal Highness some idea of what had passed previous to my being enabled to transmit copies of the examination of the Physicians, whose evidence, I will only say here, very little corresponded with the expectations I had formed of it. But not to add to your Royal Highness's suspense by detaining your servant while I repeat what I stated in the letter I presumed to address to your Royal Highness, & dispatched from hence between 5 & 6, I will desire him to ask for that letter at Carleton House before he returns to your Royal Highness with this.   (38318)

Burlington House, 10.30 p.m., Wednesday 3 Dec. 1788
The Duke of Portland takes the liberty of offering to your Royal Highness the answers of the physicians without waiting for the questions for which he sent to the Clerk of the Council[1], that your Royal Highness may be possessed as expeditiously as possible of all the information which it is in the Duke of Portland's power to submit to your Royal Highness. (38304)

Burlington House, 12 midnight, Wednesday 3 Dec. 1788
The Duke of Portland has this moment received the enclosed which he loses no time in humbly laying at your Royal Highness's feet, & takes the liberty of making Mr. Cottrell's note to himself a part of the enclosure, as it seemed in some degree necessary to explain the manner in which the references are made. (38319)

[Enclosure] STEPHEN COTTRELL TO THE DUKE OF PORTLAND

Council Office, Wednesday night [3 Dec. 1788]
Mr. Cottrell is very sorry it has not been in his power sooner to obey the Duke of Portland's commands in sending to his Grace the questions put to the physicians this morning by the Lords of the Council.

Inclosed he has the honor to transmit the questions put to Dr. Warren *at length* in the order they stood upon the minutes, and where the same questions were repeated to the other physicians, he has, in order to save time, refer'd to them by the number; and has followed the same method in regard to the additional question put to Sir Lucas Pepys and Dr. Reynolds after their answers to the question No. 2. (38320)

1. Stephen Cottrell.

403

337 EARL CAMDEN TO THE PRINCE OF WALES

3 Dec. 1788

I have the honour to send inclosed to your Royal Highness a copy of the testimony of five Physicians examined this day upon oath before his Majesty's Privy Council touching the state of his Majesty's health, & have the honour [etc.]. (38312)

338 THE PRINCE OF WALES TO THE LORD CHANCELLOR
AND THE REPLY

Carlton House, 3 Dec. 1788

I send you the inclosed for yr perusal, & if without giving yourself too much trouble you can draw up yr. sentiments within ye compass of a letter I will take care to transmit ym. to the Queen. (38315)

LORD THURLOW'S REPLY

3 Dec. 1788

In obedience to your Royal Highness's commands I have put in writing what I said to her Majesty yesterday. I have doubted whether I ought to send a letter to the Queen open, and yet I wish your Royal Highness to be apprised of what I have said.

I have represented to her Majesty that the Royal person is just as much under private care in this tedious disorder as it would be in a fever till the Legislature thinks fit to provide otherwise—that the ordering his family, including the care of his sick person, fall naturally into the hands of her Majesty—that there will be no want of confidence anywhere in her tenderness on such an occasion—that all manner of assistance and advice from every quarter will naturally be at her Majesty's commands—and that so far as responsibility of any sort belongs to the matter, it will belong to those who advise—and that in such circumstances it is unnecessary and consequently improper for me or any other to assume a different character.

If in the manner of obeying your Royal Highness's commands I have got wrong in any point of etiquette, I hope your Royal Highness will not impute it to any failure in that duty and respect, with which at all times I remain [etc.]. (38316-7)

THE DUKE OF YORK AND THE PRINCE OF WALES TO PRINCE AUGUSTUS [1]

London, 3 Dec. 1788

I am exceedingly sorry that it falls to my lot to acquaint you with the melancholy situation in which the King at present is, and from which God alone knows whether he ever will recover. You will have heard before you left Gottingen that his Majesty was ill, and for a long time we have done everything in our power to keep it secret, but it is now no more possible. His complaint, which is a total loss of all rationality, has apparently been coming upon him for some time but now is grown to such a pitch that he is a compleat lunatick. I can easily conceive how much you will be affected with this account; it is a dreadfull thing indeed, and totally unexpected. The Queen and my sisters are as well as can be expected under such unlucky circumstances. As my brother stands below me and means to add a few lines to this himself, I shall say nothing about him. I shall therefore conclude by assuring you, my dear Augustus, how sincerely I remain [etc.].

FROM THE PRINCE OF WALES

I wd. not let Frederick close his packet without adding a few lines myself to say how much oblig'd to you I am for the very kind letter I receiv'd a month ago, & wh. I shd. have answer'd long since but for the very unhappy business we have had before us for the last five weeks. Believe, my dearest Augustus, yt. there is nothing yt. can make you happy yt. is within my compass to manage for you, yt. you may not expect from [etc.]. (Add. Georgian 9/60)

340 MEMORANDUM RESPECTING DR. FRANCIS WILLIS [2] [unsigned]

[? *Late Nov. or early Dec. 1788*[3]]

In Lincolnshire there resides a clergyman with a good private fortune who, from motives of principle & charity towards his fellow creatures,

---

1. The two letters are on the same sheet.

2. Dr. Francis Willis (1718-1807), one of the few eighteenth-century physicians who were also in holy orders. He was physician to the hospital at Lincoln. The *General Advertiser* said that Willis had been recommended by the Lord Chancellor, the doctor having had several wards of the Court of Chancery similarly disordered, under his care, and they had recovered after a few months. He quickly achieved popularity at Court and with Ministers by expressing absolute confidence in the King's speedy recovery, in opposition to the gloomy views of Dr. Warren, who was cried up by the Opposition. The Queen's letter of 3 January 1789 to the Lord Chancellor well illustrates the clash between these two medical men:

'We have had another difference with the physicians about the Bulletin. I saw Dr. Warren myself & got him to alter it, but I must own that, though he was careful not to say anything

happening to have met with some cases that particularly affected him, undertook the study of the sad disease that every British heart is now lamenting. He has practiced I beleive upwards of 30 years, & his success has been beyond that of any other person in proportion to the numbers that have passed through his hands. At the request of different families of distinction he has received into his house as boarders variety of ladies & gentlemen, most of which have been restored to their families as perfectly well in every respect as before they were under the sad necessity of being separated from them. Among the number I had the experience of a near connection of my own who, after residing some months with Doctor Willis, returned home without the smallest remains of her complaint, & tho the measures used had been coercive, yet with such judgment had they ever been applied that after the cure there remained the most perfect amity between the parties, & for twelve years that the lady had the entire use of her reason she kept up a correspondence of

disrespectful to me, yet do I intend never to see him again, & told him, by what I understood below stairs, both parties have been warm, which I am sorry for, & do not intend to see Dr. Willis today; but this difference of oppinion, arising so constantly amongst the physicians, makes me the more desirous of seeing some alteration made in the mode of their attendance; &, as your very kind & amicable advice has not succeeded, may I desire that you would be so obliging as to consider with the rest of the Cabinet some means to get rid of this physical & incomprehensible calamity? I see clearly by Dr. Warren's behaviour that his ambition & those who depend upon him, look upon they two Willis's [see page 407, *n* 1] with a jealous eye, & I declare that I fear they will hurt them if they can. But I trust their characters are such that they will meet with the support of every honest man.

'I will only add, that if Dr. Guisborne was to come every evening, & make up the Bulletin the next morning, the world might depend upon hearing the exact truth of his Majesty; & any one of the other physicians coming every fortnight would be sufficient to disturb the whole house, & the world too. May I beg that my poor mind may soon be made easy upon this subject?, as the sight of that black spirit, Dr. Warren, has agitated it very much' (Egerton *MSS.* 2232 f. 71).

The Opposition even alleged that Willis had been brought in for the specific purpose of persuading the public that the King's speedy recovery was to be expected, and stigmatised him as 'a quack'. 'Willis', wrote Sir Gilbert Elliot (29 December) 'has been detected writing letters to Pitt, who has read them at White's to the M.P.'s and other people, giving assurances of the King's great amendment and of his immediate recovery, and this on the days when he had been in a strait-waistcoat. . . . Warren and the other physicians have remonstrated against this, and it has made some noise' (*Minto*, i.253).

It was said that Willis kept a pack of hounds for his patients and allowed them to hunt and shoot. He certainly trusted the King with a razor.

3. The letter must have been written a few days before 5 December, when Dr. Willis arrived at Kew (R. F. Greville's *Diary*, p. 118). The Queen wrote from Kew on 2 December, evidently to the Lord Chancellor: 'My Lord, I have this instant received your letter & return you thanks for your attention in giving me the information contained in it, & shall be anxious to hear that the Privy Council have determined to send for Dr. Willis.' (Add. MSS. Georgian 2/46). On the 4th, Fanny Burney, at Kew, heard that Willis had been sent for express. (*Diary*, iii. 118. See also, *Political Memoranda of Duke of Leeds*, p. 129).

friendship with Doctor & Mrs. Willis & expressed the greatest gratitude as due from her to them.

Dr. Willis's son[1] has for some years been joined with him in the same benevolent occupation & is supposed to have equal skill; both have the best of private characters, both have uncommon good natural under-standing, & both have had the most liberal educations. It is humbly submitted to those whose judgment on the present occasion cannot be doubted, whether coercion is not easier procured by means of strangers than from those who have been the objects of immediate command, & whether if by any means the father & son, one or both, cd. be procured as auxiliaries to the Faculty & to execute & enforce their directions, they might not be found very useful on the present lamented occasion. (38314-5)

341   THE PRINCE OF WALES TO THE QUEEN, AND THE REPLY

Carlton House, 3.45 p.m., 4 Dec. 1788
I have been so extreamly unwell since I had ye. pleasure of seeing you yesterday yt. I was obliged to be blooded last night, & ye. arm having bled of itself this morning I am advised by Dr. Warren not to go to Kew this day, wh. I assure you, my dear mother, makes me not a little uncomfortable. However, I shall certainly come down tomorrow & hope by the return of my servant to hear yt. you continue perfectly well. (41906)

THE QUEEN'S REPLY

Kew House, 4 Dec. 1788
I am extreamly sorry to hear that you continue to feel so unwell, & that I am deprived thereby of the pleasure of your company. I agree with Dᵣ Warren that this severe season would only encrease your cold & beg that unless you feel quite free of all disorder you will not even think of coming tomorrow.[2] Myself & all your sisters are thank God well except

1. Dr. John Willis (1751-1835), who accompanied his father to Kew. Both he and his father were to attend the King again in 1801.

2. The Prince was evidently well enough that day to go first, to Devonshire House (to urge the Duke to accept the office of Privy Seal), and then to Brooks's, and was still there long after 10 p.m. 'At Brooks's', wrote Sir Gilbert Elliot, 'I found the Prince of Wales—that's to say he was in the house, but I did not see him, for he had just retired to a private room with Grey, who . . . is a great favourite and is admitted to all their most private or Cabinet councils.' He added, 'We are rather afraid of his premature ambition running foul of the established heads of the party one day and doing mischief.' (*Minto*, i.244). And W. Fawkener, the Clerk of

Sophia, who still coughs a little. The King is, thank Heaven, more calm this afternoon as the physician sends word.

I hope to hear that you will soon recover & am [etc.]. (36375)

342 THE PRINCE OF NASSAU [1] TO THE PRINCE OF WALES

Kirchheim, 4 Dec. 1788

Votre Altesse Royale voudra bien me permettre de lui communiquer la nouvelle de la perte cruelle que je viens de faire le 28 Novembre dernier par la mort subite de mon pere qu'un coup d'apoplexie enleva dans la 54eme année de son age.

J'ose me flatter que votre Altesse Royale daignera prendre quelque part à ma juste douleur et qu'ella agréera le liberté que je prends de saisir cette occasion pour me recommender ainsi que le reste de ma famille dans sa bienveillance et dans sa protection.

C'est avec un devouement très respectueux que je suis, Monseigneur de notre Altesse Royale, le très humble et très obeissant serviteur, Frederic Guillaume Prince de Nassau. (38321)

343 PRINCE WILLIAM TO THE PRINCE OF WALES

Jamaica, 4 Dec. 1788

I was prevented from writing last packet by numberless engagements and by the climate, for this country so totally enervates one that it requires the greatest resolution to take up a pen. I have been near a month in this country and find myself infinitely better than I could have expected. I begin now to hope by care and attention I shall be enabled to preserve my health till next Spring when nothing but a war shall induce me to visit these islands. The existance here is at best a negative one: no European can enjoy perfect health.

I received a letter from Elphinstone which has hurt me much. He is in a dangerous way and I am afraid we shall loose him. As he, poor fellow, is unable to write, and as Charles Pole is gone to France, let me

the Privy Council, wrote to Lord Hawkesbury on the 5th: 'The meetings of the new Government, I hear, are at the Duke of York's, and the Prince of Wales held a Cabinet last night at Brooks's. Lord Egremont told me he had left him there very busy, and full of importance and whispers' (Add. MSS. 38223, f. 289).

1. Frederick William, Prince of Nassau-Weilburg (1768-1816); succeeded his father, Charles Christian (1735-88) on 28 November. Charles Christian had married Caroline (1743-87), a sister of the Stadholder, William V of Orange.

beg of you to make some other person write, for I am very anxious to hear how things are likely to go with me. Frederick wrote me word you had been ill: the newspapers indeed first informed me. For God's sake my dear brother, do take care of yourself before it is too late: remember this is the second attack you have had. You will I am afraid accuse me of preaching: so I have done.

This country affords nothing worth relating. I have sent by the packet some fruit which I hope will arrive safe. In the proper season I shall convey home plenty of turtle, and have given directions respecting the rum. As I intend to go to Windward, I shall there procure the [*illegible*]. In ten days time I hope to sail and shall be out from six weeks to two months so that it will be some time before I can write again. As soon as you know anything certain respecting my destination, I hope you will have me informed. I do not expect you to write: engagements must naturally fill up your time. Remember my good friend Winne and poor Whitehead: he has now on my account been absent from his wife three years. I certainly owe him something and wish you would provide for him. Excuse me, dear brother, I can scarcely hold the pen any longer; so God bless you, and ever believe me [etc.]. (44852-3)

344   THE PRINCE OF WALES TO SIR GEORGE BAKER

[*? Soon after 5 Dec. 1788*]
As the Prince understands yt. Sir George Baker's tour of attendance calls him to Kew tomorrow, the Prince desires to receive a *circumstantial account* of what has happen'd to the King, & how he has been in the preceeding 24 hours from Sir George & the other attending physicians. Tho' the Prince forbears to expect particulars from Dr Willis, as he inform'd him by Dr. Warren, yet he insists upon *a full account* from the King's own physicians. The Prince expects from *Dr Willis only his general* opinion each day. (38350)

345   LORD LOUGHBOROUGH TO CAPTAIN J. W. PAYNE

Sunday morning [*?7 Dec. 1788*]
I send you an account of the proceedings of the three first days of an Accession, most of which are directed by the Act of Settlement. I have likewise traced out the idea of a declaration which no one could express so well as the great person who is to make it, could his mind at such a moment be sufficiently at ease to attend to words.

It seems to me of singular importance that this act should appear entirely his own. My intention was only to mark the topicks that enter into such a paper, but I could not do it clearly without putting it into form.

I beg you would burn the paper if it ceases to be of any use, for no one ought to know of this sort of communication.

I am ever yours.

P.S. You will see by some rasures that I am not satisfied altogether wth my own words. (38234)

346 RICHARD BRINSLEY SHERIDAN TO CAPTAIN J. W. PAYNE

Sunday, past twelve [?7 Dec. 1788]

Lord Loughborough call'd on me this morning, after having sent to Weltje for a servant to take the enclosed. It contains the *sketch* Ld L. mentioned. Something of the kind ought undoubtedly to be ready to be submitted to the Prince's consideration, tho' there is as little doubt that if his Royal Highness was composed enough he would dictate it better himself. Every syllable of *the Declaration* will be canvass'd, and all sorts of *meaning* discovered in every syllable. I think the Prince, if he adopts the enclosed, will alter parts & perhaps something might be added. Lord Loughborough has not only the best intentions and the greatest zeal for the Prince's service, and certainly no one can advise with better judgement in such matters—but I own I think the wording of this stiff, and not in the style which would answer what may be expected from the feelings which will be in the Prince's mind—at the same time it cannot be too general & safe. The mention of *agriculture* &c. is not usual nor good. Lord L. made some alterations at my suggestion, but I am sure you will understand how unpleasant a thing it is to find many faults in such a matter, and as it was before a third person I did not care to do it. At the same time I cannot help observing this much to you, as I really think it of the *utmost consequence* that this *first Royal communication* should be as correct and perfect as possible—& I wish, when the necessity comes, the Prince's own attention could be drawn to it. You see, my d^r Payne, I write without reserve to you, and I am sure no caution is necessary.

I am very much obliged to you for the fulness of your communication last night. I purposely avoid being in the way of people, that my name may not be entangled in any reports.

I have certain intelligence that measures are *already taking* to give a *particular complexion* to the Address which would immediately come from the City of London in case of a certain event, and I suppose the same game is preparing elsewhere. (41924-5)

347 THE PRINCE OF WALES'S DECLARATION [draft¹]

[*? before 7 Dec. 1788*]

Gentlemen, I thank you most cordially for the affectionate and loyal sentiments you have express'd respecting the situation of my Royal father. I assure you that the greatest consolation I feel in undertaking the arduous trust to which I am call'd is founded on the affectionate proofs I receive of the zeal and attachment of his subjects to his Majesty's royal person & family. It will ever be the first pride of my life to merit the continuance of their confidence & esteem & in every situation to act on those constitutional principles which you, gentlemen, so warmly aprove and which first placed the House of Brunswick on the throne of this kingdom. (38287)

348 THE EARL OF SANDWICH TO [?] CAPTAIN J. W. PAYNE

Monday night [*?c. 8 Dec. 1788*]

I think I have secured another friend to our cause who will do us credit, the person I mean is Sir Peter Parker²; he is to dine with me on Wednesday next. I wish you would meet him, as that would certainly fix him.³

Let me beg of you to tell me when I can see you; calling at my door without an appointment can never answer any purpose, & there are some things on which I wish to have a little conversation with you. (38297)

1. This draft is evidently in Sheridan's hand. It may be Sheridan's alternative to Loughborough's draft declaration to be made by the Prince to the Privy Council, and the enclosure referred to in the previous letter, No. 346.

2. Sir Peter Parker (1721-1811), M.P. for Seaford, 1784-6; for Maldon, 1787-90. Knighted 1772. Created Baronet, January 1783. Captain, R.N., 1747; Rear-Admiral, 1777; Vice-Admiral, 1779; Admiral, 1787.

3. He voted with the Prince's party on 16 December. The 8th therefore seems a reasonable date, and clearly the latest. The 1st seems less likely as Parliament was not then sitting, the adjournment being from 20 November to 4 December. On the 17th Grenville wrote: 'I was a little mortified at finding our friend Sir P.P. among these [those who voted against Ministers]. I had no previous intimation of this till I saw him in the division . . . I am not sure that he did not think he ought to have been a Lord of the Admiralty instead of Lord Hood. It is either that, or his intercourse with some of the Independents. On the whole I think it better to leave him to himself, as I do not think I have sufficient influence over him to do any good, and the attempt might do harm' (Buckingham, *Court and Cabinets of George III*, ii. 64). His having sided with the Prince in 1788-9 did not prove detrimental to him professionally. The King wrote to Lord Chatham, the First Lord of the Admiralty, on 7 April 1793: 'I trust Sir Peter Parker will make a good Port Admiral, having from his command at Jamaica been already practiced in the business. He will be engaged in at Portsmouth' (Chatham Papers, 364).

349 EDMUND BURKE TO CAPTAIN J. W. PAYNE

[*?8 or 9 Dec. 1788*]

May I beg the favour of seeing you with as many papers relative to the King's illness as may be of use (& most may be of use) for the examination of tomorrow.[1] Will D.ʳ Warren have any objection to my having half an hours conversation with him? On reflexion I had better not. But pray do you come hither. (38212)

350 THE PRINCE OF WALES TO THE LORD CHANCELLOR, AND THE REPLY

Carlton House, 9 Dec. 1788

I am just arriv'd from Kew & the Queen has desir'd me to acquaint you that her Majesty wishes much to see you tomorrow morning & to have some conversation with you. As the Queen is a very early riser your Lordship may safely go to Kew at ten o'clock, as she desir'd me to say that she would not stir out till she had seen you. I myself shall be happy to see your Lordship on Thursday morning, any hour before the House meets that may be convenient to yourself, & beg you will name the hour, as I am very desirous of having some particular conversation with you. (38322)

LORD THURLOW'S REPLY

Tuesday, 6.30 p.m. [9 Dec. 1788]

I will attend her Majesty at Kew to-morrow morning at ten. In obedience to your Royal Highness's commands, I presume to mention one o'clock, as the hour for waiting on your Royal Highness on Thursday. But, if it is your Royal Highness's pleasure to name any other hour, I will not fail of paying my duty to your Royal Highness at that time. (38323)

351 THE QUEEN TO THE PRINCE OF WALES

Kew, 9 Dec. 1788

Dr. Willis is returned not long ago from town, & obliged to return there tomorrow early. I beg therefore that you will prevent the Chancellor's

---

1. On 10 December Pitt presented to the House of Commons the Report from the Committee appointed to examine the King's physicians (*House of Commons Journal*, xliv.6).

comming down there, as the D^r wishes to wait upon him in town, which may be more convenient to the Chancellor.

I hope to hear that you did not suffer from your ride & that you continue better, which will be a pleasure to [etc.]. (36376)

352 THE LORD CHANCELLOR TO THE PRINCE OF WALES

8.30 a.m., 10 Dec. 1788
According to the Queen's pleasure signified by your Royal Highness I shall wait for her Majesty's farther orders to attend her at Kew.

In obedience to your Royal Highness's commands I will be at Carlton House at one o'clock to-morrow. (38324)

353 THE DUKE OF PORTLAND TO THE PRINCE OF WALES

Burlington House, 11.30 p.m., Wednesday 10 Dec. 1788
Conceiving, I hope not too presumptuously, that your Royal Highness might not be displeased to see the evidence of the physicians who were this day examined by a Committee of the Lords[1], I have procured a copy to be made of it, & humbly beg leave to offer it with all deference to your Royal Highness. (38325)

354 THE EARL OF SANDWICH TO CAPTAIN J. W. PAYNE

Thursday morning [? 10 Dec. 1788]
Be so good as to inform me at what hour tomorrow morning I am to have the honour to attend his Royal Highness's pleasure. I shall endeavour to see the Duke of Portland today upon other business, but shall avoid entering into anything that concerns myself till I first have a knowledge of his Royal Highness intentions.[2] Sir P. Parker dined with me yesterday & declared before all the company that for the future his political conduct should be guided by mine: he is much fixed, & as eager in our present cause as anyone among us.

1. See *Political Memoranda of Duke of Leeds*, p. 133.

2. Fox and Portland in effect vetoed Sandwich's nomination to the office of First Lord of the Admiralty. 'Sheridan ... tells me that the Prince has given up Lord Sandwich in the handsomest way in the world,' wrote the Duchess of Devonshire on the 12th. She added, 'Lord Sandwich has behaved very well.'

Ld Exeter[1] is gone out of town & has left me his proxy, but has told me that if I write him word that his personal attendance is necessary he will come up again upon the great question. (38231)

355   THE PRINCE OF WALES TO THE EARL OF LONSDALE [2]

Carlton House, 11 Dec. 1788
Having understood yt. you was indispos'd I did not think it right to call upon you, but therefore trouble you with this note merely to say yt. I will either call upon you, or expect you at my house any hour tomorrow or any other day yt. is most agreable to you. I am, my dear Lord, most sincerely yrs. (Lonsdale MSS.)

356   EDMUND BURKE'S SKETCH OF A NOTE TO PITT

[? *Shortly before 12 Dec. 1788*]
The Pr. learns from general & uncontradicted report that Mr. Pitt intends to make certain propositions in the House of Commons relative to the office of Regent or to some office of a similar description which, during the present melancholy state of the King or for some other term, is to be held by the Prince, with various limitations & restrictions in the exercise of the functions of government.

The Prince delivers no opinion on the merits of this project to Mr. Pitt, but lest Mr. Pitt should be led to produce such a scheme, upon a supposition that the Prince is willing to lend himself to it, or lest such a proposition, coming from a Minister of State, might be supposed by

1. Brownlow, 9th Earl of Exeter (1725-93) succeeded his father as Earl in 1754. He supported the Fox-North Coalition, and voted with the Whigs against the Regency Bill.

2. Sir James Lowther, 1st Earl of Lonsdale (1736-1807); succeeded his second cousin as 5th Baronet [S.], 1751. M.P. for Cumberland, 1757-61, 1762-8 and 1774-84; for Westmorland, 1761-2; for Cockermouth, 1769-74. Created Viscount of Lonsdale and Earl of Lonsdale, May 1784 (having first brought Pitt into Parliament and given him the powerful support of his borough influence); created Viscount Lowther, with special remainder to his cousin, Sir William Lowther, 1797. 'Capricious, tyrannical, and sustained by an immense property, chiefly situate in the counties of Cumberland and Westmorland, he expended vast sums in election contests . . . Lord Lonsdale regularly brought in from five or six up to eight members of Parliament, among whom were three Lowthers; and he was known to exercise over his nominees an active superintendence' (*Wraxall*, iii. 358). There were four Lowthers in the Commons in 1783, including Sir James, and his little group numbered eight. Grenville said on the 9th that Lonsdale's attitude was 'still uncertain' (Buckingham, *Court and Cabinets of George III*, ii. 41).

others a presumption of the Prince's previous acquiescence in it, the Prince gives notice to Mr. Pitt that he does not acquiesce in his (the Prince's) being held forth as any part of the projected Government in the manner & on the terms as herein described.

Mr. Pitt is given to understand that the Prince is firmly resolved never to undertake the office of Regent or other similar office (for the term during wch. only he would undertake it, during the incapacity of his father) under any other limitations than those wise & salutary limitations & restrictions which, for the preservation of the laws, rights & liberties of the subject, the Constitution of this country has imposed upon the Crown; & that he never will accept the trust of preserving the King's power without having the means of restoring it to him in as good a condition as he found it.[1] (38421)

357 THE EARL OF SANDWICH TO CAPTAIN J. W. PAYNE

Hertford Street, 13 Dec. 1788

May I beg to inform H.R.H. that I have written to the D. of Portland to inform him that I am perfectly satisfied with the intended arrangement, as I shall ever be with whatever is thought adviseable by my great protector.[2]

I intend allso to call on Ld Fitzwilliam[3] & say everything to him that is proper upon this occasion.

In my letter to the Duke of Portland I have entered something at large into Ld Hinchingbrook's[4] case. It would be troublesome to you if I

1. The following fragment is also by Burke: 'At the beginning of this extraordinary & unprecedented plan I went as far as I could go in supplicating yr. Lordships to avoid a resolution wch. I then considered as originating from unfaithful dispositions towards his Majesty & malevolent designs towards his family, & wh. certainly was not called for by the assertion of any claim either on the part of the Prince, my brother, or on mine.

'Yr. Lordships undoubtedly looked upon the matter in another light, else you wd. not have come to that resolution. I do not call it into question. The Bill now before you is wholly unconnected with it.' (38422)

2. The Prince had promised him the Cabinet office of First Lord of the Admiralty. 'Both the Duke of Portland and Charles [Fox] refuse to have anything to do with it in that case,' wrote the Duchess of Devonshire.

3. William, 2nd Earl Fitzwilliam (1748-1833). Succeeded (1782) to the vast estates of the Wentworth family in Yorkshire and Wicklow, on the death of his maternal uncle, the Marquess of Rockingham. Lord President of the Council, July-December 1794, and February-October 1806; Lord-Lieutenant of Ireland, December 1794-March 1795. Lord-Lieutenant of the West Riding of Yorkshire, 1798-1819.

4. Viscount Hinchingbrooke (1744-1814), so styled until he succeeded his father as 5th Earl of Sandwich in 1792. M.P. for Huntingdonshire, 1768-92; Master of the King's Buckhounds, 1783-1806, and Joint Postmaster-General, 1807-14.

was to recapitulate what I have there said, but I think I have used some arguments that will make an impression, & if H.R.H. would throw in a few words in favour of them, I think I should carry my point. The short of this is, that if he loses his employment, he and his family will be distressed beyond measure, and it will throw some very unpleasant obstacles in my way of managing the county in the manner I could wish to do.[1]

I allso mentioned the Lieutenancy of the County, which surely ought to be put into my hands as soon as possible. I am told that Addresses in favour of Pitt will be attempted every where where impression can be made; & in the divided state of Huntingdonshire the appearance at the publick meetings of an active Lord Lieutenant who is used to business of that sort, will give great weight to the party we mean should predominate.

I will now trouble you no farther than to ask the hour of our dinner tomorrow. H.R.H. talked of five but I suppose he does not mean to abide by that declaration. (38328-9)

358   THE PRINCE OF WALES TO THE EARL OF LONSDALE

Carlton House, 13 Dec. 1788

As it is probable that the unfortunate circumstance of your Lordship's indisposition may prevent my having the pleasure of seeing you before Tuesday, I take this method of expressing my earnest hope that your Lordship's friendship to me will induce you to discountenance any proposition wh. may be brought forward with a view *to insult & arraign my character & conduct.*

It is in this light I most sincerely[2] assure your Lordship I regard Mr. Pitt's determination to press for a decision[3] on *a claim [which]*[4] *I have not preferr'd* & ye. discussion of wh. is both painful & injurious to me, & wholly unnecessary [to any][4] if not detrimental to the publick good.[5] I am, my dear Lord, most sincerely yours. (Lonsdale MSS and 38291[6])

1. Lord Sandwich and the Duke of Manchester each had an influence strong enough in Huntingdonshire to secure the return of one county Member. Lord Hinchingbrooke, as a placeman who could not afford to resign and go with his father, necessarily voted with the Government on the Regency; Lord Ludlow, the other county member, voted against.

2. 'seriously' in 38291.   3. 'division' in 38291.

4. The words within square brackets are in 38291. After 'which', the words 'I conceive to be' are deleted from 38291.

5. The following words originally concluded the sentence: 'any good public object' (38291).

6. The draft (38291) seems to be in Sheridan's hand.

Dr. Richard Warren
by Gainsborough

Prince William
by Cosway

Prince Edward
by Cosway

THE PRINCE OF WALES TO THE EARL OF LONSDALE [1]

[*? 14 Dec. 1788*]

The Prince conceives the *pressing a decision* on the *question of right* to be personally injurious and insulting to him, and any opportunity taken of discountenancing that proceeding will be considered as a decisive act of friendship to the Prince.

The Prince most readily acquiesces in every measure that is necessary to secure the King's repossession of the Government on the return of his health, as he conceives that as absolutely necessary, but hopes that no measures not necessary to that object, but which may tend to weaken and distract his Government at a crisis when every support is necessary, will be pursued by anyone who professes not to have a personal distrust of him, but expects *or* [2] *at least* that no limitations or restrictions whatever will be exacted as the *conditions* of Parliament's consenting to his being placed in the Regency.

The custody of the King's person, and the power of making the most liberal and respectful appointments for attendance on his Majesty is an object which the Prince expressly wishes to be in the hands of others. [3]

360 THE QUEEN TO THE PRINCE OF WALES, AND THE REPLY

Kew House, Sunday 14 Dec. 1788

I cannot make my mind easy after our conversation, which agitated me so much that I have hardly words to express it, & for fear I should not have stated my meaning sufficiently strong, I must beg to repeat *that I most earnestly desire that neither yourself nor your brother will make use of my name in any shape or upon any occasion whatever*. Nothing but the promise of that by an answer to this can or will ease my agitated mind.

The servant has orders to wait for the answer. (41907)

1. This document (a draft) was purchased by the Royal Archives in 1955. It is in Sheridan's hand. The following is a shorter version (38295):

'The Prince conceives the pressing a decision on the question of right to be personally injurious and insulting to him, & any opportunity of discountenancing that proceeding will be considered as a decisive act of friendship to the Prince.

'The Prince most readily acquiesces in every measure that is necessary to secure the King's repossession of the Government on the return of his health, as he conceives that as absolutely necessary, but expects that no limitations or restrictions whatever will be exacted as the conditions of Parliament's consenting to his being Regent.'

2. 'But expects' is a correction, and '*or*' should have been scored through.

3. The following undated and unsigned fragment (38365) is a copy of part of one of Lord Lonsdale's letters: 'That his Royal Highness may be assured that in any question which may affect or insult his character & conduct in the least degree as far as I can discountenance or avert, shall be done, and I shall desire Sir W. Lowther to speak to my friends for that purpose.'

THE PRINCE OF WALES'S REPLY

Carlton House, 8.30 p.m., Sunday, 13 [14] Dec. 1788

I have this instant receiv'd the honor of your letter, & as it is the sincerest wish of both my brother as well as myself yt. you shd. enjoy every comfort possible, & as certainly there is none in this world yt. can be greater than perfect quiet, we take ye. liberty with all duty to assure your Majesty *that we never will suffer your name to be introduc'd by our authority, in any place, or for any purpose* whatever. I hope this answer will in every respect prove ye. dutiful attachment with wh. I have ye. honor to subscribe myself [etc.].   (41908-9 [draft], and 41910)

361   LETTERS FROM THE PRINCE OF WALES
      TO THE LORD CHANCELLOR [copy]

[*5 Dec. 1788*]

I find Mr Pitt has declared his intention of proposing my being sole Regent under certain conditions which he is to lay before Parliament on Tuesday next. Mr Pitt's whole conduct towards me since the commencement of these unfortunate circumstances which have made any new settlement necessary has been such as to render it not surprising to me that he should think it decent and proper to announce to Parliament his intentions respecting my future situation, without my having received the slightest previous communication on the subject. Thinking, however, that I am entitled to a different treatment, I have to request of your Lordship that you will require from Mr Pitt the outline of that plan in which he proposes to involve my name, and in which I must on so many accounts be so nearly & deeply interested. It is my desire that this communication from Mr Pitt should be made to me in writing and if any explanations are necessary I shall be ready to receive them thro your Lordship.[1] (38333-4)

Carlton House, 14[2] [?15] Dec. 1788

I will not trouble you with many words at the present moment, therefore will immediately come to the point, which [is] that if you do not find it contradictory to your own mode of thinking I wish most sincerely you would deprecate the idea of bringing the question of right to a division

1. 'A very haughty letter,' commented Grenville on the 15th (Buckingham, *Court and Cabinets of George III*, ii. 60). There is a copy in P.R.O., Chatham Papers, 181, and one in Add. MSS. 28063, f. 332, where the date was altered from the 15th to the 14th (which seems to be more appropriate).

2. Clearly a slip; the 14th was a Sunday.

418

in either House, as considering it in the light of a question of infinite delicacy & perhaps conveying with it a most serious as well as dangerous tendency. Should this meet with yr. approbation & should you express your sentiments to this effect this day in the House of Peers I shall consider it as a personal obligation confer'd upon me.[1] (38330)

362 WILLIAM PITT TO THE PRINCE OF WALES

Downing Street, Monday, 15 Dec. 1788

The Lord Chancellor delivered to me last night a letter which he had received from your Royal Highness, from the contents of which I have the unhappiness to perceive that both my general conduct and what I have said in the House of Commons has been represented to your Royal Highness in a light which I flatter myself neither of them deserve. Nothing could give me more concern than to be thought to take any step inconsistent with the deference and respect which I owe to your Royal Highness. But I am not conscious of any conduct towards your Royal Highness during the present unfortunate circumstances, or at any former period, which has not been dictated by those sentiments, as well as by my invariable attachment and duty to his Majesty. I have certainly felt myself bound rather to wait the commands of your Royal Highness than to intrude on your Royal Highness's time, without having received a previous intimation of your pleasure. At the same time your Royal

1. During the debate in the Lords on Monday the 15th, Thurlow said he was 'averse to the discussion of unnecessary questions' (*Parliamentary Register*, xxvi. 34). Instigated probably by the Prince, Sheridan had a five-hour interview with Thurlow on the 14th. Sheridan reported that although the Chancellor had committed himself so far as the restrictions were concerned, 'he would be with us as far as he could', and that, next day, he should 'speak against the House dividing on the right'. Sheridan asked him what would be done if the Prince refused the limited Regency. 'Appoint Lords Justices,' was the reply. 'And pray,' Sheridan rejoined, 'do you consider when the Prince does come to the Crown what will become of your head?' 'They may hang the Chancellor,' Thurlow replied, 'but the law can't alter.' Sheridan declared that if Lords Justices were appointed, it would end in a civil war, and Dr. Warren thought that the decisive battle would be fought at Barnet!

One of the Duke of Dorset's correspondents wrote, whilst the debate was still in progress: 'The Opposition, to prevent the passing this question, have moved that the Chairman leave the Chair and report a progress. Their view in this is to obtain the votes of several members, particularly of what is called the Armed Neutrality, who will not vote against the question if put, but are of opinion that the question should not be put, and they want to reject all former precedents which are universally against the claims of the Prince. At a quarter past 9 Mr. Pitt and the Master of the Rolls had spoken in support of Government, and Lord North, Mr. Bastard, member for Devonshire, Mr. Powis of Northamptonshire, and Mr. Loveden of Abingdon, had spoken against the present Government. It is supposed by Government that if all the Armed Neutrality join the Opposition on this question, they may divide 203, and that Government will have about 300 in their favour.'

Highness will permit me to recall to your recollection that I more than once had an opportunity humbly to express my readiness at all times to attend your Royal Highness, and have several times at Windsor had the honor to enquire whether your Royal Highness had any orders for me, and have received for answer that you had not. I should, however, in common with the rest of his Majesty's servants have felt it incumbent on me, before any specifick plan was brought forward in Parliament, to request your Royal Highness's permission humbly to submit it to your consideration.

With regard to what I have said in the House of Commons, altho' I am satisfied that if what passed in the debate had been faithfully related to your Royal Highness, you would have formed a very different judgment upon it, I nevertheless do not think myself at liberty, even in my own justification, to state to your Royal Highness the particulars of the language used by any other Member. But I must beg leave respectfully to assure your Royal Highness that I did not declare an intention (as your Royal Highness appears to have been informed) to lay before the House on Tuesday next the particulars of such a plan as the present circumstances may require. The Motion of which I gave notice for that day relates to the question of the right of Parliament to take the measures which may be necessary and proper in the present conjuncture. At the same time, from the circumstances in the debate (to which I beg leave only to refer generally) I found it unavoidable to enter in some degree into my general ideas of the outline of the plan proper to be adopted; which (if those circumstances had not occurred) I certainly should not have stated at all, till I was enabled to do so with more detail, and till I had previously asked your Royal Highness's permission to submit them to your consideration. Those ideas were in substance, that it was in my opinion highly desireable that whatever portion of Royal authority might appear necessary to be exercised during the present unhappy interval, should be vested in your Royal Highness. That it should be exercised by your Royal Highness, unrestrained by any permanent Council, and with the free choice of the political servants to act under your Royal Highness. Precisely what portion of Royal authority ought to be given, and what ought to be withheld I conceived it would be improper then particularly to discuss, but I added in general terms the principle on which in my opinion the distinction ought to be made, with a view to the exigency of the public service during the present interval, and to the situation of the King when his Majesty should be enabled to resume the personal exercise of the Government. Until the question of right should have been considered, I expressed my wish to abstain from going into any farther particulars, especially as, if the determination of the House should be contrary to the opinion which I thought it my duty to state on that subject, it would preclude me from bringing forward the propositions which I should otherwise have to lay before them. Under these circumstances I must entreat your Royal Highness's permission not to enter at present into any farther detail of the measures to be grounded upon the principles which I have stated. If I should be fortunate enough to find the sentiments which I entertain respecting the right of Parliament sanctioned by the determination of the House, I shall think myself highly honored, in the farther progress of this business, in being permitted, according to the wish & intention which I have always entertained in conjunction with the rest of his Majesty's servants, to submit to your Royal Highness as explicitly as possible the best opinions which we find ourselves enabled to form respecting the specifick measures to be proposed for the consideration of Parliament.[1] (38335-40)

363   THE EARL OF LONSDALE TO THE PRINCE OF WALES

[*?15 Dec. 1788*]

Since the receipt of the last letter which Lord Lonsdale has been honor'd with from H.R.H. he has been considering & turning over in his mind every possible thought of means to meet what might be agreeable to his R.H.'s wish as express'd in that letter.

He therefore submits the following to H.R.H.'s consideration.

Whether it would not be adviseable for H.R.H. to send the following to the House of Commons tomorrow, either by Message to be delivered at the Bar the moment the House meets, or to be communicated to the House by a letter to the Speaker, saying, that in the present melancholy situation how very desirous H.R.H. is that everything should be carried

---

1. Pitt's second Resolution, moved in Committee of the House on Tuesday, 16 December, was the controversial one (the second paragraph constituted what became known as the Third Resolution):

'That it is the opinion of this Committee that it is the right and duty of the Lords Spiritual and Temporal and Commons of Great Britain, now assembled, and lawfully, fully and freely representing all the Estates of the people of this Realm, to provide the means of supplying the defect of the personal exercise of the Royal authority, arising from his Majesty's said indisposition, in such manner as the exigency of the case may appear to require.

'Resolved, That for this purpose, and for maintaining entire the constitutional authority of the King, it is necessary that the said Lords Spiritual and Temporal and Commons of Great Britain, should determine on the means whereby the Royal assent may be given in Parliament to such Bill as may be passed by the two Houses of Parliament, respecting the exercise of the powers and authorities of the Crown, in the name, and on the behalf, of the King, during the continuance of his Majesty's present indisposition' (*Parliamentary Register*, xxv. 61). Grenville said on the 17th that he had been employed 'very near the whole of two days' in settling the wording with Pitt and the lawyers, Amongst whom was Kenyon, the Lord Chief Justice, who wrote in his Diary on the 14th: 'I was at Mr. Pitt's to meet some of the Cabinet about the Motion to be made on Tuesday in the House of Commons.' (Kenyon MSS.)

on for the benefit & welfare of the nation—that it is his earnest wish there should be entire harmony on this occasion—and as he has reason to beleive it is the wish of the people in general that he should be Regent, he could wish to have such a communication with that honourable House for the carrying into execution & setling matters in such a manner as may conduce to the welfare & prosperity of the people.

Lord Lonsdale further proposes that a Member of the House should immediately after the letter or Message is read by the Speaker, get up & move for a Committee of the whole House to take the same into consideration—& in that Committee the same Member to move that a Committee be appointed, consisting of a few Members, either to confer with H.R.H. or such persons as H.R.H. shall appoint—& it is further proposed that in case any person of any kind should offer any extraneous matter, for that to be taken up with a high hand as tending to disturb every prospect of peace & quietness, & for the previous question to be moved upon it.

Lord Lonsdale flatters himself that this may stop any improper expressions which may proceed from the misguided zeal of any party, & will avert impertinence which may proceed from the folly of any individual—& Lord Lonsdale submits it to H.R.H. whether it would not be better for Sir W. Lowther[1] to communicate these thoughts, as from Lord Lonsdale himself to Mr Pitt, & receive his answer upon them, rather than leave it to the meeting of the House, when from ignorance of what was going to be done, a bustle & noise might ensue, which would prevent that quiet so much wish'd for.

If the above should meet H.R.H. approbation, Sir W. Lowther & his brother[2] will have the honor to move it in the House as has been requested by Lord Lonsdale—and Lord Lonsdale flatters himself this may tend to the comfort & satisfaction of the Prince & people.[3] (38412-3)

1. Sir William Lowther, Lord Lonsdale's cousin (1757-1844). M.P. for Carlisle, 1780-4; for Cumberland, 1784-90; for Rutland, 1796-1802. Succeeded to his cousin's viscountcy, 1802; created Earl of Lonsdale, April 1807. He was a staunch supporter of Pitt, to whom he wrote on 19 January 1789: 'I desired my brother to explain to you the cause of my absence on the late important occasion—but I cannot refrain congratulating you on your success in the House of Commons & on the sense the whole nation seems to entertain of your conduct. It is a matter of serious concern to me that Lord L. should have adopted sentiments in which I cannot possibly coincide. I consider it as a great misfortune that the particular circumstances of my connection with the person to whom I am indebted for my parliamentary situation, have placed me in this predicament, but you may rest assured, (however unimportant it is), of my firm attachment to you, & tho' it may not, under my present circumstances, be in my power to render you the service I wish, yet I beg to assure you I shall always remain [etc.]' (P.R.O., Chatham Papers, 153).

2. Sir John Lowther (1759-1844). M.P. for Cockermouth, 1780-6; for Carlisle, 1786, for Haslemere, 1786-90; for Cumberland, 1796-1831. Created Baronet, 1824.

3. This suggested procedure was not followed. Neither Sir William Lowther nor his brother is reported to have spoken at all during the Regency crisis.

422

[*?16 Dec. 1788*]

You may easily conceive y^t I am excessively anxious on ye event of ye day. What are y^r apprehensions about numbers? For God's sake explain yourself, *who is false*, who is staunch, *who deceive us, pray remark w^l you*, & for Heaven's sake send me word & relieve my uneasiness. Do you think y^t any of the 247[1] will desert us, or y^t most of ye doubtful are against us? Pray send word immediately. God bless you.

Do you think ye previous question will pass? The Goulds, Sir Charles[2] & his son[3] will vote as well as Morgan[4]. Will the Lonsdales vote sure?[5] (41709)

1. Possibly 249: the figure is not clear. This does not refer to the number of votes recorded in any particular division; it must merely be a considered estimate of the strength of the anti-Government vote on this question of right (approximately this number of M.P.s attended an Opposition meeting at Burlington House on the night of Sunday the 14th [*The Times*, 16 December]).

2. Sir Charles Gould (later, 1792, Morgan) (1726-1806). M.P. for Brecon borough 1778-87; for Breconshire, 1787-1806. Judge Advocate-General, 1771-1806. Knighted, 1779; created Baronet, 1792. 'His inclinations, his principles and his official employment,' declared Wraxall, 'all impelled him to support Administration. But he was brought into the House of Commons as member for the county of Brecon by the Morgan interest, and Pitt having offended that family in order to oblige the Duke of Beaufort, Gould, who beheld himself the probable heir to their vast property, quitted the Minister on some questions to follow his brother-in-law into opposition. Such was the secret history of his defection, at which the King expressed so much astonishment. . . . He . . . never could succeed in attaining the grand object of his ambition—a British peerage. Pitt created him, indeed, a Baronet in 1792. He supplicated, implored, offered to resign his employment of Judge Advocate General, and exerted during many successive years every effort in order to conciliate the Minister. Pitt remained, however inflexible, and Sir Charles died a commoner' (v. 329-30).

3. Sir Charles Gould (later, 1792, Morgan) (1760-1846). M.P. for Brecon borough, 1787-96; for Monmouthshire, 1796-1831. Succeeded to the baronetcy, 1806. In 1792 his mother inherited the estate of her brother, John Morgan: hence the change of surname that year.

4. John Morgan (1732-92). M.P. for Brecon borough, 1769-71; for Monmouthshire, 1771-92.

5. The inference is that the letter was written before the first division on the Regency—on the 16th, the numbers being 268 v. 204. According to *The Times* over 500 were present and about 50 paired off before the division (this may well have been the case, though the names of only eight members who paired off are given in *Parliamentary Register*, xxv. 95. It was said that 517 members were known to be in town—'a greater number than at any time since the King's accession.'

The Duchess of Devonshire was one of those who shared the Prince's extreme anxiety about the outcome of the debate on the 16th. 'We sat up till 4 to hear the result. . . .We had been kept in anxiety the whole day, and I had a terrible headache, yet would not go to bed. At 3 the Duke of Bedford and my brother came like Priam's messengers, and told us our defeat. This did not make me better.' She added: 'I hope Mr. Pitt will offer limitations the Prince can accept, otherways what will be the event of Lords Justices &c. having the Government and the Prince and Duke of York kept out?' (Chatsworth MSS).

17 Dec. 1788]

The Prince of Wales was sorry to learn at Lord Lonsdale's door that he still continued unwell, & upon which he feels additional concern in not being able to express to him in person the real pleasure he derives from finding that every occasion that presents itself is but an additional proof of the sincerity & friendship of Lord Lonsdale's attachment to him & which he shall never forget.

[*Lower on same page, in another hand*]

I was extremely sorry to learn at yr. door yt. you still continued so unwell, especially as I wish'd much to have an opportunity of expressing to you in person, the real comfort & pleasure I feel at finding that every occasion yt. presents itself is but an additional proof of yt sincere friendship & firm support I have always experienced from you upon all occasions & wh. I assure you I never shall forget.[1] (38294)

366 THE PRINCE OF WALES TO RICHARD BRINSLEY SHERIDAN

St. James's Street, 5 p.m. [*?c. 18 Dec. 1788*]

Charles[2] has just receiv'd a note from Sir John Sinclair[3] saying yt. he has just receiv'd a letter from Dempster relative to how they were to concert the bringing in *his* Amendment to the Address yt. is to be

1. The letter which Lord Lonsdale received, dated 17 December, ran as follows:
'My dear Lord,

I was extremely sorry to learn at your door this morning that you still continued so unwell, especially as I wish'd much to have an opportunity [of] expressing to you in person the *real* comfort & pleasure I feel at finding that every occasion which presents itself is but an additional proof of that *sincere friendship & firm support* I have always experienced from you upon all occasions, & which I assure you I never shall forget' (Lonsdale MSS.).

Grenville wrote on the 17th: 'Lonsdale's people were against us, in consequence of a letter written by the Prince of Wales himself, soliciting it as a personal favour. This, which I know *from authority*, may serve to give you an idea of the pains they had taken. They were so confident, that, on Sunday night, Fox assured the whole party, at a general meeting at Burlington House, that he had no doubt of beating us' (Buckingham, *Court and Cabinets of George III*, ii. 64).

In the first division on the 22nd the Lonsdales voted with the Prince's party, and stayed away on the second division (Buckingham, *Court and Cabinets of George III*, ii. 83).

2. Fox.

3. M.P. for Caithness-shire, 1780-4, 1790-6, 1802-6, 1807-11; for Lostwithiel, 1784-90; for Petersfield, 1797-1802. Created Baronet, 1786. He was the first President of the Board of Agriculture. He was an LL.D. of Glasgow University, but Sir Walter Scott, evidently prejudiced against him, described him as an 'unutterable idiot', a 'booby of a Baronet' (Sir Walter Scott, *Journal*, i.229).

moved by Sir John, or Sir John's Amendment into the Address yt. Dempster¹ mov'd, neither Charles nor I quite comprehend from Sir John's note wh. of the two he means. He ends his note by saying yt. he will call upon Charles any time this evening yt. is most agreable to him. Charles is not well enough to see him & therefore wishes you immediately to write him a note saying yt. he had receiv'd Sir John's note, yt. he was very sorry he neither was well enough to answer his letter nor to have ye. pleasure of seeing him; yt. therefore you write to him & wd. have ye. pleasure of seeing him any time he wd. call upon you, or else yt. you wd. call upon him *this evening*, as attention, & ye. greatest too, is absolutely necessary at the present moment. I am, dear Sheridan, ever sincerely yrs. (Add. MSS. Georgian/3, f.5)

367 THE LORD CHANCELLOR TO THE PRINCE OF WALES

19 Dec. 1788
Your Royal Highness has mentioned twelve o'clock, in terms which make me imagine it may be indifferent in point of convenience to your Royal Highness. Upon that I have presumed to suggest to your Royal Highness, not my own convenience but that of a great many persons who will be attending on the Seal at that hour. But I presume to make this suggestion only on the idea that the hour of twelve was indifferent. I can adjourn the suitors, and I will wait on your Royal Highness at any hour you will be pleased to appoint. (38345)

Lincoln's Inn Hall, 19 Dec. 1788
I am extreamly mortified at having given your Royal Highness so much trouble. I will wait on your Royal Highness the moment I can leave this Court. (38346)

368 HINTS ON THE REGENCY [unsigned]

20 Dec. 1788
What I mentioned yesterday has actually turned out to be the case. Mr. P-tt declared in the House last night² that it is his intention to propose

1. On 19 December Dempster moved an Amendment to the Second Resolution. George Dempster (1732-1818) was M.P. for the Perth Burghs, 1761-8, 1769-90, and a Director of the East India Company.

2. *Parliamentary Register*, xxv. 98.

that the two Houses of Parliament shall appoint Commissioners under the Great Seal in the King's name to open the Session; that as soon as the Session is *so opened* a Bill shall be brought in appointing a Regent, and specifying such portions of the Royal authority as shall be proper to be conferred on such Regent. I, *privately*, understand that the Act will be limited in point of time to *one year*. This mode of *resuscitating* the regal authority is, in consequence of the opinion of Councillor Hargrave, a *connoisseur* in musty records and *old seals*.

Unprecedented as this manner of holding Parliaments may be, the getting possession of a *right* which is held from one, by force, would induce me to overlook forms. When once power is obtained matters may be *legalized* and informalities be rectified. The business of Monday will, in my opinion, require much circumspection. A Motion was made, not by one of the soundest heads, that the latter words of P-tt's *third Motion* should be left out and others nominating the Prince of Wales Regent be inserted.[1] Is there not much danger in this precipitate mode of proceeding? Are the troops *numerous* enough to come, at once, to the decisive battle on which the fate of *a kingdom* depends? Will not the losing such a question be attended with fatal consequences? Will P^{tt} if he finds he has a majority, suffer it to be withdrawn? Are they not all on the watch for precipitation, error or imprudence? What if some *understrapper* should *amend* the *Amendment* by inserting the Q—n's instead of the P—ce's name? Would Mr. D[und]as permit Mr. P-tt, notwithstanding he is pledged to nominate the P—ce, in his own way, to oppose such *Amendment*? If it should be put and carried—*de republica actum foret*.

What would, in such case, remain to be done? The people, though generally right in the end, are slow in comprehension. An appeal to them in the present state of opinions would be vain and fruitless! Had even the Prince of Orange[2] appealed to the people when the House of Commons appeared hostile, amusing themselves with idle declamations on abstract questions, he would have found them deaf to his remonstrances. He must have either have returned like a good, peaceable man to Holland, or have mounted the throne as *autocrator* [*sic*] at the head of his Dutch and Scotch Guards. He was too wise to do any such thing. He complained of the conduct of the two Houses, but he had *resolved in private* to accept the boon they were to give *in their own way*. He knew

---

1. George Dempster, M.P. for the Perth group of boroughs, moved an Amendment to the Third Resolution (see page 421*n*, paragraph two of the Resolution), leaving out the words following 'determine' and substituting the following: 'humbly to address his Royal Highness the Prince of Wales, to take the care of the Administration of the civil and military Government of the Kingdom, during the continuance of his Majesty's indisposition, and no longer.' (*Parliamentary Register*, xxv. 124-25)

2. Who became King William III at the Revolution.

that authority gathers power in its progress and increases in its size; like a snowball the further it is rolled along the bigger it grows.

I would let Mr. P. proceed in his own way. He is pledged to nominate the Prince. Let me once have that nomination *ex septo dentium* and I will combat with him his limitations and negative all that is necessary of them with a high hand. Until the nomination is made many will fear the uncertainty of the times, but once it is made they will come over like a flock of sheep. My advice would be to let the question alone—if *they* will consent to its being withdrawn; if they will not, I would not divide upon it. If *they* will *insist* upon a division to shew their friends without doors their strength, I would have some *capital friends* of the P——ce vote with them to shew that this is not a trial of the force of parties.

I was told by one of the other side that the Lords boggled about imposing limitations. This may be a fetch to mislead, but be that as it may if the P——ce is once nominated the limitations will be so triffling that they may be easily borne.

I may perhaps have written much nonsense upon the matter, but as these thoughts occurred to my mind I could not avoid committing them to paper.

D——s plays the whole game, like a desperate gambler at his last stake! Beware of every thing—sic notus Ulysses! Beware of a certain quarter; no assurances of non-acceptance are a thorough security. There is something so dazzling in power that even *a woman's firmness* cannot withstand the temptation. Accept and shut the door at once. The ὁ μέγιστος αἰών *maximum rerum tempus* will do everything.[1] (38348–9)

369 RICHARD BRINSLEY SHERIDAN TO CAPTAIN J. W. PAYNE

Sunday night [*?21 or 28 Dec. 1788*]

I executed the Prince's commission tonight and left Lord Loughborough highly gratified. He is extremely fair, and I think there are some things he wishes to say which the Prince will be pleased with. He will wait on his R.H. tomorrow at two o'clock. Pray enquire if that hour is convenient, and convey the Prince's pleasure to him if it should not.

There is going to be a ministerial meeting at Manchester which will certainly be defeated.[2] (38374)

1. Nos. 379 and 384 are in the same hand.

2. On Tuesday, 30 December, there was held a general meeting of the inhabitants of Manchester, to consider the idea of presenting an address of thanks to Pitt 'for his disinterested spirit and constitutional conduct in general, and to congratulate him upon the large majority recently in the House of Commons.' Confusion prevailed at the meeting, which was dissolved by the Boroughreeve and Constables without the taking of a decision (*The Manchester Mercury*, 13 January 1789).

[*? Shortly before 23 Dec. 1788*]

It is with the greatest deference and submission that Lord Lonsdale gives his opinion—nor should he presume to do it but under his Royal Highness's commands.

Lord Lonsdale does not see what it will avail, or what advantage his Royal Highness can receive from the Motion of the Address being renew'd, as he conceives that the Members who have voted upon the former Motion[1] will think themselves pledg'd to vote the same way upon this occasion—besides Motions which have been once brought forward, being again repeated, retards matters agreable to the suppos'd wish of the present Administration.

But if the time that such Motions take up is not thought by his Royal Highness to cause too much delay, he would beg leave again to offer for his Royal Highness's consideration whether this would not be a proper moment for a Message from his Royal Highness to the two Houses in manner & form as before suggested by Lord Lonsdale.[2] It would prevent all disagreable debates—and Lord Lonsdale trusts and thinks, that it would be the means & cause of producing a happy effect.[3] (38414)

371 WILLIAM PITT TO THE PRINCE OF WALES

Downing Street, Tuesday night, 30 Dec. 1788

The proceedings in Parliament being now brought to a point which will render it necessary to propose to the House of Commons the particular measures to be taken to supplying the defect of the personal exercise of the royal authority during the present interval, and your Royal Highness having some time since signified your pleasure that any communication on this subject should be in writing[4], I take the liberty of respectfully entreating your Royal Highness's permission to submit to your consideration the outlines of the plan which his

---

1. On 16 December, when, on the question of the Prince of Wales's inherent right to the Regency, his friends were defeated by the unexpectedly large majority of 64. The division list is in *Parliamentary Register*, xxv. 90.

2. No. 363.

3. After midnight on 22 December the Government had an increased majority of 73, the numbers being 251 *v.* 178. 'We had expected to have a much better division than on the former day', wrote Sir Gilbert Elliot, 'which increases the disappointment.' He added, 'Pitt will now certainly carry his restrictions. We don't know with certainty what they will be, but heavy enough, no doubt, and the intention will be to make them such as shall prevent the Prince from carrying a Government without him.'

4. See 361, 15 December.

Majesty's confidential servants humbly conceive (according to the best judgment which they are able to form) to be proper to be proposed in the present circumstances.

It is their humble opinion that your Royal Highness should be empowered to exercise the royal authority in the name and on behalf of his Majesty, during his Majesty's illness, and to do all acts which might legally be done by his Majesty, with provisions nevertheless that the care of his Majesty's royal person and the management of his Majesty's Household and the direction and appointment of the officers and servants therein should be in the Queen, under such regulations as may be thought necessary. That the power to be exercised by your Royal Highness should not extend to the granting the real or personal property of the King (except as far as relates to the renewal of leases), to the granting any office in reversion or to the granting for any other term than during his Majesty's pleasure any pension or any office whatever except such as must by law be granted for life or during good behaviour, nor to the granting any rank or dignity of the peerage of this realm to any person except his Majesty's royal issue who shall have attained the age of twenty one years. These are the chief points which have occurred to his Majesty's servants. I beg leave to add that their ideas are formed on the supposition that his Majesty's illness is only temporary and may be of no long duration. It may be difficult to fix beforehand the precise period for which these provisions ought to last, but if unfortunately his Majesty's recovery should be protracted to a more distant period than there is at present reason to imagine, it will be open hereafter to the wisdom of Parliament to reconsider these provisions whenever the circumstances appear to call for it. If your Royal Highness should be pleased to require any further explanation on the subject and should condescend to signify your orders that I should have the honor of attending your Royal Highness for that purpose, or to intimate any other mode in which your Royal Highness may wish to receive such explanation, I shall respectfully wait your Royal Highness's commands.[1]

I have the honor to be with the utmost deference and submission, Sir, [etc.].[2] (38361-3)

1. The Duchess of Devonshire described the letter as 'very insolent', Sheridan as 'insolent and imperious', and the Prince doubtless considered it in the same light. As early as the 6th or thereabouts, he had told the Duchess that he would not accept the Regency with limited powers. Had he refused the Government's terms the Queen would have accepted the Regency, but his advisers prevented him from committing that blunder.

2. Pitt evidently sent the Queen a letter epitomizing his letter to the Prince of Wales, and she replied on the 31st:
'Sir,
    I have this instant received your letter & return you many thanks for your attention in communicating to me the particulars contained in your letter, & desire if not inconvenient to

372 J. TOWNSHEND TO CAPTAIN J. W. PAYNE

Thursday noon, 4 p.m. [*?1 Jan. 1789*]

We are very desirous at *Becket's* (in case there sh^d be no *objection*) to have as soon as possible a copy of the Restrictions, in order that we may lose no time in getting them properly circulated throughout the country, with the necessary observations on their nature & tendency, &c. &c, which it is impossible to do properly without a sight of them.

If you can oblige me in this, be so good as to send them enclos'd to Mr. Geo. Reid at Becket's, bookseller in Pall Mall.

Courteney & I call'd on you for this purpose, & not knowing exactly what time we shd find you at home, I have troubled you with this note.

P.S. I'll take care that in our accounts of them it shall be so managed that there shall be no suspicion of a correct copy having been obtain'd from Carleton House. This may be easily done by the alteration of some point, which may give it the appearance of *common report*. We only want the substance. (38375)

373 THE PRINCE OF WALES TO WILLIAM PITT (BURKE'S DRAFT REPLY[1] TO PITT'S LETTER OF 30 DEC. 1788[2])

[*?c. 1 Jan. 1789*]

It is impossible for the Prince to mistake the design & tendency, or to be insensible to the probable effect of the very extraordinary project delivered to him by Mr. Pitt. On the proceedings which have hitherto passed in Parliament the Prince is silent; nothing done by the two Houses can be a subject of his aminadversion.

The heavy calamity with which it has pleased the Divine Providence to visit the King had overwhelmed the Prince & the Royal Family with affliction & distress, & for a considerable time, sacrificed to natural affection, to filial duty & to publick propriety, the Prince had taken no steps whatsoever to counteract the designs wch. were carrying on against him. They were in a considerable degree of forwardness before he could put himself on his guard against them or indeed suspect such an intention. In that state the Prince had reason to expect a due attention to his personal dignity & to look for everything lenient & consolatory

you, that you would come here this evening, as I conclude tomorrow to be a day of fatiguing business' (P.R.O., Chatham Papers).

'I could tell you some particulars of the Prince of Wales's behaviour towards the King and her [the Queen] within these few days, that would make your blood run cold', wrote Grenville on 21 December (Buckingham, *Court and Cabinets of George III*, ii. 68).

1. These draft pages are much scored through and amended, and in places hardly legible.

2. No. 371.

to his feelings, especially from Ministers who have been distinguished by an abundant measure of the favours & benefits of the King, his father. The difficulties to Government in that melancholly situation of things were of course many & great. It was not expected that those difficulties would be aggravated by persons who were under every obligation to lessen their weight. It was not expected that attempts would have been made to render Government impracticable in the hands of any person whatsoever intended to represent the King's authority, much less in the hands of his eldest son, the Heir Apparent to his kingdom.

The Prince does not find those his natural expectations to be answered; by this part of the plan the intended Regent is to [be] deprived of the power of granting those honours, distinctions & favours which create or reward attachment; whilst all the arduous, harsh & invidious parts of government & those which in their nature are most exposed to doubt & objection are devolved upon him.

This plan appears to the Prince to have in principal three objects: first, it proposes to divide into two separate & totally independent bodies, with the Queen at the head of the one & the Prince at the head of the other, the Court & the State, & wh. can alone be intended for what alone it can produce, discord, disunion & the bitterest animosities amongst the Royal Family & debility & disorder in every part of Government. The establishments most essential to the dignity of the Crown or that of its representative are set up for its humiliation in opposition to it; he sees in this plan the revenues of the Crown employ'd, not to forward but to embarrass the administration of publick affairs.

The second part is to deprive the Prince of the power of granting any peerage, pension, or patent office for term of life.

For the consideration of a scheme so unprecedent, doubtful & perplexing & for coming to a final determination upon it, a part of one night is allowed to him. Thus limited in time & embarrassed by circumstances, the Prince is reduced to the distressing alternative, either of being obliged to accept of the trust of his Majesty's Govt. without adequate means of performing its duties & without any security for his being able to restore to his Majesty his royal authority in the state in wch. he left it; or, on the other hand, to expose himself to what of all things it is his duty, his interest & his inclination to avoid, a difference with the two Houses of Parliament. (38423)

[The following three paragraphs are on a separate sheet]
Although Mr. Pitt's sketch of a plan is ambiguously expressed in some parts & not very fully open'd in others, it is impossible for the Prince to mistake the design & tendency or to not to be [*sic*] fully aware of the effect it is calculated to produce. Concerning the steps which

431

Mr. Pitt without any notice to him has already taken in Parliament, the Pr. is silent. Nothing done in the two Houses can be a proper subject of his animadversion, but when previously to any discussion in Parliament a communication is made to him of schemes of government in which he is personally & principally concerned, & by wh. the royal authority & the publick welfare may be deeply affected, the Prince cannot be justified in withholding an explicit declaration of his sentiments; his silence might be construed into a tacit approbation & a sort of previous consent upon his part.

In the state of deep distress in wh. the Prince & the whole Royal Family were involved by the heavy calamity which has fallen on the King, the Pr. had reason to look for everything lenient & consolatory to his feelings, especially from Ministers who have been distinguished by an abundant measure of the favours & benefits of the King, his father.

The difficulties to government in that melancholly situation of affairs were many & great. It was not expected that attempt . . . (38424)

[The following paragraphs are on separate sheets]

The Prince of Wales has reason to be surprised that a plan for conducting the King's government on the principles of the project delivered to the Prince by Mr. Pitt should have been contrived by Ministers, most of whom have been loaded with the favours of the King his father.

In the state of heavy calamity under which the Royal Family is oppressed by the dreadful & unforeseen stroke of Providence wh. has fallen upon the King, the Prince must naturally have look'd for everything on the part of his Majesties Ministers, the most attentive to his person & the most lenient & consolatory to his feelings. Their conduct has not answered his expectations.

In so distressful a situation it was natural that the difficulties in the management of the publick concerns would be very considerable. It was not expected that these difficulties would, by those who had received so many & such distinguished obligations from the King be aggravated in the hands of any person whatsoever intended to represent the King's authority: it was still less to be expected that Ministers under that description would have done their utmost to render his Majesties Government impracticable in the hands of his eldest son & the Heir Apparent to his kingdoms.

The Prince is concerned to see that one principal object of the plan delivered to him is to form those Officers of the Court the most necessarily dependent on the pleasure of the King or his representative into a permanent body, to continue as long as it may please God to aflict the Prince & Royal Family by the King['s] illness. They are to be maintained in their places without any sort of connexion with the opinions

The North Front of Carlton House
from an engraving by Reeve, after Woodall

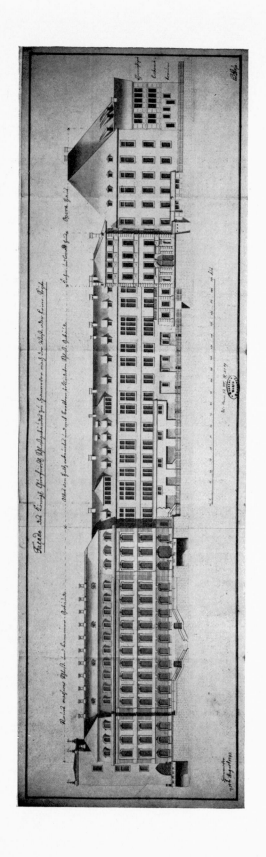

The Leineschloss, Hanover, where Frederick, Duke of York, lived from 1781 to 1783 from a drawing by I. B. Hase, 1793

or wishes of the Prince. The Prince sees that by this plan the offices of the Court & Household, instead of a mark of dignity to the Crown or its representative & the means [of] support to those stations, are intended as a matter of humiliation & as a scource of weakness. The Pr. beholds the revenues of the Crown employ'd not to forward but to embarrass its service.

By the whole of this plan taken together the Regent is to be deprived of the power of granting those honours, distinctions & favours which create or reward attachment, whilst all the arduous, harsh & invidious parts of government, & those wh. in their nature are most exposed to doubt & objection, are devolved upon him.

It is obviously the design of this project to put the Prince into a situation of all others the most perplexing; on the one hand that of being obliged to accept the trust of government without any adequate means of performing its duties, or on the other hand that of entering into discussions with either House or both Houses of Parliament.

For the consideration of a scheme of government so wholly unpre[ce]-dented, doubtful & perplexing & for his final determination upon it, he is allowed the space of one night.

In this situation, apprehensive that if more time is demanded, more material injuries can be prepared for his Majesties royal authority, & that if the Prince were to give way to what his private sentiments & personal feelings dictate on the occasion, attempts might be made to create new & unspeakable & unnatural & most disgraceful divisions in that family that even the kingdom in which the Prince only values the rank he hold as the means of demonstrating his devoted attachment to it, might suffer by delay, the Prince decides without any reserve whatsoever to throw himself upon the wisdom of Parliament; to accept the trust (created by a melancholy necessity which of all the King's subjects he deplores the most) in any way in which the two Houses shall think fit to settle it during the King's illness only, in full confidence that their loyalty to the King & their experienced affection to his house & the generosity of character which has always distinguished this nation will supply the want of so many of the usual supports of Government & carrying him thro the many difficulties attending his most critical situation. (38425–6)

[The following paragraphs are on separate sheets]

The Prince of Wales has little reason to be surprised that a scheme of government, or rather of confusion, like [that] delivered to him hands by Mr. Pitt last —— should be proposed by any combination of men, but most particularly from Ministers, all of whom are loaded with the favours of the King, his father, & some of whom have been by his gracious indulgence & condescension elevated in the earliest period of life & as

433

their very first step to those situations which have usually been cons-[ider]ed as the fruit of long & faithful service to the Crown & of tried attachment to the principles of the constitution.

The studied disrespect shewn to the Prince since the melancholy event of the King's illness (in which he ought to have looked for everything the most kind, lenient & consolatory), the withholding from him all communications on the publick affairs as if he had no concern in them, & without taking his opinion on them, all this misconduct did not prepare him for this event. The Prince now finds that the plan delivered to him tends to form a permanent body composed of certain servants of the King about his Court, officers the most directly & necessarily dependent on the pleasure of whoever is to represent the royal authority, & to station them (for a length of time but too uncertain) as a party to weaken Government & render [it] contemptible. On the other hand the Regent is deprived of the grant of all honours & favours which create or reward attachment, whilst all the arduous, critical, doubtful, harsh & invidious parts of Government are devolved upon him; thus an attempt is made by an abuse of the royal revenue to debauch the servants of the King into a settled opposition to his Government.

The Prince, overwhelmed with grief & dejection at the cruel stroke by which the Royal Family was deprived of its natural head, was (even if he could have looked for such a design from such persons) wholly disabled for a considerable time from taking any measures towards his defence against it, & now the Prince sees the plan for the ruin of the royal authority delivered to him by the King's servants before its proposed execution in Parliament. It is not long since that he knew it by report.

The Prince is well informed of the means which have been used to alienate from him, the son & heir apparent of the King, the hearts of his Majesties faithful subjects.

The P. has the greatest reason to suspect that attempts have been made by the most unjustifiable machinations towards the Prince on the Ministers' part & whilst the King's present unhappy condition requires the most cordial union in the Royal Family, to create unnatural dissentions, to destroy its peaceful order & bring it to disgrace & ruin.

This project, founded on the supposed success of these artifices, is to put the Prince in a situation either of being obliged to accept a nominal Govt. under a totel incapacity for its duties, existing only at their pleasure, or to fall into a contention with both Houses of Parliament.

Surrounded with these difficulties, brought on by the persuasion of the powers of Govt. intrusted to those who are capable of making this use of them, the Prince has no recourse but to the known loyalty of the people of G.B., their known attachment to the King, & the generosity of character wh. has hitherto distinguished this nation. (38427–8)

. . . would have been made to encrease & to aggravate these difficulties by those whom every obligation had bound to render them as few & as light as possible, much less to render government totally impracticable in the hands of any person intended to represent the King's authority, much less in the hands of his eldest son, the Heir Apparent to his kingdoms.

This plan appears to the Prince to have in view three principal objects: first, it proposes to divide the Court & the State into two separate unconnected & totally independent bodies, with the Queen to be at the head of the one & the Prince to take upon himself the risque of conducting the other. This plan can be intended for what it is fear'd it has but too manifest a tendency to produce, discord, disunion amongst the Royal Family, & debility & disorder in every part of Government, the establishment of the King's Royal Household, an object most essential to the dignity of the Crown perverted into an instrument of weakness & humiliation in the person of his Majesties son & representative.

The second part is to deprive the Prince of the power of granting any peerages, pensions or patent offices for term of life. By this part of the plan the intended Regent is to be deprived of the power of granting those honours, distinctions & favours which create or reward attachment; all the arduous, harsh & invidious parts of government & those which in their nature are most exposed to doubt & objection, are devolved upon him.

The third part of the plan concerns the King's real & personal property. In this property the Prince, the Princes his brethren, the Princesses his sisters, have an eventual interest if the King should die intestate, & it is the very first time that in similar melancholy circumstances existing in any family the estate has been taken out of the management of the nearest kindred. The Prince is above making any observation or setting up any defence against the unworthy notions upon wh. this part of the Minister's plan is founded. His brethren & sisters & all his kindred to whom he has ever shewn the most affectionate attachment & from whom he had a return correspondent to his wishes, think themselves, their rights & their properties as secure under his protection & management as under that of any other wh. his Majesties Ministers may substitute in his place, & the Prince is not afraid of being contradicted by any of them. This affair however only touching pecuniary property, he is not so attentive to this part of the arrangement as that in which the publick welfare is more directly concerned. (38418-9)

THE PRINCE OF WALES TO THE LORD CHANCELLOR,
AND THE REPLY

Carlton House, 2 Jan. 1789
Having some business of consequence to mention to your Lordship, I must request yr. attendance at Carlton House at ½ past nine o clock this evening.[1] (38391)

LORD THURLOW'S REPLY

5.45 p.m., 2 Jan. 1789
In humble obedience to your Royal Highness's commands the Chancellor will attend on your Royal Highness at half an hour after nine this evening. (38392)

375 THE PRINCE OF WALES TO WILLIAM PITT

Carlton House, 2 Jan. 1789
The Prince of Wales learns from Mr. Pitt's letter that the proceedings in Parliament are now in a train which enables Mr. Pitt, according to the intimation in his former letter, to communicate to the Prince the outlines of the plan which his Majesty's confidential servants conceive to be proper to be proposed in the present circumstances.

Concerning the steps already taken by Mr. Pitt, the Prince is silent. Nothing done by the two Houses of Parliament can be a proper subject of his animadversion, but when previously to any discussion in Parliament the outline of a scheme of Government is sent for his consideration, in which it is propos'd that he shall be personally and principally concerned, and by which the Royal authority and the public welfare may

1. There had been 'a final explanation' between the Whigs and the Chancellor on Christmas Day, which, said Sir Gilbert Elliot, 'terminated in a decided separation between him and our party, to the great joy of Fox and of every one of us except the Prince himself.' He added: 'The Prince, who has always had a partiality for the Chancellor, probably on account of his *table* qualities, has been negotiating, and intriguing, and canvassing him incessantly, with very little discretion or prudence all the time; and in spite of many disappointments and breaches of engagements which the Chancellor had made about the part he should take in the House of Lords, he still persisted in sending for him and holding long conversations with him on the business. The Chancellor, by this means, learned the interior of the Prince's affairs and intentions, and was betraying him all the time to Pitt. Fox at last, who has uniformly been against any connection with the Chancellor, of whom he thinks worse than of any man in the world, had an explicit conference with him in which he drove the Chancellor to a final and full declaration of his intention; and he is now quite off. The reason of our satisfaction on this event, notwithstanding the strength of the Chancellor's interest in the House of Lords, is that he is considered as a treacherous and dangerous character to form any connection with and to admit into a Cabinet' (*Minto*, i. 250).

be deeply affected, the Prince would be unjustifiable were he to withhold an explicit declaration of his sentiments. His silence might be construed into a previous approbation of a plan, the accomplishment of which every motive of duty to his father and Sovereign as well as of regard for the public interest obliges him to consider as injurious to both.

In the state of deep distress in which the Prince and the whole Royal Family were involv'd by the heavy calamity which has fallen upon the King, and at a moment when Government, deprived of its chief energy and support seem'd peculiarly to need the cordial and united aid of all descriptions of good subjects, it was not expected by the Prince that a plan should be offer'd to his consideration by which Government was to be render'd difficult, it not impracticable in the hands of any person intended to represent the King's authority, much less in the hands of his eldest son, the Heir-Apparent of his kingdoms, and the person most bound to the maintenance of his Majesty's just prerogatives and authority, as well as most interested in the happiness, the prosperity and the glory of his people.

The Prince forbears to reason on the several parts of the sketch of a plan laid before him; he apprehends it must have been form'd with sufficient deliberation to preclude the probability of any argument from him producing an alteration of sentiment in the projectors of it, but he trusts with confidence to the wisdom and justice of Parliament, when the whole of the subject and the circumstances connected with it shall come under their deliberation. He observes therefore only generally on the heads communicated by Mr. Pitt and it is with deep regret the Prince makes the observation that there seems to be in the contents of that paper a project for producing weakness, disorder and insecurity in every branch of the administration of affairs, a project for dividing the Royal Family from each other, for separating the Court from the State and thereby disjoining Government from its natural and accustom'd support; a scheme for disconnecting the authority to command service, from the power of animating it by reward, and for allotting to the Prince all the invidious duties of Government without the means of softening them to the people by any one act of grace, favour or benignity.

The Prince's feelings on contemplating this plan are also render'd still more painful to him by observing that it is not grounded on any general principle, but is calculated to infuse jealousies and distrust, wholly groundless, he trusts, in that quarter whose confidence it will ever be the first pride and object of his life to receive and to merit.

With regard to the motive and object of the limitations and restrictions propos'd, the Prince can have but little to observe: no light or information whatever is afforded to him by his Majesty's Ministers on these points; they have inform'd him what the powers are which they mean to refuse to him, not why they are to be with held.

The Prince, however, holding as he does that it is an undoubted and fundamental principle of this Constitution that all the powers and prerogatives of the Crown are vested there as a trust for the benefit of the people, and that they are sacred only as they are necessary to the preservation of that poise and balance of the Constitution which experience has prov'd to be the true security of the liberty of the subject, must be allow'd to observe that the plea of public utility ought to be strong, manifest and urgent which calls for the extinction or suspension of any one of these essential rights in the supreme power or its representative, or which can justify the Prince in consenting that in his person an experiment shall be made to ascertain with how small a portion of the kingly power the Executive Government of this country may be carried on.

The Prince has only to add that if security for his Majesty's repossessing his rightful government whenever it shall please Providence in bounty to the country to remove the calamity with which he is afflicted, be any part of the object of this plan, the Prince has only to be convinced that any measure is necessary, or even conducive to that end, to be the first to approve and urge it, as the preliminary and paramount consideration of any settlement in which he would consent to share.

If attention to what is presumed might be his Majesty's feelings and wishes on the happy day of his recovery be the object, it is with the truest sincerity the Prince expresses his firm conviction that no event could be more repugnant to the feelings of his Royal father than the knowledge that the Government of his son and representative had exhibited the sovereign power of the realm in a state of degradation, of curtail'd authority and diminish'd energy, a state hurtful in practice to the prosperity and good government of his people, and injurious in its precedent to the security of the Monarchy and the rights of his family.

Upon that part of the plan which regards the King's real and personal property, the Prince feels himself compell'd to remark that it was not necessary for Mr. Pitt nor proper to suggest to the Prince the restraint he proposes against the Prince's granting away the King's real or personal property. The Prince does not conceive that during the King's life he is by Law entitled to make any such grant, and he is sure that he has never shewn the smallest inclination to possess any such power, but it remains with Mr. Pitt to consider the eventual interests of the Royal Family and to provide a proper and natural security against the mismanagement of them by others.

The Prince has discharged an indispensable duty in thus giving his free opinion on the plan submitted to his consideration: his conviction of the evils which may arise to the King's interests to the peace and happiness of the Royal Family and to the safety and welfare of the nation from the Government of the country remaining longer in its present maim'd and debilitated state, outweighs in the Prince's mind every other consideration, and will determine him to undertake the painful trust impos'd upon him by the present melancholly necessity (which of all the King's subjects he deplores the most) in full confidence that the affection and loyalty to the King, the experienced attachment to the House of Brunswick and the generosity which has always distinguish'd this nation will carry him thro' the many difficulties inseparable from the most critical situation with comfort to himself, with honor to the King and advantage to the public.[1] (38341-4, and Add. MSS. Georgian/2, f.6)

376 LOOSE HINTS ON THE REGENCY [unsigned]

[*?c. 3–5 Jan. 1789*]

Mr. P[itt] & Co. had four different lines to come at their object. 1st. Delay, the best chapter in the history of doubtful politics. It was necessary to prevent this delay from *appearing* to arise from the party; therefore the *lapsus linguæ* of their opponents was seized with avidity and made the object of unmeaning but tedious and deceptious discussion. The time gained by these means was an addition to the stock of the Company, and whatever *their art* on the one side, or *chance* on the other has gained is an accession to their profit. The produce of the art is to give time to their adherents to work on the prejudices & ignorance of the people, to vote thanks and addresses whilst they take care to feed the sanguine and ignorant with hopes from Kew.

The 2d. object is pursued at the same time, although P[itt] has the human frailty of being fond of power, the manner in which he received

1. This letter was drafted by Burke, 'altered a little, but not improved,' said Sir Gilbert Elliot, 'by Sheridan and other critics' (*Minto*, i. 268. Cf. Sichel's *Sheridan*, ii. 393-6, and 422). At a meeting at Fox's house on the night of the 31st the question was discussed whether the Prince should or should not ask Pitt for the explanation which he had offered. Portland thought he should not, 'as it would be admitting the principle on which Pitt is acting.' Carmarthen wrote, on the 3rd: 'The Chancellor having received late the preceding evening a paper sealed from the Prince of Wales to be communicated to the K.'s Ministers, and being obliged to go to Kew this morning, sent it to Lord Stafford, who opened it and read it to us at the Cabinet.... It was upon the whole a strange performance, and by no means an able one; now and then there appeared something of Sheridan's language, and still more of Lord Loughborough's, tho' very far from being in either of their best manners' (*Political Memoranda of Duke of Leeds*, p. 137).

For the Cabinet discussion as to whether an answer should be sent to the Prince's letter, see *Political Memoranda of Duke of Leeds*, p. 139. And the Lord Chief Justice wrote in his Diary on 4 January: 'To town—sent for by Mr. Pitt to attend a Cabinet on the Regency.' And on the 6th: 'Attended another Cabinet Council.' He attended further Cabinet meetings on 25 January and 3 February (Kenyon MSS.).

it in 1784 was neither flattering to his talents nor did it suit his pride. He wishes now to appear to owe to his own merit what he derived before from the influence of the Sovereign, being *too great* to be any man's servant. Strange as it may be in the present age, this principle in him is supported by an enthusiasm scarcely known, at least little practised, since the beginning of the last century.

It is well known that even if the present crises had not come on, he had resolved to try his strength against the —[1]; and either through force or intimidation to gain that uncontrouled ascendency over his employer which he had reprobated with so much success as being the fixed principle of his opponents in the year 1784.

3d. If his proposed restrictions are rejected by the P—ce, he thinks another Regent, with a Council, will meet the present state of the minds of the people. If these restrictions are received by the Prince and yet are rejected by the P—ce's friends, he himself (P-tt) with his crew may rule the roast [*sic*] under the *shadow of a name*.

4th. If both the P—ce and his party will accept under the restrictions P-tt thinks he has an after-game to play. He expects that by keeping by means of restrictions a majority within doors and by retaining popularity without, he will be able to retake the citadel and to possess it on his own terms.

None of these ways to power are, in the opinion of the writer hereof, either safe or certain. The means already used would certainly have been unsafe at any other period, and he ought to recollect the fate of his opponents in 1784 before he builds any certainty of success on his own present schemes. It was an opinion that *they meant* to retain a majority in parliament against the executive power that first rouzed the jealousy of the people; and it was their being supposed to make use of that majority to obstruct the necessary business of the State that set the nation in a flame.

To the rock on which his predecessor split he *must* drive with full sail if the *Regency is accepted*. The people will soon perceive his design and will reprobate his conduct. The tide will not only turn, but set strongly the other way. *Patience*, the first of virtues, is only necessary and were her *sister Silence* but to accompany her for a short space, matters would be settled in a few months on a solid foundation notwithstanding all the arts and machinations of the enemy.

I would permit either Gr—v-lle[2] or Buckhorse [*sic*] to be their Speaker!! (38289–90)

1. The King.

2. William Wyndham Grenville (1759-1834). M.P. for Buckingham, 1782-4; for Buckinghamshire, 1784-90. Irish Secretary, 1782-3; Joint Paymaster-General, 1784-89; Speaker of the House of Commons, 5 January-5 June 1789; Home Secretary, 1789-91; Foreign Secretary, 1791-1801; created Baron Grenville, November 1790; Prime Minister, 1806-7.

Geneva, 9 Jan. 1789

Excuse my trespassing upon your time with these lines, but I certainly would not have troubled you with a letter at a moment when I well know that you have a thousand affairs of the highest consequence to attend to, if I did not think myself obliged both by my duty to you, and by what I owe to myself, not to be silent. By some letters which have been received in this town lately from England, I have been informed that there have been many reports spread there which were not only disadvantageous to me, but also highly dishonourable to my character, either as a Prince, an officer, or a man who wishes to be considered as a man of honour. Now as during the whole time I have been here, though guilty perhaps of many of those *étourderies* without which scarce any young man can live, except a perfect milksop or a *poule mouillée*, I have never suffered myself either to forget that necessary dignity which a man in my situation must always preserve, or ever to do anything which I could afterwards not look back upon but with shame, I must confess that, absent from my friends and family, it affects me cruelly to think it even possible that through false and insidious reports you should be prejudiced against me, without having it even in my power to plead my justification. You know, my dearest brother, how many false and detrimental things are said against young men when they first appear in the world, and more particularly so against those who, from their rank and position in life, draw the eyes of all the idle and curious upon them. I am not ignorant of the cruel underhand methods used by those (who from their position about me, ought rather to have concealed my faults and failings than to have trumpetted them about the world) to ruin my reputation and character with my friends and family. As it is therefore to your friendship, to your protection, and to your affection alone that I can look up for justice and assistance, judge, if it was not incumbent upon me to intreat you never to think your brother capable of base or low actions: for the past, words alone can speak for me, but for the future let my actions and those *under your eyes*, speak for me. I trust, you will ever find me to be not only a man of honour, but one whose zealous attachment to *your person* will claim that place in your affection and esteem which I shall ever strive to render myself *worthy of*. Before I conclude, you must forgive me if I express my most *earnest* desire of returning to Old England, that you may all judge by my conduct whether I *merit* or not that good opinion which I should be so proud to obtain; with the most fervent and sincere wishes for your happiness and welfare, and the most devoted assurances of attachment [etc.]. (45767–8)

MINUTES OF DOCTOR WARREN'S EXAMINATION (IN THE HANDWRITING OF LORD RAWDON[1])

Dr. Warren, Friday evening [*?9 Jan. 1789*]. Late on Wednesday night the Committee asked him if he had not seen a copy or something purporting to be a copy of a letter written by Dr. Willis to Mr. Pitt at 12 o'clock at night during the debate on the day of the first division in the H. of Commons?[2] He could not at that time recollect anything to which he could apply the word "copy". Next morning he recollected that on his arrival at Kew the day after such letter was supposed to have been written, Sir L. Pepys informed him he had a message for him from H.R.H. the Prince of Wales who had been at Kew the night before & had ordered him to deliver a message for Dr. Warren when he came next morning. Sir L. P. had taken the message down in writing from his memory soon after the P. of Wales had left him. The message was to desire Dr. Warren to enquire into the state of his Majesty's health at a particular time because the Prince had been informed a letter had been written by Dr. Willis stating the King was in a very good way at that time, when the Prince had understood he really was not so; & then recited other words of the supposed letter he (Dr. Warren) cannot recollect. He does not remember that he took this paper from Sir L. P., but in talking about this letter he made use of the word "copy" when he ought rather to have said that he had seen an account of the letter in writing. The first account of such letter being written he learned from rumour; next information he had of it was from the message delivered to him by Sir L. P. He did inform his R. Highness of the result of his enquiry, & next day, or the 2d day after, acquainted the Prince he had done wrong with respect to Dr. Willis, as he could not find any letter had been written by him at the time mentioned; that he must retract what he had said to Dr. Willis & acknowledge his error. The Prince said he thought Dr. Warren did right; he approved his intended conduct. He positively declares he knows not from whom he first heard this report, and paid very little attention to it till be received the message from Sir L. P. He declares positively from fatigue of examination or some other circumstance he knows not what he could not recollect it. He took pains about it as soon as he left the Committee, & as he was

1. This is the Memorandum copied from Loveden's notes. See No. 380 and *n*,1.

2. In the course of his re-examination by the Parliamentary Committee appointed to examine the King's physicians (Wednesday, 7 January) Warren was asked whether he had had any difference of opinion with Dr. Willis respecting letters written by Willis in which he, Willis, declared that the King was making more progress towards recovery than Warren himself could discover. In reply, Warren said that he had been informed that Willis had written a letter of that description to Pitt at midnight during the House of Commons' debate. See the evidence in *House of Commons Journal*, xliv. 53, under date 13 January.

going to Kew the next morning he gradually made it out & immediately determined to acquaint the Committee with it as soon as he had an opportunity, tho' he knew it was at the expence of appearing to have concealed the truth the night before. Soon after he got to his own house on Thursday he put into writing what he had recollected on his road to Kew. He communicated the paper he has now read to his brother this morning. He sent it to the Prince at twelve or one o'clock & read it over with his son this afternoon; does not know if he did not desire him to speak to the Chancellor on the subject. (38331–2)

379 LETTERS FROM J. ROBINSON TO SIR JOHN MACPHERSON[1]

10 Jan. 1789
Most private. I have just received your favor of last night. Your maxim *piano* et *sano* was certainly never more properly applied than to the present time; add to it an old English adage, hear all, say little and do nothing which is not absolutely called for, and *ends* wished for will be attained at no great distance of time, to the *full extent*, altho' perhaps not *immediately.* Calmness, good temper, a conduct dignified, civil, steady & firm, and an address given by Providence when brought into action in conspicuous life, will always succeed; little prejudices & party attacks must & will fall to it, and the minds of moderate and good men will by *degrees* accede and go on to *respect* and to *revere.*

What you write to me *of* the Committee is what I foresaw and foretold must be the consequence, and I was equally aware that upon the examination of physicians it must appear they had information from the surgeons and persons who sit up with his Majesty, and that unless the Commee. would permit the physicians to *state in their evidence* and *suffer to be taken down* the reports of these persons to them, they must permit such persons to be examined at the Commee., or, if it is apprehended the powers given to the Commee. from the House do not extend so far, then to come to the House of Commons for further powers for this purpose. This I said the night of Mr. B—'s forced and I thought imprudent division when *the point had been obtained.* All divisions, except *those* to *mollify* the restrictions, seem unwise; they engage and *dip* men more than is necessary, make retreat more difficult, and in the state of things are of no use. On the ground of restrictions *beyond* the first principle to keep for a while, to give time for recovery, the Crown & its prerogatives & powers from being impaired, diminished or fettered, men's minds SEEM OPENING & this delay is favourable for reflection. Conversations had on some of the points in the *minutes you had,* seem

1. Endorsed 'No. 1, from Mr. Rob—n', and 'Robinson's letter sent by Sir J. M.'

443

to be felt; appointments *pro tempore* vague, uncertain & useless; *House-hold* ought to be defined; *filling up vacancies* in its *higher* offices unnecess-ary and improper. Real estates expressed and particularized. On these points debates will arise and divisions may be had. But to ask you a question. What good reason think you can be given that the *purport* of the very proper answer given to the communication of the restrictions shd. not be LET out? If known, the effects I think wd. be that it wd. appear there is a readiness to do whatever Parliamt. shall think best and to do the most possible good to the country under it, fearing only that it may not be equal to what is wished if a Government of imbecility is formed, and it would do away the idea that the Regency would *not be accepted*. The first effect would be popular ground; the second, a certainty of the Regency, which wd. alarm some, fix the wavering and carry others. Diffidence and a fear of presumption or impropriety ever restrain me from coming too forward, but you have my sentiments freely, tho' wrote hastily. I think from your conciliating temper & mind they will not far differ from yours, and a strong presentiment possesses my mind that we shall see things turn out *fortunate and* GLORIOUSLY FOR THIS COUNTRY.[1] (38393-4)

Saturday, late at night [*?10 Jan. 1789*]
Most private. I send you the enclosed, in the utmost confidence. It is the result of *my own* most mature consideration. I think, if followed in a better manner than I have expressed it, it cannot fail of the *utmost success*. It will secure the people when clamour is over; it will secure the K. when ever he recovers, and those who lay ambitious traps in the hopes of reviviscence will be intrapped themselves. What can I say more?[2] (38384)

1. 'Paper left with Mr. Payne' (endorsement). John Robinson (1727-1802), M.P. for Westmorland, 1764-74, and for Harwich, 1774-1802, had been in office under Lord North (as Joint Secretary of the Treasury), 1770-82, but had gone over to Pitt's side in 1783 and had been appointed Surveyor General of Woods and Forests in 1787. At the beginning of January 1789 the Whigs heard that he was going to join them—but Fox, unlike Sheridan, was not anxious to have him. He would be 'a disgrace to the Party and ought not to be tried for'. The Duchess of Devonshire wrote (4 January): 'A note came to him [the Prince of Wales] from the Duke of York saying that Jack Robinson was inclined to treat, but that he should employ somebody, it being below his dignity to speak to him himself' (Sichel's *Sheridan*, ii. 423).

2. Endorsed 'No. 2, contain'd in Sir John's [?Macpherson] letter.' This must be Macpherson's note: the ending is typical.

Monday morning [*12 Jan. 1789*]

Loveden[1] told me yesterday evening that Mr Sheridan had been anxious to copy his (Loveden's) minute of part of Dr Warren's examination; hinting that it was for the information of the Prince of Wales. Loveden, from what scruple I cannot comprehend, declined imparting his notes. Tho' I am doubtful whether the communication may not be too tardy to gratify any curiosity, yet as there is still a chance of its being acceptable, I send a hasty copy from the paper which Loveden suffered me to examine.[2] You will see that the detail is inaccurately expressed, but I would not correct anything. Be so good as not to mention publickly that the account comes from Loveden, from whom indeed I have no authority for what I am doing. (38376)

381   SIR GODFREY WEBSTER TO CAPTAIN J. W. PAYNE

Brighton, Tuesday evening [*?13 Jan. 1789*]

I came to this place last night, & this forenoon went over to Lewes, & had a long conference with Mr Kempe[3]. At first he was rather shy of explaining himself, & had got some nonsense into his head that his Royal Highness had been prejudiced against him. At length he spoke out, & declar'd his perfect independence of, or connexion with the

1. Edward Loveden Loveden (*c.* 1750-1822). M.P. for Abingdon, 1783-96; for Shaftesbury, 1802-12. An independent country gentleman, he voted with the Prince's friends in the December divisions, though, he said, he had 'never spoken one word to the Prince of Wales'. 'Pitt has behaved to me with great civility, but I must own that he appears to me of the doubtful gender. . . . He is most certainly setting up a fourth estate—the Queen and himself' (Preston MSS., Berkshire Record Office). In 1783 he had reprobated the Coalition, had pledged himself to support Pitt, and, it was alleged, had caused foxes, rats and other vermin to be exhibited on a gallows for the derision of the populace, and consigned to the flames, declaring that 'they were types of what the Coalition ought to be'. But in 1788 he had joined 'the Coalition faction through private pique to Mr. Pitt, or for some other . . . reasons.' It was further alleged against him that his motion for the re-examination of the physicians was designed in the expectation of finding the King much worse than the daily bulletins seemed to indicate, 'in hopes to obtain such terms for the Prince as would enable his intended Ministers to lavish the public treasure and *splendid titles* on themselves and such *time-serving adherents* as could be tempted to betray their kind and good master in the hour of his affliction' (ibid.).

2. No. 378.

3. Thomas Kemp (*c.* 1746-1811). M.P. for Lewes, 1780-1802, 1806-11; a country gentleman. He had voted against Fox's India Bill, and with Pitt on parliamentary reform (1785) and, in December 1788, on the Regency.

present people in office—owned he was convinced of the propriety of the Prince being sole, & unfettered Regent—but said he hoped I would not press him to an unconditional promise—a thing he never yet had done—adding that he was clear from our conversation, that the more the Prince's right to the Regency, & his conduct were investigated, the stronger they would appear—but that he thought every honest & independent man should hear the Report of the Physicians &c &c.

In short I think I may venture to say you will be sure of him.[1]

Are not you too sanguine about my old friend W. G. H[amilton].[2] He is an old fox, & I know in company with Pittites has held a language within this week different from what we thought his opinion at Windsor.

If his Royal Highness chuses I will ask him plump, for if he speaks out I think he is too much a man of honor to break his word.

I shall be in town (Charles Street, Berkley Square) by 4 to morrow. If I can in any way render service, I shall most readily obey his Royal Highness's orders. Excuse haste.   (38366)

382   THE MARQUESS OF CARMARTHEN TO THE PRINCE OF WALES

Whitehall, 16 Jan. 1789

Lord Carmarthen begs leave to inform your Royal Highness that the Marquis del Campo[3] has communicated the formal notification of the late King of Spain's[4] death; & has also delivered his own credentials as Ambassador from the present King of Spain[5].

Lord Carmarthen has thought it expedient to desire the Lord Chamberlain[6] to issue orders for the Court going into mourning for the late King of Spain, the late Infanta, the late Infant Don Gabriel her

1. On 11 February, however, Kemp again voted (in effect, by pairing off) with Pitt.

2. William Gerard Hamilton (1729-96). M.P. for Petersfield, 1754-61; for Pontefract, 1761-8; for Old Sarum, 1768-74; for Wareham, 1774-80; for Wilton, 1780-90; for Haslemere, 1790-6; known as 'single-speech Hamilton'. A former supporter of Lord North, he voted against Pitt on the Regency. 'Gerard Hamilton is among the rats,' wrote Grenville on 17 December, 'which is no small amusement to me, who have frequently been abused by Pitt for my bad opinion of him, at the time that he was swallowing toads *à toute outrance*' (Buckingham, *Court and Cabinets of George III*, ii. 64).

3. The Spanish Ambassador in London.

4. Charles III, King of Spain, 1759-88 (1716-88).

5. Charles IV (1748-1819) succeeded his father on 13 December 1788. Napoleon forced him to abdicate in 1808.

6. The Earl of Salisbury (1748-1823). Lord Chamberlain, December 1783-1804; Joint Postmaster-General, 1816-23. Created Marquess, 1789.

husband[1]; as likewise for the late Margrave of Brandenburg Schewdt[2] & the Prince of Baden Dourlach[3]; the deaths of these several personages having been formally announced.

Lord Carmarthen begs leave to remark that the originals of these papers being directed to his Majesty have not been opened, but that the copies of them appeared sufficiently to justify Lord Carmarthen in troubling your Royal Highness on the subject of their respective contents. (38395)

383 J. ROBINSON'S MOST PRIVATE MINUTES

[?c. 20 Jan. 1789]

In the present situation of things any material impressions seem *not* to be made so as to have effect to prevent the Minister executing his plan. Men look on it as only to have temporary & a short existence, and therefore, altho' in conversation they allow & hold the restrictions improper in parts, to exist for any length of time, they are led to acquiesce in them, to give a time for recovery; with this idea they solve the objections made to the parts tho't harsh and a desire that the Sovereign may not in case of recovery in a little time (the probability of which is by the physicians' examination last taken fixed upon their minds) feel that his subjects have not been impatient and that his servants have not been removed, carry them and it is believed will carry most of those who have taken a part in going along with the Resolutions.

This, it is apprehended, will be verified by the result, let what can be done to prevent it. Impressions cannot be made to alter these prevalent ideas at the present moment; *time* only can accomplish that, and *that time* it is realy believed *will come* whenever the *Regent is fixed*, even with all the restrictions. If these sentim[ts] are founded, and every occurrence which arises seem to confirm them, it can only be to consider what conduct is most prudent to hold.

The second question of Friday night[4] cd. not perhaps *be let to* pass witho[t] a division for fear of many expectants taking offence, otherwise it

1. Don Gabriel (1752-88), Charles IV's younger brother, died on 23 November 1788; his wife, Maria Anna Victoria (1768-88), daughter of Peter III, King of Portugal, died eighteen days earlier.

2. Brandenburg-Schwedt.

3. William Louis, Prince of Baden-Durlach (1732-88), died on 17 December. He was the younger brother of the Margrave Charles Frederick (1728-1811).

4. The second division in the House of Commons on the night of Friday, 16 January, on the Resolution respecting the creation of Peers, was carried by Ministers, by 216 votes to 159.

might have been wise to have reserved that limitation for one general question by way of proviso *or limitation* of the Act when passing, or at the third reading, or as a rider to the Act before passed, when the whole of the plan in all its branches have been before the House.

On this a question will be asked, but then what are you to do in the meantime? The answer seems, *object* to the parts of the Resolutions which appear *objectionable*, *debate* them somewhat if *desired* by *some*, move Amendments, lay *in a claim* to *discuss* & *debate* the points in the Bill when the whole plan is *seen* & known; but do *not divide* unless it is evident that the point in discussion has struck *the House* in *those* parts likely to DETACH, and thus let the whole Resolutions pass; let the Bill be brot in,[1] discuss them again in the several proceedings on the Bill, impress on all occasions men's minds that the Bill ought to have a *short duration*, & a *limited* time for its continuance, and on this *at last* take a division, for it seems the only point likely to succeed, but avoid divisions on the others. You ask me my thots on this buss, and you have them most truly. I wish time and circumstances wd allow an attentive revision of them, but as they are only a continuance of former opinions, corrobated by the course of events in the proceedings, they wd. not I think vary in substance, altho' they might be more correct and explicit. (38370–1)

384   ? JOHN ROBINSON TO SIR JOHN MACPHERSON

3 p.m., Tuesday [*?20 Jan. 1789*]

I wrote you this morning in a kind of half sleep, but notwithstanding that I did not dream. The troops of the enemy, through management have been induced to *swear allegiance* for a limited time; that is, they were *individually* questioned and they *promised* to go *thorough stitch with the* restrictions. Their courage has been kept up in two ways. Dr. W[illi]s *was* certainly to recover the K.; if not, the restrictions were to be made so bitter that the P. would not swallow them! This latter is *still* their great hope, for some did not scrupple to whisper [to] others last night that the giving the Household to the Q. would be, probably, followed by the R[egenc]y.

If they find themselves disappointed in this *last hope*, a great number in the course of next week will go over to the opposite camp, or rather desert into the country. Notwithstanding their repeated victories, they are *low-spirited*, and nothing but perseverance is necessary to turn completely the fortune of the war. Why will not men compare the present to past times? During the recess of 1783–4, when the new

1. The Regency Bill was introduced on 5 February.

Ministry had time given them to be rechosen to Parliament, every engine was set to work to gain votes in the House of Commons. A Ld. of the Bedchamber told me, at the end of three weeks, with extacy of joy, that *thirteen* members had been *gained over* in that time. I found upon inquiry it was not *one-third* of that number, viz., 4 only, yet the King, the H. of Lords, the Ministry, the people were of one side. Don't attribute this to the steady principles of members; they had *sworn allegiance* for a *limited time*, as at present, and they were assured that a *steady opposition* in the House would overset the Ministry *in three weeks*. Week followed week & without producing the desired effect. Some became sick, several went to the country, a few, very *conscientiously*, owned they had gone too far, and they measured back their steps to the other side. In the first week of March 1784, just *three months* after the India Bill was rejected by the Lords, the Ministry, through the means mentioned in the preceeding sentence, came within a few votes of their opponents, but notwithstanding the prospect of their getting ahead, they were advised to take advantage of the temper of the people and to get a new House of Commons.

In the present times only patience and a little management are necessary. The restrictions, especially the Household, are deemed severe even by many who voted for them in their plenitude last night.[1] Give a little time to the nation and it will see them in as *abominable* a light as it was induced to look upon the India Bill. The current, be assured, will turn in a few months; there are strong principles for Monarchy in this country. This double state and influence which P-tt has chosen to create will be seen as separating what is *indivisible*, and the *double expence* will frighten away that idea which is impressed upon the minds of *unexamining* weak men.

F-x hinted, and the sentiment met with universal applause, that the Regent should not put the nation to any additional expence. If he had mentioned and explained that the state of the Regent should be supported by savings from the Household of the King, P-tt would not have an inch of ground to stand upon. Were it possible for the Regent to ask for nothing, the contrast between him and the *mock-state* kept up by P-tt would open the eyes of the world in an instant. The nation would call out "*Shame*" upon such a farce, and the pensioners of the Household would be hooted off the stage. Believe me, slow as mankind are in their comprehension, the appropriating between *two* and *three* hundred thousand pounds a year to the idle state of a personage not sensible of it will not hold water for three months. Indeed P-tt seems to think so for the only argument he made use of was the shortness of the time the arrangement would continue.

1. On the 19th Ministers had a majority of 220 *v.* 164 in one division; 229 *v.* 165 in the other.

I am still of opinion that by proper Amendments on the Bill when it comes in, the dangerous parts of this same Household may be frittered away. Men vote propositions by the lump, but I have frequently seen the most zealous give up the substance of the preliminary resolutions in the Committees upon Bills. Let no discontent be shown, though it cannot but be felt by the P——ce. To this discontent the enemy looks with avidity, for it is on the forlorn hope of his being disgusted they feed and support their party. Let him take the Gov^t., everything else will follow; the harder the restrictions the sooner they will break. Had the limitations been milder they would be more dangerous, as they might perhaps last for ever. Patience and firmness will lay the enemy completely on his back! and that very soon indeed.

Rolle[1] shot his bolt in the end of the business with respect to a certain lady[2]. He says he has pledged himself to his county to bring forward that business: let him when he will, he can make nothing of it. He was trimmed handsomely by Ld. N[orth].

By the by, I was once of opinion that the Ch[ancello]r would not venture to put the G. Seal to the act of Government. I was glad of it at the time, but I have now altered my opinion completely. The party are already on as hollow a piece of ground as their worst enemies could wish them to be. Let them go on this other *great step*, and they are undone for ever. Let them use the Seal; it will *vitiate the whole of the restrictions*! They must come for an indemnity; then will be the time to throw off the fetters. I again repeat the sentiment, that the harder the restrictions are the better, as they will the sooner be got rid of. I would certainly oppose them in all their stages, but I would neither waste many words on them nor at all divide upon them in the lump, but try only what can be taken from the Household by *judicious Amendments* in the Committee. Let me implore the P——ce's party to say little and do less against the Great Seal business. They will have their opponents in a noose and they may draw the cord as tight as they please.

I was much pleased with the conduct of *our* party last night. They were able, cool and moderate. Lord N. spoke well and Mr. F-x very ably and *unanswerably*. The light and noisy troops were kept as much as was possible in the rear of the line. This must always be done till a good footing is obtained.   (38381–3)

1. John Rolle (1756–1842), 1st Baron Rolle; peerage, 1796. M.P. for Devonshire, 1780–96; the hero of the *Rolliad*.

2. Mrs. Fitzherbert. Not later than 13 December Sheridan had asked Rolle in the Prince's name to refrain from making further inquiries about Mrs. Fitzherbert. Rolle refused to promise, saying that he was an independent member and cared little for the Prince's smiles or favours.

Göttingen, 21 Jan. 1789

Well assured how you have been since some time overwhelmed with business I did not dare trouble you with a letter, but now as the King's health is, thank God mending, according to the last accounts I have received from England, I seize this opportunity of writing to you by Dornford, a young Englishman with whom I have studied at Gottingen. My intention was to send you my shade by him, but as the man who makes it has not got it finished time enough, I must postpone the pleasure of sending it you 'till when the next messenger goes. Since the illness of the King has naturally all public diversions ceased here [*sic*], but as the King recovers they will soon take place again. Augustus has wrote to me from Hyeres, where he is now quartered, & says his health grows dayly stronger. It is one of the luckiest things possible that he has not passed this winter in Germany, for the weather has been so intensely cold that I am confident it would have certainly cost him his life. I suppose Augustus will bring back with him a cart full of minerals & stones in which he finds a great deal of amusement; he has already a pretty large collection left behind him sealed up 'till his return. As for me I do not know what amusement there can be in collecting stones, but as the French proverb says "Chacun a son gout", and it really is so for Augustus has a taste for stones & prints, the latter of which I have no objection to but however think there are more amusing ways of spending my money. It is already pretty late & I must be up early tomorrow, so believe me [etc.].   (47008)

386   SIR JOHN BLAQUIERE [1] TO GENERAL [?]

Dublin, 23 Jan. 1789

At such a crisis there need [be] no apology—I am writing to a friend, and wish to be guided by better sense than my own.

It is not in human nature to imagine that under an accumulation of insult the Prince will be at rest—nor will it be out of the way to supose

1. John Blaquiere, Lord De Blaquiere [I.] (1732-1812), son of a French Protestant refugee Lieutenant-Colonel, 17th Dragoons; Chief Secretary to the Lord-Lieutenant of Ireland, 1772-7; M.P. [I.] for various constituencies, 1773-1800. K.B., 1774; created a Baronet [I.], July 1784; peerage, for supporting the Union, 1800. M.P. for Rye, 1801-2; for Downton, 1803-6. His conduct was thought to be particularly shabby. He owed everything to the King, who had raised him from the rank of Lieutenant-Colonel of Dragoons in Ireland to that of Chief Secretary to the Lord-Lieutenant, made him a Knight of the Bath and given him some of the best sinecure appointments in Ireland. But, thinking that the King would never recover, he went over to the enemy. See *Cornwallis Correspondence*, iii. *passim.*

that the people of Ireland may be inclined to do him better justice. A little wisdom and some management may be necessary, but an host of strength will be derived from the unpopularity of our present Chief Governor[1], who is the indignation of three-fourths of this Kingdom.

The history of our prorogation last Sunday, has no example—nor will it be believed at a future day that a man whose characteristick bears no extraordinary instances of either manhood or valour, should have the temerity impudently to call us together for the purpose of pledging ourselves to support the measures adopted in England, altho it was impossible at that time for any man living to know what those measures were. That Lord Buckingham intended us this favor, altho it may be now denied, I do aver. Even on the Saturday, the very day preceeding the prorogation, his Speech from the Throne, received back in our Address, were points related by some of those who had the patience to speak on the subject, of which number I was not one—nor was it till the day following (Sunday) that this prepostrous measure was abandoned by his Excellency.

On the 5th of Feb: then, unless we are again prorogued, we shall engage: and to the points of limitting the Prince & altering the Constitution, another must be added and of which the most will be endeavoured to be made, that of seperating ourselves from England, if we suffer our proceedings to differ from what has been done there, and upon which some leading men in this country are pledged, and upon this point it is that our best exertions must issue, for as to the limitation and the injurious insult which it implies, were the question entire to us, which it is not, it would be scouted out of the House. But you are still in time for all you want, and I entertain not the smallest doubt that, with a little common discretion, aided by the unworthyness of the man in whom Mr Pitt has chose to confide, I mean the Marquiss of Buckingham, you will attain from Ireland reparation to the injured honor of the Prince, & a Regency adopted in the form it ought.

These are my principles, and this my creed—inspire me with better, & tell me how I can most usefully act, & I shall thank you—and tell me too, my dear General, are any exertions from so small a man as myself likely to be acceptable to the Prince? It would make me happy if I could think they were!

P.S. Why wont the Duke of York be our Lord Lieutenant?   (38397–9)

1. The Marquess of Buckingham.

CarltonHouse, 9.30 p.m., Friday [*? Jan. 1789*][1]

I am but this instant return'd here & find by my porter yt. you have given yourself the trouble of calling at Carlton House again this day. If there is any hour tomorrow particularly convenient to you, I will either call upon you, or wait yr. calling upon me. Pray do whichever is most agreable to yourself & for God's sake use no ceremony whatever, as there is no one can have a higher esteem or regard for you, than yr. very sincere friend.   (Lonsdale MSS.)

388   PRINCE WILLIAM TO THE PRINCE OF WALES

Barbadoes, 24 Jan. 1789

It was not till the 16th instant, when I arrived at this island, that I received the least information respecting the dreadful situation of his Majesty's health. The shock I first felt was great, but what are the King's feelings to the sensations of that dear inestimable woman the Queen? From the 16th merchantmen keep constantly coming in with fresh and worse accounts of this valuable and unfortunate Monarch. The inhabitants of all the West India Islands have behaved in the properest manner on this truly melancholy occasion. On the 23 I received a letter from the Duke of Cumberland and two from Captain Elphinstone which have fully informed me of the situation of the best of Kings and fathers.

I immediately dispatched a vessel to Commodore Gardner to signify to him that upon the intimation I had received from the Duke of Cumberland I thought it my duty to remain here either till a man of war should arrive or till 1st February, when nothing arriving I should proceed down to Jamaica. The ship is ready to proceed to England at an hour's notice. I hope you have sent my orders to return both to the Commanding Officer at these islands as well as Jamaica. That is all I have to say respecting the subject of my return.

I must now request you will say for me everything that is right and proper to the Queen. She I trust is convinced of my affection for the best of mothers. It is not for want of feeling but really for want of words that I do not write to her. Tell her, my dear brother, I feel most sensibly for her unhappy situation and have her and my sisters constantly in my mind. God grant that we may all yet have the happiness of possessing this valuable man restored to his former good health. It does the English

1. Lonsdale was ill during the second half of December 1788, and did not recover until sometime in January 1789. The letter could have been written on the 9th or the 16th or possibly the 23rd.

nation the highest honour for the manner in which they feel for their beloved King. Permit me to express myself strongly. I follow the dictates of my heart. Sincerely do I love this good and worthy man and long may he yet with his usual firmness reign over us. The poor Queen: what a situation for her.

With respect to myself I trust you know me that I am attached to you of all other of the family in the strongest manner. Situated as we unfortunately now are, you are by this time in the situation of Regent, from whence I make no doubt you will be loved and respected by everybody. I am sincerely thankful for your kind remembrance of me at all times. It gives me the highest satisfaction to find from the Duke of Cumberland, to whom I beg to be sincerely remembered, that there is so great a harmony between you four, and I only hope to be admitted of the party.[1]

Till I hear something fresh adieu, and ever believe me [etc.]. (44854-5)

389   THE DUKE OF LEINSTER[2] TO THE PRINCE OF WALES

Dublin, 28 Jan. 1789

May it please your Royal Highness to accept of my most sincere thanks for the very great honor your Royal Highness has conferred on me in giving so immediate an answer to the letter I presumed to trouble your Royal Highness with.

Nothing but a severe illness coud have prevented my acknowledging this great mark of condescension in your Royal Highness sooner. With a heart overflowing with gratitude for this particular honor I beg leave once more to trouble your Royal Highness & to assure your Royal Highness that it shall be the study of my life to deserve your Royal Highness esteem & to be ranked amongst those who are most truly attached to your Royal Highness's person, and that you will at all times find me ready to support your honor & dignity.

I hope & indeed flatter myself that you will have every reason to be content with the people of Ireland, & I trust, in spite of the machinations of the present Administration, that your Royal Highness will be placed in that situation in this country you are so justly entitled to.   (38400)

1. The Duke of Cumberland, though wholly devoted to the Prince of Wales and to his cause, was conscious of his inability to make an intelligent speech, and took no part in the Lords' debates on the Regency.

2. William Robert, 2nd Duke of Leinster (1749-1804), succeeded his father as Duke, 1773. Master of the Rolls [I.], 1788-9, and Clerk of the Crown and Hanaper [I.], 1795-7. He was an Opposition Peer. 'The Duke of Leinster has, as I suppose you know, written to the Prince of Wales, to offer himself to him,' wrote Grenville on the 19th (Buckingham, *Court and Cabinets of George III*, ii. 95).

[*29 Jan. 1789*]

Having been appointed by the two Houses of Parliament a Committee to attend his Royal Highness the Prince of Wales with the several Resolutions agreed to by the Lords and Commons for the purpose of supplying the defect of the personal exercise of the Royal authority during his Majesty's illness, we beg the favor of your Lordship to acquaint his Royal Highness the Prince of Wales therewith, and to receive H.R.H. commands at what time they may be permitted to wait on his Royal Highness in order to communicate the said Message.[1]

Camden
Stafford[2]
W. Pitt
R. P. Arden[3]
Fredk. Campbell[4]

(38288)

1. 'We have passed the Resolutions in the House of Lords,' Lord Hawkesbury wrote to the Duke of Dorset on the 26th. 'Towards the end of our proceedings our majorities decreased owing to the defection of some shabby fellows, but I think that in future we shall stand at least as well as we are at present. We shall probably improve. During the whole of this proceeding the eloquence of the Chancellor has exceeded everything I ever heard in either House of Parliament. It has raised his reputation immensely with all parties, and will give him an ascendancy in this country which few have ever attained, especially as he is to be the principal Counsellor about the Queen' (Sackville MSS. Kent Record Office).

2. Granville Leveson-Gower, Earl Gower and (1786) Marquess of Stafford (1721–1803). Succeeded his father as Earl Gower, 1754. Lord Privy Seal, 1755–7; Master of the Horse, 1757–60; Lord Chamberlain of the Household, 1763–5; Lord President of the Council, 1767–79, and 1783–4; Lord Privy Seal, 1784–94.

3. Richard Pepper Arden, 1st Lord Alvanley (1744–1804). Solicitor-General, 1782–3 and 1783–4; Attorney-General, 1784–8. M.P. for Newtown (Isle of Wight), 1783–4; for Aldborough (Yorks.), 1784–90; for Hastings, 1790–4; for Bath, 1794–1801. Master of the Rolls, and knighted, June 1788; Chief Justice of the Common Pleas, May 1801; peerage, 1801.

4. Lord Frederick Campbell (1729–1816), third son of John, 4th Duke of Argyll. M.P. for Glasgow Burghs, 1761–80; for Argyllshire, 1780–99. Vice-Treasurer of Ireland, 1787–93. Wraxall remarked that he was 'attached to the Crown, if not to the Government, by a lucrative place, the Lord Registrar [Register] of Scotland', with a salary of £2,000 a year (iv. 77). When, on 12 December, Lord Frederick declared that no one was more attached to the Prince than himself, and that he should be very happy to serve him, he raised quite a laugh in the House and Fox hinted that he was a mere place-hunter. The House of Commons nominated four, not three Members to wait on the Prince. Rather oddly, the Secretary at War, Sir George Yonge, did not put his name to the letter. He did, however, accompany the others to Carlton House.

WILLIAM, PRINCE OF ORANGE[1] TO THE PRINCE OF WALES

La Haye, 30 Jan. 1789

Je ne scaurois manquer de temoigner a Votre Altesse Royale mon desir sincere & ardent de cultiver & de cimenter autant qu'il est en moi la bonne harmonie qui regne si heureusement entre la Grande Bretagne & la Republique des Provinces Unies. C'est avec la plus grande satisfaction que j'ai eté informé des sentiments de Votre Altesse Royale au sujet de l'Alliance qui a eté contractée entre ces deux etats & de ce qu'elle a bien voulu dire a cette occasion au Baron de Nagell[2]. J'ai toujours regardé que l'interet commun de la Grande Bretagne & de la Republique exigeoient leur union & que le plus grand malheur qui pouvoit leur arriver etoit d'etre brouilleés, Il y a d'autres Puissances qui ne pouvant voir de bon oeuil la prosperité de ces deux Puissances tacherait toujours de mettre tout en oeuvre pour semer la teraine entre elles afin qu'elles s'entredetruisent, & j'ai eté ravi de voir que Votre Altesse Royale envisageoit les choses du meme oeuil. J'ai toujours eté personellement attaché au Roi son pere & Votre Altesse Royale ne sera point surprise de ma vive douleur du malheur qui lui est survenue, & des voeux que je fais pour son prompt retablissment. Je ne puis la feliciter d'avoir du prendre sur elle la Regence dans d'aussi tristes circonstances mais je prie le Tout Puissant de la combler de ses plus pretieuses benedictions & de l'assister a lui faire supporter le fardeau de l'Administration du Royaume de son Pere, & que son Administration puisse tendre au bien etre de la Grande Bretagne & a la gloire de Votre Altesse Royale & veuille l'Etre Supreme quand il lui plaira de la faire monter au trone & d'appeller a lui le Roi son Pere & de lui faire changer cette courronne perissable contre une couronne eternelle, accorder a Votre Altesse Royale un regne long & heureux. Je saisis cette occasion de me recommander avec les miens a sa bienveillance & de l'assurer du profond respect avec lequel j'ai l'honneur d'être [etc.]. (38415)

WILHELMINA, PRINCESS OF ORANGE[3] TO THE PRINCE OF WALES

Le Haye, 30 Jan. 1789

Votre Altesse Royale en chargeant Mr de Nagel de me faire part des assurances flatteuses qu'elle a bien voulue lui donner de ses sentimens favorables pour la Republique et pour son sistéme actuel, excite une

1. The Stadholder, William V, Prince of Orange (1748-1806).

2. The Dutch Minister in London since March 1788. Lord Carmarthen, the Foreign Secretary, described him as 'a very pleasant man with nothing of the bad qualities of a Foreign Minister about him, and not much of anything which could mark the *amiable*

juste reconnoissance, je prie Votre Altesse Royale d'en agréer l'expression avec bonté. Le respectueux attachement que je porte au Roi son pére, et ma vive gratitude des bienfaits signalés que nous en avons recu, sont garants à Votre Altesse Royale du vif intéret que je prens, à la triste calamité qui accable ce Prince respectable. Dans ces circonstances facheuses rien ne pouvoit m'étre plus agréable que de recevoir des preuves de la précieuse bienveillance dont Votre Altesse Royale nous honnore, je forme des voeux bien sincères pour tous ce quie peut contribuer à la gloire & à la prospérité de V.A.R.. Elle voudra bien me rendre la justice d'étre persuadée de la part que je ne cesserois d'y prendre. Ce sera une satisfaction bien douce pour moi que de voir consolider de plus en plus le sistéme auquel cet Etat doit le retablissement de sa tranquilité & de son bonheur, et je saisirai toutes les occasions de témoigner à V.A.R. combien je desire que les liens qui unissent la Grande Brètagne et la Republique soyent resseré de plus en plus. C'est avec un sincére attachement & une haute considèration que j'ai l'honneur d'être [etc.]. (38416)

393   THE PRINCE OF WALES'S DRAFT SPEECH (IN THE
       DUKE OF PORTLAND'S HAND)

[*30 Jan. 1789*]
My Lords & gentlemen, I thank you for communicating to me the Resolutions agreed to by the two Houses, and I desire that you will assure them in my name that my duty to the King, my regard to the peace & happiness of the Royal Family, & my anxious concern least the publick safety & interests of the people may be endangered if the government of the Kingdom should remain longer in its present state, will in my mind outweigh every other consideration, & determine me, in conformity to the united wishes of the two Houses, notwithstanding the difficulties which I foresee in the execution of it, to express my willingness to undertake the weighty & important trust as it is now proposed to me for my acceptance.[1]   (38402)

country he comes from' (Add MSS. 28063, f. 102). He added, a few weeks later, on further acquaintance (29 April 1788): 'I like him very much , and he certainly is not disliked here for he is chosen a member of White's (to my great astonishment)' (ibid., f. 156).

3. Princess Wilhelmina (1751-1820), daughter of Frederick the Great's brother, Prince Augustus William of Prussia, married the Stadholder in 1767.

1. At 3 p.m. on the 30th the Committee waited on the Prince of Wales at Carlton House to present the Address of the two Houses praying him to accept the Regency under limitations. He made a verbal reply, accepting. This draft speech is in the Duke of Portland's hand, but Sir Gilbert Elliot wrote on the 31st: 'The answer made by the Prince yesterday to the Address

[*? Early 1789*]

The author of the inclos'd letter to Mr. Pitt, whom it is presum'd he has address'd by his characteristic title, humbly approaches to lay it at the feet of his Royal Highness the Prince of Wales.

It will be introduc'd to the public eye tomorrow, and the writer flatters himself that it conveys in firm but decent language wholesome truths which, to be universally and willingly allow'd, need only be widely diffus'd and generally known.

It may be consider'd as the voice of a faithful people looking up with the fondness of hope and the warm wishes of expectation to his Royal Highness, the person alone proper and alone able, like the rising sun, to dispell the dark cloud which envelopes the nation.

Shou'd the sentiments of the letter, written on the spur of the occasion and produc'd rather by the emotions of a zealous heart than any pretensions to superiority of talent, shou'd this early offspring rather of strong attachment than great abilities, be so fortunate as to meet with the approbation of his Royal Highness, the writer will ever consider the auspicious effort as the prize and pleasure of his life.

To open the eyes of a kingdom that has long been mislead by an artful but dangerous Minister, to make a people sensible of the blessings they have in store, and to do away the false prejudices of ministerial insolence, is what he has attempted, however he may have fail'd in the execution.

He ventures to flatter himself that however unskilful the hand, he has touch'd the right string, and that every honest heart in the kingdom will vibrate in unison with it.

If in this or any other exertion the author can serve a Prince, the delight and future dependance of the age, he will embrace with pleasure every opportunity of devoting his pen or even his life to a cause which so powerfully calls forth every fine feeling of honour, generosity and loyalty, according at the same time with the true principles of the Constitution, the real glory and prosperity of the British Empire.

Shou'd his Royal Highness, with a spirit as manly as it is polite, excuse this intrusion and condescend to communicate any commands, he will be pleas'd to order them to be left by a written message directed to Mr. Richard Gregory, to be left at the York Coffee House, St. James's Street. (Add. MSS. Georgian/3, f.4)

... was entirely mine, and done in a great hurry half an hour before it was to be delivered' (*Minto*, i. 269).

This verbal reply was later reduced to writing, or, should one say, put into its final shape, and presented to both Houses on 2 February. The printed version (*House of Commons Journal*, xliv. 91) is identical with the Archive document (No. 403) except for two trifling differences, and it probably represents more accurately than this draft what the Prince actually said.

[*? End Jan. 1789*[1]]

The friendship you have always expressed for me makes me not hesitate of informing you of the death of Admiral Forbes[2]. You know my object was to be General of Marines on a vacancy & I have no doubt of your gratifying me in this particular.[3] (38528)

396 THE PRINCE OF WALES TO THE QUEEN, AND THE REPLY

Carlton House, 30 Jan. 1789

Before your Majesty gives an answer to the application for your permission to place under your authority the direction & appointment of the King's Household[4], thereby to disjoin from the difficult & arduous office which I am call'd upon to fill, the accustom'd & necessary support & dignity wh. have hithero belong'd to it. Permit me, with every sentiment of duty & affection towards your Majesty, to entreat your attentive perusal of the papers which I have the honor to enclose. They contain a

1. On 2 February the newspapers were reporting that the Duke had applied to the Prince of Wales for the Generalship of Marines in case of Admiral Forbes's death. The net income was said to be £1700 a year. The Duke was obviously acting on a mistaken report. See *n*2.

He had written to the King on 27 November 1786: 'Permit me to submit to your Majesty's consideration that the appointment of General of Marines is the only mark of your Majesty's favor I am eligible to receive as an Admiral & I presume, Sir, to trust in your Majesty's goodness as the only advocate I shall solicit to obtain it & to counterbalance the great interests that will be exerted whenever by the death of Admiral Forbes the Marines shall become vacant.' (54483)

2. He lived until 1796. Lieutenant, 1731; Captain, 1737; Rear-Admiral, 1747; Vice-Admiral, 1755; Admiral, 1758. He was the second son of the 3rd Earl of Granard. General of Marines, 1763. (1714-96).

3. The Duke had asked the Prince for something (its nature seems to be unknown) in 1787, and had written to him on 18 July: 'I have but one apology to make to you in not having answered yours of the 13, but knowing you would receive one on the subject I therefore rather chose to be silent & wait your answer, which I freely own was exactly what I expected; for my part I must declare that ever since I have had the happiness of being so intimately acquainted with you I never have seen but one tenor in your conduct towards me & that I am certain the refusal has given you more unhappiness, & the more so by being constructed as if you declined giving me a convenience. Rest assured of one thing, I am thoroughly satisfied, nor did I name the subject as I knew it was not in your power to comply with my request.' (54486)

4. The House of Lords nominated Lord Waldegrave and Lord Ailesbury, and the House of Commons ordered four of its members—Lord Courtown, the Comptroller of the Household, Richard Howard and Lieutenant-Colonel Manners—jointly to wait upon the Queen with the Resolution and Address agreed to by both Houses respecting the care of the King's person and the direction of his Household.

sketch of the plan now propos'd to be carried into execution as communicated to me by Mr Pitt, & the sentiments which reason & duty suggested to my mind in answer to that communication. It is also my earnest wish to be permitted to lodge authentick copies of this correspondence in your Majesty's hands, confiding that whenever it shall please Providence to remove the malady with wh. the King my father is now unhappily afflicted, your Majesty in justice to me & to those of the Royal Family whose affectionate & cordial concurrence & support I have receiv'd th[r]o' the whole of the critical situation in which I have been plac'd, will take the fittest & earliest opportunity of submitting to his royal perusal this just explanation of the true grounds & principles upon which we have acted, & I here solemnly repeat to your Majesty that among those principles there is not one which has guided or now influences my mind so much as the *firm persuasion* I have that my conduct in endeavouring to maintain unimpair'd & undivided *the just rights, prerogatives, & dignity of the Crown* in the person of the King's representative is the *only line* of conduct which would entitle me to *his Majesty's approbation*, or enable me to stand with confidence & without self-reproach in his presence, on the happy day of his recovery; & on the contrary I have the same firm persuasion that those who under colour of respect & attachment to his Royal person have contriv'd this project for weakening & degrading the executive authority of the Empire will be consider'd *by him* as having risk'd the peace & happiness of his people for the purposes of their *own interested ambition*, & as having shaken the security of the Throne by establishing a fatal precedent, which may hereafter be urged against *his own authority*, or be revived on *various pretences* against *the rights of his successors.* In speaking my opinion of the motives which may have actuated the projectors of this scheme I trust I need not assure your Majesty that the perfect duty & affection I ever have felt for your Majesty have never suffer'd me for a single moment to consider you as countenancing in the slightest degree their plan or their purposes. I have *the firmest reliance on your Majesty's early declaration to me on the subject of publick affairs,* at the commencement of our common calamity, & whatever may be the efforts of evil & interested advisers, I have the same confidence that your Majesty will never permit nor endure that the influence of your respected name should be profan'd for the purpose of *distressing the Government & insulting the person of your son.*

How far *those* who are manifestly persuing *both these objects,* may be encourag'd in their purpose by your Majesty's acceptance of the powers & state denied to me, I will not presume to say. The proposition itself has assum'd the form of a Resolution of Parliament, & therefore I leave unsaid much of what I feel & apprehend upon the subject. Your Majesty however will, I doubt not, do me & yourself the justice to weigh the opinions I form'd & entertain'd before the two Houses had adopted their present plan, & with those before you, which I have the honor to submit, will enable your Majesty's own judgment to decide upon. Actuated as I am sure you will be by your duty to my father & by your constant affection to your children, I feel the firmest reliance on those principles that nothing will ever prevail upon you to lend your countenance to any councils that can in the smallest degree be liable to even the suspicion or rumour of having consented to adopt measures that were likely to interrupt in the slightest degree that harmony & affection that has ever invariably prevail'd hitherto, & wh. it shall continue the constant object of my wish to cherish & promote.

I remain, with the sentiments of the truest affection & invincible respect, Madam [etc.].[1]   (38429–33)

THE QUEEN'S REPLY

Kew, 1 Feb. 1789
Your letter was delivered but a few minutes before the Committee of both Houses came to me by my own appointment. Considering the proposition as a Resolution of Parliament, I thought only one answer could be given to it: and, if your suggestions had come in time, they are not sufficiently particular to furnish an alternative.[2]

I saw nothing in the Address of the two Houses but their desire to charge me with a trust which, in all private respects was my duty before, with such powers as seemed to them necessary for that purpose. That tender and anxious office I have endeavoured to perform ever since the melancholy occasion arose, and I have no views beyond it.

How the King's Government is to be administered, what provisions are to be made for replacing it in his hands, and what stile of dignity

1. The Hon. Stephen Digby wrote to Pitt from Kew House on the 30 January 1789: 'I have her Majesty's commands to forward to you the inclosed, a copy of a letter her Majesty received from his Royal Highness the Prince of Wales between the hours of two and three o'clock this afternoon.

'*P.S.* If you have any wish to take a copy of this you are at liberty, but her Majesty desires you will in the course of three or four hours send the inclosed back, and may I beg you to direct it to Lady Charlotte Finch' (Add. MSS. Georgian/2, f. 8).

2. The Queen replied to the Address: 'My duty and gratitude to the King, and the sense I must ever entertain of my great obligations to this country, will certainly engage my most earnest attention to the anxious and momentous trust intended to be reposed in me by Parliament. It will be a great consolation to me to receive the aid of a Council, of which I shall stand so much in need, in the discharge of a duty wherein the happiness of my future life is, indeed, deeply interested, but which a higher object, the happiness of a great, loyal and affectionate people, renders still more important'(*House of Commons Journal*, xliv. 92). She was 'extremely affected, and fainted away when it was over.'

should attend his person in the meantime are considerations upon which I can form no adequate judgment.

If the care of so great a person is thought by the public necessarily to draw after it an Establishment which is really capable of being abused in the manner you represent, I must consider even that circumstance as a mark of their confidence that no such abuse will be attempted.

Conscious of my claim to your affection and confidence, I believe you without hesitation when you assure me that you depend upon my duty to the King, and my constant affection to my children, for preserving harmony & mutual kindness in the family. Nor can I omit to thank you from my heart for this solemn promise that it shall continue the constant object of your wish to cherish and promote it.

When it shall please God to restore the King to us and the nation, I will not fail to lay before him every paper, and make every other representation which you may wish to convey through me, for I shall resume with joy the office in which I have always delighted of conciliating and maintaining the harmony of my family.

How long our common calamity may last, God, who inflicts it, alone can foresee. In the meantime you will easily conceive how much of my consolation must depend on preserving the affection of my family.[1]
(36377–8)

397 EDMUND BURKE'S MEMORANDUM[2]

[? *Jan. 1789*]

These offices form much the most considerable part of the patronage of the Crown, notoriously those which are the most sought after by persons of the higher rank, influence & consideration in the kingdom, and as consisting rather in dignity & honour than in responsible & laborious employment. To separate them from government, the Prince apprehends, is to subvert it. That her Majesty should be principal (not exclusive) in the care & custody of the King is so far from being an arrangement apposite to the Prince's inclination that he would never have consented to any plan in wh. this was not a fundamental part. In no one particular has the Prince failed in demonstration of affection &

1. The Queen's letter was drafted for her by the Lord Chancellor, to whom she wrote, from Kew, on 31 January: 'I am this instant returned from the King, which is the reason of your servant being detained so long. I return you many thanks for the trouble you have taken in forming [?'framing' in original] so useful an answer for me to the Prince of Wales, which I intend sending tomorrow morning' (Egerton MSS. 2232, f. 72, *copy*).

2. Burke's disconnected sheets (38417-20) form a very much amended draft, hardly legible in places.

perfect duty to the Queen & he appeals to her honour . . . on the subject. But in giving proper weight to the serious concern of the King's government as manifestly as deeply affected by setting up this seperate & perhaps superior interest, the Prince hopes he does not derogate from the filial respect which is due from him to her Majesty. The Prince conceives that the entire management of so large a system, composed of many extensive & intricate departments & the disposition of so vast a patronage is not necessary, perhaps not altogether consistent with the care of the King's person in his present most melancholy condition. The distressing circumstances wh. must daily, perhaps hourly, occur to wound her Majesty's sensibility who is to have the peculiar care of the King's person, will be ill relieved by the competition & intrigue with wh. so many offices are to be sought. Such business the Prince conceives must be highly disgusting & painful to her Majesty in the present state of things, & the Prince has no sort of doubt that if her Majesty has given her consent to a plan tending to bring so much vexation on herself as well as embarrassment to the King's affairs, her Majesty has been abused by the most mystifiable misrepresentations. His duty, affection & veneration for the person of his royal parent will never suffer the Prince to believe that her Majesty has been persuaded to lend her name to a project so pernicious to the real interests of the King & of her family. Whatever steps the Queen shall take the Prince will attribute to the best motives, but he is apprehensive that this measure may be construed by those who judge rather from what commonly happens among mankind than from her Majesty's inherent goodness, from the separation of so large a part of the patronage of the Crown as her Majesty's yielding to a plan for setting up her Majesty as the head of a party agst. the administration of her son & the interests of all her children.[1] (38417)

[The next sheet seems to be missing]

398 MEMORANDUM [2]

[? Jan. 1789]

Most private. The parties are still squabbling and God only knows when their quarrels will end: I believe never as both look to one object, which is not large enough to satisfy the views and ambition of all. The pasture is not extensive enough for the cattle. The matter of right is *pro tempore* over, but mere *Resolutions* can form no part of the Constitution of this

1. This may be a draft for a letter from the Prince of Wales to the Queen (possibly that of 30 January, No. 396).

2. No. 384 (38381-3) is in the same hand (? John Robinson's).

country. Mr. Fox was in the *right* in his explanation. The Houses had no *right* but *judicially* to decide according to form where the *right* lay. They could not, in my humble opinion, create a *right*; they were only to announce where the *right* lay; no more than a court of justice can give away an estate in prejudice of the *lawful heir*. But these are matters that are now past; I mean only for a time, for whenever the whole functions of the State are restored, the streams of *right* and *justice*, which have been diverted from their proper courses, must be *legally* brought back to their former channel.

Nec Deus intersit nisi dignus vindice nodus. This is a sound maxim in policy as well as poetry. The *Gordian knot* will present itself in a few days and it must be *cut through* or untyed. Without a metaphor—a great personage must not stand much longer in the character of an indifferent spectator. A damp may fall on those who think warmly of his *rights* and they who have listened to the bold assertions of the *right* and *duty* of Parl^t will begin by too much acquiescence on the part of his R.H. to suppose that there is some foundation for what has been *resolved* through the force of pompous sounds alone!

The moment will come on in a few days for his R.H. to come forward and make a full impression on the minds of a public that, from being ignorant of his true and genuine character have been deceived by interested men. There is so much loyalty in this country that the people are artfully made the dupes of their own good principles. Let the great personage come forward, in his place, I mean in a certain Assembly; let him cloath with the garb of his natural talents and elegance the meagre skeleton which is here, with the greatest humility, presented. Let him say "That a regard to national unanimity and filial duty have hitherto possessed his mind more than an attention to the precise limits of any right he may possess as undoubted heir to the Crown: that he is still influenced by the same motives and principles which are rooted and fixed in his mind: that he has observed with much sorrow and regret that the business of the nation has for some time and perhaps too long been suspended: that his duty to his royal father and a sincere love for his native country will not permit him any longer to remain a silent spectator, or to seem, through an appearance of inattention, to withhold his offer of his best services in promoting the peace and prosperity of the nation in which he himself, his royal father excepted, is more interested than any person on earth. That considering the delay that has happened through various causes, he finds it necessary for the public good to accept the care of the Executive Government under any limitations the two Houses of Parliament, in their zealous loyalty to his illustrious father, may think proper and expedient to be laid on his temporary office; that it was not his wish, nor could it possibly be his interest, that the Crown should be impaired or lose any of its lustre or

464

legal powers when resumed by the King, whenever it will please God to restore him to his health and his people: that he trusts the two Houses of Parliament, in making the regulations, will take the proper care of reserving to him that force and energy which is necessary to make an Executive Government efficient for the public good in the internal as well as foreign concerns of the nation: that he has already communicated these his sentiments to his Majesty's Ministers, and that he expects, after this public declaration of his sentiments, the national business will not be much longer retarded by unnecessary discussions; that as his sole object is to serve the public to the utmost of his abilities during the indisposition of the King, he hopes to receive that firm support from Parliament which they have uniformly given to his royal father." (38385-6)

399   HINTS ON THE REGENCY

[1788-9]

The peculiar character of the present Chan——r has been at the bottom of every change that has happened since the beginning of the year 1782. During the war he never once approved of any measure brought forward in the Cabinet, yet he would not propose any of his own. The news of Lord Cornwallis's losing his army[1], arriving in November 1781, shook Administration to the center, and it was perceived by a great majority of the K's servants that they must give up either America or their places. His M[ajesty] was so much averse to the relinquishing any part of his dominions that Ld. N[orth] durst not press the subject, and thus matters went on during the recess 1781/2, hastening to a fall which happened about the middle of March.

The Ch——r, finding that the party with whom he had acted was to fall, began, as early as the beginning the year 1782, to break the other party by tampering with some of them. The most accessible was the E. of Shel-b--ne. Though he joined the Opposition in Parliament he was known to be united with them neither in views nor in principles. Some others, among whom was Mr. D[unda]s, made overtures of a similar kind but at a very humble distance. A treaty was so early and so firmly settled that I was assured from the best authority just *three days* after Ld. N. *agreed* to resign, and before his successors were appointed, that Lord Rock——m[2] and his party were not to remain in office after the 1st of July 1782. Such prophets were the contracting powers that the

1. At Yorktown.

2. The 2nd Marquess of Rockingham (1730-82) had been Leader of the Whig Party, and Prime Minister, 1765-6 and again, March-July 1782 (until his death).

Minister died on that very day, and that saved the Chan——r and Sh——ne the trouble of turning him out with his party.

During the discordant interval which intervened between the fall of Ld. N—th and the demise of Rock——m, Mr. D——s, although his knowledge of the *interior* was but slight, as he had not the good fortune of being trusted, came to learn something of the ground through his friend Mr. At[kinso]n¹; he therefore cultivated the friendship of Ld. Sh——ne. But the intelligence he received induced him also to look forward to his Lordship's Ch———r of Exch——r, Mr. P-tt, who from his *name* and the advantage of a very early possession of a *great situation* seemed to promise his being soon in play. Luckily for D——s the Minister and his Ch———r of Exch——r were totally ignorant of E. India affairs, and finding this, *though he was as ignorant as either of them*, he imposed upon them the knowledge of *others* for his own. This revelled [*sic*] with them an idea that he could be of the greatest service to them when India affairs should fall under parliamentary discussion. To secure his supposed talents he received the boon which he now possesses, the Treasurership of the Navy, together with the office which he holds in Scotland, for life; which had been absolutely refused to him under Ld. N.'s Administration.

In February 1783 Ld. Sh——ne, having been frightened from his office by two adverse votes of the Commons, an interregnum of Administration, if so it may be called, continued for near two months. Those who knew most of the inclinations of the K. renewed their intrigues, as on former occasions. The office of Minister was hawked about from door to door; Lord Gow-r hesitated for *one day* and P-tt for *three*; both at last refused. The other party were then brought in, but their fate was determined before they were nominated to their *offices*. Before the end of July, the day of the rejection of the India Bill, almost the very hour of the intended change of administration was prophesied by men in the secret, and the dissolution of Parliament and the introduction of another India Bill were fixed to the very dates at which both happened in the following year. D——s, who was in July in Scotland, was not in this secret, for he was *not trusted* by those who knew the *interior* of affairs.

When Mr. F-x brought in the Bill for regulating India affairs, it

1. Richard Atkinson (1738-85). M.P. for New Romney, 1784-85, an Alderman of the City of London, and a Director of the East India Company. The commercial house with which he was connected had contracted to supply rum for the army during the War of the American Revolution, and it was to him in this capacity that the *Rolliad* referred when describing Pitt's powers of eloquence in debate:

> Nor rum contractors think his speech too long,
> While words like treacle trickle from his tongue.

Atkinson had been an enemy of the Coalition and a strong supporter of Pitt.

was so open that much advantage was immediately taken by those who had formed the plan I have mentioned above. The Ch———r, and more particularly *some others*, began to form a new Administration, but how this could be done was the difficulty, for want of proper *ostensible* figures. Ld G-w-r was too timid to accept then what he had refused some months before: Sh———ne was not to be thought of on account of his *great integrity* and *direct conduct*. P-tt became the only object. But the line to be taken was rough and rugged and he did not know the way. The secret springs which move *slowly* but *surely* the State machine, were not within the reach of *his* experience, and the consequence was that he was frightened at what he did not understand. The game was thus nearly lost, though the cards had been *judiciously shuffled* to win it.

It happened that from his natural shyness and other circumstances P-tt was not sufficiently accessible to those who *could* and *were ready* to give the most judicious and most infallible advice. They were therefore obliged, *though very unwillingly*, to send their plans *at second hand* through D——s. To execute this important business Mr. Atk——n was chosen who, on account of accidental but important favours, thought himself in much request with D——s.

From day to day every difficulty that arose was removed by the sound advice given. The very spirit of prophecy seemed to animate the advisers, for nothing was predicted but punctually and literally happened. As there was no end to difficulties there could be none to advice, yet P-tt was frequently on the point of quitting till some *new project*, offered him through the medium of D——s, revived his spirits and induced him to stand.

It was afterwards found that D——s imposed the plans of others upon P-tt as merely the result of his own profound knowledge of men and things. P-tt believed him infallible and gave him his implicit confidence. D——s availed himself of the warm gratitude of his admiring friend, and obtained from him *under his hand* not only acknowledgments that it was his (D——s') advice alone that enabled him to stand, but that he would give him a *complete & perpetual* support: in short, that nothing but death itself would induce him to desert his friend. Thus, whether he remains in or returns to office, P-tt will and *must* have his friend in the line in which his injudicious precipitancy has long placed him. The truth is that D——s leads him as a nurse does a child when he first begins to walk, and there is not the least doubt but he is the first mover of all his present measures. The *Seal turned King* is D——s's crude idea, for everyone knows the wise intention of this *northern Lycurgus* in his first India Bill was to make a *Seal* Governor General of Bengal.

Although D——s runs away with the *reputation* of being the *soundest counsellor* on the present occasion, there are others who sometimes convey their knowledge of men and matters to P-tt through various channels;

but this is done *by stealth*. The jealous eye of the *dragon* forever watches the *tender plant* he has reared to maturity. The dragon is not liked, nay, he is hated by the figures in the background of the piece, but a common interest has occasioned a pause of hostilities, and the fear of proscription from the other side may make the *armistice* terminate in a treaty of friendship. Although D----s assures his dependents that *he* and *his friends* will inevitably *force* their way back into the fortress in a very short time, he is anxiously eager to keep his present hold. His vanity and ambition are even stronger passions than his avarice on this occasion. He is afraid that India ceasing once to be *rode* will not be easily *mounted* again by so clumsy a horseman, and his being out of place would break those political cobwebs he has endeavoured to spread over almost all the Scotch elections, for his hope and intention are to place relations and personal friends in some counties and several boroughs to create a bodyguard for himself with which he can treat with any enemy and ultimately, when the worst comes to the worst, obtain terms for himself.

The character of the man is well known. Although he certainly has but the *frigida dextra* in the political field, he is bold in advice to induce others to go to the front of the line. The manner in which he rouzes *his friend* at present is curious. He brings before him the example of his father. "You have been the Minister of the Crown because then it was necessary; be now the Minister of the people and spurn with indignation the step from which you mounted. You stood up against the H. of C.'s before; they now stand up for you. Keep what you have as a conquest —hold of nothing but your own popularity. This is your time to render the Sovereign, whoever he may be, subservient to yourself and your friends. This will be the way to strengthen and fix you beyond the power of whim or accident, and you will be followed and supported in proportion as the idea of your stability is established in the minds of men."

It is the fate of the most powerful and wisest nations to be misled and deceived by insignificant men whose selfish machinations could only have effect from their not being seen. Obscure and even incapable persons having the ear of the Sovereign or the confidence of a Minister have more than once moved and agitated this State. Two thousand guineas have been known to turn out a well-established Ministry, and a man who by a coarse species of artifice has rather enslaved than gained one man of popularity, bids fair to make a dangerous change in the Constitution of this country.

It would be a very humiliating circumstance indeed should a fabrick reared at such an expence of toil and time suffer detriment from so mean a cause! Captique dolis—

Quos neque Tydides, nec Larissœus Achilles,
Non anni domuere decem, non mille Carinae.

468

The scenes that may follow are connected with the farce already described, and they must be attended with more danger than the interludes played between the acts of former changes. One step of violation leads to more, for one piece of injustice requires another to protect its authors. Injury will thus succeed injury unless obviated by coolness, precaution, firmness and address. To be quiet and silently to receive what may be offered will be the best manner of preventing further breaches and of repairing those already made. The people, though they may ultimately judge aright, are slow in comprehension; to attempt to stop or stem the torrent would increase its rage. A calm ebb will soon succeed this rapid flow, and men, as awaking from some foolish dream, will be ashamed of having been so much deceived. They will see that all this mighty bustle about *right* and *claim* is but a squabble for office, and matters will be restored in a very little time to their former legal and constitutional state. (38387–90)

400 ROUGH IDEA OF WHAT MIGHT BE SAID BY THE PRINCE OF WALES
AT THE REGENCY[1] [copy]

My Lords, Conscious of the wisdom and loyalty of both Houses of Parliament, I have hitherto forborne to express any sentiments of mine upon the present unhappy state of the Government of this country: a state which has arisen from a calamity which all must lament, but which I feel with the severity of a domestic misfortune.

I would not even have risen at this time to join my thoughts to the deliberations of your Lordships, but that the duty I owe to my Royal father and my anxiety for the national wellfare, compel me to break a silence which I would have observed on any points that might concern my own personal interests; being thoroughly satisfied that the wisdom of your Lordships and of the other House of Parliament will form a better judgement upon every concern of mine than I can venture to ground upon my own opinions.

But while I leave every personal consideration, with perfect confidence, at the disposal of the Houses of Parliament, I should hold myself deficient in the duty of a loyal and affectionate son, if, during the present inability of my Royal father, I should not object to any circumstances which, according to the best of my judgement, may retard his recovery or may render government more uneasy to his

1. Draft for a possible declaration by the Prince of Wales to the House of Lords. On 10 February *The Times* advertised a correct copy of the Speech intended to be delivered by the Prince of Wales on his first appearance in Parliament as Regent. Price 6d. Sold by John Walter (the proprietor of *The Times*), No. 169, Piccadilly.

mind, when that happy period shall arrive, which is the wish of the whole world and is the ardent prayer of his dejected family.

My Lords, have we not all, one and the same object—that the sovereignty of these Kingdoms shall be preserved entire, for the exercise of those hands which alone are intitled to hold the Crown and weild the Sceptre? I disclaim not only the right, but I hope you will believe the wish likewise, to touch those ensigns of Royalty during the life of my ever respected father: but if they are to remain sacred from any approach of mine, I hope they will not be violated by any other less connected person or persons. While his Majesty lives, and long may he live and reign a blessing to his people, he alone is the King of this country: and as his regal authority is one single individual power, which cannot be separated or divided without being impaired, I think it a duty I owe to my Royal father to give my voice against parceling out and distributing his sovereign functions, which, in my opinion, wou'd be using an unnecessary, and therefore a reprehensible licence, with his royal dignity, and would be a dangerous measure for the unanimity and prosperity of the nation.

Whatever powers the necessities of State will not suffer to lie dormant for a time, let them be exercised by some one person, who, for that occasion and to that extent, shall be the Representative of his Majesty. The duration of the occasion is in the hands of the Almighty, and the extent of powers is in the wisdom of Parliament: but let me conjure your Lordships, on behalf of my Royal father, not to agree to mangle his individual powers and prerogatives by questionable distributions of his authority; a sight that would distress his reviving mind, at all times anxious to preserve entire every part of the Constitution of this country. Let me also offer the same intreaty, on behalf of the loyal people of these Kingdoms, whose quiet and happiness might be disturbed by the rise of new, distracted, and perhaps counteracting powers, in the government of the country, from whence embarrassments might ensue, which the wisdom and experience of my father, even in his firmest unimpaired health, might find difficult to disentangle.

I have understood that the partialities of your Lordships and of the other House of Parliament have supposed me qualified to exercise, as the Representative of his Majesty, those Royal functions which the affairs of State call into immediate action. This is a flattering opinion, which I receive with serious respect and cordial gratitude. I mention it in the present stage of this important business for the purpose of declaring that I most willingly join in leaving to the great Council of the Nation to determine which of the suspended powers of the Crown ought to be restored and exerted for the present government of the country. Whatever may be their number and extent, if brought to my hands, I will accept them with readiness for the good of the people. But with far greater pleasure will I surrender them again, into the hands of him to whom of right they belong, when it may please God to bestow upon us all the happiness of seeing him once more in a condition to receive them.

My Lords, where is the necessity for consuming much time on enquiries by your Lordships into ineffectual variations in my father's disabled condition; and what occasion is there for exposing to the world the venial effects of domestic hopes and anxieties for his recovery? My Lords, let the temporary representation of the Sovereign be appointed for as short a time as the wisdom of both Houses may think proper; I join my voice for as limited a duration as the concerns of State can possibly admit: and if, even within the narrowest period, his Majesty should happily recover, I trust that by the aid and support of his Parliament I shall be able, under the blessing of Almighty God, to restore his Royal prerogative, unimpaired, into his hands, and his dominions flourishing & prosperous, as they came under my management.

Why therefore should we expose any longer this Kingdom to the eyes of other nations, in the defenceless and dangerous situation of a country without a Government, while we waste our time in unnecessary deliberations, which may tend to foment dissensions at home and lessen our national consequence abroad? My Lords, I earnestly recommend a cessation of all needless investigations which tend to bring additional distress and confusion into a family already sufficiently afflicted; and, through too much delay, serve to leave the nation at the mercy of those mischiefs which cannot long fail to spring up in a country uncontrouled by any existing Government. (38284-6)

401   THE PRESENT QUESTION, IN ITS CONSTITUTIONAL POINT OF VIEW [1]

The constitution of the British Government is justly considered as the most perfect of human institutions. It is more complete, than any system of the kind hitherto reduced into practice, as a *whole*; and its *parts* are so connected, that they form both a spring and a check to each other. The *King* is the first vital principle of the body politic: he is, therefore, considered as *permanent*, in the exercise of the political functions; and, in the eye of the Law, he is deemed *immortal*. He is, in a manner, supposed to be *perfect*, as the constitution says he can do no wrong. His servants alone are responsible for the measures of his Government: and this is the great (and it is a sufficient) check on any

1. A printed pamphlet, endorsed 'Not published but ready to be distributed after the Great Seal Creation—Sir J. Macpherson.'

improper extension or exertion of the prerogative royal. Nothing can be more wise and salutary, than the following three maxims:

I. That, in a political view, as the King *never dies*, there can be no dispute about filling the throne, upon his natural demise.

II. As the constitution declares he can do no wrong, his situation cannot be liable to revolution or change: and, consequently, he remains the permanent pillar which supports the Government; whilst the two other branches of the legislature are subject to a temporary suspension or renewal of their functions.

III. As the King's servants are answerable for the measures of the King, as it is taken for granted they advise what they execute, no detriment can arise to the constitution, from the political permanency, and want of error, in the Sovereign.

This responsibility of Ministers on the one hand, gives them much power on the other, for they, in a great degree, sanctify and protect their measures, by making them those of the King. The Constitution knows of no power in the State, but what flows in a regular gradation from the sovereign; and, consequently, every act of Ministers, that is not authorized by the immediate order, command, or signature of the King, is *invalid* and *illegal*.

On these principles, the great question which agitates the nation, at this juncture, hinges. The King's Ministers, it is acknowledged on all hands, cannot act, at present, either *lawfully* or *constitutionally*, as they cannot receive either the *order* or *signature* of the King. If, therefore, they act at all, they *usurp the Regal Power* in their own persons, and are become answerable to the laws of their country for their conduct. If they *do not act at all*, or rather, if they *obstruct* and *delay* the restoration of the first vital principle of the State, they are, in the eye of the Law, guilty of *high crimes and misdemeanors*. In either of the above cases, they are bound, by the strongest of human ties, *a regard to their own safety*, to provide instantly for the restoration of the executive power, to legalize their own acts, or to obtain a legal indemnity for keeping suspended by evasion and delay, the regal functions, which the unfortunate malady of the King has interrupted.

No appeal to the people, no dependence on a majority of the two Houses of Parliament, to Ministers so situated as they are now circumstanced, will be a sufficient security. The people may be deceived. The two Houses are as incompetent as the Ministers themselves to do a *legal act*, without the sanction and signature of the Sovereign, or his representative. Mere resolutions are matters of opinion, not of Law: and what the majority of one Parliament may vote, that of another may expunge and annul. In short, there is no safety but in acts, which having passed through both Houses, have received the assent of the executive authority, which alone will make those acts a part of the Constitution of the country, and permanently binding, as far at least as personal security is concerned.

It being a fundamental law in the Constitution, that all the acts of Ministers originate with the King; it follows, that if Ministers have, in any one instance, *acted at all* during the interruption of the Royal functions, that they have USURPED THE KINGLY POWER, the greatest crime that can be committed against the State. The moment that proofs were exhibited before both Houses, that the Regal functions were interrupted, the power of action in the King's servants ceased. This is a matter of public notoriety. The ascertaining of facts and dates will, therefore, be sufficient to establish the guilt. If nothing actually has been done since the first vote passed, with respect to the interruption of the Royal authority, delay, though a less one than the former, is still a great crime.

The remedy to all our late misfortunes was obvious. Application should have been made, in the first instance, to the great personage appointed by the laws of the Constitution, in the succession, to discharge the Regal functions. He should have been requested to open Parliament according to the usual forms, which alone can render their transactions legal. No inanimate substance will ever be allowed to supply the deficiency which the hand of God has occasioned in the government of this nation. To the measure now recommended both Houses must still revert: to give a political life to themselves, they must restore, in a living agent, the Heir Apparent, the Executive authority, which is now become, in a manner, extinct. If regulations are deemed necessary, for circumscribing a little the power of the Regent in exercising the Royal Prerogative, and that for some specific and limited time, let the outlines of those regulations be communicated to his Royal Highness in the Addresses, which will request him to assume the Executive authority. This is the line pointed out by expediency and reason; and it is that which the Constitution has prescribed. The Revolution furnishes us with a precedent in point. In the Address of the Commons to the Prince of Orange[1] to accept of the throne, they prefixed the articles on which was afterwards founded the Bill of Rights. They did not say to him thus: 'Sir, we intend to confer upon you the Regal functions in this country; but your time is not yet arrived. We have some rights of the people to establish: we have some restrictions on the Royal Prerogative to frame. As we cannot *trust you*, after you are King, to give your assent to any Act that may trench upon your authority, we will make *an inanimate thing* called the Great Seal, King *pro tempore*, to answer *our* purposes.

1. William III.

473

This *inanimate King* will, in the first instance, open a Parliament, and afterwards give *its* assent to the Bill of Rights. After we have thus secured your *good behaviour*, we will make you the *Seal's Successor*.'

. . . The language of the Revolution Parliament was the contrary of the above: 'We have a good opinion of your talents; and we will not distrust your principles, so far as to suppose it possible, you will refuse your assent to such regulations, respecting the Constitutional rights of the people as we may think expedient to make after you have *legalized* our proceedings, by opening the session. We, therefore, request, that you will assume the Regal authority, and restore to life the Constitution of this country, which cannot exist, as long as the Executive Government is either *dormant* or *extinct*.' (38377-8)

402 THE VOICE OF REASON[1]

[*c. Jan. 1789*]

Without turning to the right hand or to the left, the voice of reason intends to bring before the people a series of circumstances and a state of reasonings that shall serve as a lanthorn to the public path.

So many years have elapsed since any very great constitutional question was agitated in England, that error is to be expected and confusion scarcely to be avoided on the first impulse of a case important as the present. The perplexity natural to novelty, the zeal inseparable from party, that obscurity that always grows out of tedious, entangled and mutilated debate, the eagerness on either side to magnify mistake and misrepresent truth, the melancholly condition of the sufferer whose malady furnishes the occasion, the natural leanings of the heart towards the unhappy, the painful sensations of a son situated and circumstanced as the Prince of Wales now is, and the consequences to be apprehended from dissentions and a divided government, all conspire to confound and embarrass the understandings of the people.

In such a situation, fraught with danger and scarcely to be got over without confusion, the first and wisest resolution of the people, of the whole people, for I speak not to parties, should be to keep themselves cool, collected and reserved, to have a just and manly idea of their own importance and interest, and to permit the free operation of truth on whichever side it may fall.

She who now addresses you cannot deceive you. Her influence would cease and she will no longer be the voice of reason than while she keeps within that circle which every man, however he may exceed it himself, knows and feels to be her proper and natural boundary. The daylight and the dark are equally known to the peasant and the philosopher, and

1. Endorsed 'Edmund Burke'.

in like manner that illuminating dispassionate process by which simplicity is distinguished from confusion, reallity from speciousness and truth from fiction, is equally known by all by the impression it makes. A question of law or of science may turn upon points and principles which only professional men can judge of, but a question of *national* rights as distinguished from *parliamentary* rights, a constitutional question, needs only to be held up in its own natural simplicity in order to be seen and understood by every man, let his station of life be ever so distinguished or so humble.

How often has the magic of a word, artfully applied, stolen a march on the sober senses of mankind? How often has the voice of the people and the sense of the people turned out to be two distinct things? The one was the effect of sudden impression, the other the result of information and cool reflection. That a multitude, like an individual, may speak before they think, is a truth confirmed by every day's experience, and that all hasty conclusions are subject to this error, and that the greater part of them are erroneous we need only look back and see how often the popular cry of the moment has fallen a sacrifice to the calm superiority of reason and reflection.

The history of parties at any period we will take them ought ever to put us on our guard against being taken by surprise. That which is right will strengthen by time, but that which is only the *counterfeit* of the right requires to be hurried thro' the nation before the flimsy guilding that hides, like a bad shilling, the fraudulent composition, be worn away.

Something had been thrown out by Mr. Fox respecting the right of the Prince to the Regency as founded on or running parellel with his right of succession to the Crown, the succession itself being founded, not merely on an Act of Parliament but on the known and universal consent, approbation and authority of the whole nation. This was violently opposed by Mr. Pitt and his motives for this opposition, so far as they can be deduced from his subsequent conduct, will appear in the conclusion of this work.

Much has been said about the question of RIGHTS, but whether by those rights are to be understood the original inherent rights of the whole people or merely the rights of Parliament as a branch of the Government acting originally from itself, and determining on the extent or encrease of its own power under the name of rights, deserves the most serious attention of every friend and lover of his country before he gives his opinion on the merits or demerits of this case.

Whatever may be errors of Mr. Fox, the nation, as well enemies as friends, will acquit him of hypocrisy. There is a certain openness about him not calculated to carry measures by contrivance, and he has sometimes failed by acting on a scale too broad and national for the views of Parliament. Such is the case now.

Circumstanced as England is (as will be hereafter shewn) a Parliament without a regal power to regulate and moderate it is equally as dangerous as a regal power without a Parliament, for an hereditary House of Nobles is certainly as dangerous as an hereditary Prince.

The Prince is hereditary in right of the whole nation, for the regal power itself stands on the right and authority of the nation. Therefore the difference between Mr. Fox and Mr. Pitt in this case is that Mr. Fox went on a national scale, and Mr. Pitt on a Parliamentary scale. Mr. Fox took the known consent and guarantee of the whole kingdom to the next in succession as the ground of right; Mr. Pitt, secure of a majority, took up his abode in the right of Parliament.

Could every man in the kingdom have been assembled, and could the question have been put to them, 'whether the right of the Prince as the next in succession to the exercise of the regal power stood on the great right and guaranteed authority of the whole people and kingdom or on the meer will and authority of Parliament', the ground Mr. Fox took would have been universally supported, but being brought before Parliament Mr. Pitt had no chance of losing it, for it requires but little knowledge of the human heart to judge how men will decide on a question that is to encrease their own power. Let us now proceed farther into the enquiry, taking for our guide the principles of the Constitution.

It will readily be granted, because it cannot be denied, that the great original source of all rights and of all power is the nation itself, and it will then follow that the nation has delegated thro' the means of its Constitution such parts and portions of those rights and powers to the several branches of the Government as are fit and necessary to answer all the good purposes thereof. But it certainly has not delegated away *all* its rights because where no right remains, slavery begins.

There are yet remaining to the great bulk of the nation, as well the unrepresented as the represented, parts thereof, a great body of inherent *undelegated rights*, many of which are of too sacred a nature to be made even the subject of Parliamentary discussion. The Parliament cannot alter the Constitution because the Constitution is the property of the nation and not of the Government. It cannot annihilate the religion of the country and establish an unknown one because the right to religion is a right the people hold from God. These and many other instances may be produced to shew that there are rights inherent in the nation not delegated to Parliament, and that to introduce them into Parliament under any shape whatever serves no other purpose in the end than to encrease the powers of Parliament beyond what the Constitution gives it, and to curtail and lessen the inherent undelegated rights of the people.

We have seen as many and strong endeavours in Parliament to grasp at and extend power as was formerly practised by the Crown. We have seen them set up the *omnipotence* of Parliament, the *universal supremacy* of Parliament, and sundry other titles offensive and hateful to the ear and heart of a free nation; nay, so great is the thirst for power in those who possess it that bring any question before them that has a flattering tendency to encrease that power, and they will resolve it in their own favour.

At a time that a late Parliament was profusely voting for every measure of the Crown, a majority of that very Parliament passed a resolve *influence*
'that the *power* of the Crown had encreased, was encreasing and ought to be diminished'. We now see it diminished below what is sufficient and necessary for preserving the equipoise of the three branches of the Government. We now see a majority of an hereditary House of Peers, over whom the people have no controul and who *assume* to sit in their own right independant of the people, forming a *coalition* with a Minister of the House of Commons and his adherents, and resolving (for such is the true explanation of their question of rights) that the people have no rights at all—that the Crown has no rights at all —that the powers of the three branches of Government and of the people are absorbed into the remaining two, and that neither the people nor the Prince have any right in the case.

This question of rights, so artfully and unnecessarily introduced into Parliament, and so industriously circulated thro' the nation to answer interested purposes that are now beginning to unravel themselves, is not on the very face of it a question determined on the rights of the people, as has been mistakenly supposed, but is a question of Parliamentary power and Parliamentary ambition, and may hereafter be produced as a precedent that Parliament, independant of and unauthorized and uninstructed by the people, can and may on their own will and authority alter the constitution or any part or parts thereof.

Having thus opened the outlines of the case, let us proceed, not in the spirit of party, but of reason and moderation, to investigate it clearly and fully.

In order to do this it is necessary that we exhibit the three branches of the Government, each in its proper and distinct functions, shew their relative connection and dependance on each other, and the consequences, to follow from an aggrandizement or a diminution of constitutional power in any of them.

We always say it consists of three branches, *King, Lords* and *Commons*.

The nation is composed of two orders of men, *Peers* and *Commoners*. By Commoners is *properly* meant every man in the nation who has not the title of *Peer*, and it is the existance of those two orders setting up distinct and opposite claims, the one heriditary and the other elective,

477

that makes it necessary to establish a third power or that known by the name of the regal power, or the power of the Crown.

The royal power is not the creature of the Parliament; it is not sett up by the two branches—the House of Peers and the House of Commons: it is set up by the whole nation. It originates from the womb of the nation and is that particular power in the Constitution which every man represented or unrepresented in Parliament feels an interest in and a relation to, and it is the sense of the nation distinct and separate from any powers the Parliament have or may possess, or from any opinion the House of Peers or House of Commons may or can give, *that there shall exist such a power;* for as their already exists an hereditary House of Peers, the remains of the feudal system, the aristocratical part in the Constitution which says to itself, the people have no controul over us, we are independant of them, it becomes the interest of the nation to support the regal power as being nearer related to it than what the House of Peers are, for the purpose of controuling that House, over which the nation has no other hereditary controul than thro' its King.

If therefore the powers lodged with and separately apportioned to each of those three branches is in that just proportion which the circumstances of the nation renders necessary for the equipoise of all its parts, and if two of those powers, viz., the regal power in right of the nation, and that of the Peers in right of themselves, are admitted to be herid[it]ary, it follows as a fair, just and undeniable conclusion, that if the regal power is diminished, the hereditary aristocratical power of the Peers must be diminished also, or the Constitution is violated and the equipoise so much boasted of is destroyed.

It is not the persons invested with or possessing those powers, but the powers themselves proportioned to each other that forms what is called the British Constitution, and as those three powers which compose the Constitution are executed by three distinct bodies of persons, the King, the Lords and the Commons, let us suppose that insanity, instead of taking place in the person of the King, had taken place in any of the other two branches; suppose, for instance that the whole House of Peers or the whole House of Commons had gone mad, is the powers & principles of the Constitution to be altered or suspended because of their insanity, or are the persons who are to succeed them even before the time of their natural dissolution or legal expiration to have less powers than their still existing predecessors? Those powers were not given for the sake of the persons but for the sake of the nation. The King is not King for the sake of himself but for the sake of the people. What therefore is true in any one of the branches is true in all.

There is not a light in which this question of rights, which the coalition of the Peers and Commons have determined in their own favour, and for the encrease of their own power, and the gratification of their

478

own ambition, can be placed in which it will not appear a dangerous and unconstitutional question.

That it was a question on their *own* rights and not on the rights of the people is now further evidenced by the use they are already making of it, for it has been followed up by a string of Resolutions (as will be hereafter stated) in which no man in the kingdom is interested but the actors themselves.

Let us now proceed to examine this question of rights in a further point of view.

The Parliament, as has been already observed, is composed of two Houses, the one hereditary in right of itself, the other elective.

The British Constitution naturally supposes that the regal power is that part in the Constitution which being detached from, and superior to, all the local parts, parties and interests in the nation exercises itself to preserve a constitutional equipoise and general interest in all the parts. It is not to know the landed interest, the mercantile interest, the manufacturing interest with partiality to the one more than to the other, but it is to know and promote the general interest of all and of the whole. It is not to know the House of Peers or the House of Commons with any distinctions of favour, but it is to know them equally. Agriculture, commerce and manufactures, arts and sciences are equally the object of its care and patronage. In short, it is neither more or less than the majesty of all the people collected to [a] center and is that disinterested power in the Constitution which is to arbitrate between the jarring interest of the parts. In order therefore to do this, it must not, as is before observed, be the creature of the Parliament dependant on a vote of Parliament, but must originate from the womb of the nation and stand on the broad basis of universal authority.

The Constitution and the consent of the nation have already defined and fixed what extent the regal power shall have, and it is the duty of Parliament to see that it does not misapply or exceed those powers, and likewise that it applies them rightly, and thus far and no further the power of Parliament goes with respect to the regal power, which is, as is before observed, the majesty of all the people collected to a center, and not the creature of Parliament, and whatever may be necessary beyond this either for the purpose of augmenting, diminishing, suspending or any ways altering the regal power must result back to the whole nation as the original source from whence that majesty springs. The Parliament have not a right in original cases of this kind to *assume* the right of the nation. The regal power cannot supply the place of a House of Commons; it cannot supply the place of the House of Peers; it cannot alter the constitution of either of them, neither can they alter the constitution of the regal power lodged where the consent of the nation has placed it and for the purposes for which it is established.

479

In order still farther to illustrate this point and to shew the unconstitutional inconsistency of the present measures pursued in Parliament, we will mention two other instances in addition to those already mentioned.

Often has it been noticed in the small compass of this work that we have an hereditary House of Nobles and that this House forms one of the branches of the Government.

The annals of this country furnish so many examples of the tyrannical oppression of the Nobles in former days over the people that, to free themselves from it, the Crown and the people saw it their mutual interest to form a sort of common cause, and it was by supporting the regal power against the power of the Nobles that [the people] laid in a great measure the foundation of the British Constitution. The power of the Nobles was curtailed and the power of the people encreased by the interest which the regal power found in supporting their rights. Were there no other reason than this it is sufficient to shew the danger of the conduct of Parliament in the present case. A monarch totally incapable of governing even his own person, and a Regent, the legal heir in succession, held thro the interested ambitious policy of Mr. Pitt, in the arbitary shackles of an hereditary House of Nobles.

Were this a meer work of the House of Commons the sense of the people operating at elections might correct it, but it [sic] order to prevent the effect which time and information might have on the mind of the country, the old exploded aristocratical system is resorted to and that of the most disgraceful kind, an aristocrasy of Bedchamber Lords, for to the honor of all the great families be it spoken they are on the constitutional side of the question.

The other reason why the regal power is not and ought not to be the creature of Parliament is this—

The great bulk of the people of England are unrepresented in Parliament; some of the largest towns and of the greatest national interest sends no members, while many of the inferior boroughs scarcely inhabited enjoy a large portion of the representation; but the whole nation feels an interest in the regal power which is, as [has] been before observed, the majesty of all the people collected to a center, and the person possessing the exercise of the regal power is the only personal representation [sic] they have in the Government. He is in fact their actual representative, the representative of their portion of national majesty. How little then, how derogatory to the honor of the nation must the question of rights on a Parliamentary scale appear when compared with the comprehensive rights of the nation. It is a question that ought not to have been agitated in Parliament. The constitutional line which marked out the order of succession and *that succession* standing on the known consent and authority of the whole nation included all inferior cases, for it is a known maxim that the major includes the minor.

It ought not, I say, to have been agitated in Parliament. It was purloining the rights of the nation, particularly the unrepresented parts thereof to introduce it there, for whatever appertaineth to the regal power, appertaineth to the nation in its original right and not to the Parliament.

Men always feel, tho they do not always reason, and it is not difficult to discover that the people of Manchester, tho' they might not define and analize the impulse under which they acted when they rejected the proposed address to Mr. Pitt[1], had some impression of this kind.

The minority or those who were opposed to making it a Parliamentary question acted consistently with the Constitution. It is as if they had said, 'leave it on the floor of the nation, the regal power is the majesty of the nation. It appertaineth to the nation, & Parliament are but parts of the Government'.

That the legislative power of Parliament is now incompetent to any purposes of legislation does not arise meerly from the absence of one of the branches, but because the regal power comprehending and representing the whole majesty of the nation is not present, therefore whatever they may now do is illegal and nugatory.

The majesty of the nation does not reside in the Chancellor's Great Seal, any more than in his great wig; it must reside in a sensible Being, in a Being capable of knowing whether what he is going to do is right or wrong. He is to reflect, he is to weigh consequences before he proceeds to determine.

What is consent but the action of a rational being? The Great Seal when affixed to any instrument is only the evidence of that consent and not the consent itself. Is the Lord Chancellor so bad a lawyer as not to know that a bond or a note of hand is only the evidence of a debt and not the debt itself, and that to manufacture a bond or a note of hand where no debt exists and to affix the Great Seal as an evidence of consent that never existed are equal species of forgery?

What is the Great Seal? Hath it eyes to see; hath it ears to hear; hath it a mind to judge and an heart to feel? What then is it? Is it Nebuchadnezer's golden image or Aaron's molten calf? The honest pride of nature spurns the idolatry, the enlightened mind of man disdains the deception. How must we laugh? How contemptibly must we feel at such silly impositions on ourselves? If the constitution hath laid it down as a principle that the concurrence of three distinct and separate powers in making a law is a better security than two, and therefore necessary to the perfection of a law, is the Chancellor's Great Seal one of them? Were the Chancellor's great wig put on a barber's block and made to nod consent, should not we laugh at the gallantee show? Nothing could then

1. See No. 369.

be wanted to compleat the sublimity of buffoonery than to follow in procession and huzza *vive la perruque*.

But let us return to our argument. The matter is either too silly for satire or too serious for ridicule.

From the innate love of liberty it follows as a natural and popular prejudice *that to take power from the government is to secure or add rights to the people*.

But Mr. Pitt is acting the direct reverse of this, and it is only because the subject has not had time to operate on the understanding of the people that addresses have been procured. It certainly did not strike everybody in the same light. There appeared to many discerning people an ambiguity, a misteriousness, a certain something that required consideration.

Mr. Pitt, so far from securing or adding to the rights of the people, is artfully taking them away. He is, it is true, diminishing power in one part of the Government but he is adding it not to the people but to another part of the government. Enleagued with a majority of the Peers he is diminishing the power of the Prince and adding it to the House of Peers; a House who are not the representatives of the people and over whom they have no controul. Is this an encrease of the rights of the people? Let Mr. Pitt answer for himself.

There is a Resolution wisely founded on the principles of the Constitution which, for the purpose of better securing the rights of the people, forbids any Peer of the realm interfering at elections, but Mr. Pitt has found a way to transfer by a vote of Parliament under the shape of a 'Question of Rights' the rights of the people into the House of Peers. All that has been done by our forefathers to prevent that House engrossing or possessing too great a share of power in the Constitution is done away by this delusive contrivance of Mr. Pitt.

It is well worth the attention of the nation to observe how engeniously artful this whole business is carried on, for as the event of this question of rights is to diminish the legal power and to establish a power in the House of Peers which it had not before, it is necessary that the measures to accomplish it should not make their first appearance in that House; therefore Mr. Pitt brings them forward in the House of Commons, a conference with the Peers is proposed and agreed upon; they are then carried into the House of Peers and by this manoeuvring the *rights* of the people are first absorbed into the *rights* of Parliament and transferred from the Commons to an hereditary House of Peers independant of the suffrages of the people.

In laying down those arguments the rule of Parliament in the present case has been observed. There the language has been *a* King, *a* Queen, *a* Prince, &c. so here *a* House of Peers, &c. make the objects of the argument, for it is not the persons immediately composing those bodies but the powers attached to those bodies that make up the principles of the argument.

It may serve as a quietude to the minds of the people to know that the great families in the House of Peers are supporters of the constitutional and not of the aristocratical powers of that House. It would certainly be more dangerous, tho' it does not affect the principles of the argument, if the families of Norfolk, Bedford, Devonshire, Portland, Northumberland and the Rockingham connections were aristocratical instead of constitutional, but as the caustic in those arguments, if any there is, is of a nature that will affect only the sore and not the sound flesh, it needs no apology, therefore none is offered.

On these grounds we will rest the argument. They are but a small part of what might be advanced, but they are sufficient for a beginning. The sense of the people and their reflections on the subject will supply a great part of what is omitted and time operating with reason will unravel the whole.

The part intended to follow were the restrictions alluded to in the beginning, page 3[1]. (38403-11)

403   THE PRINCE OF WALES TO BOTH HOUSES OF PARLIAMENT [2]

2 Feb. 1789

My Lords and Gent., I thank you for communicating to me the Resolutions agreed to by the two Houses, and I request you to assure them in my name, that my duty to the King my father, and my anxious concern for the safety and interests of the people, which must be endangered by a longer suspension of the exercise of the Royal authority, togr. with my respect for the united desires of the two Houses, outweigh in my mind every o[the]r consid[eratio]n, and will determine me to undertake the weighty and important trust proposed to me, in conformity to the Resolutions now communicated to me. I am sensible of the difficulties that must attend this trust in the peculiar circumstances in which it is committed to my charge, of which, as I am unacquainted with a former example, my hopes of a successful Administration cannot be founded on any past experience; but confiding that the limitations on the exercise of the Royal authority deemed necessary for the present have been approved only by the two Houses as a temporary measure, founded on the loyal hope, in which I ardently participate, that his Majesty's disorder may

1. See page 475.

2. There was what Sir Gilbert Elliot described as 'a sham' opening of Parliament on the 3rd; that is, it was done under the authority of a commission, to which Burke gave the name of the 'Phantom'. Incidentally, Canning's 'set' at Christ Church debated and carried a motion 'That Mr. Pitt's conduct in the Regency was unconstitutional'.

not be of a long duration, and trusting in the meanwhile that I shall receive a zealous and united support in the two Houses and in the nation, proportioned to the difficulty attendg. the discharge of my trust in this interval, I will entertain the pleasing hope that my faithful endeavour[s] to preserve the interests of the King, his Crown and people may be successful. (38437)

404 CHARLES JAMES FOX TO THE PRINCE OF WALES

Bath, 4 Feb. 1789[1]

I really do not know how to express my gratitude for the very kind letter which I have this day received from your Royal Highness. My health, about which you are so good as to interest yourself so much, is so good, and my amendment every day so visible, that, if Mr Pitt is not shamed out of his system of delay, I have no doubt but I shall be as well as ever I was in my life before your Royal Highness is appointed Regent.

I am not at all surprised at the satisfaction your Royal Highness expresses at the noble and manly manner in which the Duke of York has distinguished himself. Indeed it is more than a compensation for every unpleasant circumstance one can meet in life to have such a brother and friend as your Royal Highness has in the Duke.

The Duke of Portland did mention to me an idea suggested by your Royal Highness of giving the Duke of Norfolk[2] the Stannaries, which I entirely approved, and which, if it can be carried into execution, will relieve the Duke of Portland and me from considerable difficulties. I hear Pitt[3] was but eleven ahead of Howard[4] at the close of last night's

1. Fox, seriously ill, set off for Bath on 27 January.

2. Charles, 9th Duke of Norfolk (1746-1815), succeeded his father in 1786. He was styled Earl of Surrey, 1777-86. He renounced the Roman Catholic faith at the time of the Lord George Gordon riots (1780). Whig M.P. for Carlisle, 1780-6; a Lord of the Treasury, April-December 1783. For him see *Wraxall*, iii. 362-67.

3. John Pitt (1725-1805). M.P. for Gloucester, 1789-1805. On 5 February he was elected after a 15-day poll, the numbers being, Pitt 837, the Hon. Colonel Howard 836; the bye-election being caused by the death of Sir Charles Barrow. On Saturday, 31 January the numbers were Pitt 797, Howard 769. Pitt put the expenses of his return at £10,000, his opponent's at twice that sum. He himself contributed £4,500, his committee between them paid £3,000 out of their own pockets, and at the end of May, 'the electioneering spirit having evaporated', no one was disposed to subscribe the remaining £2,500, so he asked Ministers for some money. 'Should suits be commenced, the expense must fall on my Committee,' he informed George Rose, the Joint Secretary of the Treasury, who could draw on secret service money. 'I propose therefore that their Lordships [of the Treasury] should give £1,000. I will give another £1,000 both on condition that every debt be immediately discharged, and

poll and that [there] were still hopes, but I confess I am not sanguine.

I take it for granted that the vacant Regiment will be given to Lake, and I am sure I shall be as happy as any man at such a disposition of it; but I should be very ungrateful to a very worthy man if I did not take an early opportunity of representing to your Royal Highness's consideration & to that of the Duke of York the very strong pretensions of General Charles Ross[1] who had a Regiment in the war and who is one of the oldest Major-Generals upon the list. I feel myself peculiarly bound to support his claim because I am firmly persuaded that the neglect shewn towards him has been entirely owing to his political attachments and Parliamentary conduct.

I have the honour of inclosing to your Royal Highness a letter from the Duke of Leinster.

General Burgoyne[2] and Mrs Armitstead both desire me to express their gratitude to your Royal Highness for the obliging manner in which you are so good as to mention them.   (38438-9)

405   THE EARL OF CHATHAM TO CAPTAIN G. K. ELPHINSTONE

Admiralty, 4 Feb. 1789

Lord Chatham presents his compliments to Mr Elphinstone, and begs to acknowledge the receipt of his Royal Highness the Prince of Wales's dispatches for H.R.H. Prince William Henry, transmitted to him by Mr Elphinstone, and to add for H.R.Hs the Prince of Wales information that H.R.Hss commands will be obeyed and that H.R.H. Prince William Henry will be directed on his return to repair in the Andromeda to *Spithead.*   (38440)

I will follow your directions to the mode of paying it in to the committee as to secrecy, &c.'
(P.R.O., Chatham Papers, 167).

4. Henry Thomas Howard (1766-1824). M.P. for Arundel, 1790-5; for Gloucester, 1795-1818; for Arundel, 1818-20; for Steyning, 1820-4. In 1812 he assumed the additional surname of Molyneux, and in 1817 that of Howard in addition to Howard-Molyneux. His elder brother succeeded his cousin as 10th Duke of Norfolk in 1815.

1. M.P. for Dornoch, etc., 1780-4 (1729-97). He had voted for Fox's India Bill, but with Pitt on the Regency question.

2. John Burgoyne (1723-92), who capitulated at Saratoga in 1777. M.P. for Midhurst, 1761-8; for Preston, 1768-92.

Carlton House, 12.30 p.m., 6 Feb. 1789

Supposing yt. your My. had nothing particular to say to the D of Y. & myself in private owing to Ly. Harcourt's[1] continuing in yr. presence, I did not venture, having nothing particularly pressing to communicate, to request a private audience of Yr. My. Had yt. opportunity presented itself I shd. have presum'd to have inform'd you yt. from the urgency of the present times I judg'd it incumbent upon me to take upon myself ye administration of H. My.'s Hannoverian dominions. I take ye liberty of inclosing an authentic copy of the measures yt. were necessary to be taken in order to accomplish yt. point, & wh. I flatter myself I may venture to hope, yt. yr. My. will preserve, in order yt. they may be laid before my father, whenever it shall please Providence to enable him to form a judgment of my conduct in every respect, from the commencement of his malady to the present period. (38441)

407 THE PRINCE OF WALES TO THE PRINCESS OF ORANGE [copy]

10 Feb. 1789

Je saisis avec empressment la premiere occasion qui se presente pour repondre a la lettre que V.A.R. m'a ecrite en date du 30 Janvier et pour lui temoigner combien je suis sensible a la maniere dont elle s'exprime a mon egard.

Les qualites eminentes que V.A. Royale possede, ainsi que ses vertus et la la [*sic*] fermete qu'elle a scu developper dans un moment critique et epineux lui ont assures toute mon admiration et estime et je me ferai un devoir de lui en donner des preuves continuelles.

Je regarde le systeme actuellement etabli entre La G. Bretagne et les Puissances du Continent comme celui qui est le plus analogue a leurs interets comme a leur gloire reciproque et il me sera bien doux d'unir mes efforts a ceux de V.A.R. pour le consolider de plus en plus.

Je me conformerai par là pas moins a mes sentimens particuliers qu'a ceux qui animera le Roi mon Pere, a meme temps que que [*sic*] je m'acquitterai de ce que je dois a la nation dont la Regence m'est confieè jusqua ce temps qu il plairait a Tout Puissant d'exaucer mes voeux et de rendre a Sa Maj. la sante dont elle est actuellement priveè. (38442-3)

1. Elizabeth (1746-1826), daughter of George, 1st Baron Vernon, married her cousin George, 2nd Earl Harcourt (1736-1809), in 1765. He was Master of the Horse to the Queen, 1790-1809. She was appointed a Lady of the Queen's Bedchamber, August 1784.

10 Feb. 1789

Les sentiments exprimès dans la lettre de V.A.S. du 30 Janvier me sont trop agreables pour que je tarde de lui en temoigner ma satisfaction, et je me fais un plaisir de lui reiterer de cette manière les assurances que je lui a fais parvenir par la voye de Mons le Baron de Nagel.

Les liens de sang qui m'unissent a V.A. doivent lui servir de garant sur de mon affection personelle; ces liens sont renforcés par l'Alliance si heureusement contractee entre la G.B. & la Republique des Provinces Unies, et par la ferme persuasion dans laquelle je me troubre que la duree de ce systeme est essentiel a leurs interets reciproques. C'est d'apres ces principes que je le croirai de mon devoir de me comporter aussi longtemps qu'il plairait a Tout Puissant d'affliger le Roi mon Pere de la maladie dont S. Maj. est accablee convaincu que je ne scaurai observer une conduite plus analogue a ses sentimens ni plus conforme au bien etre des royaumes dont la Regence m'est confiee. (38444-5)

Hieres, 12 Feb. 1789

I take the liberty of troubling your Royal Highness with a few lines for to put you in mind of a brother who is and will always be most sincerely attached to your Royal Highness. The place here is at present vastly entertaining as the weather is become vastly fine. No day passes without my going out, which I find becomes me vastly well, being at present almost entirely recovered. I intend to stay here 6 weeks longer, about which time I intend to return by slow journeys to Gottingen unless I receive orders to the contrary. I hope soon to have the pleasure of seeing Sir Ralph Payne as he promised to come and see me before his departure. By all accounts I have heard of Sir John Deyar[1] he is in a bad way. Mr Obyrne[2] passed through here the other day but I had not the pleasure of

1. ? Sir John Dyer. See pages 37, *n*1; 168; and No. 178.

2. Possibly the O'Byrne mentioned by Wraxall as one of the Prince of Wales's boon companions. 'Without talents, morals, connections, rank or education, he contrived to attain a certain degree of celebrity, acquired a very considerable fortune, entertained with splendid profusion, and was received among persons of the highest rank, who even courted his society .... He played very successfully at almost every game, and in 1781 he won at a single sitting at the Cocoa Tree in Pall Mall £10,000 from Admiral Eliab Harvey, then a Lieutenant in the Navy.... He lived in very familiar habits with the late Duke of Orleans.... As O'Byrne passed much of his time in the capital of France between 1782 and 1788, he frequently dined with the Duke, either at the Palais Royal or at the voluptuous retreat at Monceaux' (*Wraxall*, v. 381–82).

seeing him as he only staid a day here and I was unluckily not at home then. The Court of France have been very civil to me. Hearing that I was come to remain at Hieres they ordered the Commander of the sea forces at Toulon, Monsieur le Comte d'Albert de Rion, to come over here [to] felicitate me on my safe arrival and offer me to come over and see the Port and the place where the ships lay. Accordingly after this polite invitation I went the other day to see it and was very genteely received. I went aboard the largest ship ever yet built, Le Commerce de Marseilles, a ship bored for a hundred and eighteen guns. It is a very fine ship indeed, but being no seaman I beg your Royal Highness to excuse my not making use of the proper terms; my brother William would know them better. Afterwards they took me in a very fine boat on the sea to see a Fort there called *La Malge*. All this together made me pass a very pleasant day. (47846-7)

410 ADDRESS OF THE IRISH PARLIAMENT TO THE PRINCE OF WALES

12 Feb. 1789

We, his Majesty's most dutifull & loyal subjects the Lords and Commons of Ireland in Parliament assembled, beg leave to approach your Royal Highness with hearts full of the most loyal & affectionate attachment to the person and Government of your Royal father to express the deepest & most gratefull sense of the numerous blessings we have enjoyed under that illustrious House, whose accession to the Throne of those Realms has established civil & constitutional liberty upon a basis which we trust will never be shaken, & at the same time to condole with your Royal Highness upon the grievous malady with which it has pleased Heaven to afflict the best of Sovereigns. We have however the consolation of reflecting that this severe calamity hath not been visited upon us until the virtues of your Royal Highness have been so matured as to enable your Royal Highness to discharge the duties of an important trust for the performance whereof the eyes of all his Majesties subjects of both Kingdoms are directed to your Royal Highness. We beg leave humbly to request your Royal Highness will be pleased to take upon you the Government of this Realm during the continuance of his Majesty's present indisposition & no longer, & under the stile & title of Prince Regent of Ireland in the name & behalf of his Majesty to exercise & administer according to the laws & Constitution of this Kingdom all regal powers, jurisdictions & prerogatives to the Crown & Government thereof belonging.

The Address being carried on a division it was presented to the Lord Lieutenant with the request of both Houses of Parl[t] that he would transmit the same to his Royal Highness the Prince of Wales & his Excellency have [*sic*] declined so to do, the Lords & Commons of Ireland chose the following messengers out of their own Houses—

The Duke of Leinster & Lord Charlemont[1]
Mr Thomas Conolly[2] & Mr Wm Ponsonby[3]
Mr John O'Neil[4] & Mr James Stewart[5]

Every species of indignity & disrespect having been levelled against the person & character of his Royal Highness during the progress of this whole transaction, the following persons declared their determination to sacrifice their offices rather than continue to support the Admn of Mr Pitt & the Marqs of Buckingham—

Earl of Shannon	Vice Treasurer	3500
Mr Wm Ponsonby	Postmaster	1500
Mr Lodge Morres[6]	Treasr P.O. and Clerk of Permit	1400

1. James, 1st Earl of Charlemont [I.] (1728-99). Succeeded his father as 4th Viscount Charlemont, 1734; Earldom, 1763. A consistent Whig, he opposed the Union.

2. Thomas Conolly (1738-1803), was M.P. for Malmesbury, 1759-68, and for Chichester, 1768-80, in the British Parliament; and, in the Irish, M.P. for Co. Londonderry, 1761–May 1800. In 1782 it was said of him: 'Has a very large fortune—married a sister of the Duke of Richmond—brother-in-law to Lord Buckingham and Mr. G. Byng—has the boroughs of Ballyshannon and Newtown Limavady—inclined to Government but unsteady' (*Proceedings of the Royal Irish Academy*, lvi. 256). He was naturally described in 1793 as 'against' the Government (Melville MSS., National Library of Scotland).

3. William Brabazon Ponsonby, 1st Baron Ponsonby (1744-1806). M.P. for Cork, 1764-76; for Bandon Bridge, 1776-83; for Co. Kilkenny, 1783-1806. His father was John Ponsonby, Speaker of the Irish House of Commons. Peerage, March 1806. Joint Postmaster-General in Ireland, July 1784-1789. A Foxite Whig, he opposed the Union. He was described in 1782 as 'a sensible, steady man'.

4. John, 1st Viscount O'Neill [I.] (1740-98). M.P. for Randalstown, 1761-83; for Co. Antrim, 1783-93; created Baron, 1793, and Viscount, 1795. He was murdered by the rebels in 1798. He was thus referred to in 1782: 'Supposed descendant and representative of the great Ulster family of O'Neill—has a large estate in the County of Antrim—much respected—inclined to Government—supported Lord Carlisle, Lord Buckingham and the Duke of Portland. Lord Buckingham made him Privy Councillor.' By 1793 he had gone over to the Government side.

5. At this time there were two M.P.s. in the Irish House of Commons named James Stewart: James Stewart of Fort Stewart, who sat for Inniskillen in the 1783-90 Parliament; and James Stewart of Killymoon, the member for Co. Tyrone, 1768-1800, and, in the Imperial Parliament, for that County, until 1812. Born about 1741, his date of death is unknown (he was alive in 1818). He was a consistent supporter of the Whig party, and a parliamentary reformer.

6. Lodge Evans Morres (1747-1822), 1st Viscount Frankfort [I.]. M.P. for Innistioge, Bandon Bridge, Ennis and Dingle Icouch successively, from 1768 to 1800. Under-Secretary of State [I.], February-May 1795. A Lord of the Treasury [I.], 1796-1806. Created Baron Frankfort, 1800; Viscount Frankfort, 1816. In 1782 he was said to be 'attached to Mr. Ponsonby.' In 1800 he was described as a Lord of the Treasury, 'of the family of Lord Mountmorres, and has estates amounting to £5,000 a year in the counties of Kilkenny and Wexford, and has given a warm and useful support to the measure [the Union Bill]' (*Cornwallis Correspondence*, iii. 254).

489

Mr Geo Ponsonby[1]	Councel to the Revenue	1200
Mr Wm Burton[2]	Paymaster to foreign troops	1000
M^r Jⁿ Townshend[3]	Barrack Mast^r of Dublin	800
Sr Jo^s Hoare—dead	Weightmast^r of Cork	800
M^r Jⁿ Uniacke—dead	Com^r of Bar^k Board	400
Mr Bowes Daly	Ranger of the Curragh of Kildare	500

(38446-7)

411 CHARLES JAMES FOX TO THE PRINCE OF WALES

Bath, 15 Feb. [*1789*]

I can not let the opportunity of Grenville's going to town go by without troubling your Royal Highness with a few lines. The reports of the great amendment in the King's health will I doubt not be made use of by Mr Pitt and his friends to justify the restrictions, and consequently will be much exaggerated; but I humbly submit to your Royal Highness that it is wisest for you to act precisely as if the King were in the same state as he was a month ago. To make any alteration in your conduct would be a sort of confession that your Royal Highness knew the measures you were taking would be disagreeable to him in case of his recovery.

I shall leave this place Thursday and be at St Anne's Hill Friday, where I shall stay Saturday and Sunday unless your Royal Highness has any commands for me in town.

Mrs Armitstead and General Burgoyne desire me to present their duty to your Royal Highness.   (38448)

1. M.P. for Wicklow in the Parliament of 1776-83; for Innistioge, 1783-97; for Galway Town, 1797-1800; for Wicklow, 1801-6; for Co. Cork, 1806-7; for Tavistock, 1808-12; for Peterborough, 1812-16; for Wicklow, 1816-17. Lord Chancellor [I.] in the Grenville Ministry, 1806-7; Leader of the Whig Opposition in the House of Commons, 1808-17. (1755-1817).

2. William Burton (1739-1818). M.P. for Co. Carlow, 1768-1802. He sold his pocket borough (Carlow) to a Unionist, but remained staunchly opposed to the Union himself. He was described in 1782 as of Burton Hall in his County; 'has a good estate and the borough of Carlow—is nephew to Mr. Ponsonby, with whom he has influence—always votes with Mr. Ponsonby.'

3. There was a John Townsend in the Irish House of Commons (M.P. for Dingle-Icouch, 1783-97, and for Castlemartyr, 1797-1800) who was in opposition in 1793, and, being then described as a Commissioner [? of Barracks], he voted against the Union.

Carlton House, 20 Feb. 1789

It is with infinite pleasure I received the communication made to me with great joy on his part by my brother the Duke of York. He informs me that the Chancellor has made a representation to the House of Lords of the state of the King's health so very favourable as to give just grounds for the animating hope of his Majesty's speedy recovery & of his restoration to his Government. This public blessing when it is fully realized will free me from a heavy burthen & remove me from a situation so very *perplexing & mortifying* as I never thought it possible I could be placed in. Your Majesty will easily imagine how much the prospect of this relief has added to the joy I naturally felt from my sentiments of duty & affection to the King my father.

I beg leave for myself & the Duke of York most sincerely to congratulate with your Majesty & my sisters on this comfortable view of things, the very first intimation of which I received by means of the public declaration made in the House of Lords. The Duke of York & myself are very desirous of knowing when we can be indulged with the gratification with which the Chancellor has been honor'd and at what time we may be permitted to throw ourselves at the feet of the King our father, & to pour forth our respectful joy in his Majesty's presence. We request that your Majesty will be pleas'd to consult the physicians as to the day, as we wish for many reasons that it may be as early as safety & propriety will admit, and that if unfortunately we should be debarred by professional precaution from that enjoyment tomorrow, that your Majesty will be so gracious as to direct them to send me *their opinion in writing & the grounds on which they act*.[2]   (38451-2)

---

1. The draft of this letter (38449-50) is practically identical with the letter as sent on the 20th. It is in no recognizable hand, except for the address and the date (at the end) which were clearly written by the Duke of Portland.

2. Sir Gilbert Elliot wrote on 23 February (the letter must be wrongly dated, as the 23rd was a Monday): 'The Prince of Wales and the Duke of York have for this week gone repeatedly to Kew, desiring to see the King, but were constantly refused on one pretence or the other, though the Chancellor and many other strangers were admitted to him. The Prince at last wrote to the Queen on the subject, and after many shifts and delays the Prince and the Duke of York were yesterday admitted. The meeting was extremely affecting and affectionate on both sides. The King, when he came to the door of the room where they were, stopped and said he was not yet able to go in, and cried very much, but after a little pause he said he found himself better, and came in. He embraced them both with the greatest tenderness, and shed tears on their faces, and both the Princes were much touched with the scene. The King did not touch at all on anything like business, but talked to the Prince about horses and to the Duke about his regiment. The Queen was present, and walking to and fro in the room with a countenance and manner of great dissatisfaction, and the King every now and then went to her in a submissive and soothing sort of tone, for she has acquired the same sort of authority over him that Willis and his men have' (*Minto*, i. 274-5).

THE QUEEN'S REPLY

Kew, 20 Feb. 1789

Though my head & face still continue to plague me very much[1] I will not omit any longer to return you thanks for your affectionate congratulations, of which I shall not fail to inform the King whenever a proper opportunity does offer.

I am sorry not to be able to accompany this with the physicians' oppinion about the time of your seeing the King, but you may depend upon my sending it tomorrow morning as early as I possibly can. I beg you will inform the Duke of York of this with my compliments, & believe me [etc.].[2]   (36381)

413   THE PRINCE OF WALES TO THE KING OF PRUSSIA [copy]

[Not later than 20 Feb. 1789]

La maladie dont le Roi mon Pere est affligee, etant malheuresuement d'une nature a ne pas lui permettre de diriger le Gouvernement de son Electorat d'Hanovre, je considere l'administration de cette partie de ses etats comme un devoir sacrè qui m'est devolu jusqu a ce temps qu'il plairait au Tout Puissant de lui rendre la sante.

En exercant une charge aussi importante au nom du Roi mon Pere, je crois ne pas pouvoir temoigner une attention plus respectueuse pour sa personne, ni un zele plus essential à ces interets, qu en observant le meme systeme que Sa Majeste a tracee elle-meme, et surtout en adherant aux engagemens qu'elle a contracte de concert avec Votre Majeste avec les differens princes de l'Empire pour assurer de la paix en Europe, et pour la conservation de la Constitution Germanique.

Votre Majeste me permettra a cette occasion de lui dire que je n'ai rien de plus a coeur que de cultiver son amitie personelle, que ce sentiment de ma part lui est bien sincerement devouè.[3]   (38435-6)

1. She was suffering from toothache.

2. Grenville wrote on the 21st: 'Their Royal Highnesses the Prince of Wales and Duke of York have been once or twice at Kew, to desire to be admitted to see him, which you will naturally suppose was not permitted. This morning they thought proper to make a formal demand that they should be allowed to see him; or if not, insisting that the physicians should give in writing the reasons for their refusal. In consequence of this, Warren and Gisborne, who were there this morning, sent Willis in to the King to acquaint him that the two Princes wished to see him. Willis returned with a message to them from the King, thanking them for their inquiries, but wishing to put off the seeing them till he had seen Thurlow again, which he is to do tomorrow. This was reduced to writing, and sent to them; how it will be received I know not, but it has completely defeated the avowed object of the visit, which was to prejudice his mind against the measures which have been taken' (Buckingham, *Court and Cabinets of George III*, ii. 120). The two Princes saw the King on the 23rd. The Queen was present, 'a precaution for which, God knows, there was but too much reason' (ibid., ii. 125).

3. See No. 417 for Frederick William II's reply.

492

414 THE PRINCE OF WALES TO THE QUEEN

Carlton House, 21 Feb. 1789

Allow me to express my gratitude for your Majesty's having condescended to communicate yourself to me the physicians' opinions relative to my seeing the King, & which, in obedience to your Majesty's commands, I will acquaint my brother the Duke of York with as soon as I see him.

(38453)

415 THE PRINCE OF WALES TO THE LORD CHANCELLOR, AND REPLIES

Carlton House, 21 Feb. 1789

I wish much to have the pleasure of a few minutes conversation with you at nine o'clock this evening, or at any time, *however early*, *before you* go to Kew in the morning.   (38454)

LORD THURLOW'S REPLY

21 Feb. 1789

In obedience to your Royal Highness's commands the Chancellor will not fail to attend your Royal Highness's pleasure at Carlton House at nine o'clock this evening.   (6495)

FROM THE LORD CHANCELLOR

25 Feb. 1789

In obedience to your Royal Highness's commands the Chancellor will not fail to wait your Royal Highness's pleasure at Carlton House at half an hour after five.[1]   (38457)

416 THE DUKE OF PORTLAND TO THE PRINCE OF WALES

Burlington House, Wednesday noon, 25 Feb. 1789

The Duke of Portland humbly begs leave to inform your Royal Highness that the Irish Deputies appointed to present the Address of the two

1. 'The Chancellor', wrote Sir Gilbert Elliot, 'is again getting about the Prince of Wales, persuading him that he is attached to him, and that he hates Pitt, which latter part is perfectly true; but he is the falsest and most treacherous character in the world, and is much more likely to mislead the Prince than to serve him or do anything else that is consistent or honourable' (*Minto*, i. 275). On the 24th the Lord Chief Justice wrote in his Diary: 'Dined with Lord Chancellor, who had been at Kew with the King and with the Prince' (Kenyon MSS.).

Houses of Parliament of that Kingdom to your Royal Highness[1] landed at Holyhead on Sunday night & will arrive in town tomorrow evening.[2]

(38456)

417 THE KING OF PRUSSIA TO THE PRINCE OF WALES[3]

Berlin, 26 Feb. 1789

Je prends une part aussi vive que sincere a l'indisposition du Roi qui oblige Votre Altesse Roialle de diriger le Gouvernement de l'Electorat d'Hanover en son nom, jusqu'a ce quil plaise au Tout Puissant de rendre la sante au Roi son Pere; je vois avec beaucoup de satisfaction par la lettre que Votre Altesse Roialle a eu lattention obligente de mecrire qu'elle adhére au sistéme et aux engagements que le Roi a contracté avec moi, et avec les differents Princes de l'Empire pour la conservation de la paix et pour celle de la Constitution Germanique. Votre Altesse Roialle peut etre persuadée que je desire sincerement de lui prouver en toute occasions en tout ce que dependera de moi, que je serés a jamais [etc.]. (38460)

418 ANSWER DELIVERED BY THE PRINCE OF WALES TO THE DEPUTIES FROM THE IRISH PARLIAMENT [26 FEBRUARY] 1789

My Lords and Gentlemen: The Address from the Lords Spiritual and Temporal and Commons of Ireland which you have presented to me demands my warmest and earliest thanks.

If anything could add to the esteem and affection I have for the people of Ireland it would be the loyal and affectionate attachement to the person and Government of the King, my father, manifested in the Address of the two Houses. What they have done, and their manner of doing it, is a new proof of their undiminished duty to his Majesty, of their uniform attachment to the House of Brunswick, and of their constant care and attention to maintain inviolate the concord and conection between the kingdom of Great Britain and Ireland so indispensibly necessary to the prosperity, the happiness and the liberties of both.

If in conveying my grateful sentiments on their conduct in relation to the King my father, and to the inseperable interests of the two

1. *The Times* reported that the Address was presented to the Prince at 5 p.m. on the 26th, and that the delegation dined that evening with the Duke of York.

2. Sir Gilbert Elliot wrote on 4 March: 'I dined yesterday at the Duke of York's with the Prince and the Irish deputies. We were 32 at table.' (*Minto*, i. 277)

3. This is the reply to No. 413.

kingdoms I find it impossible to express adequately my feelings on what relates to myself, I trust you will not be the less disposed to believe that I have an understanding to comprehend the value of what they have done, an heart that must remember and principles that will not suffer me to abuse their confidence.

But the fortunate change which has taken place in the circumstances which gave occasion to the Address agreed to by the Lords and Commons of Ireland induces me to delay, for a few days, giving a final answer, trusting that the joyful event of his Majesty's resuming the personal exercise of his royal authority may then render it only necessary for me to repeat those sentiments of gratitude and affection to the loyal and generous people of Ireland which I feel indelibly imprinted on my heart.

(38467-8)

THE PRINCE OF WALES'S ANSWER TO THE ADDRESS FROM
THE IRISH PARLIAMENT IN 1789.

Mr Conolly—Stated the following message—

I have it in command from his Royal Highness the Prince of Wales to return his thanks to those who maintained his rights in the Parliament of Ireland on the question of Regency.

And to those who so nobly refused to remain in office in support of a Ministry who had used him with personal disrespect he declares he will retain a lasting remembrance of their conduct & good opinion.[1] (38469)

419   THE PRINCE OF WALES TO WILLIAM ADAM [2]

Carlton House, 6.30 p.m. [endorsed 'February 1789']
Lord Loughborough wishes very much that you wd. call upon [him] this evening when the House is up, but certainly before you go to the

1. Grenville had declared (9 December) that the Addresses from Ireland could not be presented to the Prince until he had become Irish Regent (Buckingham, *Court and Cabinets of George III*, ii. 42). The Address was presented on 26 February (*Harcourt Papers*, iv. 259). The Prince was more popular in Ireland than his father because he favoured the Catholic claims, and the Lord-Lieutenant, the Marquess of Buckingham, had to admit that 'many of the great interests' in Ireland had abandoned Government (Add. MSS. 40733, f. 177).

2. William Adam (1751-1839). M.P. for Gatton, 1774-80; for Wigtown Burghs, 1780-4; for Aberdeen Burghs, 1784-90; for Ross-shire, 1790-4; for Kincardineshire, 1806-12. Treasurer of the Ordnance, 1780-82, and April-December 1783; Solicitor-General to the Prince of Wales, 1802; Attorney-General to the Prince of Wales, 1805; Chancellor and Keeper of the Great Seal to the Prince of Wales, 1806; a Councillor for the Duchy of Cornwall, and a State Councillor for the Prince appointed for Scotland, 1806. Lord Chief Commissioner of the Scottish Jury Court, 1815. He was one of the Prince of Wales's legal advisers for many years.

meeting at Burlington House, as he has something he wishes to mention to you wh. perhaps may not strike other persons, and yet one of consequence to be mention'd and well consider'd. (Blair Adam MSS.)

420 THE PRINCE OF WALES'S PROJECTED SPEECH TO PARLIAMENT [1] [copy]

My Lords & Gentlemen

Since it is at your desire that I am placed in this station to supply the defect in the exercise of Royal authority during the continuance of the calamity with which it has pleased Almighty God to afflict the King my ever honoured & beloved father, I consider it as the first act of my duty to assure you that, how difficult & painfull soever it may be for me to bear the weight which has fallen upon me by my being called to the Government of the Kingdom under such peculiar circumstances, I will use my utmost endeavours to exercise those powers of the Regal Office with which Parliament has thought fit to invest me, for the interests & honour of the King, & for the safety & happiness of his people: and I am the better prepared to meet the difficulties which must surround the execution of such a trust, by the consolation which I feel in the uprightness of my own intentions, & by the hope which I entertain, that my conduct in this temporary administration of Government will intitle me to the confidence of Parliament & of the nation, which it is & ever will be the study & the pride of my life to merit & to obtain.

I acknowledge with the deepest sense of gratitude the loyalty & affection of this free & powerfull country to the King my father, & their constant & zealous attachment to the House of Brunswick, and I can from my heart declare that no Prince of that House ever held in higher veneration than I do the principles on which our excellent Constitution in Church & State was asserted & vindicated at the Revolution, or was more fully convinced than I am that the steady adherence to those principles, the preservation of that Constitution intire & inviolate, & the maintenance of the laws which have been since made for confirming & perfecting the system formed at that glorious period will ever be found to be the best & most permanent security for the prerogatives of the Crown, the privileges of Parliament & the rights & liberties of the people.

Gentlemen of the House of Commons.

I will order the Estimates for the current year to be laid before you &c.

1. Endorsed 'Sketch of a Speech in case the Regency Bill had passed'.

My Lords & Gentlemen

On the justice & generosity which mark the character of Britons, I rely for a favourable interpretation of my actions, & of my utmost, tho perhaps feeble, exertions in their service, to promote the commerce the manufactures & general prosperity of the Kingdom to consult the real interests of the subjects of the King in all his dominions, and to preserve & secure the honour & the credit of Great Britain at home & abroad.

And when it shall be the will of Divine Providence to restore the King my Father to his former health, & to a capacity to resume the personal exercise of royal authority, I shall consider it as the happiest moment of my life to throw myself at his Majesty's feet with all the zeal & devotion of a dutifull son & an affectionate subject, & it will afford me the most cordial satisfaction as a faithful administrator & trustee for his Majesty & for the public, to surrender into his Majesty's hands the government of his Kingdom, & to see all the powers which the Constitution has allotted to the Regal Office, reunited under his authority undiminished in their lustre & unimpaired in their strength.   (38279-83)

421   THE PRINCE OF WALES TO THE DUKE OF YORK

[*1789*]

I am so anxious if it shd. be necessary for you to speak in the course of this day's debate yt. you shd. acquit yourself, wh. I am confident you will, with the same credit as you did the last time, yt. I cannot help troubling you with a few lines, to venture a few trifling ideas of my own, wh. perhaps in the hurry of the day, might not otherwise occur to yr. mind.

My particular wish is yt. you shd. be as short, concise, & pointed in yr. language as possible, to be careful not to be in a hurry, & to speak tho' slow, *in a strong tone of voice* as well as with a degree of emphasis to make people remark *yt. you feel what you are saying, & to be particularly pointed & to lay the strongest stress*, if you think it adviseable to say (wh. I confess I shd. were I in yr. place) 'Why it was a point yt. it appear'd absolutely necessary for the Minister or Ministers who had fix'd not only the Counsel for the Queen, but who mov'd also yt. ye sole care of the King's person shd. be vested in the Q. why I say it was a point absolutely necessary for *ym.* either to carry or to propose, yt. tho' there were so many & very near relations of Hs. My. who were honor'd with a seat in yt. House, yet yt. not only *ym.* but absolutely no one individual of the Royal Family were to be concerned in *yt. charge* with Hr. My. who certainly from affection as well as ye. close ties of relationship, must have as great, & as strong concerns in the personal wellfare & care of the Kg.

497

as those who were to be join'd with Hr. My. in yt. important trust as her Counsel; & yt. therefore the whole family & yt. you cd. speak for yourself in particular as an individual, & the world in general *cd. not nor wd.* not consider this great & unpardonable slight of the Ministery to the *whole Royal* Family otherwise than originating from an unfounded jealousy owing to the close & tender ties in wh. they are all most dutifully & affectionately bound to His Majesty.' Yr. own sentiments then wh. you mention'd this morning wd. follow well, respecting ye. impossibility in the present case as propos'd by ye. Ministers, for any of the Family, & yrself in particular, who on every account was most affectionately attach'd to a kind parent, to receive yt. exact intelligence of the King's health, wh. it is not only their anxious wish, but their right to expect.

Forgive me, my dearest brother, for thus troubling you, but really my anxiety originating from the boundless affection I ever have felt for you, wd. not allow me to be silent, when I thought yt. any thing yt. I cd. suggest wd. be of service to you. I think if you speak to this purport it will make an amazing impression. Pray dont burn nor lose this letter, & send me word instantly when you have spoke as I am in agonies & upon thorns till I shall hear how you have acquitted yourself, pray send me from time to time how things are going on.[1] (43906-7)

422 THE EARL OF SANDWICH TO CAPTAIN J. W. PAYNE

Hertford Street, Monday night [?1789]
I am most exceedingly obliged to you for the very communicative letter that I have just recieved from you, & you may be assured that the contents of it shall be locked up within my own breast.

I had intended to leave London tomorrow as I have business in the country with regard to a contest that has started up in the county that requires my attention if a speedy dissolution of Parliament is likely to take place; tho' I am perfectly easy about the event of that contest, & if the dissolution does take place under the circumstances that it most probably will, I have no doubt but that the four Members chosen for the county and town of Huntingdon, will be chosen by me.[2]

1. The Duke of York spoke both on 15 December 1788 and on 31 January 1789, but neither speech, as reported, bears any resemblance to that here suggested.

2. The County Members elected in 1784 were Lord Ludlow and Lord Hinchingbrooke, and they sat for the whole Parliament.

Peter, Lord Ludlow [I.] (1730-1803), was M.P. for Huntingdonshire, 1768-96. He was created a peer in 1755, and given an Irish Earldom in 1760. He was Comptroller of the Household, 1782-4. He voted with the Whigs on the Regency Bill.

Lord Hinchingbrooke (1744-1814), who succeeded his father as 5th Earl of Sandwich in

In these sort of moments it would be ridiculous to profess attachment or gratitude where it is due, & I have laughed too often at the nonsense in Mr Doddington's[1] Diary, to desire to be allowed to kiss hands for what it may never be in the power of those who honour me with their protection to realize: my attachment in that quarter will allways remain the same, whither I am a little man as I am at present, or what the world may improperly call a great one; which appellation I know I can never attain but thro' the protection allready mentioned.

I will stay in town to morrow in the idea that this melancholy affair may possibly be brought to a conclusion, & therefore I should take it as a favour if you would in the course of to morrow send me an authentick account of the state of the King's health, which I heartily hope (tho' I fear with little foundation) may be a favourable one. (38209-10)

423 LORD LOUGHBOROUGH TO CAPTAIN J. W. PAYNE [2]

Monday, 4 p.m. [?*1789*]

I shall try to discuss the various topicks that arise out of so singular a state with those whose experience, judgment & fidelity I know & write to you often, if you will direct whoever you send to call here for letters. I wish even to avoid the appearance of sending into Pall Mall. (38364)

424 STATE OF THE ATTENDANCE OF THE SEVERAL PHYSICIANS ON HIS MAJESTY IN HIS LATE ILLNESS

Sʳ Geo. Baker	25 nights & days at Windsor at £30 is	£750	0	0
	58 times at Kew .. .. .. 10 „	580	0	0
Dr. Warren	24 nights at Windsor .. .. 30 „	720	0	0
	48 times at Kew .. .. .. 10 „	480	0	0

1792, was so styled until that date. He was M.P. for Brackley, 1765-8, and for Huntingdon-shire, 1768-92; Vice-Chamberlain of the Household, 1771-82; Master of the Buckhounds, May 1783-1806; Joint Postmaster-General, 1807-14. He, as a Household official, voted with Pitt on the Regency Bill, though his father voted, in the Lords, the other way.

The Members who sat for Huntingdon borough in 1788 were Sir Walter Rawlinson and Captain J. W. Payne.

Sir Walter Rawlinson (*c.* 1735-1805) was M.P. for Queenborough, 1774-84, and for Hunt-ingdon, 1784-90. He voted with the Whigs on the Regency Bill, and so, of course, did Payne.

1. George Bubb, afterwards (1717) Bubb-Dodington, Lord Melcombe (1691-1762), the well-known diarist. M.P. for Winchelsea, 1715-22; for Bridgwater, 1722-54; for Weymouth 1754-61; a Lord of the Treasury, 1724-40; Treasurer of the Navy, 1744-9, 1755-6, and April-June 1757. Peerage, 1761.

2. The first part of this letter seems to be missing.

Dr. Reynolds	24 nights at Windsor	..	..	30 „	720	0	0
	31 times at Kew ..	..	..	10 „	310	0	0
Sr Lucas Pepys	13 nights at Windsor	..	..	30 „	390	0	0
	31 times at Kew ..	..	..	10 „	310	0	0
Dr. Gisborne	30 times at Kew ..	..	..	10 „	300	0	0
Dr. Addington	3 times at Windsor	..	..		100	0	0
Dr. Heberden	3 times at Windsor	..	..		100	0	0

(Add. Georgian/2/10)

X   c.1783-1789 Some Undated Letters

425   PRINCE ERNEST TO THE PRINCE OF WALES

I took the liberty to write this little bit of a letter to say that if you would give me a sword knot I should be much obliged. The 27 o January.[1] Your ever affectionate brother.   (46972)

426   LORD NORTH TO CAPTAIN J. W. PAYNE

[*?c. beginning of April 1784*]

Lord North presents his compliments to Captain Payne. He has no reason to believe that his wishes will have any weight with the Collector of the Customs at Dover but will apply to him thro' the medium of a friend there to whom he is just going to write. Lord North desires that Captain Payne will lay him at his Royal Highness' feet and inform him that he has already written very earnestly to his friend at Dover in favour of Mr. Trevanion and will continue to give him all the assistance in his power.[2]   (38063)

1. The year is uncertain. The letter is written in a childish hand, like the Prince of Wales's first letter.

2. 1784 is the earliest possible date, and 1789 is probably the only alternative (but much less likely). John Trevanion (*c.* 1740-1810), M.P. for Dover, 1774-84 and 1789-1806, had been 'uniformly and constantly' in opposition to Lord North's Ministry, and Lord North would

CHARLES JAMES FOX TO THE PRINCE OF WALES

St. James's Street, Wednesday morning [*?1784*]

I am so much fatigued with yesterday's exertion and am so much afraid of increasing my disorder with cold that I shall consider it as an addition to the many favours your Royal Highness has conferred upon me, if my paying my duty to day at Carleton House can be excused. I hope in the course of the day to have opportunities of conversing with our principal friends and to suggest to your Royal Highness the best plan we are able in this untoward state of affairs. I confess this House of Commons is much worse than I thought it,[1] but our cause is such that sooner or later we must succeed.   (38091)

LIEUTENANT-COLONEL GERARD LAKE TO THE PRINCE OF WALES

Clarges Street, Monday night [*before Nov. 1784*]

I have receiv'd too many proofs of your Royal Highnesses friendship and regard to doubt of your attachment to me and my family. It ever has been my wish to possess your good wishes and esteem as well as to render your Royal Highness every assistance in my power. I have only to lament (however flattering such a mark of affection must be) that any accident that may have happen'd to me should have occasion'd so much uneasiness to your Royal Highness. I think myself most infinitely oblig'd to you for the pleasing intelligence you have been kind enough to communicate to me of the health and safety of Prince Frederick[2],

not have been prepared to support him at Dover before the formation of the Coalition Ministry. John Robinson, who planned the election campaign for Pitt and his friends at the end of 1783, wrote: 'Although it is the wish of the inhabitants of Dover because it is so much their interest, and although if a good man could be found to stand there he would probably carry it, yet as Lord North is Lord Warden [of the Cinque Ports] there may be doubts about it, and therefore both members are classed as they stand now, *against*' (*Parliamentary Papers of John Robinson*, p. 80). Trevanion was defeated at Dover in 1784, James Luttrell and Robert Preston being elected on 5 April. He was described in 1806 as a broken down West Indian who had dissipated whatever property he possessed (Add. MSS. 38458, f. 180). There is a memorial to him in St. James's Church, Dover, and the inscription reads, 'Sacred to the Memory of John Trevanion, Esq., who represented Dover in several successive Parliaments. He was faithful to his electioneering colours as long as a mast remained or a shred of canvas to nail to it: in short, as long as there was a breath of air to waft the ship into port' (*Devon and Cornwall Notes and Queries*, October 1950, p. 123).

1. If, as seems likely, the reference is to the House elected in April 1784, the letter could have been written in May. Fox, who had been elected for the Kirkwall division of Burghs on 26 April, spoke in the debate on 24 May which revealed in decisive fashion the weakness of the Opposition in the division lobby.

2. In November 1784 he was created Duke of York.

in whose wellfare I must always feel myself deeply interested. I am really in so much pain with writing that I hope you will excuse my adding more than to beg your acceptance of my sincere wishes for your health, prosperity and happiness and to believe me with the truest attachment, Sir [etc.].   (38056)

429   THE PRINCE OF WALES TO THOMAS PELHAM

Brighton, twelve o'clock 1785

My dear Tom, I am excessively sorry yt. I am prevented having the pleasure of dining with you & Harry today at Lewes, as I am oblig'd to go up to London upon very particular business, & nothing but very particular business shd., I assure you, have prevented me from meeting you at the Whig Club.   (Add. MSS. 27914, f.1)

430   CHARLES JAMES FOX TO THE PRINCE OF WALES

South Street, 8 Nov. [? 1786]

I was very sorry that both in October and now I could not have the honour of seeing your Royal Highness, from your being out of town the only days in which I was in it. But although I have not had that opportunity I am sure your Royal Highness does not doubt the sincere & lively interest which I take in everything that concerns your honour & interest, and I need not say how truly in those points of view I am rejoiced at the manly step which your Royal Highness has taken, & which I have no doubt but you will pursue with the same firmness of mind which enabled you to make the resolution. Permit [me] to take this occasion of repeating to your Royal Highness the assurances of that attachment with which I am [etc.].   (38156)

431   THE EARL OF STAIR¹ TO [?] LORD SOUTHAMPTON

Berkeley Square, 21 Dec. [?1786]

As I conceive that the most respectful mode of conveying any information to the Prince of Wales is through your Lordship, I trouble you with this letter in order to request that you will be pleased humbly to lay me

1. John, 5th Earl of Stair [S.] (*d.* 1789), succeeded his cousin, the 4th Earl, in 1768. Representative Peer [S.], 1771-4.

at his Royal Highness's feet, & at the same time to inform him of the following circumstances.

The situation of the Scotch Peers who were candidates, & were not returned at the last general election, has given rise to a scrutiny of all the titles of those who voted against them on that occasion, & in the course of that investigation such grounds of objection have appeared to his Royal Highness the Prince of Wales's title to vote at the election of Scotch Peers, that I & others have been advised to state these objections in our petitions to the House of Lords. As it would be highly improper, my Lord, that his Royal Highness should be first apprised of this step by the proceedings of a public court, I thought it my duty previous to presenting the petitions to inform him of it, both in my own name, & that of the other Lords whose petitions contain similar objections, & who would have adopted the same mode if their absence from London had not prevented them.   (38157-8)

432   [?] THE PRINCE OF WALES TO [?] THE EARL OF LONSDALE

[? April or May 1787]

Accept my best thanks for the generous, active & friendly exertions I have reciev'd from yourself and your friends. It is is [sic] to men of such independent spirit as your own, & of the natural consequence you hold in the welfare of the county [sic], that I shall always look for support, and your Lordship's concurrence with me on this occasion gives me the greatest satisfaction as well as prospect of success. I was in hopes the business would have terminated without the interference of my friends, but some late unsteady conduct on the part of the negociators, make [sic] it necessary for me to beg the favour of your Lordship to sollicit the attendance of your friends in town till the compleat arrangement of the business.[1]   (38296)

433   LETTERS FROM THE DUKE OF YORK TO THE PRINCE OF WALES

[Before July 1787]

I cannot let the post go without making you my excuses for not having sent you by the last courier the letter which I promised you, but as I was

1. The letter probably refers to the discussions in Parliament on the Prince's debts and the interlinked question of his connexion with Mrs. Fitzherbert. Sir Gilbert Elliot had to admit that 'those who generally vote with Opposition' and who might have been expected to support the Prince, were divided in opinion; and, he added, 'several *of our country gentlemen* are against him' (*Minto*, i. 155.

at Brunswick at the time that he set out it was impossible for me to do it. You may however depend upon it next courier. I have not time to add any more except that I am, dear brother [etc.].

P.S. I forget to add that I had to beg you to order a sword something in the style of the Turkish hanser [?] that I had just before I set out, but not half so fine. Adieu. (43818)

St. James, 5 o'clock
I intended to have called upon you after the Drawing Room was over, but Weltje told me you was already gone out; I therefore write this to acquaint you from the Queen that she has told the King of your message concerning the keeping of your birthday, who has taken it as a great compliment and accepts of your offer, and has said that as soon as he returns he will fix a day in order to keep it upon.

I send you enclosed a letter I have just received from Mr. Pitt, which I do not think very satisfactory.

God bless you. (43929)

434   LORD AMHERST TO THE PRINCE OF WALES
[*After 1786*]
From a conversation I had this morning with Sir Wm. Fawcett[1], I thought it was not improbable that his Majesty might have honoured me with a message to your Royall Highness. And fearing, Sir, at present that your Royall Highness might be doubtfull whether anything on the subject had been mentioned by his Majesty to me, I beg leave to say that the subject was not mentioned by his Majesty or I should have seized the first moment to have waited on your Royall Highness. (38049)

435   LETTERS FROM MRS. SHERIDAN [2] TO CAPTAIN J. W. PAYNE
Crewe Hall, 8 Jan.
As I know you will not think me very troublesome, I have the less scruple to request a favour of you. Will you find out from the Prince if

1. K.B., 1786.

2. Richard Brinsley Sheridan (1751-1816) married (13 April 1773), as his first wife, Elizabeth Ann Linley, the famous singer (1754-92). She was the daughter of Thomas Linley (1732-95), the composer. 'Mrs. Sheridan', wrote Sir Gilbert Elliot, 'is really nearer one's notion of a muse or an angel, or some such preternatural or semi-divine personage, than anything I have ever seen alive' (*Minto*, i. 148).

he would have any great objection to appoint Dr Pearson his Physician Extraordinary? I understand the appointment is merely honorary and does not supercede either of the present Physicians Extraordinary. Dr Pearson is a very clever man, and as I really think he saved my father's life, I am particularly anxious to obtain this honor for him, which seems the heigth of his ambition. My father has written to me to request Mr Sheridan's interest with the Prince. Mr S. advises me to try my own, but I have too humble an opinion of my influence to venture to intrude on his Royal Highness on this occasion—but as I am not quite so much afraid of you, I really shall take it as a particular favour if you will make the request for me, if it is not an improper one, and whether it is granted or no, pray send me a letter that I can shew Dr Pearson and my father, to convince them that I have endeavour'd at least to obtain what they desire.

I am commission'd by Mrs Crewe[1] to tell you she shd have been very glad if you had put your threats into execution of coming here, and if you do not think it too late, that you may still find a welcome at Crewe Hall till the meeting of Parliament. She likewise begs you will desire Ly Payne to write to her when you see her.

I shall hope to hear from you as soon as possible, and pray excuse my giving you this trouble.   (38057-8)

Undated

I don't know whether I am right in applying to you, but as this is my first attempt at an assembly, if I am sinning against the rules of etiquette, pray excuse it, and in a proper manner inform the Prince that I mean to be at home on the 17th and 24th of this month, and that I hope his Royal Highness will honor me by his company.

There will be faro and all sorts of gambling for you, so I suppose you will come, and if there is anybody about the Prince that I don't know and ought to ask, pray do it for me.   (41828)

Tuesday [after July 1787]

I am going to give you another commission, tho' I know you will soon hate the sight of my handwriting for plaguing you so. Will you make the proper invitation for me to the Duke of York and his suite? Or tell me how to do it, for I don't know the name of anyone belonging to him. Pray forgive me.   (41829)

1. Frances (d. 1818), daughter of Fulke Greville, the grandson of Fulke Greville, Lord Brooke, married John Crewe (1742-1829) of Crewe Hall, Cheshire, in 1766, he being created Baron Crewe in February 1806. She was a famous beauty and Whig toast.

436 SIR JOHN MACPHERSON TO THE PRINCE OF WALES

Brompton, Sunday

Sir John Macpherson presumes to enclose two papers for the perusal of his Royal Highness. The writer of No. 1 has made considerable progress among his friends, as will appear in time.

The paper No. 2 contains so important a proposition that it cannot be adopted but on full consideration with the leaders who support the cause and have a right to advise. (38213)

437 THE PRINCE OF WALES TO THE QUEEN

Carlton House, 1.30 p.m. [after 1783]

I am forbid to leave my room by Sir Richard¹, but shd. be very happy to see you & the girls, if you will admit of it. I am in my dressing room. Cannot you permit my sisters to come with Miss Planta² & you do me the favor of coming & fetching ym. away when Court is over? Miss Planta can have a chair to fetch her away when you come. Shall I send my coach or do you chuse to make use of your own? (41797)

438 LETTERS FROM THE LORD CHANCELLOR TO THE PRINCE OF WALES

4.20 p.m., 13 December

In obedience to your Royal Highness's commands, with which I am at this moment honoured, I shall signify your Royal Highness's pleasure by the earliest opportunity, I hope, this evening to Mr. Pitt. If I judge right, shewing him the letter with which your Royal Highness has honoured me will be the properest manner of making that communication. This of course it will be my duty to do, unless your Royal Highness should be pleased to prefer any other manner of doing it.³ (38090)

[? Early 1789]

The Chancellor waited upon your Royal Highness with a message from his Majesty. He will either return from the country to-night or wait your

1. Sir Richard Jebb (1729-87).

2. Miss Planta taught English to the younger Princesses. She had 'a very useful understanding but no powers of entertainment', said Fanny Burney (*Diary*, ii. 301).

3. Endorsed, 'Supposed to relate to His R.H.'s debts', but it could conceivably be a 1788 letter, during the Regency crisis.

Royal Highness's pleasure at any hour to-morrow morning which your Royal Highness may be pleased to command. (38455)

439   LORD ROBERT SPENCER TO CAPTAIN J. W. PAYNE

Berkeley Square, Sunday night [*?c. Nov.-Dec. 1788*]

I have been endeavouring to meet with you for these 3 or 4 days but without success. I therefore trouble you with this note to ask you if you can propose to H.R.Highness to assist us towards paying ye remaining debts upon account of ye last Westminster election[1]. I am sure he will

1. The reference is clearly to the Westminster bye-election in the summer of 1788 when, on 4 August, after a 15-days' poll, Lord John Townshend defeated the Government candidate, Lord Hood, who had necessarily vacated his seat on being appointed a Lord of the Admiralty: the numbers were 6392 and 5569 respectively. Lord Robert Spencer informed Lord Fitzwilliam (the undated letter was probably written in September 1788) that the election expenses amounted to 'the enormous sum of' £33,000, and that only £10,000 had as yet been raised. 'I have borrowed £4,000 upon my own credit, by means of which we hope to keep the people quiet till the middle of October, but £3,000 of the money borrowed must be paid by the 12th of October. It appears to me that the not paying the debts will be absolute ruin not only to the interest in Westminster but to the Party in general, and I do not see how the money can ever be raised by small subscriptions. If it is raised it must be by falling very heavy upon a few persons'. His plan was 'to get a few persons to join in borrowing £18,000, of which I reckoned that about £4,000 would be repaid them by subscriptions. This sum, added to £1,000 from a secret friend [clearly the Duke of York], and £1,000 which (if this took place) I offered to add to my former subscription, would make up £20,000, the whole sum wanted.' He went on: 'If by the 10th of October we do not get money enough to pay £3,000 of the £4,000 which are borrowed and at least £9,000 more, in all £10,000, there will be an amazing outcry indeed.' 'The Duke of Norfolk, I hear, says that he has just cleared his estate, which is £40,000 per annum, and that he is ready to apply the whole to Party purposes, a good vapour. The Duke of Bedford subscribed £2,000 when we expected from what had passed that it would be near £5,000, but he said he would give more if it should be wanted.' Fitzwilliam was clearly staggered by the enormous cost of the election, but in a subsequent letter (18 September) Lord Robert assured him that it had been money well spent. 'Nobody can doubt that it [the election] must have an effect upon the country in general, and make all other contested elections easier on our side.' On or about 13 October he wrote again to Fitzwilliam: 'The subscription makes considerable advances, so that we shall soon think ourselves entitled to call upon you. Out of the £20,000 there is now actually subscribed,

by different persons	£2,500	
by Duke of Portland	2,500	to be paid in a few days
by myself	2,000	
promised by L. Damer	200	
" by Pelham	300	
" by Duke of Bedford	4,000	
" by yourself	4,000	
	15,500	

besides some hundreds as good as promised to the Duke of Portland, and besides the Duke of Devonshire, whose answer is not yet come.' (Fitzwilliam MSS., Northants. Record Society).

509

see how necessary it is that they should be discharged before a change of Ministry, for two reasons—viz. to secure a quiet re-election to Charles & to prevent any suspicion of the money coming from yᵉ Treasury. We have already paid above thirty thousand pounds, which you will easily imagine could not have been raised without a severe tax upon most of our friends. The Duke of York has subscribed one thousand—another thousand would compleat the business. If I had the Prince's authority, I could take £500 from Lᵈ Cholmondeley immediately or perhaps £1000: but I rather think that money may be wanted for yᵉ purposes to which it was originally intended to apply it. I therefore think I had better not take more than £500 unless it is likely to be replaced soon. Upon ye whole, if you think the Pr. of Wales will not be offended at yᵉ liberty I am taking, I wish you would lay this business before H.R.H. and let me know what are his orders upon it.   (38583-4)

440   THE PRINCE OF WALES TO CAPTAIN J. W. PAYNE

Newmarket, 10.30 a.m.

I have only time to write a few lines to thank you for yr. letter. I shall make no comments upon it as I shall be early enough in town tonight to converse all this cruelly unpleasant subject over with you. But to another subject wh. requires some dispatch. The enclos'd, wh. I receiv'd by express from Ld. Southampton, will inform you of everything. Send instantly for Sheridan to the House of Commons, or all over London, wherever he is to be found. Concert what is best to be done, but above all things let that letter be laid before Parliament in some shape or other wh. Mr. Pitt wrote three years back to me & wh. you have ever since that time had under yr. care. Parliament shd. be given to understand yt. the house¹ is not mine, yt. I am only a tenant at will, & yt. the money beyond what they granted is disbursed out of my own pocket, wh. embarrasses me much, & yt. the rest of the debt owing upon ye house by the letter I received from the Minister & upon the bona fide of yt. letter, I advanc'd the money I have done, & the tradespeople embark'd still farther. Whether a public faith of yt. sort is to be depended upon or not I must leave to Parliament to decide upon. Pray act exactly as I have desir'd you, & believe me [etc.].

P.S. All I wish Parliament to do is to reimburse me the money I have expended, & to finish the house, or else to get the King to give me a grant of the whole, & to let me finish it myself.   (41899-900)

1. Presumably Carlton House, for the completion of which the House of Commons had voted £60,000 in 1787.

441 THOMAS ERSKINE TO CAPTAIN J. W. PAYNE

Tuesday

Will you be so good as to present my humble duty to the Prince and say to his Royal Highness that I am a prisoner in the King's Bench till two, and from thence with the Scotch Peers till six o'clock. I will attend afterwards if I have the honour of knowing the Prince is at home.

(38092)

442 LORD RAWDON TO [?] CAPTAIN J. W. PAYNE

Tuesday morning

I have been so beset with intruders this morning that it has been impossible to get my papers finished; therefore as the messenger cannot at any rate reach Brighton time enough for the Prince to consider them this evening, it will be early enough for him to set out by the mail this evening, and you had better order a place to be taken accordingly.

(38372)

443 HORACE MANN[1] TO CAPTAIN J. W. PAYNE

Egerton Farm, near Maidstone, 19 Nov.

Most highly am I flattered by the gracious expressions which the Prince of Wales has condescended to use in respect to my interests, and most sensible of the very obliging manner in which you have conveyed to me his Royal Highness's sentiments. My devotion and dutiful obedience to his Royal Highness makes me regret that upon the present occasion there should be any obstacle to my exerting my interest at Canterbury in favour of Mr. Beckford[2], but when his Royal Highness is informed that upon my declining to offer my services to that City I promised to observe the strictest neutrality at the next election, the high sense of honor that animates his breast will make his Royal Highness coincide with me in opinion that mine is deeply concerned in adhering to a promise of so sacred a nature. I take the liberty of solliciting you to mention this fact to the Prince of Wales, with my sentiments of profoundest duty to his

1. Sir Horace Mann, 2nd Baronet (1744-1814), the nephew of the 1st Baronet (1701-86), Horace Walpole's friend. He was M.P. for Maidstone, 1774-84, and for Sandwich, 1790-1807. Horace Walpole wrote (11 April 1784): 'He has parted with his house in town and abandoned his borough' (Toynbee, *Letters of Horace Walpole*, xiii. 141).

2. ?William Beckford (1759-1844), the celebrated owner of Fonthill, and man of letters. M.P. for Wells, 1784-90; for Hindon, 1790-4, 1806-20.

511

Royal Highness and devoted adherence to those principles which have entitled me to the honor of approbation where only I am sollicitous to obtain it.

My particular thanks are due to you for your polite attention to me and I beg leave to assure you that I am, with the greatest truth, dear Sir [etc.]. (38087)

444 THE HON. HUGH SEYMOUR CONWAY TO THE PRINCE OF WALES [draft]

[*?1788*]

Enclosed I have the honor to send your Royal Highness a letter with which Prince William charged me on Sunday last. I should have been happy in having presented it myself but as my absence from Clanville has been longer than I expected it would have been, your Royal Highness will easily understand my wishing to pass a few days there quietly with Lady Race, and I trust your good humour will find an excuse for my deferring for a short time the honor of waiting upon you.

I am sorry to inform you that Prince William did not succeed in his wishes of avoiding the trip he had expected before he was order'd to join Adm. Leveson's Squadn., and I am still more so at saying that the way in which he received his orders to go abroad was not formed to lessen his dislike to it as he was sent away from the Squadron after he had his provisions, stores, &c. were compleated from it at sea [*sic*] without having had permission of coming into port for a few days to arrange his private affairs previous to his quitting this country—a want of indulgence which I am afraid would have disgusted many of my brother officers without there had been some appearance of service to have reconciled them to the inconvenience of sailing in such a hurry. If his Royal Highness has not expressed to you how much he was shocked at being distinguished from his brother officers by having less attention paid to him than we all have, it must have been to prevent your feelings suffering with his own, and the way in which we all were surprised at learning his destination justifyd him in thinking that people would feel for him on the occasion. Adm. Leveson was as ignorant of it as any person in the Squadron till we fell in with the persons who had been sent out with the orders to him, and was so much inclined to soften those he was charged with for Pce. Willm. that he would have consented at his own risk to have given the Prince leave to anchor at Plymh. for a few hours, but your brother, though he was sensible of the Adml.'s attention to him, decided for the most officer-like step and went off without availing himself of it. (Ragley MSS.)

Index to Letters

Index to Letters

524